KU-177-931

PENGUIN CLASSICS

# THE DIVINE COMEDY

DANTE ALIGHIERI was born in Florence in 1265 into a family from the lower ranks of the nobility. He may have studied at the university of Bologna. When he was about twenty, he married Gemma Donati, by whom he had four children. He first met Bice Portinari, whom he called Beatrice, in 1274, and when she died in 1290 he sought consolation by writing the *Vita nuova* and by studying philosophy and theology. During this time he also became involved in the conflict between the Guelf and Ghibelline factions in Florence; he became a prominent White Guelf, and when the Black Guelfs came to power in 1302, Dante was, while absent from the city, condemned to exile. He took refuge initially in Verona but eventually, having wandered from place to place, he settled in Ravenna. While there he completed the *Commedia*, which he began in about 1307. Dante died in Ravenna in 1321.

ROBIN KIRKPATRICK graduated from Merton College, Oxford. He has taught courses on Dante's *Commedia* in Hong Kong, Dublin and – for more than thirty years – at the university of Cambridge, where he is a Fellow of Robinson College and Emeritus Professor of Italian and English Literatures. His books include *Dante's Paradiso and the Limitations of Modern Criticism* (1978), *Dante's Inferno: Difficulty and Dead Poetry* (1987) and, in the Cambridge Landmarks of World Literature series, *Dante: The Divine Comedy* (2004). His own published poetry includes *Prologue and Palinodes* (1997), and currently he is working on several volumes in which notions of performance are pursued in conjunction with a range of theological considerations.

# DANTE ALIGHIERI

# The Divine Comedy

*Translated, edited and introduced by*
ROBIN KIRKPATRICK

PENGUIN BOOKS

PENGUIN CLASSICS

Published by the Penguin Group
Penguin Books Ltd, 80 Strand, London WC2R 0RL, England
Penguin Group (USA) Inc., 375 Hudson Street, New York, New York 10014, USA
Penguin Group (Canada), 90 Eglinton Avenue East, Suite 700, Toronto, Ontario, Canada M4P 2Y3
(a division of Pearson Penguin Canada Inc.)
Penguin Ireland, 25 St Stephen's Green, Dublin 2, Ireland (a division of Penguin Books Ltd)
Penguin Group (Australia), 707 Collins Street, Melbourne, Victoria 3008, Australia
(a division of Pearson Australia Group Pty Ltd)
Penguin Books India Pvt Ltd, 11 Community Centre, Panchsheel Park, New Delhi – 110 017, India
Penguin Group (NZ), 67 Apollo Drive, Rosedale, Auckland 0632, New Zealand
(a division of Pearson New Zealand Ltd)
Penguin Books (South Africa) (Pty) Ltd, Block D, Rosebank Office Park,
181 Jan Smuts Avenue, Parktown North, Gauteng 2193, South Africa

Penguin Books Ltd, Registered Offices: 80 Strand, London WC2R 0RL, England

www.penguin.com

The translation of *Inferno* first published in Penguin Classics 2006
The translation of *Purgatorio* first published in Penguin Classics 2007
The translation of *Paradiso* first published in Penguin Classics 2007
This combined edition, with a revised introduction, first published 2012

016

Translation and editorial material © Robin Kirkpatrick, 2006, 2007, 2012
All rights reserved

The moral right of the translator and author of the editorial material has been asserted

Set in 10.25/12.25pt PostScript Adobe Sabon
Typeset by Jouve (UK), Milton Keynes
Printed in Great Britain by Clays Ltd, Elcograf S.p.A.

Except in the United States of America, this book is sold subject
to the condition that it shall not, by way of trade or otherwise, be lent,
re-sold, hired out, or otherwise circulated without the publisher's
prior consent in any form of binding or cover other than that in
which it is published and without a similar condition including this
condition being imposed on the subsequent purchaser

ISBN: 978-0-141-19749-4

www.greenpenguin.co.uk

MIX
Paper from
responsible sources
FSC
www.fsc.org    FSC™ C018179

Penguin Books is committed to a sustainable
future for our business, our readers and our planet.
This book is made from Forest Stewardship
Council™ certified paper.

# Contents

## THE DIVINE
## COMEDY

# Chronology

1224 Saint Francis receives the stigmata

1250 Death of Emperor Frederick II

1260 Defeat of the Guelfs at the battle of Montaperti, leading to seven years of Ghibelline domination in Florence

1265 Dante born, probably 25 May

1266 Defeat of imperial army by the Guelfs and the French under Charles of Anjou at the battle of Benevento

1267 Birth of Giotto; restoration of Guelf rule in Florence under the protection of Charles of Anjou

1274 Deaths of Thomas Aquinas and Bonaventure

1282 The influence of the guilds starts to grow in Florence

1283 Dante begins his association with the poet Guido Cavalcanti

1289 Dante fights at the battle of Campaldino; Florence, having defeated Arezzo and Ghibelline factions at Campaldino, begins to extend its supremacy over Tuscany

1290 Death of Bice (Beatrice) Portinari

1292 Dante compiles the *Vita nuova*

1293 *Ordinamenti di Giustizia* promulgated in Florence

1294 Election and abdication of Pope Celestine V; election of Pope Boniface VIII

1295 Dante enrols in a guild

1296 For five years, Dante is actively involved in the political life of the Florence commune; *Rime Petrose* probably composed

1300 Dante elected to the office of prior; fictional date of the *Commedia*

1301 Crisis and *coup d'état* in Florence; Charles de Valois enters the city; return of Corso Donati; defeat of the White Guelfs by the Black Guelfs

1302 In his absence, Dante formally exiled and sentenced to death by the Black Guelfs

1303 Dante seeks refuge for the first time in Verona; death of Pope Boniface VIII

1304 Dante probably engaged until 1307 on the *Convivio* and the *De Vulgari Eloquentia*; birth of Petrarch

1305 Pope Clement V detained in Avignon

1307 Possible date for when Dante started the *Commedia*; accession of Edward II to English throne

1308 Henry VII of Luxembourg elected Holy Roman Emperor in Rome

1310 Dante writes his epistle to Henry: '*Ecce nunc tempus acceptabile*'; Henry enters Italy

1312 Possible (though much debated) date for when Dante started *De Monarchia*; Henry crowned Holy Roman Emperor

1313 Emperor Henry VII dies; Boccaccio born

1314 Dante begins living for six years in Verona, under the protection of Can Grande della Scala

1318 Dante in Ravenna: in close contact with Guido Novello da Polenta

1320 Dante in Latin verse correspondence with the humanist Giovanni del Virgilio; lectures at university of Verona: *Questio de Aqua et Terra*

1321 Dante dies in Ravenna, 13 September

# Introduction

## Dante: Life and Times

In January 1302, at the age of thirty-six, Dante Alighieri was exiled from his native Florence. In the five or six years before that date, he had played an increasingly important role in the political life of the Florentine commune and in 1300 was elected to the governing authority of the city, the Council of Priors. It is this period of Dante's life that is celebrated in a fresco painted by a contemporary, Giotto di Bondone (1267–1337), which depicts the poet among the most prominent citizens of his day. His look is keen, gaunt and defiant. Yet he also seems capable (almost) of smiling; and it is easy to see in Giotto's portrait something not only of the political activist but also of the delicate young poet who in the 1290s had already dedicated his poetry to 'Beatrice' – the Florentine neighbour, Bice Portinari, who married a banker and died an early death in 1290.

Under the impetus given by poets and intellectuals such as Dante himself, a highly sophisticated culture was developing in thirteenth-century Florence. But the city was also wracked by internal dissension and susceptible to pressures from the world beyond its civic boundaries. In 1301, Dante's party was ousted from power by a *coup d'état*, and the poet, 'midway on [his] path in life' (*Inferno* 1: 1), subsequently condemned to exile. He never returned to Florence. Accused – falsely, one presumes – of the corrupt exercise of his public office, Dante refused to admit to the charges or accept any ignominious offer of amnesty, preferring, until his death in 1321, to remain as a voice in the wilderness, travelling from place to place in the northern part of the Italian peninsula. He was accompanied for ɔme of this time by two of his three sons – these two being among the first people to write commentaries on their father's work – and by his daughter, who became a nun and took 'Beatrice' as her name in religion. Dante's wife appears to have remained in Florence.

Little more than this is known about Dante's life, save for what Dante himself relates – often obliquely – in the *Commedia*. It is possible that he travelled as far as Paris and visited the great schools of philosophy at the Sorbonne. He must certainly at some time, possibly before his exile, have reached Bologna, about sixty miles from Florence, and been able to develop at its civic university the interests in philosophy that he had pursued as an amateur in Florence. Subsequently, his reputation as a politician, philosopher and poet seems to have secured him a livelihood at some of the great courts of north-east Italy, notably those of Can Grande della Scala (1291–1329), ruler of Verona, and Guido Novello da Polenta (*fl.* mid-thirteenth century), in Ravenna. Indeed, within fifty years of Dante's death, Florence itself came to recognize the merits of the erstwhile outlaw – whose writings by now existed in a great many copies, though no autograph script has ever been found. By 1373 Giovanni Boccaccio (1313–75) had organized a series of public lectures in Florence on the *Commedia*. But Dante died in exile on 13 September 1321, having perhaps contracted malaria while on a diplomatic mission to Venice. He was buried in Ravenna with great honour at the church of San Pier Maggiore.

One of the most notable features of Dante's *Commedia* is the unfailing attention that its author pays to the history and politics of his day. Even in the *Paradiso*, where the reader might have expected a certain detachment from worldly concerns, Dante can speak movingly (at 17: 58–60) of how bitter it is for him as an exile to climb another man's stair each night and trace the causes of his personal tragedy to the factionalism that, by 1300, had been brewing in Florence for more than a century. Equally (at 27: 25–7), he can launch a violent attack on the late medieval papacy not only for its corruption – which has turned the sacred territory of Rome into a sewer spilling with 'blood and

pus' – but also because of its involvement in the political disrup-
tions of which he himself had become the victim.

At no stage, however, are such passages merely the product
of embittered nostalgia. Surveying the history of Europe from
the vantage point of 1300, Dante accurately identifies some of
the major forces which, at that point, were to determine the
shape and character of the modern world. There is much here
that he resists, in particular the rampant advance of capitalism
and nationalism. But always he seeks solutions of his own.
In the *Commedia* he develops a voice which, while often dra-
matically aggressive, is also quick to celebrate the possibilities
and achievements that continue to flare in the contemporary
wasteland.

Throughout the thirteenth century, the political and eco-
nomic life of the Italian peninsula was driven by the interaction
of three forces. Two of these – the Holy Roman Empire and the
Roman Catholic Church – laid claim to universal jurisdiction.
The third force, generated by the emerging economies of the
mercantile Italian city states, did not initially make any such
claim – though, in effect, the hegemony of the global market-
place that has developed over the last 700 years owes much to
its origins in late medieval Italy. From the time of Charlemagne
(742–814), crowned Holy Roman Emperor in 800, Europe had
at least a notional principle of unity in feudal allegiance to the
imperial throne. There was, of course, little hard reality to sup-
port this principle; and by Dante's time dynastic aspirations
began to display themselves in the territories of present-day
France, Spain and Italy, which, over the coming centuries, came
progressively to displace imperial authority in favour of the
ambitions of the several nation states. To Italian eyes – and par-
ticularly to Dante's – there were a few decades at the beginning
of the thirteenth century when imperial power seemed to have
gained ascendancy in the peninsula. With Frederick II (1194–
1250) as emperor, a flourishing imperial culture developed, in
which notions of the emperor as the embodiment of universal
justice were consciously cultivated. At the same time, the first
stirrings of Italian vernacular poetry were discernible at his
court and there was even some development of science. (See

*nferno* 13.) By 1265, however, the claims of Frederick's dynasty to political control in Italy had been extinguished by a lack of legitimate descendants and through the armed opposition of Church and city state. Nevertheless, as late as 1313 Dante maintained the passionate, if ill-founded, hope that the Empire would return to Italy in the person of Henry VII of Luxembourg (*c.* 1269–1313) and restore the unity and peace once enjoyed under the rule of ancient Rome.

Throughout the twelfth and thirteenth centuries, the Empire was in conflict, on both ideological and territorial grounds, with a Church that displayed increasing efficiency and appetite as a political institution. The advance of the Papal Curia as an extremely well-regulated civil service encouraged the development of bureaucratic technologies that strengthened central control and allowed the Church to respond rapidly and rapaciously to the decline of imperial power in Italy. A manifestation of what this might produce is the papacy of Boniface VIII, in office from 1294 to 1303. An aristocrat and a lawyer experienced in the wheelings and dealings of the Curia, Boniface claimed the right as pope to intervene directly (if not always successfully) in the local politics of Italy, and was an important protagonist in the coup that led to Dante's exile. Dante himself speaks of Boniface with often brilliant sarcasm. (See especially *Inferno* 19 and *Purgatorio* 20.) Nor was he alone in the odium he expressed: a posthumous trial of the pope accused him of heresy, witchcraft, embezzlement, nepotism and sodomy.

The third feature of the Italian scene was the emergence in the course of the thirteenth century of a considerable number of city states. As they gathered momentum, these urban centres increasingly asserted their independence and were inclined to forge self-interested alliances. These were established in league, sometimes, with the Empire against neighbouring city states. But cities also formed alliances with the Church against the Empire, which – though in decline – could still claim suzerainty over lands that were now increasingly subject to the influence of mercantile and banking interests. The huge energies of the city state were to find expression not only in trade but also in intellectual ambition and artistic achievement. It was in this complex and highly charged arena that Dante most directly encountered the intersecting currents that impelled and wracked the social order into which he was born. By the end of the twelfth century, Florence was expanding rapidly as a workshop for luxury goods and, increasingly, as a centre of financial expertise. Migrant workers from the surrounding countryside flooded in – bringing the population of the city from approximately 30,000 in 1200 to something like 100,000 in 1300, and leading to a corresponding expansion of the city limits. (See *Inferno* 15 and *Paradiso* 15–17.) The feudal nobility also began to set up working establishments in the city, which allowed them to share in its economic success. Energies and tensions ran high. Rivalries – often between aristocratic factions or between noblemen and *nouveaux riches* – were rife. Clan opposed clan. And, where marriage alliances failed, murder was likely to prove the alternative. In the course of the thirteenth century, two partisan groupings, along with lesser and more shifting factions, developed aggressively visible identities: the Ghibelline party, proclaiming allegiance to the increasingly beleaguered Empire, and the Guelfs, who, even though they themselves were often nobles of feudal origin, tended to look pragmatically to the future, associating with the new power of the papacy while also supporting the claims of northern dynasties such as the Angevin. Despite these turf wars – which saw ascendancy switch from Ghibelline to Guelf and back again – civic and ecclesiastical planning prospered during the period, and Florence became remarkable for the vigour and beauty of its building programme.

The 1260s, the decade in which Dante was born, saw a number of crucial developments. In 1260, the Ghibellines, riding on a final surge of imperial influence, won a military victory over the Guelfs, which was apparently so decisive that they could easily have chosen to raze the city of Florence to the ground. (See *Inferno* 10.) Yet by 1266, the influence of the Empire in Italy had been extinguished and the Guelf cause came to prevail, producing a period of stability which was to endure for at least thirty-five years. Dante's own family was a minor scion of an aristocratic Guelf clan. But political involvement had, by mid-century, come to depend upon membership of the great trade guilds that oversaw the interests of the commercial commune. Dante's father, Alighiero Alighieri (d. *c.* 1283), who died in or before the poet's eighteenth year (his mother had died much earlier), seems to have worked on the shadier margins of the banking industry, possibly as a money-lender. He did not qualify to belong to any guild. Alighiero Alighieri, though known to contemporary texts, is never mentioned by Dante himself. But Dante (unlike his father) became a nominal member of the Guild of Physicians and Pharmacists. Thus, while he came to detest many aspects of Guelf polity, he was formally qualified to take an active part in the political life of the city.

By the late 1290s, the Guelf party itself had divided into two factions, the Blacks and the Whites. The Blacks (who by 1301 were temporarily in exile) were led by Corso Donati (d. 1308), described by Dante (*Purgatorio* 24: 82–7) as the one 'most to blame dragged at a horse's tail towards the ditch [Hell]'. It is an indication of how finely drawn were the lines of internal division (and also perhaps of Dante's open-mindedness and delicacy in discrimination) that Corso's brother, Forese Donati (d. 1296), was one of Dante's closest friends – and appears as a redeemed sinner in *Purgatorio* 23 – while Corso's sister, Piccarda Donati (*c.* 1270–*c.* 1298/9?), is found among the blessed in *Paradiso* 3 delivering one of the most important accounts of love and order in the whole *Commedia*.

Corso, however, had a clearer eye for political advantage than Dante. He formed alliances with both the Church and Angevin armies, who were marching close to Florence. The city, under a supposedly non-partisan government, sought to rally the guilds, who failed, however, to muster any unified defiance to the military threat. In early November 1301, while Dante was out of the city on a last-ditch diplomatic mission to Rome, the French armies under Charles de Valois (1270–1325) came within striking distance of Florence and installed the Blacks in power. Along with members of the White Guelf faction, Dante was banished from the city.

## The *Commedia*

The dark wood of *Inferno* 1 may be thought in large part to represent Dante's own entanglement in the world of Florentine politics, a place of sterile barbarity, remote from all true civilization. But even in the midst of desolation, Dante is seeking to construct a solution: 'my theme will be the good I found there' (*Inferno* 1: 8). And the first good that he finds is an authoritative guide, encountered dramatically at lines 62–6, who will lead him forward in purposeful discovery. This is Virgil (b. 70 BC, near Mantua), author of the *Aeneid*.

To identify Virgil as the immediate source of his salvation is an astonishing decision on Dante's part. Not only is Virgil a poet and a pagan rather than some accredited Christian authority, he is also himself an inhabitant of Hell. (See *Inferno* 4.) As will be seen, the implications of these extraordinary facts resonate throughout the whole *Commedia*. Yet considering Dante's predicament, as both a politician and as a poet, there are at least two ways in which Virgil may be seen to answer directly to Dante's needs.

In the first place, as author of the *Aeneid*, Virgil points to certain political considerations that Dante will continue to explore in philosophical writings such as *De Monarchia*. The *Aeneid* tells of how, at the fall of Troy, Aeneas led his refugee band away from the ruins of the city and eventually brought them to Italy where, in founding Rome, he also lays the foundations for the Roman Empire. Dante, in *De Monarchia*, proceeds to meditate philosophically on the significance of the Roman Empire. On his understanding, it is an institution authorized by God Himself and intended to bring justice and peace to the whole human race. (See also *Paradiso* 6.) In particular, Roman justice alone can be seen as the answer to the partisan strife which the avarice and greed of mercantile cities such as Florence have fomented. Facing the bitter consequences of that strife in exile – in the dark wood – it is natural that Dante should turn to Virgil who first celebrated the principles, embodied in the hero Aeneas, that underlay the establishment of the Empire.

In the *Commedia*, however, matters of philosophy can never be seen in isolation from those of poetic form. And in choosing Virgil as his guide, Dante also signalled a radical change of direction in his poetic career. Until he began the *Commedia*, he had written almost exclusively within the lyrical love tradition of his day. Vernacular poetry, which had been developing in Italy before he began to write, had cultivated the idiom of a refined meditation on the meaning of love, deriving in some measure from the love poets of Provence. In its most sophisticated form such poetry had been intended for private circulation among an elite circle of like-minded individuals – such as those in Florence whom Dante designates the *stil novisti*, poets of the 'sweet new style'. (See *Purgatorio* 24: 57 and 26: 97–9.) But now with the example of Virgil's *Aeneid* Dante sets himself to write a public poem, a narrative work which aims to explore the political and ethical principles on which a successful society must always depend. Thus at *Inferno* 1: 85–7 Dante can proclaim that it is Virgil who has taught him his fine new style. This may be seen as an exaggeration, since there is little evidence, before the *Commedia* itself, that Virgil had influenced Dante's way of writing. These lines do, however, reflect, as a matter of pride, Dante's new intention to distinguish himself from his contemporaries by close attention in terms of style and moral purpose to the example of Virgil's Latin poem. Under the influence of Virgil, Dante now comes to see his exile, not as an occasion for despair, but rather as the stimulus to an epic endeavour comparable to that which Aeneas undertook to re-establish a homeland, at least an intellectual one, for himself and all true Florentines.

Central as Virgil proves to be in the narrative of the *Commedia*, it would be a mistake to suppose that Dante slavishly followed Virgil's example, or to suggest that he ever ceased to develop the conception of love and the lyrical modes of expression that he had first discovered in his devotion to Beatrice. It is crucial in reading the *Commedia* to take seriously the declaration, recorded in *Paradiso* 31, which speaks of Beatrice as the ultimate source of his personal salvation and the true inspiration of his poetry. Indeed, while Beatrice does not appear in the poem until the final cantos of the *Purgatorio*, she is already identified in *Inferno* 2 as the voice, speaking on behalf of Heaven, who commissions Virgil to assume his role as Dante's guide. Beyond the harmony that imperial justice might bring about, there is an ultimate harmony with the divine powers that first brought into being and now sustain the created order of the universe. The final line of the *Commedia* will speak of the 'love that moves the sun and other stars'. And on Dante's account he originally began to understand how he himself might be moved by and participate in the universal activity of love by his particular experience of Beatrice's presence. At no point in the *Commedia* is justice shown to be at odds with love. But the final fruit of justice will be a condition in which one is free to contemplate, unimpeded by faction, friction and political strife, the goodness of all creation.

If, then, Dante learns from Virgil how to be an epic poet, he also remains, as he always was, a love poet. And the goal of his epic endeavour is to reaffirm the Christian truth that our home, whether in time or eternity, is not a geographical location to be secured by territorial ambition but a revelation of the fundamental relationships that should and can be expressed in love of our neighbours and the whole of the created order. In arriving at this understanding, Dante will greatly magnify and minutely define his original conception of love. (See especially *Purgatorio* 16–18.) And in doing so, his journey will at times take on the character both of an educational syllabus and of a pilgrimage of faith, in which his understanding of Christian love will be systematically supported by reference to the most sophisticated thinkers of the late Middle Ages, including Saint Thomas Aquinas (1225–74). The heroes of his poem will prove to be not warriors such as Aeneas, but saints such as Saint Francis and Saint Dominic (*Paradiso* 11–12), along with the innumerable men and women of his own time whom Dante celebrates, in the *Purgatorio* and *Paradiso*, for the richness of their earthly lives. But in all these figures – and also in himself – he will always be seeking evidence of that joy in existence which Beatrice inspired in him. That joy, as he argues in *Purgatorio* 16, is the very condition of the lives that God, who is for Dante not a judge but a 'joyous Maker' (line 89), always intended us to pursue.

## Inferno, Purgatorio, Paradiso

To many of its readers, the *Commedia* is remarkable above all as a great intellectual synthesis, a *summa* sustained by the confidence that all things in the universe can be fully understood and all things explained. On this reading, Dante's poem has frequently been compared to a great Gothic cathedral. And those who favour such an analogy are likely to argue that the work is a characteristic product of the late Middle Ages, of a period in which Christian faith joined hands with Christian reason and confidently developed (as did the writings of Aquinas) a comprehensive account of our relationship to God and of the cosmos that He had created.

Scholars may now question whether the late Middle Ages offered as unified a picture of the world as it has sometimes been thought to do. And it is certainly doubtful whether Dante, faced with the controversies that animated the intellectual, as well as the political life, of the period, would have remained a passive inheritor of that system. (See his overview in *Paradiso* 10–14.) His thought is too individualistic and idiosyncratic for that. None the less, the overall plan that he devised for his poem – including the landscape through which he imagines himself to be travelling – reflects a mind that was devoted to the concept of order in a philosophical perspective while, at the same time, proving capable of great leaps of imagination and narrative invention.

The *Inferno*, despite the manifold horrors that Dante envisages there, differs from those depictions of Hell, common in his own time, which indulged an understanding of sin and evil as sheer ugliness and chaotic violence. Against unbridled disorder, Dante pictures a graded descent, leading from the surface of the earth (Dante knew it was round) to its dead centre, where Satan, displaying the utmost deformation of dignity and person, stands imprisoned in ice. Each successive circle of Hell reflects Dante's progressive analysis of the ways in which sin destroys the goodness that he believes to be the essential attribute of all created beings. In pursuing this analysis, he draws as much upon classical philosophers such as Aristotle and Cicero as he does upon Christian thinkers. (See notes to *Inferno* 11.) And the results of his diagnosis are often surprising, even to the modern reader. Why, for instance, are the sins of flattery and seduction deemed to be so much more heinous than those of lust and greed? Why is it that, for Dante, the worst sin of all is treachery, whether to friends, guests, nations or benefactors? In asking such questions as these, the reader is drawn to engage with Dante's own developing conception of how order, in the intellectual and ethical sphere, is finally to be understood.

Even more original than Dante's depiction of Hell is his picture of Purgatory. The doctrine of Purgatory had only recently been formulated, and such descriptions as were available generally represented it as a subterranean region in which penitents suffered punishments identical to those suffered by the eternally damned, save that their sufferings were only temporary in duration, endured as a remedial preparation for the pleasures of Heaven. Dante, for his own purposes, takes a very different view, drawing upon a talent for invention more associated today with a writer of science fiction. On this understanding, when Satan fell from Heaven, the impetus of his fall drove him to the centre of the terrestrial globe. But what, Dante seems to have asked himself, was the logical result of this? Where did the mass of earthly matter that Satan had displaced disappear to? His answer is that, since Satan struck the earth at the point which was later to be named Jerusalem, the core of matter that he gouged out was extruded into the southern hemisphere, at the antipodes of Jerusalem, to form a mountain-island – on the summit of which is the Garden of Eden. This mountain is now Mount Purgatory, where penitents will spend centuries on its slopes, recovering by their own willing efforts the happiness that was lost to humanity by the fall of Adam and Eve. Free as this flight of rigorous fancy undoubtedly is, it serves to embody some of Dante's most characteristic emphases, in the philosophical as well as the poetic sphere. Hence, for instance, Satan's fall, so far from precipitating disaster in God's universe, serves to create a realm in which sin can always be redeemed. Adam and Eve are created in Satan's stead. And even when they sin, their sins can be redeemed through penitential assimilation to the sufferings of Christ. Nor is redemption simply a matter of transcending one's human nature in pursuit of some transcendently angelic ideal. On the contrary, Dante's Purgatory as a natural environment – subject to the passage of time, the play of the senses in the diurnal alternation of day and night – invites its inhabitants to recover the human selfhood that they were always intended to enjoy through the full exercise of their intellectual and sensuous natures.

Dante's powers of architectonics and invention do not desert him in the *Paradiso*. The Heaven that he depicts is no vaguely suggestive symphony of pleasing melodies and delightful illumination. Order again is his concern; and the originality of his conception resides in a triumphant realization that the rational mind is born to enjoy the rationally appreciable ordering of the cosmic system. The journey here, until its very last phase, ascends through the planetary spheres as studied by Dante in the pages of the best astronomical science that was available to him. The planetary heavens from the moon to Saturn mark the stages of his journey, and Paradise, on the view that emerges from his poem, becomes a realization of the variety and refreshment that the created cosmos was intended to offer to the searching mind.

For all that, too strong an emphasis upon the coherence and architectural characteristics of Dante's poem can sometimes prove misleading and distort the character of his thinking and achievement. Doubt, for Dante, is a productive state of mind. This is true even in the *Paradiso*, where, if one were to suppose that Christian faith was simply a matter of comforting certitude, one might imagine that Dante would have been content to offer, faithfully, a simple reaffirmation of established doctrine. Yet at 4: 124–32, the poet declares that doubt springs like a growing shoot from the base of truth and drives the mind onwards to ever greater understanding.

## Dante's Sources

In literary terms, too, the narrative of the *Commedia* displays a dynamic interest in effects of dislocation, hesitation, surprise and sudden illumination. As most readers will testify, the poet demonstrates exceptional skill in the handling of episode, in cinematic cliffhangers, fades-to-black, unexpected changes of tempo. But these effects are never merely incidental. They encourage attention to critical moments in Dante's visions where his thinking itself needs to begin anew or pursue some new direction, as, for instance, in *Inferno* 8 and 9 where Virgil – having a mere seven cantos previously been chosen as Dante's trusted guide – proves inadequate to the task. (Compare *Inferno* 5–6, 16–17, *Purgatorio* 20–21 and *Paradiso* 6–7, 19–20 and 21–2.) But these same moments also indicate how unremittingly, as the *Commedia* advances, Dante develops and refashions language, image and motif. This is particularly evident in his handling of the sources on which he draws, whether these be classical, Scriptural or vernacular. In assimilating earlier texts Dante, at all points, is prepared to experiment, interpreting or combining these texts to serve his own artistic ends.

Consider, for instance, how subtly his treatment of Virgil – and of the *Aeneid* – gradually develops. As we have seen, Dante departs decisively from contemporary practice in claiming that Virgil has taught him 'the fine-tuned style that has, already, brought [him] so much honour' (*Inferno* 1: 86–7); and he reinforces this claim in *Inferno* 4, where he pictures himself as a new member of the ancient school of poets that includes not only Virgil but also Homer, Ovid, Horace and Lucan. Yet from the outset the very form of narrative that Dante chooses to adopt differs radically from that in the *Aeneid*, where the narrative unit – also employed by subsequent writers of epic such as John Milton – is book length, extending always to some 600 lines or more, thereby allowing for sustained and coherent development of action and atmosphere. By contrast, Dante's cantos are never more than 160 lines long, so that author (and the reader, too) is at every point challenged to re-forge connections or establish some new angle of perception. Furthermore, while the *Aeneid* is prominent in Dante's mind, especially in the early *Inferno*, he increasingly draws upon the example of Virgil's pastoral poetry – the *Eclogues* and the *Georgics*. (See, in particular, the opening of *Inferno* 24.) Indeed, by *Purgatorio* 22: 57, Virgil is referred to as 'the singer of the farming songs'. The fourth of Virgil's *Eclogues* – which speaks of the coming of a golden world of justice – was regularly taken in Dante's time to be a prophecy of Christ's nativity. Then finally, in depicting Virgil as a character in his fictional journey, Dante perpetrates a great many liberties upon the Roman patriarch. So, for example, at one point in *Inferno* 24, Virgil is shown to accelerate Dante's escape from a band of pursuing demons by hoisting his pupil on to his stomach and sliding down a precipitous cliff-face, with all the instinctual energy of a mother saving her child from a burning house. Through a series of such moments, the relationship between Dante and Virgil emerges less as a heroic companionship such as the *Aeneid* had depicted than as a matter of intimate nuance and, at times, comedy, deserving to be compared with the relationship, say, between Don Quixote and Sancho Panza.

A similar inventiveness marks Dante's treatment of other authors in the classical pantheon. For instance, Statius (d. *c.* AD 96) wrote his epic poem *Thebaid* to depict, in spectacular fashion, the corruption and divisions that arose in Thebes after the death of Oedipus. The *Inferno*, being itself the depiction of a degenerate city, draws prolifically on references to the *Thebaid*. (See *Inferno* 12, 32 and 33.) Yet when Statius himself appears in Dante's poem, it is in *Purgatorio* 21, where he joins Virgil as Dante's guide on the last stage of the penitential journey. Moreover, entirely without historical justification, Dante represents the Latin poet as a secret convert to Christianity (at the time of imperial persecution) and, indeed, the only Christian who, in a great *coup de théâtre*, is released from penance in the course of Dante's three days on the Mountain. The implications of this exuberant invention (see notes to this canto) are only complicated and deepened when Statius in the course of the episode claims to have been not only taught how to write epic poetry through observing Virgil's example but also taught how to be a Christian by reading Virgil's *Fourth Eclogue*. (See *Purgatorio* 22: 73.)

Consider, likewise, Dante's treatment of Ovid. In terms purely of narrative technique, Ovid may well be regarded as a greater influence on the *Commedia* than Virgil is. Ovid's *Metamorphoses* are deliberately anti-Virgilian in their spectacular and often amoral portrayal of a shifting and unstable world of physical transformations. The appeal of Ovid's narrative lies in its cultivation of sensuous effect, shock, horror and fictional extravagance. And Dante in *Inferno* 25: 97 – where he depicts the phantasmagoric transformation of sinners into snakes and snakes into sinners – can explicitly claim to outdo anything Ovid might have achieved. Yet Ovid's work remains an influence even in the *Paradiso*. When, in *Paradiso* 1, Dante imagines his own unimaginable transformation on entering a world of pure intelligence, the text he draws upon is Ovid's account of how Glaucus became a sea god. (See *Paradiso* 1: 67–72.) In the same canto, at lines 19–21, when the poet invokes Apollo, in addition to the Muses, he also recalls the Ovidian story of Marsyas, the satyr who challenged Apollo to a flute-playing contest and, on losing, was flayed alive. This violent act is now seen as a metaphor for inspiration, by virtue of which Dante seeks to be wholly possessed by the example and presence of Apollo, who can be understood to be Christ himself.

The two principles underlying Dante's treatment of classical literature are those of assimilation and experiment. And these principles extend also to his handling of Scriptural reference and the allusions he makes to the vernacular literature of his own day. He has constant recourse to the narratives of the Judaic and Christian traditions, in citation, particularly of the Psalms, the prophetic books, the Gospels and the Book of Revelation. Although these citations are usually less explicit than his quotations from classical texts, they are far greater in number. Commonly, Scriptural reference is combined with classical (see, for instance, *Purgatorio* 30: 10–21), and, in this regard, Dante shows himself to be syncretist, claiming to reconcile all forms of literary text – whether classical, Scriptural or Christian – in a manifestation of how divine truth is progressively revealed through history.

In his dealings with the contemporary literature in the vernacular tradition, Dante, while claiming superiority by virtue of his interest in classical literature, engages at all points with the works of poets who have immediately preceded him. At times his treatment is polemical, as in *Inferno* 28, where the troubadour poet Bertran de Born (for whom Dante had once expressed admiration) appears as a decapitated corpse in one of the most violent cantos of the *cantica*. At other points, Dante acknowledges the influence of poets of the Occitan literature of southern France (which inspired the rise of vernacular literature throughout Europe), as when Arnaut Daniel is placed at the summit of Purgatory, speaking indeed in a Dantean version of his own mother tongue (*Purgatorio* 26: 142–7). Dante, in his celebration of Beatrice, will certainly claim to have taken this tradition to a higher level. But from first to last, he can only do so, on his own account, because he has appropriated and refined the lyric poetry that preceded him. The same may be said of his references to the narrative traditions in the vernacular, whose main examples of narrative had been the prose romances in French concerning the Arthurian legends of errant and love-lorn knights. The essential form of these narratives is that of the quest. And Dante may have been conscious of having enriched this tradition and also to have seen its shortcomings. His own narrative is not only an epic poem on the model of the *Aeneid* but also a romance, a quest for lost love, an ordeal displaying the virtues and prowess of the lover in the eyes of the lady. Indeed, in *Inferno* 1, Virgil's enigmatic appearance carries with it something of the aura of a fable and far-off legend, as – refusing to name himself – he lays before Dante a series of cryptic hints as to who he is and what Dante's destiny must be.

## Human Being: Philosophy and Theology in the *Commedia*

Among the most distinctive features of Dante's narrative in the *Commedia* is its interest in the psychology, actions and fate of the human individual. It is this concern that has led readers to place the *Commedia* alongside the plays of the Elizabethan period and the great novels of the nineteenth century. Shake-speare is unlikely to have read Dante's work, but he shares with him an interest in representing people at points of crisis. Hon-oré de Balzac in his *Comédie humaine* (1842–53) consciously attempts to emulate the detail and variety that Dante brings to his observation of human beings. Dante is undoubtedly sensi-tive to the appeal exerted by the voices of particular and recognizable (usually historical) people. Supremely skilful at creating such voices, he is clearly conscious of the deep pathos that arises in contemplating the loss or destruction of these individuals. The most familiar example occurs in *Inferno* 5, where Dante represents the delicate figure of the adulterous Francesca trapped in the filigree of her own fine sentiments in a way that could be taken to anticipate Gustave Flaubert's Ma-dame Bovary. There are almost as many comparable characters in the *Commedia* as there are cantos. And many readers of the poem – especially if they are influenced by nineteenth-century styles of interpretation – are, not unreasonably, content to focus their attentions on such dominant personalities as the Florentine patriot Farinata (*Inferno* 10), the intellectual adven-turer Ulysses (*Inferno* 26) or Count Ugolino, the agonized but cannibalistic father of *Inferno* 33.

Yet for all Dante's evident interest in the details of human behaviour, he also sets himself to explore fully the ethical rela-tionships that could or should exist, in the social sphere, between one individual and another. Equally, under the impulse of his theological vision, his poem is intended to reveal the most fundamental relationship of all, that between all human beings and the source of their being 'in the hand of God'. (See especially *Purgatorio* 16.) This exploration begins, in the *Inferno*, with a realization of how disastrously human indi-viduals can be divided from their own true selves, from their fellow creatures and from their Creator. Then, progressively in the *Purgatorio* and the *Paradiso*, the poet recuperates an under-standing of what our lives were always at their best intended to be. But in the course of this long investigation, he develops a view (sometimes, it seems, to his own amazement) that directly challenges some of the preconceptions that the reader, especially the modern reader, is likely to bring to the text. The points at issue are both philosophical and theological. The first concerns the structure of the human being, in particular the connection between mind and body. The second concerns the ways in which we think about good and evil.

In philosophical terms, Dante may, in a certain sense, be regarded as a great rationalist. Virgil, as his guide in both Hell and Purgatory, is frequently taken as an allegorical representation of our rational faculties. It is also evident that Dante, as a philosopher, was deeply indebted (as was Saint Thomas Aquinas) to the Greek philosopher Aristotle, whom he describes (at *Inferno* 4: 132) as 'the master of all those who think and know'. Indeed, initially sin is diagnosed from a rational point of view, unaided or unimpeded by specifically Christian categories of thought. One might even say that sin in the *Inferno* is seen less as an offence against God than as a crime against humanity, in which the clarity of rational perception is fatally clouded or perverted. It follows from this that the worst of sins, according to the plan of Hell, is not lust or greed or even avarice but rather treachery, which is punished at the very centre of Hell. Traitors – whether to family, friends or nation – undermine the best institutions that human beings have rationally established. They are now imprisoned in ice; and this punishment is an exact indication of how, in Dante's view, treachery wholly extinguishes the fruitful capacity for love that exists in all individuals.

In speaking, however, of Dante's rationalism, one needs also to emphasize that his view of reason is by no means identical to that which has become familiar since the European Enlightenment (and still dominates the popular view). We may now suppose, taking science as our model, that hypothesis, experiment and the dispassionate assessment of evidence are the essential characteristics of rational procedure. Dante would not wholly dissent. To this understanding, however, with its emphasis upon neutrality of view and clarity of neutral analysis, he would add the realization that reason is the central factor in our ethical lives and is deeply engaged in our pursuit of happiness. On the account offered in the central cantos of the *Purgatorio* (16 and 17), the core of human personality is freedom of the will. And, for Dante, it is the will that impels us constantly to pursue those objects and purposes that bring us, individually, to fruition but also lead us to collaborate with those whose lives are lived alongside our own. As the *Inferno* demonstrates, Hell is the condition of those who refused in the course of their lives to free themselves from destructively self-imprisoning appetites. The *Purgatorio* and *Paradiso* proceed to investigate how wide the field of human possibilities might be if people set their minds upon the pursuit of rational freedom. Dantean reason, therefore, is concerned less with the production of logically valid assertions than with the search for what is truly good. It is also the common bond between all human beings engaged upon this search. In this respect the possession of reason carries with it a commitment to discourse: to argument, but also to conversation and persuasion; to logic, but also to rhetoric. Correspondingly, the characters whom Dante condemns or applauds represent the many historical figures from whom he sought to disassociate himself or towards whom, as members of the intellectual community, he owed some particular debt of gratitude.

Where the mind is expected to engage in the pursuit of rational good, what part does the body have to play in such a journey? There is scarcely an episode in the *Commedia* that does not in some way focus upon the human body, its gestures and its dynamics. Sodomites dance like greased gymnasts under a rain of fire (*Inferno* 16); blind penitents tilt back their heads – as the visually impaired observably do (*Purgatorio* 13); saints yearn towards God like babies seeking milk at their mother's breast (*Paradiso* 23). Behind such details lies a philosophical perspective, infused by Christian belief, that marks Dante off from any school of thought that disparages or recoils from the physicality of the human condition. Nothing would seem more natural than to insist upon a division between body and spirit, and to locate the core of human identity in its spiritual characteristics. But Dante is no dualist. His very conception of a human soul denies that he could be. For Dante – as for Aristotle – the soul, or (in Italian) *anima*, is neither more nor less than the *animating* form of the body. All forms of life that are capable even of minimal self-motivation are endowed with a soul, whether vegetable, animal or rational, which impels them to seek what is good for their existence, be it food, procreation or pleasure. Human beings differ from other life forms only in having more complex forms of good to pursue if they are to survive and flourish: reading, music, friendship and social cohesion are just some of these. But none of these are attainable without physical effort and thus they include and subsume animal motivations. Reading requires a healthy and attentive eye, for instance; friendship requires a handclasp. We are rational beings, but we live our lives in and through the specific stories that our physical existence in space and time demands that we should enter. This is what being human means and, for Dante, it is good that this should be so.

It remains true, of course, that human beings can themselves, however, traduce and distort the value of the body. Gluttons, for instance, are guilty of this, and are shown to have reduced the world around them to a morass of undifferentiated matter (*Inferno* 6). Gluttony is an unending and unchanging appetite for one type of object – the merely edible – and so distracts attention from the many other objects of intelligent attention to which human beings must freely choose to turn if they are to satisfy the requirements of their complex and subtle nature. For Dante the human individual is, then, best seen as neither purely rational nor fixedly material, but rather as essentially psychosomatic. The body displays its value when it moves, when it shifts, when it suffers or when it poises itself beautifully in the pursuit of some freely chosen objective.

But if these are the philosophical conclusions to which Dante's poem is pointing, then they are confirmed, in a theological perspective, by the understanding at which Dante arrives in the final canto of the *Paradiso*: human beings are formed in the image of God and the greatest mystery of existence is that, in seeking God, we are seeking what we all along have truly been. Here, at the end, Dante is simultaneously overwhelmed and enlivened as he contemplates a God who cannot be circumscribed by any intellectual or geometric construct but is simply our own image (*Paradiso* 33: 133–8) looking back at us. Pursuing the theological implications of this understanding, it needs to be emphasized that God for Dante is the infinite principle on which all other forms of existence – and supremely the human form – is always dependent. Only the goodness of God's activity can be said fully to exist. Conversely, one needs to emphasize that evil, as Dante comes to demonstrate in the *Inferno*, is nothing other than the negation of life in all its manifestations. Especially to modern ears, any such suggestion is likely to sound unfamiliar. For if we are now inclined to find sin romantically attractive (at least in literature), then so, too, we have become accustomed to the idea that evil is interesting.

This tendency has its roots in William Blake's observation that Milton in his depiction of Lucifer was 'of the devil's party without knowing it'. Since Blake first ventured this suggestion, it has become a wearisome cliché that spectacular displays of wickedness, which in real life would be abominable, are somehow more engaging in a literary work than a concern with goodness.

To Dante this would have been an utter nonsense. One of the many surprises that the *Inferno* holds for the modern reader is that the climax of the *cantica*, with its final vision of Satan, proves in effect to be an *anti*-climax. Satan is spectacularly ugly, a three-faced abomination whose gigantic limbs are covered with clumps of shaggy hair. In spite of this, he is far from being a threatening presence. He is, after all, capable only of two endlessly repeated actions: his bat-like wings flapping perpetually to refrigerate the frozen depths of Hell, and his three mouths endlessly gnawing away at the three sinners who are located between his jaws. But behind the dramatic non-event of Dante's encounter with Satan lies a theology which leads us back to a full understanding of the transcendent divine. For in Dante's view (*Paradiso* 19: 46–8), Satan fell not through an act of rebellion but rather through stupid impatience. God, as infinity of being, can and will answer the desire that finite creatures have for illumination. But Lucifer, although created to be the summit of all light-bearing beings, simply would not wait for light progressively to reveal itself, but 'fell . . . acid, unripe'. Evil, then, is pure inactivity, existing only as a distorted silhouette of divine activity. Dante himself suggests this when he chooses to endow his Satan with three gruesome faces. This feature invites us immediately to see Satan as a mere parody of the Trinity, dependent even for the minimal life he possesses on a goodness beyond his own self-imprisoned being.

All too frequently, readers are led by another modern preconception to suppose that the *Paradiso* will be nothing other than a sequence of repetitious sermons or a monotonous harping on images of music and light. But it is Hell that for Dante is the realm of banal monotony (one damned thing after another). Conversely, goodness is more original than sin. It is the prismatic source of variety in image, discourse and narrative invention. The very nature of Dante's Heaven is that it should rejoice, participating in the infinite activity of the divine, in constantly productive change. Heaven is, as Dante puts it, a 'sempiternal springtime' (*Paradiso* 28: 116), a constant reinvigoration, a purposeful new beginning and an unending refreshment.

## Dante and Beatrice

Among the innumerable figures that are represented in the *Commedia*, there is one above all who embodies the full spectrum of human possibility. This is Dante himself. And no episode more fully demonstrates this than the intensely dramatic sequence at the climax of the *Purgatorio*, where Dante describes the coming of Beatrice and the simultaneous disappearance of Virgil (*Purgatorio* 30). The arrival of Beatrice is represented as a moment of revelation or conversion in which Dante fully recognizes the grounds on which our existence as God's creatures depends. God has created Beatrice, and though to human eyes she has died an early death, He has sustained her and restored her to life. So, too, Dante now displays in the drama of the episode how he himself, having been almost lost to sin, has also been sustained and made ready to enter Heaven.

Over the space of two cantos (*Purgatorio* 30–31), Beatrice lays bare the sins that Dante has committed since the moment of her death. And the source of his sin is shown to be his failure to rejoice precisely in the existence that she as God's creature had been granted or to recognize that God, the joyous Creator, has destined all human beings to happiness. Strength of will, rational discourse and justice will never cease to be celebrated in Dante's poem, even though Virgil – hitherto the representative of such virtues – is from now on absent. Once Beatrice has drawn Dante back to a true understanding of his relation to her and the God to whom she points, virtue is to be understood as, itself, a joyous exercise of all our faculties and the fulfilment of all the potentialities that we, as creatures, were originally intended to possess. And it is precisely this joy that Virgil – and all he represents – could never, on Dante's account, be fully aware of. Tragically, Virgil is after all an inhabitant of Limbo, where, suffering no pain, he is still able to be neither happy nor sad (*Inferno* 4: 84). The converse of this tragedy, as revealed now by Beatrice, is the comically unexpected truth voiced at *Purgatorio* 30: 75 that human beings were made to be happy. And if, as has been suggested earlier, we should properly speak of the human being as psychosomatic in Dante's view, then this revelation involves the very roots of Dante's bodily as well as spiritual existence. So in the face of Beatrice Dante shows himself to be reduced to the state of an infant, wracked by sobs and sighs. Even when he wishes to agree with her condemnation of his faithlessness, he is unable to utter the simple word 'yes'. Beatrice herself is left to read it on his lips, as it forms there, unspoken. But this is also the moment of his entry into the new life. From this point, the *Commedia* is an account of his true growing up, and the *Paradiso*, in that light, is a testimony to his spiritual and intellectual adulthood. Now liberated from misconception, Dante can exercise and enjoy to the full the variety of discourse and the richness of imagination that a complete understanding of Beatrice – and happiness – inspire in him.

A footnote is necessary here. It has become a commonplace among students of the *Commedia* to draw a distinction between Dante as author of the poem and Dante as a character within its fiction. This can be useful, but it should be borne in mind that Dante as author of the *Commedia* conspicuously bequeaths to the timorous and sometimes comic character who bears his name many of the same historical figures – whether condemnable enemies or laudable associates – that he, in real life, is known to have encountered. Nor should attention to the drama surrounding the Dante character distract one from the equally dramatic and ever present voice of the poet himself, who struggles with his theme (as, for instance, at *Inferno* 1: 4, 32: 1–12 and *Paradiso* 23: 55–69), draws attention to his own achievements or intentions (*Inferno* 25: 94–102, *Purgatorio* 1: 7–12 and *Paradiso* 1: 13–33) or, indeed, speaks of his poem as a means to the restoration of his reputation among his fellow Florentines (*Paradiso* 25: 1–9).

Often, the similarity between Dante the poet and Dante the character is more significant than the difference. This is certainly the case in *Purgatorio* 30, the episode where he allows his own name to appear in the text, spoken by Beatrice. The meeting that he depicts between himself and Beatrice is, in the fullest sense, a piece of confessional writing. Dante here openly acknowledges – through the speeches he gives to Beatrice – the failings of which he is inclined to convict himself. He also confesses to the truths of the faith that are now bringing him to salvation. Saint Augustine, in his *Confessions* (AD 397–8), represents himself simultaneously as a sinner and a vessel of revelation. Likewise Dante throughout his poem offers an account his own best and worst achievements, as poet and as exile, as a confused and suffering Florentine and equally as the lover of Beatrice. The *Commedia* is no mere fiction.

## Reading the *Commedia*

When Dante speaks at *Purgatorio* 32: 103 of his purposes in writing the *Commedia*, he declares that he writes 'to aid the world that lives all wrong'. This dictum immediately points a finger at the reader – particularly, perhaps, at the modern reader, who is unused to literature that directs itself so unambiguously at the conscience. What does it mean to read a work that is driven by such an intention? What 'benefit' is likely to accrue from our doing so? Supposing there were a benefit for

Dante's original readers, is it likely to be the same for the many subsequent generations that have valued his poem so highly?

One familiar answer leads us to assume that Dante is writing an allegorical poem in which, beyond the complications of narrative surface, there are other meanings that reflect some clear and comprehensive vision of an ultimate truth. Over the centuries, such a reading of the *Commedia* has produced significant results. For instance, we should hardly be able to make the useful distinctions between Virgil as a figure for unaided reason and Beatrice as a figure for revelation if a long tradition of allegorical exegesis had not sanctioned this. Dante was clearly interested in that mode of interpretation. In the *Convivio* (*c.* 1304–7) he offers an allegorical reading of three of his own *canzoni*, and allegory is a feature of the few vernacular narratives that preceded Dante's own, as, for instance, in the French *Roman de la rose*. (An Italian version of this poem, *Il Fiore* (1285–?1295), may have been written by Dante himself.) Then, too, there is the evidence of the famous *Epistle to Can Grande*, which offers an allegorical reading of the opening lines of the *Paradiso*. This work (of uncertain date) may not after all have been written by Dante. (The debate continues.) Yet if it is not by Dante himself, it must still represent an approach adopted by of one of his near-contemporary readers.

It is, none the less, doubtful whether we can describe the *Commedia* as a medieval allegory without considerable qualification. For one thing, even in his explicitly allegorical *Convivio*, Dante noticeably tires of seeking a multiplicity of levels of meaning in his own text. Increasingly his attention falls not upon the *other* meanings that might lie beneath the text (*allegoria* means to speak 'otherwise', strangely or differently) but upon the interest of the *literal* meaning. So when Dante is speaking of the planetary system, he may indeed derive an allegorical meaning from the characteristics he observes in the planets, associating each with one of the subjects studied in the university syllabuses of his time: Venus, for instance, may, in the *Convivio*, be designated as a figure for the art of rhetoric, able to persuade and inspire others by her clarity and beauty. Even in the *Paradiso* there is some residual sense of this. (See

*Paradiso* 8–9.) Yet Venus remains, literally, a planet and as such invites the scientific eye to examine it. Such a reading, far from directing us to any hidden meaning, asks us to contemplate directly the design that God has wrought within the created universe.

The original purpose of allegorical (or typological) interpretation was to reveal in the Scriptures a providential meaning such as could then continue to nurture the life of the Church, in liturgy, prayer and pastoral practice. If Dante is indeed seeking to educate the world that lives amiss, then his aim is exactly comparable. His concern is not merely to offer in the coded form of allegory a body of doctrine or authoritative information. Rather, he seeks to engage his reader in the full exercise of all their faculties – rational, discursive, perceptual and imaginative – and to concentrate this exercise on the particular situations which might disturb, encourage or delight the attentive mind. So in *Inferno* 1, Dante may at first appear to be offering his reader a simple allegorical lesson, in depicting how his escape from the dark wood is impeded by three beasts which can, not unhelpfully, be identified respectively as Self-indulgent Pleasure, Pride and Avarice. Yet any so abstract an approach is overturned completely by the appearance of Virgil, who at once brings Dante to think about the specific and wholly literal role that Rome plays in history as the agent of divine providence. And the canto concludes with Virgil's insistence that Dante must now prepare himself to encounter, first, the 'shrill cries' (line 115) of those in Hell who have put themselves beyond the embrace of providence and then to see under Virgil's guidance in Purgatory the souls of those who live in hope of Paradise.

For Dante the most fundamental act of the mind is that of seeing. A glance at a concordance will immediately reveal that words referring to eyes and sight in frequency far exceed all others. And the educative process embodied in the *Commedia*, involving the reader no less than Dante himself on his journey, is one which reveals the widest possible spectrum of modes of perception, ranging from mystic ecstasy to nightmare surreality – and amply including, in often unexpected places, the precise observation of, say, animals wriggling in a sack

(*Paradiso* 26: 97–9) or the vibrations of an Adam's apple (*Inferno* 23: 88). Dante, as T. S. Eliot insists, is a visual poet (*Dante* (1929)), thus suggesting one of the reasons why he himself was so drawn to the *Commedia* in the imagist phase of his career. At all points, the Dantean eye moves constantly between the patterns of cosmological movement registered in the stars to the finest details of earthly life – then back again.

In parallel with such optical exercises, Dante also calls upon his readers to train themselves in the field of speech and language. While vision may ultimately rise to heights to which language cannot aspire – thus Beatrice, who leads Dante to his final epiphany, is always superior to Virgil, who from the first is seen as Dante's teacher in the use of language – words are of utmost importance. They are the medium in which Dante himself is supremely a craftsman, one of the hallmarks of his style being a readiness to drawn upon all available registers of language, whether high or low, so as to dramatize or define his meaning.

At all times, the dominant feature of Dante's text is an incisive precision of word and syntax. Indeed, he is unfailingly conscious of how words, honest, exact and finely tuned, are the best remedy against the Babel that sin and evil generate. (See *Inferno* 14: 61–3.) Above all, language well used is the necessary medium that human beings employ in all those relationships of justice and love which properly they were created to cultivate. Thus, alongside the vocabulary of sight, a crucial word throughout Dante's poem is '*rispondere*' ('to answer'). Language is a field of both response and responsibility. In Hell, all conversation is radically distorted. In Paradise, it flows freely from tongue to ear. In the *Purgatorio* – which in this regard is the subtlest sequence of the *Commedia* – conversation always represents a productive negotiation between persons, leading them towards the restoration of that harmony of understanding that human beings were originally intended to enjoy. (See, for example, *Purgatorio* 23.)

But what are the implications of this for a present reading of the *Commedia*? In one sense, when stressing the primacy of seeing in Dante's poem, it might be supposed that the *Commedia* requires us to defer to an author who, on his own account, had received the highest and most comprehensive vision of all. Does Dante assume the mantle of a prophet? There can be no doubt that, in common with the voice of prophets such as Ezekiel and Jeremiah, Dante's voice is more authoritative and, often, aggressive than any other poet's has ever been. Yet it would be wrong to suppose that this characteristic, exhilarating as it can be, is the one defining feature of his authorial stance. For this would be to disregard the fundamental commitment that Dante displays to the possibility of a restored linguistic cooperation. At all points, Dante – who has a high regard for the virtue of humility – is concerned to teach his reader by offering an invitation to an act of collaboration. As Virgil collaborates with Dante in his journey through the afterlife, so Dante collaborates with his reader. And this is nowhere more apparent than in the *Paradiso*. For too long it has been mistakenly represented as a series of magisterial expositions demanding of the modern reader as much attention to the scholarly footnote as to the text itself. Yet throughout this *cantica*, Dante repeatedly speaks to his reader in terms of collaborative endeavour, as though the theological import of his writing could only be delivered through discussion and shared enthusiasm. (See *Paradiso* 10: 7–10.) In this part of the poem Dante proves to be more experimental in his narrative and freer in his imagination than at any other point in the *Commedia*, constantly envisaging new and varied formulations of imagery and light-effect. The profit of this, for the reader, lies precisely (as, for instance, at *Paradiso* 13: 1–21) in the stretch which our own imaginations are invited to make.

A single word crystallizes the impulse behind Dante's narrative invention: 'why'. Why is it that Dante chooses Virgil as his guide? This question – which carries with it also the question of why virtuous pagans must be condemned to Limbo – continues throughout the *Commedia* (in, for instance, *Purgatorio* 6: 28–41 and 28) and is, if anything, sharpened rather than resolved when Dante finally addresses it in *Paradiso* 19 and 20. But the whole poem is punctuated by similar if lesser questions. Why is it that a great teacher such as Brunetto Latini should appear in Hell (*Inferno* 15) as if all along he had been an insidiously corrupting influence? Why is the Roman suicide Cato promoted to the guardianship of the Christian realm of Purgatory (*Purgatorio* 1)? Why is Piccarda Donati, a failed nun and the sister of Dante's most vicious enemy, triumphantly entrusted (in *Paradiso* 3) with one of the poet's most important discussions of freedom and divine harmony? We ask 'why?' in these cases (and in all the others which these exemplify), and immediately we begin to participate in the ethical endeavours of the poet himself – in the exercise of intelligence, in the attempt to see things afresh and to free our speech from confusion. The *Commedia*, then, through its constant interrogatives avoids any arrogant affirmation of certitude and acknowledges the essential relativity and interdependence of all human activity. (In this respect, it has much in common with other great comedies.) To ask 'why?' is also a source of pleasure, and this is where the benefit of reading the *Commedia* may still reside. For Dante, ethical benefit is not, in the end, the product of constraint, rule, duty or devotion to infallible principles. It is a matter, rather, of the flourishing that occurs when the possibilities latent in human nature are most fully exercised. It is a condition of pleasure. The last words that Virgil – hitherto the voice of common-sense restraint – speaks to Dante (*Purgatorio* 27: 131) include the line: 'take what pleases you to be your guide.'

## The Future of Dante's *Commedia*

Dante occupies a peculiar position in the canon of European literature. Since the beginning of the nineteenth century the poet has been recognized, with increasing confidence, as (to quote John Ruskin) 'the most central man in all the world'. Henry Cary, Percy Bysshe Shelley, Dante Gabriel Rossetti and even Alfred, Lord Tennyson and Henry Wadsworth Longfellow give colour to this view. The twentieth century, in its own more analytical and hard-headed way, added to this claim. Dante over the last eighty years has become an awe-inspiring but none the less practical model for writers as different as

T. S. Eliot and James Joyce, Osip Mandelstam and Samuel Beckett, Jorge Luis Borges, Seamus Heaney, Primo Levi and Derek Walcott. More recently still, the artist Tom Phillips and the film-maker Peter Greenaway in a *TV Dante* (1989) seem to have discovered in the *Commedia* a stimulus to visual experimentation in the modern idiom.

This is not to say that Dante's importance went unrecognized in earlier centuries. In his native Florence, especially, during the fourteenth and fifteenth centuries, the *Commedia* became an icon of the cultural and, sometimes, political prestige to which his native city increasingly laid claim. Commentaries were written on Dante's work by Florentines and others throughout the fourteenth century. Boccaccio, in the last years of his life, contributed to the cult with lectures on the *Commedia* and a *Treatise in Praise of Dante* (*c.* 1351–5). Botticelli executed a long sequence of supremely intelligent drawings illustrating the poem. Michelangelo not only drew motifs from the *Inferno* in painting his *Last Judgement* (1535–41) in the Sistine Chapel, but yearned, in his sonnets, to emulate the supposedly melancholic genius of his Florentine master. Beyond the city, Dante's reputation as a poet affected Geoffrey Chaucer very deeply – and no one has written more intelligent parodies of Dante's work than Chaucer in *The Wife of Bath's Prologue* (1387–92?) and *The House of Fame* (1379–80). Marguerite de Navarre, the brilliant sister of the French king Francis I, provides a very searching treatment of the *Commedia* in her evangelical poem *Les Prisons* (1548). Others were impressed by Dante's political and religious thinking which – especially in its anti-ecclesiastical aspect – provided ammunition to the Protestant movement. His *De Monarchia* was cited by members of the court of the English king Henry VIII.

It has to be admitted that, over a certain span of centuries – stretching from the Renaissance to the Enlightenment – Dante's voice was not as prominent as it later became. In large part, this is due to the counter-influence of his Italian successor Francesco Petrarch (1304–74), who displays towards the *Commedia* a version of that literary paranoia which Harold Bloom has called 'the anxiety of influence', refusing to keep a copy of Dante's poem on

INTRODUCTION                                                    xxxix

his shelves lest it overshadow the development of his own talent. For Petrarch, the very qualities of Dante's language and vision that recommended him to subsequent generations were the features that he himself wished to avoid and replace. Petrarch's vernacular writings, introspectively focused on the travails of his love for Laura, cultivate qualities of melodic refinement which display nothing of the controversial frictions and spurts of aggression that characterize Dante's work. Likewise, where Dante never hesitated to use a vulgarism, if that is what was needed, and, generally, developed a vocabulary of the widest possible range (see *Inferno* 21 and 22), Petrarch deliberately restricted his own lexical spectrum, in the interests of literary polish. And in doing so he established a standard of poetic diction that was to prevail for much of the Renaissance, in Italy and elsewhere.

It would be inappropriate here to pursue the debate that developed in Italy between Danteans and Petrarchans. It is enough to say that when Dante's text began to be discovered anew, this discovery was a part of that reaction against Enlightenment and Renaissance modes of thought that was initiated by the nineteenth-century Romantics. The Romantic interest in the sublime could readily be stirred by the sheer ambition of Dante's philosophical project. The minds of both author and reader are tested to the full by the scope of the poem and stretched beyond their normal competence. An energy beyond the control of urbanity or good taste was unleashed by the driving force of his vision. And to some, such as Shelley and Blake, this could be put to political use in their offensive against the constrictions of eighteenth-century culture. Meanwhile, Italian exiles and thinkers such as Ugo Foscolo (1778–1827) and Gabriele Rossetti (1783–1854) found in Dante's work a source of inspiration for political reform. Equally, an appetite for the grotesque and uncanny could easily be stimulated – as in the illustrations of Gustave Doré and Eugène Delacroix – by a reading particularly of the *Inferno*.

The twentieth century developed its own version of this initial response. In its vision of the 'heart of darkness', to borrow Joseph Conrad's phrase, the *Inferno* continued to excite the general reader. The *Commedia* as a whole could also offer a remarkable resource to many who, in their own lives, were compelled to confront those hellish consequences of supposedly enlightened thinking that were revealed in the progressivism of the early communist regimes and the industrial horrors of the concentration camps. Osip Mandelstam, persecuted by the Soviet state, not only felt a kinship with the exiled Dante (as had Fyodor Dostoevsky before him), but also embraced Dante's political vision of Rome as a just and universal authority. Later, Primo Levi took Dante's understanding of knowledge as the truest human requirement to be an indispensable source of hope amid the unremitting horrors of Auschwitz.

It is not merely the vision that Dante offers, but also his precision of thought and language that appealed to the minds of Mandelstam and Levi. As an example of how disaster may be encountered and transformed, Dante offers to both of these writers a work which succeeds because it attends with scientific honesty to the details of the world, recognizing that exactitude of observation and phrase is the precondition of all communication between human beings. The same concern with precision in language and imagination – above all when faced with the collapse of civilized order or the day-to-day evidence of malice in a divided community – accounts for the interest displayed, for instance, by writers as different as Ezra Pound and Seamus Heaney. In *The Cantos* (1917–69), Pound attempts to weld an alliance between Chinese thinking and medieval thought (drawing on Cavalcanti as well as upon Dante), which could conceivably re-animate the language of the lost tribes of Europe. Heaney – particularly in his collection from 1991, *Seeing Things* – repeatedly turns to Dante (as Joyce did also) in his attempt to record those epiphanies, or moments of revelation, that can arise from the sudden perception of value in, for instance, a dust-veined beam of light.

It is notable, however, that in the twentieth century attention shifted away from the excitements of the *Inferno* to that subtler understanding of process and the constantly renewed attention to detail that Dante pursues in the *Purgatorio*. The only remote analogy for Dante's highly original conception of Purgatory, as an island located in the southern hemisphere, is Station Island in Lough Derg, County Donegal – still a site of penitential practice. Heaney recognized this in his 1984 collection entitled *Station Island*. It was, however, T. S. Eliot and Samuel Beckett – the one a founding father of modernism, the other the acknowledged master of post-modernism – who between them made the most sustained claims for the *Purgatorio*. These two great experimentalists each discovered in Dante ways of writing and thinking that offered a release from the encumbrances of more recent cultural baggage.

At the conclusion of *The Waste Land* (1922), Eliot alludes to the episode in *Purgatorio* 26 where Dante depicts the soul of the troubadour poet Arnaut Daniel hiding himself 'in the fire that sharpens'. The way to redemption – and to linguistic vitality – lies through a constant and often agonizing return to our origins and the roots of our tradition. This becomes Eliot's Christian theme in *Four Quartets* (1943): 'We shall not cease from exploration / And the end of all our exploring / Will be to arrive where we started / And know the place for the first time.' Dante in exile discovered a similar truth and translated it into the questing experience of the second *cantica*. Beckett died with a copy of the *Commedia* at his bedside. Throughout his writing career he had taken, as his own alter ego, the character of the indolent Belacqua who appears in *Purgatorio* 4. Above all, Beckett's concern with 'waiting' as a condition of human existence exactly mirrors a major theme of the early *Purgatorio*.

If the *Inferno* dominated the response of the nineteenth century to Dante's poem, and the *Purgatorio* that of the twentieth century, we are still waiting for the *Paradiso* to take the place it deserves in defining his overall achievement. The day is perhaps not far off. In Italy, the lectures on Dante's theology given by the film-maker and comedian Roberto Benigni (b. 1952; best known for his film *Life is Beautiful*) have attracted large audiences. And the present translation in its small way is an attempt to reveal in English the vivacity of word and imagination that is still to be discovered in the *Paradiso*.

## Dante's Language and the Question of Translation

For any translator of the *Commedia* it is chastening to discover that Dante himself thought translation to be impossible. In his early philosophical treatise the *Convivio*, he declares at 1: 7 that 'nothing which is bound together in harmonious form by musical ligatures can possibly be translated from one language into another without losing entirely its sweetness and harmony'. Doomed, however, as any translator of the *Commedia* might be, he or she cannot rightly ignore Dante's discussion, in his theoretical writings, of such matters.

To read a poem by him is, in a real sense, to enter into responsible and responsive connection with another 'person', body as well as mind. There are, indeed, cases in the early *canzoni* (as for instance, the envoi of '*Tre Donne intorno al cor . . .*' (*c.* 1303–4), which expresses Dante's despairing love of justice) where the poet formally addresses the poem he has written as if it were in fact a human being, capable of independent life or even of suffering the wandering existence of the exile himself. Nor is this a vague metaphor. There are exact and technical equivalents in Dante's style to both mind and body, and to the 'harmonies and ligatures' that ensure a fully psychosomatic interaction. Grammar and syntax have their part to play in this, as do the physical patternings of metre, rhythm and rhyme. And all of these features demand close attention from the translator.

To consider first the 'mind': in the *De Vulgari Eloquentia* (*c.* 1304–5), Dante speaks of the need in poetry for tightness of structure; the poet is one who has worked 'with strenuous intelligence' on this aspect of his art, learning the principles at least from a study of Latin (*De Vulgari Eloquentia* 2: 4: 10). In English we are not accustomed to poets who are thrilled by the sequences of cause, effect, concession and logical linkage that syntax is designed to indicate, but syntax for Dante is the voice of intelligence, seeking exactitude of understanding, psychological consequence and philosophical affirmation. This is a poet who relishes the word 'therefore'. The structure of any single verse in his poem is articulated by the ways in which grammatical considerations of subordination, consequence and conclusion determine the pauses that occur at caesurae and line-endings. Translators need to be alert to such considerations. Indeed, one of the reasons why Dante is relatively easy to translate (as Shakespeare is not) is that the progress of his thought is always very clearly marked. This is also the reason why a non-Italian reader often finds it easier to arrive at an exact meaning in a verse – rather than a prose – translation. Verse that has learned anything at all from Dante will deliver the sense of the original in a clearly articulated form, with grammatical connectors always clearly indicated.

If syntax is the 'mind' of Dante's writing, then metre and rhyme are its phonetic 'body'. The standard unit of metre – throughout the *Commedia*, as in most of Dante's lyric poems – is an eleven-syllable line, which concludes (almost) invariably with a stressed followed by an unstressed syllable. It is our expectation of this final cadence that governs the musical pattern of the line, and though Dante's versification acknowledges the importance of stress, it does not rely as heavily upon it in the first nine syllables as does the English iambic pentameter. Dante's regular eleven syllables can, in most cases, only be so numbered if account is taken of elisions between adjacent vowels. Puckerings and pleatings in the metrical fabric occur as vowel flows into vowel; and by virtue of these elisions a line that contains, apparently, fourteen otherwise separate syllables can regularly be reduced to eleven. It is usual (but again not invariable) for any single line to subdivide, according to the demands of clause or phrase structure, around some midpoint, either at the fourth or sixth syllable, bringing an accent on to one or the other of these syllables. The result is a line which is very responsive to the voice as it shapes its meaning and pursues the melodic current towards the last two, rhyming syllables.

No translation is likely even to approach the voice print of Dante's verse unless it pays attention to effects such as these. But there is no real reason (save a lack of Dantean talent) why the rhythms of his eleven-syllable lines should not broadly be adopted in English. The translator needs to abandon too strong a commitment to the iamb as an organizing principle of a line. But free verse (along with Shakespeare) has taught us a great deal about how this might be achieved. The speaking voice never produces regular beats or equal stresses, but rather a constantly varied melody of half tones and quarter tones.

Rhyme, as any translator will ruefully be aware, is a different and far more complex matter. Dante devises for the *Commedia* a three-line verse form, the *terzina*, for which no plausible precursor has been found. The *terzina* aims at and makes possible a simplicity or fluidity of structure evidently desirable in a narrative poem. Yet the inherent elegance and lightness of this form is also a result of rhyme. The scheme here runs: ABA BCB CDC, and so on. That is to say, the sequence knits itself together by taking the central line-ending of one *terzina* and employing it as the initial and concluding rhyme of the following verse. The meaning of a *terzina* can sometimes be clinched as rhythm and rhyme produce an emphatic closure at the final line. It is, however, equally possible for Dante to build up larger units or verse paragraphs, all held together by the bond between the middle line of one verse and the opening line of the subsequent one. Paragraphing of this sort displays its importance when Dante sets himself to produce a sustained piece of argumentation, with logical consequences and conclusions all being grouped by the rhyming pattern (a good example would be *Paradiso* 3: 79–87). Simultaneously, such paragraphs serve the demands of narrative form, allowing for a continual variation of tempo between sustained sequences and sudden interruptions.

Some translations (such as the present) have abandoned all attempts at rhyme, tending to justify the departure by maintaining that Italian has an unfair advantage over English. Italian verse is dominated by words ending in vowels, not least because all Italian words end like this. In any case, Italian rhymes on a stressed–unstressed pair of syllables and therefore produces a far less obtrusive effect than the monosyllabic rhymes of English. (The most common rhymes in the *Commedia* are generated by the endings -*ore*, -*ia*, -*ate*, -*ente* and -*etto*.)

Others, however, have bravely contended that, granted the

use of half rhyme, translators need only gird up their rhyming loins and get on with the task ahead. There may be some virtue in this approach, and perhaps a successful version in these terms awaits us somewhere in the future. But past examples are not encouraging. All too often rhyme becomes the dominant point of interest in a line, drawing undue attention to itself and often distorting the subtleties of cadence or inflection and thrust of Dante's narrative. At worst – and the worst often happens – an obsession with regular rhyme can distract translator and reader alike from the precise implications of Dante's meaning, which is itself almost invariably precise. Conscious of such possible distortions, the translation offered here does not usually rely upon end rhyme, though at times – when a particularly conclusive effect is called for – it will produce such a rhyme. This translation has, however, been written in the conviction that the body of Dante's text is indeed of central significance. It seeks therefore to reproduce something of the aural density of the original by a consistent use of internal rhyme, assonance and alliterative patterning, seeking also, in this respect, to create a discernible phonetic design and simultaneously to replicate those effects of paragraphing and narrative orchestration which are central to Dante's enterprise.

Why did Dante decide to entitle his mature work a 'comedy'? The *canzoni* he discusses in *De Vulgari Eloquentia* are, in his understanding of the term, 'tragic' works. By this he signifies, not dramatic form or melancholic subjects, but an extreme elevation of style appropriate to the treatment of equally elevated subjects, such as love, justice or wisdom. The *canzoni* and the theory that accompanies them are also described as 'courtly' in that they speak to an elite audience of aristocratic intellects. Yet, now, attempting a work that from the first he clearly regarded as the summation of his thought and experience, Dante surprisingly chooses to write a 'comedy'. This term did not for Dante (or for medieval rhetoric in general) refer either to a theatrical genre or even, necessarily, to an interest in happy endings. It does, however, imply a new realization on Dante's part of the virtues of a moderate or median level of writing.

The comic style occupies a position from which it is possible to rise (as Dante often does) to the very summit of rhetorical display but also, as needed, to descend to the lower registers of diction and construction, either to plumb the depths of human degradation or else to demonstrate (as again he often does, at least in the *Inferno*) a perverse genius in the treatment of vulgar, scatological or obscene locutions. Such flexibility of style directly serves both a narrative and an ethical purpose. Where the lyric *canzoni* are univocal, and seek always to defend or affirm the dignity of the poet's moral *persona*, the *Commedia* dares to unleash from the echo chamber of Dante's political and intellectual memory a multiplicity of voices and tones. Many of these are vicious and contentious, as in the Babel of Hell. Many, as in the *Purgatorio*, are capable of conversational nuance. Many, too, in the *Paradiso*, are able to generate the unity and variety of a polyphonic chorus. Such diversity contributes to the dramatic impact of the *Commedia*. At the same time, the resources of common speech that Dante now claims to employ also add urgency and directness to the exposition of his philosophical understanding. With characteristic, even comic bluntness, Dante is prepared to assert, even in the *Paradiso*, that he will speak the truth boldly and openly; and as for those who resist the truth, well, 'let them scratch wherever they may itch' (*Paradiso* 17: 129).

At many points, Dante's verse can still rise to exhilarating heights of rhetoric. (See, for instance, *Purgatorio* 6 and *Paradiso* 23.) But such passages are the more remarkable in that they coexist with, and sometimes include within their orbit, the widest range of lexical choices, sometimes violent, sometimes delicate, sometimes emotively charged, sometimes bathetic. In *Paradiso* 14, the ranks of Christian philosophers respond to an extraordinarily elevated hymn, celebrating the doctrine of the Resurrection, with the shout of '*Amme*' – which is vernacular Florentine for 'Amen' – rhyming with the '*mamme*' (or 'mummies') that they hope to see again on the Day of Judgement. So, too, in *Inferno* 32, Dante will burst forth with a string of hard, exotic rhymes and locutions – '*plebe*', '*zebe*', '*converebbe*' – displaying a virtuoso delight in this extravagant sequence while also registering how dangerously far such extravagance might take him from the 'sweetness' of the poetry he wrote (and will write again) for Beatrice. The spectrum of Dante's linguistic choices is a reflection of his power to dramatize an extreme multiplicity of voices and an indication of his irrepressible virtuosity. The translator must reconcile the full range of Dante's choice of words with an orientation towards simplicity and even silence. The contemplatives of *Paradiso* 21: 81 can be described, in unexpectedly colloquial terms, as 'grindstones' 'spinning' in their circles of light. But in the following canto (line 49), Dante relies on the simplest components – the verb 'to be', the use of proper names, a central caesura – to denote the austerity and harmony that two of these contemplatives have arrived at in their monastic lives: 'Maccario is here; Romoaldo here.'

Many modern translators of the poem have recognized – just as modern critics emphasize – how 'polylingual' Dante's poetry is and have consequently sought to avoid archaism and artificiality. Not all, however, have realized that plainness is different from flatness, and that directness of address cannot always be achieved best by the adoption of merely colloquial registers. Too often those who speak most loudly of plainness have produced versions that are lexically inert and intellectually flaccid. But Dante is never loose in his choice of word, or anything less than 'strenuous' in his pursuit of meaning and effect. That, too, is a consequence of the ligatures that he seeks to tie between the mind and body of the text.

A word needs finally to be said about the figurative aspect of Dante's text, particularly in its deployment of metaphor and simile. We have come to suppose that metaphor is the supreme, even defining figure in poetic utterance, a crucible in which the imagination transforms reality as we know it to reality on some deeper level: 'Light thickens,' says Shakespeare's Macbeth, thus invoking impossible corruptions, profound pollutions and limitless evil. Dante rarely attempts such imaginative flights. His metaphors are more likely to be scarcely perceptible resurrections of long-dead tropes: a hill – in *Inferno* 1: 16–17 – has 'shoulders'. Not a striking image, yet relevant in context: Dante needs security and guidance; the hill momentarily provides it but, in the barely noticed metaphor, a space is opened that can only be filled by a guide with literal shoulders, a human being rather than a physical object, whose discourse can lead Dante, as Virgil shortly does, towards his goal.

It is, however, in simile – which to the post-Romantic reader may seem a plain and uninteresting rhetorical figure – that the Dante of the *Commedia* finds his imaginative centre. To Osip Mandelstam, Dante is 'the Descartes of simile: I compare therefore I am'. These words pithily suggest the extent to which simile, far from being a gratuitous ornament, reflects many of the essential features of Dante's vision and processes of thought. As we have seen, the created world for Dante is not (as it might be for certain Platonists) a world of illusions that we need to transform and transcend in pursuit of a higher truth. Rather, we must look clearly at the world around us, and employ the resources of sense perception and even emotional sympathy in a way that reveals the significant relationships and differences between its various phenomena. The true value of objects in the world is that they provide opportunities for the sharpening of our minds and perceptions. Thus, in *Paradiso* 14: 109–17, the souls of Christian warriors – scintillating as sparks of fire in the twin beams of a celestial cross – can be compared to motes of dust dancing in a beam of sunlight that falls through a hole in a hovel roof. We see the scene, of course, more clearly because of this homely comparison. But there is also comedy here, in the incongruity of the comparison and in the generous suggestion that even motes of dust are allowed, by association, the status of heroic beings: once perceived in relation to the Christian Crusaders, the contribution of dust particles to the created order takes on wholly unexpected significance. Comparison reveals their *raison d'être*.

A Dantean simile is, in short, an invitation to participate in a process of perception and interpretation. The task of the translator must be to allow each simile space for attention, so that the implications of the reference can unroll in parallel with the main narrative of the canto. It is usually not enough simply

to introduce this figure of speech with the sort of apparatus –
'As when . . .', 'Like as to . . .' – that, since Dante, has been
developed (as in Miltonic usage) to signal the onset of a stand-
ard epic simile. For that reason, the formula frequently adopted
in the following pages is 'Compare: . . .' The hope is that here,
as in other respects, the reader is invited into a critical and col-
laborative venture, seeing what Dante sees and constructing
along with him (as he himself asks his reader to do, for instance,
in *Paradiso* 13: 1–18) the relationships that define us humans
in our own participation in existence.

# Further Reading

Auerbach, E., *Mimesis: The Representation of Reality in West-ern Literature* (Princeton, 1953).

—, *Literary Latin and Its Public in Late Latin Antiquity* (New York, 1965). These two seminal studies, written with great critical sensitivity, identify crucial issues in regard to Dante's allegory and his relation to classical tradition.

Barolini, T., *Dante's Poets: Textuality and Truth in the Comedy* (Princeton, 1984).

—, *The Undivine Comedy: Detheologizing Dante* (Princeton, 1992). Interesting attempts to detach Dante's poem from an over-insistence on moral issues which reveal the virtuosity of Dante's fiction in creating a 'hall of mirrors'.

Boitani, P., *The Tragic and the Sublime in Medieval Literature* (Cambridge, 1989).

—, *The Shadow of Ulysses* (Oxford, 1994). Highly original studies of issues such as 'recognition' and the search for knowledge as central issues in Dante's poem.

Boyde, P., *Dante, Philomythes and Philosopher: Man in the Cosmos* (Cambridge, 1981).

—, *Perception and Passion in Dante's Comedy* (Cambridge, 1993).

—, *Human Vices and Human Worth in Dante's Comedy* (Cambridge, 2000). A magisterial trilogy expounding all the central principles of Dante's philosophical system.

Burrell, D., *Faith and Freedom* (Oxford, 2004). A major theological study of issues that concerned Dante's con-temporaries.

Curtius, E. R., *European Literature and the Latin Middle Ages*, trans. Willard R. Trask (New York, 1953). Dante seen as the culminating figure in the tradition of medieval Latinity.

Davis, C. T., *Dante and the Idea of Rome* (Oxford, 1957). An important study of Dante's political thinking.

Dronke, P., *Dante and Medieval Latin Traditions* (Cambridge, 1986). Detailed essays on Dante's use of classical and medieval motifs.

Eliot, T. S., *Dante* (London, 1929). Not in itself a particularly illuminating essay, but crucial in pointing to issues that concerned Eliot as a poet throughout his long apprenticeship to Dante.

Fergusson, F., *Dante* (New York, 1966). A stimulating introduction by a passionate Dantist.

Foster, K., *The Two Dantes* (London, 1977). The most penetrating study available of Dante's conception of free will and love.

Fowlie, W., *A Reading of Dante's Inferno* (Chicago and London, 1981). A valuable point-by-point study of the first *cantica* of the *Commedia*.

Freccero, J. (ed.), *Dante: A Collection of Critical Essays* (Englewood Cliffs, 1965).

—, *The Poetics of Conversion* (Cambridge MA, 1986). Freccero's edited volume includes extremely important essays on Dante's philosophy of love and learning and also on his poetic experimentalism.

Gilson, E., *Dante and Philosophy* (London, 1948). An indispensable study of Dante's political theory, by the most influential medievalist of the twentieth century.

Griffiths, E. and Reynolds, M., *Dante in English* (London, 2005). An exhilarating account of English versions of Dante's work beginning with Chaucer and including William Ewart Gladstone.

Hawkins, P., *Dante's Testaments* (Stanford CA, 1999). A study of Dante's indebtedness to the Scriptures, notable for many critical insights.

Holmes, G., *Dante* (Oxford, 1980). A concise introduction to the history of Dante's time and also to his political theory.

Jacoff, R. (ed.), *The Cambridge Companion to Dante* (Cambridge, 1993). Good introductory essays on a range of essential subjects.

Kirkpatrick, R., *Dante's Paradiso and the Limitations of Modern Criticism* (Cambridge, 1978). An analysis of the poetic originality of Dante's *Paradiso*.

—, *Dante's Inferno: Difficulty and Dead Poetry* (Cambridge, 1987). A canto-by-canto study of the first *cantica*.

Lansing, R. (ed.), *The Dante Encyclopedia* (New York and London, 2000). A comprehensive study of Dantean issues, drawing on the best of modern scholarship.

Le Goff, J., *The Birth of Purgatory*, trans. A. Goldhammer (London, 1984). A scholarly account of medieval doctrine which gives great weight to the originality of Dante's conception of Purgatory.

Mandelstam, O., 'Conversation about Dante', in *Collected Critical Prose and Letters*, trans. J. G. Grey (London, 1991). A poet's account – sometimes extravagant but always interesting.

Mazzeo, J. A., *Structure and Thought in the Paradiso* (Ithaca NY, 1958). A clear overall account of Dante's intellectual plan.

Mazzotta, G., *Dante's Vision and the Circle of Knowledge* (Princeton, 1993). An excellent scholarly investigation of Dante's Christian philosophy.

Moevs, C., *The Metaphysics of Dante's Commedia* (Oxford, 2005). A brilliant account of Dante's theology.

Phillips, T., *The Inferno* (London, 1985). A highly imaginative and penetrating critique of the first *cantica*, in the form of canto-by-canto illustrations and notes, from the hand of a major modern artist.

Quinones, R., *Dante Alighieri* (Boston, 1979). A good account, especially of historical themes in the *Commedia*.

Scott, J. A., *Dante's Political Purgatory* (Philadelphia, 1996). A careful account of the political themes in the *Purgatorio*.

Singleton, C. S., *Journey to Beatrice* (Baltimore, 1977).

Turner, D., *Faith, Reason and the Existence of God* (Cambridge, 2004). A searching account by a leading theologian with a particular sympathy for Dante's work of the general theological questions against which Dante's poem is to be viewed.

Williams, C., *Religion and Love in Dante: The Theology of Romantic Love* (London, 1941). A subtle but accessible introduction to Dante's theological imagination.

—, *The Figure of Beatrice: A Study in Dante* (London, 1943).

# A Note on the Manuscript Tradition

Dante appears to have published parts of the *Commedia* in manuscript form before the work as a whole was completed. The *Inferno* appeared around 1315 and the *Purgatorio* around 1320, a year before the author's death, by which time groups of cantos from the *Paradiso* may also have been available to patrons. No manuscript in Dante's own hand has ever been identified. But the immediate popularity of the work ensured that, from the earliest times, there were a great many copies available. The oldest manuscript of the work complete in all three of its parts appears to have been produced in Florence between 1330 and 1331. The success of this publication is attested by an anecdote in which a Florentine copyist active in the 1330s is said to have made provision for the dowries of his daughters by producing no less than 100 redactions of the *Commedia*. A further wave – of largely de luxe editions, produced in Tuscany, beyond the walls of Florence – began to emerge in the 1350s. This second tradition seems to have been stimulated by the interest that Boccaccio took in Dante's poem. Boccaccio himself appears to have copied out the *Commedia* at least three times, and had one of these delivered to Petrarch in Avignon in 1351. In all, something approaching 900 manuscripts were available before printed editions began to appear in 1472. These editions, too, of which there were many, were quickly sold. They included an octave edition in 1502 from the prestigious house of Aldine – important enough to be pirated in the same year at Lyons. No less than 100 of the early manuscripts were scrupulously illustrated, establishing a collaboration between poet and painter which reached its height in Botticelli's extraordinarily subtle treatment of all of the cantos of the *Commedia* produced in Florence during the 1480s, and which continued unabated in the works of William Blake, Gustave Doré and Tom Phillips.

The Italian text on which the present volume is based is that established by Giorgio Petrocchi in *La commedia secondo l'antica vulgata* (Milan, 1966–7). Petrocchi's text is based on some thirty of the earliest Florentine manuscripts. Debate continues over the detail of some of Petrocchi's readings. However, it is a testimony to the clarity of Dante's thought and style that his copyists seem only rarely to have lapsed in concentration. In very few cases do variant readings lead to significantly different interpretations. This is the more remarkable in that punctuation was negligible in early copies. Dante's use of rhyme and caesurae fulfils most of the functions that are now ascribed to punctuation. The scholarly reader, therefore, of both Petrocchi's text and the present translation may reasonably complain at the very high level of editorial punctuation that these both display. Their justification lies in an attempt to articulate and clarify the subtlety, nuance and polyphonic variety of the author's original voice.

Map of Italy, c. 1300

N

TYROLEAN ALPS

A L P S

Monte Viso ▲

Novara ○
Pavia ●
Genoa ○
Milan ○
Brescia ●
Lago di Garda
Verona ●
Mantua ●

L O M B A R D Y

Po

Trento ●
Piave
Treviso ●
Padua ○
Venice ○
Adige

ISTRIA

GOLFO DI QUARNERO

D A L M A T I A

A D R I A T I C   S E A

Bologna ○
R O M A G N A
Ravenna ●
Faenza ●
Forlì ●
Rimini ●

Campaldino ✕
Pistoia ●
Lucca ○
Pisa ○
Florence ○
Arno

T U S C A N Y

Siena ○
Montaperti ✕

Ancona ●

M A R C H E

Gubbio ●

Monte Subasio ▲
Assisi ●

U M B R I A N

Perugia ●

Lago di Bolsena

Tiber

Tagliacozzo ✕
Rome ○ ✕
Palestrina ✕
Anagni ●

L A T I U M

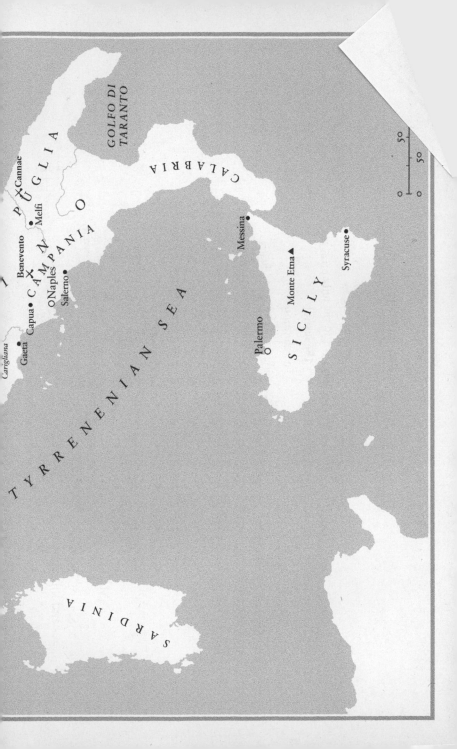

## Plan of Hell

**Sins of incontinence**

- Threshold — The apathetic
- Circle 1 — Limbo: pagans and the unbaptized
- Circle 2 — The lustful
- Circle 3 — The gluttonous
- Circle 4 — The avaricious and the spendthrifts
- Circle 5 — The wrathful and the melancholic
- Circle 6 — The heretics

**Malice: I**
**Sins of violence and inhumanity**

- Ring 1 — Violence against others: in person (murder); in property (plunder)
- Ring 2 — Violence against the self: in person (suicide); in property (profligacy)
- Ring 3 — Violence against God and nature: in person (blasphemers); in nature (sodomites); in nature and art (usurers)

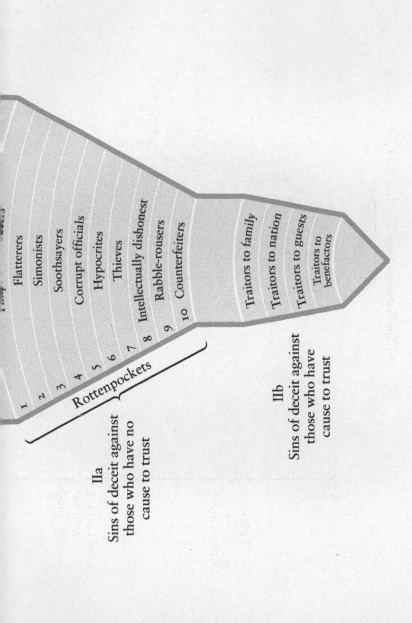

Flatterers 1
Simonists 2
Soothsayers 3
Corrupt officials 4
Hypocrites 5
Thieves 6
Intellectually dishonest 7
Rabble-rousers 8
Counterfeiters 10

Rottenpockets

IIa
Sins of deceit against
those who have no
cause to trust

Traitors to family
Traitors to nation
Traitors to guests
Traitors to benefactors

IIb
Sins of deceit against
those who have
cause to trust

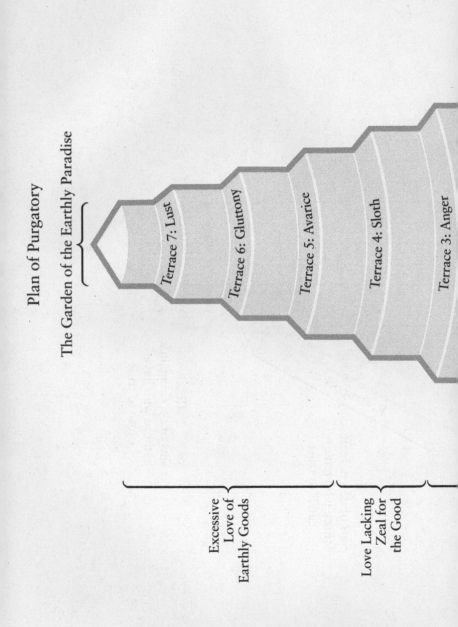

Plan of Purgatory

The Garden of the Earthly Paradise

Terrace 7: Lust

Terrace 6: Gluttony

Terrace 5: Avarice

Terrace 4: Sloth

Terrace 3: Anger

Excessive Love of Earthly Goods

Love Lacking Zeal for the Good

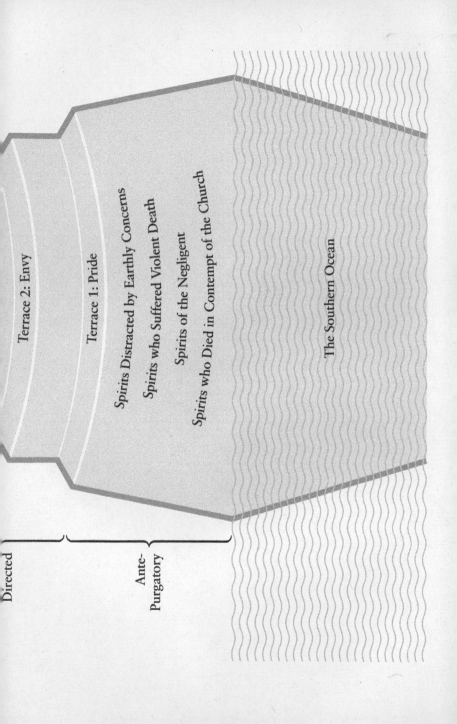

Terrace 2: Envy

Terrace 1: Pride

*Spirits Distracted by Earthly Concerns*
*Spirits who Suffered Violent Death*
*Spirits of the Negligent*
*Spirits who Died in Contempt of the Church*

The Southern Ocean

Directed

Ante-
Purgatory

# Plan of Paradise

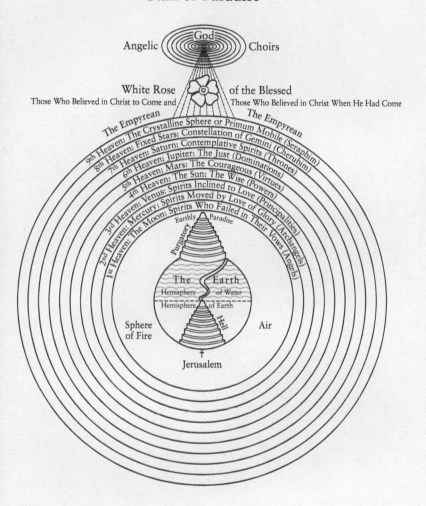

Angelic **God** Choirs

**White Rose** of the Blessed
Those Who Believed in Christ to Come and
Those Who Believed in Christ When He Had Come

The Empyrean
The Empyrean
9th Heaven: The Crystalline Sphere or Primum Mobile (Seraphim)
8th Heaven: Fixed Stars: Constellation of Gemini (Cherubim)
7th Heaven: Saturn: Contemplative Spirits (Thrones)
6th Heaven: Jupiter: The Just (Dominations)
5th Heaven: Mars: The Courageous (Virtues)
4th Heaven: The Sun: The Wise (Powers)
3rd Heaven: Venus: Spirits Inclined to Love (Principalities)
2nd Heaven: Mercury: Spirits Moved by Love of Glory (Archangels)
1st Heaven: The Moon: Spirits Who Failed in Their Vows (Angels)

Earthly Paradise

Purgatory

The **Earth**
Hemisphere of Water
Hemisphere of Earth

Sphere of Fire

Hell

Air

Jerusalem

# Commedia Cantica 1: *Inferno*

# CANTO 1

At one point midway on our path in life,        1*
I came around and found myself now searching
through a dark wood, the right way blurred and lost.

How hard it is to say what that wood was,        4
a wilderness, savage, brute, harsh and wild.
Only to think of it renews my fear!

So bitter, that thought, that death is hardly more so.    7
But since my theme will be the good I found there,
I mean to speak of other things I saw.

I do not know, I cannot rightly say,        10
how first I came to be here – so full of sleep,
that moment, abandoning the true way on.

But then, on reaching the foot of a hill       13*
which marked the limit of the dark ravine
that had before so pierced my heart with panic,

I looked to that height and saw its shoulders     16
already clothed in rays from the planet
that leads all others, on any road, aright.

My fears, at this, were somewhat quieted,      19
though terror, awash in the lake of my heart,
had lasted all the night I'd passed in anguish.

And then, like someone labouring for breath     22
who, safely reaching shore from open sea,
still turns and stares across those perilous waves,

so in my mind – my thoughts all fleeing still –    25
I turned around to marvel at that strait
that let no living soul pass through till now.

28*      And then – my weary limbs a little rested –
I started up the lonely scree once more,
the foot that drives me always set the lower.

31*      But look now! Almost as the scarp begins,
a leopard, light and lively, svelte and quick,
its coat displaying a dappled marking.

34      This never ceased to dance before my face.
No. On it came, so bothering my tread
I'd half a mind at every turn to turn.

37      The time, however, was the hour of dawn.
The sun was mounting, and those springtime stars
that rose along with it when Holy Love

40      first moved to being all these lovely things.
So these – the morning hour, the gentle season –
led me to find good reason for my hopes,

43      seeing that creature with its sparkling hide.
Yet not so far that no fear pressed on me,
to see, appearing now, a lion face.

46      This, as it seemed, came on and on towards me
hungrily, its ravening head held high,
so that, in dread, the air around it trembled.

49      And then a wolf. And she who, seemingly,
was gaunt yet gorged on every kind of craving –
and had already blighted many a life –

52      so heavily oppressed my thought with fears,
which spurted even at the sight of her,
I lost all hope of reaching to those heights.

55      We all so willingly record our gains,
until the hour that leads us into loss.
Then every single thought is tears and sadness.

58      So, now, with me. That brute which knows no peace
came ever nearer me and, step by step,
drove me back down to where the sun is mute.

61      As I went, ruined, rushing to that low,
there had, before my eyes, been offered one
who seemed – long silent – to be faint and dry.

Seeing him near in that great wilderness,
to him I screamed my '*Miserere*': 'Save me,
whatever – shadow or truly man – you be.'

His answer came to me: 'No man; a man
I was in times long gone. Of Lombard stock,
my parents both by *patria* were Mantuan.

And I was born, though late, *sub Iulio*.
I lived at Rome in good Augustus' day,
in times when all the gods were lying cheats.

I was a poet then. I sang in praise
of all the virtues of Anchises' son. From Troy
he came – proud Ilion razed in flame.

But you turn back. Why seek such grief and harm?
Why climb no higher up that lovely hill?
The cause and origin of joy shines there.'

'So, could it be,' I answered him (my brow,
in shy respect, bent low), 'you are that Virgil,
whose words (a river running full) flow wide?

You are the light and glory of all poets.
May this well serve me: my unending care, the love
so great, that's made me search your writings through!

You are my teacher. You, my lord and law.
From you alone I took the fine-tuned style
that has, already, brought me so much honour.

See there? That beast! I turned because of that.
Help me – your wisdom's known – escape from her.
To every pulsing vein, she brings a tremor.'

Seeing my tears, he answered me: 'There is
another road. And that, if you intend
to quit this wilderness, you're bound to take.

That beast – you cry out at the very sight –
lets no one through who passes on her way.
She blocks their progress; and there they all die.

She by her nature is cruel, so vicious
she never can sate her voracious will,
but, feasting well, is hungrier than before.

64\*

67\*

70

73

76

79

82

85

88

91

94\*

97

100     She couples, a mate to many a creature,
and will so with more, till at last there comes
the hunting hound that deals her death and pain.

103     He will not feed on dross or cash or gelt,
but thrive in wisdom, virtue and pure love.
Born he shall be between the felt and felt.

106     To all the shores where Italy bows down
(here chaste Camilla died of wounds, Turnus,
Euryalus and Nisus, too), he'll bring true health.

109     Hunting that animal from every town,
at last he'll chase her back once more to Hell,
from which invidia has set her loose.

112     Therefore, considering what's best for you,
I judge that you should follow, I should guide,
and hence through an eternal space lead on.

115     There you shall hear shrill cries of desperation,
and see those spirits, mourning ancient pain,
who all cry out for death to come once more.

118     And then you'll see those souls who live in fire,
content to hope – whenever that time comes –
they too will be among the blessed choirs.

121     To which if you shall ever wish to rise,
a soul will come far worthier than me.
I must, at parting, leave you in her care.

124     Reigning on high, there is an Emperor
who, since I was a rebel to His law,
will not allow His city as my goal.

127     He rules there, sovereign over every part.
There stands His capital, His lofty throne.
Happy the one He chooses for His own.'

130     'Poet,' I answered, 'by that God whose name
you never knew, I beg you, I entreat –
so I may flee this ill and worse – that you

133     now lead me on to where you've spoken of,
to find the gate where now Saint Peter stands,
and all those souls that you say are so sad.'

136     He made to move; and I came close behind.

# CANTO 2

Daylight was leaving us, and darkened air                    1*
drawing those creatures that there are on earth
from all their labours. I alone, I was
   the only one preparing, as in war,                      4
to onward-march and bear the agony
that thought will now unfailingly relate.
   I call the Muses. You great Heights of Mind             7
bring help to me. You, Memory, wrote down all I saw.
Now shall be seen the greatness of your power.
   'You,' I began, 'my poet and my guide,                  10
look at me hard. Am I in spirit strong enough
for you to trust me on this arduous road?
   As you once told, the sire of Silvius                   13*
travelled, though still in fragile flesh, to realms
immortal, and his senses all alive.
   Nor will it seem (to those of intellect)                16
unfitting if the enemy of ill
should thus so greatly favour him, recalling
   what flowed from him, his name and who he was.          19
He was ordained, in empyrean skies,
father of Rome – its noble heart and empire.
   To speak the truth: that city – and the sphere          22
it ruled – was founded as the sacred seat
for all inheritors of great Saint Peter.
   You have proclaimed the glory of that march.           25
He on his way heard prophecies that led
to all his triumphs and the papal stole.

28*  And then Saint Paul, the chosen Vessel, came –
to carry back a strengthening of that faith
from which salvation always must begin.

31  But me? Why me? Who says I can? I'm not
your own Aeneas. I am not Saint Paul.
No one – not me! – could think I'm fit for this.

34  Surrendering, I'll say I'll come. I fear
this may be lunacy. You, though, are wise.
You know me better than my own words say.'

37  And so – as though unwanting every want,
so altering all at every altering thought,
now drawing back from everything begun –

40  I stood there on the darkened slope, fretting
away from thought to thought the bold intent
that seemed so very urgent at the outset.

43  'Supposing I have heard your words aright,'
the shadow of that noble mind replied,
'your heart is struck with ignominious dread.

46  This, very often, is the stumbling block
that turns a noble enterprise off-course –
as beasts will balk at shadows falsely seen.

49  I mean that you should free yourself from fear,
and therefore I will say why first I came,
and what – when first I grieved for you – I heard.

52*  With those I was whose lives are held in poise.
And then I heard a lady call – so blessed,
so beautiful – I begged her tell me all she wished.

55  Her eyes were shining brighter than the stars.
Then gently, softly, calmly, she began,
speaking, as angels might, in her own tongue:

58  "You, Mantuan, so courteous in spirit,
your fame endures undimmed throughout the world,
and shall endure as still that world moves onwards.

61  A man most dear to me – though not to fate –
is so entrammelled on the lonely hill
that now he turns, all terror, from the way.

My fear must be he's so bewildered there          64
that – hearing all I've heard of him in Heaven –
I rise too late to bring him any aid.

Now make your way. With all your eloquence,          67
and all that his deliverance demands,
lend him your help so I shall be consoled.

For me you'll go, since I am Beatrice.          70
And I have come from where I long to be.
Love is my mover, source of all I say.

When I again appear before my Lord,          73
then I shall often speak your praise to Him."
She now fell silent. I began to speak:

"Lady of worth and truth, through you alone          76
the human race goes far beyond that bourne
set by the moon's sphere, smallest of all the skies.

To me, so welcome is your least command,          79
I'd be too slow had I obeyed by now.
You need no more declare to me your will.

But tell me why you take so little care          82
and, down to this dead middle point, you leave
the spacious circle where you burn to go."

"Since you desire to know so inwardly,          85
then briefly," she replied, "I'll tell you why
I feel no dread at entering down here.

We dread an object when (but only when)          88
that object has the power to do some harm.
Nothing can otherwise occasion fear.

I was created by the grace of God –          91
and so untouched by all your wretchedness.
Nor can the flames of this great fire assail me.

In Heaven, a Lady, gracious, good and kind,          94*
grieves at the impasse that I send you to,
and, weeping, rives the high, unbending rule.

She called Lucia, seeking her reply.          97
'Your faithful one,' she said to her, 'has now
great need of you. I give him to your care.'

100       Lucia is the enemy of harm.
Leaving her place, she came at once to where
I sat – Rachel, long-famed, along with me.

103       'You, Beatrice, are, in truth, God's praise.
Why not,' she said, 'make haste to him? He loves you,
and, loving you, he left the common herd.

106       Can you not hear the pity of his tears?
Do you not see the death that beats him down,
swirling in torrents that no sea could boast?'

109       No one on earth has ever run more rapidly
to seek advantage or else flee from harm,
than I in coming – when her words were done –

112       down from that throne of happiness, to trust
in your great words, their dignity and truth.
These honour you and those who hear you speak."

115       When she had said her say, in tears, she turned
her eyes away – which shone as she was weeping.
And this made me far quicker still for you.

118       So now, as she had willed, I made my way,
to raise you from the face of that brute beast
that stole your pathway up that lovely hill.

121       What is it, then? What's wrong? Why still delay?
Why fondle in your heart such feebleness?
Why wait? Be forthright, brave and resolute.

124       Three ladies of the court of Paradise,
in utmost happiness watch over you.
My own words promise you the utmost good.'

127       As little flowers bend low on freezing nights,
closed tight, but then, as sunlight whitens them,
grow upright on their stems and fully open,

130       now so did I. My wearied powers reviving,
there ran such wealth of boldness to my heart
that openly – all new and free – I now began:

133       'How quick in compassion her aid to me!
And you – so courteous, prompt to accede
to all the words of truth that she has offered!

You, as you speak, have so disposed my heart          136
in keen desire to journey on the way
that I return to find my first good purpose.
    Set off! A single will inspires us both.          139
You are my lord, my leader and true guide.'
All this I said to him as he moved on.
    I entered on that deep and wooded road.          142

# CANTO 3

1*     'Through me you go to the grief-wracked city.
Through me to everlasting pain you go.
Through me you go and pass among lost souls.

4     Justice inspired my exalted Creator.
I am a creature of the Holiest Power,
of Wisdom in the Highest and of Primal Love.

7     Nothing till I was made was made, only
eternal beings. And I endure eternally.
Surrender as you enter every hope you have.'

10     These were the words that – written in dark tones –
I saw there, on the summit of a door.
I turned: 'Their meaning, sir, for me is hard.'

13     And he in answering (as though he understood):
'You needs must here surrender all your doubts.
All taint of cowardice must here be dead.

16*     We now have come where, as I have said, you'll see
in suffering the souls of those who've lost
the good that intellect desires to win.'

19     And then he placed his hand around my own,
he smiled, to give me some encouragement,
and set me on to enter secret things.

22     Sighing, sobbing, moans and plaintive wailing
all echoed here through air where no star shone,
and I, as this began, began to weep.

25     Discordant tongues, harsh accents of horror,
tormented words, the twang of rage, strident
voices, the sound, as well, of smacking hands,

together these all stirred a storm that swirled          28
for ever in the darkened air where no time was,
as sand swept up in breathing spires of wind.

I turned, my head tight-bound in confusion,          31
to say to my master: 'What is it that I hear?
Who can these be, so overwhelmed by pain?'

'This baleful condition is one,' he said,          34*
'that grips those souls whose lives, contemptibly,
were void alike of honour and ill fame.

These all co-mingle with a noisome choir          37
of angels who – not rebels, yet not true
to God – existed for themselves alone.

To keep their beauty whole, the Heavens spurned them.          40
Nor would the depths of Hell receive them in,
lest truly wicked souls boast over them.'

And I: 'What can it be, so harsh, so heavy,          43
that draws such loud lamentings from these crowds?'
And he replied: 'My answer can be brief:

These have no hope that death will ever come.          46
And so degraded is the life they lead
all look with envy on all other fates.

The world allows no glory to their name.          49
Mercy and Justice alike despise them.
Let us not speak of them. Look, then pass on.'

I did look, intently. I saw a banner          52
running so rapidly, whirling forwards,
that nothing, it seemed, would ever grant a pause.

Drawn by that banner was so long a trail          55*
of men and women I should not have thought
that death could ever have unmade so many.

A few I recognized. And then I saw –          58*
and knew beyond all doubt – the shadow of the one
who made, from cowardice, the great denial.

So I, at that instant, was wholly sure          61
this congregation was that worthless mob
loathsome alike to God and their own enemies.

64     These wretched souls were never truly live.
They now went naked and were sharply spurred
by wasps and hornets, thriving all around.

67     The insects streaked the face of each with blood.
Mixing with tears, the lines ran down; and then
were garnered at their feet by filthy worms.

70     And when I'd got myself to look beyond,
others, I saw, were ranged along the bank
of some great stream. 'Allow me, sir,' I said,

73     'to know who these might be. What drives them on,
and makes them all (as far, in this weak light,
as I discern) so eager for the crossing?'

76     'That will, of course, be clear to you,' he said,
'when once our footsteps are set firm upon
the melancholic shores of Acheron.'

79     At this – ashamed, my eyes cast humbly down,
fearing my words had weighed on him too hard –
I held my tongue until we reached the stream.

82*     Look now! Towards us in a boat there came
an old man, yelling, hair all white and aged,
'Degenerates! Your fate is sealed! Cry woe!

85     Don't hope you'll ever see the skies again!
I'm here to lead you to the farther shore,
into eternal shadow, heat and chill.

88     And you there! You! Yes, you, the living soul!
Get right away from this gang! These are dead.'
But then, on seeing that I did not move:

91     'You will arrive by other paths and ports.
You'll start your journey from a different beach.
A lighter hull must carry you across.'

94     'Charon,' my leader, 'don't torment yourself.
For this is willed where all is possible
that is willed there. And so demand no more.'

97     The fleecy wattles of the ferry man –
who plied across the liverish swamp, eyeballs
encircled by two wheels of flame – fell mute.

But not the other souls. Naked and drained,                    100
their complexions changed. Their teeth began
(hearing his raw command) to gnash and grind.

They raged, blaspheming God and their own kin,                 103
the human race, the place and time, the seed
from which they'd sprung, the day that they'd been born.

And then they came together all as one,                        106
wailing aloud along the evil margin
that waits for all who have no fear of God.

Charon the demon, with his hot-coal eyes,                      109
glared what he meant to do. He swept all in.
He struck at any dawdler with his oar.

In autumn, leaves are lifted, one by one,                      112*
away until the branch looks down and sees
its tatters all arrayed upon the ground.

In that same way did Adam's evil seed                          115
hurtle, in sequence, from the river rim,
as birds that answer to their handler's call.

Then off they went, to cross the darkened flood.               118
And, long before they'd landed over there,
another flock assembled in their stead.

Attentively, my master said: 'All those,                       121
dear son, who perish in the wrath of God,
meet on this shore, wherever they were born.

And they are eager to be shipped across.                       124
Justice of God so spurs them all ahead
that fear in them becomes that sharp desire.

But no good soul will ever leave from here.                    127
And so when Charon thus complains of you,
you may well grasp the sense that sounds within.'

His words now done, the desolate terrain                       130
trembled with such great violence that the thought
soaks me once more in a terrified sweat.

The tear-drenched earth gave out a gust of wind,               133
erupting in a flash of bright vermilion,
that overwhelmed all conscious sentiment.

I fell like someone gripped by sudden sleep.                   136

# CANTO 4

1      Thunder rolling heavily in my head
       shattered my deep sleep. Startled, I awoke –
       as though just shaken in some violent grip.

4          And then once more my sight grew firm and fixed.
       Now upright and again afoot, I scanned,
       intently, all around to view where I might be.

7          I found I'd reached – and this is true – the edge
       of the abyss, that cavern of grief and pain
       that rings a peal of endless miseries.

10         The pit, so dark, so wreathed in cloud, went down
       so far that – peering towards its deepest floor –
       I still could not discern a single thing.

13         'Let us descend,' the poet now began,
       'and enter this blind world.' His face was pale.
       'I shall go first. Then you come close behind.'

16         I was aware of his altered colour.
       'How can I come, when you,' I said, 'my strength
       in every time of doubt, are terrified?'

19         'It is the agony,' he answered me,
       'of those below that paints my features thus –
       not fear, as you suppose it is, but pity.

22         Let us go on. The long road spurs our pace.'
       So now he set himself – and me as well –
       to enter Circle One, which skirts the emptiness.

25         Here in the dark (where only hearing told)
       there were no tears, no weeping, only sighs
       that caused a trembling in the eternal air –

sighs drawn from sorrowing, although no pain. 28
This weighs on all of them, those multitudes
of speechless children, women and full-grown men.

'You do not ask,' my teacher in his goodness said, 31
'who all these spirits are that you see here?
Do not, I mean, go further till you know:

these never sinned. And some attained to merit. 34
But merit falls far short. None was baptized.
None passed the gate, in your belief, to faith.

They lived before the Christian age began. 37
They paid no reverence, as was due to God.
And in this number I myself am one.

For such deficiencies, no other crime, 40
we all are lost yet only suffer harm
through living in desire, but hopelessly.'

At hearing this, great sorrow gripped my heart. 43
For many persons of the greatest worth
were held, I knew, suspended on this strip.

'Tell me, sir, tell me, my dearest teacher,' 46*
so I began, determined – on a point
of faith, which routs all error – to be sure,

'has anyone, by merit of his own 49
or else another's, left here then been blessed?'
And he, who read the sense my words had hid,

answered: 'I still was new to this strange state 52
when, now advancing, I beheld a power
whose head was crowned with signs of victory.

He led away the shadow of our primal sire, 55
shades of his offspring, Abel and Noah,
Moses, who uttered (and observed) the law,

of Abraham the patriarch, David the king, 58
Israel, his father and his own twelve sons,
with Rachel, too, for whom he laboured long,

and many more besides. All these He blessed. 61
This too I mean you'll know: until these were,
no human soul had ever been redeemed.'

64     Speak as he might, our journey did not pause,
but on we went, and onward, through the wood –
the wood, I mean, of spirits thronging round.

67     Our steps were still not far from where, in sleep,
I fell, when now, ahead, I saw a fire
that overcame a hemisphere of shade.

70     From this we were, as yet, some paces off,
but not so far that I should fail to see
that men of honour made this place their own.

73     'Honour you bring, my lord, to art and learning.
Inform me who these are – their honour great –
who stand apart in some way from the rest.'

76     He answered me: 'The honour of their name
rings clear for those, like you, who live above,
and here gains favour out of Heaven's grace.'

79     And then there came upon my ear a voice:
'Honour be his, the poet in the heights.
His shadow now returns which had departed.'

82     The voice was still and silent once again.
And now, I saw, there came four noble shades,
no sorrow in their countenance, nor joy.

85     My teacher – that good man – began to speak:
'Look on. Behold the one who, sword in hand,
precedes, as their true lord, the other three.

88*     This is that sovereign Homer, poet.
Horace the satirist is next to come,
Ovid is third. Then (see!) there is Lucan.

91     All these, by right, must duly share with me
the name that sounded in that single voice.
They do me honour thus, and thus do well.'

94     And so I saw, assembling there as one,
the lovely college of that lord of song
whose verses soar like eagles over all.

97     Some little time they talked among themselves,
then turned to me and offered signs of greeting.
On seeing all of this, my teacher smiled.

And greater honour still they paid me now:     100
they summoned me to join them in their ranks.
I came and walked as sixth among such wisdom.

So on we went to reach the dome of light     103
and spoke of things which, proper where I was,
are relegated, rightly, here to silence.

We reached the footings of a noble fort,     106
circled around by seven curtain walls
and also, as its moat, a lovely stream.

We passed this brook as though it were dry land.     109
Through seven gates I went with these five sages.
We then came out upon a verdant lawn.

Here there were some whose eyes were firm and grave –   112
all, in demeanour, of authority –
who seldom spoke; their tones were calm and gentle.

And so we drew aside and found a space,     115
illuminated, open, high and airy,
where all of these were able to be seen.

And there, across that bright enamelled green,     118
these ancient heroes were displayed to me.
And I within myself am still raised high

at what I saw: Electra, many round her.     121*
Hector I recognized, Aeneas, too,
and Caesar in arms, with his hawk-like eyes.

Camilla I saw and Penthesilea,     124
and King Latinus on the other side –
his daughter seated with him, his Lavinia.

Brutus (he drove proud Tarquin out), Lucrece     127
and Julia, Marcia, Cornelia – all these I saw,
and there alone, apart, the sultan Saladin.

And then – my brow raised higher still – I saw,     130*
among his family of philosophers,
the master of all those who think and know.

To him all look in wonder, all in honour.     133
And, closer to his side than all the rest,
I now saw Socrates, I saw now Plato,

136   and one, Democritus, who claims the world is chance,
Diogenes and Tales, Anaxagoras,
Empedocles, Heraclitus and Zeno.

139   Then one I saw who gathered healing herbs –
I mean good Dioscorides. Orpheus I saw,
and Seneca the moralist, Linus, Tully,

142   Euclid (geometer) and Ptolemy,
Hippocrates, Avicenna and Galen,
Averroes, too, who made the *Commentary*.

145   I cannot here draw portraits of them all;
my lengthy subject presses me ahead,
and saying often falls far short of fact.

148   That company of six declines to two.
My lord in wisdom leads a different way,
out of that quiet into trembling air.

151   And nothing, where I now arrive, is shining.

# CANTO 5

And so from Circle One I now went down                                    1
deeper, to Circle Two, which bounds a lesser space
and therefore greater suffering. Its sting is misery.

Minos stands there – horribly there – and barking.        4*
He, on the threshold, checks degrees of guilt,
then judges and dispatches with his twirling tail.

I mean that every ill-begotten creature,                          7
when summoned here, confesses everything.
And he (his sense of sin is very fine)

perceives what place in Hell best suits each one,        10
and coils his tail around himself to tell
the numbered ring to which he'll send them down.

Before him, always, stands a crowd of souls.                  13
By turns they go, each one, for sentencing.
Each pleads, attends – and then is tipped below.

'You there, arriving at this house of woe,'                        16
so, when he saw me there, the judge spoke forth,
(to interrupt a while his formal role),

'watch as you enter – and in whom you trust.                  19
Don't let yourself be fooled by this wide threshold.'
My leader's thrust: 'This yelling! Why persist?

Do not impede him on his destined way.                          22
For this is willed where all is possible
that is willed there. And so demand no more.'

But now the tones of pain, continuing,                            25
demand I hear them out. And now I've come
where grief and weeping pierce me at the heart.

28      And so I came where light is mute, a place
that moans as oceans do impelled by storms,
surging, embattled in conflicting squalls.

31      The swirling wind of Hell will never rest.
It drags these spirits onwards in its force.
It chafes them – rolling, clashing – grievously.

34      Then, once they reach the point from which they fell . . .
screams, keening cries, the agony of all,
and all blaspheming at the Holy Power.

37      Caught in this torment, as I understood,
were those who – here condemned for carnal sin –
made reason bow to their instinctual bent.

40      As starlings on the wing in winter chills
are borne along in wide and teeming flocks,
so on these breathing gusts the evil souls.

43      This way and that and up and down they're borne.
Here is no hope of any comfort ever,
neither of respite nor of lesser pain.

46      And now, as cranes go singing lamentations
and form themselves through air in long-drawn lines,
coming towards me, trailing all their sorrows,

49      I saw new shadows lifted by this force.
'Who are these people? Tell me, sir,' I said,
'why black air scourges them so viciously.'

52*     'The first of those whose tale you wish to hear,'
he answered me without a moment's pause,
'governed as empress over diverse tongues.

55      She was so wracked by lust and luxury,
licentiousness was legal under laws she made –
to lift the blame that she herself incurred.

58      This is Semiramis. Of her one reads
that she, though heir to Ninus, was his bride.
Her lands were those where now the Sultan reigns.

61      The other, lovelorn, slew herself and broke
her vow of faith to Sichaeus's ashes.
And next, so lascivious, Cleopatra.

Helen. You see? Because of her, a wretched          64
waste of years went by. See! Great Achilles.
He fought with love until his final day.

Paris you see, and Tristan there.' And more          67
than a thousand shadows he numbered, naming
them all, whom Love had led to leave our life.

Hearing that man of learning herald thus          70
these chevaliers of old, and noble ladies,
pity oppressed me and I was all but lost.

'How willingly,' I turned towards the poet,          73*
'I'd speak to those two there who go conjoined
and look to be so light upon the wind.'

And he to me: 'You'll see them clearer soon.          76
When they are closer, call to them. Invoke
the love that draws them on, and they will come.'

The wind had swept them nearer to us now.          79
I moved to them in words: 'Soul-wearied creatures!
Come, if none forbids, to us and, breathless, speak.'

As doves, when called by their desires, will come –          82
wings spreading high – to settle on their nest,
borne through the air by their own steady will,

so these two left the flock where Dido is.          85
They came, approaching through malignant air,
so strong for them had been my feeling cry.

'Our fellow being, gracious, kind and good!          88*
You, on your journeying through this bruised air,
here visit two who tinged the world with blood.

Suppose the Sovereign of the Universe          91
were still our friend, we'd pray He grant you peace.
You pity so the ill perverting us.

Whatever you may please to hear or say,          94
we, as we hear, we, as we speak, assent,
so long – as now they do – these winds stay silent.

My native place is set along those shores          97
through which the river Po comes down, to be
at last at peace with all its tributaries.

100     Love, who so fast brings flame to generous hearts,
seized him with feeling for the lovely form,
now torn from me. The harm of how still rankles.

103     Love, who no loved one pardons love's requite,
seized me for him so strongly in delight
that, as you see, he does not leave me yet.

106*     Love drew us onwards to consuming death.
Cain's ice awaits the one who quenched our lives.'
These words, borne on to us from them, were theirs.

109     And when I heard these spirits in distress,
I bowed my eyes and held them low, until,
at length, the poet said: 'What thoughts are these?'

112     I, answering in the end, began: 'Alas,
how many yearning thoughts, what great desire,
have led them through such sorrow to their fate?'

115     And turning to them now I came to say:
'Francesca, how your suffering saddens me!
Sheer pity brings me to the point of tears.

118     But tell me this: the how of it – and why –
that Love, in sweetness of such sighing hours,
permitted you to know these doubtful pangs.'

121*     To me she said: 'There is no sorrow greater
than, in times of misery, to hold at heart
the memory of happiness. (Your teacher knows.)

124     And yet, if you so deeply yearn to trace
the root from which the love we share first sprang,
then I shall say – and speak as though in tears.

127     One day we read together, for pure joy
how Lancelot was taken in Love's palm.
We were alone. We knew no suspicion.

130     Time after time, the words we read would lift
our eyes and drain all colour from our faces.
A single point, however, vanquished us.

133     For when at last we read the longed-for smile
of Guinevere – at last her lover kissed –
he, who from me will never now depart,

touched his kiss, trembling to my open mouth.                          136
This book was *Galehault* – pander-penned, the pimp!
That day we read no further down those lines.'

And all the while, as one of them spoke on,                            139
the other wept, and I, in such great pity,
fainted away as though I were to die.

And now I fell as bodies fall, for dead.                               142

# CANTO 6

1  As now I came once more to conscious mind –
closed in those feelings for the kindred souls
that had, in sudden sadness, overcome me –
4  wherever I might turn I saw – wherever
I might move, look around or settle my gaze –
new forms of torment, new tormented souls.
7  I am in Circle Three. And rain falls there,
endlessly, chill, accursed and heavy,
its rate and composition never new.
10  Snow, massive hailstones, black, tainted water
pour down in sheets through tenebrae of air.
The earth absorbs it all and stinks, revoltingly.
13*  Cerberus, weird and monstrously cruel,
barks from his triple throats in cur-like yowls
over the heads of those who lie there, drowned.
16  His eyes vermilion, beard a greasy black,
his belly broad, his fingers all sharp-nailed,
he mauls and skins, then hacks in four, these souls.
19  From all of them, rain wrings a wet-dog howl.
They squirm, as flank screens flank. They twist, they turn,
and then – these vile profanities – they turn again.
22  That reptile Cerberus now glimpsed us there.
He stretched his jaws; he showed us all his fangs.
And me? No member in my frame stayed still!
25  My leader, bending with his palms wide-spanned,
scooped dirt in each, and then – his fists both full –
hurled these as sops down all three ravening throats.

A hungry mongrel – yapping, thrusting out,       28
intent on nothing but the meal to come –
is silent only when its teeth sink in.

In that same way, with three repulsive muzzles,    31
the demon Cerberus. His thunderous growlings
stunned these souls. They wished themselves stone deaf.

Over such shadows, flat in that hard rain,    34
we travelled onwards still. Our tread now fell
on voided nothings only seeming men.

Across the whole terrain these shades were spread,    37
except that one, at seeing us pass by,
sat, on the sudden, upright and then cried:

'You there! Drawn onwards through this stretch of Hell,  40*
tell me you know me. Say so, if so you can.
You! Made as man before myself unmade.'

And I replied: 'The awful pain you feel    43
perhaps has cancelled you from memory.
Till now, it seems, I've never even seen you.

Then tell me who you are, and why you dwell    46
in such a place? And why a pain like this?
Others may well be worse, none so disgusting.'

And he: 'That burgh of yours – that sack of bile    49
that brims by now to overflow – I lived
as hers throughout my own fine-weather years.

You knew me, like your city friends, as Hoggo.    52
So here I am, condemned for gullet sins,
lying, you see, squashed flat by battering rain.

I'm not alone in misery of soul.    55
These all lie subject to the self-same pain.
Their guilt is mine.' He spoke no further word.

'Hoggo, your heavy labours,' I replied,    58
'weigh on me hard and prompt my heavy tears.
But tell me, if you can, where they'll all end,

the citizens of that divided town?    61
Is there among them any honest man?
Why is that place assailed by so much strife?'

64     His answer was: 'From each side, long harangues.
And then to blood. The Wildwood boys
will drive the others out. They'll do great harm.

67     But then, within the span of three brief suns,
that side will fall and others rise and thrive,
spurred on by one who now just coasts between.

70     For quite some time they'll hold their heads up high
and grind the others under heavy weights,
however much, for shame, these weep and writhe.

73     Of this lot, two are honest yet not heard.
For pride and avarice and envy are
the three fierce sparks that set all hearts ablaze.'

76     With this, his tear-drenched song now reached an end.
But I to him: 'I still want more instruction.
This gift I ask of you: please do say more.

79*    Tegghiaio, Farinata – men of rank –
Mosca, Arrigo, Rusticucci, too,
and others with their minds on noble deeds,

82     tell me, so I may know them, where they are.
For I am gripped by great desire, to tell
if Heaven holds them sweet – or poisonous Hell.'

85     And he: 'These dwell among the blackest souls,
loaded down deep by sins of differing types.
If you sink far enough, you'll see them all.

88     But when you walk once more where life is sweet,
bring me, I beg, to others in remembrance.
No more I'll say, nor answer any more.'

91     His forward gaze now twisted to a squint.
He stared at me a little, bent his head,
then fell face down and joined his fellow blind.

94     My leader now addressed me: 'He'll not stir
until the trumpets of the angels sound,
at which his enemy, True Power, will come.

97     Then each will see once more his own sad tomb,
and each, once more, assume its flesh and figure,
each hear the rumbling thunder roll for ever.'

So on we fared across that filthy blend          100
of rain and shadow spirit, slow in step,
touching a little on the life to come.

    Concerning which, 'These torments, sir,' I said,          103
'when judgement has been finally proclaimed –
will these increase or simmer just the same?'

    'Return,' he said, 'to your first principles:          106*
when anything (these state) becomes more perfect,
then all the more it feels both good and pain.

    Albeit these accursed men will not          109
achieve perfection full and true, they still,
beyond that Day, will come to sharper life.'

    So, circling on the curve around that path,          112
we talked of more than I shall here relate,
but reached the brow, from which the route descends,

    and found there Plutus, the tremendous foe.          115*

# CANTO 7

1*      *'Popoi Satan, popoi Satan! Alezorul!'*
So Plutus – shrill voice clucking on – began.
But Virgil, wise and noble, knowing all,

4      spoke out, to comfort me: 'Let not your fears
occasion you distress. Despite his powers,
he cannot steal your right to scale this rock face.'

7      And then he turned to meet those rabid lips.
'Silence, you execrable wolf!' he said.
'May fury gnaw you inwardly away.

10*      To these dark depths, with every right he treads.
All this is willed where Michael, in the heights,
avenged the rapine wrought by prideful hordes.'

13      As sails, inflated by a furious wind,
fall in a tangle when the main mast snaps,
so too he flopped, this predator, to ground.

16      Then downwards to the seventh sink we went,
advancing further down the curving wall
that bags up all the evil of the universe.

19      God in all justice! I saw there so many
new forms of travail, so tightly crammed. By whom?
How can our guilt so rend and ruin us?

22*      Over Charybdis, the sea surge swirls
and shatters on the swell it clashes with.
So must these people dance their morisco.

25      I saw, in numbers greater than elsewhere,
two factions, hollering, this one to that,
who rolled great boulders, thrust by rib and tit.

Their stones would clash. Then wheeling they'd retreat   28
and yell, across their shoulders, cry and counter-cry.
'You miser! Why?' 'Why fling it all away?'

So back along that dismal curve they went,   31
to reach, at either end, the diametric points,
still screaming shamefully insulting chants.

Arriving – each round his half-circle – back,   34
each whisked around to tilt against the next other.
At this – my heart transfixed, or very nearly:

'Sir,' I spoke up, 'make clear to me what folk   37
these are, and whether – to our left – all those
with tonsured scalps could really have been clerics.'

'Without exception, all of these,' he said,   40
'when first they lived, had such strabismic minds
they'd bear no check or measure on expense.

And when they reach the two points in the round   43*
where converse crimes uncouple each from each,
they bark their meaning out and sound it clear.

Clerics they were – all those whose heads aren't dressed   46
with shaggy hair. All popes – or cardinals.
In that lot, avarice displays its worst.'

'Well, sir,' I said, 'in any group like this,   49
I surely ought to recognize some few
who bore in life the taint of this disease.'

'You seek,' he said, 'to form an idle thought.   52
The mindless lives that made them all so foul
darken them now against all acts of mind.

Both, to eternity, will buck and butt.   55
These from their tombs will rise with fists tight shut,
the others with their curly manes cropped short.

Their frenzied sprees or febrile hoardings-up   58
have wrung from them the beauty of the world,
and brought them firmly to this ugly brawl.

You now can see, dear son, the short-lived pranks   61
that goods consigned to Fortune's hand will play,
causing such squabbles in the human ranks.

64     For all the gold that lies beneath the moon –
or all that ever did lie there – would bring
no respite to these worn-out souls, not one.'

67     'Please tell me, sir,' I said, a little more,
'what can it be, this Fortune that you touch on,
that clasps all earthly goods between its claws?'

70     And he to me: 'You idiotic creatures,
so greatly hurt by your own ignorance!
Feed on my words. I'd have you grasp their sense.

73*    He who transcends in wisdom all that is,
wrought every sphere and gave to each a guide,
so every part shines out to every part

76     always in equal distribution of light.
So, too, above the splendours of the world,
He set a sovereign minister, ordained to move –

79     in permutations at the proper time –
vain goods from tribe to tribe, from blood to blood,
in ways from which no human wisdom hides.

82     And this is why, where one race rules supreme,
another faints and languishes: they all pursue
her judgements, secret as a snake in grass.

85     Your powers of mind cannot contend with her.
She, looking forwards, will pronounce her law,
advancing, as do other gods, her own domain.

88     Her permutations never come to rest.
It is necessity that makes her quick,
so thick they come by turns to meet their fate.

91     She is the one so often crossed and cursed
by those who, rightly, ought to sing her praise,
yet vilify her name and speak her ill.

94     But she, a holy being, pays no heed.
Happy, with all the other primal powers,
she turns her sphere, rejoicing in beatitude.

97*    So let us now go down to greater pain.
The stars that rose when I first stirred now fall.
We cannot stay too long. That is forbidden.'

Cutting across the circle, we approached     100
the margins of a spring – which, seething, spilled
and ran from there along an outer sluice.

The waters here were darker, far, than perse.     103
So, on – accompanied by murky waves –
downwards we travelled by a weirder route.

Into a swamp (by name, the loathsome Styx)     106
this melancholy brook makes way, and finds
the foot of those malignant, grey-black slopes.

As there I stood, intent and wondering,     109
I saw there, plunged within that stagnant fen,
a peevish people, naked, caked with mud.

Each battered each – and not with fists alone,     112
also with head butts, kicks and charging chests.
Their teeth, too, tore them, bit by bit, to shreds.

'You witness now,' my gentle teacher said,     115*
'the souls of those whom anger overthrew.
And this I'd also have you know: be sure,

beneath the surface of this slick are some     118
whose sighs – as you can see at every turn –
now aerate that pullulating film.

So, stuck there fast in slime, they hum: "Mournful     121
we were. Sunlight rejoices the balmy air.
We, though, within ourselves nursed sullen fumes,

and come to misery in this black ooze."     124
That is the hymn each gurgles in his gorge,
unable to articulate a single phrase.'

So, on around this sour, revolting pit,     127
between the sludge and arid rock, we swung
our arc, eyes bent on those who gulped that slop.

We reached, in fine, the bottom of a tower.     130

# CANTO 8

1      And so I say (continuing) that, long before
we reached the bottom of that lofty tower,
our eyes had travelled upwards to its summit,

4      drawn by a pair of tiny flames, set there –
as now we saw – to signal to a third,
so far away the eye could hardly grasp it.

7      I turned towards the ocean of all wisdom:
'What do they mean?' I said to him. 'What answer
does the farther fire now give? Who makes these signs?'

10     And he: 'Across these waves of foaming mire,
you may already glimpse what they've been waiting for,
unless it still goes hidden by these marshy fumes.'

13     No bow string ever shot through air an arrow
rapider than now, at speed, I saw come on
towards us there, a mean little vessel,

16     within it – as pilot plying these waters –
a single galley man who strained the oar,
squealing: 'You fiend! You've got it coming now!'

19*    'Phlegyas, Phlegyas!' my master said.
'Your screams and shouts have, this time, little point.
We're yours – but only while we cross this marsh.'

22     Like someone hearing that a massive hoax
has just, to his disgruntlement, been pulled on him,
so Phlegyas now stood, in pent-up rage.

25     My lord stepped down, and, entering the boat,
he made me, in my turn, embark behind.
The hull seemed laden only when I did.

At once – my leader boarded, me as well –                                28
the ancient prow put out. It sawed the waves
more deeply than it would with other crews.

So, rushing forwards on that lifeless slick,             31*
there jerked up, fronting me, one brimming slime
who spoke: 'So who – you come too soon! – are you?'

And my riposte: 'I come, perhaps; I'll not remain.       34
But who might you be, brutishly befouled?'
His answer was: 'Just look at me. I'm one

who weeps.' And I to him: 'Weep on. In grief,            37
may you remain, you spirit of damnation!
I know who *you* are, filth as you may be.'

And then he stretched both hands towards our gunwales.   40
My teacher, though – alert – soon drove him back,
saying: 'Get down! Be off with all that dog pack!'

And then he ringed both arms around my neck.             43*
He kissed my face, then said: 'You wrathful soul!
Blessed the one that held you in her womb.

That man, alive, flaunted his arrogance,                 46
and nothing good adorns his memory.
So here his shadow is possessed with rage.

How many, in the world above, pose there               49
as kings but here will lie like pigs in muck,
leaving behind them horrible dispraise.'

'Sir,' I replied, 'this I should really like:           52
before we make our way beyond this lake,
to see him dabbled in the minestrone.'

He gave me my answer: 'Before that shore               55
has come to view, you'll surely have your fill.
And rightly you rejoice in this desire.'

Then, moments on, I saw that sinner ripped              58
to vicious tatters by that mud-caked lot.
I praise God still, and still give thanks for that.

'Get him,' they howled. 'Let's get him – Silver Phil!'  61
That crazy Florentine! He bucked, he baulked.
Turning, the Guelf turned teeth upon himself.

64     We left him there. Of him, my story tells no more.
And yet my ears were pierced with cries of pain.
At which, I barred my eyes intently forwards.

67     'Dear son,' my teacher in his goodness said,
'we now approach the city known as Dis,
its teeming crowds and weighty citizens.'

70     'Already, sir,' I said, 'I clearly can
make out the minarets beyond this moat,
as bright and red, it seems, as if they sprang

73     from fire.' 'Eternal fire,' he answered me,
'burning within, projects, as you can see,
these glowing profiles from the depths of Hell.'

76     We now arrived within the deep-dug ditch –
the channel round that place disconsolate,
whose walls, it seemed to me, were formed of iron.

79     Not without, first, encircling it about,
we came to where the ferry man broke forth:
'Out you all get!' he yelled. 'The entry's here.'

82     I saw there, on that threshold – framed – more than
a thousand who had rained from Heaven. Spitting
in wrath. 'Who's that,' they hissed, 'who, yet undead,

85     travels the kingdom of the truly dead?'
He gave a sign, my teacher in all wisdom,
saying he sought some secret word with them.

88     At which they somewhat hid their fierce disdain.
'You come, but on your own!' they said. 'Let him,
so brazen entering our realm, walk by.

91     He may retrace his foolish path alone –
or try it, if he can – while you'll stay here.
You've been his escort through this dark terrain.'

94     Reader, imagine! I grew faint at heart,
to hear these cursed phrases ringing out.
I truly thought I'd never make it back.

97     'My guide, my dearest master. Seven times –
or more by now – you've brought me safely through.
You've drawn me from the face of towering doom.

Do not, I beg you, leave me here undone.   100
If we are now denied a clear way on,
then let us quickly trace our footsteps back.'

My lord had led me onwards to that place –  103
and now he said: 'Do not be terrified.
No one can take from us our right to pass.

Wait here a while. Refresh your weary soul.  106
Take strength. Be comforted. Feed on good hope.
I'll not desert you in this nether world.'

So off he went. He there abandoned me,  109
my sweetest father. Plunged in 'perhapses',
I so remained, brain arguing 'yes' and 'no'.

What he then said to them I could not tell.  112
Yet hardly had he taken up his stand
when all ran, jostling, to return inside.

They barred the door, these enemies of ours,  115
to meet his thrust. My lord remained shut out.
With heavy tread, he now came back to me.

Eyes bent upon the ground, his forehead shaved  118
of all brave confidence, sighing, he said:
'Who dares deny me entrance to this house of grief?'

To me he said: 'You see. I'm angry now.  121
Don't be dismayed. They'll fuss around in there.
They'll seek to keep us out. But I'll win through.

This insolence of theirs is nothing new.  124*
At some less secret gate they tried it once.
But that still stands without its lock, ajar.

You've seen the door, dead words scribed on its beam.  127
And now already there descends the slope –
passing these circles, and without a guide –

someone through whom the city will lie open.'  130

# CANTO 9

1       The colour that courage failing brought out
        so quickly in me, seeing my leader retreat,
        made him, the sooner, check his own new pallor.

4       Intently, as though listening hard, he stopped.
        Eyesight unaided – in that blackened air,
        through foggy, dense swirls – could not carry far.

7*      'This contest, even so, we're bound to win.
        If not . . .' he began. 'Yet granted such a one . . .
        How long to me it seems till that one comes!'

10      I saw quite clearly how he covered up
        his opening thoughts with those that followed on –
        words inconsistent with the first he spoke.

13      Yet fear came over me at what he had said.
        And so, from these truncated words, I drew
        a meaning worse, perhaps, than he had meant.

16      'Into the hollow deep of this grim bowl
        do any make their way from that first rung
        where nothing, save for thwarted hope, brings pain?'

19      I put this question to him. 'Seldom,' he said.
        'It happens rarely that our people take
        the path that I am venturing to tread.

22*     It's true, of course, I've been here once before,
        conjured to come by bitter Erichtho –
        she who called shadows back into their limbs.

25      A short while only was I bare of flesh
        until, as she compelled, I breached these walls
        to fetch a spirit from the Judas ring.

That is the utmost deep, the darkest place,      28
the furthest from the sky's all-turning sphere.
I know the way. Be confident, be sure.

    This marsh, exhaling such a nauseous stench,      31
forms in a belt around the mournful town
and not without due anger shall we enter in.'

    He said much more. But what I can't recall.      34
My eyes in all attention now were drawn
towards the blazing summit of that gate,

    where suddenly, at one point, there had sprung      37*
three blood-stained Furies from the depths of Hell.
In pose and body they were, all three, women,

    wound round about with water snakes, bright green.      40
Fringing their vicious brows they bore, as hair,
entwining snakes. Their curls were sharp-horned vipers.

    And he – who knew quite well that these were slaves      43
who served the empress of unending tears –
said to me: 'Look! The cruel Eumenides!

    That one's Megaera, on the left-hand side.      46
Weeping there stands Alecto, on the right.
Tisiphone's between these two.' He paused.

    Each rent her breast with her own fingernails.      49
With slapping palm, each beat herself and screamed –
so loud I strained, all doubt, against the poet.

    'Come now, Medusa! Turn him – quick! – to stone!'      52*
Staring hard down they spoke in unison.
'The Theseus raid went unavenged! We're wrong!'

    'Turn round! Your back to them! Your eyes tight shut!      55
For if the Gorgon shows and you catch sight,
there'll be no way of ever getting out.'

    He spoke and then, himself, he made me turn      58
and, not relying on my hands alone,
to shield my eyes he closed his own on mine.

    Look hard, all you whose minds are sound and sane,      61
and wonder at the meaning lying veiled
beyond the curtain of this alien verse.

64       Already across the turbid swell there came
a shattering resonance that, charged with panic,
evoked great tremors down each river bank.

67       In this way, too, a driving wind – impelled
by clashing currents through the burning air –
strikes at a grove and, meeting no resistance,

70       splinters the branches flat and bears them off.
So, proudly on it goes, in clouds of dust,
shepherds and beasts all fleeing in its path.

73       He loosed my eyes, 'And now,' he said, 'stretch straight
your strings of sight across this age-old scum
to where the fumes are thickest, stinging most.'

76       Like frogs that glimpse their enemy the snake,
and vanish rapidly across the pond –
diving till each sits huddling on its bed –

79       I saw a thousand ruined souls or more
scattering in flight, ahead of one whose pace
passed, yet kept dry, across the river Styx.

82       The greasy air he wafted from his face,
his left hand drawn before him, as a fan.
And this was all the strain, it seemed, that tired him.

85       I saw full well that he was sent from Heaven,
I turned towards my teacher, and he signed
that I should bend in silent deference.

88       How full he seemed to me of high disdain!
He reached the gates. And, simply with his rod,
he opened them. For nothing held them firm.

91       'Outcasts from Heaven, driven beyond contempt!'
Thus, in that dreadful doorway, he began:
'How is such truculence bred up in you?

94       Why so recalcitrant against that will
whose aim and purpose never can be maimed,
which has so often now increased your pain?

97*      What is the point? Why kick against your fate?
Your guard dog Cerberus is still (remember?)
hairless for doing so, at chin and neck.'

He then turned back along the filthy road. 100
He spoke no word to us. He had the look
of someone gnawed and gathered up by care –
   though not the cares that here confronted him. 103
And now we set our tread towards that land.
The holy words had made us confident.
   We entered. And no force was offered us. 106
So, eager to survey what such a fort
could lock within the confines of its wall,
   when once inside, I cast my eyes about. 109
I see a plain, extending all around.
And everywhere is grief and wracking pain.
   Compare: at Arles (the Rhône there forms a marsh), 112*
or else at Polj by the Kvarner gulf,
which shuts the door on Italy and bathes its bounds,
   are sepulchres that make the ground uneven. 115
And so, too, here, a tomb at every turn,
except that all was done more bitterly.
   For flames were scattered round among these tombs. 118
The pits were therefore so intensely fired,
no tradesman needs his brand iron half so hot.
   The covers of the tombs all stood half-raised; 121
and out of each there came such cruel lamenting
these must have been the cries from pain within.
   And I to my master: 'Who can these all be, 124
these people buried in the sepulchres?
They make their presence felt in such pained sighs?'
   The answer: 'These are the master heretics, 127
with all their followers from every sect.
These tombs are filled with more than you suspect.
   Those of like mind are buried each with each. 130
The monuments are all at differing heats.'
He turned towards the right, then on we went,
   between the torments and high battlements. 133

# CANTO 10

1    Onward along a secret path – confined
     between those ramparts and the shows of pain –
     my teacher led and I was at his shoulder.

4    'You,' I began, 'true power and height of strength,
     you bring me, turning, through these godless whirls.
     Speak, if this pleases you. Feed my desires.

7    Those people lying in the sepulchres –
     what chance is there of seeing them? The lids
     are off already. No one stands on guard.'

10*   'These tombs,' he said, 'will finally be shut
     when, from Jehoshaphat on Judgement Day,
     sinners bring back their bodies left above.

13*   This circle is the cemetery for all
     disciples of the Epicurus school,
     who say the body dies, so too the soul.

16   The question, therefore, that you've put to me,
     once you're within, will soon be satisfied,
     so, too, the longing that you keep unsaid.'

19   'I never would – my lord, my trusted guide –
     keep, save for brevity, my heart from you.
     And brevity you've urged on me before.'

22*   'Tuscan! You go through the city of fire
     alive and speaking as a man of worth.
     Come, if you will, and rest in this domain.

25   Your accent manifests that you were born
     a son of that great fatherland on which,
     perhaps, I wreaked too harsh an injury.'

This sound, so suddenly, came ringing out     28
from one among the sepulchres. Fearful,
I shrank still closer to my leader's side.

'What's wrong?' he said to me. 'Just turn around!     31*
And see there, upright, risen, Farinata.
From cincture upwards you will see him whole.'

My gaze was trained already into his,     34
while he, brow raised, was thrusting out his chest,
as though he held all Hell in high disdain.

My leader (hands in animated aid)     37
drove me towards him down the line of vaults.
He counselled: 'Let your words be duly measured.'

So there, beneath his sepulchre, I stood.     40
He looked me up and down a while, and then
inquired, half-scornfully: 'Who were your forebears?'

I – always eager and obedient –     43
concealing nothing, laid all plainly forth.
At which he arched his brows a little more.

And then: 'In fierce hostility, they stood     46
against myself, my ancestors, my cause.
And so, on two occasions, they were scattered wide.'

'Scattered,' I answered, 'so they may have been,     49
but all came back from all sides, then and now.
And your men truly never learned that art.'

Then there arose, revealed before my eyes,     52*
a shadow near the first, seen from chin up,
which had, as I suppose, just risen to its knees.

It looked me all around, as though intent     55
on seeing whether, with me, was another.
But when its doubting glance was wholly spent,

weeping he called: 'If you, through this eyeless     58
prison, pass on through height of intellect,
my son, where is he? And why not here with you?'

'I come,' I said, 'though not through my own strength.     61
The man who waits there leads me through this place
to one, perhaps, whom once your Guido scorned.'

64     The way he spoke – and what he suffered, too –
had now already spelled for me his name.
And that was why my answer was so full.

67*     Upright suddenly: 'What's that you say?'
he wailed. '"He once . . ."? You mean, he's not alive?
And are his eyes not struck by bonny light?'

70     But then, in noticing that slight delay
which came before I offered my reply,
he fell back flat, and did not re-appear.

73     The other noble soul (at whose command
I'd come to rest) in no way changed expression.
He neither moved his neck nor bent his waist.

76*     But still continuing in what he'd said:
'If,' he went on, 'they learned that art so ill,
that is more torment than this bed of pain.

79     And yet no more than fifty times that face
(the moon's, who is our sovereign here) will shine
till you shall learn how heavy that art weighs.

82     If you once more would gain the lovely world,
tell me: how dare those burghers, in their laws,
oppose themselves so viciously to mine?'

85     My answer was: 'The massacre, the mindless waste
that stained the flowing Arbia with blood,
led, in our oratories, to these demands.'

88     Sighing, he did now move his head. 'In none
of that,' he said, 'was I alone. And I
would not, without good cause, have gone with them.

91     I was alone – where all the rest could bear
to think that Florence might be swept away –
and boldly stood to speak in her defence.'

94     'Well (may your seed find sometime true repose!)
untie the knot for me,' I now besought,
'so tightly twined around my searching thoughts.

97*     You see, it seems (to judge from what I hear)
far in advance what time will bring to pass,
but otherwise in terms of present things.'

'We see like those who suffer from ill light.                    100
We are,' he said, 'aware of distant things.
Thus far He shines in us, the Lord on high.

But when a thing draws near to us, our minds          103
go blank. So if no other brings us news,
then nothing of your human state is known to us.

You will from this be able to deduce                       106
that all our knowledge will be wholly dead
when all the doors of future time are closed.'

And then I said, as though my heart were pierced      109
with guilt, 'Go, say to him, that fallen soul,
his first-born son is still among the living.

And if, before I answered, I fell mute,                     112
I did so (make him understand) because
my thoughts – which you have solved – had strayed to
      doubt.'

By now, my teacher had already called.                   115
And so, with greater urgency I begged that soul
that he should tell me who was with him there.

'I lie,' he answered, 'with a thousand, more.            118*
Enclosed beside me is the second Frederick.
Cardinal Octavian, too. Of others, I keep silent.'

And then he hid: and I, towards that great             121
poet of the ancient world, turned my steps backwards,
musing on words that seemed my enemy.

He went his way and, as he walked, he asked:         124
'Why is it you're so lost in thought, so blurred by doubt?'
And I responded fully to his words.

'Keep well in mind,' my lord in wisdom said,         127
'the things that you have heard against yourself.
But now,' his finger raised, 'attend to this:

when once again you stand within the rays            130*
that she, whose lovely eyes see all things, casts,
you'll learn from her what your life's course will be.'

133      And then he swung, to tread towards the left.
We quit the wall and headed for the middle.
The path we took cut straight into a gorge,
136      and even from above the stench was foul.

# CANTO 11

Now near the brink of a sheer escarpment                                    1
formed in a circle from great, shattered stones,
we found, below, a crueller bunch of souls.

And there, against an awful overflow –                                      4
a stink arising from the utmost depths –
we huddled back together by the lid

of one vast sepulchre, inscribed, I saw,                                    7*
in words that said: 'I guard Pope Anastasius,
drawn by Photinus from the rightful road.'

'Best not descend too rapidly, but first                                    10
get more accustomed in our sense of smell
to this grim belch. We'll then not notice it.'

These were my teacher's words. To him I said,                              13
'Find something that will compensate, to waste
no time.' 'I'm thinking, as you see,' he said,

and then began: 'Dear son, within this rock-rimmed pit    16
three lesser circuits lie. And these (like those
you leave behind) go down by due degrees.

Each rung is crammed with spirits of the damned.                           19*
But listen now – so sight may henceforth serve –
and hear the "what" and "why" of their constraints.

Malice is aimed in all its forms – and thus                                22*
incurs the hatred of Heaven – at gross injustice,
and, aiming so, harms others, by deceit or force.

Deceit, though, is specifically a human wrong,                              25*
and hence displeases God the more. Liars
are therefore deeper down, and tortured worse.

28    Ring One throughout is meant for violent wills.
      But violent acts may fall upon three persons.
      And so this ring is shaped and formed in three.

31    To God, to self, to neighbours hurt is done
      (to persons, of course, but also their possessions)
      in ways that you will now hear argued out.

34    To those around us, death or grievous wounds
      are wrought by violent hands, the things we own
      ruined by outrage, extortion or fire.

37    So in the agonies of Sub-ring One,
      in different squads, are homicides and thugs,
      vandals and looters, bandits and brigands.

40    In violence, too, we turn against ourselves,
      or else our own belongings. And thus
      in Sub-ring Two are those (regret now vain)

43    who by their own free will strips off your world
      or gambles all their competence away,
      and weeps where, properly, they should rejoice.

46    Force, too, is offered to the Deity
      by hearts, blaspheming, that deny His power,
      or else scorn Nature and her great largesse.

49*   And so the imprint of the smallest ring
      falls on Cahorsian bankers, as on Sodom,
      and those who speak at heart in scorn of God.

52*   As for deceit – which gnaws all rational minds –
      we practise this on those who trust in us,
      or those whose pockets have no room for trust.

55    Fraud of the second kind will only gash
      the ligature of love that Nature forms:
      and therefore in great Circle Two there nests

58    smarm and hypocrisy, the casting-up of spells,
      impersonation, thievery, crooked priests,
      embezzlement and pimping, such-like scum.

61    Fraud of the other sort forgets no less
      the love that Nature makes, but then, as well,
      the love particular that trust creates.

So in the smallest ring of all – that point                    64
within the universe where Satan sits –
consumed eternally, are traitors, every one.

'Your explanation, sir,' I said, 'proceeds                     67
with great lucidity. You clarify
the levels of this grim abyss and all within.

Yet tell me, too: those souls in that gross marsh,             70
those swept by winds, those creatures lashed by rain,
and those that clash with such abrasive tongues,

if they all, likewise, face the wrath of God,                  73
then why not racked within these flame-red walls?
Or if they don't, why are they as they are?'

'Why,' he replied, 'do your frenetic wits                      76*
wander so wildly from their usual track?
Or where, if not fixed here, are your thoughts set?

Do you, at any rate, not call to mind                          79
the terms in which your *Ethics* fully treats
those three dispositions that the Heavens repel:

intemperance, intentional harm and mad                         82
brutality? Or that intemperance
offends God least, and least attracts His blame?

If you think carefully of what this means,                     85
and summon into thought what those souls are
who serve their sentence in the upper ring,

you'll plainly see why these are set apart                     88
from those condemned as felons, and, in pain,
less sharply hammered by divine revenge.'

'You are the sun who heals all clouded sight.                  91
Solving my doubts, you bring me such content
that doubt, no less than knowing, is delight.

But still,' I said, 'turn backwards to the point               94*
where you declared that usury offends
God's generosity. Untie that knot.'

'Philosophy, as those that read it know,                       97
takes note,' he said, 'on more than one occasion,
of how the course that Nature runs is drawn

100     directly from the mind and art of God.
        And if you read your *Physics* with due care,
        you'll see, before you're many pages through,
103     that your art takes, as best it can, the lead
        that Nature gives – as student does from master.
        Your art is nearly grandchild, then, to God.
106     From these two principles – if you recall
        the opening lines of Genesis – we're bound to draw
        our living strength and multiply our people.
109     But usurers adopt a different course.
        They place their hopes in other things, and thus
        make mock of Nature's self and her close kin.
112*    But follow on. I'm ready now to go.
        The writhing Fish have swum to the horizon.
        The Wain lies high above the Western Wind.
115     The leap we now must make lies far beyond.'

# CANTO 12

The place we'd reached – to clamber down that bank –     1
was alpine crag. No eye, considering
what else was there, would not have flinched away.

Compare: an avalanche in Adige,     4*
southwards of Trent, once struck the mountain flank,
triggered perhaps by landslip or earthquake;

and boulders from the summit shifted down     7
in steps and stages to the valley floor,
to offer those up there a downward route.

Likewise the path we trod down this ravine.     10*
And on the angle where the incline broke,
there lay stretched out the infamy of Crete,

spawned in the womb of Pasiphae's fake heifer.     13
And when he saw us there he gnawed himself,
as though flailed flat within by utter rage.

My leader in his wisdom called towards him:     16
'You may suppose that he's the duke of Athens,
who dealt you, in the world above, your death.

You monster! Move aside! This one's not come     19
provided with instructions from your sister.
He comes to see what you are suffering here.'

A stunned bull, stricken by its mortal blow,     22
wrenches, that instant, free from noose and rope.
It cannot walk but skips and hops about.

The Minotaur, I saw, behaved like that.     25
'Run!' shouted Virgil, watching out. 'A gap!
Better get down while still his fury bites.'

28      So down across the scree we picked our way.
Beneath my feet, the stones would often move,
teetering beneath the strange new weight they bore.

31*      I walked on, deep in thought. 'Perhaps,' he said,
'you're thinking of this landslide? Or that guard
whose brutal anger I have just eclipsed?

34      When once before (I'd like you now to know)
I came down here and entered lower Hell,
these cliffs had yet to suffer any rock fall.

37      But certainly, if I have got this right,
there once came One who gathered up from Dis
the stolen treasure of its highest place.

40      Moments before, a tremor in every part
disturbed these fetid depths. The universe
must then, I think, have felt that love through which

43      it often turns (so some suppose) to chaos.
At that same point, these age-old crags were rent
and left both here and elsewhere as they are.

46      But fix your eyes upon the valley floor.
We now are nearing the river of blood.
There simmer all whose violence damaged others.'

49      What blind cupidity, what crazy rage
impels us onwards in our little lives –
then dunks us in this stew to all eternity!

52      I saw there (as my guide had said I would)
a ditch of great dimensions in an arc
that stretched its wide embrace around the plain.

55*      And there, between the hill foot and those banks,
were centaurs, running in a long-drawn line,
armed – as they'd been on earth to hunt – with arrows.

58      On seeing us descend, they all reined in.
Three of that company then sallied forth,
their barbs and bow strings already well picked.

61      And one, still distant, shouted out: 'What pain
have you to meet, now making down that butte?
Tell us from there. Or else I draw my bow.'

My teacher in response then said: 'To Chiron –          64
there, just beside you – we shall make reply.
You are too headstrong. And you always were.'

'That's Nessus there,' he said, alerting me.          67
'He died for love of lovely Deianira,
but then avenged himself with his own blood.

The middle one (eyes fixed upon his chest)          70
is Chiron the Great. He nurtured Achilles.
Pholus, who lived so full of wrath, is third.

Around this ditch, in thousands these all run,          73
and loose their arrows at those souls that strain
higher beyond the blood than guilt allows.'

We drew now closer to those swift-foot beasts.          76
Then Chiron plucked a shaft and, with its notch,
he combed his beard and tucked it from his jaw.

And, once he'd made his noble mouth thus free,          79
he said to his companions: 'Have you seen
the one behind, how all he touches moves?

A normal dead man's feet would not do that.'          82
My trusted leader was now standing where,
around the waist, the double nature weds.

He answered thus: 'He is indeed alive.          85
To me it falls to show him this dark vale.
Necessity, not pleasure, leads us on.

Someone whose hymn is the "Alleluia"          88*
paused in that song to hand me this new task.
He is no robber, I no thievish soul.

Now in the name of that True Power by which          91
I move each step along this tangled way,
allot a guide to us from your own band

to show us where the ford might be, and bear          94
this man beside me on his crupper.'
He is no spirit walking through the air.

Now Chiron turned, to pivot to his right.          97
'Go back!' he said to Nessus. 'Be their guide.
Make any troop you stumble on give way.'

100     The escort by our side, we now moved on
        along the shore of boiling vermilion
        where souls, well boiled, gave vent to high-pitched yells.

103     Some, so I saw, were plunged there to the brow.
        'And these,' the mighty centaur said, 'are tyrants.
        They lent their hands to violent gain and blood.

106*    So here, in tears for their unpitying sins,
        with Alexander there is vicious Dionysius,
        who brought on Sicily such grieving years.

109     That forehead there – its quiff as black as jet –
        is Azzolino. At his side the blond
        Opizzo d'Este, who – and this is true –

112     was done to death by his own bastard son.'
        I turned towards the poet, who now said:
        'Let him go first and I'll be next to come.'

115     A little further on, the centaur stopped,
        arched over people who emerged, it seemed,
        throat high above the seething of that stream.

118     There, to one side, he pointed out a shade.
        'He stabbed,' he said, 'in the bosom of God,
        the one whose heart drips blood still on the Thames.'

121     I now saw some with heads above the flood,
        then others further on, their torsos clear.
        And these, in greater numbers, I could recognize.

124     Then, gradually, the blood race grew more shallow –
        so that by now it only stewed their toes.
        And there we found the crossing of the ditch.

127     'On this side – see? – the boiling stream grows less.
        So, correspondingly,' the centaur said,
        'I'd have you understand that, over there,

130     the bed is pressed, in process point by point,
        still further down until it finds the place
        at which in pain great despots wring out moans.

133     Justice divine on that side sharply stings
        the hun Attila – scourge of all the earth –
        Pyrrhus and Sextus. There it also milks

the tears eternally that boiling wave unlocks     136
from Renier the Mad to Renier da Corneto,
who wrought such strife upon the open roads.'
And then he turned and passed the ford once more.     139

# CANTO 13

|     |                                                              |
| --- | ------------------------------------------------------------ |
| 1   | No, Nessus had not reached the other side                    |
|     | when we began to travel through a wood                       |
|     | that bore no sign of any path ahead.                         |
| 4   | No fresh green leaves but murky in colour,                   |
|     | no boughs clean arc-ed but knotty and entwined,              |
|     | no apples were there but thorns, poison-pricked.             |
| 7*  | No scrubby wilderness so bitter and dense                    |
|     | from Cécina as far as Corneto                                |
|     | offers a den to beasts that hate ploughed farmlands.         |
| 10  | Their nest is there, those disgusting Harpies                |
|     | who drove the Trojans from the Strophades,                   |
|     | with grim announcements of great harm to come.               |
| 13  | Wings widespreading, human from neck to brow,                |
|     | talons for feet, plumage around their paunches,              |
|     | they sing from these uncanny trees their songs of woe.       |
| 16  | Constant in kindness, my teacher now said:                   |
|     | 'Before you venture further in, please know                  |
|     | that you now stand in Sub-ring Number Two,                   |
| 19  | and shall until you reach the Appalling Sands.               |
|     | So look around. Take care. What you'll see here              |
|     | would drain belief from any word I uttered.'                 |
| 22  | A wailing I heard, dragged out from every part,              |
|     | and saw there no one who might make these sounds,            |
|     | so that I stopped, bewildered, in my tracks.                 |
| 25* | Truly I think he truly thought that, truly,                  |
|     | I might have, just, believed these voices rose               |
|     | from persons hiding from us in the thorn maze.               |

Therefore: 'If you,' my teacher said, 'will wrench 28
away some sprig from any tree you choose,
that will lop short your feeling in such doubt.'

And so I reached my hand a little forwards. 31*
I plucked a shoot (no more) from one great hawthorn.
At which its trunk screamed out: 'Why splinter me?'

Now darkened by a flow of blood, the tree 34
spoke out a second time: 'Why gash me so?
Is there no living pity in your heart?

Once we were men. We've now become dry sticks. 37
Your hand might well have proved more merciful
if we had been the hissing souls of snakes.'

Compare: a green brand, kindled at one end – 40
the other oozing sap – whistles and spits
as air finds vent, then rushes out as wind.

So now there ran, out of this fractured spigot, 43
both words and blood. At which I let the tip
drop down and stood like someone terror-struck.

'You injured soul!' my teacher (sane as ever) 46
answered. 'If he had only earlier
believed what my own writings could have shown,

he'd not have stretched his hand so far towards you. 49
This, though, is all beyond belief. So I was forced
to urge a deed that presses on my own mind still.

But tell him now who once you were. He may, 52
in turn, as remedy, refresh your fame,
returning to the world above by leave.'

The trunk: 'Your words, sir, prove so sweet a bait, 55
I cannot here keep silence. Don't be irked
if I a while should settle on that lure and talk.

I am the one who held in hand both keys 58
to Federigo's heart. I turned them there,
locking so smoothly and unlocking it

that all men, almost, I stole from his secrets. 61
Faith I kept, so true in that proud office
I wasted sleep and lost my steady pulse.

64         That harlot Scandal, then (her raddled eyes
she never drags from where the emperor dwells,
the vice of court life, mortal blight of all)

67         enflamed the minds of everyone against me.
And they in flames enflamed the great Augustus.
So, happy honours turned to hapless grief.

70         My mind – itself disdainful in its tastes –
believing it could flee disdain by dying,
made me unjust against myself so just.

73         By all these weird, new-wooded roots, I swear
on oath before you: I did not break faith,
nor failed a lord so worthy of regard.

76         Will you – should either head back to the world –
bring comfort to my memory, which lies
still lashed beneath the stroke of envious eyes?'

79         Pausing a while, he said (my chosen poet),
'He's silent now, so waste no opportunity.
If there is more you wish to know, then say.'

82         'You,' I replied, 'must speak once more and ask
what you believe will leave me satisfied.
I could not do it. Pity wrings my core.'

85         And so he did once more begin: 'Suppose
that freely, from a generous heart, someone
should do, imprisoned ghost, what your prayers seek,

88         tell us, if you should care to, this: how souls
are bound in these hard knots. And, if you can:
will anyone be ever loosed from limbs like these?'

91         At that (exhaling heavily) the trunk
converted wind to word and formed this speech:
'The answer you require is quick to give:

94         When any soul abandons savagely
its body, rending self by self away,
Minos consigns it to the seventh gulf.

97         Falling, it finds this copse. Yet no one place
is chosen as its plot. Where fortune slings it,
there (as spelt grains might) it germinates.

A sapling sprouts, grows ligneous, and then                    100
the Harpies, grazing on its foliage,
fashion sharp pain and windows for that pain.

We (as shall all), come Judgement Day, shall seek         103
our cast-off spoil, yet not put on this vestment.
Keeping what we tore off would not be fair.

Our bodies we shall drag back here; and all              106*
around this melancholy grove they'll swing,
each on the thorn of shades that wrought them harm.'

Attention trained entirely on that stock                   109
(thinking, in truth, it might as yet say more),
we now were shocked by a sudden uproar,

as if (to make comparison) you'd heard some hog           112
and all the boar hunt baying round its stand –
a sound composed of beasts and thrashing twigs.

And look there, on the left-hand side, there came,        115*
at speed, two fleeing, naked, scratched to bits,
who broke down every hurdle in that scrub.

One was ahead: 'Quick, quick! Come, death! Come
        now!'                                             118
The other (seeming, to himself, too slow)
was yelling: 'Lano! Oh, your nimble heels

weren't half so nifty at the Toppo rumble!'              121
And then (it may be his breath was failing),
he sank to form a clump beside a shrub.

Behind these two, the wood was teeming, full             124
of black bitches, ravenous and rapid,
as greyhounds are when slipping from their leads.

These set their teeth on that sad, hunkered form.        127
They tore him all to pieces, chunk by chunk.
And then they carried off those suffering limbs.

My guide then took me gently by the hand,               130
and led me to the bush, which wept (in vain)
through all of its blood-stained lacerations,

saying: 'O Jacopo da Santo Andrea!                      133
What use was it to take me as your shield?
Am I to blame for your wild, wicked ways?'

136     My teacher came and stood above that bush.
        'So who were you,' he said, 'who, pierced to bits,
        breathes painful utterance in jets of blood?'

139     'You souls,' he said, 'you come – but just in time –
        to see the massacre, in all its shame,
        that rends away from me my fresh green fronds.

142*    Place all these leaves beneath this grieving stump.
        I too was from that city, once, which chose
        Saint John as patron over Mars – its first –

145     whose arts, since spurned, have always brought us harm.
        And were there not, beneath the Arno bridge,
        some traces visible of what he was,

148     those citizens who built it all anew
        on ashes that Attila left behind
        would then have laboured with no end in view.

151     Myself, I made a gallows of my house.'

# CANTO 14

Seized, in pure charity, by love of home,　　　　　1
I gathered up those scattered leaves, then bore them
towards my countryman, his voice grown dim.

And then, from there, we reached the boundary　　4
of circuits two and three and witnessed now,
in horror and awe, how skilful justice is.

To make more manifest what now was new,　　　　7
we'd reached, I'd better say, an open plain
that dusts all vegetation from its floor.

Round this, the wood of pain creates a fringe　　10
(as likewise, round that wood, the wretched ditch).
And here we halted at the very edge.

The ground beneath was brushed with coarse, dry sand,　13*
no different from those arid Libyan wastes
on which the feet of Cato marched to war.

Great God! Your vengeance must be rightly feared　16
by all who read the verses I compose
to say what there was straight before my eyes.

I saw ahead a flock of naked souls.　　　　　　19
And all were weeping, very mournfully.
But each was subject to a different law.

Some of these folk lay supine on the ground,　　22
and some sat huddling, tight about themselves.
Others again strode endlessly around.

The latter were, in number, far the more.　　　　25
Those lying flat, though fewer, were in tongue
more free at voicing their sharp miseries.

28      And over all that barren sand there fell –
as slow as Alpine snow on windless days –
a shower of broad-winged fire flakes drifting down.

31*      Recall how Alexander, on his march
across the climes of scorching India,
saw clouds of fire that fell around his troops

34      and reached the earth still whole. He therefore made
his squadrons stamp the ground, since, broken down,
these vapours proved far easier to quell.

37      So, too, eternally, the flames fell here.
The sand caught fire, like tinder under flint,
and doubled – from beneath – the upper punishment.

40      Unrestingly, their wretched hands jived on –
now up, now down, now high, now low, slap, clap! –
to shake fresh drops of ardour from their skin.

43      So I began: 'You, sir, in everything
have conquered all, though not those demons, hard-faced,
at the gate of Dis, who stopped us on that step.

46*      That hero there, who's he? Heedless he seems
of these incendiaries. Scowling in scorn,
it seems he lies unripened by the rain.'

49      The man himself roared forth (for he had seen
that I, in questioning my lord, meant him):
'What I, once living, was, so dead I am.

52      Yes! Jupiter may tire the blacksmith out
from whom he tore in wrath the thunder spear
by which I stood, on my last day, drilled through;

55*      and others, too, he may exhaust, in shifts
that stoke that black forge under Mount Jabal,
bellowing: "Vulcan! Aid, more aid! Good man!"

58      just as he did when battle raged at Flegra,
and loose his bolts at me with all his force . . .
But no! No sweet revenge he'd have on me!'

61      My leader then spoke out with greater strength
than ever I, till then, had heard him use:
'Oh, Capaneus! Pride yet uninterred!

This punishment, in consequence, is yours.                    64
No agony, except your own great rage,
would serve as proper answer to your ire.'
    And then – a better look around his lips –          67
he turned to me. 'This man,' he said, 'a king,
was one of seven laying siege to Thebes.
    God he disdained – he seems to, still – and seemed    70
to pay Him scant regard. So, as I said:
disdain alone must be his sole medallion.
    And now keep close behind. Take every care.       73
Do not set foot upon these blistering sands.
Follow the wood's verge round at every step.'
    In silence now, continuing, we came               76
to where a rill flows spurting from the grove.
Remembering its redness, I still squirm.
    As in Viterbo there's the Bubble Brook –         79*
which scarlet women, bathing, share between them –
so this stream took its course across the sand.
    That rivulet, in bed and bank, was formed         82
of stone, as also were the margins by its side.
This, I could tell, was where our best path lay.
    'Among so many other things that I –             85
since entering the gate through which
no foot is ever disallowed an entry –
    have shown to you, nothing your eyes have spied    88
has been more notable than this stream here,
above which all the sparks grow dim and die.'
    These were the words my leader spoke to me.       91
And I besought him, through his great largesse,
to grant the food in granting me the hunger.
    'Mid-sea,' he said, 'there lies a land now waste.    94*
To us, this land is known as Crete, where once,
when Saturn ruled as king, the world was chaste.
    A mountain stands there, Idaeus its name.          97
This, once, rejoiced in streams and leafy fronds,
but now stands abandoned like forbidden ground.

100     Once, Rhea – seeking for a sanctuary –
chose here to lay her boy child, Jove. And then,
to hide his wailings, called for dance and din.

103     Within those caves an aged man stands tall.
His back is turned to Egypt and Damiatta.
Rome is the mirror into which he stares.

106     His head is modelled in the finest gold.
Of purest silver are his arms and breast.
Then downwards to the fork he's brightest brass,

109     and all below is iron of choicest ore.
The right foot, though, is formed of terracotta.
On that he puts more weight than on the left.

112     And every part that is not gold is cracked.
Tears through this single fissure drizzle down,
then, mingling, penetrate the cavern wall.

115     Their rocky course cascades to this deep hollow.
They form the Acheron, Styx and Phlegethon.
These then disgorge themselves through this tight race,

118     until (since there is no way further on)
they all collect as Cocytus. But you yourself
will see that pool. So I'll not tell the tale.'

121     'If,' I now put to him, 'this gutter flows
from somewhere in our human world, then why
do we just see it at this selvage hem?'

124     'You know,' he said, 'this place is circular.
Yet, far as you have sunk in your descent,
your path has always tended to the left.

127     So you have still not spanned the circle round;
and if new things now show themselves to us,
it should not stir amazement on your brow.'

130     And I kept on at him: 'And so, sire, where
are Phlegethon and Lethe found? The one, you say,
rains down in tears. The other you are silent of.'

133     'By everything you ask,' he said, 'I'm pleased.
And yet, as one solution, you should note
the seething redness of the waters here.

Lethe you'll see, but far beyond this ditch.          136
Its waves are where the soul will go to wash,
when guilt, repented, is at last removed.'
    And then: 'It's time for you to leave this wood.     139
So come. Keep close behind me as you do.
The banks, which are not burned, provide a road.
    These vapours are extinguished over it.'         142

# CANTO 15

1  We're carried down by one of those hard shores,
while vapours from the brook rise, arching up,
to save both stream and margins from the fire.

4  Flemings, enflamed – from Wissant on to Bruges –
in terror of the floods that blast towards them,
construct great screens to put the sea to flight.

7  So, too, the Paduans, along the Brent,
attempt to shield their castles and estates,
before its source (Carinthia) is touched by heat.

10  Modelled on some original like these
(whatever master hand contrived them so)
these breaks were formed, though not that high or broad.

13  By now, we'd left the grove so far behind
that, even had I turned around to look,
I'd not have glimpsed the tract where it was found.

16  But here we came across a band of souls
who milled around the ditch and met our tread.
And each one peered at us – as people will

19  on evenings when the moon is new – their brows
towards us, wrinkled into squinting blades,
like those of some old tailor at his needle.

22*  Eyed up and down so closely by this clan,
I now was recognized, as known, by one
who plucked my hem and cried: 'How marvellous!'

25  And I – as he then stretched an arm towards me –
fixed eyes so keenly through his fire-baked look
that these singed features could not fend away

my mind from knowing, truly, who he was.                    28
And, reaching down a hand towards his face,
I answered him: 'Brunetto, sir, are you here?'

'Do not, my dearest son,' he said, 'be vexed,              31
but let Brunetto Latino turn and walk
a while along with you. The troops can run!'

'I pray, sir, to the utmost, do. Or should                  34
you wish,' I said, 'I'll sit with you, so long
as this man here agrees. I go with him.'

'Dear boy,' he said, 'if any in this herd                   37
should ever pause, he lies a hundred years
powerless to fan these searing fires away.

And so move on. I'll follow at your coat-tails             40
then catch up later with that entourage,
which, as it goes, bewails eternal loss.'

I did not dare climb down to quit the causeway            43
and walk with him on equal terms. But still,
as though in reverence, I kept my head bowed low.

'What chance or destiny,' he then began,                    46
'leads you down here before your final day?
And who is this that shows the way to you?'

'There, up above,' I answered him, 'where life            49
is halcyon, I lost myself – my path all blurred –
in some great deep before my years were full.

Only as dawn rose, yesterday, I turned                      52
aside. Then he – as yet again I turned –
appeared, and guides me on the road back home.'

'If,' so he answered, 'you pursue your star,               55
then doubtless you will reach a glorious goal,
supposing, in the happy life, I knew you well.

And I myself (had not I died too soon),                     58
seeing how kind the Heavens looked on you,
would willingly have helped you in your work.

But that malignant and ungrateful race                     61*
descending *ab antico* from Fiesole
(they still retain the taint of crag and hill)

64       will act, because you act so well, as bitter foes.
That much is logical: no luscious fig
can rightly thrive where small, sour sorbus grows.

67       The world, since ancient times, has known they're blind.
The tribe is grasping, envious and proud.
Keep yourself clean of habits of their kind.

70       Fortune for you reserves such great renown
that both these factions – Black and White – will seek
to set their teeth in you. Keep goats from grass!

73       Well may these cattle from Fiesole
make themselves straw but never touch the sprout
that springs (if any does within their dung)

76       to bring to life the sacred seed of Rome –
of those remaining when that ancient place
became the very home and nest of malice.'

79       'If all,' I said to him, 'that I might ask
were answered, and in full, then you would not
be exiled, as you are, from human nature.

82       Fixed in my thoughts, and working at my heart,
an image of you still endures – a dear, good father –
as, in the world, you were when hour by hour

85       you taught me how a man becomes eternal.
How great my gratitude must be, will show,
while I still live, in all my tongue will tell.

88       I write, as you recount it here, the story
of my future course, and keep your words with others.
A lady, if I come to her, will comment.

91       On this point only I would have you clear:
that I, so long as conscience does not chide,
am well prepared for all that Fortune wills.

94       In what you vouch, my ears hear nothing new.
Let Fortune, therefore, do as Fortune pleases –
whirl at her wheel like yokels at their hoe.'

97       My teacher, who had now turned right-about,
looked back at me and fixed me with his eye.
'Those listen well,' he said, 'who take good note.'

So on I go, speaking with lawyer Brunetto.                      100
I ask who his companions are, the great
and good, the eminent, and men of note.

'Of some,' he said, 'you're right to want to know.            103
More laudable of others not to speak.
Our time would be too short for all that din.

But all of them, be sure, were men of learning,              106*
authorities and dons of world renown,
besmirched, when living, with the self-same sin.

And so, among this dismal crowd, runs Priscian.              109
D'Accorso, too – the Prof. And if you yearn
to set your eyes on such-like mangy scabs,

you could. That bishop there! The Slave of Slaves          112
transferred him to Vicenza from the Arno.
He left his muscles, ill-distended, there.

I would say more. Yet further I may not                      115
advance nor any longer talk with you.
I see new smoke there, rising from the sand.

I can't consort with those who now draw near.              118*
My Treasury – may that commend itself.
In that, I still live on. I ask no more.'

Around he swung. To me he seemed like one                  121*
who, in the fields around Verona, runs
for that fine prize, a length of green festoon.

He seemed to be the one that wins, not loses.              124

# CANTO 16

1       I stood already where the roar and boom
of waters falling to the next great ring
could now be heard – a rumble like a beehive.

4       But then appeared, together, at the run,
three shadows, swerving from a further squad
of those in rasping torment from the rain.

7       Towards us, as they came, each cried aloud:
'Stop there! To us, it seems, you're dressed like one
who travels from our own degenerate homeland.'

10       No! No! I saw how branded by the bite
of fire their limbs all were. New wounds! Old scars!
This, though mere memory, still brings me pain.

13       My teacher paused, attending to their cries.
And then, his eyes on me, he said: 'Now wait.
We owe to these men here some courtesy.

16       Indeed, were not the nature of this place
to shoot down barbs of fire, then haste (I'd say)
should properly be shown by you, not them.'

19       And so again, as now we came to rest,
they all began the song they'd sung before
and, turning, formed among themselves a wheel.

22       Compare: prize wrestlers, with their bare skin oiled,
circle – until they clash, then punch and gouge –
in search of some advantage, grip or hold.

25       These likewise. As they wheeled around, each fixed
their glances hard on me. And so their necks
turned counter always to the track they trod.

'The misery,' thus one began, 'of these                              28
vile sands may render us, and all our prayers,
contemptible, our faces, too, now black and burned.

But let our reputations bend your heart.                             31
And who are you – now tell – whose living step,
in perfect safety, scours the paths of Hell?

This man, whose prints my own feet trample on,                       34
although he now goes naked, shorn of hair,
was once of higher rank than you'd imagine.

Grandson by birth of our good Gualdrada,                             37*
he was, by title, Conte Guido Guerra.
Much he achieved alive with mind and sword.

The other next to him who flails the sand                            40
is Lord Tegghiaio of the Aldobrands.
He ought to have more pleased the world in word.

I, in excruciating pain with them,                                   43
was Iacopo Rusticucci. And, yes,
it was my wife who did me greatest harm.'

If only I'd had cover from the fire,                                 46
I'd willingly have flung myself among them.
(I think my teacher would have suffered this.)

But since, down there, I'd soon have singed and baked,               49
fear got the better of the good intent
that stirred my appetite for their embrace.

So I began: 'Great grief, not scornfulness,                          52
to see your state was planted in my heart
(and only slowly will it shed its leaves)

the instant that my lord, in words to me,                            55
led all my inner thoughts to understand
that persons such as you might soon come by.

I am of your place, too. So, I have heard –                          58
and always with affection have proclaimed –
the deeds you've done and honour of your name.

I now take leave of galling fruits, to seek                          61
sweet apples, promised by my lord in truth,
but first must reach the centre of the circle.'

64     'Long may your soul lead forth your living limbs!'
So, in reply, said one of them. 'And – grant
your fame may long shine after you! – then say:

67     do courtesy and valour dwell, as once
they did, within the circuit of our city walls?
Or have they utterly departed thence?

70*     Report of this, from courtly Borsiere
(who only joined us here of late, and goes
with our companions there), has caused us pain.'

73     'That race of newly rich, and rapid gains,
these seeds, Fiorenza, bring to flower in you
excess and pride. And you already weep for that.'

76     With head thrown back, I cried this, all aloud,
and they, the three (accepting this response),
glanced each to each like those who've heard plain truth.

79     'If at so little cost,' they said, 'you speak
so well and satisfy what others seek,
then you may happily pronounce at will.

82     And so, should you escape from these dark haunts,
and go once more to see the lovely stars,
when you, with pleasure, say that "I was there",

85     then do, we beg you, speak of us to others.'
With this they broke their wheel and, as they fled,
their agile limbs in flight were quick as wings.

88     No 'amen' ever was so swiftly said
as these three disappeared before our eyes.
And now my teacher thought that we could leave.

91     I came behind. But now, not travelling far,
the sound of the water was so near at hand
that we could scarcely hear each other speak.

94*     Compare: a river, near its native source,
runs through the eastern Apennines due east,
and first descends the slopes of Monte Viso.

97     Its tranquil name up there is Acqua Cheta.
But then, on flowing to its lower bed,
at Forlì it assumes a different mode,

and thunders here, in one great bound, above      100
the Alp Saint Benedict, where – were it eased
from ledge to ledge – the height would need a thousand.

So, likewise, down through one great shattered force,    103
we found, resounding there, a blackened stream –
the din of which would soon have stunned our ears.

Around my waist I wore a braided cord,      106*
and had on past occasion thought, by this,
to snare the leopard with its painted hide.

My leader told me I should slip this off.      109
And when I'd got it wound from round my waist,
I handed it across in twisted knots.

And then he turned towards his right-hand side,    112
and flung it, bunched, some distance from the bank.
It fell, to find the depths of that great sink.

'Astounding things,' I told myself, 'are bound    115
to come at this astounding sign, which now
my master follows with his waiting eye.'

How cautious we must always be when faced    118
with those who, far beyond observing deeds,
can gaze in wisdom on our very thoughts.

So now he said: 'There soon shall rise what I    121
expect (what you in thought now dream) will come.
All shall be, soon, uncovered to your eyes.'

Always, to every truth that looks, in face,    124
like lies, one ought (quite firmly) bar the lip
lest, guiltless, what one says should still bring shame.

I cannot, though, be silent here. Reader,    127
I swear by every rhyme this comedy
has caused to chime (may it not lack long favour)

that now, through dark and fatty air, I saw –    130
to strike sheer wonder in the steadiest heart –
approaching us a figure swimming up,

as any diver might who'd gone below    133
to loose an anchor snagged on rocks (or something
other, hidden in the sea) and now comes back,

arms stretching high, legs drawn to make the stroke.    136

# CANTO 17

1     'Behold! The beast who soars with needle tail
      through mountains, shattering shields and city walls!
      Behold! The beast that stinks out all the world!'

4*    To me, my lord spoke thus, then beckoned up
      the monster to approach the jutting prow
      that marked the end of all our marble paths.

7     It came, that filthy image of deceit.
      Its head and trunk it grounded on the shore.
      It did not draw its tailpiece to the bank.

10    The face was that of any honest man,
      the outer skin all generosity.
      Its timber, though, was serpent through and through:

13    two clawing grabs, and hairy to the armpits,
      its back and breast and ribcage all tattooed
      with knot designs and spinning little whorls.

16*   No Turk or Tartar wove a finer drape,
      more many-coloured in its pile or tuft.
      Nor did Arachne thread such tapestries.

19    Compare: on foreshores, sometimes, dinghies stand
      in water partly, partly on the shingle –
      as likewise, in the land of drunken Germans,

22    beavers will do, advancing their attack.
      So did this beast – the worst that there can be –
      there on the rocky rim that locks the sand.

25    Out into emptiness it swung its tail,
      and twisted upwards its venomous fork.
      The tip was armed like any scorpion's.

My leader said: 'We need to bend our path          28
a little further down, towards that vile
monstrosity that's lolling underneath.'

So down we went, towards the right-hand pap.        31
Ten paces, and we'd reached the very edge,
stepping well clear of flames and burning shoals.

And then, on getting to that spot, I saw,           34
a little further on along the sandbar,
a group just sitting near the gaping waste.

And here my teacher said: 'To carry back            37
experience of the ring that we're now in,
go over there and look at their behaviour.

But do not stay to talk at any length.              40
Till you return, I'll parley with this thing,
for him to grant us use of his great thews.'

So once again, along the outward brow               43
of Circle Seven I progressed alone
to where there sat these souls in misery.

The pain they felt erupted from their eyes.         46
All up and down and round about, their hands
sought remedies for burning air and ground.

Dogs in the heat of summer do the same,             49
stung by the bluebottle, gadfly and flea,
swatting at swarms with paw pads or with snout.

On some of these – these faces under showers        52
of grievous, never-ceasing rain – I set my eyes.
I recognized no single one, but noticed

around the neck of each a cash bag hung             55
(each with its own insignia and blaze),
on which their staring eyes appeared to graze.

So I, too, gazing, passed among them all,           58*
and saw, imprinted on a yellow purse,
a blue device, in face and pose a lion.

Then, as my view went trundling further on,         61
I saw another, with a blood-red field –
the goose it bore was whiter, far, than butter.

64   And then I heard (from one whose neat, white sack
was marked in azure with a pregnant sow):
'What are you after in this awful hole?

67   Do go away! Yet you – as Vitaliano is –
are still alive. Then understand me, please:
he'll sit on my left flank, my one-time neighbour.

70   I'm Paduan, among these Florentines,
and often they all thunder in my ears:
"Oh, let him come," they'll scream, "that sovereign knight,

73   who'll bring the bag that bears three rampant goats."'
At which, in throes, he wrenched his mouth awry
and ox-like curled his tongue to lick his nose.

76   And I, who feared that, if I lingered long,
I'd irritate the one who'd said 'Be brief',
now turned my back upon these worn-out souls.

79   My leader, I discovered there, had jumped
already on that fearsome creature's rump.
'Come on,' he urged, 'be stalwart and courageous.

82   From now on we'll descend by stairs like these.
Mount at the front so I can come between,
to see the tail won't bring you any harm.'

85   Like someone shivering as the grip of 'flu
spreads over him, pale to the fingernails,
who trembles merely at the sight of shade . . .

88   well, that was me, as these words carried over.
The threat of shame, however, when one's lord
is near, emboldens one to serve him well.

91   I settled down between those gruesome shoulders.
I wished to say (my voice, though, would not come):
'Yes. Please! Be sure you hold me very firm.'

94   He, who in many an earlier 'perhaps'
had aided me, as soon as I got on,
flinging his arms around me, hugged me tight,

97   and said: 'Go on, then, Geryon. Cast out!
Wheel wide about to make a smooth descent.
Think of the strange new burden on your back.'

Slowly astern, astern, as ferries leave 100
the quay where they had docked, so he moved out.
Then, only when he felt himself ride free,

he turned the tail where breast had been before, 103
and – stretching long, as eels might do – set sail,
paddling the air towards him with his paws.

No greater fear (so, truly, I believe) 106*
was felt as Phaeton let the reins go loose,
and scorched the sky as still it is today,

nor yet by ill-starred Icarus – his loins 109
unfeathering as the wax grew warm – to whom
his father screamed aloud: 'You're going wrong!'

And then with fear I saw, on every side, 112
that I was now in air, and every sight
extinguished, save my view of that great beast.

So swimming slowly, it goes on its way. 115
It wheels. It descends. This I don't notice –
except an upward breeze now fans my face.

By then I heard, beneath us to the right, 118
the roar of some appalling cataract.
And so I leant my head out, looking down.

More timorous of falling still, I saw 121
that there were fires down there and heard shrill screams.
Trembling, I huddled back and locked my thighs.

And then I saw, as I had not before, 124
the going-down – the spirals of great harm –
on every side now coming ever nearer.

A falcon, having long been on the wing, 127
and seeing neither lure nor bird to prey on,
compels the falconer to sigh: 'You're coming in,'

then sinks down wearily to where it left so fast. 130
A hundred turns – and then, far from its lord,
it lands, disdainful, spiteful in its scorn.

So, too, did Geryon, to place us on the floor, 133
the very foot of that sheer, towering cliff.
And then, unburdened of our persons now,

vanished at speed like barbed bolt from a bow. 136

# CANTO 18

1*     There is in Hell a place called Rottenpockets,
rock, all rock, its colour rusted iron,
as is the wall that circles all around.

4     Dead in the centre of that poisoned plain
a well yawns open – empty, broad and deep.
Of that (when it's 'convenient') I'll have my say.

7     For now, between the well mouth and the clench
of cliff, a circling belt goes round, its floor
divided into ten deep trenches.

10     Compare: to guard the outer walls of castles,
moats in concentric multiples are dug,
and form the figure of a wheel around them.

13     That was the pattern that these trenches made.
And where, from fortresses, pontoons run out
to link each threshold to the other shore,

16     so, at the bottom of the precipice,
radials ride over every bank and ditch
till, at the pit, they're stopped and then sucked in.

19     This was the place where – shaken from the spine
of Geryon – we found ourselves. The poet
took the left-hand fork. I followed in his track.

22     Then, to my right, I saw fresh suffering:
new whips, new torments and new torturers,
and Pocket One, with these, was all a-flutter.

25     Down in those depths, stark naked, there were sinners
who came, on this side of a line, face on,
and faster, in our direction, on the other.

The Romans, in the Jubilee, devised                    28*
a way for pilgrims and pedestrians,
in all their multitudes, to cross the Bridge
    so that, on one side (making for Saint Peter's),    31
they faced the Castle and, conversely, took
the other lane when heading for the Hill.
    This way, that way, over the dismal rock,           34
there were (I saw them!) horny demons lashing,
lashing at the rear with vicious scourges.
    Ouch! Even at the first stroke they lifted          37
their trotters; and none of them, for certain,
stayed for second helpings – fewer still for thirds.
    But then, as I was moving on, looks clashed,        40
my own and one of theirs. I said straight off:
'There's one I've seen before. Once was enough.'
    To get him in my sights, I stopped my stride;       43
and, pausing quietly along with me,
my guide now let me turn a short way back.
    The body beaten abased its gaze, as if              46
it thought he really could hide. That didn't work.
'You there,' I said, 'Eyes-down! Bashful, are we?
    Assuming that your profile's not a lie,             49*
then you are Venedico Caccianemico.
So what brings you to this killing pickle?'
    And he to me: 'I grudge you my reply.               52
You and your bright words grind one out of me,
and make me call the world that was to mind.
    Foul tittletattle got this right. It's me;          55
I fixed it. My sister Ghisolabella
did let the marquis have his way with her.
    Don't think, though, I'm the only Bolognese         58
who's here in tears. The place is full of us.
Between the rivers Sàvena and Reno,
    far fewer tongues speak "yes" as "yeah" than here.  61*
And if you want to get this straight, recall
what money means to Bolognese hearts.'

64     And, as he spoke, a devil now struck out:
'Push off, you pimp,' he said, and swung his lash.
'There aren't tarts here for you to turn to cash.'

67     I turned to join my escort once again,
and walked with him a few steps further on,
then reached an outcrop jutting from the bank.

70     We made our way quite easily up that,
then, turning right along the splintered ridge,
we left that bunch to endless circulation.

73     So now we came to where the vault gapes wide
to let those beaten beings pass beneath.
'Pause here,' said Virgil, 'and ensure some glimpse

76     of all these woebegones now marks your eye.
They go in our direction. So, as yet,
you've had no chance to look them in the face.

79     We saw from that decrepit bridge the traces
of a second crew. These came towards us.
These, as well, were driven by whistling whips.

82     I did not prompt him, but my mentor said:
'Look at that hero there, advancing now!
He seems, for all his pain, to shed no tear.

85*    How great an air of majesty he still retains!
He is that Jason who, astute and strong,
made Colchos grieve to lose its gold-fleeced ram.

88     Journeying on, he passed the isle of Lemnos,
where cold and reckless women had, by then,
delivered death to every living male.

91     Yet he, with hints and eloquence of phrase,
beguiled the young Hypsipyle – a girl
who had herself proved guileful to the rest.

94     Alone he left her there, alone, with child.
That crime incurs for him this penalty
which also stands as vengeance for Medea.

97     Along with him go all who turned such tricks.
And that's enough to know about this vale,
or else of those who're caught within its fangs.'

We'd come already to the point at which                                     100
the tight path crosses with the second bank
and makes a shoulder to another arch.

And now we heard, from Pocket Number Two,                                    103
the groans and griping of another lot,
the snuffling of their snouts, their slapping palms.

The banks were crusted with a slime and mould                               106
that rose up in porridgy exhalations
and, scuffling, violated eye and nose.

The bottom of that pit goes down so deep                                     109
we saw it only when we climbed the ridge
and stood to see the rock rise straight above.

Reaching that point and looking down, we saw                                112
that all of them were plunged in diarrhoea
flowing, it seemed, from human cubicles.

And while my eyes were searching deep within,                               115
I noticed one whose head was foul with shit.
Had he the tonsure? It was hard to tell.

But he screamed out at me: 'Why gawp like that,                            118
so hungry-eyed for me and not the other swill?'
'Because,' I said, 'if I remember well,

I've seen you once before, with drier coiffure.                            121*
You are from Lucca. Alessio Interminei.
And that is why I've got my eye on you.'

He answered (battering his turnip top):                                    124
'I'm sunk this deep because of flatteries –
none were too sickly for my tongue to speak.'

When that was done, my leader now went on:                                 127
'Just poke your nose a little further out.
Your eyes may then be able to detect

a slut down there – filthy, with tangled hair,                             130
scratting herself with cacky fingernails,
squatting at one time, upright at the next.

Thais! She's there, the whore, the one who cooed                           133*
to her hot panting swain ("Yeees! Good for you?"),
"Angel, a miracle! My thanks indeed!"

Let that be all that here we need to view.'                                136

# CANTO 19

1*     You! Magic Simon, and your sorry school!
Things that are God's own – things that, truly, are
the brides of goodness – lusting cruelly

4*     after gold and silver, you turn them all to whores.
The trumpet now (and rightly!) sounds for you.
There you all are, well set in Pocket Three.

7      Onwards towards this yawning tomb, mounting
the ridge, by now we'd reached its summit –
the point that plumbs the middle of the ditch.

10     O wisdom in the height, how great the art
that you display in Heaven, on earth and even
in that evil world! How justly you deal power!

13     I saw how all the livid rock was drilled
with holes – along its flanks, across its floor –
all circular, and all of equal measure.

16*    To me they seemed, in radius, no more nor less
than fonts that, in my own beloved Saint John's,
allow the priest at baptisms a place to stand.

19     (Not long ago, I shattered one of those.
Someone was drowning there. I got them out.
This, sealed and sworn, is nothing but the truth.)

22     Out of the mouth of every single hole
there floated up a pair of sinner feet,
legs to the ham on show, the rest concealed.

25     The soles of all these feet were set alight,
and each pair wriggled at the joint so hard
they'd easily have ripped a rope or lanyard.

As flames go flickering round some greasy thing 28
and hover just above its outer rind,
so these flames also, toe tip to heel end.

'Who, sir,' I said, 'is that one there? That one 31
who jerks in pain far greater than his *cònfreres*,
sucked at by flames more fiercely vermilion.'

'I'll lift you down,' he answered me, 'if you 34
insist. We'll take that bank the easier.
He'll talk to you himself about his twists.'

'Whatever pleases you,' I said, 'to me is good. 37
Lord, you remain: I'll not depart – you know –
from what you will. You read my silent thoughts.'

So on we went to the fourth embankment. 40
We turned around, descended on our left,
arriving at that pitted, straitened floor.

My teacher, kindly, did not set me down – 43
nor loose me from his hip hold – till we'd reached
that fissure where (all tears) shanks shuddered.

'Whatever you might be there, upside down, 46*
staked, you unhappy spirit, like a pole,
if you,' I said, 'are able, then speak out.'

So there I stood like any friar who shrives 49
the hired assassin – head down in the earth –
who calls him back to put off stifling death.

And he yelled out: 'Is that you standing there? 52*
Are you there, on your feet still, Boniface?
The writings lied to me by quite some years.

Are you so sick of owning things already? 55
Till now, you've hardly been afraid to cheat
our lovely woman, tearing her to shreds.'

Well, I just stood there (you will know just how) 58
simply not getting what I'd heard come out,
feeling a fool, uncertain what to say.

Then Virgil entered: 'Say this – and make speed: 61
"No, that's not me. I am not who you think."'
And so I answered as he'd said I should.

64   At which – all feet – the spirit thrashed about,
then, sighing loudly in a tearful voice:
'So what is it you want of me?' he said.

67   'If you're so keen to know who I might be,
and ran all down that slope to find me out,
you'd better know I wore the papal cope.

70   A true Orsini, son of Ursa Bear,
I showed such greed in favouring her brats
that – up there well in pocket – I'm in pocket here.

73   Below me, in great stacks beneath my head,
packed tight in every cranny of the rock,
are all my antecedents in the Simon line.

76   Down there I'll sink, in that same way, when he
arrives whom I supposed that you might be,
and uttered, therefore, my abrupt inquiry.

79   But I already – feet up on the grill, tossed
upside down – have passed more time
than Boniface yet will, stuck here with red hot toes.

82*   For after him from westwards there'll appear
that lawless shepherd, uglier in deed,
who then, for both of us, will form a lid.

85   He shall be known as a "Jason-Once-Again".
We read in Maccabees: "Priest Bribes a King."
This other will score well with one French prince.'

88   I may have been plain mad. I do not know.
But now, in measured verse, I sang these words:
'Tell me, I pray: what riches did Our Lord

91   demand, as first instalment, from Saint Peter
before He placed the keys in his command?
He asked (be sure) no more than: "Come behind me."

94   Nor did Saint Peter, or the rest of them,
receive from Matthias a gold or silver piece,
allotting him the place that Judas lost.

97*   So you stay put. You merit punishment.
But keep your eye on that ill-gotten coin
that made you bold with Charles the Angevin.

And, were I not forbidden, as I am,          100
by reverence for those keys, supreme and holy,
that you hung on to in the happy life,

    I now would bring still weightier words to bear.    103
You and your greed bring misery to the world,
trampling the good and raising up the wicked.

    Saint John took heed of shepherds such as you.    106*
He saw revealed that She-above-the-Waves,
whoring it up with Rulers of the earth,

    she who in truth was born with seven heads    109
and fed herself, in truth, from ten pure horns,
as long as she in virtue pleased her man.

    Silver and gold you have made your god. And what's    112
the odds – you and some idol-worshipper?
He prays to one, you to a gilded hundred.

    What harm you mothered, Emperor Constantine!    115*
Not your conversion but the dowry he –
that first rich Papa – thus obtained from you!'

    And all the time I chanted out these notes,    118
he, in his wrath or bitten by remorse,
flapped, with great force, the flat of both his feet.

    My leader, I believe, was very pleased.    121
In listening to these sounding words of truth,
he stood there satisfied, his lips compressed.

    So, too, he took me up in his embrace.    124
Then, bodily, he clasped me to his breast
and climbed again the path where he'd come down.

    Nor did he tire of holding me so tight.    127
He bore me to the summit of that arch
spanning the banks of Pockets Four and Five.

    And there he gently put his burden down,    130
gently on rocks so craggy and so steep
they might have seemed to goats too hard to cross.

    From there, another valley was disclosed.    133

# CANTO 20

1
    I now must turn a strange new pain to verse
and give some substance to this twentieth chant
that deals (*Cantica* 1) with sunken souls.

4
    Already I had set myself to peer
intently on those now-discovered depths,
washed as they were with agonizing tears.

7
    I saw there people circling round that trench.
And on they came in silence, weeping still –
as slow in pace as litanies on earth.

10
    Then, as my gaze sank lower down these forms,
each was revealed (the wonder of it all!)
twisted around between the chin and thorax.

13
    The face of each looked down towards its coccyx.
And each, deprived of vision to the front,
came, as it must, reversed along its way.

16
    Seized by some paralytic fit, others,
perhaps, have been so turned awry. But I –
not having seen, myself – don't credit it.

19
    That God may grant you, as you read, the fruit
that you deserve in reading, think, yourselves:
could I have kept my own face dry, to see,

22*
    close by, that image of our human self
so wrenched from true that teardrops from the eyes
ran down to rinse them where the buttocks cleave?

25*
    Of this, be sure: that, leaning on a spur
of that unyielding cliff, I wept. 'Are you,'
my escort said, 'like them, an idiot still?

Here pity lives where pity's truth is dead.                    28
Who is more impious, more scarred with sin
than one who pleads compassion at God's throne?

Lift up your head! Stand straight. See, that one there?    31*
Under his chariot wheels, the earth yawned wide;
and Thebes – all eyes – yelled: "Where, Amphiaraus,

headlong away? Why leave us in this strife?"               34
Into the ceaseless void he fell, until
he came where Minos stands, who seizes all.

He's formed his chest – amazingly – from shoulder.         37
As once he wished to see too far ahead,
his tread is backward, and he stares to rear.

See there Tiresias! Male-to-female switch.                 40*
His looks, mutating, were entirely changed,
his members altering till each was each.

And then, to win once more his virile plumes,              43
he needs must strike a second time, and shake
again at coupling snakes his witch's wand.

Then, spine to gut, the prophet Arruns comes.              46
High in the Lunigiana hills – over
Carrara homesteads, so hard-hoed by serfs –

he found a grotto in the marble cliffs                     49
and took this for his dwelling place. Nothing,
from there, cuts off the view of sea or star.

And then there's one whose breasts you cannot see          52*
(since these are mantled by her flowing strands)
who shows on that side all her shaggy fleece.

She, once, was Manto, scouring many lands,                 55
until she reached and settled at my birthplace.
And so – to please me – listen for a while.

Her father, having left this life – and Thebes,            58
the place of Bacchus, being now in thrall –
for years she travelled, searching through this world.

Above, in lovely Italy, there lies a lake                  61*
(in Latin: Benacus) beneath those Alps
that lock out Germany beyond the high Tyrol.

64    From waters gathered in that standing pool
a thousand springs, I think, or more, refresh
the lands between those peaks, Camonica and Garda.

67    There is a place, the central point of these,
where pastors – if they choose to sail from Brescia,
from Verona and from Trent – have power to bless.

70    Here that brave citadel Peschiera sits,
built where the shoreline sinks to reach a low,
boldly outfacing Bergamese and Brescians.

73    Cascading from the lap of Benacus,
waters, unstayably, must run down here.
Through lush green meadows these all form a stream.

76    And this, when it begins to run, is known
by name as Mincio, not Benacus.
(It meets the river Po around Govérnolo.)

79    Moving, the Mincio at once dips down,
then, broadening in the plain, it forms a marsh –
and this in summer can be foul and brackish.

82    Manto, that bitter virgin, passing by,
saw, in the centre of that great morass,
a place unploughed and bare of population.

85    There, fleeing still from human fellowship,
she settled with her vassals, plied her arts,
in this place lived, here left her empty corpse.

88    Then other peoples came who had, so long,
been scattered all about. Because the marsh
surrounded it, the site was safe and strong.

91    They raised their city over those dead bones.
They called it Mantua (no magic charm!),
since Manto first had made the place her own.

94    Those living there were once more numerous,
before the idiotic Casalodi was
so taken in by Pinamonte's trick.

97    So, if in other stories you should hear
some tale of how my city came to be,
don't let the truth, I urge, be mocked by lies.'

'Sir,' I replied, 'to me your words are sure,                           100
and capture so entirely what I think,
that differing versions are as burned-out coal.

But let me know some more of this parade,                    103
that is, if any here still merit note.
My mind is waiting only for that word.'

And so he said: 'The one who there fans wide          106*
his beard from cheek to shadowed shoulderblade,
was – in those years when Greece was void of men,

when, even in the cradle, boys were few –               109
an augur. He, with Calchas, cast the hour
at which to cut the anchor rope in Aulis.

By name Eurypylus, there is some verse                   112
in my great tragedy that sings of him.
But you'll know where. You know the whole thing through.

And then we meet, so withered in his flanks,            115*
a certain Scotsman, Michael. In the spheres
of fraud and magic, he was full of pranks.

There's Guido Bonatti. Look! Asdente, too!          118*
The cobbler must be wishing now he'd stuck
to thread and leathers. Too late to repent.

Then see those hags? They, one and all, forsook     121
for witchcraft distaff, needle, pin and spool.
They cast their spells with weeds and ju-ju dolls.

But come, now come. The zone where hemispheres     124*
both meet by now is gripped (and, under
Seville, waves are touched) by Cain, his bush and thorns.

And yestere'en the rounding moon was full.            127
You must remember this. It shone while you,
unharmed, were deep within that first dark wood.'

And so he chatted on and we fared forwards.         130

# CANTO 21

So on we went from bridge to bridge, speaking
of things that I shan't, in my comedy,
commit to song. We gained the brow. Once there,

we paused and, down in Rottenpockets, saw
another fissure still, more empty tears.
I saw it all – a marvel of mere dark.

Compare: Venetians in their Arsenal,
in winter when their ships cannot set sail,
brew up a viscous pitch which they then smear

on ailing boards, or else lay down new hulls.
Others will plug the ribs of hulks that have,
by now, made many a long-haul trip.

Some hammer at the prow, some at the poop,
some whittle oars, where others plait the rig.
Some mend the mainsail, others patch the jib.

So here – though more by art of God than fire –
a dense black gunge was brought to boiling point,
and splashed on all the banks in sticky smears.

I saw this stuff but nothing else within
but bubbles as the boiling bubbled on,
swelling to roundness, glue-ily sinking in.

In mesmerized amazement I just gazed.
But then, 'Look out! Look out!' my leader cried,
then dragged me, where I'd stood, towards his side.

And there I turned as one who may well pause –
all swagger, in his sudden panic, gone –
to peep at what he really ought to flee,

yet, glimpsing this, does not delay his parting.                    28
I saw there, right behind us, this black demon
running the ridge around in our direction.

Eek! How ferocious all his features looked.                         31
How viciously his every move seemed etched,
wings wide apart, so lithe and light of foot.

The hunch blades of his shoulders, keen and proud,                  34
bore up the haunches of some criminal,
his hook fixed firm in tendons at each heel.

Mounting our bridge, demonically he barked:                         37*
'Get this, Rotklors! A boss man from Lucca!
You lot can dunk him. I'll get back for more.

I've got it stuffed, Saint Zita's place, with this sort.            40
They're at it there, the lot. (Oh! Not Bonturo!)
Cash on the nail, and "no" becomes "for sure".'

Dumping his load, he then dashed down                               43
and crossed the flinty slope. No mad bullmastiff
ever was loosed so fast to catch a thief.

The sinner dived, but then turned, writhing up.                     46
At which the demons, dossing by that bridge,
yelled: 'No place, black face, here for black-faced gods.

You can't swim here like bathers in the Serchio.                    49
If you don't want to know what hooks can do,
then just don't poke your nose above that tar.'

They sank in him a hundred barbs or more.                           52
'Down here,' they sang, 'you'll tango in the dark!
Get under cover! Pull what scams you can!'

Chefs do the same. They get their kitchen boys                      55
to fork the centre of a simmering pot,
so chunks of meat do not float up too high.

Here, too. 'Seem not to be here,' Sir now said.                     58
'Just hunker down behind a spur of rock.
It may still offer you some place to hide.

Yet have no fear. Oppose me as they may,                            61
my strategy – I know what's what – is clear.
I've been involved in rucks like this before.'

64  So now, beyond the bridge head, on he went,
    and needed, when he neared Embankment Six,
    the steadiest front that he could summon up.

67  With all the fury and tempestuous rage
    of dog packs rushing on some poor old tramp –
    who freezes there and pleads from where he'd reached –

70  so now those demons underneath the arch
    stormed out at him and brandished all their hooks.
    But he cried out: 'Don't even think of it.

73  Before you set on me with curving prongs,
    let one of you who'll hear me out draw near,
    and then discuss if hooking me is right or wrong.'

76  So, 'Go on, Rottentail,' they shrieked. 'That's you!'
    And he advanced (the others kept their ground
    and muttered: 'What will he get out of it?')

79  'Do you imagine, Rottentail,' my teacher said,
    'who've seen me come already once, immune
    to all your tricks, that I am here without

82  the favouring aid of fate or will divine?
    Let us pass on. For Heaven wills that I
    should guide another on the savage way.'

85  His arrogance at this took such a fall
    he let his hook slip, dangling, to his heels.
    'OK,' he told the others, 'let's not cut him.'

88  And now my leader turned and said: 'O thou
    who sittest there, squatting by that splintered bridge,
    return to me with confidence renewed.'

91  So shift I did, and reached him speedily.
    At which the demons all came pressing forwards –
    so I could not be sure they'd keep their word.

94* In this way, at Caprona once I saw
    the infantry come edging out, despite
    safe conduct, chary of the hordes around.

97  Huddled against my leader's side, pressed hard
    along him, head to toe, I could not wrench
    my eyes from them. Their looks did not look good.

They cocked their barbs. Then one spoke out:      100
'Want me to touch him on his fat backside?'
And they replied: 'Yeah, get him in the notch.'

But then that devil who was still in speech      103
with my great leader swung around at speed,
and said: 'Just cool it, cool it, Tangletop!'

'Further along this crag,' he now declared,      106
'you just can't go. Bridge Six is broken down.
It lies in ruins on the valley floor.

But if you'd care to schlepp still further on,      109
then do so round this arching cliff. Nearby,
another outcrop makes a path for you.

Just yesterday (five hours ahead of now),      112*
a thousand years, two centuries and sixty-six
from when the path was cut had then elapsed.

I'll send in that direction some of mine,      115
to watch for any sinner scenting air.
You go with them. They won't dare pull a stunt.'

'So, forward, Crackice! Forward, Flash Ali!'      118*
so he began: 'And Baddog! You as well.
And you, old Twirlitufts, can lead the squad.

Loveslot as well. And you, too, Dragonrunt,      121
Bigpig with tusks, and also Skratcherker,
Flutterby! For'ard! And you there, mad Glogob!

Search all around this pan of boiling lime:      124
until you reach the spur that arcs, unbroken,
over these dens, these two will go unharmed.'

'Sir, sir,' I said, 'what's this I see! Please, sir,      127
if you know how and where, let's go alone.
Myself, I didn't ask for this at all.

Your eyes are usually so very keen.      130
Can you not see? Just look! They grind their teeth.
Their frowns are warnings of what harm they mean.'

His answer was: 'I wouldn't have you frightened.      133
Let them scowl so, and grind as they may choose.
They mean it for the souls in this sad stew.'

136    About-face, leftwards on the rocky pass,
       each poked a tongue, teeth clenched, towards their lord,
       and he – to give the order now, 'Quick march!' –
139    in answer made a trumpet of his arse.

# CANTO 22

I, in my time, have seen brave knights strike camp,                     1
parade their power, launch an attack, and then,
at times, to save their skins, desert the field.

Yes, you, Aretines, I have seen our cavalry                            4*
charge through your heartland. Skirmishes I've seen,
cut-and-thrust tournaments and running duels,

all to the sound of horns (at times) or bells,                        7*
to beating drums or signals flashed from ramparts,
devices of our own and more exotic signs.

Yet never to so weird a pipe or whistle                              10
have I, till now, seen foot or horse fall in,
nor ship set sail to signs like that, from land or star.

So, on we went, five friends on either side.                         13
What fearsome company! Well, that's the way it is:
hobnob in church with saints, in pubs with sots.

The tar pit called for all my concentration                          16
to note each facet of this rotten hole,
and also of the persons burning there.

As schools of dolphin when they arch their spines                    19
provide a signal to the mariner,
to say the ship should soon be steered back home,

so too from time to time, to ease their pain,                        22
a sinner gave his back some air, then quick
as any lightning flash would hide again.

Likewise, in ditches at the water's edge,                            25
bullfrogs will stand, their snouts alone on show,
their feet concealed, with all their bulk below.

28    In this same way, these sinners lolled around.
      But then, whenever Twirlitufts came past,
      they swiftly dived beneath the bubbling crust.

31    I saw – at this, my heart still skips a beat –
      that one (as happens when a frog school springs,
      but one stays dallying) was left behind.

34    And Skratcherker – as being nearest to him –
      enmeshed his hook among those tar-caked locks
      and yanked him out like any floppy otter.

37    I knew them all by name, the lot of them.
      I'd noted each when they were first enrolled,
      and then, between them, heard them call out names.

40    'Get in there, Glogob! Get him with your hook!'
      (So, in damned unison, the chorus shrieked.)
      'And tear the leather off his ugly rump!'

43*   I turned, and to my master said: 'Find out,
      if you can manage it: who is that so-and-so
      who's fallen foul of these antagonists?'

46    My leader went, and stood beside him there,
      wanting to know the place where he was born.
      He answered: 'I'm a native of Navarre.

49    My mother, having borne me to a lout,
      who brought himself and all he had to ruin,
      engaged me to the service of a nobleman.

52    And then I joined King Thibaut's retinue,
      to practise arts of chartered bribery.
      For which I pay my dues in this great heat.'

55    Then Bigpig, with his boar-like jowls – a tusk
      stuck out from both his cheeks – supplied a sip
      of how well one of these could rake and rip.

58    The mouse had got among the bad cats now.
      But Twirlitufts enclosed him in his arms.
      'Stay over there!' he said. 'I'll keep him pinned.'

61    He tilted up his face towards my guide:
      'Go on, then. Ask him, if you want still more.
      But quick,' he said, 'before they do him in.'

'So tell me, then,' my master now went on,    64
'among the criminals beneath the tar,
are any – can you tell? – Italian?' 'Just now,'
    he answered me, 'I left a man from there.    67
If only I were with him still beneath the lid,
I wouldn't need to dread these hooks and claws.'

    'We've taken quite enough of this!' So said    70
the Loveslot. Skewering an arm, he sliced
a muscle out in one long hookful.

    Then Dragonrunt must also have a go.    73
He ogled the ham. But their decurion
swung round and gave them all a filthy frown.

    Then, just a little, they all settled down.    76
The sinner lay there, wondering at his wound.
My lord without delay now turned and asked:

    'Who was the one from whom, you say, you took,    79*
ill-fatedly, your leave to reach this shore?'
'Brother – as was – Gomita!' he replied.

    'Sard from Gallura, vessel of deceit!    82
Palming (well-greased) his sire's worst enemies,
he treated all so well, each sang his praise.

    He took their cash, then let them off the hook.    85
In this – as he'll admit – and everything
a total crook. Not small time, though. The King!

    Don Michael Zanche, from the Logudor,    88
still hangs around with him. Their tongues don't tire
of banging on about "Sardin-i-ah".

    Ow! Look at how that demon grinds his teeth.    91
I could tell more but (oh! I'm terrified!)
he means to come and give my scabs a scrub!'

    The high commander swung on Flutterby,    94
whose moon eyes popped in eagerness to pounce.
'Butt out!' he hissed. 'You vulture! Over there!'

    Witless with fear, he started once again:    97
'If you would witness or hold audience
with Lombards or Tuscans, I can make them come.

100 But let these Rotklors all stand well aside –
and no one need be frightened they'll attack –
while I, just sitting on this self-same spot,

103 will whistle. Now I'm here alone. Presto!
And now we're seven! That's our usual trick
when any from below gets out of it.'

106 Hearing this blag, old Baddog twitched his snout,
then shook his head and snarled: 'The little demon!
He means to take a dive and get back in.'

109 That sinner up his sleeve had snares galore.
'O yeah! That's me,' he said. 'A demon! Sure!
Really? You think I'd bring my gang more grief?'

112 Flash Ali, at these words, could not hold back.
Despite what his companions thought, 'Go on,'
he said. 'Slope off. I'll not come galloping.

115 I will, though, stretch my wings across the pitch.
Let's leave the ridge. Let's make the slope our screen.
And then we'll see if you can get off clean.'

118* O you there, as you read! Get this! Olympics!
They all then turned to face the other bank,
even the one who first was most reluctant.

121 The Navarrese chose his moment well.
Feet firmly planted, in a single flash,
he'd leapt and gone, scot-free of their intent.

124 At this, the lot of them were pierced by guilt.
Yet, undeterred, the devil most at fault
drove onwards. 'Now you're for it!' he yelled out.

127 To no avail. No wing could overhaul
the speed of fear. The sinner plunged. Square on,
the demon baulked and then shot up again.

130 So, too, a rapid duck dives down, glimpsing
a falcon closing in. The duck's foe then
returns aloft, bitter in thwarted pique.

133 Crackice, still seething at the doublecross,
zoomed ever onwards in his yen to see
the sinner free – then mix it with Flash Ali.

So, since the barrator had long since gone,      136
he turned his talons on his own best mate.
Above the ditch he locked him in his prongs.

The other, though, a right old sparrowhawk,      139
returned the hook. And so the two of them,
as one, went tumbling to the boiling pond.

The heat that instant made them come unhitched.      142
But, even so, they couldn't raise a thing,
so tightly glued together were their wings.

Then Twirlitufts, condoling with his kin,      145
sent four of them towards the inner rim,
with all their grappling tackle, at top speed.

This side and that they went to take their posts,      148
and bent their hooks towards those two, stuck fast.
By now they both were crisped within the batter.

With that entanglement, we left the matter.      151

# CANTO 23

| | |
|---|---|
| 1 | Silent, alone with no one now beside us, |
| | we went our way – the one behind, the other |
| | leading on – walking as meek Franciscans do. |
| 4* | My mind turned (thinking of that scuffle still) |
| | to Aesop and his fables, most of all |
| | the one about the frog and rat and hawk. |
| 7* | For 'now' and 'noo' are hardly more alike |
| | than this fine mess to that – if parallels |
| | are rightly drawn between the start and finish. |
| 10 | But thoughts pop up and then lead on to more. |
| | So from this first a further set was born, |
| | which now redoubled all my earlier fears. |
| 13 | 'Because of us,' the sequence ran, 'that lot |
| | have been so injured, put on, tricked and scorned, |
| | they cannot fail, I think, to be upset. |
| 16 | Suppose their bile gets tangled now with anger, |
| | then surely they'll come after us and snarl |
| | more viciously than dogs that snout a hare.' |
| 19 | I felt already that my every curl |
| | was bristling, on its end. So, gazing back, |
| | stock still, I said: 'If you, sir, do not hide |
| 22 | yourself this second, me as well . . . I dread |
| | the Rotklors gang. They're not now far behind. |
| | I hear them now, imagine it, quite clear.' |
| 25 | 'If I,' he said, 'were leaded mirror glass, |
| | I could not make your outer image mine |
| | more swiftly than I grasp your inward stress. |

Your thoughts just now came in upon my own,   28
in bearing similar, and look as well.
These, all together, formed a single plan.

Suppose that, on the right, the incline's such   31
that we can reach the pocket there beyond,
we shall elude the hunt we now imagine.'

No sooner had he offered up this thought   34
than, coming after us, I saw them, wings
stretched wide, now closer, meaning to get us.

My leader in an instant caught me up.   37
A mother, likewise, wakened by some noise,
who sees the flames – and sees them burning closer –

will snatch her son and flee and will not pause,   40
caring less keenly for herself than him,
to pull her shift or undershirt around her.

Down from the collar of that circling rock,   43
backwards he launched himself, and met the slope
that forms a bung against the other trench.

No mill race ever ran through any sluice   46
at such velocity, or streamed to meet
the scoops that drive, on land, the grinding stone,

as now my master slithered down that verge,   49
bearing me with him, bound upon his breast,
as though I were his son and no mere friend.

And hardly had his feet touched down to meet   52
the pocket floor than those were at the summit,
over us. We need have had no worries.

For that exalted providence that chose   55
such ministers to guard Ditch Five also
deprived them of the power to ever leave.

We found, down there, a people painted bright.   58
Their tread, as round they went, was very slow,
weeping, worn down and seemingly defeated.

They all wore robes with hoods hung low, that hid   61*
their eyes, tailored – in cut – to match those worn
by monks who thrive in Benedictine Cluny.

64* So gilded outwardly, they dazed the eye.
 Within, these robes were all of lead – so heavy
 those capes that melt in torture would have seemed mere s

67 What labour to eternity to wear such dress!
 We took once more the leftward path along
 with them, intent on their distress and tears.

70 Because, though, of the labouring weight they bore,
 these weary folk came on so slow that we,
 at every hip swing, joined new company.

73 'Do all you can' – I put this to my guide –
 'to find here someone known by name or deed.
 As we move onward, scan around to see.'

76 Then one who'd recognized my Tuscan words
 from close behind yelled out: 'You! Racing there
 through all this murky air, just ease your stride.

79 You'll get, perhaps, from me what you desire.'
 At this my leader turned. And, 'Wait,' he said,
 'then follow forwards at the pace he sets.'

82 I stopped and saw there two who, from their look,
 (though hampered by their load and narrow footings)
 in mind were speeding on to reach my side.

85 At last, they caught me up. With eyes a-squint,
 they gazed at me in wonder, spoke no word,
 till muttering they turned and, each to each:

88 'This one, it seems – Just see his throat! It flicks! –
 is still alive. If dead, why favoured so,
 to go uncovered by a weighty cloak?'

91 And then to me direct they said: 'Tuscan,
 you've reached the college of the hypocrites.
 Do not disdain to say who you might be.'

94 'Born,' I replied, 'by the lovely Arno,
 grown in the city that adorns its banks,
 I still am in the limbs I've always worn.

97 But who are you, in whom, as I can see,
 great pain distils such tears upon your cheeks?
 What punishment strikes out these sparks from you?'

And one replied to me: 'These orange robes 100
are thick with such a quantity of lead,
the weight of them would make a balance creak.

We're good-time friars, Bolognese both. 103*
Our names? I'm Catalano. Loderingo's there,
captured together in that town of yours –

although, by custom, there is one alone 106
whose mandate is to keep the peace. Our doings
still appear around the Watch, for such we were.'

I then began: 'O brothers! All the harm that you . . .' 109
but said no more. Straight to my sight, there sped
one crucified. Three staves fixed him to earth.

And he, on seeing me, writhed all around 112
and fluffed his beard up with the sighs he heaved.
Then brother Catalan, who saw all this,

revealed to me: 'This figure, staked, whom you 115*
so wonder at, advised the Pharisees
that one man suffer for the sake of all.

Across the road, stretched naked, as you see, 118
he first must feel, whoever passes by,
the toiling weight of those who come this way.

Here too lies Annas – father of his wife – 121
racked in this ditch with others of that house
that proved an evil seed bed for the Jews.'

Virgil, I saw, just stood there marvelling, 124
bending above that figure on the cross,
eternally in ignominious exile.

But then, towards the friar he voiced: 'Please say 127
(though not to trouble you), if you're allowed,
is there some outlet lying to the right

through which the two of us can make our way 130
without the need to call black angels here,
who might come down to further our departure?'

'Far sooner than you hope,' the answer was, 133
'we'll near a rock that, jutting from the Ring,
vaults over all these savage valley floors –

136       except it's broken here and forms no covering.
          You can, though, clamber up the ruined side.
          The slope is gentle and the base piled high.'

139       My leader stood a moment, head hung down.
          And then he said: 'He gave a false account,
          that hooker-up of sinners over there.'

142       'I, in Bologna,' so the friar said, 'have heard
          a good few stories told of devil vice,
          not least "Old Nick's a liar – falsehood's dad".'

145       At this, with lengthened pace, my lord strode off,
          clear signs of anger flitting on his face.
          And so I left these beings with their loads

148          to follow in the prints of his dear feet.

ear,                                          1*

h Aquarius,

the day,

n the ground                                  4

o endure),

pplies                                        7

t and sees

his thigh,

, as though                                   10

lo,

ug,

he features                                   13

ad.

asture.

ayed                                          16

row.

                                              19

me

oot.

hought                                        22

survey

assesse

ves                                           25

(so tha

in hauli

---

THERE, in the Broad, within whose booky house
Half England's scholars nibble books or browse.
Where'er they wander blessed fortune theirs:
Books to the ceiling, other books upstairs;
Books, doubtless, in the cellar and behind
Romantic bays, where iron ladders wind.

JOHN MASEFIELD

*Whatever book you may want, wherever you may be—
ask* BLACKWELL'S

Blackwells.co.uk

28      of one moraine, he'd see a spur beyond
and say: 'Next, take your hold on that niche there.
But test it first to see how well it bears.'

31      This was no route for someone warmly dressed.
Even for us – he, weightless, shoving me –
we hardly could progress from ledge to ledge.

34      Had not the gradient been less severe
than that which faced it on the other side,
I'd have been beat. I cannot speak for him.

37      But Rottenpockets slopes towards the flap
that opens on the lowest sump of all,
and so, in contour, every ditch is shaped

40      with one rim proud, the other dipping down.
So, in the end, we came upon the point
where one last building block had sheared away.

43      My lungs by now had so been milked of breath
that, come so far, I couldn't make it further.
I flopped, in fact, when we arrived, just there.

46      'Now you must needs,' my teacher said, 'shake off
your wonted indolence. No fame is won
beneath the quilt or sunk in feather cushions.

49*     Whoever, fameless, wastes his life away,
leaves of himself no greater mark on earth
than smoke in air or froth upon the wave.

52      So upwards! On! And vanquish laboured breath!
In any battle mind-power will prevail,
unless the weight of body loads it down.

55*     There's yet a longer ladder you must scale.
You can't just turn and leave all these behind.
You understand? Well, make my words avail.'

58      So up I got, pretending to more puff
than, really, I could feel I'd got within.
'Let's go,' I answered, 'I'm all strength and dash.'

61      Upwards we made our way, along the cliff –
poor, narrow-going where the rocks jut out,
far steeper than the slope had been before.

...ed and distributed circa 1939

Talking (to seem less feeble) on I went,      64
when, issuing from the ditch beyond, there came
a voice – though one unfit for human words.

I made no sense of it. But now I neared      67
the arch that forms a span across that pocket.
The speaker seemed much moved by raging ire.

Downwards I bent. But in such dark as that,      70
no eye alive could penetrate the depths.
But, 'Sir,' I said, 'make for the other edge,

and let us then descend the pocket wall.      73
From here I hear but do not understand.
So, too, I see, yet focus not at all.'

'I offer you,' he said to me, 'no answer      76
save "just do it". Noble demands, by right,
deserve the consequence of silent deeds.'

So where the bridgehead meets Embankment Eight      79
we then went down, pursuing our descent,
so all that pocket was displayed to me.

And there I came to see a dreadful brood      82
of writhing reptiles of such diverse kinds
the memory drains the very blood from me.

Let Libya boast – for all her sand – no more!      85
Engender as she may chelydri, pharae,
chenchres and amphisbaenae, jaculi,

never – and, yes, add Ethiopia, too,      88
with all, beyond the Red Sea, dry and waste –
has she displayed so many vicious pests.

And through all this abundance, bitter and grim,      91*
in panic naked humans ran – no holes
to hide in here or heliotropic charms.

Behind their backs, the sinners' hands were bound      94
by snakes. These sent both tail and neck between
the butts, then formed up front the ends in knots.

And near our point, at one of them (just look!)      97
a serpent headlong hurled itself and pierced
exactly at the knit of spine and nape.

100　　　Then, faster than you scribble 'i' or 'o',
that shape caught fire, flash-flared and then (needs must)
descended in cascading showers of ash.

103　　　There, lying in destruction on the ground,
the dead dust gathered of its own accord,
becoming instantly the self it was.

106*　　Compare: the phoenix (as the sages say)
will come to its five-hundredth year, then die,
but then, on its own pyre, be born anew.

109　　　Its lifelong food is neither grass nor grain,
but nurture drawn from weeping balm and incense.
Its shroud, at last, is fume of nard and myrrh.

112　　　The sinner, first, drops down as someone might
when grappled down, not knowing how, by demons
(or else some other epileptic turn),

115　　　who then, on rising, gazes all around,
bewildered by the overwhelming ill
that came just now upon him, sighing, staring.

118　　　So, too, this sinner, getting to his feet.
What power and might in God! How harsh it is!
How great the torrent of its vengeful blows!

121*　　My leader then demanded who he was.
'I pelted down' – the sinner, in reply –
'to this wild gorge, right now, from Tuscany.

124　　　Beast living suited me, not human life,
the mule that once I was. I'm Johnny Fucci,
animal. Pistoia is my proper hole.'

127　　　I to my leader: 'Tell him, "Don't rush off!"
and make him say what guilt has thrust him down.
I've seen him. He's a man of blood and wrath.'

130　　　The sinner, hearing this, made no pretence.
He fixed on me a concentrated eye,
and coloured up in brash embarrassment.

133　　　'It pisses me right off,' he then declared,
'far more than being ripped away from life,
that you have got to see me in this misery.

    I can't say "no" to what you ask of me.         136
I'm stuck down here so deep 'cos it was me,
the thief who nicked the silver from the sanctuary.
    Then I just lied – to grass up someone else.     139
You won't, however, laugh at seeing this.
If ever you return from these dark dives,
    prick up your ears and hear my prophecy:    142*
Pistoia first will slim and lose its Blacks.
Then Florence, too, renews its laws and ranks.
    Mars draws up fireballs from the Val di Magra,   145
wrapped all around in clouds and turbulence.
And these, in acrid, ever-driven storms,
    will battle high above the Picene acre.     148
A rapid bolt will rend the clouds apart,
and every single White be seared by wounds.
    I tell you this. I want it all to hurt.'       151

# CANTO 25

<sup>1*</sup> His words now reached their end. And then the robber
hoisted hands on high – a fig-fuck formed in each –
and screamed: 'Take that! I'm aiming, God, at you!'

4 From that point on, the serpents were my friends.
For one entwined its length around his neck
as if to say: 'I'd have him speak no more.'

7 And then another bound his arms down tight,
and clinched itself so firmly round the front
he could not shake or shiver in either limb.

10* Pistoia! Ah! Pistoia! Why not take a stand?
Just burn yourself to blackened ash, and be
no more. Your seed succeeds in doing only ill.

13* In all of Hell, through every murky ring,
I saw no spirit facing God so proud,
even that king flung down from Theban walls.

16 Away he fled. He spake no further word.
And then there came, I saw, a wrathful centaur.
'Where? Where is he,' he called, 'so sour and crude?'

19 Maremma, I should think – with all its swamps –
has fewer snakes than he. They writhed from rump
to where, on human features, lips begin.

22 Above its shoulders, stretched behind the nape,
there lay a dragon, wings extended wide.
And all it hits against, it sets on fire.

25* 'This centaur,' so my teacher said, 'is Cacus.
He is the one – so many times – who caused
a lake of gore to flood the Aventine.

He does not tread the path his brethren take.    28
For spying, once, a mighty herd at hand,
he made it all his own by furtive fraud.

Beneath the mace of Hercules (that god    31
rained down a hundred blows, and he, perhaps,
felt ten, no more) his devious doings ceased.'

So Virgil spoke. The centaur sped away.    34
But now three spirits had approached beneath,
though neither of us noticed they were there

until they shouted out: 'So who are you?'    37
Our story-telling pausing at this point,
we fixed attention wholly on that trio.

Among the three was none I recognized.    40
And yet it chanced – as happens many times –
that one was forced to speak another's name,

inquiring: 'Where has Cianfa got to now?'    43*
At which (to shut my leader up) I placed
a finger slantwise from my chin to nose.

If you are slow, my reader, to receive,    46
in faith, what I'll say now – no miracle.
I saw it all, and yet can scarce believe.

While, eyebrows raised, I stared at these three men,    49
a reptile hurled itself with all six feet
at one, front on, and took a total hold.

It clenched the belly with its middle claws.    52
With each anterior it seized an arm.
It sank a forked fang deep in either cheek.

Along each loin it slithered out a leg,    55
then struck its tail between the two, to take,
now upwardly, a grip around the buttocks.

Ivy in tangles never barbed to tree    58
so tight as this ferocious awfulness,
linking its limbs in tendrils round that trunk.

As though the two were formed of warming wax,    61
each clung to each and, mingling in their hues,
neither now, seemingly, was what it was.

64   Like that, a flame runs flaring up a page
and, just ahead, goes ever-darkening tints,
not black as yet, and yet the white still dies.

67   The other two, at this, stared on. And each
moaned out: 'Ohimé, Agnello, how you change!
Already, look, you're neither two nor one.'

70   And yes, those two by now were both as one.
That is: the outlines of the two appeared
in one face only, two-ness lost and gone.

73   Two arms were fashioned out of four long strips.
Thorax and stomach, loins and thighs and hips
became such organs as you've never seen.

76   In each, the primal signs were all struck out.
Two yet not either, as it seemed, this sick
apparition. So, treading slow, it went its way.

79   The great green lizard, at the summer's height,
lashed by a dog star rage from hedge to hedge,
crosses the path as though a lightning flash.

82   So, paunch high (darting at the two, of three,
who still remained), inflamed and fierce, there came
a snakelet, livid as a peppercorn.

85   This serpent pierced in one that spot where first
we draw our nourishment, transfixing him.
It then fell back, stretched out before his face.

88   The one transfixed gazed down but spoke no word.
Rather, he yawned, his feet just planted there.
Sick sleep, it seemed, had struck him hard, or fever.

91   He eyed the snake. The reptile eyed him back.
Each gave out smoke in streams – the wound of one,
the serpent's jaws. The smoke streams slowly met.

94*   Lucan! Be silent now, and tell no more
your snaky tales of poor Sabellus and Nasidius.
Give ear to what the bow will now unleash.

97   Ovid, be silent! Less 'Cadmus' and 'Arethusa'!
In turning verse, these two he may convert
to snake or stream. I do not envy him.

For he, through metamorphosis, did not　　　　100
compose two species, glance on glance, whose forms
disposed themselves exchanging actual substance.

Each answered each in working through this rule:　103
the serpent fashioned (from his tail) a fork;
the wounded human dragged his footprints to.

The legs, now fastening at their inner thighs,　　106
adhered so well that soon the join between
gave no clear sign of ever having been.

The cloven tail assumed the figure now　　　　109
of that which, over there, was lost to view.
Hide softened here, but hardened over there.

I saw each arm retract and reach its pit.　　　112
The paws, conversely, of that stubby newt
lengthened as much as human feet grew short.

The hindmost toes then curled around and clinched;　115
these formed the member that a man conceals.
The other wretch wrenched his own part in two.

As now, around this pair, the fumes still hang,　118
a gauze of stranger colours – causing hair
to sprout fresh here, while there it plucks it sleek –

the one rose up, the other fell down flat,　　　121
yet, peering out, as this snout changed for that,
neither could wrest from either evil eye beams.

Upright, the one dragged jowl across to temple.　124
And then, from leakages of surplus pulp,
a pair of ears appeared, on thinned-out jowls.

Whatever residue did not run back　　　　　127
now gelled, and gave that face its human nose.
The lips, plumped up to meet the need, gained bulk.

The other, lying flat, extends his muzzle.　　　130
Then, just like snails when pulling in their horns,
he draws his ears back, flush along his skull.

And now the tongue – once whole, and quick to speak – 133
divides in two. The other finds his fork
has closed right up. The furls of smoke now cease.

136*   The soul, transmogrified to fearful beast,
    flees – hissing, snuffling – off across the pit.
    Spot on his track, the speaking presence spits.

139    And then he turns on him his novel back
    to tell the third: 'I'll see slick Buoso go
    as I did, bellyflop, around this track.'

142    Zymotic in the seventh bilge, I saw, then,
    change and counterchange. My only plea, if here
    my pen turns vain, must be sheer novelty.

145    And though my vision was a bit confused
    (spirit quite drained of all its energies),
    these souls could not so covertly pass by

148*   that I should fail to see the cripple Puccio.
    Of three companions who had first come there,
    he, all alone, escaped from alteration.

151    The last was him that you, Gaville, weep for.

# CANTO 26

Rejoice, Florentia! You've grown so grand          1*
that over land and sea you spread your beating wings,
and through the whole of Hell your name resounds.

Among those thieves and robbers there, I found,          4
were five of your own citizens. I am ashamed.
And you do not acquire, by this, great honour.

Yet if we dream, near dawn, of what is true,          7*
then you, not long from now, will surely feel
what Prato aches to see for you – others, as well.

And were it now it would not be too soon.          10
Would it were so, as rightly it should be.
It weighs me down the more that time drags on.

We now moved off. And climbing by those stairs          13
that, going down, had bleached us ivory,
my leader, mounting up, pulled me along.

And so, proceeding on this lonely way          16
through splintered rocks and outcrops from the ridge,
feet without hands would not have gained advantage.

It grieved me then, it grieves me now once more,          19
to fix my thoughts on what I witnessed there.
Now, more than usual, I must hold mind back,

lest brain should speed where virtue does not guide.          22
Thus if, by some propitious star (or more),
I've come to good, I'd best not make it void.

A farmer, leaning on his hillside, rests.          25
(It's summer time, when he who lights the earth
least hides his face from us.) This countryman,

28  as now the fly makes way for the mosquito,
sees there, below him on the valley floor,
(where he perhaps will plough and gather grapes)

31  glow-worms in numbers such as now I saw,
glittering around the dip of Pocket Eight,
when I arrived there, looking to its depths.

34*  Compare, as also in the Book of Kings:
Elisha (once avenged by furious bears)
beheld Elijah's chariot drawn away

37  by horses rising to the Heavens, straight.
His eye, unable to pursue, could see
only the flame, like cloud whisp, rising high.

40  So, too, within the gullet of that ditch,
these fires move round. None shows its thievery.
Yet each fire stole some sinning soul away.

43  I stood there on the bridge and craned to look.
Indeed, had I not clutched a nearby rock,
I surely would (unpushed) have fallen in.

46*  My leader, who had seen how hard I gazed,
informed me now: 'In all these fires are souls.
Each one is swaddled in its inward blaze.'

49  'Well, sir,' I answered, 'to be told by you,
I am, of course, the surer. Myself, though,
I'd already thought of that. I meant to ask:

52*  "Who comes within that cloven-crested flame
that seems to rise as from that pyre where, once,
Eteocles was laid beside a brother slain?"'

55  'Within this flame,' so he now said, 'suffering,
are Ulysses and Diomed. As one, they face
their nemesis, as they in rage were one.

58  Within their flame, the crime is now bewailed
of those whose cunning wrought the Trojan horse –
the door that freed the noble seed of Rome.

61  They mourn as well the ruse by which – though dead –
young Deidamia must weep Achilles' loss.
They're punished, too, for theft, of sacred statues.'

'If they, within those tongues of fire, can speak,    64
I beg you, sir,' I said, 'and beg again –
so may each prayer be worth a thousand more –
    that you do not forbid my waiting here    67
until that flame with horns has come this way.
You see I bend to it with great desire.'
    'Your prayer,' he said, 'is worthy of great praise,    70
and I, most willingly, accede to it.
But you must keep your tongue in tight control.
    Leave me to speak. For I know very well    73*
what you desire. Nor would these two be quick,
perhaps, to hear your words. They both are Greek.'
    And when the flame had reached, in time and place,    76
a point at which my leader thought it fit,
I heard him form his utterances thus:
    'O you there, two within a single flame,    79
if I, when living, won, in your eyes, merit,
if merit, whether great or small, I won –
    in penning my exalted lines of verse –    82
do not move on. Let one of you declare,
where, lost, he went, to come upon his death.'
    The greater of those horns of ancient flame    85*
began to tear and waver, murmuring
as fires will do when struggling in a wind.
    Drawing its pinnacle this way and that,    88
as though this truly were a tongue that spoke,
it flung its utterance out, declaring: 'Once
    I'd set my course from Circe (she had kept    91*
me near Gaeta for a year or more,
before Aeneas, passing, named it that),
    no tenderness for son, no duty owed    94
to ageing fatherhood, no love that should
have brought my wife Penelope delight,
    could overcome in me my long desire,    97
burning to understand how this world works,
and know of human vices, worth and valour.

100*   Out, then, across the open depths, I put to sea,
       a single prow, and with me all my friends –
       the little crew that had not yet abandoned me.

103    I saw both shorelines (one ran on to Spain,
       the other to Morocco), Sardinia
       and all those islands that our ocean bathes.

106    I and my company were old and slow.
       And yet, arriving at that narrow sound
       where Hercules had once set up his mark –

109    to warn that men should never pass beyond –
       I left Seville behind me on the right.
       To port already I had left Ceuta.

112    "Brothers," I said, "a hundred thousand
       perils you have passed and reached the Occident.
       For us, so little time remains to keep

115    the vigil of our living sense. Do not
       deny your will to win experience,
       behind the sun, of worlds where no man dwells.

118    Hold clear in thought your seed and origin.
       You were not made to live as mindless brutes,
       but go in search of virtue and true knowledge."

121    My men – attending to this little speech –
       I made so keen to take the onward way
       that even I could hardly have restrained them.

124    Wheeling our stern against the morning sun,
       we made our oars our wings in crazy flight,
       then on, and always leftward making gain.

127    Now every star around the alien pole
       I saw by night. Our own star sank so low
       it never rose above the ocean floor.

130    Five times the light that shines beneath the moon
       had flared anew – and five times, too, grown dim –
       since we had set our course on that high venture.

133    Ahead of us, a mountain now appeared,
       darkened through distance, soaring (to my eyes)
       higher by far than any ever seen.

We cheered for joy. This quickly turned to tears.    136
For now a wind was born from that new land.
Twisting, it struck at our forward timbers.

The waves and keel three times it swirled around.    139
And then a fourth. The afterdeck rose up,
the prow went down, as pleased Another's will,

until once more the sea closed over us.'    142

# CANTO 27

1    The flame was upright now, and still. It meant
to say no more. And so (the poet gently
gave his leave) it went its way, away from us.

4    But close behind, another blaze came up,
and made us turn (a sound, confusedly,
had issued out) and glance towards its top.

7*   Compare the Torture bull of Sicily.
This bellowed its inaugural – and justly so –
with wailings from the smith who'd filed it smooth –

10   these bellows echoing its victim's moans –
so that, although, in form mere hollow bronze,
it was, it seemed, transfixed with living pains.

13   So now those words which, dreadfully, could find
no vent or outlet from their burning source,
were spoken in an accent of their own.

16   But when these sounds had made their way along,
and reached the tip which gave that flick and twist
that tongues will give to any stream of air,

19*  we heard: 'You there! I square my words at you.
I heard you say – in Lombard tones – just now:
"Be out of it! I'll rile on you no more."

22   I'm here, perhaps belatedly. But you,
I hope, will not be loath to stay and speak.
You see how far from loath I am. And I burn!

25   If you have fallen even now to this
blind world, leaving the land of lovely Italy
(from which I carried any guilt I share),

tell me: Romagna – is it peace or war?      28*
I was myself from those Urbino hills,
the mountain yoke that first unlocks the Tiber.'

I held my head bowed low attentively,      31
until my leader lightly touched my side,
saying: 'You speak. This one's from Italy.'

And I, who had indeed got words prepared,      34
began without delay to speak to him:
'You, then, below! The soul that's hidden there!

Your dear Romagna (despots all the lot)      37
is not without, nor ever was, some war-at-heart.
On leaving, though, I saw no open conflict.

Ravenna stands as she has stood for years.      40
The Eagle, blazon of the Clan Polenta,
broods in her skies; its vanes hide even Cervia.

Forlì (her towers withstood that lengthy siege      43
that left a blood-stained pile of French invaders)
goes ever on beneath the green-clawed Lion.

The Mastiffs, old and young, of Fort Verucchio,      46
vicious in lordship over Lord Montagna,
still, as is usual, gnash and suck their bone.

And where Lamone and Santerno flow,      49
the towns are schooled by Lion's-Whelp-sur-Argent.
Summer to winter, north to south, he cants.

And then that place whose rim the Savio bathes –      52
between the mountain and the plain it lies;
it lives between high tyranny and freedom.

So, who are you? I beg you now to say.      55
If you still wish your name to brave the world,
be no more stiff than others are with you.'

The flame, as was its wont, first roared a while.      58
Then, to and fro it writhed its pointed peak
and finally pronounced this speaking breath:

'Should I suppose, in answering, I spoke      61
to any person who should ever see
the world again, this flame would shake no more.

64      But since, if all I hear is true, there's none
who ever yet, alive, escaped these deeps,
I may reply without the fear of infamy.

67      I, once great warlord, was a friar next,
believing, bound by cord, I'd make amends.
And my beliefs would all have been assured,

70      had not there been (he'll rot!) that sovereign priest
who won me, firmly, back to former sins.
*Qua re* and "how" I mean that you should hear.

73      While I was still, in form, such pulp and bone
as, first, my mother gave to me, actions
of mine all favoured rather fox than lion.

76      Stratagems, wiles and covert operations –
I knew them all. These arts I so pursued
that word of me rang out throughout the world.

79      But when I recognized that now I'd come
to where we all in life ought, properly,
to furl our sail and take our rigging in,

82      whatever once had pleased me now annoyed.
I vowed – repentant, shriven – all obedience.
It might (what misery!) have worked out well.

85*     The foremost lord of our new Pharisees,
who waged in Rome a war around the Lateran
(never, of course, with Jew or Saracen;

88      his foes were faithful Christians everyone;
none had been present at the fall of Acre,
none worked as trader in the Sultan's souks),

91      did not, considering his own account,
consult his office or his holy rule,
nor mine – that cord which makes its wearer thin.

94      As once, on Mount Soracte, Constantine
required that Pope Silvester cure his leprosy,
so he, mi-lording it, commanded me

97      to cure him of his fevered arrogance.
He asked advice, and I maintained my silence.
He seemed plain drunk in what he had to say.

But still he urged: "Don't let your heart be doubtful.          100
I grant you henceforth total absolution.
Teach me how Penestrina may be razed.

The power is mine (you know it well) to unlock          103
Heaven's door. Or lock it fast. Hence these two keys.
My predecessor held them far from dear."

Such points – all weighty – drove me to the view          106
that silence now was worse than quick assent.
"Father," I answered, "since you wash away

the sin that I must now be guilty of,          109
some promise – generous though of mean extent –
assures you triumph from your lofty throne."

Now dead, Saint Francis came for me. But then          112*
a black alumnus of the Cherubim
cried out: "Don't cheat! *You* can't dispose of him.

Down must he come, to join my squalid thralls.          115
His sound advice was, after all, deceitful.
And since that hour, I've hovered round his hair.

Repentance fails? There can't be absolution,          118
nor penitence when willing ill goes on.
That is, by contradiction, *impossibile*."

The pain I felt! I shook myself awake.          121
To me he said (he took a grip): "Perhaps
you never knew: I practise logic, too."

To Minos he transported me, who then –          124
eight times! – coiled tail around relentless spine.
In utter ire, he bit this thing, and then

declared: "Condemned is he to thievish fire."          127
So that is why, as you see here, I'm lost,
and thus go dressed in inward bitterness.'

And once it reached the end of these few words,          130
grieving, the flame went off along its way,
thrashing its horn and wrenching it awry.

We now – my lord and I – went further on,          133
rounding the ridge to find another arch
to span Ditch Nine – wherein, a fee is paid,

incurred by those who force fair deals apart.          136

# CANTO 28

1*      Who could relate – even in words set loose
from rhyme, even by telling it over and over –
all that I witnessed now, the blood, the wounds.

4      There is no doubt: all human speech would fail.
Our powers, whether of mind or tongue, cannot
embrace that measure of understanding.

7      Suppose that, gathered in one single whole,
were all those people of the fated South
whose blood was shed in pain on the Apulian fields –

10      be it as victims of the sons of Troy,
or else, as Livy writes unerringly,
in that long war where rings were heaped as spoils.

13      Then add all those who suffered grievous wounds
in wars against the Norman king, Guiscardo,
and also add that band whose bones are gleaned

16      at Ceperano still (where southerners, each one,
proved traitorous). To Tagliacozzo, then, move on.
There, ageing Elard won – by guile, not arms.

19      Were every lopped-off limb or part pierced through
seen once again, that, even so, would far
from equal all the foul display in Pocket Nine.

22      One I saw riven from his chin to fart hole.
No barrel – midslat or moon rib missing –
ever, I am certain, gaped as wide as that.

25      Between his legs his guts all dangled down,
innards and heart on show, and that grim bag
that turns to shit whatever gullets swallow.

My eyes were fixed and gazed on him alone.                    28
And he gazed back. Then, opening up his thorax,
hands at work: 'Look now,' he said, 'how wide I spread!

You see how mangled is the great Mohammed.                    31*
Ali, ahead, wends weeping on his way,
cloven in countenance from quiff to chin.

So, too, the others that you here observe,                    34
all in their lives sowed schism, scandal, discord.
And that is why they all are here so splintered.

Back there a devil deftly decks us out                        37
in these cruel ornaments, and crops each page
in every quire that comes upon his sword edge.

For, as we pass around this road of pain,                     40
each wound and gash is made entire and whole
before we come to face him once again.

But who are you, who there sniff down at us                   43
and so perhaps are slow to meet the harm
that you've been sentenced to for your own crime?'

'Death has not reached him yet,' my teacher said,            46
'nor is he drawn by guilt to any pain.
I, being dead, to give him full experience,

am bound to lead him all through Hell, from gyre             49
to gyre from ring to ring through every round.
And this, I tell you, is the simple truth.'

To hear this said, a hundred (or yet more)                   52
stopped short. They looked in wonder from the ditch
at me, in awe, forgetting their own agony.

'Since you, perhaps, will shortly hail the sun,             55*
then say: If Fra Dolcino is not keen
to join me soon, he'd better stockpile well,

lest winter snow in drifts makes barriers                    58
bestowing triumph on the Novarese,
which they'd not lightly come by otherwise.'

That was Mohammed who – as now to leave –                    61
had raised his foot while uttering these words.
He placed it flat to ground and went his way.

64     Another then – his throat pierced through, his nose
       shorn off and level with his hanging brows,
       one ear alone, and only that to hear –

67     now paused with all the rest to stare at me,
       but opened up, before the others might,
       his windpipe, crimson in its outward parts.

70     'You there,' he said, 'whom guilt does not condemn,
       I've met you once on our Italian soil,
       unless I'm much beguiled by close resemblance.

73*    If you should see once more the lovely plain
       that slopes between Vercelli and Marcabo,
       then call to mind again Da Medicina.

76*    And let the two best men of Fano know
       (Guido and Angiolello, his peer),
       supposing that our foresight is not vain,

79     they'll both be slung, their necks bedecked with stones,
       from boats that coast around Cattolica,
       betrayed in this by a villainous baron.

82     From Cyprus on to the Majorcan isles,
       Neptune has never seen a crime so great
       pulled off by pirates or Argolian Greeks.

85     That traitor with his single seeing eye
       (who rules a city that another with me here
       might wish his sight had still to hunger for)

88     will work it so that they will come to parley,
       then work it so they'll need no prayer or vow
       to save them from the gales around Focara.'

91     And I in answer: 'Show me. Make it clear –
       if you so wish I'll take back news of you –
       who is that despot with the bitter view?'

94*    At which, he put his hand around the jaw
       of one beside him, prising wide his mouth,
       and yelled out: 'Here he is. And he can't utter.

97     Exiled, he drowned all Caesar's hesitations.
       For, "Anyone," he said, "who's well prepared
       will always suffer harm from titubation."'

How dismal and confused he seemed to be,       100
his tongue hacked out and hollow in his gullet,
so headstrong once, this Curio, in parley.
    Then one came round with both his hands cut off.    103
He raised his flesh stumps through the blackened air;
he made his face drip filthy red with blood,
    and yelled: 'Me too! I'm Mosca, you'll recall,    106*
who said, alas: "What's done, well, that is done."
And this sowed evil seed for every Tuscan.'
    To which I added: 'Death to all your clan!'    109
So, piling always grief on top of grief,
he went his way, a melancholic madman.
    But I stayed there and, staring at the throng,    112
I now saw something which, without more proof,
I fear that I could never hope to speak of.
    Conscience, though, lends me confidence to try.    115
That good companion renders all men free
under its breastplate, knowing we are pure.
    I saw – I'm sure – and still I seem to now,    118
in company with others in that herd,
a torso striding by without a head,
    who held that head, though severed, by the hair.    121
It swung as might a lantern from his hand.
'Alas!' it said, and stared at us in wonder.
    Himself he made a lamp for his own light.    124
So here were two in one and one in two.
How that can be He knows who orders so.
    He stood directly by the bridge foot now.    127
He raised an arm (so, therefore, head and all)
to throw his words the closer to us there.
    And these words came: 'See this, the harm, the hurt.    130
Breathing you go still, watching on the dead.
See now: is any punishment as great?
    And so you may return with news of me,    133*
then know that I'm that Bertran de Born
who gave false comfort to the youthful king.

136*      Father and son, I set at mortal odds.
         No worse, with Absalom, Ahithophel,
         whose evil promptings prodded David on.

139       Since persons so close-linked I put apart,
        so I, alas, apart now bear my brain,
         thus severed from its root in this great trunk.

142       In me, then, counter-suffering can be seen.'

# CANTO 29

This multitude, their wounds so various,                    1
had made my eyes (the lights I look by) drunk.
So now they wished to stand there, and just gaze.

    But Virgil said: 'Are you still staring on?            4
Why is your seeing plunged so deep among
such miserable, mutilated shades?

    You've not done this in any other pocket.              7
Do you imagine you can count them all?
Well, think! This trench goes twenty miles around.

    The moon already is below our feet.                  10*
The time that we're allowed to stay is short.
And much is yet to see that still you've not.'

    'If you had only cared,' I answered him,              13
'to know the reasons for that lingering look,
you would perhaps have let me stay still longer.'

    But he (my leader), and myself behind,                16
was pressing on. I answered thus,
and added, as I went: 'Within that den

    where I just now, with reason, fixed my eye,          19*
there is a spirit of my blood who weeps,
grieving the guilt that, down there, sets its price.'

    My teacher then: 'Allow no wave of thought            22
henceforth to break around his memory.
Attend to other things. And let him be.

    I saw him standing by the bridge foot there,          25
still gesturing – a threatening finger raised –
and heard his name called out: Geri del Bello.

28     You were so caught, intent upon the sight
of that one there, once sire of Altafort,
you did not care to look around. So off he went.'

31     'His violent death,' I now addressed my lord,
'which goes yet unavenged by any kin,
whose fate must be to share this lasting shame,

34     inspires disdain in him. I judge that this
is why he left, speaking no word to me.
This all the more makes clear to me my duty.'

37     Our talk went on in such-like terms until
we found the jutting spur that showed (or would,
had there been light to see) the floor beyond.

40     I stood there high above the final cloister
of Rottenpockets. All its postulants
were present and revealed for us to see.

43     A host of lamentations shot around me,
their iron barbs sharp-tipped with pain and pity.
I covered up my ears with both my hands.

46*    Such sicknesses as here there'd be if all
contagions born of summer heat – from wards
throughout Sardinia, the Chiana Vale, Maremma –

49     were brought together in one single hole.
That's what it was, the stench that came from it,
a fetor rising as from rotting limbs.

52     Veering still leftwards as we always did,
we searched that ridge and reached its final crag.
And there more vividly I came to view

55     the depths in which, unerringly, the power
of justice – minister of One on High –
will castigate those known on earth as frauds.

58*    No greater woe, as I imagine it,
was ever, even in Aegina, known – where plague
infected every citizen and air

61     so dripped malignancy, its creatures all –
down to the smallest worm – fell, sickening fast.
This ancient race was then restored (so say

those poets who believe it true) by seed      64
of ants. Such woe appeared across the dark pit floor.
See, in their different stooks, the spirits languishing.

Some sprawled across the stomach of the next,      67
some over shoulders. Others, on all fours,
dragged on (to make a change) along the road.

Without a word, we went on, step by step,      70
still gazing at and listening to the sick.
They could not lift their bodies from the ground.

I saw there leaning, one against the next –      73
propped up as pairs of saucepans are to lose
their heat – two, scabby-spotted head to toe.

And never have I seen a currycomb      76
whisked (by a groom whose boss is waiting by,
or else disgruntled to be woken up)

so brisk as these attacked that raging itch –      79
for which no salve can ever now be found –
with biting fingernails to scrape at each.

With fingernails, each tore off showers of scabs,      82
as might a fish knife when it's skinning bream,
or else, perhaps, some type with larger scales.

'You there, whose fingers tear your chainmail off' –      85
to one of them my leader spoke these words –
'employing them as pincers sometimes, too,

now tell us (may your manicure endure,      88
your nails work well to all eternity!),
are there Italians sunk with you down there?'

'We, wrecked and ruined, are Italians both.'      91
So, weeping, one of them made this reply.
'But who are you that put to us this question?'

'I'm one,' my leader answered, 'who descends      94
with this still-living man from ledge to ledge.
My purpose is to show him all of Hell.'

At this, the coupling that had held them sheared,      97
and, trembling, each one turned himself to me,
as others did who heard these words in echoes.

100     My good, kind teacher came up close to me,
        saying: 'Just tell him what it is you want.'
        And so, as he now wanted, I began:

103     'So may the thought of you be never robbed
        from human memories in the first of lives,
        but live on brightly under many suns,

106     tell me who you might be, and of what kin.
        Dread not – for all your foul and loathsome pain –
        but openly make known yourselves to me.'

109*    'I was,' one answered, 'an Aretine once.
        Albero of Siena had me burned alive.
        But I'm not brought for what I died for here.

112     O yes! It's true, in jest I said to him:
        "I've got the knowhow. I can fly through air."
        Then he – all eyes, excited, but no genius –

115     was eager that I put my art on show.
        I did not do a Daedalus. For that alone,
        he got the one who called him son to burn me.

118     But Minos – not allowed to judge amiss –
        condemned me to this final slot because,
        in life, I practised as an alchemist.'

121     'On land or sea,' I turned towards the poet,
        'was anyone as gormless as these Sienese?
        Even the French aren't that idiotic.'

124*    At which, the other leper, overhearing,
        quipped in return: 'Except, of course, for Stricca,
        who really knew what temperate spending is!

127     And Nick as well, the twit. He, in that garden
        where the clove seed grows, discovered first
        how rich the virtues of carnation are.

130     Omit, as well, those merry men with whom
        Kid d'Ascian consumed both farms and vines.
        Dazzledeye, too – who taught the boy such wisdom.

133     To see, however, who (like you) speaks here
        so anti-Sienese, just sharpen up your eye.
        My face – look hard – may give you your reply.

I am, you'll see, the shadow of Capocchio.
Alchemically, I falsified base metals
and, if I eye you well, then you'll recall
    how marvellous an ape of nature *I* was.'

# CANTO 30

1*     Think of that age when Juno – wracked with wrath,
so envious of Semele – expressed her spite,
over and over, against the blood of Thebes.

4     That was the time when Athamas ran mad.
He saw his wife who carried, as she went,
in either arm the load of their two sons,

7     and yelled: 'Come on! Let's spread those nets! I mean
to stalk them all, both whelps and lioness.'
He then stretched out his unrelenting claws.

10     He grasped one child (Learchus was his name).
He whirled him round. He dashed him on a stone.
His wife drowned, loaded with their second son.

13     When, likewise, ever-turning Fate brought down,
in flames, the Trojans from all-daring height –
and so, together, king and kingdom broke –

16     Hecuba, grieving, wretched, now enslaved,
first saw Polyxena, her daughter, dead,
and then – to find there, lain along the margin

19     of the sea, her youngest, Polydorus –
barked in her lunacy like any cur,
the pain of it so wrenched her mind askew.

22     And yet no fury known in Troy or Thebes
was ever seen, in anyone, to strike
so viciously at beast or human limb

25     as now I saw in two blank, naked shades –
who, racing round that circle, gnashed and gored
as swine do when their pigsty is unbarred.

One got Capocchio. At the very knot     28
of neck and spine, his tusks sank in. Then round
the hard pit floor he hauled him, belly scraping.

The Aretine (still there) spoke all atremble:     31*
'That banshee idiot is Gianni Schicchi.
He rages on, and treats us all like that.'

'Really?' I answered. 'Well, let's hope his fangs     34
don't pierce your rear. But (not to trouble you),
please say who's that, before it springs away.'

'That soul is known in legend,' he declared.     37
'It's Myrrha the Depraved, beyond the bounds
of love (as love should be) her father's friend.

She made her way to meet him in that sin,     40
shaping herself in counterfeit disguise.
So, too, the other, shooting off. To win

a mare (the queen of all the herd) he shaped     43
in counterfeit the guise of dying Buoso,
whose testament, attested thus, was sound.'

And now, when these two raging shades, on whom     46
till now I'd fixed my eye, had gone their way,
I turned and looked at other ill-created souls.

And one I saw was fashioned like a lute,     49
or would have been if severed at the groin,
to amputate those parts where humans fork.

Dropsy (osmosis of a morbid flux):     52
that discomposes, as the swellings rise,
all natural fit – so face and paunch mismatch –

constrained him, so his mouth hung open wide.     55
So, too, in fever victims, wracked with thirst,
one lip curls back, the lower meets the chin.

'O you who pass and know no pain (though why     58
I cannot understand) through this mean world,'
so he began, 'behold and hold in mind

the miseries of mastercraftsman Adam.     61
I had, alive, my share of all I sought;
and now I crave, alas, the merest water drop.

64     Those brooks that trickle down the high green hills
to reach the Arno from the Casentine
and, as they run, make channels, chill and moist,

67     stand always in my sight. And not in vain:
the image of them parches me far more
than this disease that strips my face of meat.

70     Unbending justice probes me to the core.
It takes its hint from regions where I sinned,
meaning the more to put my sighs to flight.

73*     Here Fort Romena stands, and here I forged
fake specie, printed with the Baptist marque.
On that account, I left, up there, my body burned.

76     Yet could I only glimpse those woeful souls –
Guido or Sandro or their brother – here,
I'd not exchange the Branda Spring for that.

79     Already in, there's one of them, if those
crazed shadows as they whirl around speak truth.
What use is that to me? My limbs are bound.

82     If only I were still so light and lithe
to travel in a hundred years one inch,
already I'd have started on that path,

85     seeking him out from all this filthy clan.
And this ditch turns eleven miles around.
Nor is it less than half a mile across!

88     I'm only in this mess because of them.
They led me on. I counterfeited florins
so each contained three carats-worth of dross.'

91     'And who,' I said, 'are those two so-and-sos,
steaming as wet hands do on winter days,
those lying tight against your left frontier?'

94     'I found them here,' he said, '(they've not turned since)
as soon as I showered down upon this midden.
I do not think they'll budge in all eternity.

97*     Joseph was falsely charged by that "she" there.
The other, just as false, is Sinon (Trojan-Greek!).
Their biting fever brews that curdled reek.'

Then one of them, who took it much amiss –                       100
or so I'd guess, to hear his name so sullied –
now thumped that tight-stretched belly with his fist.

It rumbled forth as though it were a drum.                       103
Adam (the master) countered with his arm
to strike him no less hard across the face,

and said: 'It may well be I cannot move,                         106
seeing how heavy I've become in limb.
But still my arms are free to do the job.'

The answer came: 'You weren't as free as that                   109
when, arms trussed up, you went to mount the pyre.
Your arms were free, though, in their forging days.'

'There,' the hydroptic said, 'you speak mere truth.             112
Yet, as a witness, you were not so true
at Troy, when true words were required of you.'

'Well, I spoke false, and you struck dodgy coin.                115
But I'm here,' Sinon said, 'for one plain fault.
You were accused of more than any demon.'

'The horse! Remember that, you lying cheat!'                    118
(This came in answer out of Swollenguts.)
'Tough luck on you that all the world knows that.'

'And tough on you,' the Greek replied, 'the thirst             121
that cracks your bloated tongue, the bilge that swells
that belly to a hedgerow round your eyes.'

At which: 'Yeah, yeah' (the coiner). 'Sickness                 124
has stretched your mouth (what's new?) to tearing point.
I may be dry. I'm swollen, ripe with pus.

But you're burnt-out. Your sick head throbs and aches.         127*
It wouldn't take too much – a word or so –
to make you lick the mirror of Narcissus.'

All ears, I strained to listen in – until                      130
I heard my teacher speak: 'Go on! Just gaze!
It won't take much for me to fight with you.'

And when I heard his words, so near to wrath,                  133
I turned towards him with a shame that still,
on calling it to mind, brews vertigo.

136     Like someone dreaming of a harm to come,
who, dreaming, yearns for this to be some dream,
and hence desires what is as though it weren't,

139     so was I now. For wishing I could speak,
and so excuse myself, I so excused myself,
and did not think that all along I did.

142     'Less shame,' my master said to me, 'makes clean
far greater fault than yours has been. And so
cast off the weight of all your misery.

145     Consider well. I'm always by your side.
Remember this, if Fortune leads you on
to where such spats as this are played out loud.

148     To wish to hear such stuff is pretty low.'

# CANTO 31

The self-same tongue that bit me first so hard                    1
that both my cheeks had coloured up, bright red,
now offered once again its remedy.

So, too (as I have heard the story told),                          4*
the spear that both Achilles and his father bore
would cause a wound that spear alone could cure.

We turned our back upon the dismal deep,                           7
riding the bank that circles it around,
and made our way across without more speech.

Here it was less than night and less than day,                    10
so that our seeing went no way ahead.
But then I heard a horn ring out so loud

that thunder in comparison is vapid,                               13
and, turning back to see the echoing source,
I fixed my eyes upon one single place.

After the great and grievous rout at which                         16*
was lost the sacred band of Charlemagne,
great Roland sounded notes of no such terror.

I had not held my head turned there for long                       19
when (so it seemed) I now saw many towers.
And therefore, 'Sir,' I said, 'what town is this?'

'Because,' he said, 'through all these wreaths of shade            22
you rush ahead too far from what's at hand,
you form of it a blurred and empty image.

You'll see quite clearly when you soon arrive                      25
how greatly distance may deceive the sense.
So drive yourself a little further on.'

28        Then, with great tenderness, he took my hand.
He then went on: 'And yet before we step
ahead – so all these facts may seem less odd –

31        you ought to know that these aren't towers.
       They're giants.
These stand within the well around its rim,
navel height downwards, all the lot of them.'

34        As when a mist is thinning out, the gaze
will, point by point, begin to recompose
the figure hidden by the steam-thick air,

37        so, boring through that dense, dark atmosphere,
approaching ever closer to the edge,
false knowledge fled and fear grew yet more great.

40*       For, as above its circling curtain wall,
Montereggione boasts a crown of towers,
so too above the bank that rings the well

43        stood, towering here to half their body height,
the dreadful giants, who are under threat
from highest Jove whenever he wields thunder.

46        By now I saw, in each of these, the face,
the chest and shoulders, areas of paunch,
and, down the ribcage, all their dangling arms.

49        Nature did well, desisting from the art
of forming animals like that. She thus
deprived great Mars of his executors.

52        If she, on that account, did not repent
of whales and elephants, to subtle minds
this will seem right, and most intelligent.

55        For when the powers of working intellect
are wed to strength and absolute illwill,
then humans cannot find a place to hide.

58*       In bulk and length, his face could be compared
to that bronze pine cone in Saint Peter's, Rome.
His other bones were all in due proportion.

61*       And so that bank (his fig leaf, 'zone' or apron,
hanging around his loins below) displayed,
above, up to his mane, as much of him

as three tall Frisians would boast in vain.                    64
I saw their thirty-eight-inch finger spans
down from the point where cloaks are buckled on.
   '*Raphèl maì amècche zabì almì*,'                    67
so screaming it began, that fearsome mouth,
unfit to utter any sweeter psalm.
   My leader aimed: 'You idiotic soul!                    70
Stick to your horn. With that, give vent to wrath,
or any passion that you chance to feel.
   Just fumble round your neck, you great dumb thing.    73
You'll find the cord it's tied to. There it rests.
A chevron – see? – across your mighty breast.'
   And then to me: 'He stands his own accuser.              76
It's Nimrod there. Through his sick whim
no single tongue is spoken anywhere.
   So, let him be. We'll not speak in that vein.            79
For every tongue, to him, remains the same
as his tongue is to others: quite unknown.'
   Now, turning left, we made a longer march;              82
and there (the distance of a crossbow shot)
we found a bigger ogre, fiercer still.
   Who that lord was I cannot tell, who locked           85
these shackles round him and about. He held
his right arm bound in front, his left behind,
   by one tight chain that – tangling down – was hitched  88
a full five turns around the bits we saw,
netherwards stretching from his neck to waist.
   'This one, in pride, was quick to prove his power        91
against the majesty of Jupiter.'
Thus spoke my leader. 'His reward is this.
   By name Ephialtes, his deeds were done              94*
when giants caused the deities such dread.
He can't now budge the arm he wielded then.'
   And I to him: 'If it were possible                    97
to gain with my own eyes experience
of measureless Briareus, *that* I'd like.'

100 'Antaeus,' he in answer said, 'you'll see
not very far from here. And he – unchained
and speaking, too – will lower us to sin's last floor.

103 The one whom you so keenly wish to see
is over there, a good way further on,
constrained like these but fiercer still in mien.'

106 No earthquake, rude in vigour, ever struck
a tower with such great force as Ephialtes,
writhing round suddenly, now shook himself.

109 And, more than ever now in mortal fear,
sheer terror would have done the trick, had I
not seen the fetters that restrained him there.

112 And now, as we proceeded on our way,
we came upon Antaeus, rising high
(omitting head) five yards above the pit.

115 'You there! Yes, you! In that propitious vale
where Hannibal turned tail with all his men –
and so made Scipio the heir of fame –

118 you brought as spoils a thousand lions back.
And if, like all your brothers, you had joined
in battle with the gods above, then (some

121 believe) those earthborn sons might well have won.
Then set us down – and please, no dark disdain –
deep in Cocytus, locked by freezing keys.

124 Don't make us trudge to Tityos or Typhon.
This man can give you what you yearn to have.
Therefore bend down. And do not twist your snout.

127 To earth he can still carry back your name.
He's living still – and so expects to, long,
unless grace summons him before his time.'

130 My teacher spoke. The giant in great haste
stretched out his hands – whose powerful clutch had once
been felt by Hercules – to take him in his fist.

133 And Virgil, when he felt himself well held,
now said to me: 'Come here so I can take you!'
He packed us in – one bundle, him and me.

Just as the Garisenda tower, when viewed           136*
beneath its leaning side, appears to fall
if any floating cloud should pass behind,
   so, too, Antaeus seemed to me, as there       139
I stood expecting him to bend. And now
I'd willingly have gone some other way.
   Yet lightly he set us, lightly, in those depths      142
that eat at Lucifer and Judas, too.
He did not, bowing so, make long delay,
   but swayed again up straight as ship masts do.      145

# CANTO 32

1\*  If I had rhymes that rawly rasped and cackled
  (and chimed in keeping with that cacky hole
  at which, point down, all other rock rings peak),

4  I might then squeeze the juices of my thought
  more fully out of me. But since I don't,
  not without dread, I bring myself to speak.

7  It's not (no kidding) any sort of joke
  to form in words the universal bum,
  no task for tongues still whimpering 'Mum!' and 'Dad!'

10\*  The Muses, though, may raise my verse – women
  who once helped Amphion lock Thebes in walls –
  so fact and word may not too far diverge.

13\*  You ill-begotten zombies, worst of all,
  who stand there where to utter is so hard,
  better had you been born as sheep or bezoars!

16  Now deep within the darkness of that well
  and further even than those giant feet,
  I stood and gazed sheer upwards at that wall

19  when, out of nowhere, I heard: 'Watch your step!
  Don't plant those feet of yours on some poor head;
  we're here all brothers in this sorry crowd.'

22  I turned at this, and now could see – around,
  and all beneath, my feet – a lake of ice
  that seemed far less like water than clear glass.

25  The Danube, even in winter Österreich,
  never congealed its currents to so thick
  a veil (the Don, neither, under freezing skies)

as this. And if the crags of Tambernic      28*
had crashed down here – or Pike Pietrapana –
its very fringe would not have cracked or creaked.

As frogs sit croaking in the harvest month      31
(when country girls will dream of gleaning corn),
their snouts just poking from the water line,

so too these shadows, fixed in ice lead-blue,      34
to where, in shame, we start to blush, their teeth
as rhythmic, beakily, as chattering storks.

And each one kept his face bent down. From mouths      37
the cold, from hearts their miseries force
a public testament to suffering.

I stood a while just gazing all around,      40*
then, glancing to my feet, I saw here two
embraced so closely that their head hair mixed.

'Go on,' I said, 'so tell me who you are,      43
straining so tightly, tit to tit.' Coupled,
the two eased back their necks. Their faces now

were straight to mine. Once moist within, their eyes      46
welled up. The teardrops flowed toward their lips.
But chill gripped these, to lock them in their holes.

To wood wood never has been clamped so hard      49
as these two were; and, overwhelmed with ire,
each butted each like any pair of goats.

Another in the frost had lost both ears.      52
Still gazing downwards, he was first to speak:
'Why eye us so, as though we were your mirror?

If you're so keen to know who these two are,      55
that valley where Bisenzio streams down
belonged to them, as to their father, earlier.

They issued from a single womb. And you      58*
may go, if you so please, through all of Cain
finding no shadow freeze in aspic fitter,

not Mordred, even – breast and shadow pierced      61*
by thrusts his "uncle", great King Arthur, gave –
neither Focaccia (source of strife), nor this one here,

64      whose head, annoyingly, so cramps my view.
        His name was Sassolo Mascheroni,
        and you, if you are Tuscan, know him well.

67          However, not to drag out speeches further,
        be told that I'm Camiscion de' Pazzi.
        I wait for Carlin. He'll acquit me here.'

70*         And then I saw a thousand mongrel faces
        bitten by frost. (I shiver, remembering –
        and always will – to see a frozen puddle.)

73          Trembling, as ever, in the endless nip,
        onwards we went to reach the cone's last core,
        where all the weight of everything weighs down.

76          And whether by intention, chance or fate
        (well, I don't know!) pacing among these heads,
        hard in the face of one, I struck my foot.

79          It screeched out, whingingly: 'Why stamp on me?
        Unless, of course, you're here to take revenge
        for Montaperti. If not, why do me harm?'

82          I to my teacher: 'Wait a little here.
        I'll go and free myself of doubts with him.
        Then push me on as much as you desire.'

85          My leader paused. And, turning to the one
        still spitting curses out, I now inquired:
        'So who are you, to go on scolding others?'

88          'And who are you? You trek through Antenora,
        bashing,' he said, 'at other people's cheeks.
        Were you alive, I wouldn't stand for it.'

91          'I am alive,' I answered him. 'How dear to you
        I might become, if fame is what you thirst for!
        I could well note your name among the rest.'

94          'I yearn,' he answered, 'for the opposite.
        Just go away and give me no more grief.
        You don't know how to flatter in a bog like this.'

97          And so I grasped him tight against the scalp.
        'You'll name yourself,' I said to him. 'If not,
        you'll find no single bristle on your topknot.'

'Don't think,' he said, 'because you pluck my curls,                    100
I mean to say or show you bugger all,
bomb as you may my skull ten thousand times.'

I'd got him twisted in my fingers now,                                  103
and had, already, yanked out several tufts.
He barked, but kept his eyes held firmly down.

Another yelling now: 'What's with you, Big Mouth?                       106
Not satisfied to castanet cold jaws?
You bark as well. What devil's got to you?'

And then I said: 'I'd have you speak no more.                           109
You're vile, you traitor. I'll augment your shame,
I'll carry in your name a true report.'

'Go on,' he answered, 'gossip all you like.                             112
But don't, if you get out of here, be silent
concerning him, his tongue so slick.

He weeps for having fingered French-y silver.                          115
Now you can say: "I saw that man from Duera.
He dwells where all the sinners keep quite cool."

And should you ask me: "Are there others here?"                        118
Beside you, there is Abbot Beccheria,
the one whose gizzard Florence sawed right through.

Then Ghibelline Jack, I guess, is further on,                          121
with Ganelon and Tebaldello, too.
He slid the doors of sleeping Faience back.'

By now we had already gone our way.                                    124*
But then I saw two frozen in one single hole,
one head a headpiece to the one below.

As bread is mangled by some famished mouth,                            127
so too the higher gnawed the lower head,
precisely where the nape and brainstem meet.

The dying Tydeus in this same way,                                     130
in loathing, chewed the brows of dead Menalippus,
gnawing the skull and everything besides.

'O you who by so bestial a show                                        133
make known your hatred for the one you eat,
now tell me – why? I give my word,' I said,

136    'if you complain of him with proper cause,
       then once I know his name and how he sinned,
       I'll make you in the world a fair return,
139        provided means of speech do not fall dry.'

# CANTO 33

Jaws lifted now from that horrible dish,                                    1
the sinner – wiping each lip clean on hair that fringed
the mess he'd left the head in, at its rear –

    began: 'You ask that I should tell anew                                 4
the pain that hopelessly, in thought alone,
before I voice it, presses at my heart.

    Yet if I may, by speaking, sow the fruit                                7
of hate to slur this traitor, caught between my teeth,
then words and tears, you'll see, will flow as one.

    Who you might be, I do not know, nor how                               10
you've come to be down here. But when you speak,
you seem (there's little doubt) a Florentine.

    You need to see: I was Count Ugolino.                                  13*
This is Ruggieri, the archbishop, there.
I'll tell you now why we two are so close.

    That I, in consequence of his vile thoughts,                           16
was captured – though I trusted in this man –
and after died, I do not need to say.

    But this cannot have carried to your ears:                             19
that is, how savagely I met my death.
You'll hear it now, and know if he has injured me.

    One scant slit in the walls of Eaglehouse                              22*
(because of me, they call it now the Hunger Tower.
Be sure, though: others will be locked up there)

    had shown me, in the shaft that pierces it,                            25
many new moons by now, when this bad dream
tore wide the veil of what my future was.

28*     This thing here then appeared to me as Master
        of the Hounds, who tracked the wolf – his cubs as well –
        out on the hill where Lucca hides from Pisa.

31      In front, as leaders of the pack, he placed
        the clans Gualandi, Sismond and Lanfranchi,
        their bitches hunting eager, lean and smart.

34      The chase was brief. Father and sons, it seemed,
        were wearying; and soon – or so it seemed –
        I saw those sharp fangs raking down their flanks.

37      I woke before the day ahead had come,
        and heard my sons (my little ones were there)
        cry in their sleep and call out for some food.

40      How hard you are if, thinking what my heart
        foretold, you do not feel the pain of it.
        Whatever will you weep for, if not that?

43      By now they all had woken up. The time
        was due when, as routine, our food was brought.
        Yet each was doubtful, thinking of their dream.

46      Listening, I heard the door below locked shut,
        then nailed in place against that dreadful tower.
        I looked in their dear faces, spoke no word.

49      I did not weep. Inward, I turned to stone.
        They wept. And then my boy Anselmo spoke:
        "What are you staring at? Father, what's wrong?"

52      And so I held my tears in check and gave
        no answer all that day, nor all the night
        that followed on, until another sun came up.

55      A little light had forced a ray into
        our prison, so full of pain. I now could see
        on all four faces my own expression.

58      Out of sheer grief, I gnawed on both my hands.
        And they – who thought I did so from an urge
        to eat – all, on the instant, rose and said:

61      "Father, for us the pain would be far less
        if you would chose to eat us. You, having dressed us
        in this wretched flesh, ought now to strip it off."

So I kept still, to not increase their miseries.                          64
And that day and the day beyond, we all were mute.
Hard, cruel earth, why did you not gape wide?

As then we reached the fourth of all those days,            67
Gaddo pitched forward, stretching at my feet.
"Help me," he said. "Why don't you help me, Dad!"

And there he died. You see me here. So I saw them,      70
the three remaining, falling one by one
between the next days – five and six – then let

myself, now blind, feel over them, calling                        73
on each, now all were dead, for two days more.
Then hunger proved a greater power than grief.'

His words were done. Now, eyes askew, he grabbed    76
once more that miserable skull – his teeth,
like any dog's teeth, strong against the bone.

Pisa, you scandal of the lovely land                               79*
where 'yes' is uttered in the form of sì,
your neighbours may be slow to punish you,

but let those reefs, Capraia and Gorgogna,               82
drift, as a barrage, to the Arno's mouth,
so that your people – every one – are drowned.

So what if – as the rumour goes – the great Count     85
Ugolino did cheat fortresses from you.
You had no right to crucify his children.

Pisa, you are a newborn Thebes! Those boys             88
were young. That made them innocent. I've named
just two. I now name Uguiccione and Brigata.

We now moved on, and came to where the ice            91
so roughly swaddled yet another brood.
And these – not hunched – bend back for all to view.

They weep. Yet weeping does not let them weep.        94
Their anguish meets a blockage at the eye.
Turned in, this only makes their heartache more.

Their tears first cluster into frozen buds,                     97
and then – as though a crystal visor – fill
the socket of the eye beneath each brow.

100     My own face now – a callus in the chill –
had ceased to be a throne to any kind
of sentiment. And yet, in spite of all,

103     it seemed I felt a wind still stirring here.
'Who moves these currents, sir?' I now inquired.
'At depths like these, aren't vapours wholly spent?'

106     He in reply: 'Come on, come on! You soon
will stand where your own probing eye shall see
what brings this drizzling exhalation on.'

109     A case of icy-eye-scab now yelled out:
'You must be souls of such malignancy
you merit placement in the lowest hole.

112     Prise off this rigid veil, to clear my eyes.
Let me awhile express the grief that swells
in my heart's womb before my tears next freeze.'

115     I answered: 'Are you asking help from me?
Tell me who you are. Then I'll free your gaze,
or travel – promise! – to the deepest ice.'

118*     'I,' he replied, 'am Brother Alberigo,
I of the Evil Orchard, Fruiterer.
Here I receive exquisite dates for figs.'

121     'Oh,' I now said, 'so you're already dead?'
'Well, how my body fares above,' he said,
'still in the world, my knowledge is not sure.

124*     There is, in Ptolomea, this advantage,
that souls will frequently come falling down
before Fate Atropos has granted them discharge.

127     I very willingly will tell you more,
but only scrape this tear-glaze from my face.
The instant any soul commits, like me,

130     some act of treachery, a demon takes
possession of that body-form and rules
its deeds until its time is done. Swirling,

133*     the soul runs downwards to this sink. And so
the body of that shade behind – a-twitter
all this winter through – still seems up there, perhaps.

You're bound to know, arriving only now,                      136
that this is Signor Branca ("Hookhand") d'Oria.
Years have gone by since he was ice-packed here.'
    'I think,' I said, 'that this must be a con.              139
For how can Branca d'Oria be dead?
He eats and drinks and sleeps and puts his clothes on.'
    'Recall that ditch,' he said, 'named Rotklorsville,      142
where, higher up, they brew adhesive pitch?
Well, long before Mike Zanche got to that,
    Hookhand was history. He, as proxy, left                 145
a devil in his skin (his kinsman's here as well,
the one who planned with him the double-cross).
    But please, now reach your hand to me down here.         148
Open my eyes for me.' I did not open them.
To be a swine in this case was pure courtesy.
    You Genovese, deviant, deranged                          151
and stuffed with every sort of vicious canker!
Why have you not been wiped yet from the earth?
    Among the worst of all the Romagnuoli                    154
I found there one of yours, whose works were such
his soul already bathes in Cocytus.
    His body, seemingly, lives on above.                     157

# CANTO 34

1\*      *'Vexilla regis prodeunt inferni,*
marching towards us. Fix your eyes ahead,'
my teacher said, 'and see if you can see it.'

4      As though a windmill when a thick fog breathes –
or else when dark night grips our hemisphere –
seen from a distance, turning in the wind,

7      so there a great contraption had appeared.
And I now shrank, against the wind, behind
my guide. There were no glades to shelter in.

10      I was by now (I write this verse in fear)
where all the shades in ice were covered up,
transparent as are straws preserved in glass.

13      Some lay there flat, and some were vertical,
one with head raised, another soles aloft,
another like a bow, bent face to feet.

16      And then when we had got still further on,
where now my master chose to show to me
that creature who had once appeared so fair,

19      he drew away from me and made me stop,
saying: 'Now see! Great Dis! Now see the place
where you will need to put on all your strength.'

22      How weak I now became, how faded, dry –
reader, don't ask, I shall not write it down –
for anything I said would fall far short.

25      I neither died nor wholly stayed alive.
Just think yourselves, if your minds are in flower,
what I became, bereft of life and death.

The emperor of all these realms of gloom  28*
stuck from the ice at mid-point on his breast.
And I am more a giant (to compare)
   than any giant measured to his arm.  31
So now you'll see how huge the whole must be,
when viewed in fit proportion to that limb.

If, once, he was as lovely as now vile,  34
when first he raised his brow against his maker,
then truly grief must all proceed from him.

How great a wonder it now seemed to me  37
to see three faces on a single head!
The forward face was bright vermilion.

The other two attached themselves to that  40
along each shoulder on the central point,
and joined together at the crest of hair.

The rightward face was whitish, dirty yellow.  43
The left in colour had the tint of those
beyond the source from which the Nile first swells.

Behind each face there issued two great vanes,  46
all six proportioned to a fowl like this.
I never saw such size in ocean sails.

Not feathered as a bird's wings are, bat-like  49
and leathery, each fanned away the air,
so three unchanging winds moved out from him,

   Cocytus being frozen hard by these.  52
He wept from all six eyes. And down each chin
both tears and bloody slobber slowly ran.

In every mouth he mangled with his teeth  55
(as flax combs do) a single sinning soul,
but brought this agony to three at once.

Such biting, though, affects the soul in front  58
as nothing to the scratching he received.
His spine at times showed starkly, bare of skin.

'That one up there, condemned to greater pain,  61
is Judas Iscariot,' my teacher said,
'his head inside, his feet out, wriggling hard.

64*     The other two, their heads hung down below,
are Brutus, dangling from the jet black snout
(look how he writhes there, uttering not a word!),

67     the other Cassius with burly look.
But night ascends once more. And now it's time
for us to quit this hole. We've seen it all.'

70     As he desired, I clung around his neck.
With purpose, he selected time and place
and, when the wings had opened to the full,

73     he took a handhold on the furry sides,
and then, from tuft to tuft, he travelled down
between the shaggy pelt and frozen crust.

76     But then, arriving where the thigh bone turns
(the hips extended to their widest there),
my leader, with the utmost stress and strain,

79     swivelled his head to where his shanks had been
and clutched the pelt like someone on a climb,
so now I thought: 'We're heading back to Hell.'

82     'Take care,' my teacher said. 'By steps like these,'
breathless and panting, seemingly all-in,
'we need to take our leave of so much ill.'

85     Then through a fissure in that rock he passed
and set me down to perch there on its rim.
After, he stretched his careful stride towards me.

88     Raising my eyes, I thought that I should see
Lucifer where I, just now, had left him,
but saw instead his legs held upwards there.

91     If I was struggling then to understand,
let other dimwits think how they'd have failed
to see what point it was that I now passed.

94     'Up on your feet!' my teacher ordered me.
'The way is long, the road is cruelly hard.
The sun is at the morning bell already.'

97     This was no stroll, where now we had arrived,
through any palace but a natural cave.
The ground beneath was rough, the light was weak.

'Before my roots are torn from this abyss,      100
sir,' I said, upright, 'to untangle me
from error, say a little more of this.

Where is the ice? And why is that one there    103*
fixed upside down? How is it that the sun
progressed so rapidly from evening on to day?'

And he in answer: 'You suppose you're still    106
on that side of the centre where I gripped
that wormrot's coat that pierces all the world.

While I was still descending, you were there.    109
But once I turned, you crossed, with me, the point
to which from every part all weight drags down.

So you stand here beneath the hemisphere    112
that now is covered wholly with dry land,
under the highest point at which there died

the one man sinless in his birth and life.    115
Your feet are set upon a little sphere
that forms the other aspect of Giudecca.

It's morning here. It's evening over there.    118
The thing that made a ladder of his hair
is still as fixed as he has always been.

Falling from Heaven, when he reached this side,    121
the lands that then spread out to southern parts
in fear of him took on a veil of sea.

These reached our hemisphere. Whatever now    124
is visible to us – in flight perhaps from him –
took refuge here and left an empty space.'

There is a place (as distant from Beelzebub    127
as his own tomb extends in breadth)
known not by sight but rather by the sound

of waters falling in a rivulet    130
eroding, by the winding course it takes (which is
not very steep), an opening in that rock.

So now we entered on that hidden path,    133
my lord and I, to move once more towards
a shining world. We did not care to rest.

136       We climbed, he going first and I behind,
until through some small aperture I saw
the lovely things the skies above us bear.

139       Now we came out, and once more saw the stars.

# *Commedia* Cantica 2: *Purgatorio*

# CANTO 1

Commedia: Cantica 2:
Purgatorio

1     To race now over better waves, my ship
of mind – alive again – hoists sail, and leaves
behind its little keel the gulf that proved so cruel.

4     And I'll sing, now, about that second realm
where human spirits purge themselves from stain,
becoming worthy to ascend to Heaven.

7*     Here, too, dead poetry will rise again.
For now, you sacred Muses, I am yours.
So let Calliope, a little, play her part,

10     and follow as I sing, with chords that scourged
the wretched Magpies (young girls, once) till they
despaired of pardon for their insolence.

13     Soft hues of sapphire from the orient,
collecting gently, marked the circles now
of skies serene from height to horizon.

16     And this sight – once I left the morbid air,
which weighed so heavy on my eyes and heart –
began afresh to bring my eyes delight.

19*     The lovely planet, strengthening to our love,
lit up with laughter all the orient sky,
veiling her escort, Pisces, in bright light.

22     I turned now to the right. I set my mind
up on the southern pole, and saw four stars
that none – save Eve and Adam – ever saw.

25     The heavens, it seemed, rejoiced in these four gleams.
Oh widowed North (your name means seven stars),
how great your lack, to never look on those!

I made my gaze, at last, abandon them,        28*
and turning back to glimpse the other pole –
from which the Wain, already, had gone down –

I saw nearby an old man on his own,        31*
deserving (from the air and look he had)
of all respect a son might give his sire.

The beard he wore was long and flecked with white,    34
as, too, the hair that flowed down from his head,
falling upon his breast in double braids.

The rays that shot from those four holy stars    37
adorned his brow with honour so I saw
his face as clear as if the sun shone there.

'And who are you, you fugitives who flee,    40
across the unseeing stream, eternal gaol?'
He spoke, and moved his beard in noble plumes.

'Who was your guide? What lantern led you on    43
beyond those deepest reaches of the night
that make the vale of Hell for ever black?

The laws of the abyss – do these break down?    46
Are counsels newly changed in Heaven's height
so you, the damned, approach my secret hills?'

My leader took me firmly in his grip,    49
and – urging me with gestures, hands and words
to bend my brow and knee in reverence –

'I do not, of myself, come here,' he said.    52
'A lady came from Heaven. And her prayers
led me to help this man, and be his guide.

But since your will is that the truth be told    55
more fully as to what we are and why,
I cannot of my own will say you "nay".

This man has yet to see his final night,    58
but through his own stupidity was close,
and scarcely had the time in which to turn.

Then I was sent, for his sake (as I've said),    61
and found no way to see that he survived,
save that which I have set myself to take.

64     I have already shown him all the damned,
and mean that he should see those spirits now
who, in your care, themselves seek purity.

67     Too long to say how I have brought him here.
But power comes down and strengthens me in this –
to lead him on, to see and hear you speak.

70     Look kindly on his coming, if you will.
He goes in search of liberty. All know –
who gave their life for that – how dear it is.

73     You know yourself. For, dying in that cause,
death had, at Utica, no sting for you.
Your mortal robe, on Judgement Day, will shine.

76*     Eternal laws are not through us made vain.
This man still lives, and Minos binds me not.
I'm from that circle where the modest eyes

79     of Marcia, your wife, are seen. Eyes turned,
she prays, O sacred breast, you keep her still your own.
For love of her, incline to our entreaties.

82     So let us pass through all your seven realms.
I'll take your gracious words to Marcia –
if you will grant we speak of you down there.'

85     'Once, Marcia,' he said, 'so pleased my eyes,
while I was there, that I, in gratitude,
would do for her whatever she might choose.

88     But now she dwells beyond the evil stream.
And therefore, by a law in force since I
came out of it, she cannot move me more.

91     Yet if in Heaven there is, as you declare,
a lady who commands and moves your deeds,
fine words aren't needed. Ask it in her name.

94     Go, and around this man now bind a belt,
formed from a single rush grown straight and smooth,
then wash his features clean of filth and stains.

97     It cannot be that any eye, still clutched
by mist and murkiness, should meet the first
of ministers who'll come from Paradise.

Around this little island, all around          100
its lowest reaches where the breakers beat,
are rushes, borne up by the yielding ooze.

No other plant that comes to leaf or grows      103
to form a rigid stem could ever thrive.
For none of these could bend to take those strokes.

Do not return along the way you came.           106
The sun that rises now will show the way
to take this mountain at a gentler rate.'

So saying, he had gone. Without a word,         109
I rose. And, drawing nearer to my guide,
tight by his side, I set my eyes on him.

And he began: 'Follow my steps, dear son.       112
Let's turn back now. From here the level shore,
in reaching to its boundaries, slopes down.'

Dawn was defeating now the last hour sung       115
by night, which fled before it. And far away
I recognized the tremblings of the sea.

Alone, we walked along the open plain,          118
as though, returning to a path we'd lost,
our steps, until we came to that, were vain.

Then, at a place in shadow where the dew        121
still fought against the sun and, cooled by breeze,
had scarcely yet been thinned out into vapour,

my master placed the palms of both his hands,   124
spread wide, lightly and gently on the tender grass.
And I, aware of what his purpose was,

offered my tear-stained cheeks to meet his touch.   127
At which, he made once more entirely clean
the colour that the dark of Hell had hidden.

We then came out across an empty shore          130*
that never saw its waters sailed upon
by any man who knew how to return.

There, at another's will, he girded me.         133
And this was marvellous: that, as he chose
that simple plant, another like it rose,

reborn the instant that he plucked it out.      136

# CANTO 2

1*     The sun had reached, already, that horizon
the arc of whose meridian, at its height,
covers Jerusalem as daytime ends.

4     And night, which circles opposite the sun,
was rising out of Ganges with the Scales,
which leave her hand, once she has overcome.

7     So lovely Aurora's cheeks, both red and white,
were turning, where I was, to sallow rose
as dawn grew older in the eastern sky.

10     We went on walking, still beside the sea,
as people do when pondering the road.
(Their hearts go forward, though their limbs delay.)

13     But look! As Mars – surprised, when morning breaks,
by thickening vapours – glows to burning red,
low in the west above its ocean floor,

16     there now appeared (may I see that once more!)
a light that came so swift across the sea
that nothing else in flight could equal it.

19     And, having briefly drawn my eyes away
to ask my leader what this light could be,
I saw it now grown greater and more bright.

22     And then, around it, all appeared to me
a something of I-did-not-know pure white,
and, bit by bit, another under that.

25     As long as these first whitenesses seemed wings,
my teacher spoke no word. But when he saw
and recognized who was this galley man:

'Come now,' he cried out. 'Bend your knees to him!    28
Look there! God's angel! Fold your hands in prayer.
Henceforth, you'll meet this kind of minister.

You see he scorns all human instruments.    31
He needs no oar, nor any other sail
than his own wings, to ply these distant shores.

You see he holds these upright to the skies    34
and, with eternal pinions, fans the air.
These do not shift as human tresses do.'

Then, as he came towards us more and more,    37
that holy bird, he seemed the brighter still.
My eyes could not, close to, sustain the sight.

I bent my eyes. He reached the shore – his boat    40
so swift, so quick, so light, so elegant,
no wave could swallow any part of it.

Celestial, at the stern, the pilot stood –    43
beatitude, it seemed, inscribed on him –
and, ranged within, a hundred spirits more.

'*In exitu Israel de Aegypto*':    46*
they sang this all together, in one voice,
with all the psalm that's written after this.

Then, over them, he made the holy cross,    49
at which they flung themselves upon the shore.
And he, as fast as he had come, went off.

The crowd that now remained, it seemed, was strange,    52
astray there, wondering, looking all around,
as people do, assessing what is new.

On every side the sun shot daylight darts.    55*
Its well-aimed arrows had already chased
the stars of Capricorn from middle sky,

by which time these new people raised their brows,    58
saying to us: 'If you two know this place,
point us the way to go towards the Mount.'

And Virgil answered: 'You may think that we    61
possess experience of where we are.
But we, like you, are pilgrim foreigners.

64    We came a little while before yourselves,
      taking a different, hard and bitter road.
      So now the climb will seem to us a game.'

67    The souls who were aware (because I breathed)
      that I was still alive, now blenched in awe,
      and, wondering at the sight, grew very pale.

70    And, as around some messenger who bears
      an olive branch in hand, crowds form to hear
      the news – none shy to trample to the fore –

73    so these souls, too, stares fixed upon my face,
      forgetting almost (all so fortunate!)
      to go ahead and make themselves more fine.

76*   And one drew forward now, I saw, to me
      to take me in his arms with such great warmth
      it moved me, so I did the same to him.

79    Ah shadows, empty save in how they look!
      Three times I locked my hands behind his back.
      As many times I came back to my breast.

82    Wonder, I think, was painted over me.
      At which the shadow smiled, and so drew back,
      while I, pursuing him, pressed further on.

85    Gently, he told me I had better stop.
      And then I knew who this was, so I prayed
      that he should speak and pause there for a while.

88    His answer came: 'As first in mortal flesh
      I loved you well, so, freed, I love you now.
      And so I stop. But you, why go through here?'

91*   'Casella!' I said. 'My own! I take this course
      to come once more where I have now arrived.
      But how have you been robbed of so much time?'

94    'No one has done me violence,' he said,
      'if many times my voyage was denied
      by Him Who chooses who'll He take, and when.

97    For His will stands at one with God's just will.
      Yet truly for the last three months He's picked,
      in utter peace, whoever's wished to board.

So I, who now had gone back to that shore          100*
where Tiber waters turn themselves to salt,
was, in all kindness, taken up by him.

He's set His wings back now towards that gorge,          103
since all who don't descend to Acheron
will always gather at that river mouth.'

And I: 'If no new law has robbed you of          106
your memory or skill in songs of love –
with which you once would calm all my desires –

then, if you'd care to, ease my soul a while.          109
For coming here with still its body's shape,
it is so worn, and weary of the way.'

'Love that speaks reasons in my mind to me . . .'          112*
So he began, and in a tone so sweet
the sweetness, even now, sounds in my heart.

My teacher, I myself and those who'd come          115
along with him, were so content with this
that nothing touched the mind apart from that.

So there we were, attentive to these notes,          118
entirely still, then calling suddenly,
that stern old man: 'What's this, malingering souls?

What's this neglect, this simply-standing-here?          121
Go run towards the mountain. Shed that skin
which won't let God be manifest to you.'

Compare: when doves, when gleaning grain or weeds,          124
flock all together at their feeding place,
with none of their habitual pride, at peace,

if something they are fearful of appears,          127
then suddenly they'll leave that bait behind,
assailed by greater worries as they are.

In that same way, I saw that fresh new band          130
break off their song and flee towards the cliff,
as people do, not knowing where they'll end.

Our own departure wasn't much less swift.          133

# CANTO 3

<table>
<tr><td>1</td><td>Although the suddenness with which they fled<br>dispersed the rest across the open plain,<br>turning towards the Mount, where justice probes,</td></tr>
<tr><td>4</td><td>I drew the closer to my trusted friend.<br>For how, without him, could I run ahead?<br>And who but he could draw me up that hill?</td></tr>
<tr><td>7</td><td>But he, it seemed, was gnawed by self-reproach.<br>Such dignity of conscience, clear and clean,<br>bitten so keenly by so slight a fault!</td></tr>
<tr><td>10</td><td>When once his steps had put aside that haste<br>that strips the air of honour from our deeds,<br>my mind, till now tight-reined within itself,</td></tr>
<tr><td>13</td><td>in eagerness of purpose broadened out.<br>I gave my sight to meet the rising ground,<br>higher than all, that banks towards the skies.</td></tr>
<tr><td>16</td><td>The sun that flared behind us, brilliant red,<br>broke now in front of me – my silhouette! –<br>as rays of light lay resting on my form.</td></tr>
<tr><td>19</td><td>I turned around, to one side, fearing I<br>had been abandoned there, seeing ahead<br>of me alone the earth was dark with shade.</td></tr>
<tr><td>22</td><td>And he, my strength, swung straight around to say:<br>'Why so dismayed and faithless? Don't you know<br>that I am with you and still guide your steps?</td></tr>
<tr><td>25*</td><td>The evening falls where now, within its grave<br>that body lies in which I cast a shade,<br>Napoli has it, borne from Brindisi.</td></tr>
</table>

If nothing now is shadowed at my feet,                        28
don't wonder any more than when the rays
the heavens project don't block each other out.

To suffer torments both of heat and chill,                    31*
the Utmost Power gives bodies, fit for that,
not wishing *how* it does to be revealed.

It's madness if we hope that rational minds                   34
should ever follow to its end the road
that one true being in three persons takes.

Content yourselves with *quia*, human kind.                   37*
Had you been able to see everything,
Mary need not have laboured to give birth.

You saw the fruitless yearning of those men                   40*
who might have had that yearning satisfied,
now given them eternally to mourn.

Plato, I mean, and Aristotle, too,                            43
and many more with them.' He bowed his head
and said no more, remaining darkly troubled.

We had, meanwhile, now reached the mountain foot.             46
And there we came across a cliff so sheer
that legs, though willing, were quite useless there.

Between Fort Lerici and Turbia                                49*
the wildest, steepest scarp would be, compared
with this, an easy stairway, opening clear.

'Now who's to know on which side this cliff sinks' –          52
so stopping in his tracks my teacher said –
'to let us climb, since we have got no wings?'

And while he went along, his head bent low,                   55
examining in thought the journey's scheme,
and I, in wonder, gazed around the rock,

a tribe of souls appeared, towards our left,                  58
moving in our direction (though their tread came slow
and so it hardly seemed to us they did).

'Lift up your eyes! Look, sir,' I said to him.                61
'There, over there, are some who'll give advice,
if you yourself have nothing to suggest.'

64     He looked across, his face now free from doubt,
and answered: 'Let's go there. They come so slow.
And you, dear son, be confident, take heart.'

67     Those people, when we'd gone a thousand steps,
were still, I'd say, as far away from us
as someone with a sling might reach by hand,

70     when, one and all, they clung to that hard mass
of towering rock, and stood there firm and tight,
as travellers, uncertain, glance about.

73     'You chosen ones, who met your end so well,
I ask you,' Virgil started, 'by that peace
which, as I think, is waiting for you all,

76     please tell us where the mountain angles down
to make it possible for us to climb.
For those who know the most, most hate time lost.'

79     As silly sheep come edging from their fold,
one, two and three, the rest all standing there
timidly turning earthwards eyes and snouts,

82     to do exactly what the first one does,
huddling against her if she hesitates,
quiet and meek, not knowing why they do,

85     so, too, I now saw moving out to me
the forward markers of that happy flock,
modest in look and dignified in walk.

88     When those towards the front saw shattered light
falling at my right hand towards the ground
(so that, from me, the shadow reached the cliff),

91     they stopped and drew themselves a little back.
Likewise the rest that followed on from them.
Not knowing why, they did the very same.

94     'You need not ask. I freely will confess
that what you see are truly human limbs.
That's why the sunlight on the earth is split.

97     Don't wonder at the sight but just believe
that, not without some virtue from the skies,
does he attempt to overcome this wall.'

So said my teacher. And these honoured folk 100
replied: 'Turn back! Go on ahead of us',
and signalled this to us with hands reversed.

And one of them began: 'Whoever you, 103*
thus going on your way, may be, turn round
and say if you have ever seen me there.'

I turned to him and fixed him with my gaze. 106
Fair-haired and handsome, with a noble look,
a sword stroke, though, had cut across his brow.

In all humility, I then denied 109
that I, till then, had seen him. 'Look!' he said,
and pointed out a wound high on his chest.'

Then, smiling: 'I am Manfred,' he declared, 112
'grandson to Constance, holy empress.
I pray you, therefore, when you've once returned,

seek out my lovely daughter, who has borne 115*
the honoured crowns of Sicily and Aragon.
Tell her the truth, whatever else is said:

I, broken in my person, had received 118
two mortal wounds and, weeping, gave myself
to Him who, freely, cares to pardon us.

My sins and crimes were horrible to hear. 121
God, though, unendingly is good. His arms
enfold and grasp all those who turn to Him.

And if Cosenza's pastor, who was sent 124*
to hunt me down by Clement (then our pope),
had read aright the face God turned to mine,

my body's bones would still be where they were, 127
near Benevento where the bridge head falls,
guarded by that great cairn of heavy stones.

The rain now bathes them, and they're moved by wind, 130
beyond the Kingdom down the Green Stream's bank
to which he'd carried them with torches dimmed.

No one, while hope shows any hint of green, 133
is lost beyond return to love eternal
merely because the Church has voiced its curse.

136    It is, however, true that those who die,
       although repentant, in contempt of Church,
       are bound to stay outside this mountain wall

139    some thirty times the span of years that they
       presumed to stand apart – if this decree
       is not made shorter by good works of prayer.

142    Now see if you can bring me happiness,
       revealing to my Constance that you've seen
       where I am now, and understood this ban.

145    For here we greatly gain from those down there.'

# CANTO 4

When, through enjoyment (or indeed through pain)    1*
which takes possession of some inner strength,
the soul is gathered up round that alone,

   it can't, it seems, pay heed to other powers.    4
And this refutes the error that maintains
the soul ignites in us in multiples.

When something, therefore, that is heard or seen    7
holds in its thrall the lower act of soul,
time passes by, and we don't notice it.

   For these are different powers – the one that hears,    10.
the one residing in the total soul –
the first (let's say) is bound, the other free.

I had my own experience of this,    13
hearing that spirit, marvelling at his words.
For now the sun, although I had not seen,

   had risen fully five-times-ten degrees when    16
we arrived where all these souls, as one,
cried out to us: 'It's here, what you demand.'

A farmer, when the grapes are growing dark,    19
with one scant forkful of his hedging thorn
will often stuff a wider gap than this,

   that corridor through which my lord and guide    22
now climbed – I following behind, alone
since all the company, by now, had gone.

San Leo you can scale, edge down to Noli,    25*
climb to Bismantova, ascend Cacume.
Feet serve you there. But here you need to fly –

28      with quickening wings, I mean, and pinions
of great desire, behind that leading-on
that offers me all hope and gives me light.

31      We scrambled through the bore of shattered rock.
On every side its edges tightened round.
The ground beneath us called for feet *and* hands.

34      And when we'd reached the rim above that cliff,
and came to where the slope was opening out,
'What path, sir,' I inquired, 'shall we take now?'

37      And he to me: 'Don't let your footsteps slide.
Just follow me. We'll gain ground on this mount
until some escort comes who knows the way.'

40      The summit was so high it conquered sight.
The slope stood proud, its incline far more steep
than (point to centre) forty-five degrees.

43      I was all in, and so began to say:
'Look round, my dearest father. Turn and see,
if you don't stop, I'm stuck here all alone.'

46      And he said: 'Son, just drag yourself up there,'
his finger pointing to a ledge beyond
that ran around the flank of that sheer slope.

49      His words so stirred me to renewed attempts,
I forced myself to track him, hands and knees,
till that encirclement was at my feet.

52      And there we came and sat, the two of us,
turned to the east where we had made our climb
(for looking back will often cheer you up).

55      I set my eyes on, first, the shores below,
then raised them to the sun, and was amazed
to see its light assail us from the left.

58*      The poet noticed that I stood struck dumb
so stupefied to see light's chariot
process between us and the Aquilon.

61      'If Castor,' he replied, 'and Pollux were
now standing in conjunction with the glass
that draws its mirror light both north and south,

you then would see the rose-red Zodiac 64
wheel still more tightly round the Ursa stars –
so long as it's not left its former track.

And if you need to get your mind round that, 67
imagine Zion – harvest that within –
and how that mountain stands upon the globe,

so that, though set in different hemispheres, 70
the same horizon bounds that Mount and this.
From which you'll see (if you think clearly now)

the road where Phaeton had no skill to drive 73
was bound to travel north of that mid-line,
and south, conversely, of Jerusalem.'

'Oh, sir!' I said. 'With such great certitude 76
I've never seen as clearly as I do,
(I'd not intelligence enough for that)

how that mid-circle of supernal force 79*
(in certain texts termed "Equatorial")
which always stands between the sun and chill,

veers, for the reason that you gave, as far 82
towards the northern clime of seven stars
as Hebrews see it bend to warmer parts.

But, if you please, I'd really like to know 85
how far we've yet to travel. This slope climbs
higher by far than eyes of mine can go.'

And he: 'This mountain is by nature such 88
that, down below, the start is always hard,
yet hurts far less the more one rises up.

And so when you will find the going smooth, 91
floating as lightly upwards in ascent
as boats that travel down a flowing stream,

you'll then have reached the end of this rough path. 94
Await that point to rest your weariness.
I'll say no more. I know the truth of this.'

The moment he had finished speaking so, 97*
a voice rang out close by us: 'Well, perhaps
you'll need a good sit-down before you do.'

100    On hearing this, we both of us turned round,
       and saw, towards our left, a bulky rock
       of which, at first, we'd neither been aware.

103    We drew ourselves across. Some persons there
       were sitting in the shadow of that stone,
       in postures, one might say, of negligence.

106    And one of those, who seemed to me worn out,
       was sitting with his arms around his knees,
       holding his face bowed heavily between.

109    'My dearest lord,' I said, 'just look at him –
       at that one there who seems more negligent
       than if his sister were Pure Indolence.'

112    At this he turned a bit, to pay us heed,
       moving his cheek to look along his thigh.
       'All right,' he said. 'Head up, you big, strong lad!'

115    I knew then who he was. And all the aches
       that made my breath still come a little fast
       could not prevent me from approaching him.

118    I reached him and he hardly raised his head,
       saying: 'You've seen now, have you, how the sun
       leads to the left its chariot at your back?'

121    His curt expressions and his sluggish turns
       had moved my lips, a little, to a smile.
       'Belacqua,' I began, 'I need not now

124    grieve for you any longer. But say why
       you're sat down here. You're waiting for a guide?
       Or are you back again to your old ways?'

127    'Brother' he said, 'what point in going up?'
       God's angel, sitting at the gate up there,
       would not admit me to the Penances.

130    The heavens must circle first around me here
       the length of time they did around my life
       (since I delayed good sighs until my end)

133    unless, before that, prayer has brought me aid,
       rising on high from hearts that live in grace.
       What else – since Heaven won't hear – is any use?'

The poet now was climbing further on,   136
saying: 'Come! Come! The high meridian – look! –
is touched by sun. Along the western shore,
    the foot of night is falling on Maroc.'   139

# CANTO 5

| | |
|---|---|
| 1 | Already some way past the shadow folk, |
| | I climbed still onward in my leader's track, |
| | until, below us, one of them burst out: |
| 4 | 'See that?' – a finger pointing long – 'The one behind! |
| | No sun ray shines, it seems, towards his left! |
| | And doesn't he behave as though alive?' |
| 7 | On hearing these sharp words, I turned my eyes, |
| | and saw them gazing in astonishment, |
| | at me – yes, me! – and the broken sunlight. |
| 10 | 'Why let your thoughts get tangled up like that?' |
| | (My master speaks.) 'It only slows your stride. |
| | And why be bothered by their whisperings? |
| 13 | Keep close behind me. Let them say their say. |
| | Stand straight, a mighty tower unwavering, |
| | its height unshaken by such breaths of wind. |
| 16 | When thought is bred too rampantly from thought, |
| | then, of himself, a man will miss his mark. |
| | Each mental thrust debilitates the first.' |
| 19 | What answer could I offer, save 'I come'? |
| | I said so, sprinkled by that blushing hue |
| | that, on occasion, means we merit pardon. |
| 22* | Meanwhile, across the angle of our climb, |
| | there now appeared ahead another group, |
| | intoning, verse by verse, the '*Miserere*'. |
| 25 | But when they saw my limbs would not allow |
| | a thoroughfare to any ray of light, |
| | they changed their chanting to a long, hoarse 'Oooh!' |

Then two, who acted as their nuncios,         28
hurried to meet us with the urgent plea:
'What is your standing here? Please let us know.'

My master answered: 'You may now return      31
and bear to those who sent you this reply:
"This man, in body, is true flesh and bone."

And if, as I suppose they did, they stopped     34
because they saw that shade, these words should serve.
Let them all honour him. He'll pay them well.'

Vapours, when kindled in night's early hours,    37*
flash across tranquil skies like meteors,
and August clouds are cleft by setting suns.

Yet none I've ever seen went up as quick      40
as these two messengers, who turned, once there,
with all the rest, to us – a herd in rampage.

'They'll come in multitudes,' the poet said,     43
'and mill around and pester you for prayers.
So listen as you go, but still press on.'

'You there, that soul now set for happiness'    46
(they yelled their greeting) 'with your limbs intact
as ever you were born! Slow down a bit!

Look! Is there anyone you've seen before?     49
You might, if so, bear news of them beyond.
Ah! Where to now? Ah! Why don't you stand still?

We all were victims of some violent death,    52
yet sinners till we reached our final hour.
Then Heaven's light dawned and made us see things clear,

so that, repenting and forgiving all,      55
we came from life remade at peace with God,
who heartens our desire to see Him still.'

'I stare into your eyes,' I answered them,     58
'and recognize no single one. Yet you
are spirits born anew to good. And all

you wish – and I can do – I shall. Please say.    61
I swear this by the peace that leads me on
from world to world, pursuing this great guide.'

64*     Then one began: 'You need not swear to that.
        Granted your will is not cut short by "can't",
        each of us trusts that you will bring some good.

67      May I (who'll only speak till others do)
        entreat you, if you've seen those lands that lie
        between Romagna and the realm of Charles,

70      that you, in all your kindness, pray for me
        in Fano – so entreaties offered there
        may give me strength to cleanse my grievous sins.

73      I was from Fano. But the hollow wounds
        from which the blood by which I lived ran down,
        were dealt me by the Antenorians.

76      I thought my safety was, with them, assured.
        The Estes got it fixed, their spite to me
        exceeding all that justice could require.

79      If only I had fled towards La Mira
        – they caught me as I ran to Oriaco –
        my place would be where men breathe, even now.

82      Towards the marsh I ran, where – brackish reeds
        entwining me – I fell, watching as, in this mire,
        a lake spread outwards, forming from my veins.'

85      'May your desires be met' (another spoke)
        'that draw you to the mountain height. Then, please,
        take pity. In your goodness, aid my own.

88*     I am – once Montefeltran – now Buonconte.
        Giovanna does not pray for me. None cares.
        And so, among all these, I walk, brow lowered.'

91*     'No one has ever known,' I said, 'your place
        of burial. What led you – chance? or was it force? –
        away, at Campaldino, from the kill?'

94      'Ah!' he replied. 'A stream – the Archiano – runs
        across the lower Casentino hills,
        born above Hermitage-in-Apennine.

97      I'd got to where this river's title fails,
        fleeing on foot, and wounded in my throat,
        a line of blood behind me on the plain.

And now I lost my sight. And all my words     100
ended in uttering Maria's name.
I fell – my flesh alone remaining there.

But tell the living this – I'll speak the truth –     103
God's angel laid his hands on me. Hell shrieked:
"Why do you rob me, Heavenspawn, of this?

You'd prise him from me for one little tear,     106
and carry off his everlasting part?
Well, I'll rule otherwise the other half!"

Humid evaporations (as you know)     109
collect in air, then, rising to the grip
of freezing air, return to earth as rain.

There now arrived the Evil Urge – who seeks,     112
in mind, for nothing if not ill – and stirred,
through powers its nature gives, wind, murk and fog.

And when the light of day had been put out,     115*
he draped the vale in clouds, from Pratomagno
to reach the summit of the mountain range

and made the skies condense till gravid air     118
was turned, once more, to water. Whatever
earth refused to bear ran off in runnels.

And when these streams in torrents were
        conjoined,     121
these rushed towards the sovereign river course
with such great speed that nothing held them back.

The Archiano – furious, in spate – had found     124
my body at its outlet, rigid, chill.
It drove this to the Arno, loosing there

the cross that, lost in agony, my arms had formed.     127
From bank to riverbed, it swirled me round,
then wrapped and hid me in its muddy spoil.'

'When you return, pray Heaven, to the world,     130*
and, having rested from long travelling'
(with these few words a third soul joined the group)

133     'please, do remember me. I am La Pia.
      Siena made me, unmade by Maremma.
      And he knows this who, once I wore his ring,
136       took me in marriage with his own bright gem.'

# CANTO 6

When punters split off from some gambling game,                    1
the loser stays behind, all misery,
to check the throws once more and, sadly, learn,
    while, with the winner, all the rest go off.                   4
Some buttonhole the man, some pluck his tails,
and some his sleeve – 'Just think of me,' they mean.

    Though hearing each of them, he does not pause,                7
his hands fend all away, to make them stop.
So he defends himself from this great press.

    Well, that was me, in that dense crowd of souls,               10
turning my face to this side, then to that.
By promising each one, I got away.

    The Aretine was there who met his end                        13 *
at vicious Ghin di Tacco's scything arm,
he, too, who, running with the hunt, had drowned.

    And here as well, with hands stretched out in prayer,         16
was Frederick Novello and that Pisan man
who made the clan Marzucco's power appear.

    I saw Count Orso, and the man whose soul                      19
was severed from his limbs, so he declared,
by spite and envy and no crime of his.

    I mean Pierre la Brosse – and, while still there,             22
just let the lady of Brabant (lest she
be herded with the worst for that) take care.

    As soon as I got free from all these shades –                 25
who went still praying for another's prayer
to speed them on their way to holiness –

28    I thus began: 'It seems that you, my Light,
      deny overtly in a certain text
      that prayers can ever bend what Heaven dictates.

31    And yet these folk are praying just for that.
      Could it then be the hopes they have are vain?
      Or is it that your words aren't clear to me?'

34    And he to me: 'The words I write are plain.
      And yet, if you look closely with sane thought,
      the hope that these all have will never fail.

37    God's justice at its summit does not sink
      because, in one sharp point, the fire of love
      completes what those who dwell here expiate.

40    So, in the passage where I made this point,
      no flaw could ever be redeemed by prayer.
      For prayer was then not linked or joined to God.

43    Yet do not, truly, let your question rest
      until the one who'll come as light between
      your intellect and truth declares you may.

46    I don't know if you take my sense. I mean
      Beatrice. You'll see her up above,
      smiling, in all her happiness, on the crest.'

49    'My lord,' I said, 'let's move with greater haste.
      I'm not as wearied as I was before.
      And – look – the mountain's casting shadow now.'

52    'While daylight lasts,' he answered me, 'we'll press
      our way as far ahead as we still can.
      But things have not the shape that you suppose.

55    Before you reach that height, you'll see return
      the one who now is hidden by the ridge –
      so you cannot, now, break the light he sheds.

58*   But over there you see a soul alone,
      alone placed there who stares across at us.
      This one will teach us what's the quickest way.'

61    We came towards it. O you Lombard soul!
      How proud you stood, how haughty in your look,
      your moving eye so grave and dignified.

The soul did not say anything at all.                                       64
It let us make our way, still looking on,
as hunting lions do that pause and couch.

But Virgil went across to him, and asked                                    67
that we be shown a better path to climb.
To this request, the soul made no reply.

About our origins, our towns and lives,                                     70
*he* questioned *us*. My thoughtful guide began:
'Mantua . . .' The shade – so dark-cowled, sunk within –

rose up towards him from where first he'd been,                             73
saying: 'You Mantuan! I am Sordello.
Your fellow citizen.' And each round each flung arms.

You! Vile Italia! Sorrow's resting place!                                   76
You hulk that no one steers through raging storms!
No sovereign lady, you're a cat house whore!

That noble soul was moved with such great speed                             79
to greet his fellow citizen, to hear –
no more than that! – the sweet sound of their home.

Yet those who live within your boundaries                                   82
stand nowhere free of war. Each gnaws the next,
all locked together by one wall and moat.

Search hard, you wretch, round all your ocean shores                        85
then turn towards your heart, and try to see
if any of its parts rejoice in peace.

Why should Justinian have formed your reins?                                88*
What use is that? The saddle's riderless.
The shame would be far less were there no curb.

You people! If you only understood                                          91
what God intends you'd be more reverent,
and let the saddle be great Caesar's seat.

Just look how fierce and cruel the beast's become.                         94
No spur to set it on its proper course,
since you, Italia, took the bridle up.

You German Albert! You abandon her,                                         97*
so hard to handle now, untamed and wild,
you who should sit astride her saddle bows.

100        May justice from the stars fall, rightly, down
on your tribe's blood. May that come strange and clear,
to make your heir feel all the dread of it.

103        Held back in Germany by raging greed,
your father did – as you now – tolerate
the Empire's garden to lie desolate.

106*        Come! See the Montagues and Capulets,
Monaldi, Filippeschi, reckless men,
some plunged in misery and some in fear!

109*        Come, cruel man, and see the great distress
of all your nobles. Cure them of their warts.
You'll see how Santa Fiora is eclipsed.

112        Come now, and see that Rome of yours in tears.
Widowed and lonely, day and night she weeps:
'Say why, dear Caesar, you're not with me now.'

115        Come now, and see the love between these folk.
And if no pity for us makes you move,
come, be ashamed to know what name you've won.

118        And if, great Jove, once crucified for us,
it is permissible for me to say,
then why are Your just eyes now turned elsewhere?

121        Or is all this a preparation, formed
within the chasm of Your wisdom, for some good
cut off completely from our power to see?

124*        In Italy, the cities are all full
of petty despots. Every country lout
who joins a gang is rebel Marcellus.

127        Dear Florence, you may well content yourself
with this parenthesis, which can't touch you,
all thanks, of course, to your so brilliant crew.

130        Many, though true at heart, are slow to shoot,
for fear, without advice, they'd rush the bow.
But your lot tongue-tip justice all the time.

133        Many refuse to take on public tasks.
But your lot, so solicitous, unasked,
reply with shouts: 'Let me! I'm up for that!'

Look happy now. You've every reason to,     136
rich as you are, at peace and oh-so-wise.
The outcome does not hide that I speak true.

   Athens and Lacedaemon, which first made     139*
the ancient law, and were so civilized,
made, as to living well, the faintest mark

   compared to you who make such delicate     142
provisions in your laws that what you spin
won't reach from mid-October to November's end.

   How many times within your memory     145
have you, renewing all your limbs, transformed
duties and laws and coinage and customs?

   And if you'll know yourself and see the light,     148
you'll see how like you are to some sick hag,
who finds no comfort on her feather bed,

   but shields herself from pain with every squirm.     152

# CANTO 7

1     Three or four times, with solemn happiness,
the welcome each gave each had been renewed
till, drawing back, Sordello said: 'Who *are* you?'

4     'Before the time that souls were turned, when fit,
in dignity, for God, to this great mount,
my bones were buried by Octavian.

7     I am Vergilius. And for no crime,
save lack of faith, I lost the heavenly sky.'
This was the answer that my lord then gave.

10     Like someone on the sudden who, before
his eyes, sees what he can't help marvelling at,
can't credit it but does, and says 'It is . . . It's not . . .',

13     so did Sordello, and he bent his brow,
then, turning back to Virgil, flung once more
his arms round where inferiors embrace.

16     'You glory of the Latin race,' he said,
'through you our tongue was shown what it could do.
Eternal honour of where I, once, was.

19     What merit or what grace shows you to me?
If I am fit to listen to your words,
say – if you come from Hell – what cloister's yours.'

22     'Through all the circles of the grieving realm
I've come,' he answered him, 'and now I'm here.
A power in Heaven first moved me. So I come.

25     Through nothing I had done but what I'd *not*,
my sight lost that great Sun that you desire,
known too belatedly in time for me.

There is a place down there not grim with pain        28*
but only with sad shades whose deep laments
sound not as screams but melancholy sighs.

I take my place with children – innocents        31
in whom the bite of death set lethal teeth
before they'd been made free of human sin.

And there I stay with all who were not clothed        34
in those three holy virtues – though I knew,
and, guiltless, followed all the other four.

But give us – if you know and can – some sign        37
so we can come more quickly to the place
at which the proper Purgatory begins.'

He answered: 'No fixed ground is given us.        40
I am allowed to travel up and round.
As far as I can go, I'll be your guide.

But look! The day by now is going down.        43
And none by night can ever make the climb.
Better to think of some good resting place.

There are, towards the right, souls hidden here.        46
I'll lead you on to them, if you agree,
and you'll not want for pleasure, knowing them.'

'But how is that?' the answer came. 'Would those        49
who wished to make ascent at night be checked
by someone else, or simply lack the power?'

Sordello drew his finger on the ground,        52
saying – that good man – 'There! You see that line?
You could not cross it once the sun was down.

Not, though, because there's anything to bar        55
your going up, save shadows of the night.
It's that which knots the will in powerlessness.

We could, of course, descend and walk below        58
and, while the far horizons keep day shut,
wander and take a turn around the coast.'

My lord, then, as though wondering at these words,        61
replied: 'So lead us on to where, you say,
it's possible to linger in delight.'

64      We'd only gone a little way from there
when, so I saw, the mountain hollowed out,
as, here, our valleys hollow earthly hills.

67      'Just over there!' the shade now said to us.
'We'll go to where the cliff has formed a lap,
and there await the coming of new day.'

70      Slanting between the level and the steep,
a tight path led us to the dale's low edge –
the bank's rim here diminishing to half.

73      Gold, finest silver, cochineal, white lead,
indigo, ebony polished to a sheen,
the freshest emeralds when they've just been split,

76      each in pure colour would be overcome
by all the flowers and grasses in that fold –
as by the greater any lesser is.

79      Nor had great nature worked in paint alone.
She also with a thousand perfumes wrought
a sweetness never known and indistinct.

82*      '*Salve, Regina*'. on the flowering greens,
the souls, I saw, not seen beyond the vale,
all sat together as they sang this hymn.

85      'Until what little sun remains nests down,'
the Mantuan who'd led us there began,
'don't ask me to escort you down to them.

88      You'll better see by staying on this ledge
the faces, looks and gestures of these kings
than if you'd been received within their glade.

91*      The one who's seated highest, and (in look)
neglected what his proper duty urged,
and does not move his lips while others sing,

94      was Rudolph who, as emperor, could have healed
the wounds that did Italia to death
so that no others will revive her soon.

97      The next, who seems to offer him support,
ruled in that country where those waters rise
that bear to Elbe the Moldau and the Elbe to sea.

His name was Ottakar – a better prince,                    100
even when baby-clothed, than Wenceslaus,
his son who, bearded, grazed on lust and ease.
  And that one – button-nosed – who seems so caught    103
in conversation with the kind-faced man
died, fleeing, as he stripped the lily flower.
  Look at him! how he pounds on his own breast.          106
And see the next who's spread his palm to form
a bed on which to lay his sighing cheek.
  Father these are and in-law to the Ill                      109
of France. His vicious, filthy life they know –
and hence the grief transfixing each alike.
  And that lord there – the burly type – who sings      112*
in concert with the one of manly nose,
bore, as his knightly belt, all worth and strength.
  And if that young boy sitting at his back               115
could still, succeeding him, have been the king,
true merit would have flowed from urn to urn –
  which none could argue of his other heirs.              118
For James and Frederick rule his kingdoms now
and no one holds his better heritage.
  It seldom happens that man's probity                     121
will rise through every branch. He wills it thus,
so, given from beyond, it's known as His.
  These words go out to that one with the nose          124
no less than to Pier, who sings with him,
whom Puglia and Provence already mourn.
  The tree is that much less than its own seed,          127
as Constance can applaud her husband more
than Marguerite and Beatrice can.
  See there the monarch of the simple life,              130*
Henry of England, sitting all alone.
He in his branches comes much better off.
  The one among them lower, on the ground,             133
is Marquis William, looking to the heights.
For him, the wars of Alessandria
  make Canavese and Montferrat weep.                      136

# CANTO 8

1      It was, by now, the hour that turns to home
       the longing thoughts of seamen, melting hearts
       the day they've said goodbye to dearest friends,

4*         and when by love the pilgrim, new to this,
       is pierced to hear, far off, the evening bell
       that seems to mourn the dying of the day,

7          as I began to blank my hearing out,
       and gaze in wonder at a single soul
       who, risen up, hand raised, asked all to hear.

10         This soul, first, joined his palms then lifted them,
       eyes fixed towards the orient, as though
       to say to God: 'For nothing else I care.'

13         'Te lucis ante' issued from his lips
       with such devotion and each note so sweet
       it made me wander out of conscious thought.

16         Then, sweetly and devoutly, all the rest,
       their eyes all turned to those supernal wheels,
       picked up from him and sang the hymn in full.

19*        Reader, now fix a needle eye on truth.
       The veil is, after all, so gauzy here
       you'll thread it through as lightly as can be.

22         I saw the noble army of those souls
       in silence turn their gaze towards the sky –
       as though awaiting something – meek and pale.

25         And then I saw, descending from the height,
       two angels with two swords, each flashing fire,
       the point of each was blunt and broken off.

As green as are the freshest newborn leaves,        28
so were their garments, fanned by bright, green wings
which, drawn behind them, rustled as they beat.

One came to stand a little from our heads.        31
The other lighted on the farther bank.
The people, thus, were held between the two.

Their hair was blond. And this I clearly saw.        34
But looking at their faces, sight was lost –
as natural powers fail, tested to excess.

'These two,' as now Sordello said, 'have come        37
as guardians of the vale, from Mary's breast,
against the serpent who'll soon pass this way.'

I, ignorant of where the snake would come,        40
span all around and huddled closer up,
frozen with dread, to Virgil's trusted side.

Sordello once again spoke out: 'Let's go        43
and talk down there among those famous shades.
To see you will, for them, be welcome grace.'

Three paces only had I gone, perhaps,        46
and there I was. And one of them, I saw,
stared, wondering who I was, at me (yes, me!).

The time had come when air was turning black –        49
not yet so dark, though, that, between our eyes,
what first had been locked up should not be clear.

He made towards me, as I did to him.        52[*]
Noble judge Nino, how it pleased me then
to see you weren't among the guilty souls.

No courteous welcome now remained unsaid.        55
'How long,' he asked, 'since, over distant waves,
you reached the foothills that surround this shore?'

'Oh! Through unhappy regions,' I replied,        58
'I came at dawn. I'm still in my first life –
though travelling here, I gain the other, too.'

And once the meaning of my words was heard,        61
he (and Sordello, also) drew away,
as people do when suddenly confused.

64     One turned to Virgil, while the other turned
to someone sitting there, and cried aloud:
'Conrad, get up! Just see what God's grace wills!'

67     Then facing me: 'I pray you – by the thanks,
so singular, you owe to Him who hides
His first "because" so none can pass that stream,

70     when once you're back beyond the far-flung sea,
then tell my dear Giovanna she should call,
on my behalf, to where the pure are heard.

73     I do not think her mother loves me now.
For she has changed her widowhood's white veil –
which, wretchedly, she'll yearn for once again.

76     Because of her, one readily can see
how long the fire of love in women lasts,
if eye and touch don't often kindle it.

79     The viper of the Milanese camp
will make for her less splendid burial
than my Gallurian cockerel would have done.'

82     He said all this, his face marked by the stamp
of that true zeal that burned with measured flame
within him in his truest heart of hearts.

85     My eyes still, avidly, were on the skies
fixed where the stars ran slowest in their track,
as wheels do closest to the axle tree.

88     My guide: 'Dear son, what do you see up there?'
'Those three sharp torches,' I replied to him,
'with which the southern pole is all ablaze.'

91     His answer to me was: 'The four bright stars
that you saw just this morning sink down there.
And these have risen now to where they were.'

94     As he said this, Sordello drew him close,
saying: 'Look there! You see? Our enemy!'
He stretched his finger, showing where to look.

97     From that side where this little valley had
no sheltering barrier, a snake appeared,
perhaps like that which fed Eve bitter food.

Through grass and flowers this evil smear came on,          100
rolling its head around from time to time,
licking its back as preening beasts will do.

I did not see – and so I cannot say –          103
how those celestial hawks began to move.
I did, though, see the motion that each made.

Sensing the air ripped open by green wings,          106
the serpent fled and both the angels turned,
flying at equal pace, to their high posts.

The shadow that had drawn, when called, towards          109*
the judge, had not, throughout this whole attack,
at any point released me from his gaze.

'May that great lamp that leads you to the height          112
discern in your free will sufficient wax
to light your way to that flower-studded peak,'

(so he began). 'If you have truthful news          115
of Val di Magra or the neighbouring place,
then tell me. I was once a great man there.

I was, by name, Currado Malaspina,          118
not the great ancient but of his descent.
I bore love – here refined – towards my kin.'

'Oh! I have never been,' I said, 'through lands          121
of yours. Yet who in Europe anywhere
is there to whom your name is not well known?

The fame that brings such lustre to your house          124
exalts your lords, exalts all your domains,
so that all know it, though they've not been there.

I swear to you (so may I reach the heights!)          127
that your much-honoured race goes still unstripped
of worthiness and prize in purse and sword.

Nature and how they act so honours them          130
that, though the world's vile head may twist awry,
they all walk straight, and scorn the evil way.'

And he: 'Go on like that. The sun won't sink          133
within the bed that Ram Stars – all four feet
astraddle – cover for more than seven times

136      before the courtesy that you express
is nailed within the centre of your brain
with greater nails than hearsay brings to you –
139      if judgement is not halted in its course.'

# CANTO 9

The concubine of timeworn Tithonus                                    1*
already on the eastern balcony,
out of her dear love's arms, was glimmering white.

   Her forehead shone with gemstones in the form              4
of that chill animal, the Scorpion,
that strikes then stings us with its vicious tail.

   The night which rises step by step had now,                  7
where we'd arrived, advanced by two of these,
the third already lowering on the wing,

   when I – some trace of Adam with me still –               10
conquered by sleep, bowed down towards the grass
where all the five of us had come to sit.

   In that hour when the swallow, near to dawn,             13*
begins once more her long sad chant, perhaps
recalling all the miseries she'd borne,

   and when our minds like hawks on foreign tracks         16
furthest from flesh, least caught in their own thoughts,
are near divine in visions that they see,

   as in some dream, there hovering, it seemed               19
I saw an eagle in the sky. Its plumes were gold,
its wings wide spread, its purpose soon to swoop.

   And I, it seemed to me, was where the kin                   22
of Ganymede, when he was seized – swept up
towards the highest court – remained abandoned.

   Just to myself, 'Perhaps,' I thought, 'this strikes        25*
only by habit here, perhaps it scorns
to carry things from elsewhere in its claws.'

28    And then it seemed that, wheeling slightly round,
as terrible as lightning, down it struck
and tore me upwards to the sphere of fire.

31    And there the eagle and I, it seemed, both blazed.
And this imagined fire so scorched and seared
that, yielding, dreaming sleep just had to break.

34*   Not very differently, Achilles woke,
his startled eyes now staring all around,
dazed, knowing nothing of where he might be,

37    his mother having fled with him asleep
within her arms from Chiron's care to Skyros.
(The Greeks would, after, make him leave that place.)

40    So too I shook myself as, from my face,
sleep fled, and deathly pale I then became,
turning, as terrified we do, to ice.

43    Beside me, there was only my great strength.
The sun by now was more than two hours high.
My eyes were turned back down towards the sea.

46    My lord said, 'Have no fear. Be confident.
For we have reached a good point in our way.
Do not hold back, but give your strengths free rein.

49    You've now arrived where Purgatory begins.
See over there the wall encircling it.
See there the portal where the wall is breached.

52    Just now, at dawn which comes before new day,
when still your soul was sleeping deep within,
couched on the flowers that ornament that place,

55*   a lady came. She said, "I am Lucia.
Let me take up the man who's sleeping there,
so I can make his journey easier."

58    Sordello and those noble forms stayed back.
She took you up and, once the day shone clear,
she came up here, I following in her steps.

61    She laid you down. But, first, her lovely eyes
displayed to me the entrance open there.
Then she and sleep that instant went away.'

As, doubting, people do when reassured –                 64
changing to confidence the fears they had,
once what is true has been revealed to them –
    so I, too, changed. And since my leader saw          67
that I had now no cares, he moved to climb,
with me behind him still, the wall towards its height.
    You, reader, can now see how here I raise            70
the theme my verse attempts. Don't marvel, then,
if with more craft and art I strengthen it.
    We now drew closer and were in that part             73
where, first, as I had thought, a breach appeared,
as might some fissure that divides a wall.
    And now I saw a gate and, leading there,             76*
three steps beneath, each coloured differently,
and at that gate a guardian who spoke no word.
    And as I opened more my eyes to this,                79
I saw him sitting on the highest stair.
His face was such I could not bear that light.
    A naked sword he held within his hand                82
which so reflected sun rays back at me
that many times I fixed my eyes in vain.
    'Speak from back there! And say what is your will.'  85
So he began. 'And tell me, where's your guide?
Take care, lest going up should cause you harm.'
    'From Heaven, a lady, knowing all these things,      88
told us a short time past,' my teacher answered,
'"Go forward for the gate you seek is here."'
    'May she advance your steps in doing well,'          91
once more the courteous guardian began:
'Come forward, therefore, to these stairs of ours.'
    And there we came to them. The first great block     94
was marble, white, so burnished and so clean
that I as I appear was mirroired there.
    The second, in its tint more dark than perse,        97
was rock – waste, rough to touch and scorched and dry,
cracked both across and upward to its height.

100     The third, which, massively, weighed these two down,
was porphyry, it seemed, and flamed as bright
as fresh blood spurting from a severed vein.

103     And, on this third, the angel of the Lord
had placed both feet and sat across the threshold,
which, as it seemed, was adamantine stone.

106     Up these three steps, impelled by good intent,
my leader drew me, saying: 'Humbly ask
that he undo the lock that holds the door.'

109     I fell devoutly at his holy feet
and asked that he, for mercy, open it.
But, first, three times I beat upon my breast.

112\*     He then sketched seven 'Ps' across my brow,
written with sword point. 'When you're once within,
make sure,' he said, 'you go and wash these scars.'

115     The vestments that he wore would be, in hue,
the same as ash or soil when dug out dry.
Then from beneath his robes he drew two keys.

118\*     One key was silver and the other gold.
With first the white, then yellow after that,
he worked the door so I was well content.

121     'Whenever either of these keys falls short
and fails to turn correctly in its lock,
this path,' he said, 'will not then open up.

124     One is more precious, but the other needs
much greater art and skill to make it turn.
This is the one that gets the knot undone.

127     From Peter I receive these keys – who said,
when penitents have bowed down to my feet,
"Err more in opening than in locking out."'

130     He pushed the panels of the sacred gate,
saying: 'Go in. But be aware of this,
that those who look behind return outside.'

133     And when the pivots of that sacred hall,
forged out of resonantly massive steel,
were wrenched around within their housing hinge,

no roar was heard, no harsher sound was made,                136*
by Tarpeian doors, when from them honest
Metellus was dragged – doors that were henceforth lean.

    I turned, attentive when the thunder broke,        139*
and, seemingly, '*Te Deum laudamus*'
was heard, as voices mixed in that sweet tune.

    The sounds I heard brought back into my mind       142
the same impression that we often get
when organs play, accompanying a voice.

    Now, yes, we hear the words; now, no, we don't.    145

# CANTO 10

<table>
<tr><td>1</td><td>Now, both within the threshold of that gate<br>(our souls won't use it, out of ill-bent love<br>which makes the crooked way, to us, seem straight)</td></tr>
<tr><td>4</td><td>I heard it closed, resoundingly, again.<br>Yet if I'd turned to set my eyes on that,<br>what adequate excuse could there have been?</td></tr>
<tr><td>7</td><td>We climbed now through a trough of fissured rock<br>that moved, on either side, this way and that,<br>as waves do, surging near, then running back.</td></tr>
<tr><td>10</td><td>'We'll need,' my lord began, 'a certain skill<br>to keep together tight against the curve<br>that, ebbing here and there, avoids the swell.'</td></tr>
<tr><td>13</td><td>This made our footsteps few and hesitant.<br>And so the moon, which now was on the wane,<br>had reached its bed, to lie once more at rest,</td></tr>
<tr><td>16</td><td>before we'd gone beyond that needle eye.<br>But once we did get free and opened up,<br>climbing to where the mountain gathered in –</td></tr>
<tr><td>19</td><td>I all worn out and both of us unsure<br>of where to make our way – we paused upon<br>a road far lonelier than any desert track.</td></tr>
<tr><td>22</td><td>If measured from the edge that marked the void,<br>towards the foot of that still-soaring mount,<br>the span would be three human body lengths.</td></tr>
<tr><td>25</td><td>And, be it to the left side or the right,<br>as far as eyesight could extend its wings,<br>the ledge, in circuit, seemed to me the same.</td></tr>
</table>

We'd still to move our feet towards those heights     28
when I perceived that, all around, the bank –
which, rising straight, lacked any upward route –

    was marble, brilliant white, and all adorned     31*
with carved reliefs so fine that Polyclite,
or even Nature, would have there felt scorned.

    The angel, reaching earth with that decree     34*
of peace – so wept-for over centuries –
which opened Heaven's long-forbidden gates,

    appeared so truthfully before us now,     37
carved in a gesture of pure gentleness,
he did not seem an image keeping silence.

    In truth, one might have said he spoke the 'Ave'.     40
For in that image was the one who turned
the key that opened out the utmost Love.

    And from her stance and bearing there shone out     43
(exactly as an imprint sealed in wax)
'Ecce ancilla Dei', word for word.

    'Don't keep your mind fixed only on one part.'     46
These words my teacher gently spoke to me.
(I held him where all others have their heart.)

    And so, in sight, I moved. And I could see,     49
behind Maria, on the side where he,
in urging me to make a move, now stood,

    set in the rock, another narrative.     52
Passing by Virgil, I came near to that,
so that it stood displayed before my eyes.

    Carved there – in marble, also – was the cart,     55*
with oxen, carrying the Holy Ark
(because of which we dread unsanctioned deeds).

    Before the Ark were people, as it seemed,     58
gathered in seven choirs who made my sense –
hearing and sight – say, 'No', and, 'Yes, they sing.'

    In that same way, the incense smoke, which there     61
was imaged, worked on eye and nose, so these
were not concordant as to 'no' and 'yes'.

64 Before that vessel of all holiness,
the humble psalmist danced, his robe tucked up –
both more and less than king in all of this.

67 Then Michal, opposite, was gazing down,
as from some window of the royal court,
an effigy of rancour and disdain.

70 I turned my feet away from where I'd stood
to note another story, close at hand,
its gleam beyond the 'Michal', showing white.

73* En-storied here was found the glorious deed
of that high prince of Rome whose prowess moved
Pope Gregory to win great victory.

76 I speak of Trajan, noble Emperor.
A widow there had snatched his horse's rein,
her gestures those of grief and bitter tears.

79 Around him, surging horsemen, as it seemed,
filled all the space. And eagles, wrought in gold,
were seen above, as moving in the wind.

82 The wretched widow, as these thronged around,
was saying, seemingly: 'My lord, avenge
my dearest son. He's dead. That is my heart-wound!'

85 He, seemingly, replied to her: 'Just wait.
I shall return.' And she: 'My lord' – as though
her agony were quickening all the more –

88 'but if you don't return?' And he: 'The one
who's where I am will act.' And she: 'How can
*his* good be yours when you forget your own?'

91 Then he: 'Be comforted. It's right that I
fulfil, before I move, what I should do.
Justice demands this, and compassion binds.'

94 The One who sees no thing that's new to Him
produced this form of discourse visible –
so new to us, so fresh since not found here.

97 While I, in all delight, still gazed upon
these images of great humility,
more precious being formed by that skilled hand.

'Look over here! Although their pace is slow,        100
there are,' the poet murmured, 'people there,
a crowd who'll send us to the steps above.'

My eyes, entranced in wonder, longingly,            103
still seeking happily new things to see,
turned round towards him, making no delay.

Yet, reader, I'd not have your minds bewitched,     106
hearing how God would have the debt repaid,
or drawn away from your best purposes.

Don't dwell upon the form their sufferings take.    109
Think of what follows, and that, come the worst,
it can't go on beyond the Judgement Day.

'Sir,' I began, 'it seems that what I see,          112
moving towards us, are not human forms.
I cannot tell. I rave. I look in vain.'

'Their grievous mode of punishment' (to me)        115
'so creases them and bends them to the ground
that my eyes, too, first fought at what they see.

Look, though, and fix your gaze. Let sight untwist  118
the vines of what comes there beneath these stones.
You see already how each beats his breast.'

Proud Christians, wretched and – alas! – so tired,  121
who, feeble in your powers of mental sight,
place so much faith in your own backward tread,

do you not recognize that you are worms             124
born to become angelic butterflies
that fly to justice with no veil between?

Why is it that your thoughts float up so high?      127
You, with your faults, are little more than grubs,
chrysalides (no more!) that lack full form.

As sometimes, bracing up a roof or vault,           130
a figure will be seen as corbel stone
that, bending, joins its two knees to its chest,

at which there's born, in anyone who sees,          133
from this non-truth a truly harsh distress:
that's how I saw them when I gave them thought.

136     The truth is each was hunched up, less and more,
        according to his load, some more, some less.
        The one who, from his actions, bore the most,
139     appeared in tears to pant: 'I can't do more.'

# CANTO 11

'Our Father, dwelling in the heavenly spheres,                    1*
not circumscribed by these but through that love
which you bear more, on high, to primal things,

Your name, and all the prowess of your might,                    4
be praised by every creature. It is fit
to pay all thanks to Your sweet forming power.

May peace, as in Your realm, come down to us.                    7
For we ourselves cannot attain to that,
if come it doesn't – not with all our wit.

As all your angels make a sacrifice,                             10
singing "*Osanna*", of their wills to you,
so, too, may men make sacrifice of theirs.

Give us this day the manna each day needs.                       13
Without that, exiled in this grinding waste,
all travel backwards who strive forwards most.

And just as we, to everyone, forgive                             16
the harm we bear, grant generous pardon, too.
And do not look upon what we deserve.

The powers we have (so easily subdued)                           19
do not make trial of through the ancient foe,
but free us from the one who is our goad.

This final prayer is made, O dearest Lord,                       22
not for ourselves (we now have no such need).
We speak for those behind us, who've remained.'

Then praying, for themselves and us, 'God speed',                25
these shadows made their way beneath such loads
as sometimes in our nightmares can be seen,

28      around and all around on that first ledge,
worn-out, tormented (though each differently),
purging away the murky fogs of earth.

31      If they, in that place, always speak our good,
down here what can be said and done for them,
by those whose wills are good in where they root?

34      We surely ought to help them cleanse the marks
that they bore hence – till, light in weight and pure,
they've power to rise towards the wheeling stars.

37      'May justice and compassion soon relieve
this weight from you, so you may move your wings,
which then, as you desire, may lighten you!

40      So, too, point out to us, to left or right,
the shortest way to go towards the stair.
If more than one, teach us the least steep slope.

43      For this man here who comes along with me,
burdened in being clothed with Adam's flesh,
is loath to climb, despite the will to do.'

46      The words that came, responding now to those
that he whom I was following first spoke,
rose from some source not clearly manifest.

49*      But this was said: 'Turn right, and come with us
along the bank. You'll find an upward path
where even living persons can ascend.

52      And were I not impeded by this stone
that tames the hauteur of my once-proud neck –
so I am bound to keep my head held low –

55      I'd raise my eyes to look at this man here –
alive still, though unnamed – in case I knew him,
and make him look in pity on my load.

58      I was Italian, bred of Tuscan stock.
Aldobrandesco was my noble sire.
I don't know if his name was known to you.

61      The ancient lineage and courtly airs
of my great forebears wrought such pride in me
that, heedless of the mother we all share,

I so disdained all other men, I died       64
because of that. The Sienese know this,
as do the squads in Campagnatico.

I am Omberto, and my arrogance       67
did harm to me, but not to me alone,
for all my peers were victims of that bane.

Because of this, till God is satisfied,       70
I needs must bear this weight among the dead –
since I did *not* while still with those who live.'

Still listening, I had kept my face bowed low.       73*
And one of them – not he who spoke these words –
twisted beneath the load that bore him down.

He saw and recognized, then called to me,       76
holding his eyes, with effort, firmly fixed
on me, bowed down, who went along with him.

'Oh! Aren't you Oderisi?' I replied.       79*
'Great Gubbio's glory, glory of that art,
known to Parisians as design-in-light?'

'Dear man,' he said, 'those pages smile far more       82
that Franco Bolognese smoothly pens.
The honour is all his – and, partly, mine.

Yet while I lived, I'd not, you may be sure,       85
have shown such courtesy. My heart's desire
was excellence. I yearned for that alone.

For arrogance like this one pays a fee.       88
And I'd still not be here if I had not,
while having power to sin, turned back to God.

Oh, what vainglorying in human powers!       91*
How short a time the green lasts on the height
unless some cruder, darker age succeeds.

Once, as a painter, Cimabue thought       94*
he took the prize. Now "Giotto" 's on all lips
and Cimabue's fame is quite eclipsed.

In verse, as well, a second Guido steals       97
all glory from the first. And someone's born,
who'll thrust, perhaps, both Guidos from the nest.

100    The roar of earthly fame is just a breath
       of wind, blowing from here and then from there,
       that changes name in changing origin.

103*   What more renown will you have if you strip
       your flesh in age away than if you died
       before you'd left off lisping "Din-dins!", "Penth!"

106    when once a thousand years have passed, a space
       that falls far short of all eternity –
       an eye blink to the slowest turning sphere.

109*   He who, ahead of me, takes such brief strides
       is one with whom all Tuscany once rang.
       His name's now scarcely whispered in Siena,

112    where he was Lord when Florence, running wild –
       as proud at that time as it's whorelike now –
       was left destroyed and ravaged by the war.

115    All your renown is coloured like the grass,
       which comes then goes. And He discolours it
       who made it first appear from bitter earth.'

118    And I to him: 'Your words in truth give heart
       to good humility, and puncture pride.
       But who's this man of whom you spoke just now?'

121    'Provenzan Salvani' (the answer was).
       'And he is here because he proudly claimed
       to hold Siena wholly in his hands.

124    And since his death, he's walked as now he walks,
       without repose. Like all who down there dared,
       he pays his debts in full with such-like cash.'

127    And I: 'If any spirit who delays
       repentance to life's final verge is bound
       to dwell below the gate and not ascend

130    (unless good prayers on his behalf bring aid)
       until it's passed as much time as it lived,
       how was it granted him that he should come?'

133    'When he could boast, in life, most glorious fame,
       freely he took a stand,' the answer was,
       'in Campo di Siena, free from shame,

and there, to save his friend the punishment –    136
incurred in his imprisonment to Charles –
he brought himself to tremble through each vein.

I'll say no more (I know I speak dark words,    139
but little time will pass till those near you
will act in ways that mean you can explain).

Provenzan's deed removed him from those bounds.'    142

# CANTO 12

1    Paired up, like oxen yoked to move as one,
so onward with that burdened soul I went,
as long as he – my dear, kind sir – allowed.

4    But then he said: 'Leave him and go beyond.
The best thing is that each here drives along
his craft, by oar or sail, as best he can.'

7    I made myself (as, walking, one must do)
in person stand up straight. And yet my thoughts
remained in me stripped bare, reduced, bowed low.

10    I'd now moved on, and followed willingly
the footsteps of my teacher. And we two
already showed in tread how light we were.

13    And then he said: 'Just turn your eyes down there.
That will be good for you, to ease the way.
See there the bed on which your paces rest.'

16    Compare: to serve as some memorial
for those entombed beneath, our earthly graves
bear signs of what they had been when alive –

19    at which it often happens that we weep,
responding to the spur of memories
which only strike the heel of pious minds.

22    I now saw carvings there – though finer, far,
considering the hand that crafted them –
along the path the mountain cliffs had left.

25*    Mark now, to this side I here saw the one
nobler-created than all creatures else,
thrown down in flashing thunder fire from Heaven.

Mark this, I witnessed on the other side,  28
pierced by the spear celestial, Briareus,
heavy on earth, laid low in deathly chill.

Mark this, I saw Timbreus, still in arms,  31
and Mars and Pallas round their father's side,
amazed to see the scattered Giantbones.

Mark this, I saw, beneath the tower he'd made,  34
Nimrod, as in confusion. All the tribe
of Shinar – arrogant as he – gazed on.

Ah! Niobe I saw. With grieving eyes,  37
I traced your outline carved within that road,
among your children – seven, then seven – slain.

Ah! Saul, it seemed that you were there, as dead,  40
pierced on Gilboa's hill with your own sword,
feeling no longer showers of rain or dew.

Ah! Mad Arachne, how I saw you there  43
half-turned to spider and the work in shreds
which, once attempted, brought you so much harm.

Ah! Rehoboam, as you're there portrayed,  46
you're not, now, menacing, but full of dread.
A chariot bears you off, though none gives chase.

Now also shown on that hard floor was how  49
Alcmaeon made the fatal ornament
that cost his treacherous mother very dear.

Now was displayed how Sennacherib's sons  52
flung themselves at him in the temple hall,
and how, once dead, they left him there alone.

Now there appeared the chaos, crude and cruel,  55
wrought by Thamyris, who to Cyrus said:
'You thirst for blood. With blood I'll feed you full!'

Now, fleeing, the Assyrians were shown –  58
routed when Holofernes met his death –
and showed the relics of his mortal pain.

Mark this, I saw Troy's ash and hollowed stone.  61
Ah, Ilion! How humbled and how vile,
now picked out in those signs, you seemed to be!

64      What master of the pencil or the brush
could reproduce those shadows and those strokes
which, there, would make the sharpest mind admire?

67      The dead seemed dead, the living seemed alive.
And all I trod upon – bowed low – I saw
far truer than had those who'd seen it true.

70      Strut on, you sons of Eve, with head held high.
Display your pride, and do not bend your face
to see the errors of your evil way!

73      We'd made more distance round the mountainside
(spending more time than mind, still bound, supposed,
in following the track the sun observes)

76      when he – who always kept his mind ahead –
began: 'Now straighten up, and lift your brows.
The moment's passed to go caught up like this.

79      See? Over there! An angel quickens pace.
It comes our way. Come! See! See, too, the hour,
sixth handmaid of the day, already turns.

82      Adorn your eyes and acts with reverence,
so he, to his delight, may speed our climb.
Think! This same day will never dawn again.'

85      I was well used to his admonishments –
always 'to waste no time'. So, as to that,
the words he spoke could hardly be obscure.

88      To us that lovely creature now advanced,
white-vestitured, in countenance, it seems,
trembling in air as does the morning star.

91      Opening his arms, then opening his wings,
he said: 'Now come. The steps are very near,
and now the climb could not be easier.

94      Men, though invited, come too rarely here.
O human nature! You are born to fly!
Why fail and fall at, merely, puffs of wind?'

97      He led us where the cleft was in the rock.
And here he struck his wings across my brow,
then promised me the way ahead was safe.

Compare: to scale the hill towards that church     100*
which dominates the city (so well-ruled!)
that stands around the Rubaconte bridge,

   rightwards the vaunting angle of the climb     103
is broken by a stairway built in times
when chronicles and balances were true.

   Like this, the bank which falls so steeply here     106
from where the next ring stands was gradual,
though all around the high rock shaved its sides.

   While turning (we two persons) to that slope     109*
voices sang out: '*Beati pauperes*',
as no mere speech could properly relate.

   How different from the thoroughfares of Hell     112
are those through which we passed. For here with songs
we enter, there with fierce lamentations.

   We were, by now, ascending that great stair.     115
And I, it seemed, was lighter now by far
than I had seemed while still on level ground.

   So, 'Tell me, sir,' I said, 'what weight has now     118
been lifted from me, so I almost feel
no strain at all in walking on my way?'

   He answered: 'When the "P"'s that mark your brow,     121
remaining still, though growing now more faint,
have all (as is the first) been sheared away,

   your steps will then be conquered by good will     124
and, being thus impelled towards the heights,
will feel no strain but only sheer delight.'

   And then I did what anyone would do     127
with something on their head – they can't tell what –
but, seeing people point, peer up suspiciously,

   then raise a hand to help them be quite sure,     130
to search around, to find and do the job
that sight had been unable to complete.

   So now my right-hand fingers found reduced     133
the letters there inscribed to merely six
of those the angel with the keys had cut.

   My leader, watching as I did so, smiled.     136

# CANTO 13

1      We now were at the summit of the stair.
The mountain there – which, as one climbs, takes ill
away – is chiselled back a second time.

4      And so there's, here, a ledge around the slope,
which binds it, as the first ledge also did,
except that now the arc curves faster in.

7      Shade? There's none here, nor any sign to see.
The cliffs show bare. The path looks shorn of marks,
save only for its stones of liverish blue.

10     'I fear,' the poet said, considering this,
'our choice of route may well be long delayed
if we wait here for someone we can ask.'

13     Firmly, he fixed his eyes towards the sun.
He made a fulcrum of his right-hand side,
and moved his left around that central point.

16     'You, sweetest light, in trusting you I now,'
he said, 'embark upon this strange new road.
Guide us, as guidance must be here required.

19     You warm the world. You shine out over it.
Your rays, where counter reasons have no weight,
must always lead with their authority.'

22     The distance of a mile (as earth miles count)
we travelled now from where we'd been before –
our will so quick – in little time at all.

25     Then, unseen, flying towards us now were heard
the voices of spirits, all delivering
a courteous welcome to the feast of love.

The first voice, fleeting past, declared aloud,     28*
'*Vinum non habent!*' ('Look, they have no wine!'),
and then went on behind us, echoing that.

And then, before it wholly was not heard,     31
so distancing, another voice went by,
declared, '*I'm* Orestes!' and did not stay.

'Father,' I said, 'what voices can these be?'     34
And, as I asked, there came – just look! – a third,
saying: 'Love those by whom you suffer harm.'

'This confine scourges,' my good teacher said,     37
'the sin of envious hate. And so the skeins
that form the stinging lash vibrate with love.

The bridle will elicit different notes.     40
And these, I think, as far as I can tell,
you'll hear before you reach the pardon-pass.

But fix your eyes intently through the air.     43
You'll see some people sitting there ahead,
each in their place along the mountain wall.'

My eyes far wider than before, I looked     46
and saw in front of us a group of shades,
their cloaks in hue no different from the rock.

And when we were a little further on,     49
I heard them calling: 'Mary, pray for us.'
'Michael!' they cried. 'Saint Peter! All the saints!'

I can't believe that anyone on earth     52
could be so hard that pity, at the sight
that I saw now, would not have pierced him through.

For when at last I'd come up close to them,     55
and saw for certain what these people did,
I spurted from my eyes the milk of grief.

A poor hair shirt appeared to blanket each.     58
Each let the other lean against his side,
and all were let to lean against the cliff.

In that same way, the blind, for lack of things,     61
stand begging for their needs on Pardon Days,
the head of one bent low above the next,

64  to gain from others pity for their plight
not only through the sound of their sad words
but also through the sight, which ached no less.

67  And as the sun grants nothing to the blind,
so, to the shadows that I speak of now,
the light of heaven bestowed no generous ray.

70*  For all their eyelids, pierced by iron wires,
were sewn up like an untamed sparrow hawk's
when, restively, it won't keep calm and still.

73  To me, it seemed an outrage to walk by
seeing those others who did not see me.
And so I turned to where wise counsels were.

76  He knew full well what, mute, I meant to say.
And so he did not wait to hear my words.
'Speak out,' he said, 'but briefly, to the point.'

79  Virgil beside me took the outer strip
(where, since there is no verge to garland it,
one might too easily have tumbled down)

82  while, on my other side, in constant prayer,
were shadows who, through dreadful sutures, squeezed
a press of tears to rinse and bathe their cheeks.

85  To these I turned. 'You, who are confident,'
so I began, 'to see the Light Supreme –
which your desires are set upon alone –

88  may grace soon clarify the scum that blurs
your consciences, and let the streams of mind descend –
with all of memory's power – through you once more.

91  Tell me – I'd hold your answer very dear –
if any soul among you is Italian.
It may, if I hear that, go well for him.'

94  'We are, dear brother, now all citizens
of one true place. But you must mean:
"... who winged his pilgrim life through Italy".'

97  This, in reply, I seemed to hear proceed
from somewhere just ahead of where I stood.
So further on I made my voice be heard.

Among the rest, I saw a shadow seem                                    100
to wait as though to say to me, 'Well, how?'
tilting its chin up as the sightless do.

'Spirit,' I said, 'you train yourself to rise.                         103
If you're the one who just replied to me,
then make it known. Tell me your name and place.'

'I' (so the answer came) 'was Sienese,                                 106*
and here repair the wicked life I led,
weeping so He will grant Himself to us.

Sapia (though not sapient) I was called.                               109
And I, to witness other people's harm,
felt joy far more than at my own good luck.

Listen. Don't think that this is mere deceit.                          112
Was I (then sinking down my arc of years)
as crazy as I've said I was, or not?

My fellow Sienese near Colle cliff                                     115
were joined in battle with their enemies.
And God, I prayed, would do what He then did.

Routed here, shattered, they'd turned in bitter                        118
footfalls of flight. And, seeing them hunted,
sheer happiness seized me, beyond compare,

so great I turned my reckless face on high,                            121*
yelling at God: "I'll fear you never more!" –
just like the blackbird in a sunny spell.

Then, coming to the utmost edge of life,                               124
I sought my peace with God. And even now,
my dues would not, in penance, have been paid

had I not been remembered in the prayers                               127*
that Peter Pettinaio so devoutly made
in heartfelt charity on my behalf.

But who are you, to make your way round here                           130
inquiring as to us – with, still, I'm sure,
your eyes unbound, and breathing when you speak?'

'My eyes,' I said, 'will only briefly here                             133
be taken from me. For the harm is small
that they, pursuing envy, might have done.

136    Far greater fear holds sway within my soul
of tortures suffered on the ridge below.
The burdens of that place already press.'

139    And she: 'Who, then, has led you up to us,
when you are certain that you'll head back down?'
'This one,' I said, 'with me, who speaks no word.

142    I am alive. And so please ask of me,
you chosen spirit, if you'd have me move
my living tread on earth to serve your needs.'

145    'Well, that's,' she said, 'a strange new thing to hear,
a great sign of the love God bears to you.
Do help me sometimes when you say your prayers.

148    I beg of you, by that for which you yearn,
if you should ever tread on Tuscan soil,
make my name good for those most near to me.

151*   You'll find them with that empty-headed crowd
whose hopes are set on Talamone's port.
They'll lose more there than tracing Dian's source.

154    The venturers, though, will come off much the worse.'

# CANTO 14

'Who's this one here who's circling round our Hill          1
before Death's given him the right to fly,
opening his eyes and closing them at will?'

'I don't know who, but know he's not alone.          4
*You* ask, since you are closer up to him.
And treat him gently so he'll speak to us.'

Two spirits – each one leaning on the next –          7*
thus talked about me on the right-hand side,
then laid their heads back, to have words with me.

And one now said: 'O you, that soul who goes,          10
still fixed in mortal limb, towards the skies,
gives us, in charity, some ease and say

what place you're from, and who it is you are.          13
You make us marvel at the grace you've gained –
as much as *must* be at things never known.'

And I: 'Through Tuscany, a ranging stream          16*
cuts down from Falterona where it's born –
its course not sated for a hundred miles.

I bring this body from that river's bank.          19
There'd be no point in saying who I am.
My name, as yet, produces no great sound.'

'If, in my thoughts, I swoop on what you mean,'          22
he then replied to me (the first to speak),
'you are, I take it, talking of the Arno.'

'But why,' the other asked, 'did he then hide          25
the name that designates that flowing stream,
as people do with something that they dread?'

28       To which, in offering a due reply,
that shade first-questioned answered: 'I don't know.
It's right, though, that that valley's name should die.

31*      For from its origin, where those sheer hills
(Pelorus was disseevered from that chain)
that breed more streams than many others do,

34       down to the estuary where yet once more
it pays back what the skies dry from the sea
(rivers derive their onward spate from that)

37       virtue is fled by all – an enemy!
a hateful snake! – either because that place
is fated so, or pierced by wickedness.

40*      The people dwelling in that wretched vale
are changed in nature to the point at which
it seems that Circe might provide their swill.

43       Through brute swine, firstly, who far more deserve
acorns for food than any human dish,
it points the channel of its meagre path.

46       Then, coming down, it lights on mongrel dogs
snarling far worse than ever they can bite.
From these it turns its snout in high disdain.

49       So ever downwards – and the more it swells
so much the more does this accursed ditch
hit upon bitches now transformed to wolves.

52       Then, having sunk through many a stagnant lake,
it finds out foxes that, so full of guile,
fear not at all that they might be out-tricked.

55       Nor shall I cease to speak since this one hears.
It will be good for him if he attends
to what true spirit here unknots for me.

58*      I see your little nephew now become
a hunter of those wolf packs on the bank
of that fierce stream, and he confounds them all.

61       He sells their flesh while this is still alive,
then slays them like mere cattle past their prime.
Many of life, himself of praise he robs.

He comes out bloodied from that dismal wood,    64
and leaves it so, a thousand years from now,
it won't rebranch and reach its primal state.'

As at announcements of some grievous harm,    67
whatever side the fangs of peril strike,
the faces of those listening will grow grim,

so did I see that other soul, who'd turned,    70
setting his mind to hear, cloud and grow sad,
in garnering up these words to his own heart.

The speech of one and how the other looked    73
made me the keener to be told their names,
and so, with prayers as well, I made request.

At which the spirit who first spoke to me    76
began once more: 'You'd have me bring myself
to do for you what you'll not do for me.

But since God wills that such great grace should shine    79
through all your being, I'll not grudge you this.
Know, then, that I was Guido del Duca.

My blood so fired itself with envious thoughts    82
that, if I saw some man transformed by joy,
you'd then have seen me flushed to liver green.

From such a sowing I now reap the straw.    85
You human creatures, why repose your hearts
where you are banned from mutual exchange?

This is Rinieri of the Calboli –    88
the honour of that House, their pride. No one
lays claim, as heir, to all his proven worth.

Nor has his blood alone – between the Po,    91
the hill, the sea and Reno – turned to waste,
stripped of the good that truth and pleasure need.

For all within these confines now is full    94
of poisonous thickets, so it's now too late
for cultivation to reduce their grip.

Where is good Lizio, Arrigo Mainardi?    97*
Pier Traversaro and Guido di Carpigna?
Oh, Romagnuoli, you're all bastards now.

100     When in Bologna is a Fabbro bred?
When in Faience a Bernadin di Fosco
(branching so nobly from mere creeping weeds)?

103     Don't marvel, Tuscan, if you see me weep
when I call back to mind, with Guido Prata,
Ugolin d'Azzo (who once lived with us),

106     Frederick Tignoso and his circle, too,
the Traversara house, the Anastagians,
(these last two having no descendants now),

109     the knights and ladies, all the toil and ease
that love and courtesy once made us seek,
where now all hearts are criminal and base.

112*    O Bretinoro, why not take to heel,
since your whole family has gone its way,
as others do, eluding vice and ignominy.

115     Bagnacaval, it's good you don't re-child,
and bad for Castrocaro – far worse Conio! –
so tangled up in childing worthless lords.

118     The clan Pagani, once their demon's gone,
will do quite well, but not so well that pure
account of them will ever now remain.

121     O Ugolino of the Fantolines,
your name is safe since none, demeaning you,
is now expected who could dim your fame.

124     But, Tuscan, you had better pass along.
To weep delights me more than words now can.
This talk has wrung my mind with such distress.'

127     We knew those well-loved souls could hear our tread.
Therefore, their silence, as we went our way,
gave us the confidence to take that path.

130     So, going on, when once we were alone,
just like a thunder bolt that rends the air,
a voice rang out towards us, saying this:

133*    'They'll murder me whoever captures me!'
then fled like thunder when it fades away,
the clouds abruptly being torn apart.

Then, as our hearing gained some peace from that –     136
just see! – a second with as great a crash
seemed then at once to follow that first peal.

'I am Aglauros, who became a stone!'     139
And then, to get up closer to the poet,
I stepped not forwards but towards the right.

The air was quiet now on every side     142
and, 'That was the restraint' (so Virgil said)
'that ought to keep mankind within due bounds.

You take the bait, though. So the well-barbed hook     145
of our old enemy will draw you in.
And that's why checks and lures have little power.

The heavens wheel around and summon you,     148
displaying to your eyes eternal charms.
Yet your gaze fixes merely on the ground.

For that, He strikes you down who sees all clear.'     151

# CANTO 15

1*     As much time as the childlike circle plays
between the third hour at its ultimate
and when the day had first begun to rise,

4     remained, it seemed – till evening – for the sun
to travel and complete its onward way.
There it was vespers (midnight in our clime).

7     The sun's rays struck us straight along the nose.
For now the mountain had, by us, been turned
so that we went direct towards the west.

10     But then I felt my forehead weighted down
by splendour far more bright than first there'd been.
It dazed me, wondering at these untold things.

13     And so, towards the peak of my two brows
I raised my hands and shaped myself a shield
to pare these too great visibles away.

16*     Compare: from water or reflective glass
a ray of light leaps back as opposite,
rising exactly in the same degree

19     (as tests and theory demonstrate) against
a plumb-stone line as when it first descends,
equal as measured from that vertical.

22     It seemed that I was struck by some such light
that broke, reflected back, ahead of me,
causing my eyes, in flight, to speed away.

25     'My gentle father, what is this?' I said.
'I can't protect my eyes from it enough.
It moves, it seems, towards us all the time.'

'Don't marvel,' he replied to me, 'if still                    28
the family of the heavens yet bedazzle you.
This comes as messenger, to bid us climb.

And soon to see such things as these will bring    31
not stupor, but delight to you as great
as you by nature are disposed to feel.'

And when we'd come to where the angel was,        34
the blessed creature said in tones of joy:
'Enter this stair – less steep than those before.'

And climbing now (the angel left below)            37*
behind us, *Beati misericordes!*
and 'Rejoice! You conqueror!' were sung.

Together, my teacher and I alone                   40
proceeded upward and, while going on,
I thought I'd gain some profit from his words,

so turned to him, demanding he should say:         43
'What did that spirit of Romagna mean
to speak of "mutual exchange" and "bans"?'

'He knows the damage done by his main flaw.        46
Don't therefore be surprised,' he said, 'if he
chides us, to lessen penitential tears.

Because your human longings point to where         49
portions grow smaller in shared fellowship,
meanness of mind must make the bellows sigh.

If love, though, seeking for the utmost sphere,    52
should ever wrench your longings to the skies,
such fears would have no place within your breast.

For, there, the more that we can speak of "ours",  55
the more each one possesses of the good
and, in that cloister, *caritas* burns brighter.'

'I hunger more for satisfaction now                58
than if,' I said, 'you'd not said anything.
I gather in my mind still greater doubt.

How can it be that good distributed                61
to many owners makes, in that respect,
each one far richer than if few had shared?'

64     'You thrust your mind,' he answered, 'back down there
and, thinking still in terms of earthly things,
you tease out darkness from the light of truth.

67     The Good that – infinite beyond all words –
is there above will run to love like rays
of light that come to anything that shines.

70     It gives itself proportioned to the fire,
so that, as far as *caritas* extends,
eternal Worth increases over it.

73     The more there are who fix their minds up there,
the more good love there is – and more to love –
and each (as might a mirror) gives to each.

76     And if these words of mine don't slake your thirst,
you'll see Beatrice. And she, in all, in full,
will ease this craving – as she'll others, too.

79     Press forward, then. For these five wounds that heal,
through all the pain they bring, will soon
be gone, as are by now the other two.'

82     Intending here to say: 'You've fed me well',
I saw that I had reached the upper ring.
And there my eyes, entranced, now silenced me.

85*     For, in a sudden-seeing ecstasy,
I was, it seemed, caught up and made to see
a temple, many thronging all around.

88     There at the door a lady stood who said –
sweet in her manner as a mother is:
'Why, dearest son, have you done this to us?

91     Look at how, grieving, your father and I
have searched for you!' And she falling silent,
what first appeared now disappeared from view.

94     A second woman now appeared to me.
Her cheeks were washed with streams that grief distils
when grief is born in us from angry scorn.

97     'If you,' she said, 'are lord of that great place
whose name caused so much strife among the gods,
and yet from which all knowledge sparkles out,

take vengeance on those hands, Pisistratus,　　　100
that clasped our daughter in their rash embrace.'
That lord, to me, seemed mild and generous
and – temperate in expression – answered her:　　103
'What shall we do to those that wish us ill
if those that love us are condemned by us?'

I saw, next, crowds enflamed in fires of wrath,　　106
all yelling out to all a loud 'Kill! Kill!',
stoning a young man to the point of death.

And he, I saw, bowed down towards the earth　　109
as death imposed on him its heavy weight,
yet still he bore his eyes towards the skies

(his look that look which opens pity's lock)　　112
praying in so much strife that Heaven's Lord
should pardon those who'd hunted him to death.

When once my soul turned outwards once again　　115
to beings truly there outside itself,
I'd strayed, I saw, towards not-false error.

My leader, who could see that I behaved　　118
like someone who has just escaped from sleep,
exclaimed: 'What's wrong? Why can't you stand straight up?

You've come along for half a mile or more　　121
veiling your eyes, your legs turned all askew,
like someone in the grip of sleep or drink.'

'My dearest father, if you'll hear me out,　　124
I'll tell you what appeared to me,' I said,
'during the time my legs were snatched from me.'

'Had you a thousand masks around your face,　　127
your thinking,' he replied, 'would not, to me,
be hidden, even in the least degree.

You've seen these things. So you'll have no excuse　　130
if you don't give your heart to streams of peace
which spread out from their everlasting source.

133    I did not ask, "What's wrong?" as those might do
who only see with eyes that do not see,
staring at bodies that are drained of life,

136    but rather asked to give your stride more strength.
You need to prod the indolent like this,
slow as they are to use their waking powers.'

139    Walking towards the setting sun, we stretched
to see as far beyond as eyes could reach
against the brilliance of the evening rays.

142    Then, bit by bit, a rising cloud of smoke,
as dark as night, began to form ahead.
There was no way for us to turn aside.

145    It took from us our eyesight and pure air.

# CANTO 16

Darkness in Hell, or any night stripped bare                    1
of planets under impoverished skies
(a pall of clouds as dense as these could be),

   has never formed, for me, as thick a veil          4
as did the smoke that now surrounded us,
or stretched a weave so rasping in its feel

   that eyes could not stay open to its touch.         7
Therefore, my guide, as ever wise and true,
came to my side, his shoulder lending aid.

   And, as a blind man goes behind his guide –         10
for fear he'll wander or collide with things
that might well maim him or, perhaps, could kill –

   I, too, went on through acrid, filthy air,         13
attending to my leader, who would say,
'Take care. Don't get cut off!' repeatedly.

   I now heard voices. And it seemed that each         16
was praying to the Lamb of God, who takes
all sin away, for mercy and for peace.

   The words they uttered first were '*Agnus Dei*' –    19*
the self-same text and tune from all of them,
so that, it seemed, at heart they sang as one.

   'Are these all spirits, sir, that I can hear?'      22*
I spoke. He answered: 'Yes. In that you're right.
And anger is the knot they're working free.'

   'And who are you, that cleave our smoke-filled air,  25*
and speaks of us as though (if this could be)
you still divided time by month and year?'

28    These words were those that one voice uttered now.
      At which my teacher said to me: 'Reply.
      Ask them if we can make our climb from here.'

31    And I: 'My fellow creature, who now wash
      to go once more in beauty to your maker,
      you, if you follow close, will hear of wonders.'

34    'I'll follow you as far as I'm allowed.
      And if,' he said, 'the smoke won't let us see,
      hearing instead will keep us closely joined.'

37    'Still swaddled in the clothes that death dissolves'
      (so I began) 'I make my way above,
      and come here from the agonies of Hell.

40    And if God circles me with such great grace
      that I, as He desires, should see His court,
      in ways beyond what men of our day know,

43    then do not hide who you were till your death,
      but speak and tell me: am I near the rise?
      And your words only will become our guide.'

46    'I was a Lombard, and my name was Mark.
      I knew the world and loved that noble worth
      at which all now aim slack and unslung bows.

49    To make your climb, just take the straight way on.'
      He answered thus, and added then: 'I pray
      that you should pray for me, when you're up there.'

52    And I to him: 'Through faith I bind myself
      to do what you demand. And yet I burst,
      if you will not explain, with one great doubt.

55    Though simple to begin with, what you say
      has made doubt double now. That makes me sure
      I'm right to couple things heard here and elsewhere.

58    The world is, truly, as your words declare,
      a sterile place where every virtue fails –
      pregnant with viciousness that blankets all.

61    Point me, I beg you, to the reason why,
      so I can see and then show others, too.
      Some place the cause in stars, some here below.'

A long, deep sigh that grief dragged out to 'Uhi'   64
he uttered first, then 'Brother,' he began,
'the world iṣ blind, and, yes, that's where *you're* from.

You, living there, derive the cause of all   67
straight from the stars alone, as if, alone,
these made all move in mere necessity.

Yet were that so, in you would be destroyed   70
the freedom of your will – and justice fail
in giving good its joy and grief its ill.

The stars initiate your vital moves.   73*
I don't say all. And yet suppose I did,
you're given light to know what's good and bad,

and free will, too, which if it can endure   76
beyond its early battles with the stars,
and if it's nourished well, will conquer all.

Of better nature and of greater power   79
you are free subjects. And you have a mind
that planets cannot rule or stars concern.

So if the present world has gone astray,   82
the reason lies in you, in you it's sought,
and I, on your behalf, will spy it out.

Leaving the hand of him who holds it dear   85
(before it truly *is*), it weeps and laughs,
that little simple soul, and baby-plays,

as young girls do, and does not know a thing –   88
save only, as moved by a joyous Maker,
it willingly turns to every playful thrill.

It tastes the flavour, first, of some small good,   91
and, fooled by this, it chases down its track,
unless a brake or guide bends such love back.

So law is needed to apply this brake.   94
A king is needed, with the skill to see
the towers of that true city, at the least.

The laws are there. Who sets his hand to these?   97*
There's no one. For the shepherd out ahead,
though he can chew the cud, has not split hooves.

100 So people, when they see their leader snatch
at those same goods that greedily *they* crave,
graze on just those, and do not seek beyond.

103 So – as you may well see – bad government
is why the world is so malignant now.
It's not that nature is corrupt in you.

106* Once, Rome, which made this world for us pure good,
had two suns in its sky. And these made known
both roads to take, the world's and that of God.

109 One sun has snuffed the other out. The sword
is joined now to the shepherd's crook. And ill
is bound to follow when force links these two.

112 For, once they're joined, there can't be mutual dread.
And if you don't believe this, think of crops,
where grass is known according to its seed.

115* Before the Emperor Frederick was opposed,
in regions washed by Po and Adige
all courtesy and prowess could be found.

118 Now anyone is safe to travel through
who might avoid, from sheer embarrassment,
speech or encounters with good, honest men.

121 There are, it's true, three old ones there in whom
times now long gone rebuke the new. To them,
in granting better life, God seems too slow.

124* Currado da Palazzo, good Gherardo
and Guido da Castello, better named
the "honest Lombard" – as French travellers do.

127 So you can say this now: the Church of Rome,
by mingling in itself two forms of rule,
falls in the mud, befouling self and load.'

130* 'Dear Mark,' I said, 'your argument runs well.
And now I see why Levi's priestly sons
were all excluded from inheritance.

133 But who's that "Gerard" whom you say remains
as pattern of an age that is no more,
to speak reproaches to our savage time?'

'Your words are meant to test,' so he replied,                    136
'or else to have me on. You're speaking Tuscan,
yet have no clue, it seems, about good Gerard!

I know no other name by which he's known –                        139
unless I draw it from his daughter's shame.
May God go with you. I can't come along.

You see that bright gleam, dawning through the smoke, 142
already whitening. I must now go back –
the angel's there – before I'm shown to him.'

He turned, and would not hear me any more.                        145

# CANTO 17

|     | |
|-----|--|
| 1   | Reader, recall, if ever in the hills<br>a fog has caught you so you couldn't see<br>(or only as a mole does through its skin), |
| 4   | then how, as vapours, clinging, damp and dense,<br>begin to dissipate, the sun's round disc<br>enters, and feebly makes its way through these. |
| 7   | From this, you'll easily be brought to see,<br>in your imagination, how I saw<br>the sun again, already setting now. |
| 10  | So, levelling with my teacher's trusted steps,<br>I came out from that cloud, along with him,<br>to rays, down on the shore, already dead. |
| 13* | Imagination, you at times will steal<br>the outer world from us so we can't tell<br>(even if horns in thousands blare around) |
| 16  | who makes you move when sense does not provide.<br>It's light that moves you, formed in heavenly spheres<br>by Will, which guides it down, or else *per se*. |
| 19* | The godless wrath of one who changed her form<br>to be that bird which most delights in song<br>appeared, and left its footprint on my brain. |
| 22  | My mind was now so clenched upon itself<br>that nothing was received within its bounds<br>that might have come from outside or beyond. |
| 25  | And then, within these high imaginings,<br>one crucified rained down. He, in his gaze,<br>was fierce and full of scorn and, like that, died. |

Around him were the great Ahasuerus,         28
Esther (his wife) and honest Mordecai,
who showed such probity in word and deed.

This image of itself now burst – as might         31
some rising bubble when the water fails,
beneath the surface where it first filled out.

And then, within my vision, there rose up         34
a girl who, weeping fiercely, said: 'Great Queen!
Why wish yourself as nothing in your wrath?

To keep – not lose – Lavinia, you slew yourself.     37
You've lost me now, dear mother. This is me.
I mourn yours more than any other's doom.'

As sleep is shattered when some strange new light    40
strikes, on the sudden, at our closed-up eye,
then flickers for a moment till it dies,

so, too, these images I saw crashed down,        43
as, now, a light struck hard against my face,
greater by far than those to which we're used.

I turned around to see where I might be.         46
At which, a voice spoke out: 'You go up here.'
This distanced me from any other thought,

and wrought in me that great desire to see      49
'Who was it that said this to me?' which won't
admit of rest until we're face to face.

But, as when sun weighs heavy on our sight     52
and veils its shape in overwhelming glare,
so did my inner powers at this fall short.

'This spirit is divine. Before we've asked,      55
it indicates the way to go above,
and hides itself within the light it gives.

It treats us as we like to treat ourselves.      58
For those who see a need yet wait for prayers
ill-willingly stand ready to refuse.

To this great welcome let us tune our pace     61
and strive to climb before the darkness falls –
we cannot, otherwise, till day returns.'

64     So said my leader and, along with him,
       I turned my step to make towards a stair.
       As soon, though, as I reached its lowest tread,

67*    I felt close by a movement as of wings,
       a fanning at my face and words: '*Beati
       pacifici* – of violent wrath they're free.'

70     By now the final rays, pursued by night,
       had risen over us, and gone so far
       that stars in many parts appeared to view.

73     'My strengths and powers! Why do you slip away?'
       (I said within myself.) 'A truce, I feel,
       has been imposed upon my striding thighs.'

76     We'd got to where the stairway rose no more.
       And there we stuck – as fixedly as ships
       that beach themselves, arriving at the shore.

79     I waited for a while, in case I heard
       some sign in this new ring of anything,
       then, turning to my teacher, I said now:

82     'My dearest teacher, tell me what offence
       is purged within the circle where we are.
       Our feet stand still. Don't let your words do so.'

85     'The love of good,' he said, 'when this falls short
       of what it ought to be, is here restored.
       The oar that wrongly slackened strikes once more.

88     But, so you may more plainly understand,
       turn, pay attention and, from this short wait,
       you'll carry off some truly worthwhile fruit.

91*    Neither creator nor created thing
       was ever, dearest son, without' (he starts)
       'the love of mind or nature. You know that.

94     The natural love can never go astray.
       The other, though, may err when wrongly aimed,
       or else through too much vigour or the lack.

97     Where mind-love sets itself on primal good
       and keeps, in secondaries, a due control,
       it cannot be the cause of false delight.

But when it wrongly twists towards the ill,　　　　100
or runs towards the good too fast or slow,
what's made then works against its maker's plan.

Hence, of necessity, you'll understand　　　　103
that love must be the seed of all good powers,
as, too, of penalties your deeds deserve.

Now, since love cannot turn its face away　　　106
from that which greets it with a promised health,
all things are safe from hatred of themselves,

and since no being can be understood　　　　109
as independent, separate, from the First,
effects, decidedly, can't hate their source.

*Restat*: if I've prepared the ground aright,　　112
the ill we love must be our *neighbour's* harm.
Such "love" is born in three ways from your slime.

Some hope, by keeping all their neighbours down,　　115
that they'll excel. They yearn for that alone –
to see them brought from high to low estate.

Then, some will fear that, if another mounts,　　118
they'll lose all honour, fame and grace and power,
so, grieving at success, love what it's not.

And some, it seems, when hurt, bear such a grudge　121
that they crave only to exact revenge –
which means they seek to speed another's harm.

This tri-formed love is wept for down below.　　124
But now I'd have you understand the next
which runs, in broken order, after good.

We all, confusedly, conceive a good,　　　　127
desiring that our hearts may rest in that.
And each will strive to make their way to it.

If love is slack in drawing you to view –　　　130
or win – that good, then this ledge, where we're now,
after your fit repentance, martyrs you.

And other goods will not bring happiness,　　　133
not happy in themselves, nor that good source
of being, seed and flower of all that's good.

136     The love that gives itself too much to these
        is wept for in the circles still above.
        But why "tripartite" I shall not here say,
139         so you can seek the reason for yourself.'

# CANTO 18

That great authority concluded here.                                    1
Attentively, he looked me in the face,
to see if I was pleased and satisfied.

And I (a new thirst searching through my brain)                         4
was silent outwardly but said within:
'Too many questions may, perhaps, annoy him.'

He, though, true father that he was, had seen                           7
this hesitant desire unopened yet,
and, speaking, gave me courage to speak out.

'My power to see,' I said, 'in your light, sir,                        10
grows bright, alive in me, so – yes – I'm clear
on every point your words define and stress.

And so, my dear, kind father, I entreat                                13
that you expound for me that love to which
you trace all good acts and their opposite.'

'Direct on me,' he said, 'your mind's sharp light.                     16
And I shall make quite evident to you
the error of the blind – who claim they lead.

The mind, which is created quick to love,                              19*
when roused by pleasure into conscious act
will tend towards such things as give delight.

From things that truly are, your *apprehensio*                         22
draws out an image which it then unfolds
within you, so that mind turns round to it.

If mind, once having turned, inclines to that,                         25
this bending is called love – and "nature", too –
bound up in you afresh by pleasure's knot.

28   And then, as fire moves upwards to the heights
(by virtue of its form, it's born to rise
to where it may, as matter, most endure),

31   so minds, when captured, pass into desire –
a motion of the spirit that won't pause
until the thing it loves has yielded joy.

34   From which, it's clear, you'll find how far truth hides
from those who think it true that all love is –
in all its types – deserving of our praise,

37   perhaps because its matter, seemingly,
is always good. Yet, grant the wax is good,
the seal need not be so in every print.'

40   'Your words (and, walking in their track, my wits)
disclose to me what love is,' I replied.
'Yet this, for me, gives birth to greater doubt.

43   If love is just an offering from *outside*,
and souls go forward on no other foot,
then going right or wrong involves no merit.'

46   'I can, as far as reason sees, respond.
Beyond that, faith's required' (so he to me)
'and you must therefore wait for Beatrice.

49   Forms of substantiality (distinct
from matter, though at one with that) collect,
each one within itself, specific powers.

52   These powers, unless they act, are not perceived,
nor are they known except by their effects –
as life appears in plants when leaves are green.

55   No one can, therefore, see from where there comes
the sense of primal concepts that we have,
nor our desire for prime desirables.

58*   These are in you as is the urge in bees
to make their honey. And this primal will
cannot be credited with blame or praise.

61   To group all other wills around the first,
there is a counselling power innate in you
that's meant to guard the threshold of consent.

This is the principle from which derives 64
the inward rationale of just desert
that stores or winnows good love from what's bad.

And those who argued all things to the core 67
took notice of this inborn liberty,
and so bequeathed to us a moral rule.

Suppose that love, then, of necessity 70
does rise in you, when once its fire begins,
you have within the power to rein it back.

This power, which Beatrice understands, 73
is freedom of the will. And so take care
that, if she speaks of it, it's in your mind.'

The moon at almost midnight, slow to rise 76
(formed like a copper bucket burnished red),
now made the stars seem fewer in the sky,

and ran against the heavens around those roads 79*
where sunlight flames when anyone in Rome
observes it set between the Sards and Corsicans.

That noble shade, for whom Pietola 82*
is named above all other Mantuan towns,
had now laid down the burden I'd imposed.

So, having harvested his plain, frank words – 85
which answered all the questions I had had –
I stood like someone in a drowsy blank.

But all such drowsiness was borne away 88
by people who had suddenly appeared,
swinging towards us from behind our backs.

As once the Asop and Ismenus saw, 91*
whenever Thebans needed Bacchus's aid,
orgies at night, feet pounding by their banks,

so here – from what I saw as these came on – 94
they, too, ran scything round the mountain's curve,
spurred on and ridden by good love and will.

Soon they were on us. For they moved at speed, 97
racing towards us, that great multitude.
And two ahead were shouting, weepingly.

100*  'Maria hastened up to Juda's hill!'
 And, 'Caesar, bringing Lerida to heel,
 struck at Marseilles and then ran into Spain.'

103  'Quick! Quick! Let's lose no time through lack of love!'
 so all of those behind now shouted out.
 'For zeal in doing good turns grace new green.'

106  'You people, whose keen fervour now repays
 some negligence or else delay of yours,
 through tepidness in acting for the good,

109  this man (he's living, and I tell no lie)
 desires, when sunlight shines on us again,
 to go on up. So where's the closest gap?'

112*  These were the words my leader spoke to them.
 And one among these spirits now replied:
 'Come! Follow us and you'll soon find that hole.

115  Full of desire to move ourselves along,
 we cannot pause. And therefore, pardon us,
 if what for us is right, seems crass and wrong.

118  When Barbarossa ruled – that good, true lord
 of whom Milan still speaks with pain and grief –
 I, at Verona, was San Zeno's Dom.

121  And there's a man with one foot in the grave
 who'll bitterly bewail that abbey soon,
 and grieve the power that he had over it.

124  For he, where one true shepherd should have been,
 has placed his son, diseased throughout his frame,
 and worse than sick in mind, a bastard born.'

127  He'd run so far beyond us by this time,
 I don't know if his words went on or ceased.
 This much I heeded and would gladly keep.

130  And he who helps me in my every need
 said now: 'Turn round, and look at these two here,
 who, fast approaching, put the bite on sloth.'

133*  Behind the rest, these two were calling: 'First,
 before the river Jordan saw their heirs,
 all those for whom the sea had opened, died!'

   And: 'Those who couldn't bear until the end     136
the labours that Anchises' son endured,
submitted to a life where honour lacked.'
   Then, when these shades had split so far from us     139
that neither any more could be observed,
a new thought set itself within my mind,
   from which were born yet other, differing thoughts.     142
And so I wandered round from this to that
and, dozing off, I gladly closed my eyes,
   transforming all my thinking into dream.     145

# CANTO 19

1        Now, at that hour when daytime heat cannot –
vanquished by earth and, sometimes, Saturn's rays –
sustain its warmth against the chilling moon,

4*           when geomancers in the east trace out,
before the dawn their signs of Greater Fortune
(the path these climb is only briefly dark),

7*           there came, dreaming, to me a stammering crone,
cross-eyed and crooked on her crippled feet,
her hands mere stumps, and drained and pale in look.

10          I gazed at her. Then, as to frozen limbs
when night has weighed them down, the sun gives strength
likewise my staring made her free, long-tongued,

13          to speak, and drew her, in the briefest space,
erect in every limb, giving the hue
that love desires to her blurred, pallid face.

16          And once her powers of speech were thus untied,
she then began to sing, so I could not,
except with pain, have drawn my eyes away.

19          'I am,' she sang, 'I am the lovely siren.
So full of pleasure to the ear my tune
that mariners I magic in mid-ocean.

22          And Ulysses, entranced to hear my chant,
I turned off course. Rarely do those who've learned
my ways depart. I bring them full content.'

25          And then, before that mouth closed up once more,
a lady – holy and alert – appeared
and, at my side, she crushed the other's power.

'Virgil! O Virgil!' – in the harshest tones –     28
'Who's that?' she said. And he approached, eyes set,
unwavering, on her true nobility.

He seized the Siren, ripping down her dress,     31
opened the front of her, displayed her guts,
and that, with all its stench, now woke me up.

I swung my eyes around. 'Three times, at least,     34
I've voiced this. Come!' (My trusted teacher spoke.)
'Get up! Let's find an opening you can take.'

Up I now got. And all the circles round     37
the holy hill were full of highest day.
We went along, the new sun at our backs.

Now following in his track, I bore my brow     40
as people do when – loaded down with thought –
they make themselves the half-arch of a bridge.

And then I heard: 'Come on! The crossing's here!'     43
spoken in tones more soft and generous
than ever could be heard in mortal shires.

With open wings, as, seemingly, a swan's,     46
the one who'd spoken turned us to the heights
between two walls within the granite rock.

He moved his feathers and he fanned us both,     49*
affirming that '*qui lugent*' are the blessed.
To them the gift of consolation comes.

'What's got to you? You still stare at the ground.'     52
When once beyond the angel, climbing on,
these were the words with which my guide began.

'I'm made to make my way in so much doubt     55
by that weird vision – which so wraps me up
I just can't leave off thinking back to it.'

'You saw,' he said to me, 'the ancient witch.     58
For her the penitents above us weep.
You saw how men are loosened from her grip.

Let that suffice. So strike your heels to earth     61
and turn your eyes to see the lure that's spun
in mighty wheels by one eternal king.'

64     A falcon, first, looks down towards its feet,
then, being called, will turn and stretch full length,
drawn by desire to reach the offered food.

67     And so did I. Through one split span of rock,
which served as entrance to the upward path,
I went to where the ring above begins.

70     Now loosed out on to circle number five,
I saw there people all around who wept,
each turned face downwards, lying on the earth.

73*     'Adhaesit pavimento anima mea!'
I heard them saying this, but sighing deep
so what they said was hardly understood.

76     'You chosen ones of God whose sufferings are,
by hope and justice, made less hard to bear,
direct me to the steep way we must climb.'

79     'If you come here exempt from lying flat,
and wish to find the quickest way ahead,
your right hands will be always to the out.'

82     This was the poet's prayer, and thus – a bit
ahead of us – the answer came. And I,
on hearing this, knew where the rest were hid.

85     I turned my eyes to meet my lord's own eyes.
And he assented with a happy sign
to what my face displayed as its desire.

88     So, being free to act as I saw fit,
I drew myself across and stood above
that being whose words had made first me note,

91     saying: 'You spirit who, in tears, matures
that without which no soul can turn to God,
for my sake, leave awhile your greater care.

94     Who were you? Tell me that, and why you've turned
your backs above – and what you'd have me beg
on your behalf, returning whence I moved.'

97*     'Why Heaven should turn our rears against itself
you'll shortly know,' he said to me. 'But first
scias quod ego fui successor Petri.

Between Siestri and Chiavari                          100
a lovely stream descends, and from its name
my blood derives the height of all its claims.

A month, no more than that, I knew the weight      103
of keeping papal garments from the mud.
Compared with that, all loads are feather light.

My own conversion was, alas, too late.              106
And yet, made shepherd of the Roman flock,
the lies of life revealed themselves to me.

I saw the heart will never rest in these.           109
And I could not rise higher in that life.
So love of *this* life then caught fire in me.

I was, until that point, a wretched soul.           112
Divorced from God, my all was avarice.
And I am punished, as you see, for that.

What avarice will do is now made clear              115
through penance in these souls, inverted so.
The mountain has no pain more harsh than this.

Because our eyes were fixed on earthly things,      118
at no point raised to look towards the heights,
so justice sinks them here within the earth.

Since avarice extinguished all our love             121
for any good – and so good works were lost –
justice here holds us tight within its grip.

We're captives, bound at both our hands and feet,   124
and here stretched out, unmoving, we shall stay,
as long as our just Lord may think it right.'

I'd fallen to my knees and meant to speak.          127
But he, as soon as I'd begun, took note –
simply on hearing my respectful bow.

'What makes you twist like that?' he said to me,    130
and I to him: 'Aware of your high rank,
my conscience bit me when I stood erect.'

'Straighten your knee, my brother. Just get up!     133
Make no mistake. I am – along with you
and all – co-servant of one single Power.

136*       If ever you have heard aright the sound
of Holy Gospel in '*neque nubent*'
then you can see why I should argue thus.

139       Now go away. I'd not delay you more.
You, standing there, upset the tears I shed,
by which I ripen penance as you said.

142*       I have, down there, a niece. Her name's Alagia,
good in herself – provided that our house
does not, by bad example, make her worse.

145       And she alone is left of me back there.'

# CANTO 20

Against a better will, will can't well fight.                                    1
And so, against what pleased me, pleasing *him*,
I drew the sponge still thirsty from the stream.

I moved myself. My leader moved through those                                   4
free spaces that, around the cliff, remained –
tightly, as by some castle's battlements –

since all those people, melting drop by drop,                                   7
in tears, the ill that holds the world in thrall,
encroached too far upon the outer part.

Curses on you, you wolf bitch, ages old!                                       10*
You snatch more prey than all the other beasts,
endlessly hollow in your hungering.

You heavens, whose revolutions, we believe,                                    13
alter the way things are with us down here,
when will He come to put this wolf to flight?

We went our way with slow, restricted tread,                                   16
I listening to the shadows whom I heard
weeping in piteously sharp distress,

and chanced to hear ahead of us the cry,                                       19*
'Sweet Mary!' uttered in those floods of tears
that women scream when labouring at a birth.

The voice went on: 'What poverty you knew                                      22
we all can see from that poor lodging house
in which you laid your holy burden down.'

Then, following this: 'O good Fabrizio,                                        25
you chose the way of honest penury
above the treasures that were stained with vice.'

28   To me, these words had such a pleasing sound
that I pressed forward to be clear about
the spirit who, it seemed, had spoken them.

31   He still was speaking of the generous gifts
that Nicholas once made to those young girls,
to save the honour of their threatened youth.

34   'O soul! Your words shed light on so much good.
Tell me,' I said, 'who were you – and why *you*
alone renew these words of worthy praise.

37   If I return to finish that short road
of life on earth which flies towards its end,
your answer won't remain without reward.'

40*   'I'll say,' he answered, '(though support from there
I *don't* expect) because in you yourself,
before your death, so great a grace shines forth.

43   I was the root from which that sick weed grows
that overshadows every Christian land,
so that it's rare to strip good fruit from it.

46   If Douai, though, or Ghent or Bruges or Lille
could get their way, then vengeance would be swift.
I pray for it from Him who judges all.

49   I was, down there, called Hugh Capet once.
From me were born those Louis and Philippes
by whom in these new days our France is ruled.

52   I was from Paris, and a butcher's son.
And when the line of ancient kings died out –
all gone, save one who wears a monk's dark cowl –

55   I found my hands were tight around the reins
that govern in that realm, and so empowered
in making that new gain, with friends so full,

58   that, to the widowed crown my son's own head
received advancement. And from him began
our lineage of consecrated bones.

61   Until that splendid dowry of Provence
deprived my blood of any sense of shame,
they didn't do much good – nor much great harm.

There, there began, with violence and with lies,　　64
their course of plunderings. And to put things right,
Ponthieu they seized, then Norman lands, then Gascon.

Then Charles reached Italy. To put things right,　　67
he sacrificed young Conradin, then sent
Saint Thomas to the skies, to put things right.

I see a time, not very far from now,　　70
that brings another Carlo out of France
to make his clan and him the better known.

Unarmed he comes. And simply with that lance　　73
that Judas jousted with, he aims then stabs
the guts of Florence till the belly bursts.

From this, his profit will be no mere land,　　76
but sin and shame – the heavier for him
the more he counts as light the harm he does.

The other – captured, once, on board his ship –　　79*
I now see sells his daughter, bargaining
as pirates do in deals for female slaves.

O avarice! What more harm can you do?　　82
You've got my blood so firmly in your grip,
it takes no thought about its own kin's flesh.

To make its past and future crimes seem less,　　85*
I see the fleur-de-lys besiege Anagni,
and Christ recaptured in his vicar's form.

I see them mocking him a second time.　　88
I see renewed the vinegar and gall.
I see him slain again with living thieves.

I see renewed a Pilate who's so cruel,　　91
unsatisfied, he bears with no just cause
his greedy saints towards the Temple walls.

My Lord and God! When shall I see in joy　　94
that just revenge that, hidden to our view,
makes anger in your secret counsels sweet?

Those words I spoke about the one true Bride　　97
of God's Own Spirit – those that made you turn,
seeking from me some further commentary –

100     respond, while daylight lasts, to all our prayers.
But as the darkness of the night sets in
we then sound out the contrary tune.

103*     We now call back to mind Pygmalion,
whose hankering after gold made his will turn
to treachery and theft and parricide.

106     Then, too, the misery of miser Midas,
caused by that gluttonous demand of his,
for which he'll always be ridiculous.

109     Then each recalls mad Achan's escapade,
and how he stole the spoils of Jericho –
so Joshua's anger seems to gnaw him still.

112     We blame Sapphira, and her husband, too,
and praise the hooves that trampled Heliodore.
And round the mount, in notoriety,

115     goes Polymnestor who slew Polydore.
Then finally our cry of "Crassus!" comes.
"You know. So tell us! What's the taste of gold?"

118     These words are spoken high or sometimes low,
responding to the urge that makes us move,
spurred to a greater or a lesser pace.

121     In telling – as, by day, we do – the best,
I was not, earlier, the only one.
But no one else nearby had raised their voice.'

124     We'd gone from him by now and, moving on,
struggled, as far as we were given strength,
to overcome the hardships of that road,

127     when, as though things were crashing down, I heard
the mountain tremble. And I felt the chill
that all will suffer when they come to die.

130*     Delos itself did not so fiercely shake
before Latona made a nest of it
to bring to birth the two eyes of the sky.

133     On every side there then began this cry
(my teacher turned around to me to say,
'While I'm your guide, you need not be afraid'):

'*Gloria in excelsis Deo!*' and all 136*
were speaking out these words, so I could tell
the meaning of the cry from those close to.

We stood unmoving, caught there in suspense – 139
as were the shepherds who first heard this song –
until the tremor ceased and all was done.

And then once more we took our holy path, 142
looking at those that lay there on the earth
who'd gone back, now, to their familiar tears.

Never has ignorance with so much force 145
(if, in my memory, I do not err)
driven me in my keen desire to know,

as now it seemed to, thinking and thinking. 148
Nor had I dared, in all our haste, to ask.
Nor, for my part, could I see anything.

So, timid, deep in thought, I travelled on. 151

# CANTO 21

1* The natural thirst that never can be slaked
save by those waters that, as gracious gift,
the widowed, bright Samaritan demanded once,

4 toiled in me now, while hurry spurred my steps,
behind my leader, round the cluttered path,
mourning within to see that just revenge.

7* And look! As in his gospel Luke describes
how Christ, when risen from the hollow tomb,
appeared to two who travelled on their way –

10 a shadow from behind us now appeared.
Still looking at the crowd around our feet,
we didn't notice till it spoke and said:

13 'May God, my brothers, bring to you His peace.'
We turned round suddenly. And Virgil made
a fitting gesture to reply to this.

16 Then he began: 'May that true government
which keeps me bound in exile endlessly
grant you a place within that happy court.'

19 'What's that?' he said, as we still hurried on.
'If you are shades that God won't let ascend,
who, then, has led you up this stair so far?'

22 'If you observe,' my teacher said, 'those signs
he's bearing and the angel traces out,
you'll see it's right that he reigns with the good.

25* But since the fate that spins thread day and night
has not, in his case, yet drawn out the skein
that Clotho casts and spins for every life,

his soul – a sister to both yours and mine –     28
though coming here cannot come on its own.
Its eyes as yet don't see as our eyes do.

And I was therefore drawn from Hell's wide throat     31
to show him – and I've still to show him more –
as much as my own schooling will allow.

But if you're able, tell me why the mount     34
shuddered just now so hard, and why it seemed
to cry, down to its plashy foot, as one.'

In asking this, he pierced the needle's eye     37
of all I longed to know. And so my thirst,
through hope alone, became less keen in me.

'There's nothing that this mountain's holy law     40
consents to,' so the other now began,
'that's lacking order or irregular.

This place is free from every kind of change.     43
Only what Heaven, of itself, receives
can act here as a cause, and nothing else.

Therefore no showers of rain, nor hail or snow,     46
no dew or hoar frost ever falls above
that little stairway with its three brief steps.

No clouds here – whether rare or dense – appear,     49*
no glint of lightning nor the rainbow child
of Thaumas, there so often changing place.

And dry evaporations do not rise     52
beyond the third and highest of those steps –
I spoke of them – where Peter's vicar stands.

Tremors occur below (some small, perhaps;     55
some great). At these heights, though, no tremor comes
from winds that hide (I can't tell why) in earth.

Tremors strike here when any soul feels pure     58
and rises, newly cleansed, to start its climb.
And that cry follows as the soul ascends.

The will alone gives proof of purity     61
when, wholly free to change its sacred place,
it aids and sweeps the soul up, willing well.

64  The soul till then indeed had willed ascent.
    But, set against that will there is the bent –
    which God instils – for pain as sin's equivalent.

67  And I, who've lain five hundred years and more
    in that same pain, have only felt just now
    the freedom of the better way ahead.

70  That's why you felt and heard those tremors here,
    and spirits round the mountain rendering praise,
    so God, our Lord, might send them higher soon.'

73  He said these things to us. And since we take
    a joy in drinking equal to our thirst,
    I could not say what benefit he'd brought.

76  My lord, in wisdom: 'Now I see the net
    that here entangles you – and your escape:
    why are there tremors here, why all rejoice?

79  Now tell me, at your pleasure, so I'll know,
    who were you? And your words, please, will include
    why you have lain so many centuries here.'

82*  'In those days when good Titus, by the aid
    of our exalted King, avenged the wounds
    from which the blood that Judas sold had sprung,

85  I was,' the spirit answered, 'well renowned.
    My name down there was that which most endures,
    and honours most – not yet, though, of the Faith.

88  My voice in spirit breathed so sweet that Rome
    took me to her own heart from French Toulouse,
    where merit dressed my brow with myrtle leaves.

91  My name was Statius to the people there.
    I sang of Thebes and then of great Achilles,
    but stumbled carrying that second load.

94  The seed my ardour sprang from was a spark
    which warmed me through of that most sacred flame
    from which a thousand, and yet more, are lit.

97  I'm speaking of the *Aeneid* – a mum
    to me, to me my nurse in poetry.
    Without that, I'd not weigh a single gram.

And could I live back then when Virgil lived,     100
I would agree to pass, beyond the due
that brought me out of exile, one year's sun.'

These words turned Virgil round to me – his look     103
saying, unspeakingly: 'Be silent now!'
But will power can't do everything it wills.

For tears and laughter follow on so close     106
to those emotions from which each act springs
that these least follow *will* in those most true.

And so I smiled, as though to give a hint.     109
At which the shade fell silent and just stared,
straight in my eyes where what we feel shows most.

'I wish that all your toil may come to good     112
Why did your features, though, display to me
just now,' he said, 'that sudden flashing smile?'

So I was caught on this side and on that.     115
One urges silence while the other calls
for words from me. I sigh. I'm understood

by him, my teacher. 'Do not fear to speak.     118
Speak out,' he said to me, 'and tell him all
that he so urgently desires to know.'

At which, 'You ancient spirit,' I began,     121
you're wondering maybe why you see me smile.
I'd have you gripped with yet more wonderment.

The one who guides my eyes towards the heights     124
is that same Virgil that you drew upon
to sing so strong of deities and men.

If you suppose I'd other cause to smile,     127
put that aside. It is not true. And think
those words you spoke of him were cause enough.'

He'd bowed at once to clasp my teacher's feet.     130
But he, in that embrace, said: 'Brother, don't!
You are a shadow and you see a shade.'

And he, in rising: 'Now you grasp how great     133
the love that warms my heart for you must be,
when I dismiss from mind our emptiness,

treating a shadow as a thing of weight.'     136

# CANTO 22

1

The angel had by now been left behind –
that angel who had turned us to Gyre Six,
once having shaved my brow of one more wound.

4*     Those souls who thirst for justice he had named
as 'blessed'. His words as far as *'sitiunt'* –
but not beyond that verse – had filled this out.

7     And, flowing lighter than through other bays,
I went along and, free from any toil,
followed those rapid spirits on their way.

10     Virgil, meanwhile, began to speak: 'Pure love,
provided that its flame shows outwardly,
kindled in virtue, kindles answering love.

13*     So, from the time that Juvenal came down
to dwell among us on the fringe of Hell,
and made your feeling for me plain to see,

16     my own good will to you has gripped me more
than any for a person yet unseen.
These stairs will seem, then, short for me to climb.

19     But tell me – and, in friendship, pardon this,
if too much confidence sets free my reins –
and speak with me as friendship now permits:

22     how could it be that in your breast, so full
of all the wisdom that your learning won,
a place was found for avarice as well?'

25     Statius, on hearing this, was moved to smile
(a little, anyway), but then replied:
'As marks of love, I value all your words.

It's true, though, that the way things often look          28
provides false substance for our searching doubts,
the real considerations lying hid.

Your question verifies that you believe –          31
viewing, perhaps, the circle where I was –
that I was "grasping" in the other life.

Please understand that avarice, for me,          34
ran too far off. My own extreme – the opposite –
was punished over many thousand moons.

Had I not set my spending urge to rights,          37
and seen the meaning of the line you shout
in, almost, agony at human ways:

"You, awestruck hungering for gold! Why not          40*
impose a rule on mortal appetite?"
I'd feel the rumbling turns of that grim duel.

With that, I realized our hands can wing          43
too openly in wild expense, and so
for that repented, as for all my sins.

How many will rise up with hair cropped short          46
through ignorance of vice, which takes away
repentance while we live, or at life's end.

Know, too, the guilt that butts at any sin,          49
directly counter to that first offence,
is drained here, with it, of its rampant green.

And so, if I have been (to purge my sins)          52
among those men who weep for avarice,
this came my way by rule of contraries.'

'When first you sang of vicious wars between          55*
the twofold sadness that Jocasta bore,'
so said the singer of the farming songs,

'to read the notes that Clio strikes from you,          58
it does not seem that you had then become
faithful in faith – without which good must fail.

If that is so, what sun or candlelight          61*
dispelled your shadows so that you could set
your sails to track the fisherman aright?'

64* 'You,' he replied, 'first beckoned me to drink
  from springs that rise in high Parnassian glades.
  And you first lit the way for me to God.

67  You acted then like someone who, at night,
  bears at his back a lamp – no use to him,
  but teaching those the way who come behind

70  when once you said: "The years begin anew,
  justice returns, so, too, Man's earliest time.
  A new race, born of Heaven, now descends."

73  I was, through you, a poet and was Christian, too.
  But, so you'll better see what I intend,
  I'll stretch my hand to colour in this sketch.

76  The world, by then, was pregnant, all entire,
  with true belief – an understanding sown
  by messengers of God's eternal realm.

79  And your words (which were touched on just above)
  sang, with new preachers, to a single tune.
  I therefore took to visiting these men.

82* And these soon came to seem to me such saints
  that, when Domitian's persecution struck
  their weeping did not lack for my own tears.

85  And while on earth I lived my given time,
  I aided them. And their right-thinking ways
  made me look down on other cults in scorn.

88* Even before, in verse, I'd led the Greeks
  to drink the Theban stream, I'd been baptized,
  but still, from fear, concealed my Christian faith,

91* displaying all that time a pagan face.
  And this luke-warmness made me circle round
  more than four hundred years on Terrace Four.

94  But tell me – you who lifted up the veil
  that hid from me the good of which I speak –
  while still some way remains for us to climb,

97* where, if you know, is ancient Terence now?
  Plautus, Cecilius and Varro, too?
  Tell me if these are damned, and where they walk.'

'All these, and Persius,' my leader said,                    100
'myself and more are there beside that Greek
who, more than all, the Muses fed with milk,
   within Ring One of that unseeing gaol.              103
And many times we speak of that great peak
which always keeps our nurses on its slopes.

   Euripides is with us, Antiphon,                    106
Simonides and Agathon, and Greeks
who crowned their brows with laurels, many more.

   And seen there, too (all named within your verse),   109*
Deiphile, Antigone and Argia,
Ismene also, grieving as she did.

   She, too, is seen who spied out Langia's stream.    112
The daughter of Tiresias is there,
Thetis and, with her sisters, Deidamia.'

   The poets both fell silent and, anew,              115
free from the climb and tight surrounds of wall,
gave all their thoughts to looking round about.

   Already, of the handmaids of the sun                118*
four were behind. The fifth was at the pole,
stretching its burning point towards the height.

   My leader now: 'I think that we should turn        121
our right sides to the far extremity,
and circle round the mount, as we are wont.'

   So habit was the flag we followed there.           124
We took the chosen path with lesser doubt
since that most worthy soul gave his assent.

   They made their way, I all alone behind.           127
And as we went, I listened to their talk –
which made me see what writing verse can mean.

   But then (a sudden break to soothing words!)       130*
we found there, in the middle of the road,
a tree – its fruits, in perfume, good and sweet.

   As fir trees rise and lessen, by degrees,          133
from branch to branch, so this – but lessening *down*,
lest anyone, I'd say, should try to climb.

136      And, to the side, where rock walls closed our path,
clear liquids streaming off the towering cliff
sprinkled across the surface of the leaves.

139      Both poets now drew nearer to that tree,
and then, within its leaves, a voice cried out:
'Of this dear food you'll know the bitter dearth.'

142*      And then it said: 'Maria thought far more
of how the wedding might be full and fine
than of that mouth by which she prays for you.

145      And Roman women were, in ancient times,
content to drink plain water. Daniel, too,
despising food, gained greatly in true thought.

148      The primal age – as lovely, once, as gold –
made acorns, through long fasting, good to taste,
and, thirsting, nectar of each rivulet.

151      Honey and locust were the nourishment
that fed the Baptist in the wilderness.
How glorious and great he is, for that

154        is made quite clear in the Evangelist.'

# CANTO 23

   While I, through these green boughs, fixed searching sight   1
(as might some hunter tracking little birds,
who spends his life in vain on that pursuit),
   my more-than-father spoke. 'Dear son,' he said,      4
'do come along. The time appointed us
should be more usefully divided out.'
   I turned my eyes (my footsteps came as fast)     7
to track that learned pair, who, talking on,
made going with them free, for me, of cost.
   And then, just look! Both tears and songs were heard –   10*
'*Labia mea, Domine*', so tuned
it brought both happiness and pain to birth.
   'My sweetest father, what is this I hear?'     13
so I began. And he: 'These may be shades,
who go unknotting what their debts have tied.'
   As pilgrims do when, deep in thought, they meet   16
a group along their path that they don't know
and, though they turn towards it, still don't stop,
   so, now, behind us, moving with more speed,     19
a throng of spirits, silent and devout,
reaching and overtaking us, gazed back.
   Each one was dark and hollow round the eyes,   22
pallid in feature, and so gaunt and waste
their skin was formed to show the very bone.
   Erysichthon, as I can well believe,     25*
was not so dry and shrivelled round his rind
when, hungering, his dread was at its height.

28     And I, in thought, was saying to myself,
'Just look! The folk who lost Jerusalem
when starving Mary pecked her son to death.

31*     The sockets of their eyes seemed gemless rings,
and those who read Man's 'OMO' in Man's face
would clearly have seen 'M' in all of these.

34     Who would have thought the scent of some mere fruit
could work to make a craving grow like this,
and water, too – unless he knew the 'how'.

37     Already wondering what starved them so,
I saw no reason that could well explain
such thinness and those dreadful scales of skin.

40*     Then, look! A shadow turned its eyes on me,
deep in its skull, and, peering fixedly,
cried out aloud: 'For me, how great a grace!'

43     I never would have known him from his face.
But in his voice, all now was shown to me
that had, in feature, been destroyed and lost.

46     That spark for me rekindled at a stroke
clear recognition of those much-changed lips,
and once again I saw Forese's face.

49     'Don't boggle so to see these dried-up scabs,
which drain the colour from my skin,' he begged,
'nor that I have so great a lack of flesh.

52     But speak and tell the truth about yourself,
and who these two souls are that act as guides.
Don't stand there, holding back the spark of words.'

55     'That face of yours I wept for once in death
now gives me,' I replied, 'as painfully,
a cause to weep, seeing it here so wrenched awry.

58     But tell me, in God's name, what strips your leaves?
Don't make me, wonderstruck, attempt to talk.
No one, desiring other things, speaks well.'

61     'There falls,' he said, 'from the Eternal Mind
a virtue in that water and that tree –
back there – which sharpens me and pares me down.

And all these people, weeping as they sing,        64
because their gullets led them past all norms,
are here remade as holy, thirsting, hungering.

Cravings to eat and drink are fired in us        67
by perfumes from that fruit and from the spray
that spreads in fans above the greenery.

Nor once alone, in circling round this space,        70
is agony and pain refreshed in us.
I call it pain. Rightly, I should say solace.

For that same yearning leads us to the tree        73*
that led Christ, in his joy, to say "*Elì*",
when through his open veins he made us free.'

And I to him: 'Forese, from that day        76
that you exchanged your world for better life,
no more than five years have, till now, gone by.

If your capacity to sin was dead        79
before there came to you that holy hour
of penance that remarries souls to God,

how can it be that you've got here so quick?        82
I thought that I should find you there below,
where restitution comes to time through time.'

'To drink sweet wormwood in this rightful pain        85
I'm brought,' he now replied, 'so rapidly
by broken tears that my dear Nella shed.

With her devoted prayers and heartfelt sighs,        88
she's drawn me from that shore where spirits wait,
and freed me from the other circles, too.

My little widow, whom I loved so well,        91*
to God is dearer still, and better loved,
since she so stands alone in doing good.

For, as to womenfolk, Barbagian Sards        94
are far more chaste and modest in their ways
than is that Barbary I left her in.

What, dearest brother, would you have me say?        97
A future time, already in my sight,
will come (when our time's still not history),

100      when, from the pulpit, there'll be issued bans
forbidding bare-faced Florence girls to go
with blatant breasts and both their boobs on show.

103      What mere barbarians or Saracens
required a priest or threat of on-spot fines
to make them cover up when they go out!

106      If, though, these brazen creatures only guessed
what Heaven so swiftly will bring down on them,
then they'd already howl with open mouths.

109      For if, foreseeing this, I'm not beguiled,
they'll come to grief before the cheek grows hair
on any boy now rocked by lullabies.

112      So, brother, don't still hide yourself from me.
You see? It's all of us, not me alone,
who gaze in wonder where you veil the sun.'

115      'If you bring back to mind,' I now replied,
'what you were once to me and I to you,
the memory of that will still be sore.

118*     I, from that life, was turned away by him
who walks ahead of me the other day,
when she, his sister' (here I point the sun)

121      'showed full and round. He, through the utmost depths
of night and all the truly dead has been
a guide to me, who follow in true flesh.

124      Now his encouragements have drawn me up,
ascending here and circling all round
this mount that straightens what the world distorts.

127      He will, he says, be in my company
until I'm there where Beatrice is.
And when I am, I must then be without him.

130      Virgil it is who tells me all of this.'
(I point him out.) 'That other is the shade
for whom just now, in loosing him, your realm

133     was shaken in its every slope and cliff.'

# CANTO 24

Our words did not slow down our steps (nor stride                1
end speech). So on we went, talking apace,
like ships when driven by a favouring wind.

And all those shades, who looked like things twice dead,         4
wondered – the sockets of their eyes dug out –
as they looked on, to see me there alive.

And I, continuing my former theme:                               7
'Statius's soul climbs slower than it would,
perhaps by reason of another's need.

But tell me: where's Piccarda – if you know?                    10*
And tell me, too, among those souls who gaze
at me, are any that I ought to note?'

'My sister (was she more – I do not know –                      13
in beauty than in goodness?) triumphs now,
crowned on Olympian heights, in happiness.'

This first, and then he said: 'Since we're milked dry,          16
by fasting, of the way that once we seemed,
it's not forbidden that we each be named.

And this' (he pointed out) 'is Bonagiunta,                      19*
Bonagiunta of Lucca. And, further on,
that face more raddled than are all the rest

held tight our Holy Church in his embrace.                      22*
He came from Tours, and purges, by this fast,
Bolsena eels and flagons of vernaccia.'

Then, one by one, he named me many more.                        25
And these, it seemed, were happy to be named.
I got no dark looks from them when they were.

28      I saw there, plying teeth on empty air,
        Ubaldin da la Pila and that Boniface
        who pastured many with his castled crook.

31      I saw Sir Marquis, who had far more space
        to drink at Forlì (being far less parched),
        a man who never felt he'd had his fill.

34      But, as our glance will scan around then prize
        one above all, so I with that Lucchese –
        seeming the keenest to be known by me.

37*     And he, I heard, was murmuring – I don't know . . .
        something: 'Gentucca'? – where he felt the wound
        of justice as it plucked and nibbled him.

40      'You seem, dear soul, to long to speak with me.
        So make me understand your sense,' I said,
        'and, speaking, satisfy the two of us.'

43      'A woman's born (not yet grown-up in dress)'
        (so he began) 'who'll make my native place
        a joy for you, although men talk it down.

46      You'll leave here carrying this prophecy.
        And if my murmurings made you mistake,
        then true events will make their meaning clear.

49      But tell me: do I see the man who drew
        those new rhymes forth, whose opening line ran so:
        "Ladies, who have intelligence of love . . ."?'

52      And I to him: 'I am just one who, when
        Love breathes in me, takes note and then goes on
        showing the meaning that's ordained within.'

55*     'Dear brother, nah I see,' he said, 'the knot
        that kept the Brief, Guittone, me as well,
        from reaching to that sweet new style I hear of.

58*     I see how close behind the power that speaks
        your winged pens fly, transcribing what he says –
        which certainly our own pens never did.

61      Strive as you might to see, between our styles,
        some greater difference, you'll not see it here.'
        And then, as though content, he said no more.

As birds that pass their winters by the Nile        64*
will rise at times and gather on the air,
then fly, more rapidly, to form a line,
   so now the crowd of people who were there     67
all turned their faces and increased their stride,
light-footed, driven by desire (and thin!).
   And then, like someone tired of trotting on     70
who lets the pack go by and takes his time
until the heaving of his chest is done,
   Forese, too, now left the holy flock.     73
As these raced off, he followed in my track,
saying: 'So when shall I see *you* again?'
   'How long I'll live,' I answered, 'I don't know.     76
But my return will not be sooner than
desire already brings me to this shore.
   For that place where it falls to me to live     79
grows, day by day, less meaty as to good,
and sets its mind on ruin and despair.'
   'That's right,' he said. 'I see who's most to blame     82
dragged at a horse's tail towards the ditch
where no one, ever, can be free of sin.
   That beast rampages faster with each step,     85
accelerating always, till it strikes
and leaves his broken corpse a mangled mess.
   Those wheels' (he fixed his eyes upon the stars)     88
'have little left to run till you see clear
the things that I, in words, cannot declare.
   You stay behind. For time is precious here.     91
Coming along with you and keeping step,
I, in this realm, already lose too much.'
   Knights gallop out at times from charging troops,     94
intending, as they leave the rest behind,
to claim the honours of an opening duel.
   So off he went from us at greater pace,     97
and I remained, still travelling with those two
who in the world were such great dignitaries.

100     And when he'd gone so far ahead of us
        that eyesight strained to follow in his track
        (as did my mind to understand his words),

103     there then appeared to me, ripe-branched and bright,
        a second fruit tree, not so far from us,
        just there, around the bend that we'd now turned.

106     Beneath, I saw a group that raised their hands
        and called towards the leaves I-don't-know-what,
        like silly, over-eager little tots,

109     who plead – although their target won't respond
        but rather seeks to whet their appetite,
        dangling, unhidden, what they want aloft.

112     Then off they went (as though they'd changed their
                minds).
        And we ourselves arrived at that great tree
        which turned aside so many tears and prayers.

115     'Move further on, and don't get drawn to that.
        There's, higher up, the tree that Eve once bit.
        This tree is raised from it, and flourishes.'

118     Someone – I don't know who – among its sprigs
        spoke this. So Virgil, Statius and myself
        closed ranks, to pass by on the rising side.

121*    'Recall those curséd ones,' the voice went on,
        'the centaurs, formed from cloud, who once, when
                gorged,
        fought against Theseus with doubled chests.

124     Recall those Hebrews, softened so by drink
        that Gideon would not take them in his ranks
        when he swept down on Midian from the hills.'

127     So, tightly pressed against the near-side verge,
        we passed along and heard how sins of greed
        were followed once by miserable rewards.

130     Then, broadening out, we found an empty road.
        A thousand paces bore us on (and more),
        each of us silent, each contemplative.

'And what are you three thinking as you go?' 133
A sudden voice said this – at which I shied
in terror like an untamed animal.

I raised my head to see who this might be. 136
And in no furnace was there ever seen
metal or glass that glowed as bright and red

as now I saw one, saying: 'If you wish 139
to get up there, then here's where you must turn.
All seeking peace are bound to take this path.'

The blazing face had robbed me of my sight. 142
And so behind my teachers I went on
as someone will when led by what he hears.

And as the breeze in May – first messenger 145
of whitening dawn – is moved in fragrant waves,
pregnant with grasses, greenery and flowers,

so here I sensed, mid-brow, wind touching me, 148
and sensed the moving feathers of a wing
that brought ambrosial senses to the air,

and made me sense the words: 'The truly blessed 151
are lit with so much grace that in their hearts
a love of food fumes forth no false desire,

esurient always for the good and true.' 154

# CANTO 25

1*     The hour would not allow a crippled climb.
The sun had now abandoned to the Bull
its noon-time ring, and night to Scorpio.

4     And so, like people who will not stay put
but, driven forward by some piercing need,
go on, whatever comes before their eyes,

7     so here we entered on a passageway
(so narrow it uncouples those who climb),
clambering in single file to mount the stair.

10*     Compare: a fledgling stork will lift its wings.
It wants to fly but still dares not attempt
to leave the nest, so sinks back down again.

13     That was me, too – the urge to ask, alight
and yet snuffed out, arriving at the *look*
(no more) of someone who intends to speak.

16     My dearest father, though the pace was quick,
did not hold back, but said: 'Let loose your bow.
You've drawn that arrow to its iron tip.'

19     Now, confident, I opened up my lips.
'Where there's no need for nourishment,' I said,
'how can it be that people get so thin?'

22*     'Were you to call to mind how Meleager –
a log consumed by fire – consumed himself,
then this,' he said, 'would not seem sour to you.

25     And if you thought how, when you writhe around,
your image in a mirror also writhes,
what seems so hard would seem a hoary truth.

To make you, though, at ease in your desires,                              28
Statius is here, look. I now call on him,
begging he be the healer of your wounds.'

Statius responded: 'If, for him, I free –                                  31
with you still here – a vista of eternity,
let this be my excuse: I can't say no.'

He then began: 'My son, if in your mind                                    34*
you gather up and guard my words to you,
they'll be a light that shows the "how" you seek.

Pure, perfect blood – which never will be drunk                            37
by thirsting veins – remains behind untouched,
as might some dish that's carried from the feast,

and gains there, in the heart, a power to mould                            40
the limbs and organs of new embryos –
as blood runs through our veins to form our own.

This blood, distilled as sperm, descends to where                          43
(more decent not to say) its droplets run
within the natural cup to other blood.

These two bloods meet and gather, each with each.                          46
*Menstrum* is passive. But the other acts –
the perfect place it's pressed from causes that –

and, once arrived, begins to do its work,                                  49
first to coagulate, and then to bring
the matter that it first made dense to life.

The active virtue, which is now a soul,                                    52
much like a plant (though differing in this point,
that plant souls stay as plants while this moves on),

continues in its work, to move and feel,                                   55
as do aquatic sponges, then begins
to form the organs for the powers it seeds.

And now, my dearest son, the power that flows                              58
out of the father's heart (where nature plans
for every organ) stretching, spreads to all.

This creature will become a speaking child.                                61
Yet *how*, you don't yet see. And this same point
led someone far more wise than you astray,

64 who in his teachings set the soul apart
from *intellectus* as *possibilis*,
finding no organ taken up by that.

67 Open your heart. Receive the coming truth.
Know this: when once the foetal brain is brought
to full articulation in the womb,

70 the Primal Cause of Motion turns in joy
to see so much of Nature's art, and breathes
new breath of spirit filled with power within,

73 which draws all active elements it finds
into its being and thus forms one soul
which lives and feels and turns as conscious self.

76 And – so you'll wonder less at what I say –
look at how solar warmth transforms to wine
when joined with juices flowing from the grape.

79* And when Lachesis cannot spin more thread,
the soul leaves flesh and carries, by its power,
both human and divine along with it.

82 But memory, intelligence and will,
since all the other powers are silent now,
become, in act, much keener than before.

85 Unrestingly, it falls, by its own will –
a miracle! – on one of these two shores,
and here first knows the paths it has to take.

88 As soon as it is circumscribed by place,
the power that forms it radiates around
in size and shape as in its living limbs.

91 And as the air, when drenched with vaporous rain,
is soon adorned with many different hues,
from other rays reflected in the haze,

94 so when the soul has reached this point of rest,
the air around it gathers in the form
that virtual powers of soul impress on it.

97 And, as some little flame pursues the fire
and follows where its changing heat may lead,
so this new form will go where spirit goes.

And since in this way soul appears to view,     100
that's called soul's shade. And from this there will form
the organs of all sense, including sight.

And that is how we speak and how we laugh,     103
and how we form our tears and all those sighs
that you may well have heard around this hill.

As our desires and other feelings form,     106
the shade accordingly configures them.
And that's the cause of what you wonder at.'

Our path had brought us, turning to the right,     109
to reach the final twist of punishment,
and we were now intent on new concerns.

The bank here shot out blazing bolts of flame.     112
And round the edge there breathed an upward wind
that bent these flames back, keeping them at bay.

So, one by one, we had to make our way     115
along the unprotected outer rim.
I feared the fire there. Here I feared the fall.

Meanwhile, my leader said: 'In such a place     118
we need to keep a strict check on our eyes.
It wouldn't be too hard for them to stray.'

And then I heard: '*Summae Deus clementiae*'     121*
singing within the heart of that great blaze,
which made me – no less watchfully – turn round.

I saw there spirits walking in the flames.     124
At which I looked at both my steps and them,
dividing my attentions, here then there.

And, when the ending of the hymn had come,     127*
they cried aloud, '*Virum non cognosco!*'
then, singing low, began the hymn again.

That finished, they all cried once more: 'Diana,     130
guarding her woodlands, drove out Helice
who'd felt what bitter poison Venus sends.'

And yet again they now began their song,     133
then called on men and women who were chaste –
as virtue and our marriages demand.

136     This form of song will serve for them, I think,
        throughout the time the fire is scorching them.
        With this concern and fed by foods like this,
139     sin's final wound is sewn up once again.

# CANTO 26

While on, in single file, we went around                    1
the rim – my trusted teacher saying often:
'Careful! I'll point the dangers out. Attend!' –
    the sun was beating on my right-hand side,            4
its rays illuminating all the west,
changing its face from clearest blue to white.
    And I, in casting shadows on the flame,               7
made fire seem fierier. Then many shades,
I saw, at that one hint, while walking on,
    gave thought, and came, because of that,             10
to say of me their say. So they began:
'He does not seem, in body, fiction-formed.'
    And then, as far towards me as they could,           13
they pressed to make quite sure – with constant care
lest any come where they should *not* be burned.
    'You there (who, following the other two,            16
aren't slow, maybe, but mean to show respect)
please answer me. I burn in fire and thirst.
    Nor will your answer serve for me alone.             19
For all of us are thirsting more for this
than Ethiopes or Indians for cool streams.
    Tell us: how do you make yourself a wall             22
to shield the sun, as if you had not yet
entered within the trammels of death's net?'
    These words from one of them. And I'd have said      25
already who I was, except my mind
was set on something new that now appeared.

28      For down the middle of the blazing path,
        facing the first, there came another group.
        This made me pause in answering, and gaze.

31      I saw on either side the shadows kiss.
        They did not cease, however, in their course,
        each one content to keep the frolic brief.

34      In that same way, within their darkening ranks,
        ants nuzzle other ants, when columns meet,
        to scout the road ahead or spy on fate.

37      These friends, once parted from their warm embrace,
        before their forward steps can speed them on,
        strain, each one louder than the next, to yell

40*     (the new arrivals), 'Sodom! Gomorrah!'
        'Into the cow' (the rest) 'went Pasiphae
        to let the bull calf run his lust in her.'

43*     As flocks of cranes divide – some flying north
        to find the Riphean steeps, while some seek sand
        (the second can't stand chill; the former, sun),

46      one lot went off, the other went off, too,
        all turning, weeping, to their former song,
        each to the slogan that most suited them.

49      Then those same souls who'd pleaded with me first
        came to my side, as they had done before
        and, from the look of them, were keen to hear.

52      And I (who'd now seen twice what they found good)
        began: 'You souls, quite certain to arrive –
        whenever that time comes – at perfect peace,

55      my living limbs have not remained back there,
        not aged and ripe, nor youthful green. They're here.
        They travel with me, blood and joints entire.

58      I make this climb to be no longer blind.
        A lady up above besought this grace
        that through your world I bear my mortal part.

61      Yet – may your greater longing soon be fed,
        so that you come to lodge at rest in Heaven,
        which, ranging wide and free, is full of peace –

tell me, so I may rule a page for this,                    64
who might you be, and who's within that crowd
that's going on its way behind your backs?'

These shadows in appearance now all stood          67
as mountain yokels stand – no differently –
in dumbstruck stupefaction, staring round,

when, red-necked, rough, they make it, first, to town.   70
But once they'd set astonishment aside
(it's quickly blunted in a noble heart),

'Blessèd be you, who round our border lands,'       73
the shade who first had questioned me began,
'haul in experience for your better death!

Those folk who do not follow in our track         76*
offended as did Caesar – who once heard
"You queen!", when triumphing, yelled out at him.

Then they, as they depart, are crying, "Sodom!"   79
to castigate themselves as you have heard,
bringing self-shame to aid the scorching fire.

Our sin, by contrast, was hermaphrodite.          82*
And since we paid no heed to human law –
choosing to follow bestial appetites –

ourselves we read out our opprobrium,             85
speaking, on leaving here, the name of one
who made herself a beast in beastlike planks.

So now you know our guilt and what we did.        88
But if you seek to know us each by name,
there is no time – and I don't know them all.

I shall diminish what you want of me.             91*
I'm Guido Guinizelli. Since I mourned
my sins before my end, I'm here made clean.'

Like those two sons, who, when Lycurgus grieved,  94*
were made to see their mother once again,
so I became (though I don't reach those heights),

listening as now he named himself, the sire       97
of me and all those (better men) who ever
wrote about love in sweet and well-poised rhyme.

100     Hearing and saying nothing, deep in thought,
I walked a while, just marvelling at him,
yet did not – since the fire was there – draw near.

103     Then, having pastured fully on that gaze,
I gave myself entirely to his service,
with gestures of the kind that win good faith.

106     To me he said: 'Through what I hear, you leave
so clear a trace and footprint in my mind,
Lethe won't cancel it or make it fade.

109     But, if the oath you took just now holds true,
tell me, why is it that, in word and look,
you show so frankly that you hold me dear?'

112     And I to him: 'That smooth, sweet verse you wrote
will make its very ink most dearly prized
as long as present usage still endures.'

115     'Brother,' he said, 'the one I single out'
(his finger pointing to a soul ahead)
'crafted the mother tongue with greater skill.

118*     Lyrics of love, in prose the French Romance –
all these he far surpassed. Let idiots talk,
rating that poet from Limoges ahead.

121     Their gaze is turned to chatter more than truth.
They settle their opinions long before
reason or art is heard within their thoughts.

124     That's what they did with Fra Guittone once,
proclaiming, on and on, his proven worth
until, with many more, the truth won through.

127     Now since you're granted generous privilege
to pass within those cloistered corridors,
where Christ is abbot of the brotherhood,

130     then say a *Paternoster* for me there –
as much, at least, as we, in this world, need –
where no ability to sin is ours.'

133     Maybe to give another, nearby, space,
he disappeared at this point through the fire,
as fish do going to the water's depth.

I made towards the soul he'd pointed out,                    136
and said that my desires were gratefully
disposed to find a fit place for his name.

    And, free and open, he began to speak:         139*
'*Tan m'abellis vostre cortes deman,*
*qu'ieu no me puesc ni voill a vos cobrire,*

    *Ieu sui Arnaut, que plor e vau cantan;*         142
*consiros vei la passada folor,*
*e vei jausen lo joi qu'esper denan.*

    *Ara vos prec, per aquella valor*               145
*que vos guida al som de l'escalina,*
*sovenha vos a temps de ma dolor.*'

    He hid then in the fire that sharpens them.      148

# CANTO 27

1*    As when it strikes its first vibrating rays
where once its own Creator shed His blood
(the river Ebro falling under Libra's height,

4    while Ganges' waves are scorched by noon-time heat)
at *that* degree the sun now stood. So day
was leaving when, in joy, God's angel showed.

7*    Beyond the flame, he stood there on the bank,
and sang the words *'Beati mundo corde!'*,
his voice far more alive than ours can be.

10    And then: 'None can, you holy souls, proceed
until the fire has bitten them. Go in.
And do not turn deaf ears to what is sung!'

13    he said to us, as we came near to him.
And I became, on seeing what he meant,
as though, still living, placed within a tomb.

16    Over my suppliant hands entwined, I leaned
just staring at the fire, imagining
bodies of human beings I'd seen burn.

19    And both my trusted guides now turned to me.
And Virgil spoke, to say: 'My dearest son,
here may be agony but never death.

22*    Remember this! Remember! And if I
led you to safety on Geryon's back,
what will I do when now so close to God?

25*    Believe this. And be sure. Were you to stay
a thousand years or more wombed in this fire,
you'd not be made the balder by one hair.

And if, perhaps, you think I'm tricking you,      28
approach the fire and reassure yourself,
trying with your own hands your garment's hem.

Have done, I say, have done with fearfulness.     31
Turn this way. Come and enter safely in!'
But I, against all conscience, stood stock still.

And when he saw me stiff and obstinate,     34
he said, a little troubled: 'Look, my son,
between Beatrice and you there's just this wall.'

As Pyramus, on hearing Thisbe's name,     37*
opened his eyelids at the point of death,
and (mulberries turning crimson) gazed at her,

so, too – my obstinacy softening now –     40
I turned to hear her name, which, growing still,
thrives in my thinking to my guide, so wise.

Saying 'What's this?' he shook his head. 'Would you     43
prefer we stayed on this side?' Then he smiled
as though to see a child won round by apples.

Ahead of me, he went to meet the fire,     46
and begged that Statius, who had walked the road
so long between us, now take up the rear.

And, once within, I could have flung myself –     49
the heat that fire produced was measureless –
for coolness, in a vat of boiling glass.

To strengthen me, my sweetest father spoke,     52
as on he went, of Beatrice always,
saying, 'It seems I see her eyes already.'

And, guiding us, a voice sang from beyond.     55
So we, attending only to that voice,
came out and saw where now we could ascend.

'*Venite, benedicti Patris mei!*'     58*
sounded within what little light there was.
This overcame me and I could not look.

'The sun departs,' he added. 'Evening comes.     61
Don't stop. Think hard about your speed. Keep up,
as long as western skies have not turned dark.'

64     The pathway through the rock rose sheer and straight –
and angled so I cut, ahead of me,
the rays of sunlight, which had now sunk low.

67     The steps the sages and myself assayed
were few until – my shadow petering out –
we sensed the sun behind us laid to rest.

70     Before the sky's horizon had assumed
one look in all its vast unmeasured parts
(night gathering all within its lawful bounds)

73     on separate stairs we each had made our beds.
The mountain by its natural law had wrecked
our power to climb and all delight in that.

76     Compare: goats, ruminating, mildly stand
where first, before they'd fed, they raced above
the summits of the hills, eager, untamed,

79     now, while the sun seethes, muted in the shade –
their herdsman watching over them, leaning
against his stick, so they can safely rest.

82     And shepherds, too, will lodge outdoors beside
their flocks, and calmly spend the night on guard,
so predators can't come to scatter them.

85     That is what, now, all three of us were like –
they as my shepherds and the she-goat, me –
tucked up on either side by towering rock.

88     Little was visible of things beyond.
Yet, by that 'little' I could see the stars
brighter than usual, and of greater size.

91     So, ruminating, wondering so at these,
sleep grasped me now – that sleep which often will,
before the fact appears, tell all that's new.

94*    At that hour, so I think, when, from the east,
Cytherea casts her first rays on the hill
(seeming to blaze, as always, in love's fire),

97     lovely and young, a *donna* in a dream
appeared to me and walked along the lea,
plucking its flowers and singing as she said:

'Let anyone who asks me for my name          100
know I am Leah, and my lovely hands
fashion my garland as I move them round.

I dress here so my mirror gives me joy.          103
My sister Rachel, though, entranced, won't cease
to sit all day in wonder at her glass.

She yearns to see her own delightful eyes,          106
as I desire to dress by my own hands.
Seeing, for her, is all – as doing is for me.

Driven before bright antelucan rays          109*
(which pilgrims, in returning, welcome more
since now they've lodged one night less far from home),

shadowy dark now fled on every side          112
and, with these shades, my sleep. At which I rose,
and saw my masters were already up.

'The sweetest apple that the mortal heart          115
seeks in the branches with such urgency
today will offer all your cravings peace.'

These words were those that Virgil used on me.          118
And never had such tokens of good luck
been equal in the pleasure that they gave.

Desire beyond desire came over me          121
to be up there. And so, at every pace,
my plumage grew, I felt, more quick to fly.

Below us now, the stair had run its course,          124
and we were on the highest of the steps.
Then, firmly, Virgil fixed his eyes on me,

saying: 'The temporal and eternal fires          127
you've seen, my son, and now you're in a place
where I, through my own powers, can tell no more.

I've drawn you here by skill and searching mind.          130
Now take what pleases you to be your guide.
You're now beyond the steeps, beyond all straits.

The sun, you see, is shining on your brow.          133
You see the bushes, fresh, young grass, and flowers.
The earth by its own powers brings this to be.

136      Until, in joy, those lovely eyes appear
that, weeping, made me come to be your guide,
through these you may go walking, or may sit.

139      No longer look to me for signs or word.
Your will is healthy, upright, free and whole.
And not to heed that sense would be a fault.

142      Lord of yourself, I crown and mitre you.'

# CANTO 28

Aching to search, now, in and all around       1\*
that holy forest, dense, alive and bright,
which tempered to my eyes the newborn day,

    not pausing anymore, I left the verge,       4
treading in slow, slow steps across the field.
The earth below breathed scent on every side.

    A gentle breeze, unchanging in itself,       7
struck on my forehead, yet with no more force
than would the smoothest of our changing winds.

    To this the branches, trembling in response,       10
yielded, all bending to the place at which
the sacred mountain casts its earliest shade,

    and yet not leaning so far out of true       13
that fledglings perched among the topmost boughs
were forced to leave the practice of their trade.

    But, full of happiness, they greet the dawn,       16
singing among the foliage which holds
a steady undertone to all their tunes –

    as in those notes that gather, branch by branch,       19\*
through all the pines along Ravenna's shore
when, from the south, sciroccos start to blow.

    My steady steps by now had carried me       22
so deep within the ancient wood that I
could not see back to where I'd entered first.

    Look there! A brook held back my onward pace.       25
Its course was leftward, and its little waves
swayed all the grass that rose along its banks.

28      The purest waters that down here may flow
would seem to have admixtures in their depths
compared with those, which don't hide anything.

31      And yet these waters move dark, dark beneath
a shadow that's perpetual and allows
no ray of sun or moonlight ever through.

34      My pace here checked, I passed in sight alone
beyond that stream, to see and wonder at
these May-things in abundance varying.

37      And then appeared to me – as things appear
that suddenly in wonder will deflect
the claims of every other thought we have –

40*     a *donna* all alone who walked along,
singing and choosing flowers to pluck from flowers
that painted all the way she went upon.

43      'Lady, you warm yourself in rays of love,
or so I think, to see your lovely looks –
these usually bear witness to the heart.

46      May you incline, in will, to move more close,'
sighing I said, 'towards this flowing stream,
so I may understand the song you sing.

49      You make me call to mind Proserpina,
both where and what she was – when she lost Spring
and her own mother lost all sight of her.'

52      Her feet together, firmly pressed to ground
as when a *donna* dances, she then turned
and, scarcely setting foot in front of foot,

55      she turned above the yellow and the red
of tender flowers, as virgin girls will do
when they, for decency, dip down their eyes.

58      Then she in full responded to my prayers,
bringing herself so near that that sweet sound
came to me, with the meanings that it bore.

61      And now, the moment she'd arrived at where
the grass was bathed by waves from that fine stream,
she made a gift to me: she raised her eyes.

    I do not think so great a light shone out       64*
beneath the brows of Venus when her son
pierced her with love beyond his usual stroke.

    She stood there, laughing, on the other bank     67
arranging many colours in her hands,
strewn by the mighty earth without a seed.

    The river kept us still three steps apart.      70*
And yet the Hellespont where Xerxes passed
(a bridle still on all our human pride)

    did not so much incur Leander's hate,      73
when oceans raged from Sest to Abydos,
as this did mine because it would not part.

    'You are both new,' she now began to say,     76
'in this place, chosen for the human race
to make its nest. And you stand wondering,

    perhaps because I smile, caught up in doubt.     79*
The psalm, though, *"Delectasti"* sheds a light
that may dispel the clouds around your mind.

    And you who begged me speak – the one ahead –     82
say if there's any more you wish to hear.
I'll quickly come to answer you in full.'

    'These waters, and the sound the forest makes,     85
battle within me with a newborn faith
in something I've heard contrary to this.'

    At which she said: 'I'll tell you, then, the cause     88*
from which those things you wonder at derive,
and thus will purge the fog that strikes at you.

    The Highest Good – alone its own delight –     91
made human beings good and fit for good,
and gave this place as pledge of endless peace.

    Through his own fault, Man did not dwell here long.     94
Through his own fault, to weeping and to grief
he changed his noble laughter and sweet play.

    Water and earth below breathe vapours out     97
that search, as fully as they can, for heat,
and this induces turbulence down there.

100     Yet, so that these should bring no harm to men,
this mountain climbs and reaches to the sky,
free of these swirls from where the gate is locked.

103     But now, because the circling sphere of air,
if that's not interrupted in some part,
turns altogether as the heavens turn,

106     that motion, unconstrained in living air,
will strike directly on this utmost peak
and make the forest, being dense, sound out.

     And plants here, when they're struck, have such great strength
109   that, with its natural power they seed the breeze,
which then, in circling round, will scatter this.

112     The other hemisphere – as far as soil
is right, and climate suits – conceives and bears
plants in variety with various powers.

115     And hearing this, it would not seem, down there,
a source of wonder if a plant takes root
without there being, visibly, a seed.

118     And you should know that all this holy field
is filled where you are now with every seed,
and here has fruits which, there, are never plucked.

121     The water that you see is from no well
(as rivers are that gain and lose in force)
that's freshly filled when ice condenses mist,

124     but issues, sure and steady, from a spring
that gathers all it has from God's own will,
which then it pours out, opening in two parts.

127     It flows, in this part, down with all its power
to take the memory of sin away,
restoring, on the other, all good done.

130*    Its name is Lethe here, Eunoe there.
Until a taste is had on either side,
the influence it has won't take effect.

This savour is above all other tastes                                    133
and – though your thirst would none the less be slaked
if I disclosed to you no more than this –
    I'll add one footnote, out of grace and thanks.          136
(I cannot think you'll hold my words less dear
if these soar out beyond my promised theme.)
    Those who, in times long gone, composed those poems   139*
that sang the Age of Gold and all its joys
thought, maybe here's Parnassus when they dreamed.
    Here, once, the root of man was innocent.                 142
Here, there is always spring and every fruit.
And that's the nectar they all speak about.'
    I swung around to face my poets there,                    145
and both (as I could tell) had smiled to hear
the meaning of the words that she'd spelled out.
    I then turned back to see that lovely girl.               148

# CANTO 29

<sup></sup>1*   Singing as might some *donna* deep in love,
she then went on and brought an end to words:
'*Beati quorum tecta sunt peccata*.'

4    And then, as nymphs who, once, would go alone
through woodland shadows longing, some of them,
to see the sun while others fled its rays,

7    she moved, against the course that clear stream ran,
walking along her bank while I kept up,
with small steps too, pursuing her small pace.

10   Before a hundred steps had gone (to count
both hers and mine) the banks on either side
curved equally, so I was facing east.

13   Nor did our path continue so for long,
until the lady turned direct to me,
saying: 'Dear brother, watch now and listen.'

16*  And look! A sudden radiance, darting all
around, pierced that great forest through and through,
at which I thought that lightning may have struck.

19   But lightning, when it comes, is quenched at once,
where this, enduring, shone out more and more.
So I was left, thought muttering: 'What is this?'

22   And then, through all that luminous air, there ran
a melody so fine that purest zeal
made me reprove the recklessness of Eve.

25   Where earth and Heaven displayed obedience,
a woman, one alone, formed only now,
was not content to stay beneath the veil.

Had she in true devotion stayed beneath,                    28
I should have known these pleasures, past all speech,
far sooner and enjoyed them at more length.

While on I went among these primal fruits,                  31
the pleasures yielded by eternity,
caught up, desiring yet more happiness,

ahead of us, beneath the branching green,                   34
the air blazed up like newly kindled fire,
and that sweet sound was clearly heard as song.

You holy virgin Muses, if, for you,                         37*
I've ever suffered vigils, fast or cold,
there's now all reason to beseech your aid.

Now Helicon must pour in streams for me,                    40
Urania with her choirs assist me here,
to put in verse things hardly thinkable.

Just further on were seven trees of gold –                  43*
that semblance given them, mistakenly,
by distance that, between us, intervened.

But when I'd got so near to them that now                   46
(far off, aspectuals can fool our sense)
these things lost nothing of their proper form,

that power that sends (as manna) rational thought,          49
discerned that these were candle-bearing staves,
and heard 'Hosanna' in that singing voice.

These fine devices flamed around their heights              52
far clearer than the moon in tranquil skies,
at midnight in the middle of a month.

Filled full of radiant wonder, I turned round               55
to honest Virgil, and he answered me
with looks no less weighed down by heavy awe.

I then restored my gaze to those high things                58
that came towards us now and moved so slow
that new-wed brides would quickly have gone past.

The lady reprimanded me: 'Why burn,                         61
so moved, to see alone these living lights
and fail to look at what comes after them?'

64     I then saw people guided by the flames,
now coming near to us. Their robes were white,
of brilliant purity not seen down here.

67     The water to my left reflected fire,
and rendered back to me, if I looked down,
as mirrors do, the sight of my left side.

70     When, on my own bank, I had reached a place
where I was distanced only by the stream,
I brought my steps to rest, to see them well.

73     I saw those flames, diminishing, move on,
leaving behind a paint stroke in the air,
as though they all drew pennants after them,

76*     so that, above them, there were seven streams,
their colours those the sun makes with its bow
or else the girdle of the Delian moon.

79     These pennants stretched far back beyond my sight.
The outer two, as far as I could tell,
were drawn on through the air ten steps apart.

82     And under this fine sky, as here described,
were elders – twenty-four – who walked in pairs,
and each of them was crowned with fleurs-de-lys.

85     And all of these were singing: 'You among
the daughters born to Adam are *benedicta*,
your beauty blessed to all eternity.'

88     And when, across from me, the other bank –
with all its flowers and other fresh young growth –
was free of these, who were the chosen ones,

91*     as light lights up in sequence through the sky,
there came behind them now four animals,
and each of these was crowned with boughs of green.

94     And each was fledged and feathered with six wings.
These feathers all were peacock-eyed. The eyes
of Argus would, if they still lived, be like this.

97     I'll scatter, reader, no more rhymes to trace
what these forms were. Other expenditure
constrains me; I cannot be generous.

But read Ezekiel, who paints them all          100
as once he saw them, coming from cold climes
in whirlwinds, towering clouds and folds of fire.

And as you'll find them written on his page,      103
so were they there, except that, as to wings,
Saint John is with me, and departs from him.

The space that lay between these four contained   106
a two-wheeled chariot in triumphal state.
A gryphon drew it, harnessed at the neck.

This gryphon held his two wings stretched on high  109
between the middle band and three and three,
so that, in cleaving air, he did no harm.

These wings rose higher than the eye could see.   112
The bird-limbs of that form were all of gold,
the others white, commingling with bright red.

Not only did not Rome cheer Scipio         115*
with such fine chariots (or Caesar, even!)
the sun itself beside that would look poor –

the sun that burned to nothing when it strayed   118
(here Jove for his dark reasons once proved just)
in answer to the prayers of pious earth.

Beside the right-hand wheel, three ladies came,   121*
all dancing in a ring, the first so red
that she, in fire, would hardly have been seen,

the next as if her very bones and flesh       124
were fashioned from the freshest emerald,
the third like snow just fallen from the sky.

Their steps were drawn, it seems, by first, the white,  127
then red, and from the song that this one sang
the others took their tempo, fast or slow.

Four ladies to the left, all purple-clothed,     130
rejoiced in following the melody
of one of them, whose brow displayed three eyes.

Then, close within the track of this tight knot,   133
I saw two elders, differing in their garb,
but equal in demeanour, grave and firm

136      One showed himself a close familiar
of great Hippocrates, whom Nature formed
to serve the creatures that she loved the best.

139      The other showed the opposite concern,
a well-honed sword in hand – so bright and keen
it brought me terror from beyond the stream.

142      I then saw four, each one with humble looks,
and after these, an old man all alone,
who came as though still sleeping, face alert.

145      These seven were clothed as was the first brigade
except that, as they came, around their heads,
they wore no garland formed of lilia,

148      but roses, rather, and vermilion flowers.
And, standing just a short way off, you'd swear
that all, above their brows, bore searing fire.

151      When, now, that chariot stood facing me,
thunder was heard. These people of great worth
were banned, it seemed, from going further on.

154      With standards to the fore, they halted there.

# CANTO 30

Those Seven Polar Stars that constellate                    1*
the highest sphere, and never knowing nadir
or zenith, veiled by the murk of sin alone,
    those stars that make the souls, in Heaven, aware     4
of what is right (as, by our Wain, down here,
a helmsman turns his wheel to steer for port)
    stopped and stood firm. The people of the truth –     7
who marched between the Gryphon and these stars –
turned, as though each found peace, towards the chariot.
    And one of them, as sent from Heaven, cried out:      10*
'*Veni, sponsa, de Libano!*' singing
(the others followed on) this verse three times.
    As when the Last New Day is heralded,                 13
and happy souls will rise keen from their caves,
dressed in new voice, to echo 'Alleluia'
    so now, *ad vocem tanti senis*, there arose           16
above the hallowed chariot a hundred
angels, all bearing news of eternal life.
    They spoke thus: '*Benedictus qui venis!*'            19
and, strewing petals upward and around:
'*Manibus*, oh, *date lilia plenis!*'
    I saw, once, at the opening of the day,               22*
the orient sky in colour all clear rose,
the western height still robed in tranquil blue,
    and then the sun newborn, with shadowed face,         25
hazy, in vapours that so tempered it
that eyes could tolerate its light a while.

28     So now, beyond a drifting cloud of flowers
       (which rose up, arching, from the angels' hands,
       then fell within and round the chariot),

31     seen through a veil, pure white, and olive-crowned,
       a lady now appeared to me. Her robe was green,
       her dress the colour of a living flame.

34     And I, in spirit, who so long had not
       been, trembling in her presence, wracked by awe,
       began again to tremble at her glance

37     (without more evidence that eyes could bring,
       but darkly, through the good that flowed from her),
       sensing the ancient power of what love was.

40     But on the instant that it struck my sight –
       this power, this virtue, that had pierced me through
       before I'd even left my boyhood state –

43     I turned aside (and leftwards) meaning now,
       with all the hope and deference of some child
       that runs when hurt or frightened to its mum,

46*    to say to Virgil: 'There is not one gram
       of blood in me that does not tremble now.
       I recognize the signs of ancient flame.'

49     But Virgil was not there. Our lack alone
       was left where once he'd been. Virgil, dear sire,
       Virgil – to him I'd run to save my soul.

52     Nor could the All our primal mother lost,
       ensure my cheeks – which he once washed with dew –
       should not again be sullied with dark tears.

55     'Dante, that Virgil is no longer here,
       do not yet weep, do not yet weep for that.
       A different sword cut, first, must make you weep.'

58     From stern to prow, some admiral will pace
       to see how well, in other hulls, his captains fare,
       and seek to hearten them to do their best.

61*    So, almost (left along the chariot),
       turning around to hear my own name voiced
       (I here record it of necessity),

I saw my *donna* – who'd at first appeared 64
hidden in garlands of angelic joy –
fix, from beyond the brook, her eyes on me,

though still the veil descending from her brows, 67
encircled with Minerva's olive fronds,
did not allow, distinctly, any sight of her.

Her look was stern and proud. With sovereign strength, 70
she then went on, and spoke as though she still
held back, until the last, her fieriest words.

'Look. I am, truly, I am Beatrice. 73
What right had you to venture to this mount?
Did you not know that all are happy here?'

My eyes fell, glancing to the spring-clear brook, 76
but, seeing *me* in that, shame bent my brow.
I dragged my gaze back to the grassy bank.

A mother, to her son, looks stern and proud. 79
So she appeared to me. For true concern
is bitter to the taste and quick to sting.

She did not speak; but suddenly, as one, 82*
the angels sang: '*In te, Domine, speravi*',
but did not go beyond the '*pedes meos*'.

Compare: the snow that falls through growing eaves 85
freezes the spine of Italy in drifts
blown and compacted by Slavonian winds.

But when the southern lands (where shadow fails) 88
breathe once again, within itself it thaws,
then trickles down, as candles melt in flames.

So, too, until those beings sang – their notes 91
are all concordant with the heavenly spheres –
I'd been there uttering no sigh or tear.

And yet, on hearing, through these harmonies, 94
their pity on me (it seemed they had said:
'Why, *donna*, cause him discord such as this?'),

the ice, so tightly stretched around my core, 97
turned now to breath and water, issuing,
at mouth and eye, in spasms from my heart.

100     Then she (still leftwards on the chariot),
unmoved and standing firm, addressed her words
to these true beings, so compassionate:

103     'You wake, in vigil, through eternal day.
So neither night nor sleep can steal from you
a single step that time takes, travelling by.

106     Thus, answering, my greater care must be
that he, in tears there, grasps what I intend,
and brings to balance all his grief and guilt.

109     Not only by the work of Heaven's great wheels
that send, with its companion stars, each seed
along the road towards its rightful end,

112     but also by those holy generosities
that rain in grace from clouded powers so high
that human sight can come in no way near,

115     this man through all his new life, fresh and young,
in virtual power was one who might have proved,
in all of his behaviour, wonderful.

118     Yet there, on earth, the richer soil may be,
the more – untilled or sown with evil seed –
its vigour turns to wilderness and bane.

121     I, looking on, sustained him for a time.
My eyes, when bright with youth, I turned to him,
and led him with me on the road to truth.

124*     Then, on the threshold of my second age,
I changed, took different life, and he at once
drew back and yielded to another's glance.

127     Risen from body into spirit-form,
my goodness, power and beauty grew more strong.
Yet I to him was then less dear, less pleasing.

130     He turned his steps to paths that were not true.
He followed images of failing good
which cannot meet, in full, their promises.

133     And when I prayed that he might be inspired,
seeking to call him back – by dreams and other ways –
all *that* came to nothing. He paid little heed.

He fell so far that every other means                          136
to save this man, by now, came short, unless
he saw, himself, those people who are lost.

   I went, then, to the doorway of the dead,                   139
and, weeping, my entreaties there were borne
to one who, since, has brought him to these heights.

   God's high decree would shatter, though, if he              142
should pass by the Lethe and go on to taste
the food of life, yet leave unpaid the tax

   of penitence, which pours out flowing tears.'               145

# CANTO 31

1
'You, who are there beyond the sacred stream,'
turning the sword point of her words on me
(the edge alone had seemed quite keen enough),

4
so, without lapse continuing, she began,
'Say, say, if this is true. To such a charge
your own confession needs to be conjoined.'

7
My natural powers by now were so confused
that voice began to move, and yet gave out
before it cleared the larynx and the throat.

10
She bore this for a while, and then she said:
'Respond to me. Your wretched memories
have not been struck through yet by Lethe's stream.'

13
Fear and confusion, intermixed in me,
drove from my lips a 'yes' so hard to hear
it needed sight to make it understood.

16
A crossbow triggered under too much stress
snaps its own string and splinters at the arc.
Its shaft thus hits the target with less force.

19
I burst in that same way beneath the load
and, shedding streams of sighs and sobs and tears,
my voice came slack and slow along its course.

22
And so: 'In your desire for me,' she said,
'which then was leading you to love the Good
beyond which we cannot aspire to reach,

25
what ditches or what chains across your path
did you discover that led you to strip
the hopes you had of getting further on?

What easements, profits, gain or benefit 28
displayed themselves to you on other brows
that you preferred to flounce within their sight?'

I drew the bitterest of sighs, but then 31
I hardly had the voice left to respond.
My lips were labouring to give to words some form.

Weeping, I said: 'Mere things of here and now 34
and their false pleasures turned my steps away
the moment that your face had hid itself.'

'Had you,' she said, 'been silent, or denied 37
what you confess, your guilt would equally
have been observed. It's known to such a judge!

But when the plea of guilty, in this court, 40
bursts, freely uttered, from the sinner's cheek,
the grindstone here will turn against the blade.

And yet – so you may bear the proper shame 43
your error brings and, hearing, once again,
the siren call you may show greater strength –

put to one side the seed that nurtures tears. 46
Listen and hear how down a different path
my flesh, when buried, should have made you move.

Never had art or nature shown to you 49
such beauty and delight as did those limbs
in which I was enclosed, now strewn in earth.

And if that great delight, because I died, 52
did fail for you, what other dying thing
should then have drawn you to desire of it?

Pierced by the arrows of fallacious things, 55
you should at once have raised yourself on high,
to follow me, I being none such now.

You ought not to have weighed your feathers down 58*
just waiting to be stricken by some girl,
or other novelty of short-lived use.

A newborn chick will take a blow or two. 61
But arrows fly, and nets are spread in vain,
before the eyes of any fully fledged.'

64     As little boys who stand there dumb with shame,
eyes on the ground and listening to what's said,
aware – very sorry – of what they are,

67     so I, too, simply stood. And she said: 'Since
you grieve at what you're hearing, raise your beard
and, looking up, you'll feel still greater pain.'

70*     With less resistance some well-sinewed oak
is rooted out by northern winds of ours,
or blasts from savage Iarbas' Libyan realm,

73     than I at her command raised up my chin.
And when she spoke of 'beard' (to name my face),
I knew the venom that her meaning bore.

76     But as I stretched to show my face to her,
those primal creatures, as my eyes observed,
had ceased in scattering their arc of flowers.

79     Those lights of mine, still very far from sure,
saw Beatrice turn towards the beast,
being two natures and, in person, one.

82     Beneath her veil, beyond the flowing stream,
she overcame, it seemed, what once she'd been,
when once, as here, she overcame all women.

85     The nettle of remorse now stung so sharp,
whatever else had drawn me most to love
became for me my utmost enemy.

88*     It gnawed my heart – the consciousness of this –
that, overwhelmed, I fell. What I became,
she knows who is the cause of why I did.

91     Then when my heart gave back my outward powers,
the *donna* whom I'd found there all alone,
I saw above me, saying: 'Grip me! Grip!'

94     She'd drawn me up to throat height in the stream,
and, pulling me behind her, went her way
across the wave as light as any skiff.

97*     And then, when I approached the blessed shore,
'*Asperges me*' was heard, so sweetly sung
I can't remember it, still less can write.

That lovely lady, opening wide her arms,     100
circled my head, submerging me so far
I could not help but swallow from the stream.

From there she took and led me, bathed, still wet,     103
to join the dance of those four lovely ones.
And each one raised an arm to cover me.

'We, here, are nymphs and, in the heavens, stars,     106
given to Beatrice as her maids,
before she first descended to the world.

We'll lead you to her eyes. Yet to that light,     109
so jubilant, within, those three beyond –
their gaze still deeper – will make yours more keen.'

So, singing, they began and, moving on,     112
they brought me with them to the Gryphon's breast,
where, turned towards us, Beatrice stood.

'Make sure,' they said, 'you do not spare your eyes.     115
We've placed you here before these emeralds,
from which Love aimed his arrows at you once.'

A thousand longings, fiercer far than flame,     118
wrestled my eyes to her eyes, shining back,
fixed on the Gryphon, never wavering.

No differently from sun in mirror glass,     121
the twyform beast shone rays into her eyes,
displaying one and then the other kind.

Reader, just think how great my wonder was     124*
to see that creature stilled within itself
and yet – within that icon – altering.

And, while astounded, yet so full of joy,     127
my soul received the savour of the food
that feeds us full and makes us thirst for more,

the other three who showed, in all they did,     130
that they were scions of a greater tribe
came forward, to their angel's chant, *en loure*.

'Turn, Beatrice, turn your holy eyes'     133
(their song went thus) 'on your most faithful one
who, for your sight, has moved so many steps.

136  In grace, we beg, do us the grace to lift
the veil that veils your lips so he can tell
the second beauty that you still conceal.'

139  Splendour of living and eternal light!
Who would not seem – though pale from studying
deep in Parnassian shade, whose wells he drinks –

142  still to be much encumbered in his mind,
endeavouring to draw what you then seemed,
where heavens in harmony alone enshadow you,

145  as you came forth and showed yourself in air?

# CANTO 32

My eyes were now so fixedly intent                                    1*
to free themselves from that decade-long thirst
that every sense but sight had been eclipsed.

This side and that, my eyes were walled about         4
with 'I-don't-care-at-all' (the holy smile
so drew them to it with its age-old net!),

when, by sheer force, my face was turned around     7
towards my left by all those deities,
hearing from them a 'Far too fixedly!'

And that debility that's found in eyes                        10
when just now stricken by a blinding sun
here left me, for some moments, without sight.

But when my eye refocused on the less                      13
(the 'less' I mean in contrast to that great
thing seen from which, with strain, I'd turned away)

the glorious army had, I saw, right-wheeled –        16
those seven flames ahead – to face the sun,
and so to make its march towards the east.

As, to protect itself, a squadron turns,                      19
wheeling beneath its shields around the flag,
till every man has made a turnabout,

so, too, those troops of that celestial realm             22
that marched in front went by us, rank by rank,
before the chariot had turned its pole.

The *donne* then went back beside its wheels.           25
The Gryphon drew its blessèd burden on.
And not a single feather stirred or fell.

28      The lovely one who'd drawn me through the pass,
        Statius and I now followed – at that wheel
        which, in its orbit, traced the lesser arc.

31      So passing through that deep yet empty grove
        (the fault of her who trusted in the snake),
        our steps were measured to the angel song.

34      The distance that, perhaps, we travelled so,
        was three flights of an arrow when discharged.
        And Beatrice now, at last, came down.

37      I heard them murmur 'Adam', all as one.
        And then they circled round a leafless tree.
        Its every branch was stripped of greenery.

40      The crested peak which broadens out the more
        the more it rises, would, for height, inspire
        wonder in Hindus in their own great woods.

43      'Blessèd are you, the Gryphon. With your beak
        you did not spoil this wood, so sweet to taste.
        For, after tasting, bellies writhe, all sick.'

46      Around the mighty tree they made this cry.
        And then the creature, two-formed in its birth:
        'In this way, all that's true and just is saved.'

49      Then, turned towards the pole he'd drawn before,
        towards the foot of that long-widowed sprig,
        he tugged it and then left it bound to that.

52      Compare: in spring the great light of the sun
        cascades on earthly trees conjoined with that
        which shines out following the astral Carp.

55      These trees then swell. The colour is renewed,
        in each and all, before the sun moves on
        to yoke its horses to some other star.

58      So did this tree, whose boughs had hung bereft,
        take on new strength, in colour opening
        to more than violet and to less than rose.

61      I did not understand (it's not sung here)
        the hymn these people sang, nor could I bear
        in full the beauty of its harmonies.

If I could trace the drowsiness that came 64
on hearing Syrinx sung to ruthless eyes –
those eyes that wakefulness cost very dear –

  then, from that model, as a painter paints, 67
I'd draw in my design how I now slept.
But that needs someone who can feign sleep well.

  So I speed on to when I came awake, 70
and say how splendour tore apart sleep's veil
and this cry: 'Rise! What *are* you doing there?'

  When brought to see the budding apple flowers 73
which make the angels greedy for their fruit,
and makes in Heaven perpetual marriage feast,

  Peter and James and John were overcome 76
but, waking once again, they heard that word
which shattered greater sleeps than theirs had been,

  and saw the school they'd sat in two souls short – 79
since Moses and Elijah both had gone –
their teacher with his robe now much transformed.

  So, too, I woke, and saw, above me there, 82
the one who in compassion led my steps
along the river sometime earlier.

  And, full of doubt, I said: 'Where's Beatrice?' 85
At which, 'See there,' she said, 'beneath the leaves –
now new – she's seated on the root of that.

  And see the company that encircles her! 88
The rest behind the Gryphon go on high,
singing a deeper, ever sweeter song.'

  And if her speech flowed further on than this, 91
I do not know. My eyes were set, by now,
on her. She'd closed my mind to other thoughts.

  Alone, she sat upon that one true earth 94
as guard, left there to watch the chariot
which, as I'd seen, the two-form beast had tied.

  The seven nymphs encloistered her around 97*
and in their hands all carried lights, secure
from Aquilonian or Austral winds.

100     'With me a while you'll be a woodsman here
and then, with me, a citizen eternally
in that new Rome where Christ is Roman, too.

103     And so, to aid the world that lives all wrong,
keep your eyes firmly on the chariot.
And what you see write down when you go back.'

106     Thus Beatrice. I myself, devout,
touching the feet of all that she ordained,
gave eye and mind to where she said I should.

109*     No fire that rains from regions farthest off
has, from the densest vapours, struck
as rapidly in motion as I saw

112     the Eagle, bird of Jupiter, swoop down
straight through the tree, to rip off all its bark –
the flowers as well, and all its new green leaves.

115     It struck the chariot with all its force,
making it lurch – a ship in jeopardy,
vanquished by windward and then leeward gusts.

118     Within the cradle of the Victory Car
I saw a vixen headlong hurl herself,
starving, it seemed, for any healthy food.

121     And yet, reproving all her loathsome faults,
my lady sent that vixen off in flight –
or such flight as her fleshless bones could bear.

124     But then from where the Eagle first had come,
I saw it swoop down on the chariot-ark
and leave it feathered as it was itself.

127     And then, as coming from some grieving heart,
a voice came from the heavens. This voice said:
'My little ship, what ill load weighs you down!'

130     And then, it seemed, the earth beneath both wheels
gaped wide. I saw a dragon coming out
that thrust its tail deep in the Chariot.

133     And then, as wasps do, drawing out their sting,
so did the dragon its malignant tail –
tearing out planks – then went off, wandering.

What wood remained, like grass in living earth,    136
with eagle feathers – offered, as may be
with generous purpose kindly meant to heal –
    covered itself once more and covered all,    139
both wheels and pole, within the time it takes
for open mouths to breathe the longest sigh.

    Then, so transformed, the sacred structure sent    142
new heads out all along its many parts,
three on the pole and one on all four sides.

    The first three heads were horned as oxen are.    145
The four, though, on their brows bore single horns.
No monster like this ever has been seen.

    As confident as strongholds in the hills,    148
sitting there now, a loose-wrapped whore appeared,
her flickering lashes quick to look around.

    And then I saw a giant standing by,    151
lest she should ever lift her eyes from him.
And every now and then these two would kiss.

    But since her wandering and cupidinous eye    154
was turned on me, that rabid paramour
whipped her ferociously from head to foot.

    Then, full of jealousy and raw, wild wrath,    157
he loosed the beast and led it through the wood,
so far the wood itself now formed a shield

    between the whore and weird new beast and me.    160

# CANTO 33

1*     *'Deus, venerunt gentes,'* – alternating
three, then four – the seven *donne*, weeping
gently, sweetly, began to chant that psalm.

4     And Beatrice, sighing in compassion,
listened and changed, to hear them, hardly less
than Mary did when she stood by the Cross.

7     But when those other virgins granted her
a place to speak, she, rising to her feet,
responded, fiery in her colour, thus:

10     *'Modicum, et non videbitis me;*
*et iterum*, my most beloved sisters,
*modicum, et vos videbitis me.'*

13     She then sent all those seven on ahead
and, with one gesture, brought along behind
myself, the lady and the sage who'd stayed.

16     And so she went her way, but had not placed
her tenth step on the earth (or so I think)
before her glance had pierced me, eye to eye.

19     And, calm in countenance, 'Come on. Be quick,
so if I choose,' she said, 'to speak to you,
you'll be well placed to hear what I may say.'

22     As soon as I was with her, as I ought,
'Dear brother, now you're walking by my side,
why don't you seek to question me?' she said.

25     It happened now to me (it often does
to those too reverent with superiors,
who can't get living voice behind their teeth)

that I began without a full, clear sound:     28
'My lady, what your need is, you well know,
and also what is good to meet that need.'

And she to me: 'From dread and shame alike,     31*
I'd have you now at once unknot yourself,
so you no longer speak as in a dream.

Know this: the vessel that the serpent broke     34
was and is not. But let the guilty one
be sure God's vengeance need not fear grave-sops.

The eagle, leaving feathers on the Cart –     37
through which it, first, was monster then the prey –
will not for ever be without an heir.

I see with certainty, and therefore say     40
that stars, secure from obstacle or bar,
are drawing near to give to us the hour

in which will come FIVE HUNDRED TEN AND FIVE     43
as messenger of God to slay that thief –
the giant, too, whom she makes mischief with.

It may be that my narrative – as dark     46*
as those of Themis and the Sphinx – will blunt
(as theirs did), not persuade your intellect.

Yet real events will soon prove Naiades,     49
who'll free you from this enigmatic knot
yet bring no harm to grazing sheep or grain.

Note well. And, as these words are borne from me,     52
inscribe them for a sign to those who live
the life that rapidly runs on to death.

And take good care, when you write all this down,     55
that you don't hide how you have seen the tree,
twice over now, stripped bare and robbed of green.

Whoever steals from it, or tears its trunk     58
blasphemes, by doing so, against the God
who made it sacred for His use alone.

Five thousand years and more, the first of souls –     61
condemned to yearning pain for biting it –
hungered for Him whose own self scourged that bite.

64      Your wits lie sleeping if you do not judge
that soaring height, inverted at the top,
to be occasioned by some unique cause.

67*      And if, around your mind, your own vain thoughts
had not been calcifying Elsa streams,
their joys like Pyramus to mulberries,

70      then, from its many attributes alone,
you, in this allegory, might well have seen
that tree to be God's justice known in bans.

73      But since I see that you, in intellect,
are turned to stone and petrified, pure black,
hence dazzled by the light of what I say,

76      I wish, as well, that you'll bear this within –
at least as image, not yet written script –
as pilgrims bring their staves back wreathed with palms.'

79      And I: 'No less than wax, I'll bear the print
and never change the shape impressed on it,
seeing my brain has now been signed by you.

82      But why so far above my powers of sight
does your word, so much longed for, take its flight
so that the more it strives it loses more?'

85*      'I ask,' she said, 'so you will know how far
that school of yours can follow what I say,
and see what its philosophy can do,

88      and also that you see how all your ways
diverge, as distant from the ways of God
as your world is, untuned, from swiftest spheres.'

91      'I cannot call to mind,' I answered her,
'that I have ever been estranged from you.
My conscience sets sharp teeth in me for that.'

94      'And if you cannot bring that back to mind,'
smiling, she answered me, 'then just recall
you've drunk, this very day, from Lethe's stream.

97      And if, when smoke appears, it proves there's fire,
then this oblivion will itself conclude
that guilt once drew your will away, elsewhere.

My words must be as naked, after this,                                    100
as far as they may fittingly unveil
themselves to your as-yet-untutored sight.'

Its spark more brilliant and with slower step,                           103*
the sun now held the circle of the noon,
which moves (from what one sees) from side to side,

when, stopping – as a guide will stop, who goes                          106
before the rest as escort if he finds
some novelty or traces of the strange –

the *donne* reached the edges of that shade                              109
cast, as in mountains, over chilly streams
beneath green leaves and boughs of ebony.

Ahead of them, as from a single spring,                                  112
it seemed I saw the Tigris and Euphrates
rise and then part, like friends, reluctantly.

'You light and glory of the human race,                                  115
what are these waters that, from one sole source,
rise up then, spreading, distance each from each?'

To this demand: 'Best ask,' the answer came,                            118
'Matelda. She'll reply to you.' She did –
meaning, it seemed, to free herself from blame,

saying, that lovely lady: 'I have told him why.                         121
Both this – I'm sure of it – and other things
are not concealed from him by Lethe's stream.'

And Beatrice: 'Maybe greater cares –                                     124
which often take the memory away –
have made his mind grow darker in its view.

But see Eunoe, which is flowing there.                                   127
Lead him to that. And, as you always do,
bring back his fainting, half-dead powers to life.'

As noble souls incline to do – they make                                130
another's will, without excuse, *their* will
as soon as any sign of that appears –

so, too, when I was taken by the hand,                                   133
the lovely lady made her way and said
to Statius, as a *donna* does: 'Come, too.'

136    If, reader, I'd more space in which to write,
       then I should sing in part about that drink,
       so sweet I'd never have my fill of it.

139    However, since these pages now are full,
       prepared by rights to take the second song,
       the reins of art won't let me pass beyond.

142    I came back from that holiest of waves
       remade, refreshed as any new tree is,
       renewed, refreshed with foliage anew,

145        pure and prepared to rise towards the stars.

# *Commedia* Cantica 3: *Paradiso*

# CANTO 1

Commedia Cantica
Paradiso

1*    Glory, from Him who moves all things that are,
penetrates the universe and then shines back,
reflected more in one part, less elsewhere.

4*    High in that sphere which takes from Him most light
I was – I was! – and saw things there that no one
who descends knows how or ever can repeat.

7    For, drawing near to what it most desires,
our intellect so sinks into the deep
no memory can follow it that far.

10    As much, though, truly of that holy realm
as I could keep as treasure in my mind
will now become the substance of my song.

13*    O high Apollo, in this final work, make me
a vessel of your worth as fine as you
demand, in granting longed-for laurel crowns.

16    So far, one summit of Parnassus' heights
has been enough. In this arena, though,
the task, as I now enter, calls for both.

19    Enter my heart and breathe in me, as when
you flayed defeated Marsyas, and drew
that satyr and his limbs from sheathing skin.

22    If you can lend me, from your holy power,
enough so I may manifest the shade
of that rejoicing realm which marks my head,

25    then to the foot of your beloved bough
I'll come and crown myself with victory leaves –
as you and this great theme will fit me to.

So seldom (fault and shame of human wills!) 28
are these leaves, greatest Father, gathered up
to celebrate an emperor or poet.

If any, thirsting, freely seeks these fronds 31
(peneian-branched) there must be, in that joyful
deity of Delphi, joy born anew.

A minute spark precedes a towering flame. 34
Others may be who, after me, will pray
with better voice towards Apollo's hill.

Rising, the beacon of the world will come 37*
to mortal eyes through many estuaries,
but shines where four spheres join three cruciforms

with better impetus and better stars, 40
all in conjunction, and, with its own mark,
more clearly seals and tempers earthly wax.

That surge of sun made morning there, dusk here, 43
and all that hemisphere was almost white
while, equally, this other part was dark,

when Beatrice turned, as I saw now, 46
towards her left and, turning, set her eyes –
no eagle so intent – towards the sun.

As any falcon's searching flight will dive, 49*
then strike back up, or else like reflex rays,
which, angled from the first, return on high,

so, too, her gesture, pouring through my gaze 52
into imagination, made me turn
and fix my eyes – beyond our norm – straight at the sun.

Much is permitted there that here, on earth, 55
is not permitted to our human powers,
thanks to that place made, properly, our own.

I could not bear it long yet did not fail 58
to see, in that brief time, sparks fly around,
as iron from a fire when brought to boil.

Then suddenly it seemed that day and day 61
were joined, as though – adorned by Him who can –
the skies were lighted by a second sun.

64    Beatrice remained, her eyes fixed wholly
on the eternal wheels. And my bright glance,
turned back from that above, I fixed on her.

67*   Held in her look, I, inwardly, was made
what Glaucus, tasting grass, was made to be,
consorting with the other ocean gods.

70    To give (even in Latin phrase) a meaning
to 'transhuman' can't be done. For those whom grace
will grant experience, let my case serve.

73*   Whether I was no more than soul (which love,
in governing the spheres, made lastly new),
You know, who raised me up through Your pure light.

76*   When that great wheel – which You, desired by that,
make sempiternal – had, with harmonies
proportionate and clear, made me attend,

79    the skies of Heaven, it seemed to me, blazed out
so lit by solar flame no lake on earth,
flooded by rain or river, spread so wide.

82    The newness of the sound and that great light
kindled in me desire to know the cause
sharper than any I have ever felt.

85    And she who saw me as I am, at this,
to bring some calm to my excited mind,
before I asked her, opening her lips,

88    began to speak: 'With false imaginings
you make yourself so dull you fail to see
what, shaking off this cloud, you'd see quite well.

91    You are not still on earth as you suppose.
No thunderbolt that flees its proper place
ran at such speed as you return to yours.'

94    If I, by these brief, smiling words of hers,
was disinvested of initial doubt,
then now by new and greater I was caught.

97    'I rest content,' I said, 'in utmost wonder.
So *requievi*. Yet I wonder now
how *I* climb through these light embodiments.'

At this, in deep, affectionate concern,     100
she sighed and set her eyes on me,
as mothers do when silly sons rave on.

'There is,' she now began, 'an ordered ratio     103*
between all things there are. It's this – such *form* –
that makes the universe resemble God.

The highest creatures see the footprints there     106
of God's eternal prowess and his worth,
the end to which (as mentioned here) the rule is made.

Within the order I am speaking of,     109
all things, according to their kind, will veer
towards their origin, some near, some far.

Therefore, across the ocean of "to be",     112
all natures move towards their different ports,
each moved by import of a given drive.

One instinct bears the fire towards the moon.     115
Another moves all death-bound creatures on.
Another grips and unifies the earth.

Nor is it only such created things,     118
beyond intelligence, that this bow sends,
but also those possessed of love and mind.

The providence that integrates the whole     121*
makes limpid with its light that heavenly sphere
within which rolls the sphere of greatest speed.

It bears us now to our appointed place –     124
that bowstring with its power to aim aright
whatever it lets fly to happy targets.

It's true, though, just as, often, form will fail     127
to be attuned to what the art intends,
since matter, being deaf, will not respond,

so, too, a creature which can freely bend     130
will, sometimes, though impelled entirely straight,
desert that course and wander off elsewhere.

As lightning flashes fall from thunder clouds,     133
so likewise that first impetus strikes down,
wrenched wrong by false delight, towards earth.

136     You ought not, if I'm right, be more amazed
        at rising up than when you see a stream
        descending from a hill's crest to its base.

139     The wonder would, in your case be, when free
        of all impediment, you sat down there –
        as though live flames on earth were ever still.'

142     With this, she turned once more to face the sky.

# CANTO 2

You in that little boat who, listening hard,                    1
have followed, from desire to hear me through,
behind my bowsprit singing on its way,

now turn, look back and mark your native shores.               4
Do not set out upon these open seas
lest losing me you end confused and lost.

The waves I ride have never yet been crossed.                  7*
Minerva breathes. Apollo leads me on.
The nine bright Muses point the Ursa-stars.

You other few who have already stretched,                      10*
straight-necked, through time to reach for angel-bread
(the food we live by here, unsatisfied)

may to good purpose set your vessel out                        13
across the deep salt swell, and plough my wake
before the waters level once again.

The Argonauts, in glory, Colchis-bound,                        16*
were not so wonder-struck as you will be
when they saw Jason yoked-up to his plough.

In-born in being, our perpetual thirst                         19*
to reach the deiform domain now bore us on
as rapid, almost, as the spheres you see.

Beatrice looked up. I looked at her.                           22
Then maybe in the time an arrow takes
to hit the target, fly and slip the notch,

I saw I'd come where something marvellous                      25
tugged me in sight towards itself. So she
(no thought of mine could be concealed from her)

28 turning to me, as happy as lovely,
'Direct your mind in thanks,' she said, 'to God.
For he has made us one with this first star.'

31 To me it seemed a cloud now covered us,
shining and solid, dense and burnished clean,
almost as diamond when the sunlight strikes.

34 Into itself the eternal margarite
took us as water will receive a ray
of light, remaining, even so, all one.

37 If I was there in body (we can't grasp
how one dimension takes another in,
as – body snaked in body – needs must be)

40 that should ignite in us still more desire
to see that being where, as can be seen,
our human nature is at one with God.

43 There we shall see what here we hold in faith,
not argued through but known for what it is,
as is the primal truth that all believe.

46 'My lady, as devoutly as I can,
I offer Him all thanks,' I now replied,
'since He here parts me from the mortal world.

49* But tell me what those dark signs are that mark
the body of the moon? Down there on earth
some folk are led by these to speak of Cain.'

52 She smiled at this a little. Then she said:
'If mortals make mistakes in what they think
when sense won't turn the key of evidence,

55 no dart of wonder ought to pierce you through
when you observe, as now, that rational thought –
which has to follow sense – is weak of wing.

58 But tell me what your thoughts about this are.'
'That variance,' I said, 'so I believe,
results from matter being rare or dense.'

61 'Well,' she replied, 'you'll shortly come to see
how deeply out of true your thinking is.
If you'll attend, I'll put the counter case.

The constellations, wheeling, show you many 64
lights. And these, as one may easily discern,
present as different, both in size and kind.

If that were merely caused by "rare" and "dense" 67*
there'd be in all one single power of life,
distributed at par or more or less.

But virtues, in differing, have to be the fruits 70
of different formal principles. And these,
if you were right, would all, save one, be lost.

Consider, too: if rarity explained 73*
the dark that you have asked about, then either
in part this planet would be starved of stuff,

or else, as fat and lean are layered in meat, 76
so this, throughout its volume and extent,
would change as pages do within a book.

Suppose the first were true, then this would show 79
in all eclipses of the sun – as light
shines through, behaving as it does in rarities.

It doesn't. So let's take your second thought. 82
And if, maybe, I also prove this void,
then this will give the lie to all you've said.

If rarity does not extend throughout, 85
it must at some point terminate as, there,
its opposite prevents its onward path.

The second ray returning from that depth 88
reflects like coloured images in glass –
when glass has lead plate hidden at its back.

But now, you'll tell me, solar rays shed gloom 91
because in certain parts, at these set points,
the light, returning, breaks from further back.

Now if you'll try experiment – from which 94*
the rivers of your knowledge always flow –
from that objection you will free yourself.

Take three reflective surfaces. Move two 97
an equal distance off, the other more,
and set your eye between the former two.

100    Now facing them, arrange, behind your back,
a source of light to kindle all these three
so that it comes struck back to you from each.

103    Although the image in the further glass
is less extensive, you are bound to see
it shines back equal in intensity.

106    When warming sun rays strike a mass of snow,
aqueous valencies will then remain
naked of colour and their former chill.

109    Since you in intellect are like that now,
I want to form in you a light so live,
its shimmering look will tremble to your sight.

112*   Circling within the sphere of holy peace,
an astral body turns whose power sustains
the virtual life of all that it contains.

115    The next sphere (where so many stars are seen)
shares out such being into different modes,
each one distinct from, and contained in, that.

118    The seven spheres below in different ways
dispose the essences each has within
towards their proper *telos*, seed and aim.

121    These living organs of the world thus go,
as you can see them now, from grade to grade,
receiving from above, forming below.

124    Look closely at the steps I'll take from here
to reach the truth that you so much desire,
so you'll know how to cross this on your own.

127    Motion and virtue in these holy gyres
rightly draw breath (as hammer-skill from smith),
in turns deriving from angelic moves.

130    The sphere of stars, so fine with all its lights,
receives from that deep mind which rolls it round
the image that it has, then prints that seal.

133    And as your soul within the dust you are
diffuses and resolves through different limbs,
adapting thus to various powers of life,

so too angelic intellect unfolds                                        136
(while turning still round its own unity)
its goodness multiplied through all the stars.

So different virtue forms a different bond                              139
with all those precious bodies that it brings
to life – as life in you its strength is bound.

Deriving as it does from happy kind,                                    142
the virtue, fused with body, shines throughout,
as joy does in the pupil of the eye.

From *this* there comes – and not from rare or dense –                  145
apparent differences from light to light.
That is the formal principle that makes

(according to its goodness) clear and cloud.'                           148

# CANTO 3

| | |
|---|---|
| 1 | She – as the sun who first in love shone warm |
| | into my heart – had now, by proof and counterproof, |
| | disclosed to me the lovely face of truth. |
| 4 | And being ready, as was only right, |
| | to own my errors – and new certainties – |
| | I flung my head back, and I meant to speak. |
| 7 | But then, it seemed, a vision came to me |
| | and bound me up so tightly to itself |
| | that these confessions would not come to mind. |
| 10 | Compare: from clear and polished panes of glass, |
| | or else from glinting waters, calm and still |
| | (but not so deep their depths are lost in darkness), |
| 13 | we see reflections that reveal a hint, |
| | though faint, of our own looks and reach the eye |
| | less strongly than a pearl on some white brow. |
| 16* | So I saw many faces, keen to speak, |
| | and ran now to the opposite mistake |
| | from that which fired the love of man and stream. |
| 19 | No sooner had I noticed – and supposed |
| | that these were seemings in a looking-glass – |
| | I turned my eyes to see who these might be. |
| 22 | I saw there nothing, so returned my glance |
| | straight to the shining-out of my dear guide, |
| | who, smiling at me, blazed in her own look. |
| 25 | 'You baby!' she said. 'Don't worry or wonder, |
| | to see me smile at all these ponderings. |
| | Those feet are not yet steady on the ground of truth. |

Your mind, from habit, turns round to a void.     28
And yet those beings that you see are true,
bound here below for vows they disavowed.

So speak to them. And hear and trust their words.     31
The light of truth that feeds them with its peace
will never let their feet be turned awry.'

Now turning to the shadow who most yearned,     34*
in love and pure delight, to speak to me,
I said, nearly entranced by eagerness:

'You spirit, well created in the rays     37
of this eternity of life, you feel
a sweetness never known, if not by taste.

Then let me, in your kindness, hear your name,     40
and tell me what all here are destined for.'
To which – eyes smiling – she at once replied:

'We, living in God's love, can no more lock     43
our doors against true-minded aims of will
than God's love does, which wills this court like him.

I was a virgin sister in the world.     46
Search deep in memory. My being now
more beautiful won't hide me from your eyes.

I am Piccarda – as you'll know I am –     49
and blessed among the many who are blessed,
within this slowest moving of the spheres.

The flames of what we feel are lit in us     52
by pleasure purely in the Holy Spirit,
dancing for happiness in that design.

And though the part allotted us may seem     55
far down, the reason is that, yes, we did
neglect our vows. These were in some part void.'

'A wonder shining in the look you have     58
reveals,' I said, 'an I-don't-know of holiness
that alters you from how you once were seen.

So recognition did not speed to mind.     61
Yet all you say has helped me understand.
Your image speaks precisely to me now.

64      But tell me this: you are so happy here,
        have you no wish to gain some higher grade,
        to see and be as friends to God still more?'

67      Smiling a moment with the other shades,
        she then, in utmost happiness, replied,
        blazing, it seemed, in the first fires of love:

70*     'Dear brother, we in will are brought to rest
        by power of *caritas* that makes us will
        no more than what we have, nor thirst for more.

73      Were our desire to be more highly placed,
        all our desires would then be out of tune
        with His, who knows and wills where we should be.

76      Yet discord in these spheres cannot occur –
        as you, if you reflect on this, will see –
        since charity is *a priori* here.

79      In formal terms, our being in beatitude
        entails in-holding to the will of God,
        our own wills thus made one with the divine.

82      In us, therefore, there is, throughout this realm,
        a placing, rung to rung, delighting all
        – our king as well in-willing us in will.

85*     In His volition is the peace we have.
        That is the sea to which all being moves,
        be it what that creates or Nature blends.'

88      Now it was clear. I saw that everywhere
        in Paradise there's Heaven, though grace may rain
        in varied measure from the Highest Good.

91      But then, as often happens over food
        (though satisfied with one, we crave the next,
        reaching for that while still we're saying 'thanks'),

94      so now in word and gesture I betrayed
        an eagerness to hear from her what weave
        her spool had not yet drawn out to the end.

97*     'Perfect in life, her merits raised on high,
        there is a lady – more in-heavened than we –
        who wrote, on earth, a Rule of dress and veil,

that lets its wearer sleep and wake till death  100
beside a husband who accepts those vows
that charity conforms to his delight.

To follow her, I fled – a girl, no more –  103
out of the world. I pulled her cowl to me,
and promised my obedience to that Rule.

Men now arrived, more set on harm than good.  106
They dragged me from the cloister I had loved,
and God well knows what then my life became.

But, over to my right, there shows to you  109
another splendour who, enkindled now
with all the light that gathers in our sphere,

knows from her own life what I say of mine.  112
She was our sister. And from her head, too,
was torn the shadow of her pure, white hood.

This is the light of Constance, that high queen  115*
who bore to Swabia's second storm a son,
the third – and ultimate – of that great line.

And yet – although against her will, against  118
all decency – she went back to the world,
she never let the veil fall from her heart.'

Those were her words to me. But then 'Ave  121
Maria' began, singing. And, singing,
she went from sight, as weight sinks deep in water.

My eyes pursued as far as eyesight can,  124
but, as I lost her, so I turned once more
to target a desire far greater still.

Now all my thoughts were fixed on Beatrice.  127
But she, as lightning strikes, so stunned my gaze,
my eyes at first could not support the sight,

and this was why my question came so slow.  130

# CANTO 4

1*     Between two equidistant portions, equally
moving, if free to choose, you'd starve to death
before you'd carried either to your teeth.

4     So, too, some lamb might stand between the bite
of hungry wolves, fearing them both alike.
So, too, a hound would stand between two does.

7     If, therefore, I kept silence now, I neither
criticize nor praise myself. Driven by doubts
of equal measure, this was necessity.

10     I still kept silent. Yet my keen desire
was painted – and my questions, too – within my eyes,
warmer by far than well-formed words could speak.

13*     So Beatrice did as Daniel did
to free Nebuchadnezzar from the rage
that made him cruel beyond all rational need.

16     'I clearly see,' she said, 'how two desires
fret you as you take aim. Your own concerns
constrain themselves. You cannot breathe them out.

19     Your thinking runs: "If will-to-good endures,
how, then, can violence wrought by other hands
reduce in me the measure of desert?"

22*     A further reason for your doubt is this:
our souls return, or so it may appear,
as Plato in his teaching says, to stars.

25     These are the questions that, with equal weight,
point, in volition, hard upon your mind.
I'll first treat that which is more poisonous.

The most in-god-ed of the Seraphim,                    28*
Moses and Samuel – and either John
you care to mention – even Maria,
    none is enthroned in any other sphere          31
than those souls are who've just appeared to you.
Nor are their years, existing, more or less.
    All add in beauty to the highest gyre.        34*
Some sense the eternal breathing more, some less.
So life is sweet to all in differing ways.
    They did, here, show themselves, but not because   37
this sphere has been allotted them as theirs.
They signify celestial power least raised.
    To speak in this way fits the human mind.     40
For you can only grasp through things you've sensed
what mind will then present as fit for thought.
    For this same reason, Scripture condescends    43
to your capacities, and says that God
has hands and feet – though meaning otherwise.
    So, Holy Church will also represent            46
Michael and Gabriel with human face,
the other, too, who helped heal Tobit's sight.
    But Plato in *Timaeus* "On the soul"           49
argues a case at odds with that seen here.
For what he says, it seems, has literal force.
    He says that souls go back to their own stars,  52
believing them to be excised from these,
when Nature granted each its proper form.
    This doctrine, though, perhaps conceals a sense  55
quite other than these words of his pronounce,
with implications we should not deride.
    If Plato means that, back to join these wheels,  58
there comes the blame or honour of their power,
perhaps his bow shot hits upon some truth.
    And yet, misunderstood, this principle         61
wrenched almost all the world off course. So Jove
and Mars and Mercury were named as gods.

64*    The other doubt, so troubling you, is not
       as venomous. The injury it does
       can't lead you elsewhere and away from me.

67     That justice in our realm, to mortal eyes,
       should seem unjust concerns you in regard
       to faith. It's not some vicious heresy.

70     But since you have the subtlety of mind
       yourself to penetrate the truth of this,
       I shall, since you desire it, tell you all.

73     If "violence" is done when those who're harmed
       bring nothing of their own to outside force,
       these souls, though blessèd, aren't exempt from blame.

76     Free will, unless it wills, cannot be quenched
       but acts like Nature in a rising flame
       even though torn by force a thousand times.

79     But if it bends – whatever the degree –
       it follows force. These women, though they could
       have fled to holy ground, did bend like this.

82     Had they, in what they willed, stood absolute,
       as did Saint Lawrence on the burning coals,
       or Mucius – harsh towards his own right hand –

85     their wills would then have thrust them, once released,
       back on the road from which they'd just been drawn.
       But will as firm as that is very rare.

88     These words (suppose you've listened as you ought)
       will leave the case regarding what is just
       – which often would have irked you – null and void.

91     Yet now, across the path before your eyes,
       appears another obstacle. And you yourself –
       you'd quickly tire – could not get free from this.

94     I've fixed within your mind this certainty:
       that souls in Paradise can never lie.
       They all are, always, close to primal truth.

97     But then you might have heard Piccarda say
       that Constance kept her heart set on the veil,
       And so, it seems, she contradicts me here.

It has, my dearest brother, often been     100
that things, in fleeing danger, have been done,
counter to choice, that were not right to do,
   as when, responding to his father's prayer,     103*
Alcmaeon slew his mother for revenge,
and, not to fail in piety, proved pitiless.
   I want you, in such cases, to be clear     106
that will conjoins with violence. And so,
for these offences there is no excuse.
   Will does not, in the absolute, consent to harm.     109
It does consent, however, in degrees of fear,
lest, drawing back, it falls to more distress.
   So when Piccarda makes the point she does,     112
she means the will as absolute while I
intend the other. We, as one, speak truth.'
   These waves came flooding from that holy stream     115
that rises at the source of every truth.
As such, they set my two desires to rest.
   'Goddess, belovèd of the loving First!     118
Your words in waves,' I said, 'flow into me.
They warm me through, and light me more and more.
   No feeling I possess is deep enough     121
to make return to you, in grace for grace.
But He who sees – and can – will answer so.
   I see full well that human intellect     124
can never be content unless that truth
beyond which no truth soars shines down on it.
   When once they come to it, as come they may,     127
minds couch in truth as beasts do in their lairs.
Were that not so, then all desire would fail.
   Born of that will, there rise up, like fresh shoots,     130
pure doubts. These flourish at the foot of truth.
From height to height, they drive us to the peak.
   This beckons me. This makes me very sure     133
that I, my lady, may in reverence seek
another truth that still is dark to me.

136   I want to know if we can make amends
with other goods when vows go unfulfilled,
so these will not seem meagre in your scale.'

139   Now Beatrice looked at me with eyes all full
of sparks of speaking love, and so divine
that, overwhelmed, I turned my back on her

142   and, eyes bowed down, I almost lost myself.

# CANTO 5

'If I flame out in warmth of love to you                                    1
beyond all measure that is seen on earth,
and so defeat the prowess of your eyes,
   don't wonder why. This light in me proceeds           4
from perfect sight, which, once it apprehends
the good, will dance on, apprehending that.
   Already I see well in your own mind                          7
the mirrored splendour of eternal light
which seen will kindle – only, always – love.
   And if your love is teased to other things,            10
then these are nothing but the merest trace,
ill understood, of that light shining through.
   You wish to know if, when a vow falls short,       13
some other service might be rendered up
to keep that soul secure from legal charge.'
   So Beatrice's song began this canto,                        16
and then, as one who makes no break in speech,
continued in the sacred process thus:
   'The greatest gift that God, in spacious deed,    19*
made, all-creating – and most nearly formed
to His liberality, most prized by Him –
   was liberty in actions of the will,                             22
with which all creatures of intelligence –
and they alone – both were and are endowed.
   Now there'll appear, if you pursue this thought,  25
the value and nobility of vows,
when framed so God's consent consents with yours.

28       For in a pact confirmed by God and man
the treasured gift I speak of is itself
made sacrifice, made thus by its own act.

31       And so what restitution can there be?
You think you'll make good use of what you gave?
Well, that's to try good works with stolen cash.

34       So now you're certain of the major point.
But since our Holy Church can loose a vow –
which seems quite counter to the truth I've told –

37       you'll need to sit a while more at this feast.
The meat that you have taken on is tough.
It needs some help if you're to get it down.

40       Open your mind to what I'll now declare
and grasp it inwardly. To understand
won't count as knowledge if it's not retained.

43       Essential in a sacrificial vow
are two considerations: what we'll *do*,
then, formally, the fact that we *agree*.

46       *Per se*, agreements, save when carried through,
cannot be nullified. And that, above,
was what, precisely, was made clear to you.

49*      The Hebrews of necessity were thus
required to make appropriate offerings,
though some, as you should know, were modified.

52       The second aspect ("substance", as defined)
may properly be varied, so no blame
attaches in the change to other things.

55       Do not, though, shift the burden from your back
by any mere decision of your own.
A priest must turn both white and yellow keys.

58       All changes – please believe – are idiotic
unless the principle and substitute
stand in a ratio of four to six.

61       When first vows, therefore, are of so much weight
that they, in value, twist the scales awry,
one cannot quit the charge by substitutes.

So mortals should not take facetious oaths. 64\*
Be faithful. But in being so, don't squint –
like Jephthah, pledging his "good day" to death.

Better for him if he had said: "I'm wrong," 67
than do worse doing it. Stupid as well,
the chieftain of the Greeks, as you can see.

For him, in sacrifice, Iphigenia rinsed 70
her lovely face in tears, and caused to weep
both foolish men and wise at such observances.

Christians, be weightier in moving vows. 73
Don't flutter on every breeze like feathers.
And don't suppose that every vow will cleanse.

You have the Testaments, both Old and New, 76
a shepherd in the Church to be your guide.
That is enough for your salvation here.

If wrongful appetites yell otherwise, 79\*
you are still human, not such brain-dead sheep
as make the Jews among you laugh aloud.

Don't imitate those silly, wayward lambs 82
who wander from their mother's milk, and fight
only against themselves for sheer delight.'

So Beatrice (as I write) to me. 85
And then she, all desiring, turned once more
to where the universe shines liveliest.

Her saying nothing now and changing look 88
imposed a silence on my avid mind,
which had already new demands ahead.

And so, as when some arrow hits its mark 91
before the string that shot it comes to rest,
we ran on swiftly to the second realm.

And here, on entering that heavenly light, 94
I, on the instant, saw in her such joy
the star itself at that shone brighter still.

And if the planet changed its form and laughed, 97
then what of me, being, as mortals are,
so prone in every way to transmutation.

100     Compare: in fish pools that are still and clear,
        the fish are drawn – as though they guess at food –
        to anything that comes there from outside.

103     So now I saw a thousand splendours plus
        drawing towards us. And in each was heard:
        'Look there! He'll make our many loves grow more.'

106     And then, as each came near to us, each shade
        was seen – within the flash of clarity
        that came from each – full of pure happiness.

109     Readers, just think if what we've now begun
        did not go on, what torment it would be
        to hunger, wanting further information.

112     Imagine that, and then you, too, will see
        my great desire, when these came to my eyes,
        to hear from them what their conditions were.

115     'O you, born well! To you is granted grace
        to see the thrones of triumph in eternity
        before your soldiership on earth is done.

118     The ray that soars through all these heavenly skies
        sets us ablaze. And so, if you desire
        clear words concerning us, please take your fill.'

121*    These words were uttered by one holy soul.
        From Beatrice: 'Speak! Just get it said.
        Be confident. Believe them as though gods.'

124     'You make your nest, as I can see, within
        a light that, drawn from your own eyes,
        is yours alone. It glitters as you smile.

127     But still I do not know, you honoured soul,
        who you all are, why ranked in Mercury,
        the sphere that sun rays veil from mortal eyes.'

130     I spoke directly to that source of light,
        the first to speak to me. And this itself now shone
        with far more brilliance than it did before.

133     Compare: the sun, when heat has worn away
        the tempering influence of a vapour cloud,
        conceals itself in overwhelming light.

So now, in greater joy, that holy form                    136
hid himself from me in his own bright ray
and, thus enclosed, enclosed he spoke to me
    to chant the chant the following canto sings.          139

# CANTO 6

1*     'Since Constantine first turned the Eagle's flight
against the path, east–west, that Heaven's course takes,
(once followed by the Patriarch who chose, as wife,

4          Lavinia) a hundred years and then a hundred more,
God's bird had kept to Europe's farthest bounds,
close by the mountains of its origin.

7          Under the shadow of its sacred plumes,
from hand to hand it governed all the world,
and came by due succession into mine.

10          I, emperor once, am now Justinian.
And by the will of primal love – which I know here –
I purged our laws of emptiness and dross.

13*          Before I set my mind upon this work,
I'd thought of Christ as single and divine –
not truly man – contented in that faith.

16          But then the blessed Agapetus – shepherd
supreme – led me, by words of his, aright,
to find pure faith, unsullied and complete.

19          I trusted him, believed him, and now see
what he in faith upheld – as clear as you,
by logic, prove one thought is false, one true.

22          As soon as I walked onward with the Church,
then God so pleased, through grace, to breathe in me
the great design on which I set all thought.

25          My troops I gave in trust to Belisarius
and Heaven's right hand allied itself with his.
These triumphs were a sign to settle thus.

This answer punctuates your first demand.     28
But, even so, these words imply much more.
I'm therefore bound to add a further note,
   so you can see how right those are (Oh yes!     31*
So right!) to move against that holiest of signs,
to challenge it or claim it as their own.

   Look at its powers! These make all reverence due,     34
these virtues that were born in that same hour
when, dying, Pallas gained the Sign its realm.

   The Eagle dwelt in Alba (as you'll know)     37
three hundred years or more until, at last,
Three fought with three, to win that Sign for Rome.

   You also know what deeds, through seven reigns,     40
the great sign wrought (the Sabine wound,
Lucretia's grief), defeating tribes around.

   You know its exploits, borne by Roman pride,     43
against the Brenner Gaul and Pyrrhus, too,
against all other princedoms, states or guilds.

   Torquatus, Quintus (known, for unkempt hair,     46
as "Tousel-head"), the Decii and Fabians,
all these won fame which here I gladly laud.

   The Eagle, too, laid low the Arab boast     49
that passed, in steps that followed Hannibal,
the alpine cliffs from which, great Po, you glide.

   Beneath that Sign, young Scipio won his crown,     52
young Pompey, too. And bitter it appeared
to that great hill beneath which you were born.

   Then near the time when all the heavens willed     55
to lead the world back to serenity,
Caesar, by will of Rome, took up the Sign.

   And then Isère and Loire and Seine beheld,     58
from Var to Rhine, what that could do – and all
those streaming valleys that supply the Rhône.

   And then it left Ravenna and achieved,     61
leaping the Rubicon, such things in flight
that neither tongue nor pen could seek to trace.

64     Next, towards Spain it swung its warrior might,
then to Durazzo in Albania.
It struck Farsalia. And hot Nile felt the pain.

67     Atandros, then, and Simois (whence it sprang)
it saw once more, and Hector's resting place.
And then to Ptolemy's harm it shook its wings,

70     then fell on Juba, flashing thunder bolts.
From there it turned towards your western realms
and heard Pompean trumpets sounding there.

73     For all it bore through its next stewardship,
Brutus in Hell and Cassius both bark.
And Modena – Perugia, too – once grieved for that.

76     Sad Cleopatra also weeps for it.
By snake bite, fleeing as that Sign advanced,
she met her sudden and atrocious death.

79     Then, carried in Augustus' hand, it ran
towards the Red Sea coast and brought such peace
to all the world that Janus's shrine was locked.

82     Yet everything that Sign (which moves my speech)
had done till now, or then went on to do,
throughout the mortal realm that lies in thrall,

85     is seemingly but little and obscure
if now, clear-sightedly, with heart made pure,
you look in wonder at Tiberius' hands.

88     For, to the hands of that third emperor,
the Living Justice that inspires me now
granted the glory to avenge His ire.

91     Now look in wonder at my counter charge:
the Sign then ran, in Titus's reign, to take
due vengeance for the ancient sin avenged.

94     And when the godless teeth of Lombard hordes
bit deep in Holy Church, then Charlemagne,
victorious beneath its wings, brought aid.

97     You can now pass a judgement on all those,
with all their faults, whom I accused above,
the cause of all the ills that fall on you.

Some set, against that universal Sign,                          100
their tinsel lilies, while the rest will claim
the Sign's their own. Hard, this: who's more to blame?
Let them go on, the Ghibellines, and ply                        103
their craft beneath some other sign than this.
All, prising it from justice, serve it ill.
Nor let the Guelfs of upstart Charles Anjou                     106
assail that Sign but rather fear those claws
that ripped the hide from prouder whelps than these.
Children, as often happens, rue in tears                        109
the crimes their fathers did. Don't think that God
will change his lawful arms to lily flowers.
This little star is finely fitted out                           112
with souls who, noble in their deeds, still sought
that fame and honour should live after them.
But when desires incline to aim at that,                        115
the rays of truthful love – thus wandering off –
must needs incline, above, to lesser life.
To calculate the balance, though, between                       118
reward and merit is a part, for us,
of happiness, seeing there's neither more nor less.
Thus Living Justice sweetly shapes and fits                     121
a longing for the good within our hearts,
so this cannot be wrenched to any wrong.
As, differing, voices sing a sweet-tuned chord,                 124
so, too, in our life here, from differing thrones,
sweet harmonies are sent through all these wheels.
And here, within this pearl that flowers for you,               127*
there shines the shining light of Romeo,
whose deeds, so fine and good, were ill-received.
Those lords, though, of Provence, opposed to him,               130
well, they've no cause. They'll come to grief,
taking amiss another's virtuous deeds.
Four daughters had he, Raymond Berengar.                        133
Each was a queen. And everything was done
by Romeo, that strange and humble traveller.

136    Then slanderous tongues led Raymond to demand
       a full account of this most honest man,
       who'd paid him back for ten at seven plus five.
139    So, destitute and aged, he left that shore.
       But if the world had only known his heart,
       begging his life away from crust to crust,
142    then, praise him as they do, they'd praise him more.'

# CANTO 7

'*Osanna, sanctus Deus sabaòth,*                    1*
*superillustrans claritate tua*
*felices ignes horum malacòth!*'

Thus – circling on himself, to his own tune –     4
was seen by me the singing of that *ens*,
a double light as two-ing over him.

Into their dance they moved, this light and all.    7
And then with utter speed, like sparks of fire,
they veiled themselves from me in sudden distance.

I, still in doubt, was saying: 'Tell her! Tell her!'   10*
within myself still saying: 'Tell my lady!
Her words drop sweet and take my thirst away.'

Yet awe of her – its power en-ladying           13
the whole of me, hearing no more than 'Be—' or '—ice' –
kept me, as though some drowsy soul, head down.

She did not suffer me to be so long,              16
but now began, arraying round me there
a smile to make men happy in Hell's fire:

'As I, to look at you, can tell unerringly,        19*
a doubt has fixed in you: how vengeance might,
in justice, fall on vengeance justly wrought?

But I shall quickly free your mind from knots.      22
Attend to me. The words I am to speak
will bring you doctrine of the greatest weight.

Because the unborn first of men would bear        25
no curb, for his own good, on power of will,
damning himself, he damned all born to him.

28      The human race, because of this, lay sick –
great error deepening down the centuries –
until it pleased the Logos to descend

31      to where our nature, long abandoning
its maker, was made one, as *person*, with Him,
by action solely of eternal love.

34      Now fix your eye on what we're now to say.
This nature, with its maker once at one,
once was, without addition, pure and good,

37      but then was banished of its own accord
from Paradise. For, of itself, it turned aside
from its own life, from truth – its proper road.

40      The sentence, therefore, that the Cross imposed,
if measured by the nature thus assumed,
was just and true. No pain was ever more.

43      Conversely, none, unjustly, did such harm,
considering what person bore the pain,
conjoined within a nature such as that.

46      Thus from the self-same act flowed different things.
One death delighted both the Jews and God.
At this earth trembled, Heaven opened wide.

49      You should not, therefore, find it hard to see
why vengeance, in itself completely just,
was then avenged by action of just court.

52      But now once more I see that mind of yours
is knotted up, and snags from thought to thought.
You wait in great desire to be set loose.

55      "I understand," you say, "what I have heard.
But this to me is hidden still, why God
for our redemption willed this way alone?"

58      That ordinance, dear brother, lies entombed,
unseen by anyone whose mind, as yet,
is immature, untempered by love's flame.

61      For all that – since so many aim at this,
yet very few are clear about their mark –
I'll tell you why that way was right and finest.

The generosity of God which scorns                          64
all spite and meanness burns within itself,
yet, flaring out, unfolds eternal beauties.

Whatever – without second cause – distils                    67
directly from the source of good can have
no end. Stamped thus by good, the print won't move.

Whatever – without a second cause – rains down               70
from good is wholly free, and does not lie
subjected to the power of things new-made.

Conformed to good, it pleases good the more.                 73
That holy fire, whose rays strike everything,
lives brightest in what most resembles it.

The human creature thrives, endowed with all                 76
these gifts and benefits. But if one fails
it must be that its dignity will fall.

And sin alone deprives it of its freedoms                    79
by rendering it unlike the highest good,
so that it whitens little in that gleam.

Nor can it ever regain dignity                               82
without replenishing what guilt makes vain,
with just amends to match its false delight.

Your nature in its seed sinned *totally*,                    85
and so from all these honours was removed –
as was it also out of Paradise.

Nor could these honours ever be restored                     88
unless – if you will note this subtlety –
it made its way through one of these two fords:

either that God, in all his courteous grace,                 91
should freely pardon us, or man himself
should offer satisfaction for such madness.

Now point your penetrating eye within                        94
the chasm of eternal Mind, and fix
on what I say as tightly as you can.

Mankind could not, within its natural bounds,                97
give satisfaction, ever; none could fall,
obedient in humility, as far

100    as, disobeying, it had sought to rise.
That is the reason why the way was closed
for man to offer proper satisfaction.

103    So this was right: that God by His own means
should bring us back to fullness in our lives,
by one way or – I'd say – by both at once.

106    But since an act will please the agent more
the more it represents to view the heart
of generosity from which it flowed,

109    so, too, that holy generosity
which stamps the universe chose happily
in all His ways to raise you up once more.

112    Between the last great night and first of days
there's never been nor shall be, either way,
a process soaring, so magnificent.

115    For God, in giving of Himself to make
humanity sufficient to restore itself,
gave more than, granting pardon, He'd have done.

118    All other means, in justice, would have come
far short, had not the very Son of God
bowed humbly down to take on human flesh.

121    So now to make you see as I do here
and bring to their fulfilment your desires,
go back and clarify a certain point.

124*    "I see," you'll say, "the waters. And I see
fire, air and earth and all their compounds fail,
come to decay and last no time at all.

127    Yet these were creatures in creation, too.
And so, if what you've told me is the truth,
these likewise should be safe from gross decay."

130    The angels, and this pure place where you are,
rightly are known, dear brother, as "created" –
their being formed complete as they are now.

133*    But all those elements that you have named,
and everything that might be made from them,
are formed as such by some created power.

Matter, which they possess, was thus "created",    136
"Created", too, the power informing them,
descending from the stars that circle round.

As mere "complected" possibility,    139
the very souls of beasts and growing things
draw light and motion from the sacred stars.

But your life – through no second cause – is breathed    142
by Highest Goodness which then brings that life
to love such good and always long for it.

And from this principle you may infer    145
the resurrection you yourselves will have.
Return and think how human flesh was made

   when our first parents were themselves made live.'    148

# CANTO 8

1*     The world, while still in danger, once believed
that Venus (lovely Cyprian), whirling
through Epicyclon Three, rayed down mad love,

4     so that, in age-old error, folk of old
did her all honour. And not her alone.
In sacrifice and cries of supplication,

7     they, for her sake, would honour Dione
(mother to her), and Cupid, too (her son,
who sat, their stories said, in Dido's lap).

10     From her – as I now pluck my opening line –
they took her name, and gave it to the star
whose love-looks at the sun touch nape then brow.

13     I had no sense of rising there. And yet
my faith at being now within, she made
quite sure: I saw my lady lovelier.

16     As fire-flecks in a flame can still be seen,
as voices voiced in chorus sound distinct
when one, while others vary, holds its note,

19     so in that light I now saw torches lit
that ran in moving spirals – quick, less quick,
according, I suppose, to inward sight.

22*     From chill-compacted clouds no wind – unseen
or seen – has ever shot so swiftly down
as not to seem arrested, loaded, slow,

25     to anyone who'd seen these holy lights
(as they came up to us) who left the gyre
that starts among the highest Seraphim.

And deep in those who earliest appeared 28
there sounded an 'Hosanna', so, then on,
I lacked no urge to hear it once again.

Then one of these, approaching closer still, 31*
began, alone: 'We all are quick to hear
what you might please, so you'll delight in us.

We turn at one with royal celestial lords, 34
one single spire, one spiralling, one thirst.
You, in the world, addressed those angels thus:

"*O you whose intellection moves Sphere Three . . .*" 37
We, being full of love, are no less pleased
to rest a while, to please you, than to move.'

Towards my lady, first, in reverence 40
I bowed my eyes and, once she'd granted them
agreement and assurance of herself,

I turned again towards that source of light 43
which had, before, made promise of so much,
my voice impressed with longing warmth: 'Who *are* you?'

How, with new happiness, in strength and kind, 46
that light, when I addressed it, now increased,
adding more happiness to what it had!

So, altered now, he said to me: 'The world 49
held me, down there, no time at all. Had that
been more, much ill to come would not have been.

My happiness conceals me from you still. 52
Its rays shine round me, and they keep me hid,
as though some creature swathed in its own silk.

You loved me well – and with good reason, too. 55*
For were I still down there, I would have shown
far more of how I love you than leaf-green.

The leftward bank rinsed clean by flowing Rhône 58*
(before that river mingles with the Sorgue)
awaited me, my hour now come, as lord,

so, too, the Ausonian Horn (its fortresses 61*
are Bari, Croton and Gaeta) stretched
between where Tronto and Verde reach the sea.

64* There gleamed already on my brows the crown
of regions that the Danube irrigates –
when once it leaves behind its German shores.

67 Trinacria (lovely Sicily) where fumes
of sulphur, born from Etna's core – so *not*
breathed out by giant Typhoeus – form

70 in that gulf, whipped up by Eurus gusts,
between the capes Pachynus and Peloras,
would still have looked for princes born as heirs,

73 through me, to Charles and Rudolph, had misrule –
which chafes upon a subject race – not stirred
Palermo's scream: "Death to them French. Death! Death!"

76 And would my brother only look ahead,
he'd learn to flee the tight-wad neediness
of Catalonian ministers and not get hurt.

79 For he – or someone – ought to take that view,
lest loading up his now well-laden ship,
his cargo of extortion prove too great.

82 His temperament, the mean descendant
of a generous race, has need of officers
who do not strive to line their treasure chests.'

85 'Because, my lord, the soaring happiness
your words pour into me is seen, I think,
by you, where all that's good begins and ends,

88 as clearly as I see it in myself,
it's yet more welcome, and I prize it well,
since you behold it gazing back to God.

91 You've made me light of heart. Now make me clear,
since, speaking, you have brought this doubt to me:
how can it be that sweet seed leads to sour?'

94 So I to him. He in reply: 'If only
I can show you truth, you'll hold your eyes
to what you ask where now your shoulders are.

97* The Good, which turns the whole domain you climb
and brings it joy, forms from its providence
the power that works in all these cosmic limbs.

Nor is the *way* things are alone foreseen  100
within that mind, which of itself is whole,
but equally *how* each thing best may thrive.

And so, whatever bolt this bow may shoot  103
will arc down, shaped towards an end foreseen,
as things do when directed to their mark.

Were this not so, the spheres you journey through  106
would bring all their effects about in ways
that count as chaos, not as skill or art.

And that can't be – unless the angel-minds  109
that move these stars were failing in their acts –
the first as well, for not perfecting them.

This truth – you'd have me make it shine still more?'  112
I: 'Not at all. It is, I see, impossible
that Nature, at that need, should ever tire.'

So he once more: 'For those who live on earth,  115*
would it be worse if they weren't citizens?'
'Yes,' I replied. 'And here I don't ask why.'

'And could it be that men should live down there  118
except by difference in their different tasks?
By no means – if your teacher writes the truth.'

He'd reached this point by formal argument,  121
and then, concluding: 'It must therefore be
that there are differing roots for what you do.

So one is born as Xerxes, one as Solon.  124*
One is Melchizedek, another still
the craftsman, borne on air, who lost his son.

All-circling Nature who imprints the stamp  127
on mortal wax performs her function well,
and won't distinguish hostels high and low.

So Esau happens, by his astral seed,  130*
to differ from his twin, while Romulus
was born so low that Mars was made his sire.

The course of generated things would run  133
unchanged in nature from their generants,
if not defeated by God's providence.

136  Now that which lay behind you stands ahead.
But so you'll know your joyous use to me,
I'd have you robed in this corollary:

139   like any seed not sown in native soil,
Nature, on finding fortune out of tune,
will always give poor proof of what it is.

142   And if the earthly world would set its mind
to fundamentals set by Nature's hand,
pursuing these, you'd make a happy end.

145*  But you will twist to some religious role
a man who's born to buckle on the sword,
and make a king of someone who should preach.

148   And so your track goes wholly from the road.'

# CANTO 9

Lovely Clemenza, your dearest Carlo –          1*
once having made that clear to me – went on
to tell the treacheries his seed would face,

    but said: 'Be silent. Let the years move by.'          4
So there is nothing I can say, save this,
that grief deservedly will follow harm.

    The heart, already, of that holy light          7
had turned to meet the sun that filled it full,
the Good that is the All of all that is.

    You self-deceiving souls! Mere things-gone-wrong!          10
Twisting your hearts away from that true good,
you strain your brows direct to nothingness.

    Look now! Another of those splendours came          13*
making towards me there, and signified,
in flares of brightness, it would do my will.

    The eyes of Beatrice, firm on me          16
as earlier, confirmed me in desire,
giving beloved assurance as before.

    So, longingly, I said: 'You happy soul!          19
Quickly, in answer, balance what I will.
Prove that in you I can reflect my thought.'

    At which the light, still new before my eyes,          22
out of those depths from which it first had sung,
went on as though rejoicing in good deeds.

    'In that degenerate, that *evil* part          25
of Italy that lies between Rialto
and the fountain-springs of Piave and Brent,

28          a hill starts up – though not to any height –
from which there once came down a burning brand
who ravaged all the countryside around.

31          From one same root, this torch and I were born.
Cunizza was my name, and I blaze here
because the light of Venus vanquished me.

34          But gladly I myself forgive myself
that influence. It does not brood on me –
which will, to humdrum minds of yours, seem hard.

37          Of this deep gleaming jewel that, nearest me,
rejoices in our heavenly sky, great fame
remains, nor will it die on earth until

40          the full en-fiving of this hundredth year.
You see, then? Shouldn't men seek excellence,
bequeathing from their first a *second* life?

43          The present crowd, well, they don't think of that,
shut up between the Adige and Tagliament,
who even when they're beaten don't repent.

46*         But Padua, whose folk so bitterly
resist what's right, will see its marshes change
as, soon, the streams that bathe Vicenza blush.

49*         And where the Sile and the Cagnan join,
a lord, his head held high, struts brashly on.
The web is stretched already for his ambush.

52          Feltre will soon bewail the treacherous fault
of its own bishop whose offence stinks more
than crimes that land you in a slimy Clink.

55          The tub you'd need for Ferrarese blood
would have to be, in size, an extra-big,
and if you syphon it by drops, you'll flag.

58          It's all that bishop's gift – and how polite! –
to prove so well his Guelf allegiances.
Such gifts will suit how people there all live.

61*         Above are mirrors – you will call them Thrones –
where God, in judging all, shines back to us,
so that my bitter words are signs of good.'

She now fell silent, and the look she gave                    64
suggested that her thoughts had passed elsewhere,
returning to the wheel where she'd been first.

That second happiness – of which, by now,                     67
I knew the price – came on, to meet my sight,
like some fine ruby that the sun's rays pierce.

As laughter here breeds laughter, there above                 70
sheer happiness shoots brilliant flares. Below,
a darkening shadow marks the saddened mind.

'God sees,' I said, 'all things, and your own sight,          73
you happy souls, in-hims itself in him
so no desire can steal away from you.

Why, then, does not your voice (which so delights             76*
these spheres with that same song from holy fires
who make themselves a hood of six great wings)

bring my desires the satisfaction due?                        79
If I in-you-ed myself as you in-me,
I would not still await what you might ask.'

'The greatest ocean-trench that water fills'                  82*
– in this way he began his words to me –
'except that sea which garlands all dry land,

travels so far between opposing shores,                       85
against the sun, that where the horizon
at first had been it makes its meridian.

I dwelt once on the shores of that great lake                 88*
between the Ebro and the Magra – whose stream
briefly divides the Genoan and Tuscan realms.

Almost at one same point of dawn and dusk                     91
sit both Boughia and the place I was,
which made its harbour warm with its own gore.

Folco they called me, those who knew my name.                 94
This heaven now bears my imprint, as once I,
on earth, beneath its influence, carried *its*.

For Dido – Belus's daughter – in her love,                    97
harming Creusa and Sichaeus too,
never burned more than I when young, untonsured.

100* Nor did the Rhodopeian girl, so tricked
by her Demophoon, nor did Alcides –
heart around Iole so closely locked.

103 Yet here we don't repent such things. We smile,
not, though, at sin – we don't think back to that –
but at that Might that governs and provides.

106 In wonder, we here prize the art to which
His power brings beauty, and discern the good
through which the world above turns all below.

109 But so that you should take back satisfied
the doubts this sphere has bred within your will,
I need to make my way still further on.

112* You wish to know who shines within that lamp
here close against my side and scintillates
as sun rays in the purest waters do.

115 Then understand that Rahab in these depths
grows bright with peace. And she, at one with us,
has set the highest seal upon our ranks.

118* She to this heaven, where earth's shadow points,
was lifted up before all other souls,
drawn there by Christ in his triumphal march.

121 This much was right, for Rahab to be set
in some such heaven as a martyr's palm,
to mark the victory won by Christ's two palms.

124 She looked with favour on that proud assault
of Joshua as victor in the Holy Land –
a place that hardly stirs the papal conscience.

127* That town of yours, a thriving weed that he,
the first of all to shun his own creator,
has planted there (his meanness stirs complaint)

130 breeds and distributes that accursèd flower
that, since the shepherd has become a wolf,
leads from their proper path both sheep and lambs.

133* The Gospels and the teachers of the Church
are, for sheer greed, abandoned. Decretals
(their margins show as much) are all one reads.

   The pope and cardinals are set on that.      136
Their thoughts will never turn to Nazareth,
where Gabriel once opened angel wings.
   The Vatican and other parts of Rome      139[*]
which, chosen well, have been the burial ground
for all who followed Peter as his troop
   shall soon be free of this adultery.'      142

# CANTO 10

1      Looking within his Son through that same Love
that Each breathes out eternally with Each,
the first and three-fold Worth, beyond all words,

4      formed all that spins through intellect or space
in such clear order it can never be,
that we, in wonder, fail to taste Him there.

7*      Lift up your eyes, then, reader, and, along with
me, look to those wheels, directed to that part
where motions – yearly and diurnal – clash.

10      And there, entranced, begin to view the skill
the Master demonstrates. Within Himself,
He loves it so, His looking never leaves.

13      Look! Where those orbits meet, there branches off
the slanting circles that the planets ride
to feed and fill the world that calls on them.

16      And were the path it takes not twisted so,
then many astral virtues would be wasted,
and almost all potential, down here, dead.

19      And were the distance any more or less
from that straight course, then much – above and here –
so ordered in the world, would be a void.

22      Now, reader, sit there at your lecture bench.
And, if you want not tedium but joy,
continue thinking of the sip you've had.

25      I've laid it out. Now feed on it yourself.
The theme of which I'm made to be scribe
drags in its own direction all my thoughts.

The greatest minister of natural life 28\*
who prints the worth of Heaven on the world,
and measures time for us in shining light,

conjoined with Aries (as we've called to mind), 31
was spinning through those spirals where, each hour,
its presence is revealed to us the sooner.

And with him I was there, but no more knew 34
of making that ascent than anyone
will know a thought before it first appears.

It's she – Beatrice – who sees the way, 37
from good to better still, so suddenly
her actions aren't stretched out in passing time.

How brilliant they must all, themselves, have been 40
seen in the sun where I now came to be,
not in mere hue but showing forth pure light.

Call as I might on training, art or wit, 43
no words of mine could make the image seen.
Belief, though, may conceive it, eyes still long.

In us, imagination is too mean 46
for such great heights. And that's no miracle.
For no eye ever went beyond the sun.

So shining there was that fourth family 49
that's always fed by one exalted Sire
with sight of what He breathes, what Son He has.

And now, 'Give thanks,' Beatrice began. 52
'Give thanks to the Him, the Sun of all the angels.
In grace, He's raised you to this sun of sense.'

No mortal heart was ever so well fed 55
to give itself devoutly to its God
so swiftly, with such gratitude and joy,

as now, to hear her words ring, I became. 58
I set my love so wholly on that Sun
that He, in oblivion, eclipsed even Beatrice.

This did not trouble her. She smiled at it. 61
And brightness from the laughter in her eyes
shared out to many things my one whole mind.

64       Bright beyond seeing, I saw, now, many flares
         make us their centre and themselves our crown,
         still sweeter even in voice than radiance.

67*      Sometimes, in that same way, we see a zone
         around Latona's daughter – lunar rays,
         held in by gravid air, which form her belt,

70       There in that heavenly court from which I come
         are found so many jewels, so fine, so rare,
         they cannot be abstracted from that realm.

73       The singing of the lights was one of these.
         So minds who don't, self-winged, coming flying here,
         must wait to gather news from tongues struck mute.

76       And when, still singing, all these burning suns
         had spun three turns around us where we were –
         as stars more swift the closer to fixed poles –

79       girl-like in formal dance they looked to me,
         in figure still but silent, pausing now,
         listening until they caught the next new note.

82*      And deep in one of these I heard begin: 'When
         rays of grace igniting love in truth –
         those rays through which, in loving, love still grows –

85       reflect in you so multiplied that you
         are led along with them to climb this stair,
         which none descends who will not rise again,

88       whoever, seeing this, should then withhold
         the wine flask that you thirst for counts as free
         no more than rain *not* streaming to the ocean.

91       You wish to know what plants these are – enflowered,
         entranced – a garland round that *donna* who,
         in beauty, strengthens you to dare the skies.

94*      I was a lamb within that holy flock
         that Dominic conducts along the road
         where "All grow fat who do not go astray".

97*      This one, who here is nearest on my right,
         was master to me, and a brother, too –
         Albert of Köln. I'm Thomas Aquinas.

And if you wish to know the rest as well,                              100
then follow with your eyes the words I speak,
circling around this interwoven string.

The next flame blazes out from Gratian's smile.      103
He's loved in Paradise for having served
both civil and ecclesial courts so well.

Then next, that Peter ornaments our choir            106
who, like the widow in Saint Luke's account,
offered his treasured all to Holy Church.

The fifth light, and the loveliest of us all,        109
breathes with such love that everyone down there
hungers to have fresh word if he is saved.

A mind so high is there, to which was sent           112*
knowledge so deep that, if the truth is true,
no second ever rose who saw so much.

You see a candle shining by him there                115
that saw, while in the flesh, most inwardly
the nature of the angels and their works.

Then in the very smallest of these lights            118
there smiles the one who spoke for Christian times.
Augustine cited him in what he wrote.

Now if, to track my words of praise, you draw        121
the eye of intellect from light to light,
already you'll be thirsting for the eighth.

Rejoicing, deep within, to see all good,             124
the blessèd soul is there who made quite plain
the world's fallaciousness – to all who'd hear.

The body he was driven from lies, now,               127
below in Golden Heaven Church. He came
to peace from exile, from his martyrdom.

Burning beyond, you see the breathing fires          130
of Bede, then Isidore and Richard, too –
in contemplation he was more than man.

The one from whom your glance returns to me          133
is light born of that spirit who, oppressed
in thought, saw death, it seemed, come all too slow.

136*   This is the everlasting light of Siger,
whose lectures, given in Straw Alleyway,
argued for truths that won him envious hate.'

139*   And now, like clocks that call us at the hour
in which the Bride of God will leave her bed
to win the Bridegroom's love with morning song,

142   where, working, one part drives, the other draws –
its 'ting-ting' sounding with so sweet a note
that now the spirit, well and ready, swells –

145   so in its glory I beheld that wheel
go moving round and answer, voice to voice,
tuned to a sweetness that cannot be known,

148   except up there where joy in-evers all.

# CANTO 11

Those idiotic strivings of the human mind!     1
How flawed their arguments and logic are,
driving our wings to flap in downward flight.

Some follow Law. Some drift (great tomes in hand)     4
to Medicine, others train in priestly craft.
Some rule by force, as others do by tricks.

Some choose to steal, some trade in politics,     7
some toil, engrossed in pleasures of the flesh,
and others concentrate their minds on ease,

while I, released from all that sort of thing,     10
was gathered up on high with Beatrice
in glorious triumph to the heavenly spheres.

When each soul, dancing, had returned to that     13
position on the circle where it once had been,
all paused, like candles in a chandelier.

And in that flare which spoke to me at first,     16
I, hearing, sensed these words begin, smiling
as in their brilliance they became more pure.

'As I am here a mirror to the radiance     19
of everlasting light, so, looking back,
I grasp, in that, the wherefore of your thoughts.

You have your doubts. You want me to define –     22
with sharper and more open explanations,
directed at your human ear – the words

I uttered earlier: "Where all grow fat . . ."     25 *
and where I said: "No second ever rose."
We need to make distinctions as to that.

28      The providence that rules the universe,
in counsels so profound that all created
countenance will yield before it finds its depth,

31      intended that the Bride of Christ (He wooed her
with His sacred blood, His cries raised high)
should go to her Belovèd in delight,

34      sure of herself and truer still to Him,
and so ordained two princes that, on either side,
should walk along with her and be her guide.

37      The one was seraph-like in burning love,
the other in intelligence a splendour
on the earth that shone like Heaven's cherubim.

40      I'll speak of one. For – take whichever man –
in prizing him, you'll praise the other, too.
Their different actions served a single plan.

43*     Between the Tupin and the stream that runs
down from the hill that saintly Ubald chose,
a fertile slope hangs off that mountainside

46      from which Perugia, through its Sun Gate, feels
both heat and chill. Behind that ridge are, weeping,
Nòcera and Gualdo, bowed by wind and shade.

49      And where its swiftest incline crashes down,
another sun was born to light the world –
as our sun ranges, sometimes, from the Ganges.

52*     Let those, inventing words to suit that place,
not voice "Assisi" as "Ascesi" or "Arisen"
(*these* words all want) but properly the "Orient".

55      Nor was he far from his own rising dawn
when he began to make his country feel,
by his true powers, a certain strengthening.

58*     Headlong he ran – a callow boy – to war
and fought, against his father, for a girl
to whom – as though to death – all lock joy's door.

61      So, *coram patre* in the bishop's court,
he joined himself with her and, ever on,
from day to day he loved her all the more.

She, sad and widowed of her first beloved,    64
remained a thousand years (and more) till he
came on to her – obscure, undated, scorned.

Nor did it count to hear how Caesar – terror    67*
of the world – had found her true, unwavering,
with Amyclas, not moved by his command.

Nor did it count to hear that, likewise, she,    70
so fierce, so constant, wept (Mary herself
remained below) with Christ upon his Cross.

But lest in what I say I prove unclear,    73
then understand, in all I've just poured out,
this loving pair are Francis and pure Poverty.

The harmony, the looks of happiness    76
between these two, their tenderness and care,
their love, so wonderstruck, became the cause

of holy thoughts in Bernard (now revered),    79*
the first who flung his shoes away and raced –
running, he thought himself too slow – for peace.

Such rampant goodness, riches yet untold!    82
Egidio flung his shoes away, Sylvester his,
chasing the groom, the bride so pleased them all.

So off he goes, Saint Francis, father, lord.    85
His bride was Poverty, his family these –
their waists already bound with simple cord.

Nor in abjection did it weigh his brows    88
to be Pietro Bernadone's kid,
nor when, amazingly, he faced disdain.

Rather, in sovereign manner he revealed    91*
his stern intention to Pope Innocent,
who granted this devotion its first seal.

And when his little pauper-company    94
had grown (the wonder of his life would sound
far more when sung in glory in the skies),

this archimandrite in his holy will    97
was crowned now with a second diadem,
breathed by Eternal Spirit through Honorius.

100*     Then after, thirsting for a martyr's fate,
he preached (before the Sultan's prideful throne)
his faith in Christ and all who followed him,

103*     but found these people loath and far too sour
to change their ways. So, not to wait in vain,
he soon returned, to tend Italian vines.

106     A rough crag splits the Arno's course from Tiber.
There Francis took from Christ the final seal,
and on his limbs for two years bore that sign.

109     And when the one who'd dealt him so much good
was pleased to draw him up to that reward
which Francis earned through his great lowliness,

112     he then bestowed his *donna*, held so dear,
on followers and brothers, his true heirs,
commanding them, in faith, to love her well.

115     And from her bosom this illustrious soul
then chose to part, returning to his realm,
and chose no other bier for his own corpse.

118*     Think of the other now, what *he* was like
if fit to work with Francis and maintain
the Ship of Peter on its rightful track.

121     Such was our patriarch, Saint Dominic.
And those who follow him as he commands
will bear, as you can tell, a precious freight.

124     But now this pastor's flock turns ravenous
for weird new fodder, so they cannot fail
to scatter wide through many different leas.

127     The further – wilful, wandering and wild –
his sheep desert him, so the emptier
they are of milk, returning to the fold.

130     It's true that some are fearful of such harm,
huddling against their shepherd still. They're few.
There's not much cloth now needed for their cowls.

133     Now if my words in meaning aren't too faint,
if you have been attentive, hearing them,
if you call what's been said to mind once more,

in part what you desire will be content.                    136
You'll see why that firm plant is torn to shreds,
and see the strict correction that contends:
  "Where all grow fat that do not go astray."'            139

# CANTO 12

1 *     The moment that this consecrated flame
had plucked the string to sound its final word,
the holy grinding stone began to wheel.

4     Nor had it gone a whole rotation through
before a second circle closed around,
and coupled move to move and song with song –

7     songs that defeat, in gentle trumpet calls,
our muses and all siren-songs as much
as primal splendour does its mirrored light.

10     Compare: when haughty Juno bids her maid,
then double rainbows arch through fine-spun cloud,
concentric and the same in all their hues,

13     the inner brings the outer into life
(as, too, the words, astray, entranced, of Echo,
whom love dispersed as sun consumes the mist)

16     and these arcs show, for people here on earth,
as tokens of the pact God made with Noah
the world would never suffer flood again.

19     So, too, these swirls of sempiternal rose
circled around us in their double band.
So too the outer answered that within.

22     When once their galliard – their festal joy,
their singing and their flame-darts each to each,
light meeting light, wooing and rejoicing –

25     all at one point, together in one will,
at last were quieted (as eyelids, too,
both moved by one delight, are closed and raised)

then from the heart of one of these new lights       28
there moved a voice which made me turn to there,
it seemed, as needle to magnetic star.

'The love that makes me lovely,' this began,          31*
'draws me to speak about that other lord
whose aide has spoken here so well of mine.

It's right, where one is, that we name his peer,      34
for these two soldiered to a single end
and so their glorious triumphs shine as one.

Christ's fighting force (so costly to re-arm)         37
was marching on beneath its battle sign,
but slow and watchful now, and much worn down.

But then that Emperor who will always reign,          40
through grace alone and not through their desert,
provided for His soldiers, so perhaps-ed.

He raced to aid His bride (as said before)            43
with two great heroes by whose words and deed
the people who had strayed came running back.

Westward, in regions where mild Zephyrs rise –        46
to open out the fresh new foliage
with which all Europe sees itself reclothed –

not far from where those breaking waves resound       49
beyond which, when the time comes round, the sun,
its long course over, sinks and hides from men,

there stands, so blessed by fortune, Calaruega        52
protected by that great Castilian shield
which, quartered, bears the lion, high and low.

And here, impassioned by the Christian faith,         55
the love-sick knight was born, a champion,
kind to his own, but harsh to enemies.

And mind in him no sooner took on form                58*
than mind was filled so full of living strength
he made, while still enwombed, his mother prophesy.

Then wedded, at the well of baptism,                  61
to Faith (where Faith and he, as marriage gift,
each vowed salvation mutually to each),

64      the lady speaking as his sponsor there
saw in a dream the fruit to wonder at
that he and his inheritors would bear.

67      And so that all he was might show in words,
a spirit moved from Heaven to form his name –
the adjective of whose he wholly was.

70      They called him Dominic. I speak of him
as farmer – called and singled out by Christ,
to work His orchard and to help it thrive.

73      He seemed one sent, in truth, to follow Christ.
The first love that was manifest in him
obeyed the first command that came from Christ.

76      And many times his nurse discovered him,
awake, unspeaking, stretched out on the ground,
as though he meant to say: "For this I came."

79      Felix, O truly happy, his father!
O truly blessed, his mother Giovanna –
her name in Hebrew, rightly read, means "grace".

82*      Not craving worldly wealth (like those who ape
the Ostian lawyer or a Doctor Tad)
but loving, purely, manna of God's truth,

85      he soon became a scholar of great worth,
and hence determined to patrol those vines
that white-rot strikes when growers are no good.

88      Before the papal throne – more generous once
(not now) to poor, true hearts, grown so diseased
through his fault reigning now, and not its own –

91      he sought no leave to pay mere halfs and thirds,
no first shot at some well-paid vacancy,
no tax rebated *quae sunt pauperes*,

94*      rather, against a world of wilful lies,
licence to battle for the seed of truth,
whose saplings – twenty-four – here bind you round.

97      And then he moved with learning and with zeal,
as also with his mandate from the pope,
like some fierce torrent surging down a hill.

And at the thicket of the heretics                           100
he struck with all his impetus,
the stronger where resistance was the worse.

Then many streams were formed within his wake     103
to irrigate the orchard of the Church
and keep the shrubs there growing better still.

Take this to be the chariot's second wheel,              106*
mounted by Holy Church, in self-defence
to drive all civil nuisance from the field.

And then you'll see laid plain before your eyes        109
how excellent the other is – to whom,
before I came, Saint Thomas was so courteous.

The track, however, that the wheel-tread leaves      112*
has gone all wrong at its circumference.
Where once the wine-crust crisped, it's musty now.

His retinue – which once, in his own prints,            115
trod straight and true – has done a turn-about.
So toes now spring where once the heels had been.

And soon we'll see what crops bad farming yields,    118
when tares and weeds, complaining, will all whine,
being denied safe storage in the barn.

Granted, whoever browsed through, page by page,    121
our master-roll would find there still and read:
"I in myself am what I always was."

But not the Acquaspartan or the Casalese.              124
For these are such as either flee, or take
too strictly, text and rule *ad litteram*.

I am the living heart of Bonaventure –                   127
Bagnoregensian. In public works
I set aside all underhand concerns.

The first who joined our barefoot band, and twined  130*
the cord, as friends to God, around their waists,
are here – Illuminato, Agostino, too.

Along with them is Hugo of Saint Victor,              133
Peter of Spain – who glitters there below
in twelve fine tomes – and Peter Mangiador,

136     Nathan the Seer, the Bishop Metropolitan
Chrysostom, Anselm and Donatus next,
who set his hand to write the grammar rules.

139     Raban is here and, shining by my side,
Dom Joachim, Calabrian by birth,
endowed with all his gifts of prophecy.

142     To praise (and envy!) of Count Dominic
I'm moved by that same burning courtesy
of Brother Thomas and his well-judged words,

145     which moved this company along with me.'

# CANTO 13

Imagine, if you truly want to know      1*
what I saw now – and while I'm speaking grip
this image firm, as though a steady rock –
     some fifteen stars, from various demesnes,      4
that bring the heavens to life with light so clear
they overcome the thickest weave of air.
     Imagine, too, the Wain which needs, by day or night,      7
no arc more ample than our lap of sky –
its turning plough shaft never lost to view.
     Imagine, too, the bell mouth of the Horn,      10
its point beginning at the axle end
round which the wheel that starts the cosmos rolls.
     Imagine these all forming, in the sky,      13
two signs among themselves (as when the child
of Minos, Ariadne, felt death's chill)
     so that the rays of one contained the next      16
and each was now revolving differently,
one set in this direction, one in that,
     you'll have a shade, then, almost, of that true      19
constellation – the dance that, doubled there,
circled around the point where I was now.
     That goes as far beyond the norms we know      22*
as does that sphere which outruns all the rest
beyond the sluggish current of Chiana.
     Those songs there praised not Bacchus nor Peana.      25*
They sang three persons all divine in kind,
and in one person human and divine.

28    The singing done, the measured round complete,
these holy lights stretched out their thought to us,
rejoicing in themselves at this new care.

31    The silence, then, of these concordant powers
was broken by that light in whom I'd heard
the story told of God's dear down-and-out.

34*   'When once,' he said, 'one crop of straw is threshed,
and once the grain from that is gathered in,
then love calls gently that I flail the next.

37    Your view is this, that, firstly, in that breast
from which a living rib was drawn to make
Eve's lovely cheek (her taste once cost us all),

40    and then in Him – His side pierced by the lance –
who paid full satisfaction, first and last,
and so outweighed the scales of guilt and sin,

43    were poured infusions of the greatest light
that we in human nature rightly have,
drawn from that Worth that first made these two men.

46    Thinking all this, you wonder at my tale
when I declare: "No second ever rose"
to match the good enclosed in that fifth light.

49    Now clear your eyes to what my answer is.
Then what you think and what I say, agree,
you'll find, in truth, as circles round one point.

52    Those things that cannot die and those that can
are nothing save the splendours of the One
Idea that, loving, brought our Lord to birth.

55    For Living Light, which, from the Fount of Light,
cascades in ways that do not disunite it,
from Him or from the Love en-three-ing them,

58    in generosity collects its rays,
as mirrored in nine ranks of life anew,
itself eternally remaining One.

61    Down to the outermost of what can be,
from act to act descending, it becomes
maker of, merely, brief contingencies.

And, here, by "brief contingencies" I mean 64
those things produced – in seed or mineral –
by generative influence of moving spheres.

The wax of these – as, too, the hand that guides – 67
is never steady in some single mode,
but gleams, here more, here less, beneath the ideal sign.

It happens, therefore, that the self-same wood 70
bears, in its species, better fruit or worse.
So humans, too, are born with different gifts.

And were that wax point-perfectly embossed, 73
and were the heavens at the height of power,
the light of that first seal would show in full.

Yet Nature, as created, falls far short. 76
It operates as any craftsman will
who knows his trade and yet has trembling hands.

If Love, though, in its fervent warmth arrays 79
and prints the clear regard of Primal power,
entire perfection will be here acquired.

The earth was once made worthy in this way 82
of all that creatures perfectly may be.
So, too, the Virgin was made big with child.

I do, therefore, commend the view you take, 85
that human nature never was before,
nor was to be, as, once, in these two men.

But now suppose I did not follow on, 88
"How is it, then, that he can have no peer?"
these are the words that you'd begin to speak.

And yet to clarify what is not clear, 91
think who this was, and what – when "Ask!" was said –
moved him, in prayer, to ask as he then did.

My words have not been such that you can't see 94
this man was once a king who simply asked
for wisdom to fulfil his kingly role,

and not to know how many astral drives 97*
there are up there or whether, logically,
*necesse* and contingents prove *necesse*,

100     or *si est dare primum motum esse*
    or if half-circles can contain a shape
    that is a triangle but not a *"right"*.

103     It follows, if you note all I have said,
    that what I meant my arrow-shot to strike
    is kingly wisdom, matchless mode of sight.

106     And if you look, clear-eyed, on that word "rose",
    you'll see the phrase applies to kings alone –
    so many, yet so few who're any good.

109     So, hearing what I say, make that distinction,
    and all will stand at one with what you hold,
    as to our father Adam and our best Beloved.

112     And let this be a lead weight on your feet,
    so that you move as slow as if worn out
    to any "yes" or "no" unclear to you.

115     For no fool is as low a fool as one
    who taking either of these steps will fail
    affirming or denying in distinction.

118     So often when our judgement rushes on,
    it happens that we veer in false directions
    and then emotions bind the intellect.

121     In fishing for the truth without that skill,
    it's worse than useless to cast off from shore.
    You'll not return the same as you set out.

124*     And patent proof of this throughout the world
    are Bryson and Parmenides, Melissus and all,
    who went their way not knowing where they went,

127*     as Arius did, Sabellius, too, and all those fools
    whose heresies have gashed the Holy Word,
    returning from its rightful gaze sheer wrong.

130     And then again, don't let folk be too sure
    in passing judgement as do those who price
    the harvest in the field before it's ripe.

133     For I have seen, at first, all winter through
    a thorn bush shows itself as stark and fierce,
    which after bears a rose upon its height.

And I have seen a keel, steered swift and well,    
speed over oceans all its voyage through,
then perish at the entrance to the dock.
    And so when Mrs Smith and Mr Jones    139
see one man steal, another offer alms,
don't let them think they see this in God's plan.
    The thief may rise, the other take a fall.'    142

# CANTO 14

1     Centre to circle or circle to centre:
water in a round container moves like that,
depending where the rim is struck, inside or out.

4     I utter here the instant thought that chanced
across my mind when now, in all its glory,
the life of Thomas Aquinas fell silent,

7     born from resemblances that now arose
between his words and these that, after him,
were voiced by Beatrice. She began:

10     'This man still needs – although he does not say,
nor is he even thinking it as yet –
to trace another truth down to its root.

13     Tell him: that light in which, as what you are,
your being in its substance is in-flowered,
will that remain eternally with you?

16     And if it does remain, then tell him how,
when once you are remade as visibles,
it cannot spoil your eyesight, being so.'

19     Compare: as dancers – wheeling, drawn and pressed
by keener happiness at certain points –
exult in voice, their gestures quickening,

22     so now, to hear her prompt, devoted prayer,
the holy circles showed new joy, in turns
of flashing speed and notes to wonder at.

25     Whoever mourns to think we here must die,
to live our lives up there, has never seen
the cool refreshment of the eternal shower.

The one and two and three who always lives 28
and always reign in three and two and one,
uncircumscribed and circumscribing all,

    had, three times now, been lauded in the songs 31
of every spirit there, the melody
a condign prize, however great the worth.

    Then, in the holiest of lights among 34*
the lesser ring, I heard a voice (as modest
as the angel's, maybe, to Maria was),

    answering: 'As long as this great festival 37
of Paradise goes on, so, too, our love
will cast these robes in rays around us all.

    That brightness follows from their inward fire, 40
that fire from vision. And their sight extends
as far as each, beyond their due, has grace.

    But when the glorious and sacred flesh 43
is clothing us once more, our person then
will be – complete and whole – more pleasing still.

    For then whatever has been granted us, 46
by utmost good, of free and gracious light
(the light through which we see Him) will increase.

    Hence, as must be, our seeing will increase, 49
increasing, too, the fire that vision lights,
the ray increasing that proceeds from that.

    But just as burning coal may give out flames, 52
yet overcome these with its own white light,
keeping, within, its shape and semblance whole,

    so, too, the shining-out that rings us round 55
will, in appearance, be surpassed by flesh
which all day long the earth now covers up.

    Nor can it be that so much light will tire. 58
Our organs, physically, will have the strength
for every pleasure that can come to us.'

    So ready and alert they seemed to me – 61
those double choirs – to add their plain 'Amen'
they showed their keen desire for long dead bones,

64     not only for themselves but for their mums,
their fathers, too, and others dear to them,
before they were these sempiternal flames.

67     Look! Round those circles, matched in clarity,
a lustre, more than what was there, was born,
as though a new horizon, brightening.

70     When early evening hours are drawing in,
new things begin to show across the sky
so that the sight both seems and seems not true.

73     There, too, it seemed to me that newer things
began to rise to view and form a ring
beyond the circumscription of those two.

76     True spark shower flying from the Holy Breath!
How suddenly it flared, how incandescent!
My eyes, defeated, could not bear the sight.

79     But Beatrice showed herself to me –
laughing, so beautiful she must be left
among things seen that memory can't pursue.

82*     And so my eyes, regaining their right strength,
lifted once more. I saw myself alone,
borne with my lady to a higher good.

85     Seeing the flares of laughter in that star,
which seemed now far more fiery than before,
I knew full well that I'd been lifted higher.

88     With all my heart and with that tongue – flaming
alike in all our thoughts – aflame, I made to God
burnt offerings that fitted this new grace.

91     Nor had the ardour of that sacrifice
been drained still from my heart before it was,
I knew, propitious and acceptable.

94*     For shining so – a ruby in its hue –
splendour appeared to me in two crossed rays.
'Eliosun!' I said. 'You grant this accolade.'

97     The galaxy, distinctly marked by lights,
both great and small, between the earth's two poles,
glistens and makes the learnèd wonder why.

So too, like constellations in the depths 100
of Mars, these rays composed the honoured sign
that quadrants (joined within a circle) form.

And here remembering surpasses skill: 103
that cross, in sudden flaring, blazed out Christ
so I can find no fit comparison.

But those who take their cross and follow Christ 106
will let me off where, wearily, I fail,
seeing in that white dawn, as lightning, Christ.

From horn to horn, from summit down to base, 109
there moved here scintillating points of light,
bright as their paths met, bright in passing on.

So minute specks of matter can be seen – 112
renewing how they look at every glance,
straight in their track, oblique, long, short, swift, slow –

moving through sunbeams that will sometimes streak 115
the shade that people, to protect themselves,
have won through their intelligence or art.

As harp or viol – in tempered harmony, 118
their many strings stretched tight – still ring and sing,
even to those who do not catch the tune,

so, though I did not understand their hymn, 121
an air now gathered that enraptured me
from lights appearing there throughout the cross.

I realized full well it sang high praise 124
for, as to one who does not understand
yet hears, there came to me, 'Rise up!' and 'Win!'

At which, I sank so deep in love of this 127
that never till that time had anything
entrammelled me in such delightful bonds.

These words of mine may seem perhaps too bold, 130
slighting the pleasure of those lovely eyes,
in which, when gazing, my desires all rest.

Whoever thinks, though, that the living prints 133
of every beauty grow the more they rise,
and notices I did not turn to these,

136        will make excuse for what I here confess
to win excuse, and see me speak the truth.
Holy delight is not excluded here.

139        Rather, in rising it will grow more pure.

# CANTO 15

Good will (to which the love that breathes aright     1 *
will always in its distillation flow,
as does cupidity to wickedness)
    brought silence to that sweetly sounding lyre,     4
and stilled the motion of its holy strings,
which Heaven's right hand both plucks and modulates.
    How can it be that those true beings there     7
whose choir of silence urged me on to pray
will ever turn deaf ears to honest prayer?
    It's only right that all know endless grief     10
who, loving only things that can't endure,
steal from themselves, eternally, true love.
    Sometimes, across a pure, untroubled sky,     13
there runs an instantaneous flash of fire,
moving our steady eyes to trace its course,
    from which, it seems, a star is changing place,     16
except that, at the point it caught alight,
nothing is lost, nor does it last for long.
    So, from the right extension of the cross     19
down to its foot, there ran an astral spark
which left the constellation shining there.
    Nor did that gem stone leave its bezelled rim,     22
but ran a length along the radial beam,
as fire behind some alabaster screen.
    So, too, the shadow of Anchises showed     25
(if we give credence to our greatest muse),
seeing his son approach him in Elysium.

28\*     *'O sanguis meus, o superinfusa*
        *gratia Dei, sicut tibi cui*
        *bis unquam celi ianua reclusa?'*

31\*     The light spoke thus. I gave my mind to him,
        then turned to see my lady's countenance,
        amazed at what I saw on either side.

34      For laughter in her eyes now burned so bright
        that, as I thought, I touched the very depths
        of all I gloried in – and Paradise.

37      Then, full of joy, in hearing as in sight,
        the spirit added to those opening words,
        which I'd not understood – he spoke so deep –

40      though he'd not hidden from me out of choice,
        but rather of necessity, his thought
        so set itself above our mortal mark.

43      And when the bow shot of his burning love
        had so far settled that his speech came down
        to reach the target of our intellect,

46\*     the first thing that I came to understand
        was: 'Blessèd be Thou, the Triune and the One
        who's graced my seed with so much courtesy.'

49      He then went on: 'My son, a long, glad fast –
        drawn out in reading from the noble book
        where there can be no change of white and black –

52      you now relieve me of, within this light
        from which I speak. All thanks be hers
        who clothes you in the wings for this great flight.

55      You think that all your thoughts come down to me
        from that which is the First – as five and six
        come forth as rays, if clearly seen, from one.

58      And therefore why, myself, I am and seem
        to you more jubilant than others here
        who form this happy throng, you don't inquire.

61      You think the truth. Within this rank of life,
        the greatest and the least all gaze upon
        the glass where thought, before you think, is shown.

But (may the holy love wherein, with sight     64
perpetual, I watch and whence, with sweet
desire, I thirst, be all the more fulfilled!)

be confident in voice, be brave and glad     67
to sound your will, to sound your best desire,
to which my answer has been long decreed.'

I turned to Beatrice, who had heard     70
before I spoke. She smiled me such a sign
that made the wings of will in me grow strong.

And so I now began: 'In you, each one,     73*
the heart was balanced equally with mind
when Primal Equipoise appeared to you.

The Sun that gleams and burns in you     76
itself is, equally, both light and fire,
so finely gauged comparison falls short.

But will and intellect in mortal minds     79
(for reasons that are manifest to you)
are different in the plumage of their wings.

And I discern, since I am mortal, in     82
myself the same unequalness. My heart
alone must thank you for your father-words.

Truly I beg you, Topaz live and bright,     85
in-gemmed so joyfully within this jewel,
to bring your name to me in satisfaction.'

'My branch and leaf (in whom I was well pleased,     88
waiting until you came) I was your root.'
His opening words, as he replied, were these.

And then he said: 'The one from whom your clan     91*
takes its cognomen has trodden now the first ring
of the hill below a hundred years or more.

He was my son, to you great-grandfather.     94
It's right that, by your works on his behalf,
you render short the time of his long labour.

Florence, within the ancient ring, from which     97*
she takes the bell-sound still of terce and nones,
lived on in modesty, chasteness and peace.

100　　No bangles had she, nor a showy crown,
no exquisite, embroidered skirts, no sash
more meant for viewing than the person was.

103*　As yet the birth of daughters did not bring
fear to the father: since no wedding dower
nor early marriage passed the proper norm.

106*　As yet, no house too roomy for its clan –
no Sardanapalus had yet arrived
to show what you can do in private rooms.

109*　As yet, no Monte Mario in Rome
was beaten by your Aviary which wins
in rising high – as well as sinking low.

112*　Bellincion Berti I saw girded there
with leather and bone, and, leaving her mirror,
his lady, her face without cosmetic.

115　　I saw the Nerli and del Vecchio
content to wear the plainest skin and hide,
their women occupied with loom and flax.

118　　How fortunate these were, each being sure
of where her grave would be! None yet was left
alone in bed by men who'd gone to France.

121　　One, still awake, would watch around the crib
and soothe the baby, babbling in the tongue
that parents thrill to in the early days.

124　　Another, drawing tresses from the spool,
sat with her family and told them tales
of Trojans, of Fiesole and Rome.

127*　Lewd Cianghellas or sly Salterells
would then have seemed a marvel just as great
as Cincinnatus now or proud Cornelia.

130　　To this so tranquil and composed, so *fine*
a life of citizens, to such a true
civility, so sweet a resting place,

133*　Maria gave me (birth-pangs called her name).
And in your ancient Baptistery, I was
a Christian, and was Cacciaguida, too.

My brothers were Moronto and Eliseo.  136
My honoured wife came down from Val di Pado,
and hence derived the surname that you bear.

I followed Emperor Conrad on crusade  139*
and, rising in his favour by my deeds,
he bound me with all dignities of knighthood.

I went behind him to oppose the wrong  142
of that misguided law whose devotees
usurp (it is your pastors' fault) true justice.

There at the hand of this foul horde was I  145
unravelled from this world of vanities,
through love of which so many are besmirched,

and came from martyrdom to this pure peace.'  148

# CANTO 16

1*     Nobility of blood, that whim of ours!
If here on earth, where feeling is so frail,
you make us boast the glories you bestow,

4     to me henceforth that's nothing wonderful.
For there – in Heaven, I mean – where appetite
is never skewed, I, too, have boasted so.

7     You are, of course, a mantle that soons shrinks.
So if you're not patched up from day to day,
Time with its pinking shears will circle you.

10*     So with that 'Thou' that ancient Romans used –
its clan, though, doesn't keep the usage up –
the words began once more to come from me.

13     At this Beatrice (some way away)
smiled in the manner of the one who coughed
to mark the first mistake of Guinevere.

16     Thus I began: 'Thou art indeed my father.
In me thou hast inspired my daring speech.
Thou raisest me so I am more than I.

19     Filled by these many streams of happiness,
my mind rejoices in itself to bear
so much and not be shattered by the surge.

22     Tell me my earliest, my dearest growth,
who were your own progenitors? Also,
what years were marked for you as boy and youth.

25*     Tell me how great the sheepfold of Saint John
at that time was, and which inhabitants
deserved the most to sit on highest thrones.'

As coals, when breezes breathe them into flame,                    28
brighten and live, this incandescence now
responded to my own persuasiveness.

And as his beauty in my eyes increased,                            31
so too his voice grew gentler, sweeter still,
though not in speech we moderns might employ.

'From when,' he answered, 'the "*Ave*" was said,                   34
to when my mother, sainted now, gave birth –
lightening herself of me, the weight she bore –

five hundred times and fifty and thirty,                           37*
this fire of Mars had come to strike new flame
beneath the paws of constellation Leo.

My ancestors (like me) had all been born                           40*
within that district where your yearly race
begins to enter on its final course.

That's all you need to hear of my great sires.                     43
Of who these were and from what place they came,
silence has greater dignity than speech.

Between the Baptistery and Mars, the sum                           46
of those who rightly could bear arms was then
a fifth of those who live there nowadays.

That population, though (now intermixed                            49*
with Campi and Fegghine and Certaldo folk),
was, to the merest craftsman, pure in blood.

Better by far that those of whom I speak                           52
were distant neighbours still, so you maintained
Galluzzo and Trespiano as your outer bounds,

than have within you – and so bear the stench –                    55
of peasant Aguglione or that Signa cad,
sharp-eyed as ever for a shady quid.

If some – the very worst, degenerate priests! –                    58*
had been as kind as mothers to their sons,
and not played step-dame to Imperial rights,

there's one, now Florentine, who wheels and deals                  61*
who'd soon have gone to Semifonte again,
where all his forebears did their daily rounds.

64    The Montemurli would be Conti serfs,
the Cerchi still Acone villagers,
the Buondelmonti maybe still mere Grievians.

67    Miscegenation has at all times been
the origin, in cities, of all ills,
as when you gorge on undigested foods.

70    A blinded bull falls quicker to the ground
than any blinded lamb. A single sword
at times cuts cleaner and more sure than five.

73*   Consider Urbisaglia and Luni, too,
how both these towns have gone, and how, behind,
go also Chiusi and Sinigaglia.

76    And when whole cities have, in this way, died,
it won't seem strange or hard for you to hear
that tribes and clans can likewise be unmade.

79    All human things have their own deaths to meet,
as you do also (though in some, long-lived,
the truth of this lies hid). And lives are short.

82    And, as the turning of the moon above
covers the shore unrestingly, and then
uncovers it, so Fortune does with Florence.

85    This should not, therefore, seem remarkable –
all I shall tell of noble Florentines,
whose fame lies hidden now in passing time.

88    I saw the Ughi, I saw the Catellini,
Filippi, Ormanni, Greci e Alberichi,
already in decline, illustrious men.

91    As great as they were ancient, I saw, too,
Bostichi, Soldanieri and Ardinghians,
the Arca and Sannella here as well.

94    Nearby the gate – in present times so filled
with novel felonies of such great weight
that soon the vessel will unship its load –

97    were once the Ravignani, from whom sprang
Count Guido, and, in later times, the clan
that takes its name from great Bellincion.

La Pressa knew already what it meant          100
to serve in government. The Galigaio house
displayed the golden hilt and sword of chivalry.

The Pale of Vair already had grown great,          103
Giuochi, Sacchetti, Barucci, Fifanti,
the Galli, too – and those who blush for salt-fraud.

The stock that bore Calfuccians by now          106
was great, and also to the seats of power
Sizii and Arrigucci had been drawn.

How well I saw them then, those now destroyed          109
by their own pride! Armorial orbs of gold
made Florence flower in all its enterprise.

So did the fathers, too, of those who now,          112
on finding that your bishop's church is free,
grow fat as proxies in consistory.

That bullying crew – which dragons over those          115
who run, but acts the very lamb when tooth
or even purse is flashed before its eyes –

they had arrived, though humble in their roots –          118
so Ubertin Donato looked askance
to be their kinsman through his own wife's line.

The Caponsacco of Fiesole          121
had now come down to join the Market Place.
Giudi and Infangati were good citizens.

I'll tell you this – incredible though true:          124
the gate through which one reached that little ring
was named in honour of some Pera clan!

Each of that House that bears upon its coat          127
the name of that great baron who's renewed,
in worth and fame, at annual Thomas feasts,

received from him chivalric rank and dues,          130
though he who binds his fringe around this sign
makes common cause with lower orders now.

The Importunes and Gualterotts were here.          133*
The Borgo would have been a calmer place
if they'd still lacked the neighbours that then came.

136    The House from which your flowing tears were born –
driven by rancour, rightfully, that slew
and put an end to your so-happy life –

139    was honoured then, itself and all its kin.
O Buondelmonte! You so wrongly fled,
as others urged, your marriage promises.

142    Many would now rejoice who now are sad
if God had yielded you to Ema's stream
when you arrived a first time in this town.

145    Yet this still had to be, that Florence made –
at Mars's battered stone which guards the bridge –
in her last days of peace, this sacrifice.

148    With all these people and with others, too,
I saw Florentia in such repose
that nothing could have caused it to lament.

151*    With all of these, so true and glorious,
I saw your citizens, the lily-flag
not dragged, reversed upon its conquered pole,

154    nor coloured in the conflict bright blood red.'

# CANTO 17

As Phaeton once, approaching Clymene, 1 *
to know for sure that news about himself
which still makes fathers chary of their sons,

so was I, too – and so was understood 4
by Beatrice and that holy lamp
which had, because of me, first left its place.

At which my lady said: 'Send out the flare 7
of your desire, as clear in coming forth
as, inwardly, the fire is stamped in you,

not to increase, by saying what that is, 10
the knowledge we already have, but more
to find, when speaking out, we slake your thirst.'

'You, the dear soil in which I thrive. You so 13
on-high yourself that you see well (as sure
as mortals know, in triangles, two angles

aren't obtuse) contingencies before 16
they come to be, your eye set wondering on
the point at which all times are present time.

While I was still in Virgil's company, 19
climbing the hill that remedies our souls,
so, too, descending to the dead, waste world,

he spoke to me in grave and weighty words 22
about my future life, so I should feel
four-square against the blows that were to come.

I'd therefore willingly receive sure words 25
that told what fortune now draws near to me.
Those arrows that we know will come fly slower.'

28     I said all this to that same light that, first,
had spoken out to me, and thus confessed,
as Beatrice wished, what I desired.

31     Not in those enigmatic words that once
entrammelled pagan fools, like birds in lime,
before the Lamb of God bore off their sin,

34     but clear, precise and solemn in his speech,
that father-love now gave me his reply,
enclosed, yet shown, in his own laughing light.

37*     'Contingency, whose sphere does not extend
beyond the margins of your earthly things,
is framed and painted in eternal sight.

40     This does not, though, imply necessity,
except, as might be when some glass reflects
a ship swept onward by a raging stream.

43     From that same view there comes before my eyes
(as to the ear sweet melodies may come)
the time that now prepares itself for you.

46*     As once Hippolytus was driven out
of Athens by his father's wife, perverse
and pitiless, so you'll leave Florence, too.

49*     This much is willed, this much already sought.
And soon he'll see it through, who thinks it up,
where all day long Christ's self is bought and sold.

52     Shrill cries of blame will chase the ones who lose –
they always do. But vengeance, when it falls,
will speak of that same Truth that deals it out.

55     You'll leave behind you all you hold most dear.
And this will be the grievous arrow barb
that exile, first of all, will shoot your way.

58     And you will taste the saltiness of bread
when offered by another's hand – as, too,
how hard it is to climb a stranger's stair.

61*     Yet what will weigh upon your shoulders worst
is all the foul, ill-minded company
that you, in that dark vale, will fall to keep.

For that ungrateful, crazy, vicious crew                    64
will turn as one against you. Yet it's them
whose brows before too long will blush with shame.

Their deeds will prove what animals they are.             67
And so much so, the finer course for you
would be to form a party on your own.

Your refuge and your safe abode will be                   70*
the courtesy at first of that great Lombard
whose blazon is a stair and holy bird.

And he will hold you in such high regard                  73
that "ask" and "do" between the two of you
will place as first what others put behind.

You'll see, along with him, his brother, too,             76
so strongly marked, when he was born, by Mars
that all his deeds will prove remarkable.

People as yet know nothing of this man.                   79
He is still fresh and young. The astral wheels
have worked around him for a mere nine years.

Before the Gascon tricks great Henry, though,             82*
the sparks of his high virtue will appear,
scornful of silver and the toils of war.

His proud liberality will make its mark,                  85
and even enemies, in seeing that,
will have no power to mute their tongues in praise.

Await him, and the good he'll bring to you.               88
By him a multitude will be transformed,
the poor exalted and the rich brought low.

Now carry, written in your memory                         91
(don't speak!), report of him.' He then said things
that even witnesses will not believe.

He added, then: 'It was of this, dear son,                94
they spoke. These are the wiles and snares that lie
concealed by some few circlings of the stars.

Yet I'd not have you envy those around.                   97
Your life and fame en-futures far beyond
the punishment their perfidy receives.'

100    Now falling silent, that most sacred soul
       declared his hand unburdened of the thread
       of that taut weave which I had stretched for him.

103    So I began – as anyone in doubt
       goes on and craves good counsel from the one
       who sees, whose will is right, whose love is strong.

106    'I now see clearly, Father, how the years spur down
       on me – and how the blow they mean to strike
       is worse to those who, fleeing, flinch aside.

109    It's better, then, I arm myself with foresight,
       so if that dearest place is snatched away,
       my verses do not lose me all the rest.

112    Down through the world of endless bitterness,
       around the mountain where my lady's look
       raised me so I could reach its lovely peak,

115    then through these heavenly spheres, from light to light
       I've learnt of things which, if I now repeat,
       will leave in many mouths an acid taste.

118    And if I prove a timid friend to truth
       I shall, I fear, forego my life among
       those souls who'll count as ancient our own time.'

121    The light in which the treasure I found there
       was smiling still, first blazed in coruscations
       as will a ray of sun in golden mirrors,

124    and then replied: 'All murky consciences,
       who feel their own or any other's shame
       are bound to baulk at your abrasive words.

127    But none the less, all lies put clean aside,
       make plain what in your vision you have seen,
       and let them scratch wherever they may itch.

130    For if at first your voice tastes odious,
       still it will offer, as digestion works,
       life-giving nutriment to those who eat.

133    The words you shout will be like blasts of wind
       that strike the very summit of the trees.
       And this will bring no small degree of fame.

For you've been shown in all these circling wheels –     136
around the mountain, in the sorrowing vale –
only those souls whose fame is widely known,
    since those who hear you speak will never pause     139
or give belief to any instances
whose family roots are hidden or unknown,
    nor demonstrations that remain obscure.'     142

# CANTO 18

1 Already, whole in happiness, that mirror
had turned, rejoicing, to its own true word.
I tasted mine – and tempered sour with sweet.
4 And then that lady, leading me to God,
spoke out: 'Revise those thoughts. Think this, that I
am near to Him who lifts all wrongs away.'
7 I turned towards that sound so full of love
(my strength, my comforter!) but saw, within
those holy eyes, a love I leave unsaid,
10 unsure not only of my powers of speech,
but Memory, as well – which cannot, if not led,
return, above itself, to that degree.
13 This much of that one point I can repeat:
my heart, in awe now looking back at her,
was free of all desires, save that alone –
16 as long, at least, as eternal pleasure,
shining in Beatrice's lovely eyes,
made me, in its reflected view, content.
19 A smile – its light defeating me – she now
addressed me: 'Turn around. Pay heed to him.
Heaven is found not only in my eyes.'
22 As sometimes here on earth a face is seen
displaying all its feelings – when the soul
is caught completely in these sentiments –
25 so in the flaming of that holy flare,
as now I turned to it, I recognized
a will to have some further words with me.

'In this, the fifth espalier of that tree                               28
that thrives,' so he began, 'from summit down,
bears constant fruit and never loses leaf,

are spirits of the blessed who, there below,                           31
won such renown before they reached these spheres
that any muse which sang of them would thrive.

So look in wonder on this Cross's horns.                                34
Each one I name to you will act as does
the swift fire darting through a thunder cloud.'

I saw, along the Cross-tree's beam, a light,                           37*
drawn all along that length by Joshua's name.
Nor did I note the name before the deed.

Then at the name of great Maccabeus,                                    40
I saw another, wheeling as it moved,
a spinning top whipped round by happiness.

Then, as the eye will track a falcon's flight,                         43
my own attentive gaze now followed two,
seeking out Roland and great Charlemagne.

And then along the Cross my sight was drawn                            46
to William, Reynald, Godfrey of Bouillon,
and with them, too, Roberto Guiscardo.

Then moving, mingling with the other lights,                           49
the soul that first had spoken now displayed
his own great art with these who sang the skies.

I turned to Beatrice at my right,                                      52
to see in her some gesture, word or sign,
to show me what my duty now must be,

and saw the light within her eye so clear,                            55
so full of laughter that her look and air
defeated all that these, before, had been.

And, as we recognize from day to day                                  58
that we, in doing good, have now advanced
when, doing good, we feel a greater joy,

so, too, as with the skies I circled round,                           61
I knew the arc through which we swung had grown,
seeing that miracle yet more adorned.

64     Compare: within the briefest span of time,
a lady pale in countenance will change,
when once she frees her blushing cheeks from shame.

67     At that same speed, turning, my eyes received
the candour of the temperate star – the sixth –
which now collected me within its sphere.

70     I saw in that great torch of Jupiter
the scintillations of a love that, here,
sparked signs before my eyes in human speech.

73     Like birds that rise above a river bank
and, chorusing in joy at food they find,
form flying discs and various other shapes,

76     so, deep in light, these holy creatures sang
and, as they winged around, they now assumed
the figure of a D, then I, then L.

79     Singing, at first, the notes of their own tune,
they then (becoming one of these three signs)
paused for a moment and let silence fall.

82*     You holy Pegasean Muse, who grants
to intellect its glory and long fame –
as, through such minds, to realms and cities, too –

85     inspire me with your light, so I may draw
those figures as I first conceived they were.
In these brief verses let your power appear.

88*     In five times seven vowels and consonants
it fashioned this display. And I took note
of all these parts as they appeared to me.

91     *DILIGITE IUSTITIAM*: these first –
main verb and noun of all that bright design.
*QUI IUDICATIS TERRAM* – these came last.

94     And then they gathered on the final M,
arranged so Jupiter seemed silver now
picked out in painted ornaments of gold.

97     And then I saw, descending, other lights
to mount the summit of the M and pause,
singing the Good, I think, that drew them to him.

Then, as when burning logs are struck, and sparks,      100
beyond all number, rise around (from which
fools, once, in pagan times drew auguries),
   it seemed that from this more than a thousand      103
lights rose surging up, some higher, some less,
as God's sun, kindling them, ascribed their place.
   And, once each rested at its proper point,      106
I saw, distinctly shown in golden fire,
the image of an Eagle's head and neck.
   He who paints there needs none to guide his hand.      109
He is the guide. From Him, we recognize,
derives the power that forms in our own nests.
   Those others in beatitude who, first,      112
in-lilying the M, had been content,
now joined, with no great movement, that same sign.
   Sweetest of stars! So many gems, so fine,      115
to make this known to me! Our justice is
produced by that great sky that you in-gem.
   So I beseech the Mind, in which begins      118
the motion and the strength you have, now look
at where the fumes arise that taint your rays,
   so that a second time He should now rage      121*
at 'buy' and 'sell' within those temple walls,
once built by miracles and martyrdom.
   You heavenly army that I gaze on now,      124
pray earnestly for those who are, on earth,
led by this vile example all astray.
   War was at one time waged with swords alone.      127*
But now it's done by snatching, here and there,
the bread our loving Father locks from none.
   But you – I write of you to blot you out –      130
just think that Paul and Peter who both died
to serve the vine that you lay waste, live still.
   You may well say: 'I'm firm in my desire      133
to be like John who lived his life alone,
drawn to his martyrdom by sprightly dance,
   and so don't know this fisherman, or Paul.'      136

# CANTO 19

It showed before me now with open wings   –
that lovely emblem which those happy souls
composed in utmost *frui*, interwoven.

4 Each soul showed forth as minute rubies might.
In each a sun ray burned with such new fire
its light, reflected, broke back from my eyes.

7 But now there's something I must draw to mind
that no voice ever carried, ink inscribed,
or great imagination ever grasped.

10 I saw and heard that Eagle's beak form words
that rang, in what they voiced, as 'I' and 'mine',
although in meaning they were 'we' and 'us'.

13 'I am' – beginning so – 'through being true
and just in all things, raised to glorious heights
that no desire could ever overcome.

16 On earth I leave so great a memory
that even evil-minded men down there
who don't take up the tale still honour it.'

19 From many coals we feel one wave of heat.
So, too, from all these many loving souls,
a single sound came issuing from its form.

22 So I at once: 'You are, perpetually,
the flowerings of eternal happiness.
And all your perfumes are, to me, as one.

25 Breathing upon me, set me free, untie
the hankering that's held me now so long,
On earth I find no food for it at all.

God's justice, as I know from all I've seen,                                     28
is mirrored, in these spheres, by other realms.
But your sphere comprehends it, through no veil.

And you know how attentively I've come,                                          31*
prepared to hear. You know the doubt as well,
the old, long hungering I suffer from.'

As falcons, shaking free from training-hoods,                                    34
will move their heads, applauding with their wings,
to show their zeal and make themselves look fine,

so did this emblem, woven out of praise                                          37
that sang the glory of God's grace, in hymns
that those who celebrate above will know.

'The One who turned His compass,' it began,                                      40
'around the reaches of the universe,
and marked, within, things clear and dark to view,

might blaze His worth upon that cosmic plan,                                     43
yet could not fail, in doing so, to leave,
as infinite excess, His truest word.

As proof of this, that being, first in pride,                                   46
the summit, once, of all creation, fell –
he would not wait for light – acid, unripe.

From which it's clear that natures less than his                                49
are all too shallow to contain that Good
which has no end and measures self by self.

Therefore, the powers of sight that you possess –                               52
which must exist as rays from that one Mind
with which all things that are are brimming full –

cannot, in their own nature, be so great                                        55
that their Original should not have sight
of much beyond what, there, appears to them.

It follows that the sight your world receives                                    58
in sempiternal justice sinks itself
three-fold as deep as eyes in open sea.

Although you see the bottom near the shore,                                      61
the ocean floor you *can't*. And yet it's there.
Its depths conceal its being so profound.

64     There is no light except from that clear calm,
changeless, untroubled. Others are tenebrae,
the shadows or the venom of the flesh.

67     It's open now enough, that brooding deep –
where, hidden from you, living justice lay –
of which so frequently you've made demand.

70     "A man is born," you've said repeatedly,
"beside the Indus. And there's no one there
who speaks of Christ, or reads or writes of Him.

73     And all he does and all he means to do –
as far as human minds can tell – is good,
sinless alike in living and in word.

76     Then, unbaptized, beyond the faith, he dies.
Where is the justice that condemns him thus?
Where is his guilt, if he does not believe?"

79     Well, who are you to sit there on your throne,
acting the judge a thousand miles away,
eyesight as short as some mere finger span?

82     Of course, all those who seek to pin me down
might find amazing reasons for their doubts,
except the Scriptures are set over you.

85     You earthbound creatures, dense in thought and head!
The Primal Will, which of itself is good,
has never from its own high good been moved.

88     What counts as just will ring in tune with that.
No creature-good draws that will to itself.
But *that* – its rays projecting – causes *this*.'

91     Compare: a mother stork has fed its young
and, while its chick, well-nourished, gazes up,
it flies in circles high above the nest.

94     So, too, it rose – I raised my brows to it –
that emblem in its blessedness, which moved
with wings supported on the truths it spoke.

97     Wheeling, it sang and, singing, said: 'To you
our melodies – which you don't understand –
are as eternal justice is to mortal minds.'

And then these glowing fires of Holy Breath　　　　100
grew quiet once again within that sign
which, in the world, made Romans so revered,

　　then spoke anew: 'There is, in this realm, none　　103*
who ever rose that had no faith in Christ
since, or before, they nailed Him to the wood.

　　But see this: many cry out: "Christ! Christ! Christ!"　106
Yet many will, come Judgement, be to Him
less *prope* than are those who don't know Christ.

　　And Christians such as these the Ethiopian　　109
will damn when souls divide between two schools,
some to eternal riches, some to dearth.

　　What will the Persians say about your kings,　　112
when once they see that ledger opened up
in which is written all their praiseless doings.

　　Peer at that page, and see in Albert's deeds　　115*
one – which will shortly stir God's pen to write –
by which the realm of Prague lies waste and dead.

　　Peer at that page, and see there one who grieved　118
the Seine in uttering his worthless coin,
dying when toppled by a wild boar's hide.

　　Peer at that page, and you'll see there the pride　121
that sharpens in mad Englishmen and Scots
such thirst that neither keeps their native bounds.

　　O there you'll see the lust and lecherous lives　124
of Spanish and Bohemian sovereigns,
who know no honour, nor desire to know.

　　O there you'll see the Cripple of Jerusalem　127
scoring mere "one" for virtuous effect,
and *thousands* in the column opposite.

　　O there you'll see the weak-kneed graspingness　130*
of one who governs in the isle of fire
where once Anchises ended his long days.

　　'Xcept, to show how paltry his deeds are　133
the writing here will be in brief, maimed words,
and thus will note down much in little space.

136     'Xcept, to all the loathsome acts will show
of nuncle and his brud, those two who turned
so great a race to cuckolds – and two crowns.

139*     'Xcept, the Portuguese and Norway kings
will there be recognized, the Rascian, too,
who set eyes falsely on Venetian coin.

142     O blessèd Hungary, if you resist
further bad government! Blessèd Navarre,
if you can arm the hills that swaddle you!

145     And that is pledged, as all should well believe,
by French-ruled Nicosia and Famagosta,
lamenting, shrieking in their agony

148     against their beast, who huddles with the rest.'

# CANTO 20

When he whose flame casts light round all the world     1
goes down and leaves our northern hemisphere –
and daylight therefore fades throughout these parts –
  the sky, once lighted by the sun alone,     4
seems suddenly made new by many flares,
reflections kindled from that single source.
  These movements of our sky here came to mind     7
as now the world's great sign – true guide of kings –
fell silent at its blessèd raptor-beak.
  For all those lights, so vividly alive,     10
shining more brightly still, began a song
that glides like falling leaves from memory.
  Love, which in laughter sweetly clothes itself,     13
how ardent in those piercing pipes you burned,
voiced by the breath of holy thoughts alone.
  When all those lucid and so precious gems     16
with which, I saw, the sixth great light was set
had brought to silence their angelic peal,
  I heard, it seemed, the murmur of a river,     19
falling from rock to rock in limpid streams
that show the swelling richness of its source.
  Compare: guitar notes sound from where the fret     22
gets pressed – as, likewise, at its apertures
a reedy flute when pierced by breaths of wind.
  So here, the moment of delay now done,     25
that murmur, as in hollow columns, rose
through all the length of this great Eagle's neck.

28      It formed there as a voice and, through the bill,
        the phrases came, in words which I, at heart –
        where I inscribed them all – was waiting for.

31*     'This,' it began, 'is now required of you,
        to look, eyes fixed, upon that part of me
        that sees, in earthly eagles, yet endures, the sun.

34      Of all the fires from which I frame my form,
        those sparks that make the eye shine in my head
        appear as highest of the many grades.

37*     There, at the centre of the pupil, see
        David, the singer of the Holy Ghost,
        who bore the Ark of God from place to place.

40      And now he knows the merit of his song –
        as far as his own thought produced such verse –
        here seeing how he's paid in equal kind.

43      Then, of those five whose circle forms my brow,
        he who is closest to my bill's high bridge
        consoled the widow for her murdered son.

46      And now he knows how great a price is paid
        by those who aren't by choice Christ's followers.
        He's known life's sweetness and its contrary.

49      The one who's next in that circumference –
        forming, I mean, around the upper brow –
        made death, by his true penitence, come slow.

52      And now he knows eternal justice stands,
        and does not alter when a worthy prayer
        down there procrastinates quotidian things.

55      There follows next the one who, though his aims
        were good, brought forth bad fruit, surrendering –
        now Greek – with Law and Eagle-signs to Popes.

58      And here he knows that, though the world is wrecked,
        the ill deriving from his well-meant act
        has here for him no baneful consequence.

61      The one you see in that declining arc
        was William, long-lamented by the land
        that weeps that Charles lives still – and Frederick, too.

And here he knows what love this heaven feels     64
for righteous kings, and here he still displays
that understanding by his brilliant light.

And who, in that erroneous world down there,     67
would ever think that Trojan Ripheus
was fifth within that round of holy lights?

Here, he now knows far more about God's grace –     70
although his vision does not pierce the depths –
than any in the earthly world can see.'

A lark, as first it mounts through airy space,     73
soars upward singing but is silent then,
flush with the sweetness of its highest reach.

So, too, it seemed, that image of the print     76
of everlasting joy, at whose desire
each thing becomes what truly each thing is.

And though, in what I meant to ask, I was,     79
maybe, as glass that shows the hue it clothes,
these doubts could bear no silent waiting time,

but forced from my tensed lips: 'What is all this?'     82
with all their weight and gathered impetus.
At which I saw a fête of coruscations.

And after – as its eye burned brighter still –     85
that blessèd sign then gave me its reply,
so I'd not hang there long in wonderment.

'I see that you, because I say these things,     88
believe they're so and yet cannot see why,
so these are hidden even though believed.

You act like someone who may know quite well     91
the name but not the essence of a thing,
unless by demonstration made to see.

*Regnum celorum* will submit to force     94*
assailed by warmth of love or living hope,
which overcome the claims of God's own will,

not in the manner that men beat down men     97
but win because will wishes to be won
and, won, wills all with all its own good will.

100    The first life and the fifth that mark this brow
       cause you to wonder. You're amazed to see
       the realm of angels painted with these lights.

103    They left their bodies, *contra* your belief,
       as Christian souls, not Gentiles, firm in faith
       that His feet paced to past or coming pain.

106    Trajan from Hell – from where, to exercise
       good will no soul returns – came back to bone,
       this mercy granted him for living hope.

109    For living hope committed all its powers
       in prayer to God to raise him up once more,
       so that he could, in will, be made to move.

112    The glorious soul that we're now speaking of,
       returning even briefly to his flesh,
       believed in Him whose power could bring him aid,

115    and, so believing, blazed forth in such fires
       of love in truth that he, on second death,
       was fit to make his way to this great game.

118    The other, by that grace which drops like dew –
       its source so deep that no created eye
       can ever penetrate the primal wave –

121    set all its love, down there, on righteousness.
       God, therefore, opened Ripheus's eyes,
       grace upon grace, to when we'd be redeemed.

124    In that redemption, he believed. And so
       he did not suffer any pagan stench,
       but stood as blunt reproof to those who strayed.

127*   Those three pure *donne* from the right-hand wheel
       which you saw once were his as baptism,
       a thousand years before baptizing came.

130    Predestination! How remote your root
       from all those faces that, in looking up,
       cannot *in toto* see the primal cause!

133    And so you mortals, in your judgements show
       restraint. For even we who look on God
       do not yet know who all the chosen are.

Yet this deficiency for us is sweet.  136
For in this good our own good finds its goal,
that what God wills we likewise seek in will.'

So from that sacred sign was given me,  139
to bring to my short sight new clarity,
a gentle draught of soothing medicine.

As good guitarists with good singers make  142
the string vibrate in answer to the beat,
because of which the song gains more delight,

so as it spoke, as I recall to mind,  145
I saw the lights of those two blessed souls,
concordant as the flickering of our eyes,

move at these words the bright sparks of their flames.  148

# CANTO 21

1     Now once again my eyes were fixed upon
my *donna*'s countenance, and drawn away,
with all my thoughts, from any other aim.

4*    She did not smile. But: 'If I were to smile,'
so she began, 'you would become what once
Semele was, when she was turned to ash.

7     For if my beauty (which, as you have seen,
burns yet more brightly as it climbs the stair
that carries us through this eternal hall)

10    were not now tempered, it would shine so clear
that all within your mortal power would be
a sprig, as this flash struck, shaken by thunder.

13*   We're lifted to the seventh splendour now,
which here, beneath the fiery Lion's breast,
combines its rays, in brave strength, with that sign.

16    Fix your mind firm behind those eyes of yours,
and make them both a mirror for the form
that in *this* mirror will appear to you.'

19    Whoever knows the pasture, for themselves,
that my eyes grazed on in that blessed sight,
when once I'd altered to that other care,

22    will recognize the pleasure that I took
in bowing down to that celestial guide,
weighing consent against the sight of her.

25*   Within the crystal, circling round the world,
which bears the etymon of that dear lord –
under whose sway all evil thoughts lie dead,

I saw, as gold in which a ray shines through,    28 *
a ladder stretching upwards – and so far –
my eye-lights could not follow where it led.

I also saw descending, rung by rung,    31
so many brilliancies that every flare
the sky displays I thought was flowing down.

Compare: by instinct, as the day first breaks,    34
jackdaws will flock and stir their wings as one
to bring some warmth once more to icy plumes.

Then some will make away and not return,    37
while others *do* go back from where they'd come,
and some will stay and wheel round that same spot.

In just that way, these sparks appeared to me,    40
combining in their scintillating showers
as each one struck upon a certain step.

The light, then, tightest at our side, shone out    43 *
so clear that, thinking to myself, I said:
'I see full well what love you show to me.

But she from whom I wait to hear the "when"    46
of silence and of speech, and "how", stays still.
Against my will, it's well that I don't ask.'

So she who saw my silence in the sight    49
of Him who sees the all of everything
said now: 'Unloose the knot of warm desire.'

'No merit I may claim,' so I began,    52
'can make me fit to hear what you will say.
But, for the sake of her who lets me ask,

make known to me, you happy living soul,    55
hiding within the heart of your own joy,
the reason you have set yourself so near me.

And tell me why the symphony    58
of Paradise, which sounds in sweet devotion
through the other spheres, is muted in this wheel.'

'In hearing, you are mortal, as in sight.    61
So, just as Beatrice does not smile,
likewise,' he answered me, 'there's no song here.

64     I have descended down the holy stair
as far as this to bring you only joy,
with speech and with the light that mantles me.

67     Nor does more love to you make me more quick.
For that same love, and more, seethes upwards here
as all this flaming-out displays to you.

70     But *caritas* on high that makes us serve
so readily the wisdom of the spheres
allots the places here as you observe.'

73     'I truly see,' I said, 'O sacred light,
how love – the freedom of this holy court –
is all one needs to trace God's providence.

76     But this, for me, seems hard to penetrate:
why, among those who share your destiny,
are you alone predestined to this task?'

79     Nor had I reached the last of all these words
when that light took its centre as a hub,
spinning around itself as grindstones do.

82     The love within it then replied to me:
'Divine light drives its point upon me here.
And, penetrating that in which I'm wombed,

85     its virtue, joined with my own powers of sight,
lifts me so high above myself, I see
on high the essence where that light is milked.

88     Hence comes the brightening joy in which I flame.
Equal to what I see in clarity
is this clear flame that I myself display.

91     But still the soul in Heaven that brightens most –
that seraph with its eye fixed most in God –
could never satisfy your last demand.

94     For what you ask so in-beyonds itself
within the chasm of divine decree,
it's cut off wholly from a creature's sight.

97     And so when you return to mortal things,
bear this with you, so none there may presume
to move their feet to any suchlike aim.

Minds that shine here, on earth give off mere smoke.    100
So just consider whether those down there
could do what, raised to Heaven, no mind can do.'

His words so cut and limited my thoughts    103
that I gave up the question, holding back,
to ask him, very humbly, who he was.

'Between the littorals of Italy    106*
not far from your own fatherland, hard rocks
surge up so high the thunder sounds beneath.

These form a hunchback ridge called Catria.    109
Below that lies a consecrated cell
devoted, once, to God's unending praise.'

So he began for me his third address,    112
and then, continuing: 'Here I remained
so steadfast in the service of our Lord –

oil, simply, of the olive dressed my food –    115
that I lived lightly through both heat and chill,
contented with contemplative intent.

That cloister once would render to the skies    118
a fertile crop, but now – and this will soon
be all revealed – is hollow, empty, vain.

In that place, I was Peter Damian,    121*
and otherwise, within Our Lady's house,
Peter the Sinner on the Adriatic shore.

Little, for me, of mortal life remained    124
when I was called and forced to wear the gear
that's handed down, these days, from bad to worse.

Once Cephas came – as did that vessel, too,    127*
of Holy Inspiration – shoeless, lean,
taking their meals in any mere hotel.

Our modern pastors, though, have put on weight.    130
They need some propping up on either side,
someone to hoist their backsides up, or lead.

The robes they dress in cloak their steeds as well,    133
so two beasts go within a single skin.
What patience, God! to bear a sight like that.'

136      I saw, as this was said, more little flames,
ascending and revolving, step by step,
more beautiful at every turn they took.

139      They came and circled round this soul, then stopped,
and gave a cry so piercing in its sound
that nothing here on earth could equal it.

142      And, thunderstruck, I did not understand.

# CANTO 22

Astounded, overwhelmed, I turned to her,        1
my constant guide, like any little boy
who'll run to where his greatest trust is found.

    And rushing there, as mothers always do,        4
with words to help and set once more to rights
her shocked, pale, sobbing son, she said to me:

    'Do you not know that you're in Heaven now?        7
Or know the heavens are holy everywhere,
and all that here is done is done from zeal?

    Just think of this: how much that song and I,        10
in smiling, would have wrought in you a change
when you are so much moved by that great cry –

    in which, if you had understood their prayers,        13
you might have heard the vengeance clearly sung
that you will come to see before your death.

    That sword raised here will strike, though not in haste,    16
nor yet too slow, save only in the view
of those who wait in fear or keen desire.

    But now turn round to look on other souls.        19
If, as I ask, you turn your face to these,
you'll see the shining honour of their hearts.'

    Once more, as she desired, I turned my eyes,        22
and saw a hundred bright particular spheres
that all grew lovelier in their mutual rays.

    So there I stood, like someone driving back        25
the point of his desire within himself,
not daring out of fear to question more.

28       And now the fullest of those orient pearls,
most brilliant in its lustre, made to come
and make my will content with what it was.

31*      Within, I heard: 'Were you to see, as I,
the *caritas* that burns among us here,
you would by now have pressed your thoughts to voice.

34       But lest, in pausing, you too long defer
the road to your high goal, I'll make reply
directly to your thought, since that's your care.

37       The mountain on whose sides Cassino is
was thickly peopled round its summit once
by tribes, deluded, of a stubborn strain.

40       And I am he who bore first to that height
the name of Him who carried down to earth
the truth that bears us to transcendent realms.

43       And grace to that extent shone down on me
that I retrieved the townships all around
from false devotions that seduce the world.

46       These other fires were all contemplatives,
men brightly kindled by the ardent warmth
that brings to birth the holy flowers and fruit.

49*      Maccario is here; Romoaldo here.
Here are my brothers, who within the cloister
steadied their steps and kept their hearts entire.'

52       And I to him: 'The feeling you display
in speaking thus to me, the looks
I note so well-disposed in you, and all these fires,

55       have caused in me my trust to open wide
as sun does to the rose when this becomes
as fully open as its power can be.

58       Therefore I pray, do, Father, make me sure
that I may come to take such grace that I
might see your face, uncovered, as you are.'

61       At which, he said: 'Brother, your high desire
will be fulfilled within the final sphere,
where all desires, as mine too, are fulfilled.

All our desiring is perfected there, 64
complete and fruitful in that sphere alone
where every part is where all parts have been.

For that is no mere place. It has no pole. 67
Our ladder, rising, spans across to that,
and therefore steals in flight away from view.

Up there, to where its highest part extends, 70*
the Patriarch beheld it all – Jacob
who saw the angels loading all its length.

But no one lifts their feet, now, from the earth 73
to climb those rungs. My Rule remains a waste
of all the vellum that it's copied on.

The walls that once encircled abbey grounds 76
are turned to dens and lairs. Monastic cowls
are bursting sacks stuffed full with rotten flour.

But even usury at its worst does not 79
distract so much from all that God finds good
as that fruit does, which maddens monks at heart.

For everything the Church is there to guard 82
belongs to those who ask it in God's name.
It is not meant for kinsmen – worse still, brutes.

The flesh of mortals runs to yielding flab. 85
So good beginnings aren't enough to last
to acorn time from when the oak is born.

Peter began – no silver and no gold! – 88
as I did, too, with fasting and with prayers.
And Francis built his order on humility.

But if you look where each of these began, 91
and then consider where their track has run,
you'll see the white original turned dark.

And yet, to see the Jordan turning back 94*
or, as God willed, the ocean flee apart
is more miraculous than God's aid here.'

All this he said, and then once more drew back 97
to join his cell, and that cell tightened in.
And then, as whirlwinds do, it spiralled up.

100\*  My sweetest lady with a single sign –
the powers she had so vanquished what I was –
drove me to mount the ladder after them.

103  Nor where, in natural terms, we climb or sink
is any motion ever swift enough
to match the speed of what my wings could do.

106  So may I, reader, sometime join once more
that prayerful march of victory (for which
I often weep my sins and beat my breast),

109  you'd not so swiftly have withdrawn and thrust
your finger in the fire as I first saw
the sign that follows Taurus . . . and was in!

112  You stars in glory! Light enwombing here
those virtuous powers from which, I recognize,
whatever talents that are mine derive,

115  with you, the father of all mortal life
was born, conjoined, then hidden in your span,
when first I felt the bite of Tuscan air.

118  And then when, free and wide, grace granted me
high entry to the wheel that turns your sphere,
yours was the region here allotted me.

121  My soul in all devotion breathes to you,
seeking from you the virtue and the strength
to meet the test the heavens now draw it to.

124  'You are so close,' so Beatrice said,
'to your salvation here that you must keep
the light within your eye acute and clear.

127  And so, before you further "in" yourself,
look down and wonder at how great a world
already you have set beneath your feet,

130  so that your heart may show itself, as full
as it may be, to this triumphant throng
that rings in happiness the ethereal round.'

133  I turned about to look once more through all
the seven spheres and, seeing there the globe,
I smiled to find how small and cheap it seemed.

I thoroughly approve as best the thought          136
that earth is least. Those, then, who set their minds
on other things are known as right and able.

I saw, on fire, the daughter of Latona,          139*
free of the shadow that had made me once
believe the moon to be both rare and dense.

I now could bear, Hyperion, the look          142*
of your bright son. I saw there movements, too –
Dione, Maia – that were circling near.

And there, between his sire and son, appeared          145
the tempering influence of Jupiter
and, clear to view, the varying 'where' of each.

And all these seven spheres displayed to me          148
their magnitude, their speed, the distance, too,
that lay between the dwelling place of each.

That little threshing floor that makes men fierce,          151
myself now turning with the eternal Twins,
was seen entire – to river-mouths from hills.

My eyes I then turned back to her fine eyes.          154

# CANTO 23

1     Compare: a bird, among her well-loved boughs,
has rested all night long while things lie hid,
poised where her dear brood sleeps within their nest;

4     and then, to glimpse the looks she's longed to see,
and find the food her fledglings feed upon
(these efforts weigh with her as pure delight)

7     before dawn comes she mounts an open sprig,
and there, her heart ablaze, awaits the sun,
eyes sharpening, fixed, till day is truly born.

10*     So, too, head raised, tall, straight, my *donna* stood,
attention wholly on that stretch of sky
where, under noon, the sun displays least speed.

13     And I, to see her stand enraptured so,
became like one desiring still what he
has not – and yet in hope is satisfied.

16     But little time went by between these two –
I mean my waiting, and my seeing now
the skies that, brightening still, grew yet more bright.

19     And 'Look!' said Beatrice. 'Triumphing,
the soldiery of Christ, and all the yield,
brought from the orbit of the farthest spheres!'

22     Her face, it seemed to me, now burned so bright,
her eyes so filled with utmost happiness,
that I must needs pass on and frame no word.

25*     As in the calm, clear skies of moonlit nights,
tri-form Diana smiles (eternal nymphs,
around her, paint all Heaven's curving spheres),

above a thousand lanterns or still more,　　　　　　28
I saw one sun that, soaring, lit them all,
as our sun lights the stars seen over us.

And through this clear and living light there shone　　31
the being that creates that glow, too bright
within my eyes for me to tolerate.

My sweetness! Beatrice, guiding me!　　　　　　34
She spoke: 'This power that overcomes your sight
is one from which no shelter can be sought.

Here is all wisdom, and the strength that cleared　　37*
the open road that runs from Heaven to earth,
for which so long was once such deep desire.'

As bolts of fire, unlocked from thunder clouds,　　　40
expand beyond containment in those bounds,
then fall to ground (as fire, by nature, can't),

so, too, surrounded by this solemn feast,　　　　　43
my own mind, grown the greater now, went forth
and can't remember what it then became.

'Open your eyes and look at what I am!　　　　　46
You have seen things by which you're made so strong,
you can, now, bear to look upon my smile.'

I was like one whose waking sense returns　　　　49
yet strives in vain – his dreaming now oblivion –
to bring once more that vision back to mind,

as I now heard that utterance which deserves　　　52*
a gratitude that never should be dimmed
from that great book that tells of things long past.

Even if all those voices were to sound　　　　　55*
that Polyhymnia and her sister muses
fed on their sweetest milk so richly once,

and aid me, singing of that holy smile　　　　　58
and how her holy look grew purer still,
I'd still not reach one thousandth of the truth.

And so, imagining this Paradise,　　　　　　61
the sacred epic has to make a leap,
as when we find the road ahead cut off.

64      Yet no one if they've gauged that weighty theme –
and seen what mortal shoulders bear the load –
would criticize such trembling backing-out.

67      The waves that my adventurous prow here cleaves
are no mere sea-loch that some skiff might cross,
or helmsmen lacking in the proper skill.

70      'Why is it that my face in-loves you so
that you don't turn to see the garden where,
beneath Christ's rays, such beauty is en-flowered?

73*      The rose in which the Word of God became
our flesh is here. And here those fleurs-de-lys
whose perfume marks the path we rightly tread.'

76      So, Beatrice. And I, quick to read
whatever she might counsel, gave myself
to battle, feeble though my eyelids were.

79      My eyes have seen at times – though wrapped in shade –
a ray of limpid sunlight, filtering
through broken cloud, across a field of flowers.

82      So here I saw a swirling crowd of splendours
flung out like thunderbolts down burning beams,
and could not see from where these flashes came.

85      You, Generous Strength! You leave your imprint here.
To open this arena to my eyes (powerless
to see You otherwise) You rose on high.

88      The naming of that lovely flower which I,
at dawn and evening, call upon, compelled
my mind to face in full the greatest fire.

91      And as my eyes, together, now portrayed
the scope and nature of that bright, live star,
victorious there, victorious here below,

94      straight through the skies another torch came down
spun in a circle, as a crown might be,
and formed a ring around her, turning there.

97      The sweetest melody that sounds on earth,
or that which most attracts the soul to it,
would seem like cloud ripped wide by thunder claps

when heard beside the sounding of that lyre 100
whose notes now crowned the lovely sapphire-stone,
through whom the skies en-sapphire clearer still.

'I am the angel-love called Gabriel, 103
encircling here the height of joy that breathes
around the womb our Longed-for sheltered in.

Lady of Heaven, I shall spin these turns 106*
till, in procession, you, behind your son,
make the High Sphere, on entering, more divine.'

And so the perfect circling of that tune 109
sealed its conclusion, while the other lights
rang out the sound of Maria's name.

The regal surcoat of those rolling spheres 112
that form our universe, alive with stars,
all shimmering at the breathing of God's rule

now stretched its inner shore so far above 115
that nothing of it showed from where I was,
no glimpse of that First Mover came to view.

Therefore my eyes could not command the power 118
to follow as that flame, within its crown,
rose up so close behind the seed she'd borne.

A baby, suckling, once it's full of milk, 121
will hold its arms out wide towards its mum
to make known outwardly its inner flame.

So, at their incandescent peaks, these gleams 124
stretched up. And this, to me, made clear what depths
of heartfelt love they bore towards Maria.

But all remained there, still within my sight, 127*
singing in such sweet tones 'Regina coeli'
delight at that will never leave my heart.

What richness, what abundance now well-stored 130
within such overflowing barns – which were
good husbandmen who sowed the seed below.

Here life is lived rejoicing in that hoard, 133*
gained ever weeping in the exile years
of Babylon, when gold was put aside.

136*     And here beneath the most exalted Son
        of God and Mary, in His victory,
        with all the new and all the ancient court,
139      triumphs the one who holds such glory's key.

# CANTO 24

'You chosen confrères of the Blessèd Lamb                    1
who feeds you at his solemn feast so well
that you are full in all you wish and will,

   if this man here should taste, by grace of God,          4
the crumbs and morsels falling from your board
before his death prescribes for him due time,

   direct your mind to his unmeasured zeal.                 7
Let dew refresh him for a while. You drink
that spring for ever where his thought derives.'

   Thus Beatrice. And those happy souls                     10
became like spheres revolving round fixed points,
flaming in spinning turns as comets do.

   The well-tuned wheels of gold chronometers               13*
will seem (to those who check) to whirl in gear,
the first cog steady and the last in flight.

   So, too, with all their measures swirling diff-          16
erently, they, dancing, let me estimate
the riches – slow or rapid – each possessed.

   Then, from the one I'd marked of dearer worth,           19
I saw a fire flare out with so much joy
that none now left behind it was so clear.

   Three times it circled Beatrice round,                   22
the song it sang too deeply divinized
for my imagination to recount.

   And so my pen will leap, and I'll not write.             25
Such pictures as we form – and words, of course –
are far too garish for those subtle pleats.

28      'My holy sister. You have prayed for this
with such devotion and such ardent prayers
that you unloose me from that lovely sphere.'

31      Then, when that blessèd fire had come to rest,
it breathed directly to my lady there
in words of fire, as I have spoken them.

34      And she: 'Eternal light of that great man
to whom Our Lord bequeathed the keys (which He
first bore below) of this high jubilation,

37      try him, as you may please, on any point –
weighty or light – in matters of that Faith
by which you came to walk across the sea.

40      Whether he loves, believes and has good hope,
cannot be secret. For your eyes here turn
where all things are depicted, clear to see.

43      But since this realm has gained its citizens
through one true faith, it's good that he should come
and speak of that, to glorify its name.'

46*     Compare: at vivas students hold their fire
until, to test and not conclude the proof,
professors lay their questions out to them.

49      So I, while she was speaking, armed myself
with every argument, to be prepared
for questions, and professions of my own.

52      'Tell me, good Christian (and make clear you *are*):
what is this faith?' At which, towards the light
from which he breathed these words, I raised my brow,

55      then turned to Beatrice. Quick in glance,
she urged me, from my deepest inward source,
that I should pour these spreading waters out.

58      'Let grace, which grants that I confess my faith
to you, the noblest of centurions,
make,' I began, 'my thoughts be well expressed.'

61*     And next: 'As written by the truthful pen,
Father, of your dear brother Paul, who set,
with you, great Rome upon its rightful track:

"Faith is substantial to the things we hope,      64
the evidence of things we do not see."
And such, in essence, I believe it is.'

   And then I heard: 'You understand aright –      67
so long as you can tell why he classed faith
as "substance" first, and then as "evidence".'

   I followed on: 'All those deep mysteries      70
which here so freely show themselves to me
are, to the eyes of those down there well hid,

   so what they are lies wholly in belief,      73*
on which is posited the highest hope.
Faith, for that reason, falls in *substance* class.

   And we are bound to form, from that belief –      76
with nothing seen beyond – sound arguments.
It's therefore classed as *evidence* as well.'

   And now I heard: 'If everything down there,      79
wrung out of doctrine, were so understood,
there'd be no room for showy sophistries.'

   This breathed from that enkindled love. And then,      82
'In alloy,' he went on, 'and legal weight,
the coin you produce has passed assay.

   But tell me, have you got it in your purse?'      85
At which, 'I have!' I said. 'Yes! Round and bright.
Nothing in how it's minted p'rhapses me.'

   And then came flowing from that deepest light      88
which there shone out: 'That precious gem of joy
in which all other virtues find their ground –

   whence does that come to you?' And I: 'The rain      91
(so generous!) of the Holy Ghost that flows
between the leathered texts, both old and new,

   in logic is, I think, conclusively      94
so sharp a proof that, when compared with that,
all formal arguments appear obtuse.'

   I heard then: 'All these premises, both old      97
and new, that bring you to conclude this, *why*
are these, you think, the light of holy tongues?'

100 And I: 'The proof, for me, that unlocks truth
is found in deeds that followed from that faith.
Nature can't heat or hammer steel like that.'

103* 'But say,' came this riposte, 'who gave to you
assurance of these deeds? That very Book
asserted this which still, itself, needs proof.'

106 'Suppose the world had turned to Christian faith
without these miracles,' I said, 'then that
would be a hundred times the miracle.

109 For you were poor and needy in the field,
when you went out to sow this fertile crop.
Once there were vines where now are only thorns.'

112 When this was done, the holy court on high
echoed through all the spheres its 'God be praised!'
sung to the melodies they sing up there.

115 That lord who, in examining my work,
had drawn me out, then onward branch to branch
(so that we now drew near the last, fresh leaves)

118 once more began: 'The play of grace that woos
your mind has opened up, till now, your lips
exactly as it's right to open them.

121 So, what emerged I seal and certify.
But now you need to say what you believe,
and say what source first gave this faith to you.'

124* 'Most Holy Father, Spirit who now sees
what once you so believed that you outdid
the younger feet that ran towards the grave'

127 (thus I began) 'you'd have me now make plain
the formal essence of my ready faith,
seeking as well its rationale and cause.

130 I answer: I believe in one true God,
sole and eternal who, Himself not moved,
moves all the spheres by love and with desire.

133* For this belief I have – beside those proofs
that physics gives, and metaphysics, too –
the truth that comes to me, as rain from here,

    through Moses, through the prophets and the psalms,   136
through Gospel writings and the words you wrote
when once the ardent Spirit raised you high.

    And I believe in three eternal persons,   139
believing these one substance, one and three,
to whom, grammatically, apply both "is" and "are".

    This deep condition of divinity,   142
which I here note, is many times impressed
by Gospel teachings on my intellect.

    This doctrine is the origin, the spark   145
that spreads to light the living flame,
which flashes out in me as stars in heaven.'

    Like some great man, who, pleased with what he hears,   148
rejoicing at his servant's news, will fling
his arms, as silence falls, around his neck,

    so, singing as its blessings fell on me,   151
three times – my words now mute – it circled me,
the light of that apostle at whose will

    I'd spoken thus, the speech had pleased it so.   154

# CANTO 25

1*     If ever it should happen that this sacred work,
to which both Earth and Heaven have set their hands,
(making me over many years grow gaunt)

4     might overcome the cruelty that locks me out
from where I slept, a lamb in that fine fold,
the enemy of wolves that war on it,

7     with altered fleece, with altered voice, I shall
return as poet, taking, at my fount
of baptism, the laurel for my crown.

10     For I first entered there within the faith
that makes us known, in soul, to God, and then,
for that same faith, Saint Peter ringed my brow.

13*     Towards us now there moved a light
drawn from the sphere where that first fruit of all
the ministers of Christ had issued out.

16     And, filled with happiness, my lady said:
'Look there! The wonder of it! Look! The Lord
for whom the pilgrims travel to Galicia.'

19     Compare: a dove will settle by its mate
and, each to each, both turning, murmuring,
make proclamation of the love they feel.

22     So, too, I saw in glory each great prince
made welcome, each by each, in that high realm,
praising alike the feast at which they sat.

25*     But when their greetings reached their formal end,
they stood in silence firmly *coram me*,
their sudden fire defeating my turned eyes.

And smiling, Beatrice now spoke out:    28
'You living excellence! Your written scrolls
record the spacious giving of our hall.

Make hope now echo in these generous heights.    31*
You well know how. Whenever Jesus graced
his favoured three, you figured hope from that.'

'Raise your head high and gather confidence.    34
For all that rises from your mortal world
will grow to ripeness in these rays of ours.'

Such comfort reached me from the second fire.    37
I therefore raised my eyes towards the hills,
which first had bowed them down too heavily.

'Because our Emperor in grace desires    40
that you, before your death, should come to greet
his nobles in these secret audience rooms –

so that, once truth is seen in this high court,    43
the hope that stirs you in good love down there
may gather strength in you and others, too –

say what hope is, and how, within your mind,    46
it comes to flower, and how it came to you.'
The second light, in this way, followed on.

And she who guided, in all holiness,    49
the pinions of my wings to fly so high
answered, before I could myself, with this:

'The Church, at war on earth, has not a child –    52
and this is written in that Sun whose rays
here shine upon our ranks – more full of hope.

It has, therefore, been granted him to come,    55*
before his term of soldiership is through,
from Egypt to behold Jerusalem.

The next two points at which your questions strike –    58
seeking not knowledge but that he report
how greatly hope, as virtue, pleases you –

I leave to him. These won't prove difficult,    61
and yet won't tempt him into mere display.
Let him reply. May God's grace bear him on.'

64     A bright, keen student who has done his work
is quick to answer to his lecturer's hint,
and thus disclose to her how good he is.

67*     'Hope is sure expectation,' I declared,
'of glory that will come. The grace of God
and precedent good works produce this power.

70     From many stars its light comes down to me.
But David first instilled it in my heart,
that highest singer of the highest Lord.

73     "Let those have hope in you who know His name."
So David, in his psalmody, sings out.
And who cannot know that who shares my faith?

76     Then you in your epistle – as with drops
of dew – distilled my hopes. So I am full,
and rain your cooling shower on other lives.'

79*     While I spoke on, within the living breast
of that fierce blaze, repeated tremors flashed,
as rapid as in any lightning storm.

82*     'The love by which,' it breathed, 'I still am fired
towards that virtue which came with me till
I won the martyr's palm and left the field,

85     wills that, to you who take the same delight,
I breathe once more. My pleasure is: you say
what promises your hope has made to you.'

88     And I: 'The Scriptures, both the old and new,
define and indicate that goal for me:
the friendship God concludes with certain souls.

91*     Isaiah says that each, in his own land,
will be arrayed in two-fold vestiture.
And "his own land" is here, this sweetest life.

94     And yet more fully your own brother makes
this revelation clear to us. He speaks
(in the Apocalypse) of pure white dress.'

Then, first, when once these words had reached their
97       end,
'*Sperent in te*' above us could be heard,
and all the circling choirs replied to that.

And then, amid them all, one light shone clear.     100*
(Were such a crystal held in star sign Crab,
winter would have a month of sunlit day.)

Young girls will rise light-heartedly and go     103
to join in dancing and (so far from shame)
intend an honour to the newly-wed.

So I saw now that ever-clearer gleam     106
approach the two who spun to their own notes
in keeping with the ardour of their love.

This set itself within the wheeling song.     109
My lady kept her eyes fixed firm on these,
as silent as a bride, as motionless.

'He is the one who lay upon the breast     112*
of Christ, our Pelican. And he it was
elected, at the Cross, for one great task.'

My lady spoke, and yet she did not cease,     115
before or after, to maintain her gaze
where first it was, attentively, so fixed.

Like someone peering, doing all he can,     118
to see some moment of the sun's eclipse,
who, seeing, grows unseeing all the more,

so I became, as this last fire appeared,     121*
while words were said: 'Why dazzle your strained eyes
to see things in this place that cannot be?

My body lies as earth in earth, and shall     124
(as others shall) until our numbers mount
to equal what's eternally decreed.

Two lights alone have risen in both robes –     127*
in soul and body – to this cloistered joy.
You'll carry word of this to your own tribe.'

As this was said, the flaming wheel grew still,     130
as did the lovely mingling of those sounds
that formed within that breathing three-in-one.

(Compare: to put an end to strain or risk,     133
oars that repeatedly had struck the waves
all stop the moment that the whistle sounds.)

136    Ah! What great turmoil in my mind to turn,
       thinking to see where Beatrice was,
       and yet not see – although so near to her,
139       despite my being in that happy sphere.

# CANTO 26

As I stood wavering, all seeing gone,                              1 *
out of the flashing flame that quenched my sight
a breathing stirred that won my whole attention,

    saying: 'While you have yet to re-awaken         4
the sense of sight that spent itself in me,
it's good that you, with words, should compensate.

    Begin, then. Say what point the soul of you      7
is aiming at, and know, with reason, that your powers
of sight, blurred and confused, are not extinct.

    The lady who now leads you through this god-     10 *
like realm has, in the glance she gives to you,
the power that lay in Ananias' hand.'

    'As now or later pleases her,' I said,           13
'may healing fall upon these eyes – the gates
through which she came with fires I burn from still.

    In every text that Love reads out to me –        16 *
voiced low or strong – the Alpha and Omega is
the Good that brings content to all this court.'

    The voice that first had freed me from my fear   19
when that bedazzlement had struck my eyes
now sharpened my concern to speak once more.

    It said to me: 'You must, for certain, clear     22
in thought a stricter path. You need to tell
who is it aims your bow towards its mark.'

    And I: 'By reasons in philosophy,                25
as by those Scriptures that descend from here,
Love, of necessity, is stamped in me.

28     For good *per se*, once recognized as good,
sets love on fire – the fiercer still as love
holds more of good within its proper self.

31     Towards that essence, then (which holds such sway
that any good that's found beyond its reach
is nothing save a beam of that one ray),

34     the mind, in loving, will more rightly move
than elsewhere – or those minds, at least, that see
the truth on which this demonstration stands.

37*     To my own mind that truth is first proclaimed
by one who demonstrates the primal love
of all the sempiternal forms of life.

40     Proclaimed as well by our true Font and Rule,
Who, speaking of Himself, to Moses said:
"I shall indeed ensure you see all good."

43     Proclaimed, no less, by you in your first lines –
that trumpet call that shouted the arcane
clearer than any fanfare down from here.'

46     And then I heard: 'Through human intellect,
and through authorities well-tuned to thought,
the highest of your loves looks up to God.

49     But say, as well, what other ropes you feel
that draw you to Him and so, too, sound forth
how many teeth love's cog wheel bites you with.'

52     Nothing lay hidden in the holy mind
of Christ's great Eagle. And I saw at once
where he meant my avowals to advance.

55     So I began: 'As many ratchet-teeth
as ever turn the human heart to God,
all run as one with my own charity.

58     My being, and the being of the world,
the death that He sustained so I might live,
the hope that all, with me, confess in faith,

61     the living knowledge I have spoken of –
all drew me from the waves of wrongful love
and set me on the shores of righteousness.

And every leaf, en-leafing all the grove 64*
of our eternal orchardist, I love
as far as love is borne to them from Him.'

As I fell silent, through the sky there rang 67*
the sweetest song – my lady and these souls
all saying now the 'Holy, Holy, Holy'.

A piercing light will startle us from sleep – 70
eye-pulses racing as they meet the glare
that passes through the lens from skirt to skirt –

and, shocked awake, we muddle what we see, 73
a blank, mere nescience, at this alert,
until our faculties restore their aid.

So, too, the eyes of Beatrice shone – 76
their ray would reach a thousand miles or more –
routing the maculae that tainted mine.

I saw now better than I had before. 79
And, all but stunned, I asked who that light was,
appearing as the fourth amongst us there.

My *donna* answered me: 'Within those rays, 82
the Maker looks with love upon the first
of souls that primal power had ever formed.'

As fresh-leaved branches, when a breeze goes by, 85
bend at their tip, and then – through inner strength
which points them high – will straighten once again,

so I did, swaying, wavering at her words, 88
to be re-made, complete in confidence
that flowed from my own burning urge to speak.

'You are the single apple,' I began, 91
'produced as full and ripe. In kin and law,
to you all brides are daughters, first of men.

I beg, with all the reverence I can bring, 94
that you should speak to me. You know my will.
And so – to hear you sooner – I'll not say.'

A beast will sometimes wriggle in a sack, 97
and so display the feelings that it has
from how the wrapping follows what it does.

100     In that same way, the first of human souls
made me see clearly, through his covering,
how light of heart he was to meet my will.

103     And then he breathed: 'Without your offering,
I understand what you desire to know
better than you know all you hold most sure.

106     I see this shining truly in the glass
that holds the pure pareil of other things,
and yet in nothing finds its parallel.

109     You wish to hear how long God had me stay
within that garden rising to the heights
where she, your *donna*, set you on this stair;

112     how long that garden gave my eye delight,
and what the reason was for God's fierce scorn,
and what the language was I formed and used.

115*     My dearest son, the tasting of the tree
was not itself the cause of banishment,
but rather our transgression of the mark.

118     From where your *donna* once sent Virgil out,
four thousand revolutions of the sun,
two hundred more then two, I craved this court.

121     I'd seen the sun, with all its lights, return
along the starry road, nine hundred times
then thirty, in the years I passed on earth.

124     The language that I spoke was wholly spent
before the tribe of Nimrod set their minds
on work that could not, ever, reach fulfilment.

127     For nothing that our natural powers effect
(since human pleasures, as the years pass by,
are always new) was ever durable.

130     It's Nature's work that human beings speak.
But whether thus or thus, man's nature leaves
to you to fashion as you may best please.

133*     Before I sank to Hell's deep agonies,
the Highest Good – from which derives the joy
I'm swathed in here – was known on earth as "*I*".

Then afterwards we called it *El*. Needs must.     136
With mortal usages, like leaves along
a branch, one goes and then another comes.
  On that mount rising highest from the sea     139*
I was – in pure, and then dishonoured, life –
from when the first hour dawns until the hour
  that follows, as the sun moves zone, the sixth.'     142

# CANTO 27

1      'To Father and Son and the Holy Ghost,
       glory on high!' all Heaven here began,
       till I, at that sweet song, reeled drunkenly.

4          And what I saw, it seemed, was now the laughter
       of all the universe. So drunkenness, for me,
       came in through hearing and, no less, through sight.

7          The joy of that! The happiness beyond all words!
       A life of peace and love, entire and whole!
       Riches all free of craving, troubleless!

10         The faces of the four before my eyes
       were bright with fire. That soul (the first who came)
       began to grow more brilliant still at this.

13*        And now, in how it looked, this face became
       what Jove would be if he and Mars were birds,
       and both exchanged their plumage, white for red.

16         The providence that makes division here
       of duties, tasks and offices imposed
       a perfect silence on the holy choir.

19         And then I heard: 'If I change colour now,
       don't be amazed at that. For all of these,
       as I go on, you'll see change colour, too.

22*        He who on earth has robbed me of my place,
       my place, my place – which therefore, in the sight
       of God's dear Son, stands vacant now – has made

25         of my own burial ground a shit hole
       reeking of blood and pus. In this the sod
       who fell from here down there takes sheer delight.'

With that same colour that a cloud takes on,          28*
morning or evening, when it meets the sun,
I saw, in every part, the heavens flush.

And as some innocent – herself quite clean          31
in conscience – when she notes another's fault
may still, on hearing this, grow chaste and shy,

so Beatrice changed in countenance.          34
So, too, I think the heavens were once eclipsed
when Utmost Power submitted to the Cross.

And then Saint Peter's words went on, his voice          37
transformed so utterly from what it was
that he, in look, could not have been more changed.

'The Bride of Christ was not brought forth and raised          40*
on blood of mine – of Linus, too, and Cletus –
to be made use of in pursuit of gold,

but rather, to pursue here living joy,          43
Sixtus and Pius, Urban, Calixtus,
after harsh tears all shed their blood for this.

We did not mean that some of Christ's own race          46*
should sit in favour on our heirs' right hand,
and others, to the left, incur disgrace;

nor that the keys entrusted to my hands          49
should serve as battle emblem on the flag
that fought against those marked by baptism;

nor that, myself, I should become the stamp          52
that seals the sale of untrue privilege.
I flare and redden often at this thought.

Down there, in every pasture, ravening wolves          55
are seen dressed up as shepherds and as priests.
God our defence, why are you still unmoved?

Gascons along with bankers from Cahors          58*
prepare themselves to drink our martyr blood.
To what corrupted ends good starts may sink!

But Providence on high that made defence          61*
through Scipio at Rome of this world's fame
will soon, as I conceive it, offer aid.

64    And you, my son, whose body weighs you down
      so you'll return below, speak openly
      and do not hide what I don't hide from you.'

67*   When sun and Goat Horn touch as winter signs,
      the air in our terrestrial atmosphere
      floats down in falls of frozen vapour flakes.

70    So now I saw, with *upward* sweeping flakes,
      the aether decked in those triumphant airs
      that first had passed their time with us below.

73    My eyes, in following these semblances,
      followed until the space between became
      so great it took away sight's power to pass.

76    At which my lady, seeing me absolved
      from all attention to the heights, now said:
      'Now sink your gaze, and see how far you've turned.'

79*   I saw that since the time I'd first looked down
      I'd moved in those six hours through all the arc,
      mid-point to end, the first zone makes on earth,

82    so that I saw, beyond Cadiz, the mad
      sea-jaunt of Ulysses and, east, the shore
      where soft Europa once was borne away.

85    And more still of that eastward threshing floor
      would have been shown me but, beneath my feet,
      the sun, processing, reached a farther sign.

88    My mind, so deep in love that always woos,
      as *donna*, my *donna*, burned more fiercely still
      to turn its eyes once more to where she was.

91    Though art or nature, to possess our minds,
      may, in its paintings or in flesh itself,
      produce beguiling pastures for our eyes,

94    these all would seem as nothing when compared
      with that divine delight which shone on me
      when I turned round to see her smiling look.

97*   The inward powers her glance bestowed on me,
      uprooting me from Leda's lovely nest,
      impelled me to the swiftest of the skies.

Its regions so exalted, living bright,                          100
are all so uniform I cannot say
which Beatrice chose to be my place.

But she, who saw the strength of my desire,                     103
laughing with such great happiness
that God appeared rejoicing in her face:

'The order in the natural spheres that stills                   106
the central point and moves, round that, all else,
here sets its confine and begins its rule.

This primal sphere has no "where" other than                   109
the mind of God. The love that makes it turn
is kindled there, so, too, the powers it rains.

Brightness and love contain it in one ring,                    112
as this, in turn, contains the spheres below.
And only He who binds it knows the bond.

Its motion is not gauged by other marks.                       115
All other marks are measured out from this –
as ten is factored by its half and fifth.

So now it will be clear to you how Time                        118
takes root within the humus of this bowl,
and shows its fronds in every other part.

Crass, itching greed! You plunge our mortal sense              121*
so far within your depth that none can drag
their eyes above the mounting turbulence!

Intention blossoms well in human hearts.                       124
But rain, unending rain, will render down
the true, ripe plum to shrivelled pods of blight.

Good faith and innocence are only found                        127
in infant schools. And both will long have fled
before the cheek is covered with a beard.

There's one kid, burbling still, awaiting food,                130
who when he's fluent in his speech will gorge
on every dish, beneath whatever moon.

There's one there (burbling, too) who loves his mum            133
and heeds her words, who, when his tongue grows whole,
will long to see her buried in her grave.

136*    And so the whitest skin is scorched pitch black
merely to glimpse the lovely child of him
who brings the dawn and leaves behind the dark.

139    And you – so you should not suppose this strange –
think that on earth there's no one who will rule,
and so the human family goes astray.

142*    But those neglected hundredths in our dates
will make of January a spring-song month
before these circling heights send down such rays

145    that storms of fortune, so long waited for,
will spin the stern to where the prow is now,
so all the fleet will run a proper course,

148    and fruit will follow truly from the flower.'

# CANTO 28

In contradiction of the life now led                         1
in mortal misery, she – the in-paradizer
of my mind – had thus laid open Truth to me.

Then, as in mirrors, when the light's behind,               4
we see, although in sight and thought we've yet
to grasp the fact, the flame of some twin torch

(so turn around to see if that smooth glass                 7
has told the truth and see it does accord,
as words in song when sung upon their beat),

so too did I – my memory now records –                      10
still looking back towards those lovely eyes,
from which, to snare me, love had made the cord.

And once I'd turned – and once my eyes were touched         13
by what appears within that scroll to those
who look aright within its turning sphere –

a single point I saw, that shot out rays                    16*
so sharp the eye on which it fixes fire
is bound to close against that needle-strength.

Even the star that, seen from here, seems least            19
would seem, when set beside that point (as star
is set by star), a moon in magnitude.

As close as, perhaps, coronae appear                        22
around the lights that shape and colour them
when halo-bearing vapours are most dense,

around that point, to similar extent,                       25
fire in a circle whirled at such great speed
its motion would surpass all clasped round earth.

28   This was, in orbit, bounded by the next,
by that, a third, the third, then, by a fourth,
by five that four, and then by six that five.

31   Then, round all these, a seventh ran, so stretched
to generous breadth that Juno's messenger,
the rainbow arc, would hardly hold the all.

34   Likewise, the eighth and ninth. And each of these
moved still more slowly as the count went on,
running, in number, outward from the one.

37   And that possessed the clearest flame of all
from which the purest spark stood least far off,
because, I think, that flame in-truthed the most.

40   My lady, seeing me caught up in hard
concerns, spoke out: 'From that one point
depends both Heaven and all of Nature's world.

43   Look, in pure wonder, at that circle joined
most nearly to the point, and know it moves
so fast impelled in point of burning love.'

46   'Suppose the universe,' I said to her,
'were ordered as I see these wheels to be,
then I would rest well fed with your proposal.

49   But in the realm of sense experience
the orbits, we can see, are more divine
when these stand furthest from the earth's mid-core.

52   And so if, in this temple, set apart,
its confines marked by love and light alone,
my own desires will ever reach their end,

55   I need to hear how type and prototype
are not configured in a single mode.
For that I contemplate quite fruitlessly.'

58   'It's hardly any miracle if you,
with your own hands, cannot untie that knot.
It's got so stiff since no one works at it!'

61   These were my lady's words. And then: 'Just get
what I'll now tell you if you want your fill,
and sharpen thought to subtlety round that.

The circling of these bodies, wide or strict,    64
follow proportioned to the power that flows
diffused in all their parts, here more, here less.

A greater goodness means a greater health.    67
A greater health is held in greater limbs,
if these, throughout, are perfect equally.

Therefore this sphere – the *Primum Mobile* –    70
which draws the universe entire along
answers the circle that most loves and knows.

And so if, with your rule, you compass round    73
the virtue and the strength of what these are,
and not their look, which shows as circular,

you'll see a wonderful coincidence –    76
according to intelligence in every sphere –
between the less and least, greater and more.'

Compare: when Boreas, the northern wind,    79*
blows from his milder cheek, our hemisphere
is left serene, its air bright, sparkling, clear.

The crusted scum of clouds that swirled there first    82
is freed and clarified. The whole sky laughs.
Its many beauties smile round every steeple.

So I became, as – caring for my good –    85
my lady answered with such clarity,
and truth was seen as stars are in the sky.

And when these words of hers had come to rest,    88
then, as when boiling iron sparks and spurts,
so, too, these circles flung off their own sparks.

This surge of fire was following every glint.    91*
These glints, en-thousanding, outnumbered far
progressive doubling of the chessboard squares.

And rising, choir to choir, I heard 'Hosanna'    94*
sung to that point which, fixed there, holds them all,
and always will, *ubi* they've always been.

And seeing in my mind what doubts I had,    97
she now declared: 'The circles that I first
made known are Cherubim and Seraphim.

100      Each runs so swiftly round its twining hoop,
to be as like that point as possible,
succeeding, through sublimity of sight.

103      And round these run those other forms of love,
known as the Thrones, receiving God's regard.
With these, the first of triads terminates.

106      And all, as you must know, have their delight
according to how deep their sight goes down
into the truth that calms all intellect.

109*      You'll see from this that being truly blessed
resides upon the act by which we see,
and not in act of love. This follows that.

112      And seeing takes its measure from the worth
that grace and truest purpose bring to birth.
And so the scale proceeds from step to step.

115*      The second triad where the sap thus flows
within this sempiternal springtime season –
which night-ascendant Aries never spoils –

118      sings out perpetually that winter's done,
"*Osanna!*" in three tunes that sound in three
orders of happiness, each one en-threeing here.

121      The other gods in this hierarchic rank
are firstly Dominations, Virtues next,
then, thirdly, there's the Order of the Powers.

124      In three-some reels the two penultimates
are Principalities, Archangels, too.
The last of all is all Angelic games.

127      This order all in wonder gaze above
and triumph so, beneath, that up to God
they all are drawn and draw up all to all.

130*      And Dionysius with such desire
set out to contemplate these nine-fold ranks
that he defined and named them as I do.

133      But Gregory departed from his view.
And so, the moment that he reached this sphere,
opening his eyes, he laughed, self-mockingly.

And if, on earth, a mortal could display     136
a truth so secret, please don't be amazed.
This was revealed by one who saw up here –
and much else of truth of these great gyres.'     139

# CANTO 29

1*      When moon and sun, the children of Latona,
covered by Libra and the spring-starred Ram,
each takes, to form its belt, the same horizon,

4      the length of time from when the zenith comes
to equipoise to when these two, in change
of hemisphere, unbalance in that zone,

7      was all the time that Beatrice stayed
silent – her laughter brushed across her face,
fixed on the point that first defeated me.

10      Then she began: 'I'll say – though ask, I won't –
what you now want to hear. I've seen it there
where every "when" and "where" attains its point.

13*      Not seeking any good that He had not –
there can be none – but so his shining-out
could in return shine back and say: "I am",

16      in His eternity beyond all time,
beyond our understanding, as He pleased,
to new loves Love Eternal opened out.

19      Nor had He lain in torpor till that time,
for neither "then" nor "now" could come before
the flowing-forth of God above these waves.

22      Real form and matter (both conjoined and pure),
issued in being where there was no flaw,
as from a three-string bow three arrows fly.

25      Light rays that enter amber, crystal, glass,
display such luminescence that, from when
they reach, then *are* there wholly, there's no pause.

Likewise, the three-fold action of light's lord          28
shone brightly through all being, all as one,
without distinction in that opening word.

Rank and relationship were co-create          31
with these true beings who, within the world
(pure act produced in them), stand at the height

where, at the lowest, there's pure potency,          34
between these two an intertwining binds
pure potency to act – and never disentwines.

Jerome proposed to you a long elapse          37*
of centuries of angels from creation's point
before the other world was ever formed.

The truth is written, though, in many parts –          40
by writers listening to the Holy Ghost –
as you, if you look carefully, will see.

And even reason can see some of this,          43
refusing to concede that motive-powers
should be so long without full carry-through.

And now you know the where and when and how          46
that led to the creation of these loves.
And so, in your desires, three flames are spent.

Counting, you would not get to twice times ten          49*
as quickly as the angels, in some part,
clouded those elements on which you feed.

The rest remained, and then began their art          52
with such great pleasure that, as you can tell,
they never choose to leave their circlings.

The first cause of the fall was that cursed flounce          55
of arrogance, in one whom you have seen
gripped tight below the weight of all the world.

The angels you see here restrainedly          58
acknowledged of themselves the utmost good
who made them quick to understand all this.

Their intellectual sight was, therefore, raised          61
through merit and illuminating grace
so high that they, in will, are full and firm.

64*    And here I would not have you be in doubt.
It is a merit to receive God's grace,
in measure as hearts open up to that.

67    By now, there's much in this great council hall
that, if my words are safely gathered in,
you may well contemplate without more aid.

70    But since, down there, your universities
argue that angels are of such a kind
as understand, have memories and free will,

73*    I'll still continue till you see pure truth –
which, in ambiguous lectures there on earth,
is doubtful and so easily confused.

76    These beings, full of happiness to see
the face of God from which there's none who hide,
at no point turned their eyes away from that.

79    And so their line of vision is not cut
by new-formed objects, and they, therefore, need
no memory (thought dividing these from thought).

82    And so, down there, not sleeping, still they dream,
thinking they speak the truth – or thinking *not*.
The latter brings more guilt and greater shame.

85*    Philosophizing, you, down there, do not
proceed by any one true path. You're swept
along by show and love of showy thoughts.

88    Yet even this is tolerated here
with less contempt than when God's Holy Writ
is put aside or twisted out of true.

91    No thought is given to what blood it cost
to sow that seed on earth, nor what delight
is given when we humbly stick to that.

94    All bend their wits to mere display, and strive
for bright ideas. Then preachers flick-read these,
and, as to what the Gospels say, are mute.

97    One argues that, when Christ died on the Cross,
the moon turned back to form an obstacle,
so sunlight could not show itself down here.

All lies! The light hid by its own free choice.                    100
And that is why the same eclipse replied
to Indians and to Spaniards as to Jews.

There aren't, in Florence, half so many wops          103
as all around in pulpits every year,
such poppycockeries get blurted out.

And so the sheep, who don't know *anything*,          106
come from the pasture pastured full of wind.
It's no excuse that they don't see the harm.

Christ did not say, to his first holy band,          109 *
"Go out and preach pure prattle to the world."
He gave them true foundations that would stand.

And these resounded in their cheeks so well          112
that, fighting to ignite the fire of faith,
they used the Gospel as both shield and lance.

Now preachers go with feeble jokes and gags          115
and, just so long as they can raise a laugh,
their hoods puff up. They ask for nothing more.

A devil bird, though, nestles in their cowls.          118
Were folk to see this, they would see (they must!)
what sort of pardons these are they so trust.

And so such idiocy grows on earth          121
that all, without good evidence or proof,
chase after every promise they hear made.

Pigs of Saint Anthony grow plump on these –          124 *
and many others, too, still bigger pigs –
paying with currency that bears no stamp.

But we've digressed enough. So turn your eyes          127
once more towards the road that lies ahead,
so that we cut our path to suit our hours.

In number, the angelic natures climb          130 *
so far beyond us that no mortal tongue
nor human thought could ever reach to that.

And if you note what Daniel has revealed,          133
you'll see, while speaking of the "thousands" there,
the final number is concealed from view.

136    The primal light, whose rays shine out on all,
is taken up in ways as numerous
as there are splendours that it couples with.

139    Therefore, since depth of feeling follows act,
in each of these the sweetness of their love
seethes differently – and different, too, in warmth.

142    See now the height and all the generous breadth
of God's eternal worth. These mirrors all
were made by Him, where He Himself now breaks,

145    one in Himself remaining as before.'

# CANTO 30

Maybe, around six thousand miles away,　　　　　1*
the sixth hour, close to noon, flares out, while earth
inclines its shadow-cone to rest, near level.

At this same time, the mid-point of the sky　　　4
will start, so deep above us, to transform,
and some stars lose their semblance in those depths.

Then brightest Aurora who serves the sun　　　　7
advances and, dawning, the skies, vista
by vista, are closed till even the loveliest is gone.

In this way, too, the victories that play　　　　10
for ever round the point that conquered me –
enclosed, it seems, by that which they enclose –

was, little by little, quenched before my gaze.　13
And so, from seeing nothing – and in love –
I turned my eyes towards Beatrice.

If all that has, till this, been said of her　　　　16
were now enclosed to form one word of praise,
it would not, even so, fulfil my need.

The beauty I saw, transcending every kind,　　　19
is far beyond us here – nor only us.
Its maker, I think, alone could know its joy.

From now on, I'll admit, I'm overwhelmed,　　　22
defeated worse than all before – in comic
or in tragic genre – by what my theme demands.

As sunlight trembles in enfeebled eyes,　　　　25
calling to mind how sweet to me her smile was,
itself deprives my mind of memory.

28    Not since the day that I, in our first life,
      first saw her face until this living sight,
      has song in me been cut so cleanly short.

31    It is, however, right that I stand down –
      as every artist, at the utmost, does –
      and no more trace her beauty, forming verse.

34    And so what then she was I now will leave
      to clarions far greater than my trumpet sounds,
      and draw my vaunting line towards its end.

37    As she then was – a guide in word and deed,
      her work all done – she spoke again: 'We've left
      the greatest of material spheres, rising

40    to light, pure light of intellect, all love,
      the love of good in truth, all happiness,
      a happiness transcending every rapture.

43    Here you will see the two great heavenly ranks,
      angels and saints – the saints in countenance
      as you, on Judgement Day, will see them stand.'

46*   As lights, when flashing suddenly, disperse
      the spirits of the retina, and rob
      the eye of seeing even strong, bright things,

49    so, bright around me, shone a living light
      that left me, baby-like, in swaddling weaves
      of brilliance, so that nothing showed to me.

52    'The love that gives this Heaven its quietness
      will always make its saving welcome thus,
      to form a candle ready for its flame.'

55    No sooner had these brief words entered me
      than I rose up – as truly I could tell –
      above the summit of my natural powers.

58    New seeing-strength I kindled in myself,
      so that no light, however crystalline,
      could cause my eyes to close in self-defence.

61    I saw light form a river in full spate,
      fire-dazzle-gilded, flowing through verges
      painted afresh in colours of wonderful spring.

And rising from that flood, alive, were sparks 　　　64
that everywhere alighted on the flowers,
like rubies set in gold encirclements –

then all, as though the perfumes made them drunk, 　67
plunged in that swirling miracle once more.
And yet where one sank in, still more spun out.

'The fine desire that fires and urges you 　　　70
to gain still fuller news of all you see,
delights me more, the more the longing swells.

And yet before your thirst is satisfied, 　　　73
you'll need to drink these waters to the full.'
Those words were hers, the sunlight of my eyes.

Then following: 'The river and the glint 　　　76
of topaz, in and out, the smile of grass – these all are
shadowed prefaces that hint at their own truth.

That does not mean that any is, itself, 　　　79
unripe, acid or green. The lack is yours.
Your sight as yet cannot move proudly on.'

No baby, waking later from its nap 　　　82
than normally it would, so hurled itself
face down to mother's milk as I did now.

To make my eyes, as mirrors, better still, 　　85
I bent towards the wave that, flowing there,
will sweep us always onward to in-bettering.

I drank to the arching eaves of my brow, 　　88
and then saw all anew, as though that length
of light had now, in form, become a round.

If masqueraders, hidden in their veils, 　　　91
undress those features (not their own) in which
they'd vanished once, their look seems somehow changed.

So now, it seemed, these flowers and flecks of light 　94*
altered, to join and celebrate still more.
And I saw, now made known, both heavenly courts.

Splendour of God! Through you I came to see 　　97
triumph exalting in the realm of truth.
Grant me true strength to say what then I saw.

100     There is, above us there, a light that makes
the All-Creator in creation seen
by those who only seeing Him have peace.

103     This light became a circle in its form,
extending its circumference so far
as might a belt too generous round the sun.

106     All that appears is made there by a ray
reflected from the curve of that First Sphere
which draws its life and movings from that light.

109     It is as though the incline of some hill
were mirrored in a lake below, as if
to view itself adorned in flower and richest green.

112     Above that light, and standing round, I saw
a thousand tiers or more as mirrorings
of those of ours who've now returned up there.

115     Imagine, when the least of all these grades
could gather to itself so great a light,
how great the wealth is at the rose's fringe.

118     My eyes, despite such breadth and altitude,
were not confused or blurred but took all in –
the kind and sum of this light-heartedness.

121     Nothing's gained here or lost by 'near' and 'far'.
For where God rules without some means between,
the law of nature bears no weight at all.

124     Into the gold of that now-always rose,
which grows from arc to arc, dilates and breathes
the scent of praise to always-springtime Sun,

127     she drew me – Beatrice – like someone
yearning, while silent, to say: 'The wonder!
Look there, how great this white-caped gathering is!

130     Our city, look! And see how wide it sweeps.
The honoured places – look! – they're almost full,
and few we long to see are still to come.

133*     Your eyes are fixed upon a single throne,
drawn by the crown already set on that.
And long before you join this marriage feast,

the soul will sit – imperial in the world –
of noble Arrigo, who came to rule
an Italy unready for him yet.

The blind cupidity bewitching you          139
has made you all akin to little brats
who – famished, dying – still beat off their nurse.

And in the Sacred Forum one presides          142*
whose public and whose covert deeds will not
accord or travel in a single groove.

But not for long. God will not suffer him          145
to keep that sacred role. He'll soon be flung
where Simon Magus gets what he deserves.

The Anagnese pope will sink still further down.'          148

1      In form, then, as a rose, pure, brilliant, white,
       there stood before me now the sacred ranks
       that Christ, by His own blood, has made His bride.

4      The other force that, flying, sees and sings
       the glory that so stirs their love of Him –
       the goodness, too, that makes them all they are –

7      came down, as might a swarm of bees that first
       en-flower themselves, returning, afterwards,
       to where their efforts are made sweet to taste.

10     They search the utmost depths of that great flower,
       with all its many petals. Then they rise
       once more to where their love will always dwell.

13     Their faces all were bright with living flame,
       their wings of gold, their other parts so white
       that snow has never reached to that extreme.

16     Descending in the flower from tier to tier,
       they offered peace and all the burning love
       that they won there (wings fanning down their flanks).

19     Nor, interposed between the flower and height,
       did all that multitude in flight impede
       that radiance or the faculties of sight.

22     Divine light pierces through the universe –
       to be received, as fit, in all degrees –
       in such a way that nothing can oppose.

25     That realm – its *gaudeamus* free of strife –
       where chosen, past and new, such crowds resort,
       aims all its love and seeing at one sign.

O three-fold light that, in one single star,                    28
so flashing in their sight brings them content!
Look down upon our world of squalls and storms.

If savages from northern shores (where skies                    31*
are dark, day in, day out, under the Helicean sign
that gazes, wheeling, on her well-loved son)

at seeing Rome and her aspiring works                           34
are stupefied to view the Lateran,
soaring so high above all mortal things,

then what of me – from human to divine,                         37
coming to this eternal realm from time,
from Florence to a nation sane and true –

what pure astonishment must I have felt?                        40
Indeed, between that shock and solemn joy,
I, gladly, did not hear or speak a thing.

As pilgrims gaze, enthralled at their new life,                 43
around the temple that they'd vowed to reach,
hoping to tell, already, where they've been,

so, pacing upwards through the living light,                    46
I drew my eyes through every step and grade
now up, now lower, circling all around.

I saw there faces swayed to *caritas*,                          49
arrayed in their own smiles and light not theirs,
and all they did adorned with dignity.

The general form of Heaven had by now                           52
been grasped entirely as my glance swept round,
fixing, though, firmly no particular.

And so I turned – my will once more on fire –                   55
to ask that she, my lady, should respond.
(For here and there, some doubt in me remained.)

I'd looked for one thing. Something else replied.               58*
I'd see Beatrice, as I believed,
and saw an elder, robed like all in glory.

Around his countenance and eyes there flowed                    61
the generosity of joy, his look
a gentle father's, firm and virtuous.

64     And I at once: 'Where is she?' And at this:
'So I can bring an end to your desire,
Beatrice moved me from the place I keep.

67     If, to the highest round of that third step,
you'll raise your eyes, you'll see her on the throne
to which her merits have allotted her.'

70     Without reply, I raised my eyes up there
and saw her, mirroring eternal rays,
to form a crown or aureole around.

73     From that high region where the thunder rolls,
no mortal eye could ever be so far –
though sunk beneath the ocean's utmost depth –

76     as my sight was from Beatrice now.
Yet that meant nothing. For her image came
not blurred or lessened by the space between.

79     'In you, beloved, my hope grows strong. All this
you bore: to greet me and to make me whole,
you left your footprint in the depth of Hell.

82     The inward strength and grace of everything
I since have seen has come to me, I know,
through you, your goodness and your grace and power.

85     From servitude you've led me to be free
by all those pathways and by all the means
you have within your power to exercise.

88     Keep safe in me your own magnificence,
so that my soul, since you have made it well,
should leave the knot of body, pleasing you.'

91     My prayer was thus. And she, as far away
as she might seem, smiled and looked down at me,
then turned again towards the eternal spring.

94     The holy patriarch: 'So you may perfectly
attain the summit of the path you take
(for that I'm sent, by prayer and holy love),

97     fly through this garden with your wings of sight,
for seeing this will make your gaze more fit
to climb towards the radiance of God.

The Heavenly Queen – I burn in all my soul                100
for love of her – will bring us every grace.
I am Bernardo, her most faithful one.'

Like someone coming from Croatia, say,                    103*
to view our Veil – the Saint Veronica –
who still can't satisfy the age-old ache

and, while the image is displayed to him,                 106
will murmur in his thoughts: 'My Lord, Christ Jesus,
was this the way, true God, you looked on earth?'

so I – with wondering eyes on that bright life            109
of *caritas* who, contemplating, caught
some taste, within our world, of final peace.

'Child born of grace' (so he began) 'if you              112
continue with your eyes still fixed below,
you'll hear no note of this bright, joyful state.

Look through these circles to the furthest off           115
so far that you shall see, enthroned, the queen
to whom this realm is subject in its vows.'

I raised my eyes. And, as when morning dawns,            118
the orient horizon in new light
defeats the part in which the sun goes down,

so too, as though my eyes were travelling                121
from valley up to mountain peak, I saw
the rim outdo, in brightness, every other part.

As sky flares fiercest where the chariot pole –          124*
mis-turned by Phaeton once – is waited for,
the light diminishing on either side,

so did that oriflamme (peace-pennant now)                127*
grow bright within its central spur, as flame,
elsewhere, in equal measure, slacked and dimmed.

And, in the central band, their wings outspread,         130
I saw, in thousands, angels – feasting, dancing –
in blaze and chosen deed all differing.

I saw there, smiling on their games and songs,           133*
the height of Beauty who, as height of Joy,
was there in all the eyes of all the saints.

136    And even if, in words, I had such wealth
as, in imagining, I did, I'd still not dare
attempt to say the least of that delight.

139    Bernardo, seeing where my eyes were set,
fixed, won, attentive to her warm regard,
now turned his own so feelingly to her

142    that mine in wonder blazed out all the more.

# CANTO 32

Heart-whole in pleasure, the contemplative      1*
freely took on himself the teacher's role,
beginning thus the holy words he spoke:
   'The gash that Mary healed and soothed with oil    4*
was opened first, and then made worse, by her
who sits, so beautiful, at Mary's feet.
   Ranked in the order that the third thrones form,    7*
lower than Eve, there Rachel sits. Along
from her there is, as you see, Beatrice.
   Sara, Rebecca, Judith and the one      10
who bore the mother of the man who sang,
mourning his fault, the "*Miserere mei*".
   Descending step to step, you see all these      13
as I, in giving each her name, proceed,
now travelling down this rose from leaf to leaf.
   And downward from the seventh of these tiers    16
(as down to that) the Hebrew women come,
dividing all the curls within that flower.
   And these (according to the way their faith    19*
in Christ looked back or forth) here form the wall
that separates the sacred steps in two.
   On that side, where the flower is fully grown,    22
with all its petals at their full extent,
sit those who showed belief in Christ to come.
   There on the other side, where unfilled space    25*
still intersects the hemispheres, are those
who turned their countenance to Christ now come.

28    And where, on this side, there's the glorious throne
of Heaven's own Lady and, below, those seats
that, under hers, divide the rose in two,

31*    so, too, across from that, there sits great John.
That saint bore desert and cruel martyrdom,
then, after – till Christ came – two years in Hell

34*    And under him, elected to divide,
Saint Francis, Benedict, Augustine, too,
with others down to here, from rank to rank.

37    Look up in wonder at God's providence.
He'll fill this garden to the same extent
with those who kept the faith in these two ways.

40    Know, too, that from the rung that, midway, strikes
the line that marks these two divisions off,
no one will sit by merit of their own –

43*    of others, rather, where conditions hold.
For all of these are spirits loosed from earth
before they, truly, could conceive free choice.

46    And this, if you will look and listen hard,
will be entirely clear to you. Just note
their faces. Hear, as well, their children-voice.

49    Now you're in doubt and, doubting, do not speak.
But I shall disentangle this tight knot,
which your own subtle reasonings have tied.

52*    Within the broad expanse of all this realm
there cannot be a single point that's chance,
nor any hunger, thirst or misery.

55    For all that you may see is here decreed
by God's eternal law. Hence, right and fit,
all corresponds as finger to a ring.

58    And so it is that, not without good cause,
these children – sped too soon to this true life –
are in their excellences less and more.

61    The king, through whom this kingdom is at peace,
in such great love, and in such pure delight,
that nothing in our wills dare aim so high,

creating, in his look of happiness,                                          64
all minds, bestowed, as he best pleased, his grace
in different ways. The outcome says enough.

And this, expressed and clear in Holy Writ,                                  67*
is noted in the case of those two twins
who, in their mother's womb, were moved to wrath.

It follows from the colour of their hair                                     70
to what degree of grace the highest light
encrowns most fittingly the head of each.

Therefore, with no regard to how they act,                                   73
these are placed here in differing degrees
by difference only of their first sharp sight.

In earliest times, it used to be enough,                                     76
to gain salvation, that with innocence
parental faith alone should be conjoined.

Then, when these early epochs were complete,                                 79*
all males were circumcised to win them powers
appropriate to their wings of innocence.

But, later, when the age of grace arrived,                                   82
such innocence – when baptism in Christ
was not fulfilled – was bound on Hell's first rim.

Return now. See that face resembling Christ                                  85
closer than all. For that bright light alone
can make you wholly fit to look on Christ.'

I saw such happiness rain down on her,                                       88
borne by those holy intellects – made first
to fly with wings across that heavenly height –

that nothing I had ever seen before                                          91
had brought my wondering eyes to such a poise,
nor shown so much to me of how God looks.

And that first angel-love, descending there,                                 94*
was singing – wings extended in her sight –
'Ave Maria gratia plena'.

There answered this the sacred cantilene                                     97
from every region of the happy court.
At which, their faces showed the more serene.

100      'O holy father, who for me could bear
to be down here and leave that lovely place
where, as eternally decreed, you sit,

103      which is that angel who, with such delight,
looks at our Queen and gazes in her eyes
so deep in love he seems to be on fire?'

106      I went, in this way, back to learn from him
of one who drew his beauty from Maria,
as, from the sun, the morning star draws light.

109      'All prowess, charm and elegance of heart
as may appear in angels or men's souls
is found in him, and we all wish it so.

112      For he it is who carried down the palm
to Mary when the only Son of God
chose to take on the weight of human form.

115      But come now, note and follow with your eyes,
as I go speaking, all the noble sires
of this supremely true imperium.

118      These two who sit above – the happiest,
in being nearest to the Empress throne –
are as the double root-stock of this rose.

121      He who sits next in justice, to her left,
is that first father through whose reckless taste
the human species tasted so much gall.

124      There on the right you see the honoured sire
of Holy Church to whom Christ left in trust
the keys to this most delicate of flowers.

127*      And he who saw, before he came to die,
the heavy times of that beloved bride,
first won upon the Cross with lance and nails,

130      sits next to him, and next to him now rests
that lord beneath whose guidance there once lived
a race ungrateful, shifting, obstinate.

133*      Across from Peter, as you see, sits Anne,
so happy as she wonders at her child
she does not move her eyes to sing "Hosanna".

And facing Adam, father of our tribe,       136
Lucia sits. When you, in ruin, bent your brows,
Lucia moved that *donna* to your aid.

But since your time of slumber races by,      139
at this point we shall end, as tailors do –
who skilfully make skirts from little cloth.

And turn your eyes towards the Primal Love,      142
so that, in looking there, your eye should pierce
as far as possible His dazzling light.

But lest it be, perhaps, on your frail wings,      145
thinking you rise beyond, you sink back down,
it's best that, praying for the gift of grace,

you beg for grace from her who can assist.      148
And here you'll follow me with such good heart
that from my words your feelings won't depart.'

And so he now began his holy prayer.      151

# CANTO 33

1     'Virgin and mother, daughter of your son,
greater than all in honour and humility,
you are the point that truth eternally

4     is fixed upon. And you have made the nature
of the human being proud. Its maker, then,
did not disdain to make himself his making.

7     Love, in your womb, was fanned to fire again.
And here, in this eternal peace, the warmth of love
has brought the Rose to germinate and bloom.

10     You are, for us, the noon-time torch of love.
You are, among those mortals there below,
the clearest fountain of their living hopes.

13*     You are, in dignity and power, Our Lady.
All who, in wanting grace, do not seek help
from you, might wish to soar yet lack the wings.

16     Nor in your kindness do you give your aid
to those alone who ask, but often run,
before they ask, to them in generous freedom.

19     In you is pity, in you compassion,
in you all-giving power. All good in you
is gathered up that creature-form can bear.

22     This man is one who, from the deepest void
in all the universe, has seen thus far,
and one by one, all lives in spirit-mode.

25     To you, a suppliant, he comes, and asks
that, by your grace, he gains the strength to rise
in sight more, still to greet the final peace.

I never burned for visions of my own     28
more than I do that he might see. To you
I offer all my prayers – praying my prayers

    are not too few – that you should free this man     31
from all the clouds of his mortality,
so highest happiness be shown to him.

    Our Queen, to you, who may do what you will,     34
I also pray you keep him (he has seen
so much!) healthy in all his heart intends.

    Watch, and defeat the impulses of man.     37
See! Beatrice with so many saints
closes her hands in prayers along with mine.'

The eyes – which God both loves and venerates –     40
attentive to these orisons, made clear
how welcome to her were these holy prayers

    and then turned straight to the eternal light     43
in which (we're bound to think) no creature's eye
inwardly travels with such clarity.

    And drawing nearer, as I had to now,     46
the end of all desires, in my own self
I ended all the ardour of desire.

    Now Bernard, smiling, made a sign to me     49
that I look up. Already, though, I was,
by my own will, as he desired I be.

    My sight, becoming pure and wholly free,     52
entered still more, then more, along the ray
of that one light which, of itself, is true.

    Seeing, henceforward, was far more than speech –     55
yielding before the sight I saw – can show.
Mind's memory yields, outraged at that beyond.

    Like those who see so clearly while they dream     58
that marks of feeling, when their dreaming ends,
remain, though nothing more returns to mind,

    so I am now. For nearly all I saw     61
has gone, even if, still, within my heart,
there drops the sweetness that was born from that.

64*    So, too, in sunlight, snow will lose its seal.
       So, too, the oracles the Sibyl wrote
       on weightless leaves are lost upon the wind.

67     You raise yourself so far, O highest light,
       above our dying thoughts! Now lend once more
       some little part of what it seemed you were,

70     and make my tongue sufficient in its powers
       that it may leave at least one telling spark
       of all your glory to a future race.

73     Returning somewhat to my memory,
       re-echoing a little in my verse,
       your triumph over all will be more known.

76     As I believe, the sharp light I sustained
       in that live ray was such that, if I'd turned
       away, eyes blurring, I'd have lost my track.

79     And therefore (I remember this) I grew
       the braver as I bore that light, and joined
       the look I had to that unending might.

82     Grace, in all plenitude, you dared me set
       my seeing eyes on that eternal light
       so that all seeing there achieved its end.

85     Within in its depths, this light, I saw, contained,
       bound up and gathered in a single book,
       the leaves that scatter through the universe –

88     beings and accidents and modes of life,
       as though blown all together in a way
       that what I say is just a simple light.

91     This knotting-up of universal form
       I saw, I'm sure of that. For now I feel,
       in saying this, a gift of greater joy.

94*    One single point in trauma is far more,
       for me, than those millennia since sail
       made Neptune marvel under Argos-shade.

97     And so my mind, held high above itself,
       looked on, intent and still, in wondering awe
       and, lit by wonder, always flared anew.

We all become, as that light strikes us, such          100
we cannot (this would be impossible)
consent to turn and seek some other face.

For good – the only object of our will –          103
is gathered up entire in that one light.
Outside it, all is flawed that's perfect there.

And now my spark of words will come more short –          106
even of what I still can call to mind –
than baby tongues still bathing in mum's milk.

But not because that living light on which,          109
in wonder, I now fixed my eyes showed more
than always as before and one sole sight.

Rather, as sight in me, yet looking on,          112
grew finer still, one single showing-forth
(me, changing mutely) laboured me more near.

Within the being – lucid, bright and deep –          115*
of that high brilliance, there appeared to me
three circling spheres, three-coloured, one in span.

And one, it seemed, was mirrored by the next          118
twin rainbows, arc to arc. The third seemed fire,
and breathed to first and second equally.

How short mere speaking falls, how faint against          121
my own idea. And this idea, compared
to what I saw . . . well, 'little' hardly squares.

Eternal light, you sojourn in yourself alone.          124
Alone, you know yourself. Known to yourself,
you, knowing, love and smile on your own being.

An inter-circulation, thus conceived,          127
appears in you like mirrored brilliancy.
But when a while my eyes had looked this round,

deep in itself, it seemed – as painted now,          130
in those same hues – to show our human form.
At which, my sight was set entirely there.

As some geometer may fix his mind          133*
to find a circle-area, yet lack,
in thought, the principle his thoughts require,

136    likewise with me at this sight seen so new.
I willed myself to see what fit there was,
image to circle, how this all in-where'd.

139    But mine were wings that could not rise to that,
save that, with this, my mind, was stricken through
by sudden lightning bringing what it wished.

142    All powers of high imagining here failed.
But now my will and my desire were turned,
as wheels that move in equilibrium,

145    by love that moves the sun and other stars.

# Notes

For each canto in these notes, the reader will find broadly factual information and cross-references to texts cited by Dante that are worth reading alongside Dante's own. The asterisks in the poem text show the beginning of the *terzina* to which such a note applies. Sometimes this points to a sequence of *terzine* in which, by consolidating these references, readers may discern some pattern of concerns – with, say, the minutiae of thirteenth-century politics – that will better emerge than in a strictly line-by-line treatment. Where an indeterminate number of *terzine* are covered by a note, the first line number is cued along with 'f' ('following [lines]') to indicate that a substantial section of the canto may be included. Fuller commentary on the text may be found in the three-volume edition of this translation of *The Divine Comedy* – also published in Penguin Classics (London, 2006–7) and containing Dante's original Italian text – from which the notes here have been compiled. This edition attempts to disturb as little as possible the reader's enjoyment of the narrative flow of Dante's poem. Traditional annotations in sequential form are to be found in the excellent editions by Robert Durling and Ronald Martinez (Oxford, 1996) and the well-conceived apparatus by David Higgins in his commentary on C. H. Sissons's translation (London, 1980). To both of these editions the present editor is glad to acknowledge a warm debt of gratitude. Quotes from the Bible are from the Authorized Version.

## *INFERNO*

### CANTO 1

*The dark wood and the sunlit hill. The appearance of
Virgil. The beginning of the path down through Hell.*

1–6  Biblical references to the span of human life as threescore years
and ten are to be found in Psalm 90: 10, which Dante quotes in
*Convivio* 4, where he discourses at length on the four ages of
human life and the characteristics proper to each of them. The
notion of a road of righteousness is contained in Psalm 23, along
with that of the 'valley' of death. Isaiah 38: 10 reads: 'in the cut-
ting off of my days I shall go to the gates of the grave'. The wood
recalls the Romance wood that in, say, Arthurian legend the hero
may encounter in his search for the Holy Grail.

13–18  The hill is a figure for hope in Psalms 24: 3, 43: 3 and 121: 1.

28–30  Dante's obscure reference to his 'firm foot' has provoked much
discussion. The best explanation is that he has in mind Aris-
totle's observation that our stride is led by the *right* foot, leaving
the *left* foot to impel our movement forwards. The line may also
be taken as an example of the extreme precision of mind which
leads Dante to note exactly where, in any narrative scene, his
own body is placed and what lies to left and right of him.

31–60  The three beasts seem to be drawn from Jeremiah 5: 6, an Old
Testament book to which Dante showed particular devotion.
Allegorically, the leopard has been taken to represent false (and
possibly sexual) pleasure, which fascinates but also irritates the
mind. The lion may stand for pride, haughty but in reality a dan-
gerous void. The wolf may be taken as avarice and is of particular
importance, being the only beast of the three to which Dante
refers in his appeal to Virgil. (See also *Purgatorio* 20: 10–12.)
Avarice, for Dante, characterizes the corrupt culture of capitalist
Florence, and is above all a pointless and never-ending pursuit of
false and unsatisfying goods. In this sense it is a *'bestia sanza
pace'* ('brute which knows no peace' (line 58)), a restlessness of
mind that erodes the harmony of civic life.

64–6  Though Dante, without yet realizing it, is speaking to a pagan
figure, he invokes here the great penitential psalm *'Miserere
Domine'* (Psalm 51: 1): 'Have mercy upon me, O God, accord-
ing to thy lovingkindness: according unto the multitude of thy
tender mercies blot out my transgressions.'

67–75  Virgil (70 BC–19 BC) links his own success as a poet with the
major themes of his narrative in the *Aeneid*, which tells of the
fall of Troy (Ilion being its great citadel), the travels of Aeneas
and the foundation of Rome as a new homeland (lines 106–8)
which achieves imperial glory under Augustus. Virgil will act as
Dante's guide and companion until his disappearance in *Purga-
torio* 30. In the *Inferno*, Dante is especially influenced by – and

competes with – book 6 of the *Aeneid*, which describes the descent of the epic hero Aeneas into the underworld in pursuit of prophetic vision (see especially *Inferno* 3). The *Purgatorio* pays particular attention to Virgil's pastoral poems, the *Eclogues* (see *Purgatorio* 21–2).

94–105 The 'hound' ('*veltro*') has been variously identified as Can Grande della Scala (1291–1329), one of Dante's patrons in exile; Emperor Henry VII (*c.* 1275–1313), whom Dante hoped, vainly, would restore imperial rule to Italy; and even as Dante himself. The phrase 'between the felt and felt' may refer to geographical location (between the towns of Feltre and Montefeltro in northern Italy). The mythological Gemini, the 'twins', were thought to wear felt caps, so that anyone born under that star sign – as Dante was – would have been born 'between the felt and felt'. Scholarly ingenuity (of a kind which henceforth these notes will not indulge) can, however, all too easily diminish the imaginative impact of enigma itself. Dante is rarely enigmatic. But when he is, it is with poetic purpose.

# CANTO 2

*Virgil explains how Beatrice chose him as Dante's guide.*

1–9 These lines, like others in the canto, make liberal reference to Virgil's *Aeneid* (see also lines 127–9). Here, in delicately responsive pastiche, Dante recalls the many passages where Aeneas is left alone at night wondering how best to serve his needy companions: 'Night it was and night through every land held the weary creatures, the creatures of flight and the flocks while the father . . .' (*Aeneid* 8: 26–7). For Virgilian invocations to the Muses, see *Aeneid* 1: 1–11.

13–27 Like Virgil in *Inferno* 1, Dante adopts here an elevated circumlocutory style: the 'sire of Silvius' is Aeneas himself. Aeneas's vision in the underworld of the future glories of Rome – revealed to him by his own father, Anchises – is combined, syncretically, with a Christian vision of Rome's future. Cf., as a parallel to the meeting of Aeneas and Anchises, Dante's own meeting with his forefather Cacciaguida in *Paradiso* 15–17.

28–30 Like Aeneas, Saint Paul – while still in his human body – was granted a vision of divine glory:

I knew a man in Christ above fourteen years ago, (whether in the body, I cannot tell; or whether out of the body, I cannot tell: God knoweth;) such an one caught up to the third heaven.

And I knew such a man, (whether in the body, or out of the body, I cannot tell: God knoweth;)

How that he was caught up into paradise, and heard unspeakable words, which it is not lawful for a man to utter.

2 Corinthians 12: 2–4

For Dante's treatment of his own bodily vision, see *Paradiso* 2: 37–9.

52–81 Beatrice, who here speaks to Virgil, is (in Dante's account) the central figure in the *Commedia*, and also of his Christian understanding. The *Vita nuova* is Dante's early account of his love for her, of the poetry he wrote in her name and of the way in which he responded to her death. An example of the style of this early poetry, which exerts a strong influence over the present passage, is the last sonnet in that work, which anticipates Dante's attention here to both universal spaces and intimate effects of emotion, to tears, sighs and the light of eyes: 'Beyond the sphere that circles most widely, / there passes the sigh that leaves my heart / a new understanding which Love, / weeping, imparts to him, draws him ever higher' (*Vita nuova* 41).

94–126 The first lady to speak in Heaven is the Virgin Mary. Dante talks of his devotion to her at *Paradiso* 23: 88, and a sustained prayer to the Blessed Virgin prepares for his vision of God in *Paradiso* 33: 1–39. Saint Lucy is the patron saint of sight. According to an anecdote in the commentary written by Dante's son Jacopo, Dante was especially devoted to this saint, and Dante himself in *Convivio* 3: 9 records how he prayed to her when his eyesight had been endangered by too much study. Saint Lucy has an important role in *Purgatorio* 9 and appears in *Paradiso* 32: 13–18. Rachel is the second wife of Jacob (Genesis 29). She was frequently regarded as a figure for contemplation, and fulfils this role in *Purgatorio* 27: 104–8. (See also *Paradiso* 32: 8–9.)

# CANTO 3

*The entry into Hell. Charon and the apathetic sinners.*

1–9 The originality of Dante's treatment of Hell may be gauged by comparing these lines (and the plan of Hell offered in *Inferno* 11) with visual representations such as Giotto's in the Scrovegni chapel at Padua or in the mosaics of the Baptistery. Where, traditionally, Hell is pictured as chaos, violence and ugliness, Dante sees a vision of terrifying order expressing the underlying structure of a world that God has created but sinners have refused to contemplate. Hell Gate is not simply an awe-inspiring threat, but a demand that intelligence and understanding should be engaged anew in the analysis and exploration of divine purpose. (See also the Plan of Hell on p. lx, and Dante's own discussion of the moral categories of Hell in *Inferno* 11.)

16–18 '[T]he good that intellect desires to win' is a phrase much influenced – as is so much of Dante's thinking – by Aristotle's *Ethics*. Aristotle writes in the *Nicomachean Ethics* 6: 2: 1139a:

> What affirmation and negation are in thinking, pursuit and avoidance are in desire; so that since moral virtue is a state of character concerned with choice, and choice is deliberate desire, therefore must the reasoning be true and the desire right, if the choice is to be good, and the latter must pursue just what the former asserts. Now this kind of intellect and of truth is practical. But of the intellect which is contemplative, not practical nor productive, the good and bad state are truth and falsity respectively ... The origin of action ... is choice, and that of choice is desire and reasoning with a view to an end.
>
>                    D. Ross (trans.), *The Nicomachean Ethics of*
>                              *Aristotle* (Oxford, 1954, p. 92)

(Cf. Dante, *Convivio* 4: 7, 12.)

34f For the apathetic, see Revelation 3: 15–16: 'I know thy works, that thou art neither cold nor hot: I would thou wert cold or hot. So then because thou art lukewarm, and neither cold nor hot, I will spue thee out of my mouth.'

55–7 T. S. Eliot alludes to these lines in *The Waste Land* (1922): 'Unreal City, / Under the brown fog of a winter dawn, / A crowd flowed over London Bridge, so many, / I had not thought death had undone so many' (lines 60–63). For Eliot's continuing engagement with Dante's poetry, see especially *Inferno* 27 and *Purgatorio* 26. His phrase in *Four Quartets* (1943) 'human kind / Cannot bear very much reality' accurately interprets Dante's thinking about the apathetic.

58–60 The apathetic are unlike almost all other sinners in Hell in being unnamed. It is a mark of particular contempt for their wasted lives that names should be denied them. It is, however, generally accepted that Dante refers here to Pietro da Morrone (1215–96), who became Pope Celestine V in 1294, rather than other candidates such as Pontius Pilate or Judas Iscariot. History (if not Dante) speaks well of Celestine. A saintly figure, known to be a spiritual reformer who founded the Order of Celestines, he was canonized shortly after his death. But the 'great denial', which in Dante's eyes seems to have damned him, was his abdication after only five months, under pressure from the Curia and his successor, Boniface VIII (c. 1235–1303). This act of *viltà* (or cowardice) put an end to the possibility of reform, and opened the way to the election of the pope whom Dante hated and despised above all others. (For Boniface, see especially *Inferno* 19.)

82–111 Dante offers an animated variation on Virgil's treatment of Charon: 'A terrifying ferryman is guardian of these waters. His filth is fearsome; his chin is covered with a thick straggle of grey whiskers; his eyes are flames' (*Aeneid* 6: 298–300).

112–14 As at *Inferno* 2: 127–9, Dante deliberately alludes to the *Aeneid* 6: 309–12 and suggests the measure of both his stylistic and moral differences from Virgil. Milton makes comparable use of the autumn leaf simile in *Paradise Lost* 1.

# CANTO 4

*The First Circle of Hell. Limbo. Unbaptized children.*
*Virtuous pagans.*

46–63 The Harrowing of Hell – when Christ entered Hell and broke open its gates on Easter Saturday – brought salvation to those among the Hebrew patriarchs who had anticipated or prophesied Christ's coming, but not to the noble pagan. This event is also much in Dante's mind in *Inferno* 12 and 21–2. Attention is drawn here to Jacob (named Israel), father of the twelve tribes of Israel, who served fourteen years to win the hand of Rachel. (See Genesis 29: 9f; also *Purgatorio* 27: 100–11.)

88–90 Of the four classical poets who welcome Dante and Virgil, Homer alone was unavailable to Dante, who knew no Greek. But Dante did know of his reputation through his reading of Cicero, Virgil and other Latin poets; and in canto 26 of the *Inferno* he offers his own, highly revisionary account of the Odysseus legend. The other three are Quintus Horatius Flaccus (65–8 BC), Publius Ovidius Naso (43 BC–c. AD 17) and Marcus Annaeus Lucanus (AD 39–65). The influence of all these poets upon Dante's *Commedia* is evident at later points, notably in *Inferno* 25, where Dante claims he can outdo anything that Ovid and Lucan can achieve.

121–9 This Electra is not the daughter of Agamemnon but of Atlas. As the mother of Dardanus, one of the legendary founders of Troy, she occupies a legitimate position – alongside Hector, Aeneas and Julius Caesar – among the heroes of the Trojan line which eventually founded Rome. Camilla and Penthesilea, queen of the Amazons, are both virgin warriors mentioned by Virgil (*Aeneid* 1: 490–93, 7: 803–17 and 11: 648–835). The former was supposed to be an ally of Latinus, the latter of the Trojans. Brutus and Cornelia, as figures in Roman history, were known to Dante from Livy, Lucan and others. Brutus was first consul of the Roman republic after the expulsion of the kings. Lucrece or Lucretia, wife of Collatinus, committed suicide after being raped by the son of King Tarquin. Julia, daughter of Julius Caesar, married Pompey the Great, who later became her father's greatest enemy. For Marcia, wife of Cato of Utica, see *Purgatorio* 1. Cornelia was the wife of Scipio Africanus. Saladin (Salah ad-Din, 1137–93), sultan of Egypt, drove the Crusaders out of the Holy Land. But many legends concerning his heroism and generosity proliferated in the west.

130–44 The 'master of all those who think and know' is Aristotle (384–322 BC). Dante knew about Plato (427–347 BC) and his treatment of Socrates through Latin texts. Diogenes the Cynic (fourth century BC) rejected the claims of supposedly civilized existence. Anaxogoras (fifth century BC) was both philosopher and mentor of Pericles. Thales (seventh century BC) was considered the founder of Greek philosophy. Empedocles of Sicily (fifth century BC) was both a rhetorician and the inventor of the notion of the four elements. Heraclitus of Ephesus (fifth century BC) held that fire was the fundamental element. Zeno of Citium (third century BC) is praised by Dante in *Convivio* 4, and is considered the founder of the Stoic school. Dioscorides of Anazarbus (first century AD) founded pharmacology. Orpheus and Linus are mythical poets. Tullius is Marcus Tullius Cicero (106–43 BC), Roman statesman and philosopher, whose *De Amicitia* and *De Officiis* were acknowledged influences on Dante's thought. Seneca (d. AD 65) influenced Dante through his Stoic philosophy.

Euclid (fourth century BC) is the Greek geometrician. Ptolemy of
Alexandria (second century AD) devised the astronomical system,
posited on a geocentric universe, that Dante adopts in imagining
the universe of the *Commedia* (see P. Boyde, *Dante, Philomythes
and Philosopher* (Cambridge, 1981)). Hippocrates (fourth cen-
tury BC) founded medical studies. Avicenna (d. 1036) was an
Arabic physician and philosopher. Galen of Pergamum (second
century AD) wrote medical textbooks. Averroes (d. 1198) was one
of the most important philosophers of the Middle Ages. Born in
Arabic Spain – his name in Arabic is Ibn Rushd – his great com-
mentary on Aristotle won him the name of 'the commentator' (see
also *Purgatorio* 25: 63–5). Scholasticism – and Dante – owed
much to his influence, even if inclined to resist its implications.

# CANTO 5

*Minos, judge of the underworld. The lustful.
Francesca da Rimini.*

4–6 In classical legend, Minos, king of Crete, is the son of Zeus and
     Europa. He appears as the terrifyingly sombre judge of the
     underworld in Virgil's *Aeneid* 6: 566–9.
52–67 Semiramis, widow of King Ninus, the legendary founder of
     the Babylonian Empire, was, according to Saint Augustine of
     Hippo, Paulus Orosius and Brunetto Latini (see *Inferno* 15),
     guilty of incest with her son and used her political position to
     make this crime legitimate. Dido, queen of Carthage, deserted
     the memory of her first (dead) husband Sichaeus out of love for
     Aeneas, but committed suicide when Aeneas left Carthage to
     continue his journey to Italy and found Rome. The marriage of
     Cleopatra, queen of Egypt, to Mark Antony precipitated a civil
     war between Antony and Octavius, who was to become Roman
     emperor. Helen of Troy was the wife of Menelaus, king of Sparta,
     and her abduction by Paris, son of the Trojan king Priam, led to
     the Trojan War. Achilles, the Greek warrior, was ready to betray
     his countrymen when he fell in love with Polysena, daughter of
     Priam, but was ambushed and killed by Paris before he could
     complete his act of betrayal. Tristan – in love with Iseult, wife of
     his uncle King Mark of Cornwall – was killed as a traitor by the
     king's poisoned spear.

73f Dante focuses on two figures from thirteenth-century Italian history – Francesca da Rimini, wife of Gianciotto Malatesta (marriage *c.* 1275), and Paolo, Gianciotto's brother. Francesca was married by political arrangement to Gianciotto, a member of the ruling family of Rimini, but began an affair (as described here) with Paolo. When he discovered this, Gianciotto murdered both his wife and his brother. This was a great scandal in its day. Remarkably, Dante, having consigned Francesca to Hell, was supported between 1317 and 1320 by the patronage of her nephew, Guido Novello da Polenta.

88f Francesca may declare at line 91 that if the Sovereign of the Universe were her friend, she would pray for Dante's peace of mind. But God, who condemns her to Hell, is not her friend; and so the prayer must fail. Likewise, the sweetness of Francesca's rhetorical repetition (in Dante's Italian original) of '*Amor*' is matched by an emphasis on violent actions hidden in the second line of each of these *terzine*. Francesca displays a continuing evasiveness, seeking to shift the blame for her fate away from her own person. It is 'Love' which takes possession of her and it is the book (see lines 133–4 and 137) rather than her own passion which leads her into adultery. Thus the particularly mellifluous line 103, '*Amor, ch'a nullo amato amar perdona*' ('Love, who no loved one pardons love's requite'), reveals itself on examination to be a morally dubious justification of love as an obsessive submission to fate, in which no one who is the object of love has the right to deny love in return to the person that projects that love. On this view, Dante does not condemn Francesca for lust alone. (Among those redeemed in the *Purgatorio* and *Paradiso* are figures who submitted to lust, including the sodomites and bestialists of *Purgatorio* 26 and the courtesans and whores in *Paradiso* 8 and 9.) Her sin is rather one of moral apathy and failed intelligence.

106–7 Caina in the geography of Hell is the region in the lowest circles (see *Inferno* 32) assigned to those who, like Cain, murdered members of their kin (Genesis 4: 1–15).

121–38 Francesca and Paolo are here reading a version of *The Book of Launcelot of the Lake* (an early thirteenth-century prose account of the Arthurian legend). The 'single point' which overcame them is Lancelot confessing his love to Guinevere, under persuasion from Galehault (Galeotto in Italian). '*Galeotto*' thus came to mean the type of a go-between or pander. Note that, whereas Francesca claims to have been kissed by Paolo, Guinevere is always presented as giving the first kiss to Lancelot.

# CANTO 6

*The circle of the gluttons, guarded by Cerberus.*
*Ciacco. The politics of Florence in 1300.*

13–32 Cerberus (like Charon in *Inferno* 3, a modification and inten-
sification of Virgil's original) is to be found as the watchdog of
Hades in *Aeneid* 6: 417–22.

40–73 Ciacco – though a historical figure who is the subject of a
lively anecdote by Giovanni Boccaccio in the *Decameron* 9:
8 – is allowed no name save a nickname which means 'porker'
or 'hog' (line 52). He has no standing or stable position within
the order of society; and, indeed, when he speaks of his fellow
citizens, he divisively relishes the fate they will suffer. Such
Schadenfreude extends even to his attitude to Dante. Through
Ciacco's mouth Dante alludes for the first time to his own polit-
ical exile (lines 64–84). The exchange here between the two
Florentines and Dante provides a (sometimes allusive) account
of the factional strife between White and Black Guelfs which
came to a head around 1300–1302 and brought about Dante's
exile (see Introduction, pp. xiii–xiv). The Blacks had rioted in
1301 and Dante, in his role as one of the priors of Florence, had
been obliged to exile members of both Black and White factions.
The Whites were the 'country' party – hence 'Wildwood'; their
leaders, the Cerchi, came from the rural environs of Florence –
and in 1300 the Whites had won a temporary superiority. But
the Blacks regrouped, and within the span of three years ('three
brief suns' (line 67)) they returned to power. Their cause was
supported by the 'one who now just coasts between' (line 69) –
that is, Pope Boniface VIII – keeping open the option of alliance
with both Blacks and Whites.

79–84 All the great Florentines that Dante here disingenuously
inquires about are found in the lower circles of Hell. Notes on
Farinata can be found in *Inferno* 10, on Rusticucci and Tegghi-
aio in *Inferno* 16 and on Mosca in *Inferno* 28. Arrigo – whose
identity cannot be determined – is not mentioned elsewhere.

106–8 This principle is enunciated by Aristotle in the *Nicomachean
Ethics* 10: 4.

115 Plutus, the god of riches, dominates the first phase of *Inferno* 7.

# CANTO 7

*The avaricious and the spendthrift. The doctrine of
fortune. The wrathful and the melancholic.*

1–9 Dante imagines Plutus as a combination of the god of wealth and
the god of the underworld. Plutus's speech is impenetrable gib-
berish. At line 8, the wolf referred to recalls the she-wolf of
*Inferno* 1: 49–60 and anticipates a further reference in *Purgato-
rio* 20: 10.

10–12 The archangel Michael leads the attack that drives Satan from
Heaven.

22–7 Cf. Virgil, *Aeneid* 3: 420–23. Charybdis is the mythological name
for the whirlpools in the Straits of Messina. The reference to the sea
recalls Anicius Boethius's *Consolation of Philosophy* (524–5). For
Boethius, it was merchants who originally disturbed the harmony
of the Golden Age by their maritime enterprise. The punishment of
the rocks evokes the labours of Sisyphus in *Aeneid* 6: 616.

43–5 Avarice is punished alongside its opposite, prodigality. Aristotle
suggests this coupling in the *Nicomachean Ethics* 4: 1: 1121a.
Following Aristotle here, as elsewhere, Dante would identify
virtue as a mean between two vicious extremes. In this case,
liberality would constitute the virtuous mean.

73–96 This picture of Fortune draws upon but modifies the concept
developed by Boethius in the *Consolation of Philosophy*, in which
the world is subject to a constant shifting of Fortune's wheel:

> So with imperious hand she turns the wheel of change
> This way and that like the ebb and flow of the tide.
> And pitiless she tramples down those once dread kings,
> Raising the lowly face of the conquered –
> Only to mock him in his turn.
> Careless she neither hears nor heeds the cries
> Of miserable men.
>
> *Consolation of Philosophy* 1: 1

Dante, by contrast, attributes to Fortune angelic powers and a
providential function. Angels (on the understanding that Dante
offers in *Paradiso* 28) are the purest forms of created intelli-
gence, and are set as governors over the movements of the
physical cosmos.

**97–9** The reference to the stars establishes the hour as just past midnight on Good Friday.

**115–29** The swamp formed by the river Styx contains within it two groups of sinners, the wrathful and the sluggardly. (One etymology for 'Styx' suggests the word means 'sorrow', which can be taken as the source of both anger and hatred.) Again, Dante is using conceptions of the Aristotelian mean to identify anger and wrath as vicious extremes.


# CANTO 8

*The swamp of the Styx. Encounter with Filippo*
*Argenti. Arrival at the city of Dis.*


**19–24** Phlegyas is drawn (much altered) from *Aeneid* 6: 618–20, where he appears as king of Thessaly. His anger there is a response to his daughter's rape by Apollo.

**31f** In this highly problematical episode, Dante encounters a fellow Florentine, the notoriously arrogant Filippo, a member of the Black Guelf Adimari clan, which is condemned by Dante in *Paradiso* 16: 115–20. Though now so caked in mud – so full of it that it seems to flow out of him – Filippo was in life nicknamed Argenti, the Silver One, apparently because he had his horses shod in silver. Concentrated in this figure is the spirit of pride and divisiveness that Dante constantly identifies among the sources of Florentine corruption. This episode is illustrated in all its violence by Eugène Delacroix in his *Dante and Virgil in Hell* (1822), now in the Louvre.

**43–5** In the passage in Luke 11: 27–8 to which these lines allude, Christ replies by rejecting the praises offered to him.

**124–6** This refers to the gate of Hell (*Inferno* 3) which since the Harrowing of Hell has always stood open.


# CANTO 9

*Entry into Dis secured by the Messenger*
*from Heaven.*


**7–9** Because (in Italian) the verb 's'offerse' and its subject 'Tal' have no gender, this broken utterance ('Yet granted such a one . . .')

may be taken to refer to Beatrice or the Messenger from Heaven who in fact arrives to open the gate.

22–30 Dante – drawing on Lucan's *Pharsalia* 6: 507 – seems to have invented the story of Virgil's earlier journey through Hell to the depths where Judas is punished, conjured to do so by the witch Erichtho. Throughout the Middle Ages, Virgil had a reputation for witchcraft – which Dante repudiates implicitly in *Inferno* 20.

37–51 Cf. Virgil, *Aeneid* 6: 570–75. The Three Furies, or Eumenides, or Erinyes, specifically pursue those who are guilty of crimes of blood. Hecate is the queen of Hell ('empress') spoken of here.

52–4 The story of the Medusa and of her power to turn men to stone is told in Ovid's *Metamorphoses* 6: 606: 249. The Furies at line 54 show regret that they did not kill Theseus (see also notes to *Inferno* 12), when they had him in their power, and thus dissuaded other travellers from passing through Hell.

97–9 Hercules is said to have defeated and chained Cerberus, who appears in *Inferno* 6.

112–15 The Roman cemeteries at Arles, near the mouth of the river Rhône, and at Pola (now Pulj) on the Istrian peninsula.

# CANTO 10

## *The heretics. Farinata and Cavalcante.*

10–12 Jehoshaphat, according to Joel 3: 2, is where the Last Judgement will be announced and conducted.

13–15 Dante speaks of the Greek philosopher Epicurus with admiration in *Convivio* 4:7: 6, but here as elsewhere (see *Inferno* 12: 40–43) resists the implications of materialist metaphysics.

22f The canto is dominated by Dante's encounter with two Florentine figures, Farinata and Cavalcante – the former a Ghibelline, the latter a Guelf – from the generation preceding Dante's own, when the tensions between the Ghibelline (pro-imperial party) and the Guelf (anti-imperial party) were at their height. Dante's family was broadly Guelf in their political orientation. These men are likely to have held heterodox views, and are associated here with those 'heretics' who believe that as 'the body dies, so too the soul' (line 15). But the conversation that unrolls concerns the divided state of Florence. In particular, Farinata degli

Uberti (d. 1264), who is the first to speak, displays a deeply patriotic, if flawed, devotion to the Florentine cause.

**31–51 and 76–93** Underlying Farinata's first speech and, explicitly, his concluding speech are references to the events surrounding the battle of Montaperti, near Siena – where the battlefield is traversed by the river Arbia (line 86) and where in 1260 the Florentine Guelfs were defeated by a coalition of Tuscan Ghibellines. It was Farinata who at the subsequent war council in Empoli persuaded his allies to refrain from destroying Florence. When the Guelfs recovered their supremacy, Farinata and his descendants were excluded from the amnesties of 1280. The Uberti palace, occupying the present Piazza della Signoria in Florence, was pulled down and left in Dante's lifetime as rubble, *pour encourager les autres.*

**52f** It is here that Dante encounters Cavalcante de' Cavalcanti (d. *c.* 1280), a Guelf aristocrat and one-time chief magistrate of Gubbio, who was the father of Guido, Dante's closest friend in his early years as a poet.

**67–9** Dante has used the past remote '*elli ebbe*' ('He once . . .'), which in Italian signifies an action in the past that has no continuing connection with the present, hence implying Guido Cavalcanti's death. Dante also gives Cavalcanti's speech a Bolognese inflection: '*lume*' ('light') here becomes '*lome*'.

**97–108** Dante imagines a form of myopia by which the sinners are condemned to have no knowledge of present things and to see more clearly into the distant future than into the past.

**118–20** For Frederick II of Hohenstaufen (1194–1250), Holy Roman Emperor, see Introduction, pp. xi–xii. The cardinal is the Ghibelline Ottaviano degli Ubaldini (d. 1273), who is said to have declared: 'If I have a soul at all, I have lost it a hundred times in the interests of the Ghibellines.'

**130–32** The reference, as at line 63, is to Beatrice in Heaven.


# CANTO 11

*The plan of Hell.*

**7–9** The references to Anastasius and Photinus are not entirely clear, historically or syntactically. Pope Anastasius II (d. 498) was believed by medieval historians (though not by modern scholars) to have been led into an heretical denial of the divinity of Christ by his friend Photinus, deacon of Thessalonica.

19f Dante enunciates, through the mouth of Virgil, some of the major philosophical principles on which the moral plan or geography of Hell has been constructed. Note that his points of reference are as frequently classical as they are Christian or Scriptural. The categories do not correspond to the familiar scheme of the Seven Capital Vices, which is reserved for the plan of the *Purgatorio*.

22f The three forms of sin that are treated in *Inferno* 12–33 – violence, deceit and treachery – are defined in lines 22–64. All of them – unlike the sins of appetite considered in *Inferno* 5–8 – involve a conscious and 'malicious' misdirection of human intelligence. The upper circles (visited in *Inferno* 12–17) contain various forms of violent behaviour, all of which in some way – as in gang warfare, suicide or blasphemy – set the mind against the sustaining relationship it should enjoy with others, with its own being, with nature or with God. But fraud – or, better, deceit – which underlies sins such as flattery, fallacious leadership and, ultimately, treachery – is judged by Dante to be worse than violence, in that it turns the best faculties and capacities that God has given to human beings (reason and rational speech) to destructive ends.

25–7 Human beings share with beasts a capacity for violence. But only human beings are capable of fraud – which therefore more severely offends a higher principle. (Cf. *Convivio* 3: 2: 14–19.)

49–51 The destruction of Sodom as an archetypal city of corruption is described in Genesis 13: 10. Cahors (a city in southern France) was notorious as a centre of money-lending and usury. Blasphemers are here included among those who commit violence.

52–66 Fraud can only be practised against our fellow human beings, since God is omniscient. In its worst form, as treachery, fraud violates the special bonds of love and trust that have been established between particular persons (lines 61–6). Simple fraud is somewhat less heinous but still violates the relationships that exist between people by virtue of their common humanity (lines 55–60). As defined by lines 61–6, fraud of the other sort is treachery, an offence against the principle fundamental to all human order which is that we should love our neighbours.

76–90 Citing Aristotle's *Nichomachean Ethics* 7 explains the relative leniency with which Dante treats the sins of lust, greed, avarice and anger.

94–111 Dante insists upon the sinfulness of the practice of usury, which lay at the heart of the economic developments in thirteenth-century

Florence that he viewed with such disfavour. The Italian term *'arte'* (line 100) may be taken to mean 'intelligent and purposeful work'. In this sense, divine art creates nature. Human art, operating in the natural sphere, may and – properly – must affiliate itself harmoniously with the divine original. Usury, however, makes the artificial commodity of money itself a 'second' or parodic form of creation. Here Dante draws simultaneously on Aristotle's *Metaphysics* 12: 7 and *Physics* 2: 2, as well as Genesis 3: 19f.

112–14 References to the constellations of the Fish and the Great Wain and also to the north-west wind establish – in an 'artful' reading of the natural order – that the time on the April morning of Dante's journey is about 4 a.m.


# CANTO 12

*The Minotaur, centaurs and those who are guilty of violence against the person or possessions of others.*


4–9 These lines probably refer to the Lavini di Marco, twenty miles south of the city of Trento in northern Italy.

10–27 The Minotaur (part human, part bull) was the offspring of the union between Pasiphae, wife of King Minos of Crete, and a white bull with which she became infatuated. (Cf. *Purgatorio* 26: 40–42.) Minos ordered Daedalus to construct the labyrinth in which the Minotaur would be confined. With the aid of the Minotaur's sister, Arianna, the duke of Athens, Theseus, entered the labyrinth and slew the monster. (See Ovid, *Metamorphoses* 8: 152–82 and *The Art of Love* 2; also Virgil, *Aeneid* 6: 14–33.)

31–45 These lines alert the reader to a Christian myth, understanding of which lies beyond the world envisaged in classical legend. Here Virgil focuses (as does Dante's narrative elsewhere – for instance, *Inferno* 4 and 21–2) on the effect of divine power which – with Christ's entry into Hell on Easter Saturday – sent a great earth tremor through the region, leading to landslides and ruin in this, as in every other, circle of Hell. The tremor, however, is a redemptive power which shatters the hold exerted by human violence on humanity itself, in the restoration of universal harmony. A compressed but startling reference to this occurs at lines

40–45, where Virgil speaks of how, according to certain philoso-
phers, any touch of love would paradoxically reduce the world
to chaos. The philosophy that Virgil alludes to here is the
atomistic school (representatives of which are found in Limbo
at *Inferno* 4: 136–8), which maintained that the existence of
created forms depended upon the constant collision of streams
of atomic particles. On this view, violence is essential for the
creation of all that we know. But Dante will eventually end his
poem with a vision of how the harmony of the created order
depends upon the 'love that moves the sun and other stars'.

55–72 The centaurs are treated at length in Ovid's *Metamorphoses*
12. Nessus is slain by Hercules when the hero finds the centaur
stealing his wife Deianira. As he dies, Nessus plans his revenge,
offering a shirt dipped in his own blood to Hercules's wife, declar-
ing it to be a fitting love token for Hercules, and when later she
offers him the shirt, the poisoned blood begins to consume Her-
cules's flesh. To maintain command over his own destiny, he
builds a funeral pyre and immolates himself, thus becoming a
god. In this canto of two-fold beings, there are clearly parallels to
be drawn between Dante, himself painfully in search of divinity,
and the demi-god Hercules.

Chiron is reputedly the wisest of the centaurs, said (in Statius's
*Achilleid* 1) to be the teacher of both Hercules and Achilles. Pho-
lus (Virgil, *Georgics* 2: 256 and Ovid, *Metamorphoses* 12: 306)
is renowned for his violence. Another centaur, guilty of violent
theft and also slain by Hercules, appears in *Inferno* 25: 17–33.

88 It is Beatrice – the inspiration for Dante's heroic journey and for
his poem – who sings this alleluia.

106–38 This list of tyrants surveys history from the time of Dionysius
of Syracuse (d. 367 BC) to Alexander the Great (356–323 BC)
and Pyrrhus (319–272 BC) on to Sextus Pompeius (75–35 BC),
son of Pompey the Great (106–48 BC), and Attila (d. AD 453),
who was thought (incorrectly) to have destroyed the city of Flor-
ence. These remote figures are interspersed with men from the
history of Europe in Dante's time. Opizzo d'Este, lord of Ferrara,
who was famous for his cruelty, died in 1293 at the hand of his
(probably) illegitimate son and heir, Azzo. The assassin of line
119 is Guy de Montfort (d. *c.* 1288), who murdered a cousin of
the English king Edward I in 1271 in a church at Viterbo where
the cardinals had gathered to elect a pope. Renier the Mad and
Renier da Corneto were notorious brigands.

# CANTO 13

*Suicides and squanderers. Pier delle*
*Vigne – transformed into a thorn tree – tells his story*
*as later the anonymous Florentine suicide tells his.*

7–9 The Cécina is a stream and Corneto a village, in the swampy area on the borders of Tuscany and Lazio.

25–30 Line 25 depends (in Italian) on a contorted repetition of the verb *'credere'* ('to believe or think'). At line 30 the Italian metaphor (*'monchi'*) refers to the 'chopping off' of human limbs. Dante's doubts will end, chopped off like a hand at the wrist, if he puts his hand forward to pluck a twig.

31f This episode throughout runs parallel to that in Virgil's *Aeneid* 3: 3–65, where Aeneas encounters Polydorus, youngest son of the Trojan king Priam, transformed into a tree.

The suicide Pier della Vigna was one of the most important figures in the political and cultural life of the early thirteenth century. Born in Capua around 1200 in modest circumstances, Piero became the spokesman and chief minister of Emperor Frederick II (1194–1250), while also contributing, in verse and political rhetoric, to the development of Italian as a literary language. But in 1249 he fell victim to scandal; and though (as Dante seems to allow at lines 73–5) innocent of any treachery to his overlord, he was still disgraced. He appears to have committed suicide by beating his brains out against his prison walls.

In the symbolism and imagery of the canto, there are remote references to the central stories of the Christian faith. The tree (especially a thorn tree) points to the Crucifixion and the Crown of Thorns, and thus to Christ's Atonement, which could have made sense of sufferings such as Piero's. Equally, Piero's name reminds one of the disciple Peter, who did betray or at least deny his master (although Piero did not betray Frederick) and yet still formed the rock of the Church.

More immediately, the wood, along with the selection of Piero as an illustration, draws to mind the situation of the poet Dante himself. He, too, once found himself in a dark wood; and the wood of the suicides represents an intensified version of that *'selva oscura'* of *Inferno* 1: 2. Like Piero, Dante suffered political disgrace, yet could not follow Piero's desperate example. Nor, it seems, could the poet in Dante allow himself to be content with

Piero's *poetic* example. It is typical of Piero's poetry that it should cultivate a theme of desperation and death as attributes of the experience of love, as, for instance, in the opening verses of '*Amando con fin core e con speranza*':

> Loving with loyal heart and with hope,
> I was promised by Love a greater joy
> than I deserved,
> for Love exalted me in my very heart
> And I would never be able to separate from it,
> however much I longed to do so,
> so deeply is her image imprinted in my heart,
> even though Death has parted me
> in body from her –
> Death, bitter, cruel and violent.

106–9 Early commentators objected that Dante is guilty of heresy here, in suggesting that a body can be hung, at resurrection, from a tree and hence divided from its soul.

115–23 The spendthrifts are: Arcolano da Squarcia di Riccolfo Maconi (murdered 1288 near Pieve al Toppo), who, according to Boccaccio, was a member of the Sienese 'spendthrifts' society; and Jacopo da Santo Andrea (also the victim of murder), who was, like Pier della Vigna, a member of Frederick II's court and is said in an early commentary on the *Commedia* to have set fire to his own property out of a desire to witness a good blaze.

142–50 This speech obliquely recalls legends of the violent history of Florence in the early Middle Ages. As a Roman city, Florence had been founded under the influence of Mars (its first patron). But the pagan god was displaced by the Christian Saint John, to whom the Florentine Baptistery is dedicated. Yet enough of Mars's temple remained in the city for his influence to continue. The city was destroyed, in the account given by the anonymous suicide, by Attila (in fact it was besieged by Totila in AD 410) and, traditionally, refounded by the emperor Charlemagne in 801. The suicide thus suggests that without the warlike strain in its inheritance – represented by a fragment of statuary near the river Arno – the city would not have survived.

# CANTO 14

*The blasphemers. Capaneus. The Old Man of Crete.*
*The source of the rivers of Hell.*

**13–15** Cato the Younger (95 BC–AD 46) (as described in Lucan's
*Pharsalia* 9: 382f) crossed the northern Sahara in Libya during
his campaign in support of Pompey the Great against Julius Caesar.
Further references to Lucan's account occur in *Inferno* 25.

**31–6** This reference to an incident in Alexander the Great's campaign
in India draws on Albertus Magnus's *De Meteoris* 1: 4: 8, which
in turn cites a description of this event that Alexander is said to
have written to his tutor, Aristotle.

**46f** The (apparently) heroic figure of Capaneus is drawn from Statius's
*Thebaid* 3: 605, where the mythical Greek king – laying siege
to the city of Thebes – is described as the great 'contemner' of
the gods, and is finally struck down at 10: 935–9 by Jupiter's
thunderbolt.

**55–7** 'Mongibello' or Mount Jabal (a compound of the Latin *'mons'*
and the Arabic *'jabal'*, both signifying 'mountain') is the popular
name for Mount Etna. This is imagined as the smithy in which
Jupiter prepares his thunderbolts.

**79–81** The Bulicame (literally, 'the boiling thing') is the name of a
stream near Viterbo that runs red with sulphur. Early commenta-
tors said it was reserved for the prostitutes of the town to bathe in.

**94–120** Though the detail of the allegory has never been fully explained,
Dante, in constructing the image of the Old Man of Crete, draws
on a wide variety of sources. The primary one is the dream of
Nebuchadnezzar recorded in Daniel 2: 31–5, which Daniel inter-
prets as representing the successive rise and fall of world empires,
beginning with Nebuchadnezzar's own. Christian interpreters
such as Richard of Saint Victor took the dream as a representa-
tion of the corruption of humanity – the head of gold being
symbolic of the freedom of the will – and the coming of Christ.
Other sources include Ovid's *Metamorphoses* 1: 89–150, which
offers an account of the ages of gold, silver and brass, and Saint
Augustine's *The City of God* 15, which draws on the account of
the excavation of a statue in Crete offered in Pliny's *Natural His-
tory* 7: 16. Dante's own references to Crete see it as the birthplace
of Zeus/Jove (lines 100–102), where his mother Rhea had fled
to save her son from the murderous rage of his father Chronos/

Saturn. It is she who caused dances and music to be performed to conceal the cries of her baby boy. In *Inferno* 12, the troubled history of Crete as the realm of King Minos is recorded. Minos, as judge of the underworld, appears in *Inferno* 5.

# CANTO 15

### *The sodomites. Brunetto Latini.*

22f In the Guelf republic of Florence, Brunetto Latini (*c.* 1220–*c.* 1294) occupied a political and cultural position comparable to that which Pier della Vigna held in the imperial court of Frederick II. He was not – as is sometimes thought – Dante's 'old school master', but an administrator, intellectual and one-time exile of the first importance; and Dante seems to have had some association with the circle that gathered around Brunetto, gaining from him an interest in classical rhetoric and, perhaps, French literature.

The elder Florentine and Dante here concern themselves – as did Dante and the Ghibelline Farinata in *Inferno* 10 – with the divided state of their native city and the consequences of this for Dante's own future. (It is notable that Virgil, who is now Dante's chosen model of political and rhetorical practice, remains silent throughout the canto, save for a tight-lipped, sardonic intervention at line 99.)

Dante would have undoubtedly agreed with some of the principal tenets of Brunetto's thinking. Thus, in his commentary on Cicero's rhetoric writings, Brunetto writes: '*What is a city?* A city is a coming-together of persons as one to live according to reason: citizens are not those who live simply in the same community surrounded by the same city walls but those rather who are brought to live according to rational principle.' A city, on this understanding, is not merely a marketplace or defensive stronghold but the expression of common interest in rational values. Dante's own devotion to the life of a small city, understood in such terms, persists into *Paradiso* 8 and, especially, 15–17. It is even possible that Brunetto's writing suggested to Dante the ways in which he might begin his quest in the dark wood. For Brunetto – himself suffering exile – had written in his vernacular verse allegory *Tesoretto* (lines 190–94) of how in 'a dark wood,

coming back to conscious mind', he turned his thoughts to the
ascent of a great mountain. (Cf. *Inferno* 1: 1–18.) But Brunetto
would not be in Hell if, in some way, he had not failed to live up
to the principles that he expresses here. He has been displaced as
teacher, in respect of civic understanding, companionship and
intellectual exploration, by the figure of the Roman Virgil.

61–3 The legend (recorded in Brunetto's *Livres dou Trésor* 1: 37: 1–2
and also in Giovanni Villani's *Cronica* 1: 37–8 (*c.* 1322)) is that
the hilltown of Fiesole was a hotbed of revolt against Rome dur-
ing the Catiline conspiracy of 62 BC and was razed to the ground
by Julius Caesar. Florence was then founded in the valley as a
loyal imperial colony, while the remnants of the original Fie-
soleans gathered themselves over the centuries in continuing
opposition to the native inhabitants whom Dante considered to
be the 'sacred seed of Rome' (line 76). (Cf. *Inferno* 16 and *Para-
diso* 15–17.)

106–14 The charge of sodomy was commonly levelled against intel-
lectuals and academics, as in the important medieval text *De
Planctu Naturae* (1160–70) by Alain de Lille. But Brunetto is
known to have spoken out against sodomy and no direct charge
is laid against him in this canto. Dante's silence here has led crit-
ics to look for a variety of other ways in which Brunetto may be
thought to have committed a sin against divinely created nature.

Priscian (*fl.* 491–518) was the author of the most influential
Latin grammar of the Middle Ages. Francesco d'Accorso (1225–
93), doctor of civil law, acted as counsellor to the English king
Edward I. Andrea de' Mozzi (d. 1296), member of an important
banking family in Florence, was appointed bishop of that city in
1287; when accused of various abuses, he was transferred by
Pope Boniface VIII (see *Inferno* 19 and 27) from Florence (the
Arno) to Vicenza (identified in the Italian text by the river Bac-
chiglione which runs through it). Boniface is here ironically
given the traditional appellation of the popes: '*servus servorum*'
('Slave of Slaves').

118–20 In his *Tesoretto* Brunetto writes: 'I send and present to you
this rich Treasure worth its weight in silver and gold.'

121–3 The race is a *palio* for naked athletes, run in the environs of
Verona on the first Sunday in Lent.

# CANTO 16

*The sodomites continued. The Guelf nobles.*
*The call to Geryon.*

37–44 Guido Guerra (1220–72) came from the noble family of the
Conti Guidi and was leader of the Tuscan Guelfs. He was the
grandson of Gualdrada di Bellincione Berti de' Ravagnani, who
is mentioned, along with her husband, in the great account of
Florence in her golden age that Dante offers in *Paradiso* 15: 97–9.
His companions in sodomy are the Guelf aristocrat Tegghiaio
Aldobrandi (d. before 1266) and the minor nobleman Iacopo
Rusticucci (*fl.* 1235–66). The words that 'ought to have more
pleased the world' are a speech he made to dissuade the Floren-
tines from engaging in the battle of Montaperti. (Cf. Farinata in
*Inferno* 10: 88–93.) The presence of all these figures in Hell was
first announced by Ciacco in *Inferno* 6.

70–73 Nothing is known of Guglielmo Borsiere, save for the picture
of his courtesy and generosity that Boccaccio offers in *Decam-
eron* 1: 8.

94–102 Here, as frequently, Dante displays the exact knowledge of
landscape that he no doubt acquired in the course of his exile.

106–114 The significance of this episode has never been satisfactorily
explained. Though Dante declares that he had once sought to
lasso the *lonza*, or leopard, of *Inferno* 1 with this cord, there is
no mention of it there. (In *Purgatorio* 1 Dante girds himself
again with a reed.) A great variety of interpretations have been
offered – the most convincing of which suggests (none too con-
vincingly) that Dante may have had some association with the
Franciscan Order, whose corded belts might be taken to signify
chastity.

# CANTO 17

*The usurers. The descent on the back of Geryon*
*to lower Hell.*

4f Geryon (only named at line 97) originally was one of the monsters
overcome by Hercules (see Virgil, *Aeneid* 6: 288). Yet Dante here

draws equally upon Revelation, where Satan, scorpion-like, horse-like, rises out of the abyss (9: 2–7):

> And [the fifth angel] opened the bottomless pit; and there arose a smoke out of the pit, as the smoke of a great furnace . . . And there came out of the smoke locusts upon the earth: and unto them was given power, as the scorpions of the earth have power . . . And the shapes of the locusts were like unto horses prepared unto battle; and on their heads were as it were crowns like gold, and their faces were as the faces of men.

From this point on, the *Inferno* in its imagery and religious thinking continues to refer to the Apocalypse as depicted in Revelation. The imagery and punishments from *Inferno* 18 to 30 often reflect the images of disaster that will appear in the days preceding the Last Judgement: fire (26–7); war (28); disease (29–30).

16–18  In Ovid's *Metamorphoses* 6: 1–145, a Lydian girl, Arachne, challenges the goddess Athene to a weaving contest and, losing, is transformed into a spider. (Cf. *Purgatorio* 12: 43–5.)

58–73  Identified by their armorial bearings these figures are members of the following families: the Yellow Purse – the Gianfigliazzi, of Florence Guelfs, becoming Black Guelfs after 1300; the White Goose – the aristocratic Florentine Ghibelline Obriachi; the Blue Sow ('*scrofa*') – the Scrovegni of Padua; the Three Goats – the Florentine Buiamonte, of whom Giovanni di Buiamonte de' Becchi became Gonfaloniere (chief of police) in 1293.

106–11  Phaeton, driving the chariot of the sun, loses the reins in terror at the sight of the constellation of Scorpio (Ovid, *Metamorphoses* 2: 200), while (*Metamorphoses* 8: 226) Icarus, climbing towards the sun, finds that his wax wings melt.


# CANTO 18

*The plan of Malebolge where deceit is punished.*
*Pimps, seducers and flatterers.*

1  The invented word 'Rottenpockets' here translates the word that Dante himself invents to describe this region of Hell, '*Malebolge*' ('Evil Pockets'). *Inferno* 18–30 describe the ten '*bolge*', or 'pockets',

that contain the various sinners of deceit 'against those who have no cause to trust'.

**28–33** In 1300 Pope Boniface VIII (see especially *Inferno* 19 and *Purgatorio* 1) proclaimed a jubilee year which brought an influx of some 200,000 pilgrims to Rome. Dante refers to the methods of crowd control devised at the time: central barriers were erected on the Ponte degli Angeli to divide those pedestrians approaching Saint Peter's from those who were leaving it – that is, those who were heading towards the papal fortress of Castel Sant' Angelo from those who were going in the direction of Monte Giordano, a small hill opposite the fortress.

**49f** Venedico Caccianemico (d. *c.* 1302) was a Bolognese noble of the Guelf party and military governor of various cities. No record remains as to how or to whom he prostituted his sister Ghisolabella. At line 51 the word translated as 'pickle' is *'salse'*, which as well as meaning a hot sauce may also refer to an area of Bologna in which the bodies of excommunicants and suicides were buried.

**61** 'Yeah' translates Dante's *'sipa'* – Bolognese dialect for 'yes'.

**85–96** The story of Jason and Hypsipyle appears in Ovid's *Metamorphoses* 7: 1–424, his *Heroides* 6 and also in Statius's *Thebaid* 5: 29–485. Jason, the first sea traveller voyaging in pursuit of the Golden Fleece, becomes an important point of reference for Dante in *Paradiso* 2: 16–18 and 33: 94–6. His appearance here is accounted for by his acts of infidelity and seduction. When Jason and his Argonauts arrive at the island of Lemnos, they find that the women of the island have resolved to kill all men – but that Hypsipyle has enabled her father, the king, to escape. The Argonauts are accepted as husbands by the women of Lemnos. Hypsipyle (see also *Purgatorio* 22: 112 and 26: 95) marries Jason, only to be deserted and left pregnant when he leaves. Medea, at line 96, after bearing two children to Jason, is outraged when Jason abandons her for Glauce, daughter of the king of Corinth, and, in revenge, murders both Glauce and her own children in the sight of Jason.

**121–2** Alessio Interminei (*fl.* 1295) was a White Guelf of Lucca. For further satirical references to Lucca, see *Inferno* 21: 37–51.

**133** Thais the prostitute appears in Terence's comedy *The Eunuch* (161 BC), but Dante would have found references to her in Cicero's *De Amicitia* (45–44 BC) and John of Salisbury's *Policraticus* (1159), where flattery is treated as a form of fraud.

# CANTO 19

*Simony exemplified by papal corruption.*
*Dante reproves Pope Nicholas III.*

1f The sin punished in this pocket is simony: the abuse of sacramental
authority for the purposes of gain. This sin is traced to the apos-
tolic era: in the Acts of the Apostles 8: 9–24, Simon of Samaria
(the 'Magus') is condemned by Saint Peter when he seeks to buy
from the Apostles the sacramental powers of their priesthood
(lines 1–4). The apocryphal Acts of Saint Peter represents Simon
as chief magician to Emperor Nero, defeated in miracle-working
contests by Saint Peter. The punishment that Dante devises for
the followers of Simon – plunged absurdly one above the other
in a well, with the soles of their projecting feet set alight – involves
a continuous line of corrupt pontiffs which parodies the apos-
tolic succession.

4–6 The trumpet call – a feature of the military epic – is translated
into the prophetic instrument that will sound, once and for all,
on Judgement Day. See Hosea 8 and Matthew 24: 31.

16–21 The Baptistery in Florence contained octagonal fonts into
which four pits were built, where the priest would stand to
administer the sacrament of baptism. Dante makes elliptical ref-
erence to an episode when he seems to have damaged one of the
fonts in the Florentine Baptistery in order to save a child from
drowning. There exists no independent corroboration, but the
implications are consistent with Dante's concerns in this canto:
he has attempted to act as the true priest in saving life; and for
doing so, his own name and reputation have been attacked by
materially minded Church authorities.

46–51 The upturned sinner is Pope Nicholas III (*c.* 1225–80), a
member of the noble Orsini clan, whose family emblem was the
Bear (see line 70). Under Florentine law, hired assassins were
condemned to be executed by being buried head downwards in
the earth.

52–7 Boniface VIII was born into the noble clan of the Caetani in
1235, became cardinal in 1281 and pope on the resignation of
Celestine V (see note to *Inferno* 3: 58–60) in 1295. In his
attempts to advance the temporal ambitions of the Church he
came into conflict with Philip IV (the Fair) of France over the
right of the king to tax the clergy. He excommunicated Philip

and issued the bull *Unam sanctam* (1302). Philip replied by declaring his election invalid and arresting Boniface at his birthplace, Anagni, in 1303. On both philosophical and perhaps personal grounds, Dante reserves a particular odium for this pope. (See especially *Inferno* 27 and *Purgatorio* 20.)

82–96 The 'lawless shepherd', the third pope, is Bernard Le Got (*c.* 1260–1314) (a Frenchman from Gascony), who became Pope Clement V. His election seems to have depended upon the influence of Philip IV (the Fair) of France. Clement immediately appointed a considerable number of French cardinals and then established the Papal Curia in Avignon, preparing for the long period in which, under French dominion, the papacy was 'exiled' from Rome. Dante is referring here not to Jason the Argonaut, who appears in *Inferno* 18, but Jason Maccabaeus, who attempted to bribe the Seleucid King Antiochus IV Epiphanes (2 Maccabees 4: 7f). Clement V is the 'new' Jason in that he may have bribed Philip into supporting his election as pope.

97–9 There is a (now discredited) story which suggests that Nicholas accepted a bribe to join the conspiracy that led to the expulsion of the Angevins from Sicily in 1282.

106–11 Saint John the Evangelist in Revelation speaks of the utter corruption which will immediately precede the Second Coming (see notes to *Inferno* 17). The Whore of Babylon is a great sign of this corruption, as at Revelation 17: 3–6:

> I saw a woman sit upon a scarlet coloured beast, full of names of blasphemy, having seven heads and seven horns. And the woman was arrayed in purple and scarlet colour, and decked with gold and precious stones and pearls, having a golden cup in her hand full of abominations and filthiness of her fornication … And I saw the woman drunken with the blood of the saints, and with the blood of the martyrs of Jesus …

The seven heads may be taken to represent the seven sacraments, the ten horns the Ten Commandments that were once a source of virtue and have now been polluted. Dante shares with the 'spiritual Franciscans' of his time a willingness to identify this monstrosity with the corruption of the Church. (Cf. *Purgatorio* 32–3.)

115–17 Emperor Constantine (*c.* 274–337), having been converted to Christianity (see also *Inferno* 27: 94–5 and *Paradiso* 20: 55), was thought to have donated the temporal power of the western part of the Empire to the Church. The document of donation was proved during the sixteenth century to be an eighth-century forgery. Dante had already argued that the donation was legally invalid and an offence against the spirit of Christian poverty. (See *De Monarchia* 3: 10: 1.)

# CANTO 20

*The soothsayers. Virgil's account of*
*the founding of Mantua.*

**22f** Samuel Beckett meditates on the painful meaning of line 28 in his early story 'Dante and the Lobster' (1934). He also realized that 'pity' depends upon the double meaning (in Italian) of '*pietà*', which derives from a tension between the Virgilian notion of '*pietas*' as the public duty of a Roman to the gods and to the State and the Romance understanding which indicates compassion and sentiment.

Beckett must also have this episode in mind in *The Unnamable* (New York, Grove 1958), p. 279:

> If I am, I am but lightly. For I feel my tears coursing over my chest and all down my back. Ah yes I am truly bathed in tears. They gather in my beard and from there, when it can hold no more – no, no beard, no hair either, it is a great smooth ball I carry on my shoulders, featureless, but for the eyes, of which only the sockets remain.

**25f** Virgil speaks for most of this canto, even suggesting at lines 112–14 that Dante can remember the *Aeneid* better than he, its own author, is able to. The sinners whom Virgil introduces are soothsayers drawn mainly from the pages of classical texts. There is an implicit contrast here between his position and that of others in the classical tradition. In Dante's time, Virgil had often been regarded as a soothsayer or magician. He was thought to have journeyed to the depths of Hell at the behest of a witch. But Dante here implies a contrast between sinful soothsaying and the legitimate activities of his Virgil, who is guided by providence. Virgil was the author of the *Fourth Eclogue*, which Dante in *Purgatorio* 22 explicitly takes to be a prophecy of Christ's nativity and the coming of a new age of justice.

31–9 In Statius's *Thebaid*, the Amphiaraus episode runs to over 250
lines, 7: 688–8: 126. Amphiaraus, one of the Seven Against Thebes,
is an augur who has foreseen his own death in battle and yet,
against his better judgement, is driven to participate in the war by
his wife. His death and arrival in the underworld are described by
Statius in characteristically spectacular and ornate style:

> Behold in a gaping chasm the ground yawns sheer and deep, and
> stars and shade feel mutual terror. The huge abyss engulfs him and
> swallows the horses as they try to leap across it ... When on the
> sudden the prophet fell among the pallid shades and burst into the
> homes of the dead and the mysteries of the deep-sunken realm and
> affrighted ghosts with his armed corpse, all were horror struck ...
> *Thebaid* 7: 816–19 and 8: 1–4

Statius (a poet whom Dante read with especial attention) appears
as an important character in the *Commedia* in *Purgatorio* 21–5.
(Cf. also Dante's references to Thebes in *Inferno* 32–3.)

40–46 Tiresias and Arruns appear respectively in Ovid's *Metamor-
phoses* 3: 324–31 and Lucan's *Pharsalia* 1: 585–638. The Theban
seer Tiresias is asked by Jove and Juno whether men or women
take greater pleasure from lovemaking – Tiresias would know,
since he has been both a man and a woman. Ovid then recounts
how 'once with a blow of his staff Tiresias had outraged two
huge serpents while mating; and immediately was changed from
man to woman. Eight years later he saw the same serpents again,
struck them once more and was changed back into a man.'

Lucan describes Arruns as 'one who dwelt in the deserted city
of Lucca: the course of thunderbolts, the marks on entrails yet
warm and the warning of each wing that strays through the sky
had no secrets from him'. Arruns foresees the disasters of civil
war between Caesar and Pompey but conceals the whole truth.

The references here anticipate the great description of meta-
morphosis in *Inferno* 25, where Dante claims to outdo both
Ovid and Lucan.

52–60 Manto is the daughter of Tiresias and herself a sorceress, who
at the fall of Thebes – the city sacred to the god Bacchus – searched
over many lands for a new home (as Aeneas did at the fall of
Troy), eventually settling in the marshes around Mantua. Dante's
(modified) account draws on Virgil's *Aeneid* 10: 198–201.

61–99 This lengthy account of the foundation of Mantua follows the
downward course of the river Mincius, or Mincio, and attempts

to dissociate the city from any taint of sorcery. It is founded for good military and defensive reasons. The words that Dante attributes to Virgil contain topographical references to an Italian landscape that Dante himself may have travelled through, and define the place in terms of modern and Christian history. Garda is a city on the shores of Lake Benacus (the Latin name for Lake Garda). The 'central point' is, presumably, the island of Lechi, at which the dioceses of Trent, Brescia and Verona meet. Peschiera in Dante's time was controlled by the Scaligeri, lords of Verona; Govérnolo is a mile north of the point at which the Mincio meets the Po; in 1291 Pinamonte dei Bonacolsi (d. 1293) tricked the then-ruler of Mantua, Alberto de Casalodi, into withdrawing his nobles from the city. Pinamonte then stirred up the populace in rebellion and massacred most of the noble families.

106–12 Eurypylus is mentioned along with Calchas in Virgil's *Aeneid* 2: 114, which Dante seems to have misread, assuming that Eurypylus was an augur associated with Calchas in deciding when the Greek fleet should cast off for Troy from Aulis (where the oracles of Apollo were heard). In the period of the Trojan War, Greece was 'void of men', in that all its males had gone off to battle.

115–17 Michael Scott (d. *c.* 1235) was employed by Emperor Frederick II (see *Inferno* 10: 119) as a futurologist. He also translated from Arabic and from Aristotle's Greek texts.

118–20 Guido Bonatti (b. *c.* 1220) was, like Michael Scott, an astrologer at Frederick II's court and influential in Ghibelline circles. Asdente (meaning 'the Toothless') was a soothsaying shoemaker, whom Dante refers to in *Convivio* 4: 16: 6 as the most famous man in Parma.

124–30 As seen from Jerusalem, the moon is now setting south of Seville. The time is 6 a.m. The moon had been full when Dante entered the dark wood, and had cast an imperfect light that hindered rather than guided him. Dante's language briefly turns enigmatic in its references to the moon. There is a touch of the uncanny (and some archaism of language) in mentioning the folk tale of Cain as the man in the moon, carrying a bundle of thorns on his back. (See note to *Paradiso* 2: 49f.) But the purpose of this reference is not necromantic. Rather, it is an attempt, by reference to natural phenomena, to establish a timetable for Dante's onward journey. To speak of Virgil 'chatting' here reflects Dante's use of the Florentine dialect word *introcque* (meaning 'meanwhile') which Dante in *De Vulgari Eloquentia* 1: 13: 1 declares unsuitable for poetry in the high, tragic style. This usage is the more striking in view of the mention of Virgilian 'tragedy' (line 113) and of Dantean 'comedy' in the opening verse of the following canto.

# CANTO 21

*The sinners here have been guilty of corruption in public office (barratry). The mock epic of the demon guardians of the circle.*

**7–18** The Arsenal, or shipyard, of the Venetian empire had been in existence about 200 years when Dante visited it. It developed very early a form of production-line manufacture, accurately depicted by Dante in contrast to the unproductive activity of Hell.

**37–49** Rotklors (*'Malebranche'*) is an invented collective noun referring to the devils of this pocket. (Cf. *'Malacoda'*, 'Evil Tail', translated at line 76 as 'Rottentail', and *'Malebolge'*, 'Evil Pockets' – see note to *Inferno* 18: 1.) This sequence is punctuated by reference to the Black Guelf city of Lucca, in north-western Tuscany, which had a reputation for rampant civic corruption. Santa Zita (d. *c.* 1272) is the patron saint of Lucca. The Holy Face of Lucca is a crucifix – still on show in the city – carved in ebony (hence reference to 'black-faced gods'), supposedly by the Apostle Nicodemus. Its face is said to have been completed by a miracle while the Apostle slept. The Serchio is a river popular with bathers a few miles from Lucca.

The speaker (newly arrived in Hell) has been identified as Martino Bottaio, a political boss in Lucca, who died on the night of Good Friday 1300 – and hence at the same time as Dante's journey through Hell supposedly began. Exception from judgement is here made, ironically, on behalf of one of the most infamous of the Lucchese politicians, Bonturo Dati (d. after 1324), who, while ostensibly leader of the people's party, was driven out of the city by a popular uprising in 1313.

**94–6** Caprona, a Pisan fortress, surrendered to Florence in August 1289. Dante was probably present at the siege, as a member of the Florentine cavalry.

**112–14** Since the Passion of Christ and the Harrowing of Hell, which on Easter Saturday broke down the bridges of Rottenpockets through the aftershock of the earthquake, 1,266 years have passed to noon of Good Friday 1300, which is now 'yesterday' in the timetable of Dante's journey. If noon is five hours later than the present time, the hour is now Saturday, 7 a.m.

118-23 Some of the names given to the Malebranche may be deformations of family names from Lucca. Most are purely fantastical. A roughly literal translation of each would be as follows: *Alichino* – Harlequin; *Barbariccia* – Curly Beard; *Cagnazzo* – Nasty Dog; *Calcabrina* – Trample Frost; *Ciriatto* – Big Pig; *Draghignazzo* – Big Little Dragon; *Farfarello* – Flutterby; *Graffiacane* – Scratching Dog; *Libicocco* – (following suggestions by Robert Durling) Love Notch; *Malacoda* (lines 76 and 79) – Evil Tail; *Rubicante* – Red Face; *Scarmiglione* (line 105) – Tangled Hair.

# CANTO 22

*Corrupt officials, demon guardians*
*(and mock-heroic farce) continued.*

4-6 In a letter now lost, but recorded by the leading fifteenth-century historian Leonardo Bruni, Dante writes of his participation in the battle of Campaldino (11 June 1289) between the Florentine and Aretine Guelfs (see also *Purgatorio* 5: 93). 'Tournaments' involved group fights with hand weapons, as contrasted with jousts, which were mounted 'duels' with lances in the lists.

7-9 Medieval armies would go into battle with bells borne on great war wagons. The 'signs' are drawn from the constellations, from which appropriate auguries might be read.

43-54 Though commentators traditionally give this figure the name of Ciampolo (Jean-Paul) he is, perhaps significantly, not named in the text but simply identified by the king under which he was born, Thibaut II of Navarre (1255-70).

79-90 Between 1275 and 1296, Brother Gomita (a member of the *frati godenti* – see notes to *Inferno* 23: 103-8) acted as deputy to Nino Visconti (see *Purgatorio* 8) as governor of Gallura, one of the four administrative districts of Sardinia. Logodoro was another district, governed, it seems, by Lord Michel Zanche as deputy of King Enzo (1239?-72). At *Inferno* 33: 134, Michel Zanche is said to have been murdered by his son-in-law, Branca d'Oria.

118–20 To designate the 'sport' which Dante now describes to his readers, the poet ironically uses the elevated Latinism '*ludo*' (*ludus*). (Cf. his address to the reader at *Inferno* 16: 127–8.)

# CANTO 23

*The conclusion of Dante's encounter with the devils.*
*The hypocrites. Caiaphas.*

4–6 Aesop's *Fables* circulated widely in the late Middle Ages. In the fable to which Dante refers here, a frog offers to transport a mouse across the water and ties its leg to his, meaning to dive and drown it. As frog and mouse struggle together, a hawk descends and carries off both of them.

7–9 The Italian words used here, '*mo*' and '*issa*', both mean 'now' or 'soon' – '*issa*' being a form used in the dialect of Lucca.

61–3 Cluny was the Benedictine monastery in Burgundy, founded in 910, which by the twelfth century possessed the largest church in Christendom – but also a growing reputation for easy living.

64–6 Emperor Frederick II (see *Inferno* 10) punished traitors by encasing them in leaden cloaks, then melting these encasements around them, over a slow fire.

103–8 '*Frati godenti*' (here translated as 'good-time friars') was the disparaging nickname given to the religious order of the Knights of Saint Mary, founded in Bologna in 1261, which allegedly devoted itself to civic peace but was notorious for corruption. Two of its founding members – Catalano dei Malavolti (1210–85) and Loderingo degli Andalo (1210–93), the first a Guelf, the second a Ghibelline – were appointed to the governorship of Florence in 1266 by Pope Clement IV (d. 1268), ostensibly to maintain a troubled peace. Dante clearly suspected their motive. It was they who ordered the demolition of many Ghibelline houses in the Gardingo ('Watchtower') district of Florence, close to the present Palazzo della Signoria, including the dwelling of Farinata degli Uberti. (See *Inferno* 10 and Villani's *Cronica* 7: 13.)

115–23 Caiaphas, the High Priest of Jerusalem (son-in-law of Annas (line 121)), judges Christ and declares that it is expedient that 'one man should die for the people' (John 11: 45–52), thus ignoring the redemptive significance of Christ in favour of a partial, pragmatic judgement.

# CANTO 24

*Climbing from the pocket of the hypocrites, Dante
and Virgil arrive at a point where they can look down
into the pocket of the thieves.*

1-3 Aquarius (the zodiacal sign of the Waterbearer) is in the ascend-
ant between 21 January and 21 February. Thus the winter
solstice has passed and night has begun to come closer in length
to day – or else, in some interpretations, 'runs southwards'.

49-51 Virgil's heroic exhortation may owe something to *Aeneid*
5: 740.

55-7 For the geography of Purgatory (conceived as a mountain in the
southern hemisphere), see note to *Inferno* 34: 103–33, and the
Introduction, p. xix.

91-3 The heliotrope is a stone that was believed, in medieval studies
of the properties of minerals, to render its possessor invisible.

106-11 Dante's description of the phoenix draws directly on Ovid's
*Metamorphoses* 15: 392–407. But it is also a familiar medieval
figure for the Resurrection – in which, according to Christian
belief, human beings are finally assured of the eternal possession
of their own physical identities.

121-6 Vanni Fucci was a member of the White Guelf faction in Pis-
toia. He was responsible for the murder of a fellow White Guelf
in 1293 or 1294. In 1293 (lines 137–8), he stole two silver tab-
lets bearing images of the Blessed Virgin and the Apostles from
the sacristy of the church of San Zeno at Pistoia. Rampino di
Francesco Foresi was arrested for the crime and only released in
1295, when Vanni Fucci informed on one of his accomplices
(line 139), who was subsequently executed in Rampino's place.

142-51 This violent and perhaps deliberately enigmatic prophecy
pictures the factional conflicts of the Tuscan Blacks and Whites
in terms of the geography of the region. Mars, the god of war,
stirs up the leader of the Blacks of Lucca, Moroello Malaspina,
from his native place in the Val di Magra. (For Dante's eulogy of
the Malaspina family, see *Purgatorio* 8.) The 'clouds' (line 146)
are probably the Tuscan White Guelfs. Conflicts flared in 1302
and in 1306, when, in alliance with the Blacks of Florence,
Moroello defeated the Whites of Pistoia.

# CANTO 25

*The thieves continued, their punishment to be
constantly metamorphosed from human form to
reptile and back again.*

1–3 The obscene sign of the figs is made by thrusting the thumb
between the two forefingers. The Florentine chronicler Villani
reports (*Cronica* 6: 5) that in 1228 Pistoia set up a marble repre-
sentation of the figs aimed at Florence. The name Pistoia is derived,
says Villani (*Cronica* 1: 32), from the Latin *'pestis'* ('pestilence').

10–12 These lines represent the first of a series of polemical outbursts
against the cities of Tuscany, including Florence itself (cf. *Inferno*
26 and 33, and also the satire against Siena that concludes
*Inferno* 29). In his authorial voice, Dante enters vigorously into
the political animosities of the period.

13–18 Dante here employs the elevated and Latinate locution
*'verbo'* – which he also uses in referring to the 'Word of God' or
Logos. (See note to *Paradiso* 7: 19–123.) The rhyme *'verbo'*
('word') and *'acerbo'* (here, 'sour') also occurs in the account of
Satan's fall in *Paradiso* 19. It is a further sign of the literary self-
consciousness that characterizes this canto that Dante should
introduce two cross-references to earlier passages in his own
fiction: Capaneus (who was 'flung down from Theban walls'
(line 15)) appears at *Inferno* 14: 49–75; the centaurs from whom
Cacus is separated are guardians of the circle of Hell described in
*Inferno* 12.

25–33 Virgil recounts the outline of the story of Cacus as he himself
had told it in *Aeneid* 8: 193f. Dante has greatly transformed the
Virgilian account, in which Cacus appears not as a centaur
but simply as a monstrous half-man, who steals the cattle of
Hercules and butchers them on the Aventine Hill in Rome.

43f Though little is known about the historical lives of the five figures
who participate in these metamorphoses, all were Florentines.
The first two to appear may have been Agnello, of the prominent
Brunelleschi family, and Buoso Donati, who is referred to again
in *Inferno* 30. Cianfa (who is, presumably, the lizard that
responds to the question posed by Agnello and Buoso) was
another member of the important Donati clan. For the last two
men, see note to lines 148–51.

94–9 For Lucan's *Pharsalia* – an account of the Roman civil wars
fought in the deserts of Libya – see notes to *Inferno* 20. In Ovid's
*Metamorphoses* 6: 571–603, Cadmus, founder of Thebes, is
transformed into a serpent as a punishment for impiety, along
with his wife Harmonia. Arethusa, in *Metamorphoses* 5: 572–
641, is transformed into a stream while escaping the advances of
Alpheus – who is himself transformed into a stream and so min-
gles with her. For a fuller account of the thinking underlying the
metamorphoses of *Inferno* 25 and the differences between Dante
and Ovid, see notes to *Purgatorio* 25.

136–8 Human spittle was thought in Dante's day to be venomous to
snakes.

148–51 The last two Florentines are probably Puccio Galigai, who
was nicknamed '*Sciancato*' ('the Lame') and Francesco de' Cav-
alcanti – originally the 'snakelet' of line 84 – whose nickname
was '*Guercio*' ('Cross-eyed'). Francesco was murdered by the
inhabitants of the village of Gaville, on whom the Cavalcanti
clan took extreme vengeance. In that sense Gaville weeps on his
account.

# CANTO 26

*The first of two cantos describing the eighth pocket,*
*where the sinners, transformed into flames, are those*
*who have made deceitful or destructive use of their*
*intellectual gifts.*

1–3 Behind this sarcastic encomium one may discern the words
inscribed in 1255 on the walls of the Bargello Palace in Florence
claiming for the republic (ironically enough) imperial dominion
over the world and the right to make its Tuscan subjects 'happy':
'*Que mare, que terram, que totum possidet orbem*' ('Who pos-
sesses land, sea and all the earthly globe'; a phrase from Lucan's
*Pharsalia* 1: 109, describing the self-destructiveness of Rome,
also quoted in Dante's *De Monarchia* 2: 8). A connection is
clearly drawn between intellectual appetitiveness and commer-
cial greed. (See *Convivio* 4: 12: 11.)

7–9 As with the reference to Pistoia in *Inferno* 25, this allusion points
to the strife, particularly between Black and White Guelf fac-
tions, that had arisen in the last decade of the thirteenth century

between Florence and the Tuscan cities, such as Prato, that were
its immediate neighbours.

34-9 These lines refer, in highly compressed form, to the two Old
Testament prophets Elijah and Elisha, contained in 2 Kings 2.
Elijah is, like Ulysses, hidden in flame, but ascends to Heaven
(as, of course, Ulysses does not):

> And it came to pass, as they still went on, and talked, that,
> behold, there appeared a chariot of fire, and horses of fire, and
> parted them both asunder; and Elijah went up by a whirlwind into
> heaven.
>
> And Elisha saw it, and he cried, My father, my father, the chariot
> of Israel, and the horsemen thereof.
>
> 2 Kings 2: 11-12

Elisha is 'avenged by furious bears' for being mocked by the
urchins of Bethel:

> there came forth little children out of the city, and mocked him, and
> said unto him, Go up, thou bald head; go up, thou bald head ...
> And there came forth two she bears out of the wood, and tare forty
> and two children of them.
>
> 2 Kings 2: 23-4

46-8 The destructive fire within is now displayed in the outward fire
that consumes the sinners.

52-63 Statius describes how the two sons of Oedipus, Eteocles and
Polynices, kill each other in mutual hatred and are laid on the
same funeral pyre, their hatred dividing its fire (*Thebaid* 12:
429-32). Drawing on a number of classical sources, including
Virgil's *Aeneid* 2 and Ovid's *Metamorphoses* 13: 123-380, Dante
puts into Virgil's mouth references to three events in Ulysses's
life, all of which might be taken as evidence of a destructive or
impious intellect worthy of damnation. First, Ulysses devises the
stratagem of the Trojan horse, which allows the Greeks to enter
Troy and destroy it – thus opening the way to the ultimate foun-
dation of Rome. (Both Ulysses and Diomed entered Troy in the
wooden belly of the horse.) Secondly, Ulysses persuades Achilles
(in Statius's *Achilleid* 1) to abandon his love for his wife Deidamia,
daughter of the king of Scyros, and go off to the Trojan War, in
which he meets his death. Thirdly, in both the *Aeneid* and the
*Metamorphoses*, Ulysses is held to have been guilty of profanity,

when he stealthily enters Troy and steals from its inner sanctum the sacred image of Pallas Athene (the Palladium) on which the security of the city depends. (See also note to lines 85f.)

73–84 The rhetorical devices that Dante attributes to Virgil reflect features of Virgil's own usage in, for instance, *Aeneid* 4: 317–18.

85f Continuing the challenge to classical literature that he issued in *Inferno* 25, Dante undertakes to represent the figure of the famously intelligent Ulysses. He did not know Homer's Greek original, and so relied on references in Latin sources, including Cicero, Seneca and, above all, Horace's *Ars Poetica* and Ovid's *Metamorphoses* 14: 157. But these sources all tend to represent Ulysses in terms of low cunning rather than intelligence – as does Virgil in lines 55–63 of this canto. Nor has any precedent been found that anticipates the account which Dante puts in Ulysses's own mouth of a last journey beyond the limits imposed by the gods upon human endeavour (lines 108–9), a journey which ends in death but is impelled by a desire for knowledge of the world and of the vices and virtues of human beings (lines 98–9 and 116–20). In subsequent cantos of the *Commedia*, Dante makes more frequent mention of, or allusion to, the Ulysses story than of any other episode in the poem. (See *Purgatorio* 1: 131 and 19: 22–4; *Paradiso* 2: 1–6 and 27: 82–4.)

91–9 The sorceress Circe, daughter of the sun, demanded that Ulysses – on his adventurous return from the Trojan War – should remain with her on the island of Aeaea, near Cumae, for a full year after she has transformed his men from swine back to human form. (See Ovid, *Metamorphoses* 14.) Aeneas on his more purposeful and 'pious' journey renames a promontory in the vicinity Gaeta, in honour of his nurse who died there. (See also Virgil, *Aeneid* 7: 1–4, 97–9.) In attributing to Ulysses this burning intellectual curiosity, Dante draws directly on phrasing in Horace's *Ars Poetica* 141–42, which in turn refers to the opening lines of Homer's *Odyssey*.

100–42 The geography of this invented journey represents Ulysses as travelling through the Mediterranean – seeing both its northern and southern shores and the island of Sardinia – and then passing through the Straits of Gibraltar (the rocks of which were supposed, since Pindar's *Fourth Nemean Ode*, to have been set up by Hercules as a limit on human travel), leaving Seville on the right and Ceuta in Morocco on the left. Turning south – and therefore left – Ulysses journeys for five months, telling time by the phases of the moon; and as he enters the southern hemisphere, he sees the stars around the northern pole disappear as those stars of the southern hemisphere (never before seen by human eyes since the fall of Adam – see *Purgatorio* 1: 22–4) gradually appear to view. The mountain that Ulysses encounters is Mount Purgatory. This is, in Dante's view, the only land mass in the southern hemisphere. It stands at the antipodes of Jerusalem and its formation is described in the final canto of the *Inferno*. (See notes to *Inferno* 34 and Introduction, p. xix.)

## CANTO 27

*Abuse of intellect continued; the case of*
*Guido da Montefeltro.*

7–12 Phalarus, the despot of Acragas in Sicily, had a bronze bull made by Perillus of Athens. Within the bronze bull, the tyrant's victims would be roasted alive; a mechanical larynx translated the roars of the victim roasted within its hollow body into the bellowing of a bull. The first victim was the artificer himself. The passage in the Italian is syntactically disturbed and marked by unusual repetitions. But the essential message is clear: 'the biter bit', a villain hoist with his own petard.

19f The damned soul is not, as Ulysses was, a legendary pagan but a historical figure from the Christian era who enjoyed a close working relationship with the pope – the Ghibelline warlord and politician Guido da Montefeltro (1223–98). There had been a time when Dante admired Guido. In the *Convivio* 4: 28: 8, he spoke of him as 'the most noble Guido of Montefeltro', and praised him for the wisdom he displayed at the end of his life. Guido, after a history of excommunications, finally reconciled himself with the Church, and, having associated himself with the Franciscans, died in Assisi. In this early work, then, Guido is taken to exemplify an important point in Dantean ethics that human life goes through four phases and each has its characteristic virtues, which the intellect should seek to cultivate to the full. For instance, in what we should now call middle age and Dante calls youth – or '*gioventute*' – we should usefully be involved in practical and public affairs (since etymologically the word '*gioventute*' can be derived from '*giovare*' – 'to be useful'). Both Ulysses and Guido continue to behave as though they were, in this sense, youthful and useful. Yet both were old men at the time of their deaths, and by that time should have begun to develop the virtues of contemplation, considering the life-to-come.

Lines 19–21 may be taken as a sign of Guido's political divisiveness (see note to lines 28–54) in that, far from recognizing in Virgil a representative of true imperial authority, he focuses, perhaps disparagingly, on Virgil's Lombard accent and turn of phrase: '*Istra*' ('now') being used in the Italian text instead of the word '*issa*' which might have been expected here. (Note that Virgil at line 33 may respond by allowing Dante to speak to this mere Italian in the vernacular.)

28–54  Where most of the cities of Italy in the last decades of the thirteenth century had come under Guelf control, the Romagna, in the north-east, had remained Ghibelline in sympathy, largely through the military and strategic efforts of Guido, who locates his birthplace at lines 29–30 between Urbino (where he became duke in 1293) and the source of the Tiber. But Ghibelline control had begun to slip, leaving in its wake Guelf despotisms. In response to Guido's question, Dante ascribes to himself a survey of the political state of the seven major cities of the Romagna. Notably, they are described as despotisms (line 37), suggesting – against the claims of true empire – the assumption of violent and unlawful rule. Despots, as Aristotle (quoted in *De Monarchia* 3: 4) declares, 'do not follow laws for the common good but attempt to wrench them to their own benefit'. Dante then proceeds to describe these cities in terms, usually, of the heraldic emblems and coats-of-arms of their leading families. Since 1275 Ravenna had been ruled by the Guelf Guido Vecchio da Polenta (father of Francesca, who appears in *Inferno* 5) and in 1283 Guido da Montefeltro lost control of the town of Cervia to the Polenta, whose family emblem was a red eagle on a golden field. Forlì had been defended successfully by Guido against troops dispatched by Pope Martin IV. These troops included French mercenaries whom Guido massacred, leaving a 'blood-stained pile' (line 44) of the dead. In 1296, however, the city came under the control of the Guelf Ordelaffi. Their shield bore a green lion with prominent claws in its upper half. Rimini was ruled by the Malatesta, whose ancient stronghold was Verucchio and whose emblem was the bull mastiff – its teeth sucking the life blood out of its opponents. Ferocious adversaries of Guido, the Malatesta had driven the Ghibellines from Rimini in 1295 and imprisoned and murdered their leader, Montagna de' Parcitati, in 1296. Faenza and Imola are identified by the rivers that flow through them, the Lamone and the Santerno. These cities were ruled by the Pagani family, under the emblem of a blue lion on a white field. Maghinardo Pagani (d. 1302) fought as a Ghibelline in Romagna, north of the Apennines, and as a Guelf to the south, in Tuscany. The last of the seven is Cesena on the river Savio, which was governed nominally by Guido's nephew Galasso, but in 1300 was a Guelf commune, living politically – as it did topographically – between the high mountains of tyranny and the plains of republican democracy.

85-97 The 'lord of our new Pharisees' is Pope Boniface VIII (see notes to *Inferno* 19). He had called on Guido for advice in prosecuting his quarrel with the Colonna clan of Rome, who refused to admit the legitimacy of his election in 1294. The Colonna had retreated to their fortress at Penestrina (or Palestrina, formerly Praeneste), twenty miles east of Rome. Boniface's campaign against this citadel is contrasted with what Dante might have considered more legitimate objects of military action, particularly the recovery of Acre in the Holy Land, which had been seized by Muslim forces in 1291. Further ironies in the corrupting complicity of Church and State are identified by the parallel drawn between the emperor Constantine (see notes to *Inferno* 19) and Pope Sylvester I (314-35) and Boniface himself and Guido. The legend is that Constantine was stricken by leprosy for his persecution of the Christians, was cured on Mount Soracte, north of Rome, by Sylvester and subsequently converted to Christianity. Boniface's disease is not leprosy but a frenzied political ambition. The 'cure' is not a conversion but the involvement in an intrigue and abuse of absolution that leads Guido to Hell.

112-23 The devil identifies the false logic that runs through lines 101-11: that absolution cannot be given in advance of the crime that it is intended to pardon. Willing a sin and not willing it cannot, logically, be simultaneous. In *Purgatorio* 5, a scene occurs that exactly parallels the farcical tussle over Guido's soul at the gate of Heaven. But in this case, Guido's son, Buonconte da Montefeltro (d. 1289), receives unexpectedly the salvation which his father, for all *his* expectations, is firmly denied. Buonconte was no contemplative. He was a warrior who died in battle, fighting on the opposite side from Dante. Yet Buonconte's final act on earth is pictured as an infinitesimally small moment of repentance in which he weeps a penitent tear and locks his arms over his chest in the form of a cross.

# CANTO 28

*The ninth pocket, where those whose words have*
*deliberately fomented discord between others are*
*punished by the suffering of wounds.*

1-21 '[S]et loose' ('*sciolte*') in line 1 points to a distinction between tightly disciplined verse and the laxer form of prose, as used by historians such as Livy. Apulia in Dante's day was the whole of southern Italy, forming the kingdom of Naples. The following lines make rapid but detailed reference to the wars that were fought in this territory from ancient times up to the present. These include the battles fought between the Trojans (that is to say, the original Romans) and the native Latin tribes. The 'long war where rings were heaped' (line 12) refers to the Punic Wars of 264-146 BC, fought between Rome and Carthage for dominion over the Mediterranean, as recounted by Livy; it is reported by Saint Augustine of Hippo and Paulus Orosius that, following the battle of Cannae (216 BC), the Carthaginians gathered three bushels of rings as spoils from the Roman dead. Robert Guiscard (*c.* 1015-85) was the first of a line of Norman rulers of Sicily and southern Italy invited to stake a claim to these territories by Pope Nicholas II (d. 1061) in 1059. Southern domination of Italy was extinguished with the death of Emperor Frederick II's natural son, Manfred, at the battle of Benevento in 1266. (See *Purgatorio* 3.) On Dante's understanding, the battle was lost when Apulian barons deserted their positions near the Ceperano pass. At Tagliacozzo, in the Abruzzi hills north-east of Rome, the last remaining hopes of the imperial cause were extinguished in 1268 with the defeat of Coradino, Frederick's grandson, by Charles of Anjou (1227-85), following tactical advice from 'Alardo' (Érard de Valéry, Constable of Champagne (*c.* 1220-77)).

31-3 The Prophet Mohammed (*c.* 570-632) was thought to have been a Nestorian Christian before arriving at his own religious vision. He may thus be judged a schismatic. Ali (*c.* 600-661) was Mohammed's cousin and son-in-law.

55-60 These lines refer to the agitated religious scene – evoked powerfully by Umberto Eco in *The Name of the Rose* (1980) – which developed in Italy around 1300. Dolcino de' Tornielli (in some measure similar to Dante in his radical view of social order) was leader of the band of Apostolic Brothers and preached that possessions should be held in common. Pope Clement V moved against him 1305, with soldiers drawn from Dolcino's native Novara. Dolcino was captured and burned at the stake in 1307.

73–5  Though little is known about Pier da Medicina, early commentators suggest that he was responsible for sowing strife among the members of the Polenta and Malatesta families in the 1280s. (See notes to *Inferno* 27.)

76–90  Guido del Cassero and Angiolello da Carignano, leading figures in the city of Fano, were drowned between 1312 and 1317 (with stones slung around their necks) off the coast of Cattolica, near Rimini, on the orders of Malatestino, the despotic lord of Rimini. The currents and winds were particularly dangerous on this coastline. But since these two men were doomed to be murdered, there was no point in their praying for safe passage.

94–102  Gaius Scribonius Curio (d. 49 BC) first advised Caesar to cross the river Rubicon near Rimini, thus precipitating the Roman civil wars.

106–8  Mosca de' Lamberti (*fl.* 1200), a Florentine, first mentioned by Ciacco in *Inferno* 6, is thought to have stirred up the strife that ran through the families of Florence throughout the thirteenth century. When Buondelmonte de' Buondelmonti (*fl.* 1200) rejected the wife from the Amidei clan to whom he was betrothed, Mosca – whose Lamberti family were allied to the Amidei – incited his allies to revenge with the words: 'What's done, well, that is done.' On Easter Sunday 1215, Buondelmonte was dragged from his horse and stabbed to death.

133f  The final figure is the troubadour poet Bertran de Born (*c.* 1140–*c.* 1215), lord of the castle of Altaforte in Périgord. Famously, the poetry of Bertran displays a positive relish in the destructive energies released by warfare and battle, as for instance in his '*Be·m plai lo gais temps de pascor*' with its great, ironic crescendo of blood lust:

> How pleased I am with the season of Easter, which makes leaves and flowers flourish. And I am pleased when I hear birds in all happiness send their song ringing through the woodland. And I am pleased when across the fields I see tents and pavilions pitched and am greatly cheered when I see lined up on the plain the ranks of horsemen and horses. And I am pleased when the skirmishers put crowd and all

their possessions to flight, and cheered when after them I see a great host of men in arms come in pursuit.

In *De Vulgari Eloquentia* 2: 2: 8, Dante speaks highly of Bertran. Lamenting that the Italian vernacular has yet to provide an example of military poetry, he points to Bertran's poetry as an exemplar of what the Occitan vernacular has already achieved. Now, however, this surreal picture of the brilliant Bertran carrying his own severed head like a lantern markedly modifies the earlier celebration. If Bertran is in Hell, it is because – in a spirit of political realism – his interference in the affairs of the English court has led to acrimony between father and son. An exact correspondence of crime and punishment is observed.

Dante puts in Bertran's mouth, in the final line of this canto, the one use of the word '*contrapasso*' ('counter-suffering'), which is sometimes taken to characterize the whole vengeance system of the *Inferno*. One way in which Dante may be thought to have moved on is in his realization that only God's apparent vengeance is a guarantee of wholeness.

136–8  In 2 Samuel 15–19, Ahithophel, the friend and adviser to King David, incites David's son Absalom to rebel against his father.

# CANTO 29

*Conclusion to the ninth pocket. Entry into the tenth and last pocket, where deceit in the form of false science, counterfeiting and impersonation is punished.*

10–12  This establishes the time as about 1 p.m. on Holy Saturday. Dante must hurry on if he is to arrive at Purgatory by Easter Sunday morning.

19–21  This is Geri del Bello (lines 25–7), the first cousin of Dante's father, who was murdered by the Sachetti clan around 1280 and (according to the commentary on the *Commedia* written by Dante's son Pietro) eventually requited in 1310.

46–51  The Valdichiana and Maremma areas in Tuscany were, along with Sardinia, notorious for malaria in Dante's day.

58–65  Ovid tells in *Metamorphoses* 7: 523–660 how the people of Aegina (an island off the coast of Athens) were struck by a plague visited on them by Juno. Aeacus, king of Aegina, prayed for help to Jupiter and in a dream saw ants becoming men. The new inhabitants of the island, the Myrmidons, were transformed into human form from the ants that lived in an oak sacred to Jupiter. (See also *Convivio* 4: 37: 17.)

109–20 This speaker is the alchemist Griffolino of Arezzo, executed in 1272, whose claim to be able to fly like Daedalus was taken seriously by a Sienese nobleman, Alberto of Siena, who was greatly favoured by, and possibly the son of, the bishop inquisitor of Siena. When Griffolino failed to perform the promised miracle, Alberto persuaded the bishop to have him burned at the stake.

124–39 Continuing his satirical attack on Sienese folly, Dante – through the mouth of Capocchio, who is said in one early commentary to have been a student friend of Dante's in Florence – names a group of prominent figures who formed the '*Brigata Spendereccia*' ('Spendthrifts Club'). Of these it has been possible to identify Caccia d'Asciano (d. after 1293) and Bartolommeo dei Folcacchieri (d. 1300), also known as '*l'Abbagliato*' ('Dazzledeye'), who held important posts in the Guelf administration of Tuscany, and Caccianemico degli Scialenghi d'Asciano. The unidentified 'Nick' (line 127) seems to have dabbled in the expensive trade of spice cloves. Capocchio himself, according to contemporary anecdotes, was discovered, one Good Friday, painting the whole story of Christ's Passion on his fingernails. Dante caught him in the act and, when Capocchio hurriedly erased these images, berated him for having destroyed such a wonderful work of art. Capocchio was burned at the stake as an alchemist in Siena in 1293.

# CANTO 30

*Falsifiers continued: Master Adam, the counterfeiter;*
*quarrels between Adam and Sinon, Virgil and Dante.*

1–21 In Ovid's *Metamorphoses* 4: 465–542, Juno is stirred to jealousy by Jove's adultery with Semele, daughter of Cadmus, founder of Thebes. She takes revenge by driving Athamas (husband of Ino, another daughter of Cadmus) to bring about the deaths of both his wife and sons in a fit of madness. (For Semele, see *Paradiso* 21: 6.) Hecuba, queen of Troy at the fall of the city, sees her daughter Polyxena sacrificed on the tomb of Achilles and then finds the mutilated body of her son Polydorus, murdered by

King Polymnestor, thrown up on the seashore. Driven mad, she barks like a dog and kills Polymnestor by thrusting her fingers into his eyes. (See Ovid, *Metamorphoses* 13: 408–575.)

31–45  Gianni Schicchi (d. before 1280), a Florentine noble famous for his arts of mimicry, was persuaded to imitate a dying man, climbing into his deathbed to dictate a last will and testament in favour of Simone Donati (father of Forese: see *Purgatorio* 23 and Piccarda in *Paradiso* 3). In fact, Gianni employed the occasion to utter a will in his own favour, 'bequeathing' to himself the best mare in the dead man's stable. The dead man, Buoso Donati, appears as a serpent in *Inferno* 25. (See note to *Inferno* 25: 43f.) Myrrha is the legendary mother of Adonis, and in Ovid's *Metamorphoses* 10: 298–513 is said to adopt a disguise in order to seduce her own father, King Cinyras of Cyprus.

73–90  The gold florin of Florence carried on one side the lily, emblem of the city, and on the other the mark of Saint John the Baptist, its patron saint. By adding three carats of dross, Adam reduces the florin from its official twenty-four carats to twenty-one. The Branda Spring has not been securely identified. It may refer to the well of that name in Siena or another in the Casentino.

97–9  Sinon and Potiphar's wife are both guilty of false testimony. Sinon persuaded the Trojans to accept the gift of the Trojan horse. Potiphar's wife, in Genesis 39: 7–21, accused Joseph of rape when he rejected her advances.

127–9  The 'mirror' into which Narcissus looked (Ovid, *Metamorphoses* 3: 370–503) is the water in which he drowned. (See also *Paradiso* 3: 17–18.)


# CANTO 31

*The giants Nimrod, Ephialtes and Antaeus. Antaeus*
*lowers Dante into the last region of Hell.*

4–6  An epic reference dominates the opening of this canto, comparing Virgil's words in the moment of friction that ended *Inferno* 30 to the spear that Achilles inherited from his father which alone could heal the wounds it caused. (See Ovid, *Art of Love* 4: 43–8.)

16–18  Dante recalls the disaster, described in the eleventh-century French epic poem *Chanson de Roland*, that overcame the troops of Charlemagne in 778 at the battle of Roncesvalles in the Pyrenees, supposedly against the forces of Muslim invaders. Betrayed into an ambush by Ganelon, Roland, leader of Charlemagne's rearguard, blew his horn until his brains spilt out, but to no avail. The flower of Charlemagne's 'sacred band' (line 17) received no help. (See especially *La Chanson de Roland*, lines 1765f.)

**40–43** Montereggione was a fortress with fourteen towers rising above its circular curtain wall, eight miles north-west of Siena, built as a defence by the Sienese after their victory over Florence at Montaperti in 1260.

**58f** Nimrod was the builder of the Tower of Babel and, as such, has been in Dante's mind since *De Vulgari Eloquentia* 1: 7, in which false pride, in merely material domination, is associated with the confusion of tongues and the creation of vernacular languages. The canto confirms this emphasis, attributing to Nimrod the nonsense that he speaks at line 67. (Cf. Plutus in *Inferno* 7.)

The bronze pine cone (line 59), some four metres high and cast in antiquity, is now to be seen in the Vatican.

**61–6** Here (at a point when he is shortly to register the nonsense language of Nimrod) Dante employs the word '*perizoma*', which in the sacred tongue of Hebrew is used to refer to the apron or fig leaf with which the first humans modestly covered themselves. From folklore and encyclopedias, Dante gained the impression that the northern Frisians were especially tall.

**94–124** The giants named in this sequence are: Ephialtes, son of Neptune, who was sent by his father to pile up the mountains of Ossa and Pelion (in Macedonia) so as to reach Mount Olympus and challenge the gods, and is noted for his ferocity (Virgil, *Aeneid* 6: 583–4); Briareus, who is spoken of here as being nothing special – similar to Ephialtes – contrary to Virgil's account of him in *Aeneid* 10: 564 (see also Statius, *Thebaid* 2: 596); Antaeus, who does not speak, though he is able to do so, did not attack the gods, and so is not bound, but did, however, ruin crops and attack men and cattle in the vale of Zama in northern Africa, until Hercules arrived to conquer him by lifting him clear of contact with his mother – the earth – from whom he drew his strength (see Lucan, *Pharsalia* 4: 593–660; it was in the vale of Zama that the Roman general Scipio defeated Hannibal (lines 115–17) and ended the Carthaginian attempt to dominate the Mediterranean); Tityos, who attempted to rape Latona, the mother of Apollo and Diana (see Servius on *Aeneid* 6: 595), and in punishment was stretched out over the earth, his body covering nine acres, as a vulture fed on his liver (*Aeneid* 6: 595–7);

Typhon, who was struck by a thunderbolt sent from Jupiter and buried under Mount Etna (Ovid, *Metamorphoses* 4: 303 and 5: 354f; cf. *Paradiso* 8: 68–9).

136–41 Antaeus is compared to the Garisenda tower in Bologna (still standing), which looks as though it is about to fall when a cloud passes behind it.

# CANTO 32

*The first two subdivisions of treachery, Caina
(treachery against kin) and Antenora (treachery
against party or state). The Ninth Circle of Hell.*

1–6 The opening lines develop a thought from Cicero's *Somnium Scipionis* 4: 9, which speaks of the distribution of the planetary spheres: 'The earth is the lowest sphere and does not move. So it bears the weight of all the other heavens.' Following this logic, Dante sees the centre of the earth as the point at which all weight is concentrated.

10–12 The city of Thebes (for Dante, the image of violence and corruption; see *Inferno* 33: 88–90) was built by the poet Amphion, whose verses, aided by the Muses, caused the rocks to move and become the city walls (Statius, *Achilleid* 1: 13).

13–15 The exotic reference to '*zebe*' – 'goats' or, more exotically still, 'bezoars' – recalls the Scriptural separation of sheep and goats at Judgement Day. (See Matthew 25: 32.) In the Italian the whole of the opening passage, lines 1–15, is marked by an unusual complication of style, in its rhyming and wide range of diction.

28–30 Tambernic and Pietrapana (now called Tambura and Pania della Croce) are mountain peaks in the Apuan Alps, near Lucca.

40–57 The two figures here are the brothers Alessandro and Napoleone degli Alberti, who killed each other around 1282 in a quarrel over inheritance. The Conti Alberti, including their father Alberto, owned lands and castles – Vernia and Cerbaia – in the valley of the Bisenzio, which flows into the Arno at Signa, some ten miles downriver from Florence.

58–60 Caina, the setting of the present episode, is the region of the lowest circle of Hell reserved for those who treacherously murder their kin.

61–9 In the French prose work *Mort le roi Artu* (*c.* 1237), King
Arthur kills Mordred (officially his nephew; actually his illegit-
imate son by Morgan le Fay). The other figures are historical, all
belonging to the last decades of the thirteenth century. Focaccia
is Vanni de' Cancellieri of Pistoia, who is said variously to have
murdered his cousin or possibly his uncle in a tailor's shop, and
to have been responsible for the division of the Guelfs into the
Black and White factions (see *Inferno* 24: 142). Sassolo Masch-
eroni, probably of the Florentine Toschi clan, murdered his
cousin for an inheritance and was beheaded after being rolled
through Florence in a barrel of nails. Alberto (or Uberto) Cami-
scione de' Pazzi, from the Val d'Arno, killed his kinsman
Ubertino for his castles. But his crime is outweighed (hence 'He'll
acquit me here' (line 69)) by another of the Pazzi (the name
means 'the Mad') who more grievously betrayed a fortress of the
White Guelf faction for money during the campaign of the White
exiles in 1302.

70–123 At this point Dante passes from Caina into Antenora, where
those who betray their country are punished (see note to *Purga-
torio* 5: 64–84). The penultimate sinner at line 122 is the
archetypal traitor Ganelon, who in *La Chanson de Roland* (see
notes on *Inferno* 31: 16–18) betrayed his stepson Roland into
the hands of the Saracen king Marsilio at the massacre of Ronc-
esvalles. Among the contemporary traitors is the major
protagonist of this phase of the canto, Bocca degli Alberti ('Big
Mouth' (line 106)), who, as a Ghibelline treacherously assuming
the role of a Guelf, showed his true colours at the battle of Mon-
taperti in 1260 (see *Inferno* 10), when he conspired in the defeat
of the Guelfs by cutting the Florentine standard from the hand of
its bearer. Hence the reference to 'revenge for Montaperti' (lines
80–81). Buoso da Dovero (Duera) was a Ghibelline leader of
Cremona who was bribed (line 115) to allow the armies of
Charles of Anjou to pass through his territory in a campaign
against the imperial representative, Manfred (see *Purgatorio* 3).
Tesauro dei Beccheria, abbot of Vallombrosa and papal legate in
Tuscany (lines 119–20), was beheaded in 1258 for treachery
towards the Guelfs. Gianni de' Soldanier ('Ghibelline Jack' (line
121)) became a Guelf after the defeat of Manfred in 1266 in his
attempt to secure power. Tebaldello, a member of the Ghibelline
Zambrasi clan of Faenza (line 122), opened the gates of Faenza
on the morning of 13 November 1280 to allow in the enemies of

a certain family – the Bolognese Lambertazzi, who had taken ref-
uge there – against whom he bore a grudge.

124–39  This episode will dominate the first phase of *Inferno* 33. The
reference to Tydeus and Menalippus at lines 130–32 draws on
Statius's *Thebaid* 7: 745–64, where the hero Tydeus, who is
dying by a wound from Menalippus's spear, asks that the severed
head of Menalippus, whom he himself has slain, should be
brought to him. Spurred on by the Furies, he sets his teeth into
the skull, just at the moment when the goddess Minerva is about
to honour his victory with a laurel crown.


# CANTO 33

*Antenora continued. Ugolino. The passage to
Ptolomea. Treachery against guests.*

13f  Count Ugolino (?1230–89) was descended from an ancient
Longobard Ghibelline family with possessions in the region of
Pisa. He had been the imperial representative in Sardinia but,
with the fall of the Hohenstaufen dynasty, he returned to Pisa
and, changing his allegiances, joined the Guelf party, in the hope
of gaining control of the city. While military governor of the city,
he gave up certain Pisan fortresses (see lines 85–6) to the Guelf
cities of Lucca and Florence, meaning to weaken the antagonism
to Pisa which these cities displayed in alliance with Genova.
When the Ghibelline party, under Archbishop Ruggieri degli
Ubaldini (who is now Ugolino's victim in Hell), came once again
to dominate Pisan politics, it was this action that led them to
accuse Ugolino of treachery and to imprison him along with his
children.

22–4  The prison in which Ugolino was confined was the *Muda* (or
'Mew') where, it is thought, the hunting birds and civic eagles of
Pisa were kept during the moulting season.

28–36  Ruggieri is the 'Master' of the hunt. The Gualandi, Sismondi
and Lanfranchi were powerful families belonging to the Ghibel-
line faction in Pisa.

79–90  Thebes, the city of Oedipus and subject of Statius's epic *The-
baid*, is regularly regarded by Dante as the archetypal city of
corruption. (See *Inferno* 32 and *Purgatorio* 22.) Pisa was also
thought to have been founded by Theban travellers. Capraia and

Gorgogna are islands off the coast of Pisa at the mouth of the Arno. If they were to drift together, Pisa would be flooded with river water.

118–20 Frate Alberigo was a leading member of the Guelf families of Faenza and also a member of the lay order of *frati godenti* (see note to *Inferno* 23: 103–8). In 1285, he invited several members of his family with whom he was in dispute over land rights to dinner – and had them murdered. The sign he gave for the assassination was, 'Let the fruits be brought in.' Hence his reference to figs and dates. Figs are a poor fruit, dates are exotic and expensive: for his act of treachery Alberigo now receives more than abundant recompense in Hell.

124–6 The name for the second lowest circle of treachery derives from that of Ptolemaeus, who, in 1 Maccabees 16: 11–16, is said to have assassinated Simon Maccabaeus and both of his sons at a banquet. Atropos is one of the three Fates: Clotho spins the thread of life; Lachesis measures it; Atropos severs it.

133–8 Branca d'Oria, member of a noble Genovese family, invited his father-in-law Michel Zanche to dinner (see note to *Inferno* 22: 79–90) and had him murdered. Branca (a personal name, but also the Italian word for 'hook' and 'branch') was still alive in 1325, some four years after Dante's death.

## CANTO 34

*Giudecca, where treachery against sovereigns and benefactors is punished. Satan. The climb out of Hell through the centre of the earth.*

1–3 These lines offer a burlesque version of the hymn '*Vexilla regis*', by Venantius Fortunatus (AD 535–600), sung in Holy Week before Easter: 'The battle standards of the King advance, / the mystery of the Cross shines out, / by which the very creator of flesh / was hung in flesh upon the gallows.' Line 1 of this canto may be translated as 'The battle standards of Hell advance'.

28f Satan is seen. He has betrayed the just purposes of God. But above all, like Judas, he has betrayed the creative love that is enacted in the divine relationship of the Trinity. Thus Dante's Satan is a parasitical figure, existing only as a negative image of the ultimate truth. His three faces are parodic reflections of the

Trinity. His movements are wholly different from the harmoni-
ous and productive movements of the universe that finally gather
Dante up in the concluding moments of the *Paradiso*. Evil, for
Dante, is pure negation (see Introduction, p. xxix). In the course
of the *Commedia*, Dante does not say much about Satan. But
when he does, for instance in a final brief reference in *Paradiso*
19, he stresses not rebellion but stupidity, impatience and passiv-
ity. Satan was once Lucifer (*Inferno* 34: 89), the highest being in
Creation, who would progressively have been given as much
light as any finite creature could possibly receive. Instead of
'waiting' for light he falls '*acerbo*' ('unripe' (*Paradiso* 19: 46–8)).
It is for this reason that, in this canto, Satan is represented in a
peculiarly mechanical and negative form.

64–7  It is said of Judas Iscariot, the Apostle who betrayed Christ, that
'Satan entered into him' (John 13: 27). Marcus Junius Brutus
(85–42 BC) and Gaius Cassius Longinus (d. 42 BC) led the
conspiracy to assassinate Julius Caesar in 44 BC, when Caesar
sought to become emperor. Dante's view of this conspiracy is
significantly different from Shakespeare's, and it is consistent
with his increasingly imperial sympathies that he should con-
demn it as treachery. However, it is remarkable that in the next
canto of the *Commedia*, *Purgatorio* 1, a fellow opponent of
Caesar, Cato, who like Brutus and Cassius committed suicide in
defeat, should appear as the first soul in Purgatory and the
'guardian' of the purgatorial mountain. In the *Purgatorio* Dante's
standards of judgement are by no means identical to those in the
*Inferno*.

103–33  Space and time in this canto are measured from Jerusalem,
which in medieval cartography was thought of as the central
point of the northern hemisphere. It was at Jerusalem, through
Christ's crucifixion in the city (lines 112–15), that humanity was
redeemed from sin. In the southern hemisphere, at the antipodes
of Jerusalem, there is, on Dante's view, the mountain of Purga-
tory, where human beings as described in the second *cantica* of
the *Commedia* purify themselves from their earthly sins. The
formation of Purgatory is discussed at lines 121–6. On this
understanding, when it is midnight in Jerusalem, it is night in the
northern hemisphere from the Ganges to Gibraltar. Dante's jour-
ney down through Hell, which lies directly beneath Jerusalem,
began on the evening of Good Friday. It is now at the end of its
first full day, about 6 p.m. on the evening of Holy Saturday in
Jerusalem (line 68). The journey up through the empty subterra-

nean sphere, described in the second half of this canto, continues until just before dawn on Easter Sunday. The 'highest point' (line 114) is the zenith or place in the sky directly above any terrestrial point, in this case Jerusalem.


# PURGATORIO

## CANTO 1

*Dawn rises in Purgatory. Dante encounters
Cato, guardian of the mountain, and, at Cato's
command, Virgil binds Dante with a reed plucked
from the seashore.*

7–12 Calliope is the Muse of epic poetry. The 'Magpies' appear in Ovid's *Metamorphoses* 5: 294–678, in which the daughters of Pierus challenge the Muses to a singing contest and, even though they lose, persist in their defiance. As punishment for this, they are transformed into magpies. (Cf. *Paradiso* 1: 19–21 for a similar reference to violent contests between mortal musicians and the gods.)

19–21 The 'lovely' planet is Venus, whose brilliance here rises in company with but outshines, or 'veils', the constellation Pisces. Venus is both the morning and the evening star, and Dante seems to be mistaken about the position of the planet in April 1300, when it would in fact have risen in the evening.

28–30 The constellation is Charles's Wain, otherwise known as the Plough, which is located in Ursa Major.

31f The 'old man' is Marcus Porcius Cato Uticensis (95–46 BC). Historically, he was descended from a senatorial family famous for its rigorous defence of ancient Roman values. To him, Julius Caesar's ambition to establish his own imperial power would have seemed the equivalent of enslavement, and his death by his own hand after the battle at Utica, near Carthage, can readily be viewed as a Stoic affirmation of the freedom of conscience. Dante responds warmly to Cato's example. In the *Convivio* – written before the poet's imperial sympathies were fully formed – Dante says that Cato is illuminated by an especial light of divine goodness, and supremely demonstrates, as all Romans should, a capacity for self-sacrifice, ensuring that justice and the public good should always be of paramount importance. (See *Convivio*

4: 5 and 4: 27.) In *Convivio* 4: 28, Cato is even compared allegorically to God. In that passage, Dante refers (as he does here at lines 85–7) to the story of how Cato's wife Marcia willingly returns to him, after a second marriage, in her final years (see note to lines 76–84). So, too, the soul in the last phase of its existence on earth should turn to the contemplation of God. No mention is made in the *Convivio* of Cato's suicide. However, in *De Monarchia* 2: 5 – possibly written after the *Purgatorio* – it is seen as an act, not of cowardice or evasion (which would certainly attract condemnation), but rather of self-sacrifice, which stands among the many signs and 'miracles' that demonstrate how Rome has been chosen providentially to foster righteousness in the world. It remains surprising that Dante has chosen to make a pagan and a suicide the first figure whom he meets in Purgatory, especially considering that Cato fought against the Empire that Dante so greatly admired. Only a canto ago, in *Inferno* 34, he has placed two other opponents of the Empire, Brutus and Cassius, alongside Judas in the jaws of Satan.

76–84 For Limbo, see *Inferno* 4, and for Minos, see *Inferno* 5. Dante's account of Marcia and her relation to Cato may derive from Lucan's *Pharsalia* 2. Marcia when past the age of child bearing was given in marriage to a close friend (so that Cato should be free to father more virtuous Romans). On the death of her second husband, she successfully pleaded with Cato to take her back as his wife.

130–32 It is to Ulysses (see *Inferno* 26) that Dante alludes when he declares that no one who has seen these shores before has ever returned to tell the tale. Dante is distinguished from Ulysses exactly in his capacity to benefit from the experience of purgation. But Ulysses as a pagan is also to be distinguished from Cato and Virgil. His pursuit of knowledge reflects nothing of that self-sacrificing concern with conscience and the public good that inspires Cato's moral severity.

# CANTO 2

*The arrival of penitents in a boat impelled by an angel. Dante meets Casella. The singing of a canzone composed by Dante.*

1–9  Time in Purgatory is told in relation to the time in Jerusalem. As night falls over Jerusalem, so day begins to dawn ('Aurora') in Purgatory. The mouth of the Ganges marks the extreme of the known world. Libra – the Balance or Scales – disappears from the night sky ('leaves her hand') at the autumn equinox, when nights become longer than days.

46–8  The opening words of Psalm 114, which begins: 'When Israel went out of Egypt, the house of Jacob from a people of strange language; Judah was his sanctuary, and Israel his dominion. The sea saw it, and fled: Jordan was driven back. The mountains skipped like rams and the little hills like lambs . . .'

55–7  At dawn the constellation Capricorn was located directly above Purgatory. Capricorn descends as the sun rises with Aries, the Ram.

76–83  The figure who leaves the crowd is Casella, who appears to have been a friend of Dante's in Florence. Nothing more is known of him, though one of his musical compositions is to be found in the Vatican Library. The allusion is to a melancholic scene in Virgil's *Aeneid* 6: 700–702, where Aeneas attempts to embrace the shade of his father, Anchises, but fails as his physical arms prove unable to grasp the insubstantial ghost. Momentarily, there is a comparable note of sadness in Dante's lines. Yet the 'empty' shadow of Casella finally smiles at Dante's baffled attempts at an embrace (line 83).

91–9  Casella's speedy arrival in Purgatory is attributed to the pardon or plenary indulgence that was granted in the jubilee year of 1300 (effective from Christmas 1299) to all who travelled to Rome and visited certain specific churches. (Cf. *Inferno* 18.) Pope Boniface VIII (*c.* 1235–1303), who inaugurated the jubilee, is the object of Dante's unremitting hatred. (See especially *Inferno* 19 and 27.) But the poet still respects the office that Boniface occupies. (Cf. *Purgatorio* 20: 85–93.)

100–105  Dante imagines that the voyage to Purgatory begins at the mouth of the river Tiber, near Rome.

112f  The song sung here is Dante's own '*Amor che ne la mente mi ragiona*' from *Convivio* 3, where this *canzone* speaks of the way in which the human mind can contemplate the wisdom of God as displayed in the structure of the created universe. This theme is of central importance in Dante's thinking, and will continue to be so as late as *Paradiso* 10. Originally, it is unlikely that '*Amor che ne la mente mi ragiona*' would have been set to music. It was, rather, intended as a contribution to the elite poetic circles seemingly initiated in Florence by Guido Cavalcanti (*c.* 1255–1300) (see *Inferno* 10) and devoted to the development of philosophical and scientific discussion.

## CANTO 3

*Virgil speaks of why Dante alone casts a shadow in Purgatory. The excommunicates appear, among them King Manfred.*

25–7 Emperor Augustus had Virgil's body transported in from Brindisi, where Virgil died in 19 BC, to Naples for an honourable burial.

31–3 For an explanation of how the penitents come to possess 'ghost' bodies, see *Purgatorio* 25.

37 '*Quia*' is a term drawn from technical argumentation in Scholastic philosophy. The implication here is that human beings should not concern themselves with speculative questions as to *why* things exist, but confine themselves to the examination of things as they actually *do* exist.

40–44 See *Inferno* 4.

49–51 Lerici (just north of La Spezia) and Turbia (east of Nice) are towns lying at opposite ends of Liguria. The cliffs of these two towns go straight into the sea but landslips provide some pathways.

103f The figure here is Manfred (*c.* 1232–66). The illegitimate son of Emperor Frederick II (1194–1250) – whom the thirteenth-century Church frequently referred to as the Antichrist – he was himself excommunicated on three separate occasions, twice by Pope Alexander IV in 1258 and again by Pope Urban IV in 1261. As with Cato, Manfred's presence in Purgatory challenges any simple conception of moral norms and regulatory codes. Yet the challenge is driven to an extreme, even scandalous degree at lines 106–8, in which Dante all but explicitly compares the figure of Manfred to the risen Christ: where Christ showed his wounds to the doubting Saint Thomas (at Luke 24: 40 and John 20: 27), Manfred calls upon the uncomprehending Dante to acknowledge his own wholly unexpected salvation.

The daring of Dante's treatment in some measure reflects a political motive. Manfred was the last representative in Italy of the cause of the Holy Roman Empire to which Dante himself was committed. He acted as regent to the legitimate heirs of Frederick II, and was as deeply involved as his father in political contests with the Church. Manfred had himself crowned king of Sicily, in August 1258, but the Church had its own favoured candidate, Charles of Anjou (1227–85), who was also crowned king of Sicily, at Saint Peter's, Rome, in 1263. In the ensuing struggles between Manfred and Charles, Manfred was slain at the battle of Benevento in 1266, and with him died the ambitions of the Holy Roman Empire (and the Ghibelline cause which was associated with it) to rule in Italy. (For Dante's views of empire and for Guelfs and Ghibellines, see Introduction, pp. xi–xiv. For Charles of Anjou, see note to lines 124–32 and *Purgatorio* 6 and 7.)

115–16 Manfred's grandmother (d. 1198) was queen of Sicily and wife of Emperor Henry VI (1165–97). Manfred's daughter was Constance (d. 1302) by his first wife, Beatrice of Savoy. Constance married Peter III of Aragon (1239–85), who laid claim through her to the throne of Sicily. (See notes to *Purgatorio* 7: 91–111 and *Paradiso* 8: 72–5.)

124–32 Charles of Anjou (see *Purgatorio* 7 and 20), on defeating Manfred at the battle of Benevento and thus destroying the imperial cause in Italy, had his enemy buried honourably (though not in consecrated ground) under a cairn of stones. Pope Clement IV (d. 1268) ordered the bishop of Cosenza in Calabria to exhume the body and throw it irrecoverably over the border of the kingdom of Naples which is marked by the river Verde. (Significantly, green ('*verde*') is the colour of hope; also Manfred is said to have preferred green clothing.) The same pope confirmed Charles's claim to the crown of Sicily and Naples.

# CANTO 4

*Dante and Virgil begin to climb Mount Purgatory and encounter Dante's Florentine acquaintance Belacqua among those who have delayed their final acts of repentance.*

1–12 These lines reflect a controversy which originally arose between Platonists and Aristotelians over the nature (and number) of the human soul. For Plato, there were three souls that governed the activities of the human being – the vegetative, the animal and the rational, ascending in such a way that the rational could assert its superiority over and transcend its lower counterparts. For Aristotle, there was only one soul, though this single soul possessed three distinct functions pertaining to the activities of growth and instinct (in which humans are involved, as are plants and animals), as well as the activities of reason which are unique to the human being. It is Aristotle that Dante follows (though the compression of his thinking leads to a certain confusion over the metaphors of binding and loosing, which at lines 3–8 refer to the soul in its single nature and at lines 10–12 mean the three separate functions of the single soul). To paraphrase: when one aspect of the soul is engaged in thought, the unified soul still continues to carry along with it the other two functions – as here Dante continues to move along his path. Thought does not transcend what might, in platonic terms, be considered its 'lower' functions. Aristotelian unity continues to operate, even when, physically, we do not notice the passing of time. Here, as at every point in his thinking, Dante follows Aristotle and Aristotle's Christian followers in asserting that the soul, or '*anima*' in Latin and Italian, is nothing more or less than the power which 'animates' a specific form of life – which in human beings is always an *embodied* form of life. (See notes to *Purgatorio* 25.)

25–7 San Leo is a mountain fortress near Urbino. Noli is a city on the Ligurian coast, which is reached via a stairway cut in the cliff. 'Bismantova' probably refers to a fortress that once sat on a crag near Canossa in Emilia. Cacume is a peak near Anagni.

58–75 Aquilon is the North Pole. The reader – supplied with introductory maps and plans – is aware from the first that Purgatory is located in the southern hemisphere, whereas Dante as traveller only becomes fully aware of it, and of its implications, in the course of this canto.

At lines 61–6, Castor and Pollux are the twins of the constellation Gemini. The sun moves through this constellation in May and June. The 'Ursa stars' are Ursa Major and Ursa Minor, otherwise known as the Bears. The sun is a 'mirror' in so far as it reflects God's power into the universe. That part of the Zodiac which is heated by the sun is 'rose-red'. It 'wheels' as the sun moves north along the ecliptic, reaching further across the sky each day at noon. To paraphrase: if the present month were May or June, you would see the sun moving still further towards the north.

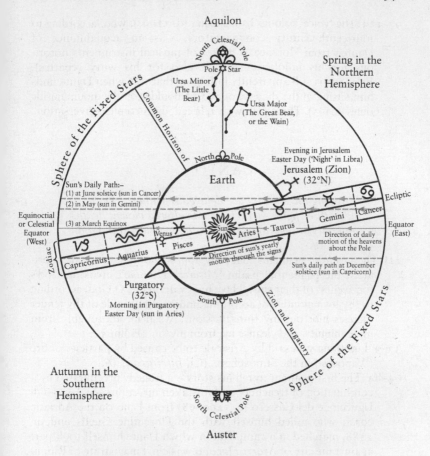

Path of the Sun

Jerusalem (Zion) in the northern hemisphere stands diametrically opposite Purgatory in the southern hemisphere (lines 67–75).

79–84 The celestial equator stands at 90 degrees from the North and South Poles. It is around this that the daily revolutions of the heavens take place. The seven stars form part of the constellation Ursa Major, seen in the northern sky. Reference to these stars regularly signifies the northern regions, as in the Italian adjective 'settentrionale'.

97–139 The 'voice' belongs to Belacqua (d. 1299?), who, according to
     fourteenth-century commentators, was an acquaintance of
     Dante's from Florence, a maker of musical instruments notori-
     ous for his indolence (though also for his witty repartee).
     Belacqua is still apparently indulging that vice when Dante finds
     him sitting in the shadow of a great boulder on the mountainside
     (lines 101–5). There follows a relaxed, even comic conversation.


# CANTO 5

*Among those who have delayed repentance, Dante
meets three figures who have all suffered violent deaths
and only at the moment of death have turned to God.*


22f The group of penitents that now approaches is singing, appropri-
     ately, the penitential psalm '*Miserere Domine*', invoking God's
     forgiveness of their sins: 'Have mercy upon me, O God, according
     to thy lovingkindness: according unto the multitude of thy tender
     mercies blot out my transgressions. Wash me thoroughly from
     mine iniquity, and cleanse me from my sin' (Psalm 51: 1–2).
37–9 Lightning was said by Aristotle to be caused by particles of fire
     ('Vapours') in the atmosphere. (Cf. *Inferno* 14: 36.)
64–84 The first penitent to tell his story – a tragedy precipitated by a
     combination of treachery and mistaken directions – is Jacopo di
     Uguccione del Cassero (*c.* 1260–98) from Fano on the Adriatic
     coast, who allied himself with the Florentine Guelfs and, in
     1288, marched in a campaign in which Dante himself took part
     against the city of Arezzo. Jacopo was chief magistrate of Rimini
     in 1294 and of Bologna in 1296, during which time he opposed
     the ambitions of Azzo VIII of Este (d. 1308). (See note to *Inferno*
     12: 106–38.) Jacopo, while travelling through Paduan territory
     en route for Milan, where he was to take up a similar office, was
     ambushed at Oriaco and scandalously murdered by Azzo's hench-
     men. 'Antenorians' (line 75) here means 'Paduans'. (Antenor, who
     according to legend betrayed Troy to the Greeks, was also said to
     have founded Padua. Antenora is the third deepest subsection of
     the circle of treachery in Hell. (See *Inferno* 32–3.))
88f The second episode, though as violent as the first, unrolls more
     slowly and is more complex, particularly in its reference back to
     a parallel episode in *Inferno* 27. The protagonist here is Buon-

conte da Montefeltro (*c.* 1250–89), a Ghibelline general – and the son of Guido da Montefeltro, who appears in *Inferno* 27 – who died leading the armies of Arezzo against the Florentine Guelfs at the battle of Campaldino in 1289. Dante (and Jacopo del Cassero, also) fought in this battle on the Florentine side. It is this which gives point to Dante's inquiry at lines 91–3 as to why Buonconte's body was never discovered on the battlefield and initiates Buonconte's own account (lines 109–129) of his final hours and of the struggle that follows his death between his body (arms tightly formed in a cross) and Satan, who raises a storm against him. At lines 103–8, Dante draws a contrast between the stories of Buonconte, the son, and Guido, the father, who appears in *Inferno* 27. (See note to *Inferno* 27: 112–23.) Where devils claim Guido's soul at the gate of Heaven, angels defeat Satan in the contest for Buonconte's soul. Giovanna (line 89) was Buonconte's wife.

91–6 Campaldino is situated in the Casentino, a mountainous region of Tuscany east of Florence, forming a plain between the Apennine peaks of Giogana and Pratomagno. The Hermitage is the monastery above Camaldoli, situated on Giogana.

115–17 Pratomagno ('the Great Meadow') lies in the south-west of the Casentino.

130–36 The 'third soul' is Pia dei Tolomei, who married Nello dei Pannocchieschi, a member of the lesser nobility in the Sienese Maremma (a notoriously swampy and insalubrious region in southern Tuscany) and was murdered by her husband in 1295. It is well worth comparing Dante's treatment of La Pia with his characterization of Francesca in *Inferno* 5 and of Piccarda, who speaks of *caritas* in *Paradiso* 3.

# CANTO 6

*A discussion of the efficacy of prayer. Dante and Virgil encounter Sordello. Dante launches a diatribe against the political confusion of Italy resulting from a lack of support for the imperial cause.*

13–24 It is not certain whom Dante intends by 'the Aretine', though it may be Benincasa da Laterino, who was beheaded around 1297 by the notorious highwayman Ghin di Tacco of Siena. Federigo

Novello was a member of the Tuscan clan of the Conti Guidi and
was killed around 1290 by a member of the Guelf Bostoli faction
of Arezzo. The 'Pisan man' is the son of Marzucco degli Scorni-
giani, whose murderer was forgiven by his father. Count Orso
degli Alberti was murdered in 1286 by his cousin in the course
of a long-lasting family feud. When Pierre la Brosse, chamberlain
to Philip III of France (1245–85), accused Philip's queen, Marie
of Brabant, of poisoning the heir to the throne, Philip's son by
his first wife, he was arrested and hanged in 1278.

58f This figure (not named until line 74) proves to be the poet Sor-
dello (c. 1200–c. 1269), who was born at Goito near Mantua
and emigrated to the court of Provence in 1229, fleeing a scandal
which probably involved an adulterous liaison with Cunizza da
Romano, the wife of his feudal lord. (Cunizza occupies an
important place in Heaven – see *Paradiso* 9: 22–66.) Sordello
prospered in his adopted country, was knighted and endowed
with lands in both northern and southern Italy. His extant poetry
is all written in the Occitan language. And, most famously, these
poems include the *Lament for Blacatz* (1237), declaring that
now his patron Blacatz is dead, his heart should be cut out so
that the great nobles, 'who now live disheartened', can eat
it – 'and then they'll have heart enough!' It seems likely that
Sordello's *Lament* was in Dante's mind as he approached the
question of faint-hearted kingship in *Purgatorio* 7 and, specific-
ally, when he wrote the polemical verses that constitute the
second half of this canto.

88–93 The Roman emperor Justinian (AD c. 482–565) appears among
the blessed in *Paradiso* 6, where he is celebrated for his achieve-
ment in codifying the Roman law. It is this body of law that
rulers in Dante's day are accused of ignoring. The 'saddle's rider-
less' in that, since the time of Frederick II (see Introduction,
pp. xi–xii, and notes to *Purgatorio* 3), no Holy Roman Emperor
had taken an active interest in the government of Italian affairs.
For Rudolph, see note to *Purgatorio* 7: 91–111.

97–105 Albert I of Habsburg (1255–1308) was elected Holy Roman
Emperor in 1298 but remained uncrowned, and here stands
accused (in common with his father Rudolph I (1218–91)) of
abandoning his rightful domains to political confusion. Albert
was murdered on 1 May 1308 by his nephew John of Swabia.
His successor was Henry VII (c. 1275–1313), on whom Dante
pinned his (disappointed) hopes for the restoration of imperial
rule in Italy.

106–8 The four families were all involved in the rivalry between the Guelf and the Gibellines in thirteenth-century Italy. The Montecchi (translated as 'Montagues') were Ghibellines from Verona, while the Cappelletti ('Capulets') were Guelfs from Cremona. The Monaldi and Filippeschi fought for control of Orvieto, the former being Guelf, the latter Ghibelline.

109–17 Cf. Dante's rhetoric with Virgil's account of the admonition that Jupiter directs at Aeneas in *Aeneid* 4: 272–6. Santa Fiora (line 111) is a town which lay under the control of the Ghibelline Aldobrandeschi (condemned for pride in *Purgatorio* 11: 52–72) until he was defeated by the Sienese in 1301.

124–6 'Marcellus' refers to Marcus Claudius Marcellus (consul 51 BC), an opponent of Julius Caesar (see Lucan, *Pharsalia* 1: 313), and thus the prototype for the rebel against imperial authority.

139–41 In his *Institutes* 1: 2: 10, Justinian recognizes Athens and Sparta (Lacedaemon) as the cities that first established both common and statutory law.


# CANTO 7

*Virgil identifies himself to Sordello, who speaks of
how journeying at night is impossible in Purgatory.
Entry into the Vale of Princes.*


28–36 Virgil speaks of his condition as a dweller in Limbo far more directly than he does anywhere else in the *Commedia* (though cf. *Purgatorio* 21: 31–3 and 22: 100–115).

82 '*Salve, Regina*' is a hymn to the Virgin Mary: 'Hail to the Queen, Mother of Mercy ... To you we cry, poor banished children of Eve. To you we send up our sighs, mourning and weeping in this valley of tears. Turn then, most gracious advocate, your merciful eyes toward us. And after our exile, show us the fruit of your womb, Jesus.'

91–111 Rudolph of Habsburg (1218–91) was elected emperor in 1291, but would not come to Italy to be crowned. Ottakar II of Bohemia (*c.* 1230–78) (whose realms are designated here by the courses of the rivers Moldau and Elbe) was in life an especially dangerous opponent of Rudolph – whom in Purgatory he now comforts. Wenceslaus II was Ottakar's successor (reigned 1278–1305) and son-in-law to Emperor Rudolph. The 'button-nosed'

prince is Philip III the Bold (1245-85), who succeeded Louis IX
(1214-70) as king of France in 1270. When Angevin rule in Sicily
was ended by the Aragonese in 1282 during the rebellion known
as the Sicilian Vespers, Philip's fleet was defeated in the gulf of
Rosas by that of Peter III of Aragon (1239-85). This defeat may
be implied in the reference to stripping the lily flower – since the
lily appears on the French royal coat-of-arms. Line 104 refers to
Henry I (the Fat), king of Navarre (reigned 1270-74). Henry's
daughter married Philip IV of France (1268-1314; reigned
1285-1314), the 'Ill' or 'plague' of France, who was thus son-in-
law to Henry and son to Philip III, who are the two figures
described in lines 106-8. The crimes of Philip IV included a mili-
tary attack on Pope Boniface VIII. (See *Purgatorio* 20: 46, 66 and
85-90, and the notes to that canto.) For other criticisms of Philip,
see *Inferno* 19: 87 and *Paradiso* 19: 118-20.

112-29 The 'burly type' is Peter III of Aragon. The marriage of his
daughter to King Manfred (*Purgatorio* 3: 115-16) provided him
with a claim to the Sicilian crown which he made good at the
time of the Sicilian Vespers. (For the Sicilian Vespers, see note to
91-111; also *Purgatorio* 20: 70-78 and *Paradiso* 8: 73-5.) Lines
115-20 refer to Peter's sons and heirs. The 'young boy' (line
115) is probably Peter's eldest son, Alfonso III the Magnificent,
who died in 1291 after a reign of only six years. Peter's second
and third sons are here accused of degeneracy. James (line 119)
is James II (the Just), king of Catalonia and Sicily (reigned 1285-
95) and king of Aragon (reigned 1291 until his death in 1327).
James was forced to abandon control of Sicily in 1296 when
the Sicilians renounced their allegiance to him and his puppet
government and installed his younger brother Frederick (also
mentioned here) as king. (See *Purgatorio* 3: 115-16, and *Para-
diso* 19: 131 and 20: 63.) The king with the 'manly nose' (line
113; cf. line 124) is Charles I of Anjou (1227-85). Though
receiving only a cursory mention here, Charles was a figure of
great importance in the history of mid-thirteenth-century Italy,
frequently mentioned by Dante, who, despite the fact that he
advances Charles to Purgatory in this canto, deplored his polit-
ics. Son of Louis VIII of France and Blanche of Castile, and
brother of Louis IX, Charles married Beatrice of Provence in
1246, thus becoming count of Provence. (See notes to *Purgatorio*
20.) His realm became still greater when on the death of Beatrice
he married Margaret of Burgundy. (See *Purgatorio* 20: 61-6.) In
1266-7 he defeated Manfred and Conradino, thus also becom-

ing king of Naples and Sicily. (See *Purgatorio* 3: 124–9.) Charles,
like Peter III, suffered unworthy heirs, particularly Charles II of
Anjou, who inherited Naples (Apulia) and Provence in 1285. For
a manifestation of Dante's consistent antipathy to the second
Charles, see *Purgatorio* 20: 79–81. The sense of lines 127–9 is
that the sons of Charles I are as inferior to him as Charles I was
inferior to Peter III of Aragon – to the same extent that Con-
stance values her husband Peter more than Beatrice and Margaret
(the two wives of Charles) value Charles himself.

130–36 The 'monarch of the simple life' is Henry III of England
(1207–72). His offspring is Edward I, who reigned at the time
the *Commedia* is set, in 1300. (See also *Paradiso* 19: 121–3.)
William VII (1254–92), marquis of Monteferrato, served as
imperial representative but took advantage of political disorder
to subject the cities of Lombardy to his rule. He moved his alle-
giances from Charles of Anjou when Charles attempted to
subjugate Lombardy. Eventually, William was captured while
attacking Alessandria in 1290 and died after being put on dis-
play in a cage. His marquisate extended from Monferrato (lying
between the Po and the Ligurian Apennines) to Canavese (between
the Pennine and Graian Alps in north-west Italy). William's son
attacked Alessandria, whose citizens, aided by the Visconti clan
of Milan, counterattacked Monteferrato and other towns in Wil-
liam's marquisate, which is why Canavese and Monteferrato
now 'weep'.

# CANTO 8

*While Dante speaks to Nino Visconti and Conrad*
*Malaspina, the Vale of Princes is defended by angels*
*from the incursions of the satanic serpent.*

4–15 The 'evening bell' is rung at the hour of Compline, which, con-
cluding the religious offices of the day, commits the soul to God's
safe-keeping, as in the hymn (sung by a figure who remains
anonymous) *'Te lucis ante'* sung at line 13: 'To You before the
end of light we pray, O Lord, / creator of all things, that You
watch over and protect us. / Keep far from us the dream and
fantasies of night, / defeat our enemy, so that our bodies may
remain without taint.'

**19–21** The address to the reader alerts us to the allegorical signifi-
cance of the coming episode. (Cf. *Inferno* 9: 61–3.) The allegory
is said to be easy to penetrate – divine truth being now very close
at hand. But it involves nothing less than a history of the Fall and
the Redemption from the Fall that the penitents are now sure of
enjoying. The setting in a place of natural beauty that foreshad-
ows the Earthly Paradise (referred to at line 114) that Dante will
enter in *Purgatorio* 28. A snake – clearly referring to Satan – enters
at lines 97–102. But the Vale of Princes is protected by angels
who have all along been at their post (lines 25–33 and 103–8).
An angel with a fiery sword had driven Adam and Eve from the
Garden of Eden. But the swords of the angels here are broken at
the tip, no longer threatening harm to human beings.

**52–81** The figure with whom Dante converses is Nino Visconti, who
(at line 109 – see note) alerts a second figure, Currado Malaspina,
to Dante's arrival. Nino (d. 1296) was a man of considerable
importance in the public life of thirteenth-century Tuscany and
the son of a daughter of Count Ugolino who appears in *Inferno*
33. He became judge (or chief magistrate) of Galluria in Sardinia
and collaborated with Count Ugolino in the government of Pisa,
but fled the city when his grandfather joined the Ghibellines.
After this, between 1288 and 1293, he was frequently to be
found in Florence, where, as seems likely, Dante became
acquainted with him. Nino speaks of his wife, Beatrice d'Este,
daughter of the infamous Opizzo da Esti (1247–93) (see *Inferno*
12: 111 and 18: 55–7), and of the emotions of loss and hope that
she and his daughter Giovanna inspire in him. His wife (lines
73–81) has been caught up in the power play of the period. At
Nino's death, she abandoned 'my Gallurian cockerel', which was
the emblem of Nino's clan, and married into the Visconti clan of
Milan, whose emblem was a viper. Beatrice came to regret her
marriage when her new husband was driven out of Milan and
into poverty in 1302. She returned to Milan when her son Azzo
was recalled in 1328. Nino's melancholy at losing the affection
of his wife is registered in line 73, in which he states simply that
he does not think she 'loves me now'. But the point of reference
in this moment of desolation is his daughter, on whose prayers
and constancy his progress up through Purgatory in part depends;
she (lines 70–81) was orphaned on Nino's death and later married
Rizzardo da Camino. (See *Paradiso* 9: 49–51.)

109–39 The 'shadow' is Conrad (Currado) Malaspina (d. 1294), marquis of Villafranca. Dante stayed with the Malaspina family for a time and in 1306 was chosen to represent them in successful peace negotiations with the bishop of Luni. In 1307 or 1308, Dante addressed his fourth Latin epistle to Moroello Malaspina, speaking in grateful terms of Moroello's hospitality. The Malaspina clan controlled the Lunigiana region – between Tuscany, Liguria and Lombardy – from their ancestral home in Val di Magra. Where Dante so often sees division and enmity within families (cf. *Purgatorio* 14), he seems to see in the Malaspinas an example of great solidarity persisting over the generations. For an equally eloquent passage in praise of Dante's patrons, see *Paradiso* 17: 70–92, in which Dante eulogizes at length about the Della Scala family of Verona.

# CANTO 9

*Dante dreams of being lifted to the skies by a golden eagle. On waking, he discovers that he has been carried to the gate of Purgatory, where the angel guarding the gate inscribes the letter 'P' seven times on his brow, to signify the Seven Capital Vices which have now to be purged.*

1–9 There has been some scholarly debate as to whether Dante means the dawn of the moon or of the sun. However, the reference to the constellation Scorpio indicates that the time is 9 p.m. The personifications are of the goddess of the dawn, Aurora, who fell in love with Tithonus, the brother of King Priam of Troy. Aurora won for Tithonus the gift of immortality but failed to ensure that he would never age. (See Virgil, *Georgics* 1: 446–7.)

13f In *Metamorphoses* 6: 424–674, Ovid tells of how Philomela was raped by Tereus, the husband of her sister, Procne. Tereus cuts out Philomela's tongue to prevent her identifying him. But she weaves a tapestry which depicts the scene and sends it to her sister, who, in revenge, murders Tereus's son Itys, cooks him and feeds him to his father. When Tereus discovers what his food is made of, he pursues both Philomela and Procne, but, before he can murder them, all three are transformed into birds. Tereus becomes a hoopoe, Procne (following the commentator Servius) becomes a swallow and Philomela (whose name means 'lover of song') becomes a nightingale. (Cf. *Purgatorio* 17: 19–21.) *Metamorphoses* 10: 155–61 retells the classical legend of how Jupiter falls in love with the beautiful boy Ganymede, descends on him in the form of an eagle and carries him to Heaven to be the cupbearer to the gods. The eagle in Dante's poem is regularly associated with justice, especially as exercised by the Roman Empire. (See, in particular, *Paradiso* 6 and 18.) Virgil explains in lines 49–63 that Dante lifted to the gates of Purgatory not by an eagle, like Ganymede, but by his own Christian patron saint, Lucy (Lucia) (see also note to 55–7). Dante also regards her as his guardian saint, and she is associated with light, love and God's providential concern for the fulfilment of Dante's appointed task. (See, in particular, *Inferno* 2: 97–100.)

In line 16 the adjective '*peregrine*', as Dante uses it here (translated as 'hawks'), suspended in an unusually prominent position at the end of the line in the original Italian, carries three possible meanings: 'pilgrim', 'stranger' (or 'wanderer') and 'falcon'. All three are relevant here, to Dante's pilgrim state in a foreign land and to his readiness to ascend in his pursuit of purity. (For comparisons between the spirit and hawks and falcons, see *Purgatorio* 14: 148–51 and 19: 61–9.)

25–33 Geoffrey Chaucer wrote a pastiche in *The House of Fame* 2 (1379–80).

34–9 This refers to an episode recorded in Statius's *Achilleid* 1: 104. (See *Purgatorio* 21 and *Inferno* 26.) The sleeping Achilles is taken away from his teacher Chiron by his mother, Thetis, to the court of Lycomedes at Scyros. While there Ulysses persuades him to join the Greeks on their way to besiege Troy.

55–7 Saint Lucy expresses the action of grace, the wholly unexpected liberation that underlies our eventual freedom. (See also note to lines 13f.)

76–108 There are readings of this canto that regard it as an allegory of the act of confession and apply particularly to these lines, where Dante climbs the three steps leading to the gate, signifying the three stages of confession: recognition of sin, contrition and satisfaction in penance.

112 The seven 'P's inscribed on Dante's forehead as marks of penance are erased one by one as he reaches the end of each of the cornices through which he has now to climb.

118–29 These are the keys entrusted to Saint Peter by Christ in Matthew 16: 19. The gold key represents the power of the Church, gained by Christ's Atonement, to forgive sins. The silver key represents the intelligence and discretion needed to unlock the hardness of the human heart.

136–8 The story of Caesar's assault on the treasury is told in Lucan's *Pharsalia* 3: 153–68. A simile here recalls the age of pagan conflict: at the foot of the Tarpeian rock was the public treasury of Rome; when its guardian, Metellus, attempted to defend it from attack, Julius Caesar drove him away and, forcing the door of the treasury, proceeded to loot it.

139–41 The *'Te Deum'* is said to date back to the fourth century AD, and was supposedly sung spontaneously by Saint Augustine and Saint Ambrose at the former's baptism: 'We praise thee, O God: we acknowledge thee to be the Lord. All the earth doth worship thee: the Father everlasting. To thee all Angels cry aloud: the Heavens, and all the Powers therein . . .' Subsequently the hymn has been sung when novices first leave the world to enter a religious order.

# CANTO 10

*On the terrace where pride is being purged, Dante and Virgil first come to see examples of humility carved on the cliff face of the mountain, and then encounter the first group of penitents.*

31–3 Polyclitus (*c.* 452–412 BC) was, along with Phidias, the most famous of the Greek sculptors, known to Dante through references in Cicero's writings.

34–54 This refers to the Annunciation, in which the Virgin Mary submits to the divine will and accepts her role as the mother of God. Luke 1: 38: 'And Mary said, Behold the handmaid of the Lord; be it unto me according to thy word.'

55–69 Having brought the Ark of the Covenant into Jerusalem, King David dances in humility before it (tucking up his robe and so displaying his naked legs), and is despised by his wife Michal (lines 67–9) for his undignified display. (See 2 Samuel 6: 16.) Uzziah sins by presumptuously touching the Ark when it seems about to fall. (See 1 Chronicles 13: 9.)

**73–93** This refers to the humility of Emperor Trajan (d. 117), who was persuaded (according to John of Salisbury's *Policraticus* (1159) and other medieval texts) to postpone a military campaign at the behest of a widow whose son had just been murdered and to pursue the justice that she claimed. For acts such as this, Trajan, although he died as a pagan, has a place of honour in Heaven (see *Paradiso* 20), his salvation having been secured by the intercession of Pope Gregory the Great (*c.* 540–604). The legend suggests that Gregory had seen the act of charity depicted on Trajan's column (which stood close to Gregory's palace on Celian Hill in Rome) and prayed so movingly for the emperor's salvation that he was restored to life long enough for him to become a Christian.

# CANTO 11

*The proud (continued). Dante speaks with Omberto*
*Aldobrandeschi, known for his pride in family, and*
*with Oderisi da Gubbio, an illuminator of manuscripts*
*who concludes the canto by speaking of the humility*
*displayed by the Sienese nobleman Provenzan Salvani.*

**1–21** Paraphrase of the Lord's Prayer as found in Matthew 6: 9–13.

**49–72** The speaker is Omberto Aldobrandeschi, son of Guglielmo, scion of a powerful family from south Tuscany and lord of Campagnatico who fought against Siena and the Empire in alliance with the papacy in 1243. Omberto was assassinated by the Sienese in 1259.

**73f** The speaker – with whom Dante seems to have been acquainted in life – is Oderisi da Gubbio (*c.* 1240–99), an illuminator of manuscripts and a friend of the painter Giotto di Bondone (1267–1337), who is said to have been employed in the Vatican Library by Pope Boniface VIII.

**79–81** The term Dante uses here for the illumination of manuscripts, '*alluminar*', is formed from the French word '*enluminer*' and thus preserves a reference to light. The more usual word in Italian is '*miniare*', derived from the noun '*minio*', meaning 'red cinnabar' – the material used for creating the red (vermilion) pigment.

**91–3** Cf. this and the whole of Oderisi's speech with the sentiments expressed, particularly, in Ecclesiastes 1: 4 and 6: 11.

94-9  Dante was alert to the changing artistic fashions of his day. In the visual sphere, the (relatively) realistic art of Giotto is said to have replaced the (relatively) iconic art of his master Cimabue (1240–1302). In the sphere of poetry, he sees, within his own literary circle, how Guido Cavalcanti (c. 1255–1300), whom Dante in the *Vita nuova* named as the first of his friends, displaced Guido Guinizelli, poet and jurist (d. before 1276). (See notes to *Purgatorio* 26, where this same theme is treated further.) It also seems likely that when Dante refers to a third poet, already born, who will supersede both of these Guidos, he is modestly, perhaps, referring to himself.

103-8  Dante's text uses here the baby word for 'food', '*pappo*', and '*dindi*' for '*denaro*' ('money'). The astrological calculation that follows refers to the movement of the fixed stars which, on Dante's reckoning, move imperceptibly 360 degrees in the course of 36,000 years. This complete revolution was referred to by Plato as 'The Great Year'.

109-38  Provenzan Salvani (c. 1220–69) at his height exercised tyrannical power over Siena. He was responsible for the military expansion of the city which led to the absorption of the lands of Omberto Aldobrandeschi. (See note to lines 49–72.) Provenzan was associated with Farinata (*Inferno* 10) in the Ghibelline cause, and supported the proposal (which Farinata opposed) that, after the battle of Montaperti in 1260, Florence should be razed to the ground. He was captured by the Florentines and beheaded at the battle of Colle di Val d'Elsa (1269). (See *Purgatorio* 13: 106–38.) The act of humility that wins Provenzan an entry into Purgatory concerns his willingness to save a close friend who had been captured at the battle of Tagliacozzo (1268). To pay the required ransom, Provenzan dressed in sackcloth and went begging through the streets of Siena.

# CANTO 12

*Examples of pride carved in the marble pathway of the mountain. An angel brushes one of the penitential marks from Dante's brow.*

25-63  Dante constructs an acrostic in these lines, which, in the Italian, spells out the word '*uom*' (here translated as 'man'), formed from the initial letters of each verse. 'VOM' (an abbreviated form of 'uomo') is spelled out progressively by the initial letters of twelve *terzine*, starting with 'V' ('M' in this translation) in lines 25, 28, 31 and 34. Its final appearance is in the opening letters of the lines of the thirteenth *terzina* (61–3). Dante substituted 'V' for the 'U' to make possible a fourfold repetition of 'Vedea' ('I saw'), to be followed by a fourfold repetition of the grief-stricken exclamation 'O' and then of 'Mostrava' ('[the pavement] showed . . .'). This sequence (in which humanity is seen, penitentially, to be summed up in a sequence of acts of pride running all through history) pictures, first, the example of Satan (lines 25–8). Then comes Briareus, one of the Titans or giants who were defeated in their challenge to the gods. (See Ovid, *Metamorphoses* 1: 151–62 and *Inferno* 31.) Mars and Pallas are referred to (line 32) as fighting alongside their father Zeus. Nimrod is the builder of the Tower of Babel. (See Genesis 10: 9–10, 11: 1–9 and *Inferno* 31: 46–81.) Niobe boasted that her seven sons and seven daughters made her superior to Latona, who only had two children, Apollo (here referred to as Timbreus) and Diana; Latona sent her offspring to murder Niobe's children, and Niobe was transformed into a stone from which tears continually ooze. (See Ovid, *Metamorphoses* 6: 142–312.) Saul, first king of Israel, fell on his sword after his defeat at the battle of Gilboa, during which three of his sons were slain. (See 1 Samuel 31: 1–6.) Arachne challenged Athene to a competition in tapestry-weaving and, when she proved to be the winner, was turned by Athene into a spider. (See Ovid, *Metamorphoses* 6: 1–145.) Rehoboam, king of Israel, was unwilling to lift the taxes imposed on his people by his father Solomon; the Israelites rose up in revolt and stoned Rehoboam's general Adoram to death, at which the king fled. (See 1 Kings 12: 1–19.) Eriphyle, Alcmaeon's mother, was bribed with a necklace to betray her husband Amphiaraus and was murdered in revenge by her son. (See Statius, *Thebaid* 2: 265–305 and 4: 187–212; also *Inferno* 20: 32–6 and *Paradiso* 4: 103–5.) Sennacherib, king of Assyria (704–681 BC), was murdered by his sons after his defeat in a campaign against Israel. (See 2 Kings 18: 13–37, 19: 1–37.) The words at line 57 are attributed to Thamyris, queen of the Scythians, who took revenge on Cyrus II (founder of the Persian Empire) for the murder of her son by decapitating him and flinging his head into a container full of blood. (See Paulus Orosius, *Historiae Adversus Paganos* 2: 7: 6.) Holofernes, general to the Assyrian king

Nebuchadnezzar, was decapitated by the Jewish widow Judith while besieging Bethulia. (See the apocryphal Judith 8–14.) Troy is designated by the name of Ilion, its great palace tower. (See Virgil, *Aeneid* 2 and Ovid, *Metamorphoses* 15: 422–5.)

100–105 On a hill above Florence there stands the ancient church of San Miniato al Monte, which is approached by a particularly steep stairway. The Rubaconte bridge over the Arno, named after the official who first began its construction, was later called the Ponte alle Grazie. When this bridge was built (around 1237), Florence was free from the scandals which later affected it, which included (in 1299) the tampering with official records and (in 1283) the selling of salt by monopolists with dishonest measures.

109–11 'Blessed are the poor [in spirit]' (Matthew 5: 3).

# CANTO 13

*Envy. Examples of generosity carried on airborne voices. The envious are compared to blind beggars. Dante meets Sapia of Siena.*

28–36 The words of Mary, '*Vinum non habent!*' (literally, 'They have no wine!'), refer to the Miracle at the Marriage at Cana, related in John 2: 1–12. Dante would have known the story of Orestes and Pylades from Cicero's *De Amicitia* 7: 24. Christ's command that we should love our enemies appears in Matthew 5: 43–5.

70–72 The penance performed by the envious is compared to the 'seeling' of a sparrow hawk's eyes (sometimes with a silk thread, and supposedly without pain), which was intended to tame the bird and make it dependent on its master. Yet the simile of the sparrow hawk also contains the symbolism that Dante invariably attaches to the hunting bird. (Cf. *Purgatorio* 19: 64–7 and *Paradiso* 19: 34–9.) The bird is inherently noble, and its nobility is only enhanced when it participates in sport with its master. Properly disciplined, the sparrow hawk is all the freer to fly in pursuit of appropriate goods.

106–54 Born around 1210 and dying between 1274 and 1289, Sapia was the aunt of the Sienese grandee Provenzan Salvani. (See *Purgatorio* 11: 121–38.) At line 109, Sapia introduces herself by alluding to the pun implied in her name: 'Sapia' being a form of '*savia*', meaning 'wise'. She describes her temperament as being so eroded by envy that she would rejoice more in the misfortunes of others than at any good fortune she might herself enjoy, and offers a particular example. As she neared the end of her life, she was present at the battle of Colle di Val d'Elsa, in which the Sienese, under her nephew Provenzan, were routed by the Florentines. Looking down on the battlefield from the great cliff where the town of Colle is located (fourteen miles north-west of Siena), she prayed (for no reason save a delight in destruction) that God would bring defeat upon her own compatriots.

121–3 In what may have been a thirteenth-century Tuscan proverb, the blackbird begins to twitter, mistakenly supposing that a single fine day in midwinter is the beginning of spring.

127–9 Peter Pettinaio (d. 1289) was a hermit and tertiary of the Franciscan Order who had once been a comb-seller. He was revered by the Sienese, who erected a tomb for him in the church of San Francesco and in 1328 instituted a feast in his honour.

151–4 This refers to two business ventures that went disastrously wrong: a proposal to buy the port of Talamone from the count of Santafiora to give Siena trading access to the sea; and an attempt to locate a water supply in the Diana, an underground stream. (Dante attributes similarly hare-brained schemes to the Sienese in *Inferno* 29.)

# CANTO 14

*The envious continued. Guido del Duca inveighs
against the corruption of the present age in Tuscany
and the decline of courtly virtue in the Romagna.*

7–9 The speakers are later identified as: first, Guido del Duca (*c.* 1170–*c.* 1250), a Ghibelline nobleman from Bretinoro (line 112) in the Romagna, who was chief magistrate of Rimini in 1199; and, second, Rinieri dei Paolucci da Calboli (*c.* 1225–96), Guelf leader of the Romagna, who was chief magistrate of various cities in northern Italy and uncle of Fulcieri (lines 58–71).

16–18 The Arno rises south of Mount Falterona in the Apennines.

31–3 The Apennines were thought once to have extended into Sicily, continuing to Mount Pelorus on that island, until they were broken off by an earthquake.

40–45 The witch Circe, daughter of the sun, changed the followers of Ulysses into swine. (See Ovid, *Metamorphoses* 14: 248.)

58–66 Guido speaks of the nephew of his silently weeping companion. But this nephew is no comfortingly domestic figure. Though unnamed, he can be identified as Fulcieri dei Paolucci da Calboli (*c.* 1270–*c.* 1340), military governor of Florence in 1303 and a Guelf supporter of the papal cause, who is reported to have persecuted, tortured and killed White Guelfs of Dante's party at the behest of the Black Guelfs.

97–111 This is a catalogue of honourable but sometimes obscure figures from the age preceding Dante's own. (At *Purgatorio* 16: 138, Dante is criticized for not knowing the name of the long-dead Gherardo.) Lizio (*fl.* 1260) was a Guelf from Valbona whose family controlled certain abbeys in that area and who fought with Rinieri (see note to 7–9) against the Ghibellines of Forlì. Arrigo Mainardi – a friend of Guido del Duca (see note to 7–9) and, like him, a native of Bretinoro – is known to have died around 1228. Pier Traversaro (1145–1225) was a Ghibelline lord of Ravenna and an ally of the emperor; in 1170 Piero and Arrigo were held prisoner together by the citizens of Faenza. Guido di Carpigna (d. 1283), a Guelf opponent of Frederick II, was chief magistrate of Ravenna in 1251. Fabbro de' Lambertazzi (d. 1259) was leader of the Ghibellines in the Romagna and Bologna. Bernardin di Fosco rose from humble origins to become a leader in Faenza, which he defended against Frederick II. Guido da Prata was probably a dignitary of Ravenna in the early thirteenth century. Ugolino d'Azzo (d. 1293) was probably a member of the Tuscan Ubaldini who settled in the Romagna. Federigo Tignoso was a nobleman associated with the Traversari of Ravenna in the early thirteenth century. The Traversari and Anastagi were Ghibelline (and Byzantine) clans important in Ravenna.

112–23 Bretinoro was a castle near Forlì held by the Manardi family, who had become extinct by 1300. The Ghibelline family of Malvicini were counts of Bagnacavallo but were also nearly extinct in 1300. The degenerate Ghibelline counts of Castrocaro in the region of Imola were, however, thriving at this time, as were the Guelf counts of Conio in the same region. The Pagani, Ghibelline lords of Imola and Faenza at the end of the thirteenth century, produced a particularly vicious offspring in Maghinardo, known as 'the demon'. (See *Inferno* 27: 50–51.) The speech concludes with praise for Ugolino dei Fantolini (d. 1278), a

Guelf nobleman of Cerfugano and of castles near Faenza, whose
line died out (and therefore can no longer be disgraced) when his
sons were killed in campaigns against Guido da Montefeltro.
(See *Inferno* 27.)

133–41 Cain murders his brother Abel out of envy and utters these
words when he receives God's curse. (See Genesis 4: 14.) The
story of Aglauros is told by Ovid in *Metamorphoses* 2: 708–832.
She envies her sister Herse, with whom Mercury is in love. He
eventually turns Aglauros into a statue of murky-hued stone.

# CANTO 15

*Dante, leaving the circle of the envious, has the
second penitential mark removed from his forehead,
and, moving to the circle of the angry, experiences
visions displaying the virtue of mildness.*

1–6 The time is three hours before sunset. In liturgical terms, this is
the hour of Vespers. In astronomical terms, the angle of the sun
above the horizon is the same now as it was a full three hours
from the beginning of the day. If it is three hours until sunset in
Purgatory, it is three hours before sunrise in Jerusalem. Since
Florence ('our clime') is 45 degrees west of Jerusalem, it is mid-
night in that city. The circle of the sun plays like a child in that,
during the course of any one year, it changes latitude and follows
different paths according to the hour and the season.

16–24 The theorem, known since the time of Euclid's *Optics*, that the
angle of reflection is equal to the angle of incidence. In medieval
optics the terms 'reflection' and 'refraction' were not clearly dis-
tinguished. Dante, as traveller, mistakenly assumes that the laws
of reflection apply to the light emanating from the angel – where
in fact the angel is a medium through which the light of God is
refracted.

37–9 These lines refer to the fifth Beatitude: 'Blessed are the merciful'
(Matthew 5: 7). Mercy, according to Aquinas, is one of the vir-
tues that stand in opposition to envy.

85–114 The episode of Christ in the Temple is related in Luke 2:
42–51. The story of Pisistratus is told in Valerius Maximus,
*Facta et Dicta Memorabilia* 5: 1. The naming of Athens (line 98)
was the cause of a dispute between Pallas Athene and Poseidon, as

related in Ovid, *Metamorphoses* 6: 70–82. The last example of meekness is that of Stephen, the first Christian martyr, dying probably in AD 36. Accused of heresy in the councils of the Jews, Stephen persists in his belief and preaches sermons that denounce the pride of the Israelites. A mob is roused in Jerusalem, who pursue him (in Dante's dramatic and somewhat altered version) with cries of 'Kill, kill!', which recall the calls for Christ's crucifixion (Luke 23: 21). He dies, according to the Acts of the Apostles, asking forgiveness for his persecutors and saying, in words that recall Christ's final words on the Cross: 'Lord Jesus, receive my spirit' (Acts 6: 6–15 and 7: 54–60).

# CANTO 16

*Anger. Dante encounters Marco Lombardo, who –*
*purging the sin of anger – identifies the abuse of free*
*will as the source of human misery and insists upon*
*the proper exercise of law as a remedy.*

19–21 This hymn is the '*Agnus Dei*' – 'Lamb of God that takes away the sins of the world' – sung as communion in the Eucharistic liturgy begins.

22f Dante's interlocutor, Marco Lombardo (*c.* 1250–*c.* 1290), a minor noble probably from the Venetian territories, insists that human beings alone are responsible for the disasters that have befallen them (lines 67–72). His tone is mainly angry and aggressive, but it becomes lyrical (lines 85–91) where he speaks of the origins of the human soul in the hand of God who creates human beings in joy and intends them joyously to follow their truest desires. What these desires are will be examined in *Purgatorio* 17. But for Marco the proper regulation of such desires to productive ends is the deepest expression of human freedom. If unregulated desire is the cause of moral disaster, human beings can still provide the remedy. Law exists, after all (lines 97–111), and, though no one pays attention to it, they *could*, and, if they did, they would be able to safeguard justice and moral freedom for all. Here Dante the poet – in the person of Marco Lombardo – expresses the main principles of his political thinking, which always points to the ways in which peace and order can be restored to the world through the implementation of imperial justice. And as always, Dante sees papal interference in matters of imperial jurisdiction as a source of malignant confusion. (See notes to lines 97–9 and 106–8.)

25–7  The Italian text speaks of telling time '*per calendi*', which is to say by the civil calendar employed in ancient Rome and still in use in thirteenth-century Italy.

73–5  To assess how far Dante is prepared to admit the influence of the stars, see *Paradiso* 22: 111–17.

97–9  Dante draws his metaphor from the dietary laws of the Jews, as laid down in Leviticus 11: 3–4, which stipulates:

> Whatsoever parteth the hoof, and is clovenfooted, and cheweth the cud, among the beasts, that shall ye eat. Nevertheless these shall ye not eat of them that chew the cud, or of them that divide the hoof: as the camel, because he cheweth the cud, but divideth not the hoof; he is unclean unto you.

106–8  Papal propaganda argued that the Empire was subject to the papacy and stood in the same relation to the Church as the moon does to the sun. However, believing that Church and Empire are equal agents of God's will, Dante speaks here and elsewhere of Rome uniquely possessing two suns in its sky. (Cf. *De Monarchia* 3: 4 and *Epistle* 5: 1: 3.)

115–17  The land watered by the Adige and the Po rivers comprises most of northern Italy, in particular Lombardy–Emilia and the march of Treviso. These territories began to oppose Emperor Frederick II (see Introduction, pp. xi–xii) in the 1220s, and thus contributed to the disastrous (in Dante's view) diminution of imperial power in Italy.

124–6  Currado da Palazzo served as representative of Charles I of Anjou in Florence in 1276 and was captain of the Guelfs in 1277, becoming *podestà* (or chief magistrate) of Piacenza in 1288. Gherardo da Camino is known to have been captain-general of Treviso from 1283; he was a supporter of the White Guelfs and a patron of poets. Gherardo's daughter Gaia married Tolberto da Cammino in 1311. Sources differ as to whether she lived a notoriously wicked or a famously virtuous life. Guido da Castello (*c.* 1235–*c.* 1316) was a member of the noble Roberti family of Reggio Emilia, and is named 'honest Lombard' by the French because of his honesty in dealing with French travellers who passed through Lombardy.

130–32 At Numbers 18: 20–24, the tribe of Levi is established as the source of priests among the Jews but is denied any territorial portion of the Promised Land.

# CANTO 17

*Visions of anger punished. The arrival at the terrace of sloth. Virgil discusses the bonds of love between creator and creature (in passages which closely reflect the philosophical discussions of such topics in Aquinas and Aristotle) and outlines the Seven Capital Vices.*

13–16 The German philosopher and theologian Albert Magnus writes of the imagination in Aristotle's *De Somno et Vigilia* 3: 1: 8–9: 'The celestial forms directed at us, when touching our bodies, move them with great strength and impress their powers, though they are not perceived because of the tumult of outward distractions. When the soul is separated from the senses, in whatever way, then the motions are perceived' (quoted in T. Gregory, *Mundana sapientia* (Rome, 1992)).

19–39 Three examples of anger are offered here. The first refers to the story of Philomela and Procne, involving infanticide and cannibalism. (See notes to *Purgatorio* 9.) Dante's source – much compressed and altered – is Ovid's *Metamorphoses* 6: 412–676. The second is drawn from Esther 3–7 and 10. Here, the 'one crucified' (line 26) is Haman, chief minister of Ahasuerus, king of Persia, whose wife is the Jewish queen Esther, daughter of Mordecai. When Mordecai refuses to bow to Haman, Haman orders all the Jews in Persia to be exterminated. Esther intervenes and persuades Ahasuerus to execute Haman. The third is the story of Lavinia, drawn from Virgil's *Aeneid* 7: 341–53 and 12: 595–607. Lavinia, daughter of the king of Latium, was promised as wife to Aeneas (who fought against the realm of Latium) in preference to Turnus. Amata, Lavinia's mother, is incensed by this decision, having vowed never to agree to such a marriage, and kills herself.

67–9 'Blessed are the peacemakers' (Matthew 5: 9).

91–139 In a similar vein, Saint Thomas Aquinas writes in *Summa Theologiae*: 'God, as he is the universal good from which all natural

goods depend, is naturally loved by all' (1a q. 60a. 5 and 4) and
'As natural cognition is always true, so natural love is always
right, since natural love is nothing other than the natural inclin-
ation grafted in us by the author of nature' (1a q. 60a. 1 and 3).
Aristotle had written: 'We are lords of our own actions, in so far
as we can choose this or that' (*Nichomachean Ethics* 3: 2: 1111b).
(Cf. *Purgatorio* 27: 142.)

There can be no suggestion that by 'natural love' (line 94)
Virgil means to indicate some instinctual or lower urge that
needs to be repressed. On the contrary, 'natural love' here is the
love of, and desire for, existence which is unconsciously present
in all created things – whether vegetative, animal or rational – and
unfailingly operates within them, impelling them towards the
fulfilment of their goals in existence. Dante never ceases to cele-
brate the action of this 'natural love' (see, for instance, *Paradiso*
1: 109–42), and there are echoes throughout this sequence of
Virgil's initial proposition. But intellectual love is another matter.
This in its rational (rather than angelic) form is unique to human
creatures. And, properly exercised, intellectual love can lead us
consciously to appreciate and bring to fruition the potentialities
that we enjoy in the scheme of existence. We shall be given credit
by our Creator for having done so, and be condemned if we fail
to do so. In this sense – though there are problems here which
Dante goes on to address in *Purgatorio* 18 – we are free (as
plants and animals are *not*) to form our own place in existence
and collaborate in our own making. But we are also free to work
against our maker (line 102). This, in the final analysis, is an
illogical thing to do. But it is the origin of sin. And, in parallel
with Marco's account of how the 'little simple soul' can be dis-
tracted from God by lesser forms of good (*Purgatorio* 16: 87 and
91–3), Virgil proceeds in the concluding part of this canto to dis-
cuss the ways in which sin can lead the soul away from its natural
orientation.

Sin, as Virgil presents it, is not directly an offence against God
but rather against ourselves, in so far as rational love chooses to
ignore the promptings of the natural love that, unfailingly, impels
our existences. In fact, even in committing sin, when rational
love abandons its innate sense of direction, we are still, confus-
edly, seeking an ultimate good (lines 127–9). This confusion also
distorts our perception of the many lesser goods – the legitimate
pleasures of the world – which rightly have their own contribu-
tion to make to our lives. In sin, however, we lose the capacity to

recognize how destructive – and self-destructive – our misapplied freedom might be. Love in its natural form can never seek its own destruction (lines 106–8), since by definition all things have a natural disposition to sustain themselves in existence. We are thus safe from self-hatred. Equally, we know, as rational beings, that we do not bring ourselves to life or are ever wholly 'independent, separate' (line 110). And since the source of our existence is God, we, strictly speaking, cannot hate God either. (In the *Inferno* 3, where 'the good that intellect desires to win' has been entirely lost, the sins of suicide and blasphemy are represented as delusional expressions of hatred against self and hatred of the divine.) So sin, in the worst cases – as in pride, envy and anger – is hatred displaced in its destructive effects from ourselves and God towards our neighbour. And sin in every form is a misapprehension of inherent goodness.

The scheme that Virgil offers in the course of this canto, detailing the nature of the Seven Capital Vices, corresponds to the scheme that Dante adopts in the *Purgatorio*, where, terrace by terrace, the effects of these seven vices are fully dramatized. However, Virgil's words are an attempt to reinvigorate the exercise of rational love, and to provide a point of reference for all the surrounding sequences of the narrative. Pride, envy and anger, as we have seen in previous notes, mistake the true nature of excellence. Pride directs itself in hatred against a neighbour in the mistaken belief that one person's good requires that it be exalted above all others. Envy, somewhat similarly, yearns for the destruction of all forms of excellence, for fear of being overshadowed by any of them. Anger perceives the damage that others wrongfully inflict upon the good, and mistakenly seeks to take revenge for that wrong – as if two wrongs could make a right. Sloth – which is the fourth of the vices, and is to be purged on the terrace at which Dante has now arrived – is a particular case which emphasizes that sin can be the result of ill-regulated love, whereby we do not set our minds with sufficient zeal to pursue the course along which natural love impels us. The remaining three sins are greed (an excessive love of things), avarice (an excessive love of power and money) and lust (an excessive love of persons). These are dealt with only cursorily (lines 124–7), and, as with sloth, there is a misregulation of our energies, expressed in these cases as excess, and, in each case, the mind apprehends a good – in things, in social efficiency or in persons – but distorts the good by making it an end in itself. These goods are only good when

seen in the perspective of the divine goodness that created them.
Dante is left to work out this diagnosis for himself. The canto
ends with that question in mind, stimulating further inquiry on
the part of Virgil's pupil.

At line 112, the technical term '*restat*' draws attention to the
method of Scholastic argument that Dante attributes to Virgil,
and means roughly 'after careful analysis there remains . . .'.

# CANTO 18

*Virgil continues his discussion of love and free will.*
*The penitent slothful appear. Visions of zeal.*

19f The argument laid out in lines 19–75 draws its principles from
Aristotle's *De Anima* and from Scholastic followers of the Aris-
totelian school. The process of 'apprehension' (line 22) is one
that humans share with all other forms of animal life and is a
direct response to impressions received from external things
(which are said to be true in that they do not exist as a result only
of such mental activity as Dante describes in, say, *Purgatorio* 19:
7–15). Apprehension takes place in the 'common sense' – which,
for Scholastics, was a physical organ thought to be located in the
frontal lobe of the brain. It is 'common' in so far as it is able to
create a synthesis from the various sensations that are conducted
along the nerves from external stimuli. In the act of apprehen-
sion, these disparate impressions are drawn together in terms of
such general features as shape, size and number. (They are
described as 'common sensibles' so as to distinguish them from
such specific manifestations of sensation as colour, sound, odour,
taste and texture.) This composite is usually referred to as an
'image'. Apprehension then delivers the image to the centre of
the brain where a distinct faculty 'estimates' the image. It is
important again to emphasize that this 'estimation' takes place
in all animals, and equally important to emphasize that the 'esti-
mation' performed will tell the animal that performs it whether
the object ahead of it is good or bad for it, whether it is some-
thing to be feared and avoided or something that will prove
nutritious, comfortable or in some other way pleasurable. The
mind thus forms 'intentions' – which are 'intent' on what is good
or bad about the object. To love something 'intentionally' is thus

rightly and inevitably rooted in our animal nature, and, if we take seriously Dante's conception of 'natural love' (see note to *Purgatorio* 17: 91–139), it will not seem strange to say that even good and bad, in their primary sense, refer not to abstract moral qualities but rather to those properties in an object that are likely to contribute to, or else damage, the proper operation of specific modes of existence. Good nourishes us, as good soil nourishes a plant. Bad contaminates us, as poisoned water might. It is true that human beings, endowed with rational as well as animal attributes, have more complex natures to nourish or protect than do animals or vegetables. Still, the principle remains the same, and may even be compared (lines 28–30) to the natural actions of fire burning upwards. (Cf., again, *Paradiso* 1.) So, when the human mind 'inclines' consciously to what pleases it, the desire for that object will be entirely legitimate. This is love, and love will be satisfied when the objects of its intentions (line 33) is reached and feeds it to the full. It should not, however, be supposed that human minds – or even the minds of animals – are unerring or immune to error. This itself is a philosophical error which Dante probably attributes (lines 34–6) to the Epicurean school of philosophy. The 'wax' (lines 38–9) may be taken to mean the raw material of the senses, while the 'seal' is the perceptual machinery which has already been discussed. The metaphor of wax and seal derives from Aristotle's *De Anima* 2: 12: 42a and was also taken up by Scholastic philosophers such as Aquinas and Albertus Magnus. Both the material and the process are inherently good – in the sense that they contribute to the furtherance of existence. But in particular situations, the seal applied to this wax may waver and produce a false result – and animals are as capable of making mistakes as human beings are. (Virgil does not say why this wavering occurs. But in *Paradiso* 13: 76–8 Dante speaks of how nature is an artist whose hand, in the fallen state of the world, may sometimes tremble in applying its intended signature.)

After receiving an answer so rigorously concerned with the natural workings of the mind, Dante's next question seeks assurance that our specifically human freedom of choice remains, and that, consequently, just rewards may be allocated after an assessment of our conscious decisions (lines 40–45). As before, Virgil says nothing directly about the actions of divine justice, nor about grace, redemption or charity. His approach is again philosophical, indeed scientific, and aims to demonstrate this by

inductive reasoning from observable evidence. Our freedom is to
be inferred from the way that human beings act. The argument
concludes with a reference to how the moral laws that were first
worked out by classical philosophers depend upon the existence
of the inward freedom that Dante is now asking to have defined
(lines 67–9). Moral laws are possible only because we are free
and responsible beings. But in arguing this case, Virgil recognizes
that there are areas of thought – eventually to be filled by the
certainties of revealed religion – in which invisible realities can
properly be known by arguments from visible effects.

The terms of this argument are once more Aristotelian in
origin, and three in particular will henceforth be of especial
importance whenever Dante debates the structure of created
things. These are substance, form and '*virtù*'. (Cf., for instance,
the account of the creation of the world offered in *Paradiso* 29.)
'Substance' for Dante and his Scholastic sources emphatically
does not mean, as in modern usage, a material substance, but is
rather the potentiality to be an independent, 'subsisting' being.
'Form' is the shaping power (which might now be explained as
DNA) that gives a specific character to independently existing
beings. '*Virtù*' does not refer solely to moral virtue but also means
the power imbued in all members of a species to operate in con-
formity with their specific nature. In the case of human beings,
this power is the discursive intellect. (See *Purgatorio* 25: 67–75.)

Applying these terms in this canto, Virgil first of all establishes
that the characteristic actions of the 'form' and '*virtù*' that make
each specific thing what it is cannot themselves be seen but are
known only from their effects. This is true of trees, where the
virtue of growth as such cannot be seen, but the green of their
foliage, as the result of that growth, can be seen, and growth
inferred from that (lines 52–4). It is the same with the action of
the human will on which our freedom depends (55–60). A more
fully theological understanding of where the mind comes from
and how it operates is offered in *Purgatorio* 25. But working
within his philosophical limit, Virgil here posits – but does not
name – a set of 'primal concepts', or 'prime desirables'. These are
ultimate realities such as beauty, truth and goodness. The mind,
set on these intellectual compass points, shows its powers of rati-
ocination by working towards the unknown from the known. In
that respect, ratiocinative action is analogous to the unseen
power that drives bees to make honey. But in bees that power is
a direct expression of the primal will. In human beings, whose

minds are consciously set upon the prime desirables, there exists a power which allows them to collect all their thoughts into one to move in harmony with their primal natures as unerringly as the zealous (but not conscious) bee might do in making honey. This power provides the measure which can be applied to all possibly divergent thoughts and which thus acts as a censor or arbiter of intellectual aims. We are, according to Virgil's account, free in so far as we can apply this censor (lines 70–75).

58–60 Virgil's natural imagery recalls the language of his *Georgics*, poems concerning various forms of farming, including bee-keeping.

79–81 The moon travelling from west to east (and thus in a direction opposite the daily motion of the heavens) has reached the same point in the Zodiac that the sun occupies when, viewed from Rome, it sets between Corsica and Sardinia.

82–4 Pietola (in Roman times known as Andes) is the village near Mantua where Virgil was born. (Cf. *Purgatorio* 6: 72.)

91–3 The rivers Ismenus and Asopus ran close to Thebes, where Bacchus was worshipped in the ecstatic dances of the Bacchantes.

100–111 The penitential 'whips' and 'bridles' that frame every episode in Purgatory, encouraging virtue and restraining presumption, are in the case of sloth notably abbreviated as this episode is so short that it occupies only the last fifty-seven lines of the canto. The first encouraging example (line 100) refers to the excitement and urgency with which the Virgin Mary, after the Annunciation, ran to tell her cousin Elisabeth about her pregnancy. (See Luke 1: 39–40.) The second refers to an episode from the Roman civil wars, as recounted in Julius Caesar's *De Bello Civili* 1: 34–87 and Lucan's *Pharsalia* 3: 453–5, which is probably the source of Dante's wording. In 49 BC Caesar showed characteristic rapidity and decisiveness when he organized the siege of Marseilles (held by his opponent Pompey), and then marched his legions into northern Spain, conquering Pompey's stronghold at Ilerda (modern Lerida), securing, within forty days, the whole western region of the Roman world.

112–26 The figure who now appears is a certain Gerard (d. 1187). Little is known about him except that he was an abbot of the opulent and strategically powerful abbey of San Zeno in Verona (a city in which Dante spent several years of his exile) during the reign of Emperor Frederick Barbarossa (1122–90). Alberto della Scala, the local overlord of Verona, later installed his illegitimate son (lines 125–6) as abbot of San Zeno. Alberto already has 'one foot in the grave' (line 121), as he was mortally ill in 1300 – the date at which Dante's journey through the other world takes place – and died in 1301. Alberto's two legitimate sons, Bartolommeo and Can Grande, became Dante's patrons, of whom he speaks with elevated praise in *Paradiso* 17: 70–92.

133–8 The 'bridles', as examples of feebleness of spirit, refer first to Numbers 14: 20–23, where the Israelites who are shown to have offended God by their lack of faith are prevented from living long enough to enter the Promised Land. The second, parallel example refers to Virgil's *Aeneid* 5: 604–776. As Aeneas is journeying to his own 'promised land', the women among his band of refugees set fire to his ships – on the anniversary of the death of Aeneas's father – in the hope of ending their wanderings. Jupiter extinguishes the flames with a rainstorm. Those who are unwilling to travel with Aeneas are left behind in Sicily in disgrace.

# CANTO 19

*Dante dreams of the Siren and witnesses the exposure
of her fallaciousness. The avaricious, including Pope
Hadrian V, engaged in their penance.*

4–6 Geomancy involves the drawing of omens from signs made in the earth, usually by the random tapping of sticks on sand. The Greater Fortune, thought to be the most favourable sign, is seen when these marks resemble six of the stars in the constellations Aquarius and Pisces.

7–33 The Siren that Dante sees in the second of his three dreams on Mount Purgatory can be seen as a powerful visualization of the false goods that Virgil has spoken of, philosophically, in the preceding cantos. The Siren's attraction is in fact a projection of the deluded mind that contemplating her repellent figure transforms her by its attentions to an object of desire. A deeper and truer desire – pointing forward to the intervention of Beatrice in *Purgatorio* 30 and back to her role in *Inferno* 2 – alerts Virgil to the danger in which Dante now stands. The *donna* at line 26 is not Beatrice herself but one of a number of female figures who now begin to foreshadow her arrival. (See especially *Purgatorio* 27 where, in his final dream on the mountain, Dante sees the figures of Rachel and Leah.) For Ulysses (line 22), see *Inferno* 26.

49–51 '*Qui lugent*' is the Latin text of the second Beatitude of the Sermon on the Mount: '[Blessed are those] who mourn' (Matthew 5: 4).

73 Translated as 'My soul cleaves to the ground', this quotes Psalm 119: 25, which in Latin reads '*pavimento*' ('ground' or 'floor') where the Hebrew text may be rendered more accurately as 'dust'. This verse, in the commentary tradition, was taken as a warning against any attachment to riches.

97–126 The magisterial Latin phrase may be translated: 'Know that I was the successor of Peter.' The speaker is Ottobono dei Fieschi (*c.* 1215–76), nephew of Pope Innocent IV, who became Hadrian V in 1276, dying after only thirty-eight days in office. The river Lavagna (lines 100–102) runs between Sestri Levante and Chiavari in Liguria. Hadrian's family, the Fieschi of Genoa, were counts of Lavagna.

136–8 These words – translated as 'neither shall they marry' – are spoken by Jesus to the Saduccees (who denied physical resurrection of the body) in Matthew 22: 30, and may here be taken to mean that in Heaven there will be no social ranks.

142–5 Alagia dei Fieschi, daughter of Ottobono's brother Niccolò, married to Moroello Malaspina of the Lunigiana, whose guest Dante had been around 1306. (See notes to *Purgatorio* 8.) Women of the Fieschi clan were otherwise notorious for their licentiousness.

# CANTO 20

*Avarice. Dante listens to Hugo Capet's attack on the*
*political ambitions of the French. Mount Purgatory*
*is shaken by an earthquake.*

10–15 For avarice as the 'she-wolf' and the need for divine deliverance from her appetites, cf. *Inferno* 1.

19–33 The three examples of willing poverty are: the Virgin Mary, who gave birth to Christ in a stable (Luke 2: 7); Gaius Fabricius Luscinus, Roman general and consul in 282 BC, who refused a bribe offered him by Pyrrhus, King of Epirus in Greece, intending to lead him to betray Rome, and subsequently died in poverty and was buried at the expense of the State, which also paid the dowries of his daughters (cf. *De Monarchia* 2: 5: 11); and Saint

Nicholas, the third–fourth-century bishop of Myra, in modern
Turkey, who saved the three daughters of an impoverished noble-
man from prostitution by dropping gold through their window,
and thus providing them with dowries.

40f The speaker is the founder of the French dynasty of Capetian
kings, Hugo (Hugues) Capet (*c.* 940–96). Hugo was never him-
self king but was powerful enough to act as kingmaker on behalf
of his son Robert II (the Pious) (972–1031). (Hugo was '*cap-
pato*' or Ciappetta, in the sense of being a lay abbot, and possibly
because he inherited the *cape* of Saint Martin, the popular saint
who divided his cloak with a beggar.) The Capetian dynasty
replaced the Carolingians in 987–8 (line 53) and ruled until
1328, seven years after Dante's death. Hugo's ascent from hum-
ble Parisian origins (line 52) was a legend widespread in Dante's
day, though in fact Hugo and his father were dukes of the Franks
and counts of Paris and Orléans. With only two exceptions, the
monarchs of this dynasty were named Philip or Louis (four of
the former, five of the latter). Line 54 refers to Charles of Lor-
raine, who should have succeeded to the throne in 987 but was
displaced by Hugo. (Charles was not, as suggested here, a monk.)

Hugo's penitent speech recalls the three main phases through
which Capetian ambition evolved:

Lines 46–8: Between 1297 and 1304, the Capetian Philip IV
(the Fair) (1268–1314) invaded the Flemish towns of Douai,
Ghent, Lille and Bruges, often using treachery to attain his ends,
as when he promised the count of Flanders liberty in exchange
for the surrender of Ghent and promptly broke his word, impris-
oning the count. Vengeance came in 1302 when the Flemish
defeated the French at the battle of Courtrai. (Cf. *Purgatorio* 7:
109 and *Paradiso* 19: 118–20.)

Lines 61–9: The southward expansion of French power, with
each violent act, is registered by an ironic repetition of the phrase
'to put things right'. Normandy, Ponthieu, Gascony and Aqui-
taine had been in English hands until they were re-appropriated,
the first two from King John in 1206, the latter two from Edward
I in 1294.

Lines 70–79: The involvement of French princes in the politics
of thirteenth-century Italy (which Dante deplored) and their some-
times stormy alliance with the papacy against the Empire, with
particular prominence given to Charles I of Anjou (1227–85), the
youngest child of Louis VIII of France. The turning point in
Charles's fortunes came in 1246 when, through marriage, he

became count of Provence. It was at this point, too (lines 61–3), that Capetian power – hitherto malignant but ineffectual – began to menace Italy. Supported by Pope Clement IV, Charles was invested as king of Sicily in 1266, which brought him into direct conflict with the Hohenstauffen rulers of Sicily descended from Emperor Frederick II – whose imperial cause Dante broadly supported. Though Charles, like Hugo, is granted a place in Purgatory (*Purgatorio* 7: 113), his campaigns in the Italian peninsula led ultimately to the extinction of imperial claims. During these campaigns he first defeated Manfred in 1266 (see *Purgatorio* 3: 118–29) and then kidnapped Conradin, grandson of Frederick II, and ended the Hohenstauffen dynasty by having him publicly beheaded in Naples in 1268. It was rumoured (baselessly) that when Saint Thomas Aquinas, who came from a southern Italian family, threatened to reveal the truth about Charles's behaviour he was poisoned by agents of the king (lines 68–9). The prophecy at lines 70–78 foretells the entry of Charles of Valois (1270–1325), brother of Philip the Fair, into Italy in 1301, with the intention of recovering Sicily for the French kingdom. Charles allied himself with Pope Boniface VIII and favoured the Florentine Black Guelfs in the coup that ousted Dante's White Guelf party – an event referred to here as the bursting of the Florentine 'belly'.

79–81 The 'other' Charles (1254–1309) – the second of that name (see *Purgatorio* 7: 126) – son of Charles I (see previous note) and king of Naples, was captured during the war of the Sicilian Vespers by Ruggiero di Lauria (*c.* 1245–1305), the admiral of the Aragon claimant, and imprisoned 1284–7. Though he was crowned king of Sicily in 1289, he never exerted control over the realm. Charles II (represented as a pirate at line 81) is condemned here for arranging an advantageous marriage between his daughter Beatrice and the infamous Azzo VIII d'Este (d. 1308). (See *Inferno* 18: 55–7.)

85–96 These quarrels broke out between Philip the Fair and Boniface VIII concerning a papal ban on payments by the French priesthood to the French exchequer. The notable feature is that Dante should envisage Boniface's humiliation at the hands of Philip as a second crucifixion. Despite his contempt for Boniface, Dante maintains an understanding of the papal office as the true representative of Christ, and Philip is referred to as a new Pilate in abandoning Boniface, as Pontius Pilate abandoned Christ, to the mercy of a violent mob (lines 91–3). When, in September 1303, Boniface was threatening to excommunicate Philip, Philip's agent Guillaume de Nogaret (*c.* 1260–1313) – here identified by the 'fleur-de-lys' – seized the pope at the papal palace of Anagni, to the south-east of Rome. Boniface was rescued by the townspeople, but died – presumably of trauma – within a month. The papacy itself now fell under French control, and removed to Avignon in 1309 under the papacy of Clement V. In 1307 Philip IV accused the Knights Templar of heresy, and acquired their enormous wealth – and remission of his enormous debts to them – when, in 1312, Pope Clement V (who as pope was titular sovereign of the Templars) suppressed the Order.

103–17 Pygmalion, king of Tyre, murdered his uncle Sychaeus (husband of his sister Dido) in an act here referred to as parricide. (See Virgil, *Aeneid* 1: 340–59.) The story of Midas, king of Phrygia, occurs in Ovid's *Metamorphoses* 11: 85–179. Midas asks Bacchus that all he touches should be turned to gold, and repents when his food is so transformed. Having pilfered the booty won at Jericho, including a 'wedge of gold', the soldier Achan is stoned to death by his comrades-in-arms (Joshua 7: 21, 25–6). In Acts 5: 1–11, Sapphira and her husband Ananias, members of the early Christian community, keep back for themselves some part of the profit on a land transaction and, when accused by Saint Peter, fall down dead. When ordered to steal the treasury of the Temple in Jerusalem, Heliodorus, the treasurer of the Syrian king Seleucus IV, was assailed and struck down by the hooves of a mysterious horse and rider (2 Maccabees 3: 2). Priam, king of Troy, entrusted his son Polydorus, along with a great weight of gold, to Polymnestor, king of Thrace, who, when Troy fell, treacherously murdered the boy and retained the gold. (See *Aeneid* 3: 19 and *Metamorphoses* 13: 429. Cf. *Inferno* 30: 13–21.) Crassus (115–53 BC), third member of the triumvirate of Rome, along with Julius Caesar and Pompey, was famous for his riches; when he was defeated by the Parthians in 59 BC, he was killed while attempting to surrender, and the king of the Parthians had molten gold poured into his corpse's mouth. (See Cicero, *De Officiis* 1: 30.)

130–32 Delos, the birthplace of Apollo and Diana, was originally a floating island, unstable and subject to earthquakes. However, because it proved to be a place of shelter for Latona, mother of Apollo and Diana, Apollo ensured that the island should be made to stand firm. (See Virgil, *Aeneid* 3: 73–7.)

136–41 'Glory to God in the highest!' The '*Gloria*' is here associated with the Nativity (Luke 2: 14). From the first lines of the canto (especially 19–21) penance has been compared to childbirth (a motif that is connected to the recurrent references to children from *Purgatorio* 15 onwards). Purgation, in its positive aspect, is viewed as a way of bringing new life to birth, as a form of conversion. But this birth depends upon another birth, which is the redemptive birth of Christ in the Incarnation. And it is Christ's nativity that is recalled at the conclusion of the canto when, as the mountain shakes, Dante compares the event directly (136–41) to the moment at which, at Luke 2: 8–14, the shepherds in the fields at the first Christmas were stopped in their tracks by the sound of the angels singing '*Gloria in excelsis Deo*'. The new life for which the penitents strive will only come about because a divine birth has interrupted the seemingly inevitable advance of decadence and corruption in the earthly sphere.

## CANTO 21

*Dante discovers that the earthquake in Purgatory
announced the end of Statius's purgation.*

1–6 At John 4: 4–26, Jesus engages in a long and spirited conversation with a woman of Samaria – and therefore from a people alien to the Jews – in the course of which he extends the offer of the waters of grace even to those (like the Samaritan woman and, implicitly, Statius) who are not of the chosen race. Jesus concludes:

> God is a Spirit: and they that worship him must worship him in spirit and in truth.
> The woman saith unto him, I know that Messias cometh, which is called Christ: when he is come, he will tell us all things.
> Jesus saith unto her, I that speak unto thee am he.

The confident expectation that the Samaritan woman displays in the coming of a Messiah is compared to Dante's thirst to know the meaning of the earthquake that has just struck Mount Purgatory. This event itself marks a moment of salvation.

7f At Luke 24: 13–32, after his resurrection, Jesus encounters two disciples on the road to Emmaus, who do not recognize him until he breaks bread eucharistically at supper. Remarkably, the figure whose appearance is here compared to that of Jesus is the

Latin poet Statius (not named until line 91), who henceforth will accompany Dante throughout his journey up the mountain. But from line 7 onwards a very complex set of considerations is brought into play, concerning the relationships that exist between the Christian and the classical world, between vernacular poetry and classical poetry and also between historical fact and the fiction that Dante is here constructing.

Publius Papinius Statius (*c.* AD 45–96) was born in Naples (not Toulouse as stated at line 89). He was the author of the epic poems *Thebaid*, concerning the disasters that befell Thebes after the death of Oedipus, and the unfinished *Achilleid* (see line 92). There is no evidence that Statius was a Christian – still less that his salvation can be compared to the appearance of Christ on the way to Emmaus. (Cf. Dante's surprising representation of Manfred in *Purgatorio* 3.) But he did live in the Christian era, and Dante builds on the possibilities that this suggests, creating a narrative of his own in which Statius was a secret convert, at a time when Christians were subject to imperial persecution. (See note to *Purgatorio* 22: 67–81.)

**25–7** The three Fates are Clotho, Lachesis and Atropos, who respectively allot the thread of a person's life, spin it and cut it off.

**49–60** Thaumas's daughter is the rainbow (lines 50–51). (See Ovid, *Metamorphoses* 14: 845.) The highly decorative style that Dante attributes to Statius may be a reflection of his view of the Latin poet's own style. The word '*tremare*' ('tremble') in the Italian, thrice repeated in lines 55–8, is always associated in Dante with the impact of love. (See especially *Purgatorio* 30: 36 and 47.)

**82–4** The emperor Titus (AD 39–81) is said to be 'good' in that he is thought to have carried out God's will, avenging the death of Christ by his brutal destruction of Jerusalem in AD 70. Dante returns to this theme in *Paradiso* 6.

# CANTO 22

*Statius comes to accompany Dante to the Earthly*
*Paradise, and discusses the influence that Virgil exerted*
*over his poetry and Christian belief. Arriving at the terrace*
*of gluttony the three travellers come across a second tree*
*from which examples of moderation are heard.*

4-6 The fourth Beatitude speaks of those who hunger and thirst after justice (Matthew 5: 6). Dante attributes a 'thirst' (*'sitiunt'*) to the avaricious and prodigal, thus (unusually) dividing the Scriptural verse so as to attribute a 'hunger' to the penitent gluttons of the next terrace.

13-15 The poet Juvenal (AD *c.* 60–*c.* 130) is famous for his satires against the extravagant vices of imperial Rome (although he also writes scornfully of Statius at *Satires* 7: 82).

40-48 Statius quotes Virgil's *Aeneid* 3: 55–8, in which Aeneas condemns the avarice that induced Polymnestor to murder the boy Polydorus (see also *Purgatorio* 20: 115 and *Inferno* 30: 13–21), crying out against the *'auri sacra fames'* – where *'sacra fames'* could be translated as both 'an accursed hunger' for gold (*'auri'*) and 'a sacred hunger'. In keeping with his emphatic Aristotelianism in this sequence, it seems that, for Dante, an appetite for riches may be productive (a divine as well as a cursed appetite) if it follows rule or measure. The reference to 'hair cropped short' (line 46) directly recalls the punishment reserved for avarice and prodigality in *Inferno* 7. In *Purgatorio* the same penance 'drains' (line 51) both sins of their original vitality.

55-60 Jocasta, queen of Thebes, unwittingly married her own son Oedipus. The sons born to their incestuous liaison were Eteocles and Polynices, who became sworn enemies. (See Statius, *Thebaid* 12.) Clio is the Muse of history, whom Statius calls upon in *Thebaid* 1: 41–2.

61-3 The 'fisherman' is Saint Peter. (See Mark 1: 16–17.)

64-81 Statius attributes his conversion to the influence of Virgil's *Fourth Eclogue*. This pastoral poem was regularly supposed in the Middle Ages to prophesy the birth of Christ, and bears resemblances to Isaiah in the picture it offers of an age of peace restored. Virgil speaks of how the birth of a child will issue in an age of perfect justice, when the earth will effortlessly bear all the fruits we need. Greed and labour will both be unnecessary:

> But for you, young boy, the first fruits of the earth without any ploughing will pour abundantly forth. Wandering ivy will be everywhere, with a scattering of berries and lotus mingling with smiling acanthus. The she goats will bring home their milk of their own accord ... The ram in the meadow will change his fleece of itself first to reddish purple, then to saffron yellow. Vermilion will freely clothe the lambs at pasture.
>
> Virgil, *Eclogue* 4: 17–22 and 43–4

In inventing the story of Statius's conversion, and especially in emphasizing the importance of Virgil's contribution to this conversion, Dante seems deliberately to raise the question of why noble pagans such as Virgil should be condemned to Limbo. This question continues in his mind until at least *Paradiso* 19 (and may not be resolved even there).

Within the *Purgatorio*, the theme of the Golden World (as anticipated by poets such as Virgil) now grows stronger until we reach the Earthly Paradise in *Purgatorio* 28 (see especially lines 139–48).

82–4   Domitian, emperor of Rome AD 81–96, initiated a particularly severe persecution of Christians.

88–91   In Statius's *Thebaid* 4: 670–844, the Greek armies marching on Thebes are close to dying of thirst when Hypsipyle leads them to the one stream still flowing, the Langia. (See also line 112.)

91–3   Thus, before spending more than 500 years in purging his prodigality (*Purgatorio* 21: 67), Statius had spent over 400 years purging his 'luke-warmness'. (His name has sometimes been taken as a pun on the word *status*, meaning 'delay'.) Where he was for the other 300 or so years since his death, Dante does not say.

97–108   The Latin authors here, given that Dante does not know their work directly, are likely to have come to his attention through his reading of Cicero, Horace and Saint Jerome. Most are comic dramatists and satirists. Terence (d. 159 BC) was a writer of comedies (see *Inferno* 18: 133–5), as were Caecilius (d. *c.* 166 BC) and Plautus (d. 184 BC). 'Varro' is unknown (and may be the result of a misreading), save from references in Horace's works. Persius (d. AD 62) was a satirist not directly known to Dante. The second part of the list transfers attention to Greek authors whom Dante, not knowing Greek, would have heard about through his reading of Cicero. Most of these are tragedians and dramatists, except Simonides, a lyric poet (556–467 BC). Of the works of Euripides (484–406 BC), eighteen tragedies survive, along with fragments of sixty more. Agathon (448–402 BC) was a friend of Socrates and Plato who speaks in Plato's *Symposium*, but nothing of his work survives. Antiphon was a poet at the court of Dionysius I of Sicily (405–367 BC).

109–14   These are Greeks who are protagonists in poems by Statius. Antigone and Ismene are the daughters of Oedipus and Jocasta. Antigone dies immured at the order of Creon. Ismene witnessed the murder of all her family and her lover Cyrrheus (line 111). Deiphile is the wife of Tydeus. (See *Inferno* 32: 130.) Argia is the daughter of Deiphile and wife of Polynices. The 'one who spied out Langia's stream' is Hypsipyle, who at *Inferno* 18: 92 is mentioned as the deserted lover of Jason and is also referred to in *Purgatorio* 26: 94–6. The daughter of the Theban seer Tiresias is Manto, who, confusingly, is placed among the soothsayers in *Inferno* 20. In Statius's *Achilleid*, Thetis is Achilles's mother and Deidamia his wife. (See *Inferno* 26: 61–2.)

118–20  The 'handmaids of the sun' are the passing hours of the day. It is now within the fifth hour.

130–38  This tree is the first of two (see also *Purgatorio* 24: 112–17) that stand at the beginning and end of Dante's encounter with the gluttons. These trees, though rooted in the ground, taper strangely like inverted pyramids. They immediately take on symbolic implications that are explored further in *Purgatorio* 23. The trees are grown from seed generated in the Earthly Paradise (*Purgatorio* 24: 117), and their shape is clearly intended to deter any such presumptuous attempt to 'climb' that led Adam and Eve to their fall. At the same time, the pleasures of the senses are sharply aroused by the freshness of the perfumes that come from these trees which are constantly sprayed by a shower of water from the cliffside. The penance of the gluttons is to experience this pleasure without being able to satisfy their appetite for it. But the promise is also implied here of the legitimate pleasure that will be experienced once penance is concluded. The voices that come out of the foliage, citing examples of restraint, point to this ultimate, if paradoxical, consummation.

142–54  The virtue of restraint is illustrated by the Virgin Mary at the Marriage at Cana; she prays for us and so thought less of the needs of her own appetite (hence the 'mouth' that intercedes on behalf of all Christians) than that of others. (See John 2: 1–11 and cf. *Purgatorio* 13: 29.) The legendary restraint shown by the women of ancient Rome is recorded by Aquinas in *Summa Theologiae* 2a 2ae q. 149 a. 4. Daniel at Nebuchadnezzar's court persuades the children of Israel to live on lentils and water. 'As for these four children, God gave them knowledge and skill in all learning and wisdom: and Daniel had understanding in all visions and dreams' (Daniel 1: 17). The 'primal age' is the Golden Age. (See Ovid, *Metamorphoses* 1: 89–150.) In Matthew 3: 4, Saint John the Baptist is described as living off honey and locusts. At Luke 7: 28, Jesus says of Saint John: 'there is not a greater prophet than John the Baptist'.

# CANTO 23

*The penance for gluttony. Dante's meeting with his*
*one-time friend Forese Donati, who speaks out*
*against the corrupt manners of modern Florence.*

10–12 The hymn '*Labia mea*' quotes Psalm 51: 15: 'O Lord, open
thou my lips; and my mouth shall shew forth thy praise.' An
obvious contrast arises here between the misuse of lips of which
the gluttons, in their earthly lives, have been guilty and the pos-
sibilities that they now pursue through prayer and praise.

25–30 Erysichthon, prince of Thessaly, cut down a sacred oak which
had within it a wood nymph and, as punishment, was made to
suffer a hunger so terrible that he finally consumed his own body.
The story is told by Ovid in *Metamorphoses* 8: 738–808, to
which Dante's phrases here closely correspond. The second refer-
ence is to the siege of Jerusalem by the Romans in AD 70, at the
command of Titus (Roman Emperor AD 79–81), as described by
Flavius Josephus in *De Bello Judaico* 6 (*c.* AD 75). During this
siege, a Jewish woman by the name of Mary was driven to eat
her own child. (See also Paulus Orosius, *Historiae Adversum*
*Paganos* 7: 9 (417).)

31–3 Dante alludes to a familiar medieval notion which declared that
the word 'man' – '*omo*' in the original text ('*uomo*' in modern
Italian) – could be read in the bone structure of the human face.
The brow and nose can be seen as an 'M', the sockets of the eyes
form the two 'O's. Such body art reminds the reader that Dante's
own brow is still inscribed with two 'P's.

40f Dante encounters his close personal friend Forese Donati (*c.* 1260–
before 1296), a distant cousin of his wife Gemma Donati. Forese
is not known for any sustained work of poetry, but historically
the closeness of his relationship with Dante is attested by an
exchange of scurrilous banter – in the form of a *tenzone*, or poetic
dialogue, in which they trade spectacular insults – that took place
between the two. Forese, so Dante's poem implies, is hopeless in
bed and, in any case, his wife Nella (see lines 87 and 91–6) has a
perpetual cold and does nothing, even on a summer night, except
wear socks and cough. Dante, according to Forese, will end up
wearing a smock in a pauper's hospital. In any case, his father
was a money-lender. Forese, according to Dante, is a scar-faced
thief, the bastard son of a licentious mother whose supposed

father stands in the same relationship to Forese 'as Joseph did to Christ'. Nowhere, except in the depths of *Inferno* 29 and 30, does Dante display comparable violence of sentiment and diction.

73–5 Christ's words on the Cross are recorded at Matthew 27: 46 (also Mark 15: 34), a quotation from Psalm 22: 1: 'Eli, Eli, lama sabachthani?' ('My God, my God, why hast thou forsaken me?') Note the emphasis upon Christ's joy in accepting crucifixion.

91–6 Praise for Forese's wife Nella (once roundly insulted in the poems that Dante exchanged with Forese: see note to line 40f) now precipitates condemnation of the shamelessness of Florentine womenfolk. The Barbarigia is a mountainous region in central Sardinia, noted for the barbarity of its inhabitants.

118–20 The allusion is to the moon, Diana, twin sister of Apollo, the sun.

# CANTO 24

*Among the gluttonous, Dante meets the poet Bonagiunta da Lucca, and speaks of his poetic success, as well as of the deficiencies of earlier poets. Forese Donati continues the conversation that began in the previous canto, speaking of his saintly sister and of his brother Corso, who is to die violently and be dragged to Hell.*

10–15 Forese's sister, Piccarda Donati, now in Heaven (the 'Olympian heights') has a principal role to play in *Paradiso* 3. (See notes to that canto.)

19f Bonagiunta Orbicciani degli Overardi (*c.* 1220–*c.* 1300), a judge and notary from Lucca in Tuscany, a city of which Dante spoke with contempt for the corruption of its public life in *Inferno* 21 and 22. In the course of their conversation, Dante draws a distinction between the successful principles on which his own early poetry was founded and the constraints of style that deny to Bonagiunta any comparable success. Bonagiunta is made to confess that his own writings are affected by a certain knottiness (line 55), probably of rhetorical exaggeration. In Dante's view, they share this defect (line 56) with the poetry of Guittone d'Arezzo (*c.* 1230–94: see *Purgatorio* 26: 124), whom historically Bonagiunta acknowledged as master, and the early Sicilian poet and lawyer, or 'Brief', Giacomo da Lentini (*c.* 1200–*c.* 1250). Bonagiunta quotes the first line of a poem from the *Vita nuova* 20: '*Donne ch'avete intelletto d'amore* . . .' (line 51), which in the *Vita nuova* itself is said to inaugurate Dante's characteristic 'praise style'. He now offers an explanation of his practice which is regularly cited as the key to the poetics of his early love poetry. While Bonagiunta and others like him are given to wordy display, Dante follows the dictates of the heart: love speaks in him and he, as poet, faithfully records its promptings in praise of his lady. Thus, Dante claims a degree of spontaneity in his writing but equally stresses the humility which makes him an accurate scribe of the revelations that love inspires. 'Praise' develops in Dante's writing to the point at which it becomes the dominant mode of his poetry in the *Paradiso*. It is in praise of others that we unknot our obsession with ourselves (as in any burst of spontaneous applause), and acknowledge an inspiration or illumination that comes from beyond.

22–33  The first person alluded to is Pope Martin IV (in office 1281–5), one-time treasurer of the cathedral of Tours. Though Dante would have criticized Martin as being a supporter of Charles of Anjou (see *Purgatorio* 20: 67) and disapproved of his meddling in Italian politics, he now he finds reasons of his own for allowing Martin's salvation – somewhat as he retracts here his earlier sweeping condemnation of the Guittonian school. Bolsena is a lake near Viterbo famous for its eels, and Martin is thought to have had eels drowned as a delicacy in the vernaccia wine. The second person (line 29) is Ubaldino da la Pila (d. 1291), father of the notorious Archbishop Ruggieri who is cannibalistically consumed by Ugolino in *Inferno* 33. This Boniface (to be distinguished from Dante's great enemy, Pope Boniface VIII) was archbishop of Ravenna between 1274 and 1295. The bishop's crook in Ravenna is not hook-shaped but carries a rook (as in the chess piece) at its extremity. Messer Marchese degli Argoglesi (line 31) from Forlì was related to the da Polenta clan of Ravenna, Dante's patrons.

37–9  'Gentucca' appears to be a woman's name, but no further identification has proved possible, though some commentators associate her with the woman at lines 43–5.

55  In the Italian text, Bonagiunta employs the archaism or dialectic word for 'now', '*issa*' – as in English it might be 'nah' or 'noo'. (Cf. *Inferno* 23: 7; like this canto, *Inferno* 23 contains certain anti-Guittonian elements.) This might be seen as an attempt to mark his speech with a certain provincialism. Similarly, at line 43, he fails to employ the courtly term *donna* or 'lady', in favour of the coarser term '*femmina*' – 'woman'.

58–60 In speaking of love dictating to him, Dante alludes to an office of high importance in medieval courts, where the Italian '*dittator*', or 'dictator', was a man trained in eloquence who often acted as head of the administrative council and drafted all legal documents, dictating them to lesser officials.

64–6 For the importance of this bird simile in the vernacular love poetry, see note to *Purgatorio* 26: 43–5.

82–87 These lines are generally taken to refer to Corso Donati, Forese's brother and a leader of the Black Guelfs who drove Dante into exile. See Introduction p. xiv.

121–6 The first examples of gluttony are the centaurs, who drunkenly attempted to rape the women guests at the wedding of Pirithous and Hippodamia, but were defeated by Theseus and the Lapiths. (See Ovid, *Metamorphoses* 12: 210–535.) The second example is from Judges 7, in which Gideon, the Hebrew general, forbids certain of his soldiers who have yielded to their physical appetites from participating in the battle against Midian and sharing the spoils of victory.

# CANTO 25

*On the way to the final terrace of Purgatory, where the lustful are purged, Statius explains how the foetus develops in the womb from conception to birth.*

1–3 The time designated by this reference is around 2 p.m. in Purgatory and 2 a.m. in Jerusalem.

10–12 Cf. this simile with the references to birds in *Purgatorio* 24: 64–6 and 26: 43–5.

22–7 Throughout the canto there are certain precise parallels and contrasts with *Inferno* 25, where Dante described a parody of procreation and claimed to outdo Ovid in his description of metamorphosis. Ovid is again in Dante's mind here, for *Metamorphoses* 8: 260–525 tells how Meleager's life was connected, by decree of the Fates, to the continued existence of a log which his mother had snatched from the fire at birth but flung back into the flames when in later life he murdered her brothers. As a consequence, Meleager died. Virgil's use of the mirror analogy here to explain the mystery of the relation of soul and body is not especially lucid, suggesting possibly the need for the philosophical and theological clarification that follows.

**34–78** This passage (requiring lengthy paraphrase) is probably the most dense and technical piece of philosophy in the whole *Commedia*, and also, probably, the most important in that it directly explores the relationship between God and the human being and equally the relationship in the human being between body and soul. The argument runs in two phases: lines 37–60 explain the physiological and biological operations that may be observed in the development of any mammal within the womb, while 61–78 look at the unique conditions that pertain in the development of a human being.

Lines 37–45 describe the process by which, in any animal, food becomes blood and blood becomes semen. On the Aristotelian view, food is received in the stomach where body heat causes it to divide into a nutritious substance, known as 'chyle', and waste matter, which is expelled as excrement. Chyle then passes to the liver where 'imperfect' – though still nutritious – blood is formed, some of which passes into the right ventricle of the heart, where it comes into contact with air from the lungs and becomes 'perfect' blood (line 37). This blood possesses a power which is formative in that it can be transformed into the tissues and organs of the body. However, in the sexually mature adult, a small part of this perfect blood remains in the heart and undergoes a third and final refinement. It is this small remainder that Dante refers to at line 39, in a somewhat strained simile, as food carried away from a banquet – thereby emphasizing, at least, that there is a continuous connection between what we eat and what we are.

The formative power of perfect blood is intensified in the course of this final transformation, so that now it can actually transmit form and generate new and independent forms of life. In the case of females, where natural warmth is supposed to be lacking, this final form of 'perfect' blood is menstrual, and possesses the power to assume, but not initiate, independent forms of life. In the male, perfect blood in its final form descends to the testicles ('more decent not to say') and becomes semen.

When active semen joins with the receptive menstrual blood, a coagulation or clotting occurs, brought about by the activity of sperm, and the embryo begins to develop (lines 47–60). In becoming a human foetus, the embryo will pass through a number of different phases, from the vegetative or nutritive phase to an animal form of life. Statius pays particular attention to the phase in which the embryo is comparable to a sea sponge (lines 55–7) – the sponge being a standard example in Aristotelian biology of a form that has some sensation without possessing organs or limbs. When the term '*anima*' – 'soul' – is used here (as at line 52) – it is employed, in a way discussed in the notes to *Purgatorio* 4, 17 and 18, to mean the 'animating' principle that gives shape, or, as one might now say, genetic character to any form of life which is capable of growth, be it vegetable, animal or rational. It is not only human beings that have souls, as Aristotle understands the word 'soul'. A sea sponge, on this account, would have its own kind of soul.

In his description of this process, as it proceeds over the next seven months, Dante favours the views of Albertus Magnus over those of Aquinas. Broadly speaking, Aquinas emphasized the discontinuities in the development of the embryo as it moves from one stage to another, whereas Albertus looked to their continuity. (See P. Boyde, *Dante, Philomythes and Philosopher* (Cambridge, 1981), pp. 270–95, for further discussion.) However, Dante, in his emphasis on continuity, does prepare for the crucial point in his argument, which is the radical discontinuity that exists in the human being between its vegetative and animal phases and its final human form (lines 61–78).

The process of embryonic generation is now complete. The limbs are formed, and so is the foetal brain. However, we do not yet know (lines 61–6) how humans come to possess an intellect, and are thus able to participate in an intellectual experience which associates them with the angels and ultimately with God. The distinction between human beings and other forms of animal life resides in the possession of an intellect. Animals possess cognition of particular objects and thus may have a mental image of a stone as being large, heavy or brown. (Cf. the discussion of intellection in the notes to *Purgatorio* 18.) What they do not have, according to Aristotle and Dante, is conceptual understanding of size, weight and colour. Human beings are capable of such understanding, a capacity that is usually referred to as the '*intellectus possibilis*' (line 65) and is not to be located in any particular organ of the body. Vision is an activity of the eye, hearing of the ear. But intellectual understanding is an abstraction which makes abstraction itself a possibility. It is by this that we give meaning to the experiences that our physical faculties deliver. It is by intellection, too, that we attain self-conscious knowledge of our own existence and, as Statius emphasizes, the ability to communicate in speech (lines 61–3). So in what way is this intellect acquired and how are its powers exercised?

It is here that Dante confronts the radical difference between his own position and that of the much respected Islamic philosopher Averroes (see note to *Inferno* 4: 130–44). Responding to Aristotle's argument that intellect cannot be located in any particular organ, Averroes came to the conclusion that the soul must be entirely separable from the particular physical form that a human being assumes, existing as a substance, somewhat in the manner of a pure Neoplatonic intelligence. In this case (to quote Boyde, p. 277), 'knowledge could be rented but not owned. Each individual could participate in the pool of intellect', but intellect was not in any way an essential part of its individuality. Nor would the intellective soul enjoy personal immortality. At death, the *intellectus possibilis* returned to the communal pool of intelligence.

No view could be less consistent with Dante's own. The Aristotelianism that he himself espouses insists that the human soul is the animating form of a physical form of life and inseparable from the body of a particular individual. (See Introduction, pp. xxvii–xxviii.) His theology is sustained by the belief – first inspired by Beatrice's death – that human beings live beyond their earthly death. The dramatic fiction of the *Commedia* involves at all points individuals who retain the marks of their intellectual and physical lives. So, a great deal depends upon the rebuttal of Averroes which Statius now utters. With appropriate solemnity of phrase (lines 67–72), Statius prepares to open up the truth, and for the first time brings God, the 'Primal Cause of Motion', into consideration. So far Statius has described the development until the point where it is complete in all its organs and limbs, as well as (Dante emphasizes) in its brain. But now God looks down on the excellent work that biological process has performed and breathes into it an intellective soul which renders it a new and particular human individual. This human being remains in certain aspects a vegetative and animal being. However, as was established in the opening lines of *Purgatorio* 4, there are not three animating principles at work in the individual but only one, which draws all others into its sphere of operations and exerts a self-conscious influence over all its activities, cerebral, animal or vegetative (lines 73–5). This soul, henceforth, can never be separated from the human being, nor can the body be seen (as Virgil suggests at lines 25–7) merely as a mirror image of the soul. As the heat of the sun combines with the juice of grapes to make wine (lines 77–8) and can never, afterwards, be distinguished from the wine itself, so the rational soul, granted by divine intervention, works in the individual as the absolute ground of what that individual is.

An important distinction is implied here (to be pursued in *Paradiso* 7: 67–9 and 124–44) between two modes of coming into being: generation and creation. Things can be 'generated' by the natural processes that God as Creator has set in motion or 'created' by a direct act of the Creator. Human beings are uniquely a product of both of these modes – body being generated, soul being given by God – and, again, once body and soul are united, their ultimate destiny at the Last Judgement and resurrection of the body is that body should never be separated from soul.

79–108 For Lachesis, see note to *Inferno* 33: 124–6. Statius here addresses Dante's initial question concerning the emaciation of the penitent gluttons and applies the preceding science to the 'science fiction' of Dante's narrative.

121 The hymn is the seventh-century '*Summae Deus clementiae*', usually sung late on a Saturday night in preparation for the Sabbath:

> O God of highest mercy, maker and ruler of these earthly workings, one in substance and in persons three, majestic Trinity in Unity. In love do graciously accept our songs mingled with our prayerful weeping, and so that, free at heart from stain and error, we may delight more fully in Thee. Burn out our loins and livers, diseased. And with appropriate fire put away all sinful lust, so that it may ever after be girded up. As we all interrupt the hours of night with our singing, so may we be enriched beyond desire with the riches of our homeland. Hear our prayer, Almighty King. And hear our praises while we sing, adoring with the heavenly choirs, the Father, Son and Holy Ghost.

The relevance of this to the lustful is immediately obvious. This is a prayer for sexual restraint, its message confirmed by the examples (lines 133–5) which conclude the canto in praise of married love. However, the introduction of the hymn at this stage also implies a theological parallel to the philosophical analysis that occupies the central verses of this canto. The point here is not simply to preach a lesson in conjugal fidelity. Dante, rather, is beginning to consider how human love may conjoin and collaborate with the divine love that is first displayed in the Trinity. '*Summae Deus clementiae*' is first and last concerned with the

action of the Trinity, with God as the maker of the universal sys-
tem and with the delight that is possible when we come home to
our proper place in the divine order. And sexuality, far from being
repressed, is viewed here – and, by implication, in Dante's text – as
a way of furthering divine action in the sphere of generated and
created existence.

**127–39** The examples of chastity are drawn, first, from the words of
the Virgin Mary to the Archangel Gabriel in Luke 1: 34: 'I know
not a man.' The second comes from Ovid's *Metamorphoses* 2:
401–507, which tells the story of Helice (or Callisto), a nymph of
Diana's company who is raped and made pregnant by Jupiter,
then driven from Diana's woods so that she cannot corrupt their
purity. When Callisto gives birth to a son, she is transformed by
the jealous Juno into a bear. But Jupiter further transforms her
and her son into the constellations of the Bear, Ursa Major and
Ursa Minor.

# CANTO 26

*The lustful. Dante meets with Guido*
*Guinizelli – whom he acknowledges as the father*
*of the sweet new style – and the Occitan*
*poet Arnaut Daniel.*

**40–42** For Sodom and Gomorrah as cities of decadence and corrup-
tion, see Genesis 18: 16 and 19: 1. For Pasiphae – who had an
artificial cow made which she could enter and so couple with a
young bull – see *Inferno* 12: 13 and Ovid, *Metamorphoses* 8:
738–40; also *Ars Amoris* 1: 290–326 and 2: 21–4.

**43–5** The metaphor of bird flight belongs to a rich vein of ornitho-
logical reference which began with the images of larks rising in
Occitan poetry and continues in Guinizelli's '*Al cor gentil . . .*'.
These references take a savage turn in Dante's own *Rime Pet-
rose*, where he is concerned in '*Io son venuto . . .*', as here, with
bird flight in the winter season. (Cf. *Inferno* 5: 46–8; *Purgatorio*
24: 64 and 25: 10–12; also *Paradiso* 18: 73–5 and 21: 34–6.)
The Riphean mountains, not recognized by modern geography,
are thought to have been located by classical geographers north-
west of the Carpathians, and are taken, for example by Orosius,
to have marked the northern boundary of Europe.

76–8 From Uguccione da Pisa (d. 1210), Dante may have heard recorded the story told by Suetonius of Julius Caesar's homosexuality, and of how he became the passive partner in a relationship with the king of Bithynia, so that his own troops greeted him with the cry of 'Queen!'

82–7 'Hermaphrodite' here means heterosexual. The story of Hermaphroditus is found in Ovid's *Metamorphoses* 4: 285–388. The son of Hermes and Aphrodite, he is loved by, but repels the advances of, the nymph Salamcis. She embraces him when he swims in her pool and, though he resists, she is granted her wish to be fused with him, producing a half-man.

91f Dante speaks to two poets, Guido Guinizelli and Arnaut Daniel (see note to 139–148), whom Guido designates the better maker in 'the mother tongue' (line 117). Guido Guinizelli (*c.* 1230–*c.* 1276) – who leads the discussion for most of this canto – was an academic jurist and judge from Bologna who in his early years had been associated with Guittone's circle of poets, and was reproved by Bonagiunta da Lucca (see note to *Purgatorio* 24: 19f) for 'changing his master's style' in favour of a supposedly oversubtle interest in matters of intellectual debate. To Dante, on the contrary, Guinizelli was responsible for a new and elevated conception of love, expressed with greater fluency than Guittone could command, particularly in the *canzone* '*Al cor gentil rempaira sempre amore*': 'Love always returns to the noble heart, as does the bird in the woodlands to the foliage. Nor did nature create love before it made the noble heart, or the noble heart before it created love.' These lines directly inspired Dante's own conviction, expressed in the sonnet '*Amor e 'l cor gentil sono una cosa* . . .' (*Vita nuova* 20), that love is the defining feature of true nobility, and that love itself can only exist where the heart is truly noble.

94–6 This very condensed and allusive reference recalls the story – which has been described as a 'romance' – told by Statius in the *Thebaid* 5: 499–753. The son of Lycurgus, king of Nemea, is left unattended by his nurse Hypsipyle. (Cf. *Purgatorio* 22: 88–9 and notes to *Purgatorio* 22.) Lycurgus demands that she be slain but she is recognized by two of Lycurgus's men who prove to be the sons whom she had deserted twenty years before, born to the Argonaut Jason who earlier had deserted her. (See *Inferno* 18: 88–94.) The sons, reunited with their mother after long separation, save her from the threat of death.

118–20 The 'poet from Limoges' is Giraut de Bornelh (*c.* 1150–1220), also referred to in *De Vulgari Eloquentia* 2: 5.

139–48 The Occitan poet Arnaut Daniel (*c.* 1180–*c.* 1210). An example of his often harsh virtuosity is to be found in the *canzone* '*Lo ferm voler* . . .' (cited by Dante in *De Vulgari Eloquentia* 2: 2: 9), which concludes:

> For thus my soul cleaves and clings with its nail to her, as close as the bark to the rod. For she is to me joy's tower, and palace and bedroom, and I love her more than I do cousin and uncle. Hence in Paradise will my soul have twofold joy, if ever a man through fine loving enters.
>
> Arnaut sends his song of fingernail and uncle for the pleasure of her who arms him with his rod to his desired One who with merit in bedroom enters.

Dante now at lines 140–7 offers verses of his own in the Occitan language, to dramatize Arnaut's voice. A literal translation is:

> So pleasing to me is your courteous request that I neither can nor will hide myself from you. I am Arnaut, who weeping and singing go on my way. With sadness I see my past foolishness and rejoicing I see ahead the joy for which I hope. Now I beg you by the power that guides you to the summit of the stair, remember my suffering.

Though these lines are much simpler in style than Arnaut's own poetry would have been, they do reflect a feature of his poems, which frequently conclude with a statement of his name and usually fraught identity: as in '*En cest sonnet coind' e leri* . . .', which ends with a picture of a distracted Arnaut ('I am Arnaut'/'*Ieu sui Arnaut*') who 'swims against the tide', 'seeks to catch the wind in a net' and goes out hunting on the back of a cow, not a horse.

# CANTO 27

*Dante passes into the fire that purges the lustful,*
*where he spends his final night on Mount Purgatory*
*and dreams of Rachel and Leah.*

1–6 If it is sunset in Purgatory, it is sunrise in Jerusalem and therefore midnight over the river Ebro in Spain and noon over the Ganges.

7–9 'Blessed are the pure in heart' is the sixth Beatitude (Matthew 5: 8).

22–4 For Geryon, see *Inferno* 17.

25–7 In Daniel 3: 27, Shadrack, Meshach and Abednego, placed by Nebuchadnezzar in a furnace, remain unharmed. Not a hair on their heads has been touched by fire.

37–9 In Ovid's *Metamorphoses* 4: 51–166, Pyramus, finding Thisbe's body mauled by a lion, supposes that she is dead and stabs himself. Thisbe, reviving, repeatedly calls his name, but he only responds when she utters her own. Pyramus's blood stains with red the hitherto white berries of the mulberry – a detail which led medieval allegorists to speak of Christ's death on the Cross. (Cf. *Purgatorio* 33: 67–9.)

58–60 'Come, ye blessed of my Father' (Matthew 25: 34). In the mosaics of the Baptistery in Florence, these words are depicted in the mouth of an angel at the Last Judgement.

94f Cytherea is Venus, who rose from the sea near Cythera in the Peloponnese. In Dante's Italian, the especially complex syntax of these lines delays '*donna*', as the subject of the sentence, in such a way as, first, to allow 'lovely and young' to refer, grammatically, either to Venus or the *donna* and then to replace Venus by attention to the *donna*. The primary allusion in lines 97–108 is to Genesis 29–30 where Jacob visits his uncle Laban and falls in love with his younger daughter, Rachel. Laban demands that Jacob should serve him for seven years, at the end of which time Rachel will be given to him in marriage. However, on the marriage night, Laban substitutes his elder daughter Leah, and only allows the marriage of Rachel and Jacob to proceed when Jacob has served a further seven years. Many children are born to Leah, but only two, the especially beloved Joseph and Benjamin, are born to Rachel after a long period of childlessness.

Dante must also have in mind here the allegorical use to which the Genesis story was put by Scriptural exegetes throughout the Middle Ages. He was probably thinking of Richard of Saint Victor's *Benjamin Minor* (*c.* 1160), in which Leah represents the active life of practical concern and Rachel the contemplative life of pure intelligence. Thus Richard writes that, after Leah had given birth to her sons, Rachel's desire for children of her own grew stronger:

As it is Leah's part to love, since she is the affection of the soul, so it is Rachel's part to know, for she is reason. The former gives birth to order and affection; the latter to the reason or the pure intelligence ... And when Judah is born, that is, when desire and love of unseen good things is rising and growing strong, then Rachel begins to desire children passionately, for she wants to know. Where love is there is vision. We like to look upon him whom we love greatly, and certainly he who can love invisible things will immediately desire to know and see them by intelligence.

> *Richard of Saint Victor: Selected Writings on Contemplation*
> trans. Clare Kirchberger (London, 1957), p. 91

109 In Dante's text '*antelucani*' – meaning 'before dawn', as does the rare English word 'antelucan' – is one of several rare words or neologisms that appear in this canto (others being, at lines 76, 78 and 83: '*manse*' ('tame' or 'mild'), '*pranse*' ('fed') and '*pernotta*' ('spend the night')).


# CANTO 28

*Dante arrives at the Earthly Paradise and encounters
a girl (later identified as Matelda) dancing and
gathering flowers on the far side of a stream. The girl
explains to him how the meteorological conditions of
the Earthly Paradise derive directly from the perfect
workings of the heavenly circles.*

1f The 'holy forest' (contrasting directly with the dark wood where Dante began his journey in *Inferno* 1) is the setting for the next six cantos. Dante describes it as the Earthly Paradise, which is significant considering in *De Monarchia* that he declares it is possible for human beings under a rule of perfect justice to enjoy beatitude on earth as well as in Heaven. But this place is also the Golden World that classical poets speak of and the site of the Garden of Eden (lines 139–44). The region is traversed by two rivers, issuing from a single source (121–6; see also *Purgatorio* 33: 127). However, the waters from that source are produced, not by the natural cycles of evaporation and precipitation, but directly at the will of God. Dante cannot cross this stream – on the other side of which he first sees Matelda (see note to line 40f) and then a great procession (*Purgatorio* 29) heralding the approach of Beatrice (*Purgatorio* 30). In *Purgatorio* 31: 94–105, he is drawn through the first of these streams – Lethe, the classical river of oblivion – in a form of baptism, freed from any memory of sin. In *Purgatorio* 33, he is refreshed in the second stream, Eunoe – a word of Dante's own invention based on the Greek lexis, '*eu*-' signifying good or well and '*-noesis*' signifying knowledge, hence translatable as 'happy thinking and remembrance' – and recovers the memory of the good deeds he has performed in his lifetime.

19–21 These pine woods, extending more than eighteen miles along the shore around Ravenna, can be identified from Dante's reference in the Italian text to Chiasso ('*Chiassi*'), the port of Roman and medieval Ravenna, now abandoned save for the basilica of Saint Apollinare. The scirocco is the warm southerly wind blowing from the coast of Africa.

40f The '*donna*' is Matelda (named at *Purgatorio* 33: 119). Where the Earthly Paradise represents the natural order in its perfect state, Matelda represents the enjoyment that human beings may derive from a full participation in that order, which they acquire by the exercise of their moral and intellectual virtues. In this sense, she is the new Eve, showing what Eve would have enjoyed if she had not been distracted from the path of obedience and justice. In this sense, too, she is an embodiment of all that Virgil would have been if he had been capable of taking 'what pleases you to be your guide' (*Purgatorio* 27: 131) or if (to put it differently) his own virtues had not been severed from fulfilment by the as-yet unredeemed repercussions of the Fall.

It is for reasons such as this that some critics (including Dante's son, Pietro, in his notes of about 1340) identify this dancing figure as Matelda, countess of Canossa (1046–1115), a powerful supporter of the Church, in whose courtyard the emperor Henry IV (1050–1106) was obliged to kneel in the snow and display his allegiance to the pope. The Earthly Paradise is a realm of justice such as Dante, in his political philosophy, regularly supposes might be brought about in temporal circumstances by the ideal emperor. However, once established, the order of justice is consistent with, and prepares for, the revelation of the order of grace, which the Church is commissioned to announce. Debate continues as to the validity (or usefulness) of so precise an identification of Matelda. None the less, this reading is broadly consistent with the allegorical role that she performs in subsequent cantos.

Though Beatrice, throughout these cantos, profoundly calls into question the competence of the human intellect in making any approach to the mysteries of divine existence, it is Matelda who stands surety for the enduring value of these virtues, once their relation to God's mystery is properly recognized. Dante must lose himself in the river Lethe. It is Matelda who acts as his baptismal advocate and sponsor, drawing him through the stream while she herself walks on its waves as the transfigured image of perfected humanity. (See *Purgatorio* 31: 91–102.)

Such a reading should not obscure the significance that derives from Matelda's position in the developing narrative, and from the lyric appeal of the verses in which Dante describes her. In narrative terms, her presence confirms the modulation that occurred at the end of *Purgatorio* 27, where feminine presences begin to displace the male guides on whom Dante has so far been dependent. (Virgil is henceforth silent, while Statius remains a vestigial figure, only intermittently visible.) Matelda is the first of the *donne* – or nymphs, as the poet frequently describes them – who now bring Dante to perfect readiness for Heaven.

In imagining the garden as a pastoral scene, Dante draws not only on classical and Virgilian models but also upon the *pastorelle* of the vernacular tradition, which concentrates less upon the perfections of the natural landscape than upon those of the people that inhabit it, and is frequently erotic in its implications. A poet will see a peasant girl or shepherdess, describe her beauty, recognize that she is ready for love and proceed to a (delicately veiled) consummation. An example that Dante would have known is Cavalcanti's '*In un boschetta trova' pastorella . . .*' (lines 3–8 and 26): 'Her sweet hair was blonde, with little curls, her eyes full of love, her complexion rosy; with her staff she was pasturing lambs; her bare feet were wet with dew. She was singing as if she were in love. She was adorned with every beauty . . . [She took me by the hand] . . . and there I seemed to see the god of love.'

64–6 Venus was accidentally wounded by Cupid's arrows and consequently fell in love with Adonis. (See Ovid, *Metamorphoses* 10: 525–739.)

70–75 Xerxes crossed the Hellespont (now known as the Dardanelles) in 480 BC to launch an attack on Greece, but was defeated at Salamis and put to flight. Leander swam across the narrowest part of the strait between Sestos and Abydos to meet his secret lover Hero, until, risking the winter storms, he drowned. Hero then drowned herself. (See Ovid, *Heroides* 18–19 and Virgil, *Georgics* 3: 258–63.)

79–81 In *Purgatorio* 28, a constant point of reference is the verse '*Delectasti* . . .', to which Matelda here alludes, where (in the Vulgate if less so in the Authorized Version of the Bible) the singer speaks of the all-consuming delight that God offers to those who take pleasure in His creation: 'For thou, Lord, hast made me glad through thy work: I will triumph in the works of thy hand' (Vulgate, Psalm 91: 5–6).

88f In the second phase of the canto, Matelda discusses the way in which winds and weathers are regulated in this place. This is the site of Eden – the garden that God intended humanity to enjoy, undying, to eternity (lines 91–6). Rising far above any mountain in the northern hemisphere, the garden is unaffected by the confusions that occur in the lower parts of the physical world and is governed only by the perfect movements of the heavenly spheres that God has set in motion. These movements generate, without impediment, the entirely harmonious and fertile conditions that prevail here. The reference at lines 103–5 is to the *Primum Mobile* (see *Paradiso* 27–30), the transparent outer heaven which, while itself unmoving, creates motion, east to west, in all heavens below it and in the sphere of air that surrounds the earth.

130–32 The river Lethe is spoken of by name in classical literature as, for instance, by Virgil at *Aeneid* 6: 748. For the word 'Eunoe', see note to lines 1f.

139–41 Parnassus is the hill sacred to Apollo and the Muses near Delphi. (Cf. *Purgatorio* 31: 139–45 and *Paradiso* 1: 16–18.) For the Age of Gold as foretold by classical poets, see the notes to *Purgatorio* 22.

# CANTO 29

*Led by Matelda from the far side of the stream,*
*Dante witnesses a procession representing the*
*revelation of divine truth.*

1–3 The Latin verse – 'Blessed are those whose sins are [covered] taken away' – is a version of the first verse of Psalm 32, a penitential psalm which looks forward, like the procession of revelation depicted here, to the redemptive action of God in history.

16f The burst of light (defeating Virgil's powers of comprehension,
enlivening Dante's own (lines 55–7)) heralds the beginning of a
procession – rich in allegorical detail – that will unroll through-
out the final cantos of *Purgatorio*, reaching its climax with the
arrival of two figures that, each in their own way, represent the
presence and being of Christ. The first is Beatrice, Dante's 'God-
bearing image' (to use Charles Williams's famous phrase in
*The Figure of Beatrice* (London, 1943)), who has borne to him
throughout his life an understanding of God's presence in the
world. The second, who draws the triumphal chariot, symbolic
of the true Church, in which Beatrice rides, is the Gryphon, the
mystic emblem of Christ in his twofold nature, both human and
divine. The head and spine of the Gryphon are those of an eagle,
as are its wings, and are gold, designating its incorruptible nobil-
ity. Its other parts are those of a lion, coloured red and white, to
betoken Christ's passionate and vulnerable humanity and his
total purity (lines 113–14).

In the climax to *Purgatorio* 31, these two images of Christ are
brought into harmony when Dante sees the Gryphon reflected in
Beatrice's eyes. In this canto, Dante's concern is with the ways in
which, as a preparation for the coming of Christ, God – through-
out history and in the traditions of Scripture – has progressively
revealed His truth to the world. The Christian Church is the
inheritor of this tradition (though often failing in its mission, as
*Purgatorio* 32 and 33 make clear). The allegory in which this
vision is expressed over the next five cantos displays, in more
concentrated form than any other episode of the *Commedia*,
Dante's close and original reading of Scriptural texts and his
sensitivity to the imagery of the Christian liturgy.

Over the whole procession run seven streamers of light in the
seven colours of the rainbow, trailing back from seven candle-
sticks at the head of the column (lines 76–8), referring to
Revelation 1: 12–13. Allegorically, these bands of light are usu-
ally taken to represent the seven gifts of God's Holy Spirit, which
fall upon human virtue and bring it to perfection. These gifts are:
wisdom, understanding, counsel, fortitude, knowledge, piety
and fear of the Lord. (See also Isaiah 11: 2.) The poet imagines
very precisely how the central streamer of the seven flows
between the Gryphon's wings, with three streams on either side
of each wing (lines 109–11), so that these eternal gifts are not
interrupted but centred and directed by the incarnate presence of
Christ.

The vanguard of the procession is formed by twenty-four venerable old men (lines 83–4), who represent the twenty-four books of the Old Testament (on Saint Jerome's reckoning), through which, in anticipation of Christ's coming, God first spoke to the Jewish people. (See Revelation 4: 1–8.) The lilies on their heads are symbols of faith in the Redeemer still to come, and of justice. (Cf. *Paradiso* 18: 92–108.) The lily is also the flower associated with the Virgin Mary, whose faith in God is the highest expression of the Jewish tradition and makes the Incarnation possible. The '*Benedicta*' which the elders sing (at line 85) is a part of the greeting offered by the Angel Gabriel to Mary at the Annunciation, repeated by Elisabeth, mother of John the Baptist, at Luke 1: 42.

Lines 91–153 represent the arrival of the Christian era. The chariot in which Beatrice rides is drawn by a cruciform pole – which is symbolic of Christ's Cross and will play a significant part in subsequent cantos, particularly at *Purgatorio* 32: 49–60. The wheels of the chariot probably represent (as at *Paradiso* 1: 106–8) the two mendicant orders of friars, the Franciscans and the Dominicans, which Dante regarded as the supreme defenders of the true faith in his own day. Dante alludes to the four-winged creatures that surround the chariot (lines 91–6). These are the four evangelists, Matthew, Mark, Luke and John, who expound the meaning of Christ's life on earth. As the poet says, he has in mind here Ezekiel (line 100) and Revelation (line 105), which establish the traditional symbolism that sees Saint Mark as a lion, Saint John as an eagle, Saint Luke as an ox and Saint Matthew as a man – all winged, even though Ezekiel and Saint John differ as to the number of their wings, Dante claiming that his version is supported by Saint John's.

37–42 The virgins are the Muses. Helicon is the mountain sacred to Apollo and the Muses. (Cf. *Paradiso* 1: 13–27.) Urania is the Muse of geometry and celestial things. (Cf. the invocation to Calliope at *Purgatorio* 1: 7–9.)

43–8 This refers to the medieval concept of common sensibles (number, size and shape), which are perceived by many of the senses – as contrasted, say, with colour or perfume, which are perceived particularly by the eye or the sense of smell.

76–8 Delia, in classical mythology, is Diana, associated with haloes round the moon.

91–105 Argus was the hundred-eyed monster who guarded Io in Ovid's *Metamorphoses* 1: 622–723. (Cf. *Purgatorio* 32: 64–6.)

115–20 Scipio Africanus the Younger (185–129 BC) defeated Carthage in 146 BC; Scipio the Elder (235–183 BC) defeated the Carthaginian Hannibal at Zama in 202 BC. (It is not certain which of these two Dante is referring to.) Augustus Caesar (63 BC–AD 14) was the first emperor of Rome; for his triple triumph, see Virgil, *Aeneid* 8: 715. For Phaeton, see Ovid, *Metamorphoses* 2: 107–9 and *Inferno* 17: 106–8.

121–48 It is part of the function of the evangelists, represented here as winged creatures (see note to lines 16f), to carry forward and accompany the mysteries of Christ's presence on earth. For that reason, it is appropriate that even Matthew, symbolized as a man, should be rendered mysterious by the wings with which he is endowed. But now (line 121) the procession begins to return to the representation of recognizably human forms. The era depicted is that of the Holy Spirit, which, descending to earth after Christ's resurrection, lives with and strengthens human intentions. Available in this new age are the theological virtues, here represented in the surrealistic but liturgical colours of the three nymphs on the right of the chariot (lines 121–6), where Faith is pure white, Charity is red and Hope is green. On the left of the chariot (lines 130–32) are the moral virtues – Wisdom (bearing a third, all-seeing eye on her brow), Courage, Justice and Temperance – which are acknowledged as necessary if any social order is to flourish, and therefore clothed in Roman purple to associate them with the rectitude that is assured by the rule of imperial justice.

The figures that follow at lines 133–42 represent the Scriptural books that were written in the earliest years of the Church. In the first pair of elders are the Acts of the Apostles, written by the physician Saint Luke and clothed accordingly in the manner of the founder of Greek medicine, Hippocrates. With him is a figure identified by the sword he bears as Saint Paul – since in his letter to the Ephesians 6: 17 he speaks of 'the sword of the Spirit, which is the word of God' – and representing the fourteen Epistles of Saint Paul. The four men with 'humble looks' (line 142) signify the minor Epistles, written by James, Peter, John and Jude. The last figure (line 143) represents Revelation, and is sleeping 'face alert' to signify the mystic rapture of Saint John's vision.

# CANTO 30

*Dante encounters Beatrice and realizes that Virgil has disappeared. Beatrice speaks to the angels surrounding her, explaining why she needs to be harsh in her treatment of Dante.*

1–6 The seven gifts of the spirit (represented in the procession by the seven-branched candlestick: see *Purgatorio* 29: 73–5) are viewed, in Dante's metaphor, in terms of the seven brightest stars of the constellation Ursa Minor. As these seven stars give guidance to earthly seafarers, so too do the gifts of the spirit sustain and guide the Church.

10–21 *'Veni, sponsa, de Libano!'* ('Come with me from Lebanon, my spouse'), uttered three times (lines 11–12), is a cry of love and desire from the Song of Solomon 4: 8 – the great expression of erotic love which, by Dante's time, had come to be read allegorically as an account of the loving relationship between God and His creation. (See notes to *Paradiso* 14.) Here the cry expresses a yearning for the mystic marriage that will only come when Christ is reunited with His Church. This moment will be marked by the victory cry of 'Alleluia' (line 15), which greets the resurrection of Christ at Easter, and which, in the liturgy of the Mass, immediately precedes the reading of the Gospel. This is appropriate if Dante is alluding in this episode to the drama of the Mass, in which Christ's continual presence in time is realized anew. (The Latin phrase at line 16 – 'at the voice of the great elder' – appears to have been devised by Dante himself.) *'Benedictus qui venis!'* ('Blessed is he who comes [in the name of the Lord]!') at line 19 is sung in the Mass at the end of the *'Sanctus'*, in which the congregation on earth joins with the song 'Holy, holy, holy' sung by the angels in Heaven, and immediately precedes the transubstantiation of bread and wine into the body and blood of Christ. The *'Benedictus'* is thus another cry of anticipation, in this case directed to the mystery of Christ's continuing presence on earth in the Eucharist. Finally, these expressions of longing and faith are daringly juxtaposed at line 21 with phrases adapted from Virgil's *Aeneid* 6: 883: *'date manibus lilia plenis . . .'* ('give me lilies with full hands . . .'), which describes the eager (but frustrated) desire of the spirits in the underworld to celebrate the beauty and goodness of Marcellus (42–23 BC), nephew of Emperor Augustus, lamenting that he (like Beatrice) died all too young. Placing Virgil's words here suggests how deeply indebted Dante is to Virgil's text but also how far we have travelled from the depths of a Virgilian underworld – the inhabitants of which are all reduced to melancholic shadow – to a realm in which the human person is nourished by the presence of Christ.

22–39 Attention shifts from the workings of providence and revelation to focus directly upon Dante's perception of and involvement in the unfolding scene with the emphatic 'I saw . . .'. These lines also call into consideration the whole development of Dante's love poetry from the time of the *Vita nuova*. There are recognizable affinities in the diction and rhythmic effect of the Italian text between this and his earlier work, particularly in recording the extreme refinement of visual perception that his love for Beatrice has brought – as, for instance, in '*Vede perfettamente onne salute . . .*' ('He sees perfectly all health and salvation . . .') (*Vita nuova* 26). In particular, lines 34–9 recall those phases of the *Vita nuova* when the poet was still under the influence of Guido Cavalcanti's melancholic understanding of love (see *Inferno* 10), and love was, as here, a power that shook the self-possession of the lover to the point of fear and trembling. In picturing Beatrice's dress, Dante alludes to the colours of red, green and white that were associated with her in the *Vita nuova*. Now, in the allegorical setting of the procession, he endows them with emblematic significance as references to faith, hope and charity and also – in his newly developed devotion – to classical literature. Dante now produces a fusion of Christian and classical symbolism, in that the olive crown that Beatrice wears associates her with Minerva, the Roman goddess of wisdom and warlike defender of civic order.

46–8 The final words that Dante addresses to Virgil are an exact translation of Virgil's Dido when in the *Aeneid* 4: 23 she recognizes her feelings of love for Aeneas. Virgil's '*agnosco veteris vestigia flammae*' becomes '*conosco i segni de l'antica fiamma*' ('I recognize the signs of ancient flame'). Notice that these words are never actually spoken, since Virgil has now disappeared. In quoting Dido, Dante is associating himself with a figure for whom love proves to be a force of utter destruction when, deserted by Aeneas, she commits suicide. Even as she speaks, Dido experiences guilt at the thought that she is betraying her first husband, the long-dead Sichaeus. The love that Dante has to record, however, is the redemptive kind which displays itself in the resurrection of the once-dead Beatrice. If Dante has reason to feel guilty – as he does – this is because he has diverted his eyes from the true significance of Beatrice's death on earth.

61–3 In *Convivio* 1: 2: 13–14, Dante argues that there are only two occasions on which an author may legitimately name himself in his own writings: when he seeks to clear his reputation of blame (as Boethius did in his *Consolation of Philosophy*), and when he may offer an improving example to others (like Saint Augustine in his *Confessions*). Both reasons apply here. Granted the privilege of returning to Eden – the original homeland of humanity – Dante implicitly demonstrates the injustice of his exile from Florence, but, in allowing Beatrice to lay bare his failings, he makes an example of his own transgressions.

82–4 The quotation is from Psalm 31: 1–8, which speaks of the 'large room' into which God's mercy will liberate the afflicted:

> In thee, O Lord, do I put my trust; let me never be ashamed: deliver me in thy righteousness … Into thine hand I commit my spirit: thou hast redeemed me, O Lord God of truth … I will be glad and rejoice in thy mercy: for thou hast considered my trouble; thou hast known my soul in adversities; And hast not shut me up into the hand of the enemy: thou hast set my feet in a large room.

The 'large room' here is hope – the theological virtue that will bring Dante through the confusions and shame of the present moment into the spaciousness, inhabited already by the angels, of God's providential presence. (See notes on *Paradiso* 25.)

124–6 The 'another' referred to here may reasonably taken to be the '*donna gentile*' who in the *Vita nuova* offers Dante consolation after Beatrice's death. On Dante's own allegorical interpretation (as developed in the *Convivio*), this 'lady' may be taken as an embodiment of all those consolations of philosophy and scientific inquiry to which Dante now turned. Necessary as these were to him – in the way that Virgil is necessary – they could also be seen as a betrayal of Beatrice in that they distracted Dante from the religious significance of her life and death.

# CANTO 31

*Turning to Dante, Beatrice elicits a confession from
him, after which he is drawn through Lethe. He then
sees the Gryphon reflected in Beatrice's eyes, and she
finally turns her unveiled eyes upon Dante himself.*

58–60 The *'pargoletta'* (translated as 'girl') may be associated with the
'stony lady' of Dante's *Rime Petrose*. Beatrice has now assumed
some of the characteristics of this daunting and resistant figure. Of
the *'pargoletta'*, Dante writes in *'Chi guarderà già . . .'* (1–4): 'Who
will look into this lovely girl's eyes that have so affected me that
all I can do is await death, which is so harsh to me?'

70–72 Iarbas, king of the Gaetulians in the vicinity of Carthage – known
for their savagery (Virgil, *Aeneid* 4: 196) – once wooed Dido.

88–90 A direct echo of *Inferno* 5: 142 and also *Purgatorio* 5: 135.
Having earlier emphasized that love is the way to death unless
it involves conscious and intelligent responsibility, Dante now
recognizes that it can also be expressed in surrender. God's love
requires no less than this. (See *Paradiso* 33: 76–102, where there
are also echoes of *Inferno* 5.) Dante's passivity in his response to
Beatrice anticipates this final surrender.

97–8 The words *'Asperges me'* ('Sprinkle me [that I may be clean]'),
from Psalm 51: 7, were at one time used by priests in giving
absolution after confession.

124–41 The reader is asked to recognize how far beyond the reach of
words Dante's experience is, even for those who have studied
long and hard at the school of the Muses on Mount Parnassus.

# CANTO 32

*Beatrice prepares Dante to carry the understanding
he has gained in the other world back to the earth,
showing him both the history of how the sin of Adam
was redeemed and also how corrupt the Church and
political order of the world have subsequently become.*

1f The allegorical procession that began in *Purgatorio* 29 takes on a
range of new meanings, raising many of the issues concerning

events in ecclesiastical and political history that, in preceding parts of the *Commedia*, have been the subjects of explicit and precisely focused attacks – as, for instance, in the assault on the corruptions of particular popes in *Inferno* 19. These attacks will resume in the *Paradiso* – very violently in cantos 27 and 29. But here, in place of open polemic, Dante creates a phantasmagoria of often grotesque metamorphoses, which require a sustained attempt at coherent interpretation. A related aspect of the sequence is Dante's continuing reflection on his own poetic mission. Most notably, at lines 103–5, Beatrice speaks of how, in contemplating the present vision, Dante should prepare himself to return to the temporal world that 'lives all wrong', and speak of what he has seen for the moral benefit of his fellow men. Cf. *Paradiso* 17: 124–42, in which Dante's ancestor, the Crusader Cacciaguida, prepares his descendant for the crusading mission that he will pursue on earth, and urges Dante to name those who corrupt the world.

The canto divides into four movements:

Lines 1–30: The first movement describes the changed direction of the procession as it turns to march towards the rising sun – and thus, symbolically, towards its origins in God's light.

Lines 31–60: The second movement evokes the mystery of the Fall and the Atonement, as the parade contemplates the tree where Adam committed the first of sins, now redeemed through Christ – here represented by the Gryphon. So, at lines 49–60, the effects of Christ's Atonement for Adam's sin, in the Crucifixion, are pictured, when the cruciform pole by which the chariot is drawn is attached to the leafless tree, which at once bursts into new life. (Legend has it that the wood of the Cross derived from the tree of knowledge.) Finally, when life surges back into the tree (lines 52–60), the flowers that are produced are symbolic in their coloration. Their scarcely perceptible mingling of rose red and blackish violet produces a dark crimson hue. Red is the colour of charity, and violet purple is the colour of imperial justice. The dark crimson is associated with the blood of Christ's Passion, in which just retribution for Adam's sin is combined with the absolute charity of God as Creator.

Lines 61–85: The third movement speaks of how sleep overcomes Dante – of a *lacuna* in which his powers as a poet desert him, and of when, on waking, he finds that Beatrice has momentarily left him. Dante does not understand the hymn that is sung as the tree comes to life, and, unable to bear the sweetness of the

song, he falls asleep. The reader, too, is here drawn away from
the immediate action by two cryptic and highly allusive similes.
The first involves a story told in Ovid's *Metamorphoses* 1: 622–
723, to which Dante has already made an equally oblique
reference, at *Purgatorio* 29: 95–6. Argus – who has a hundred
eyes all round his head and is described by Ovid as 'star-
eyed' – has been commissioned to guard Io, the victim of Jupiter's
lust, whom Juno, out of jealousy, has transformed into a cow.
Jupiter, however, sends Mercury to rescue her. He decapitates
Argus, having charmed him into sleep by telling him the tale of
Syrinx (line 65), who herself had been transformed, when fleeing
from the danger of rape, into the shape of pan pipes. The second
refers to the Transfiguration of Christ – as recorded in Luke 9:
28–36, Matthew 17 and Mark 9: 1–8. Saint John was present at
the Transfiguration, and is thought to be alluding to it when, in
his Gospel, he speaks of how 'we beheld his glory, the glory as of
the only begotten of the Father' (1: 14). Luke records the episode
as follows:

> [Jesus] took Peter and John and James, and went up into a moun-
> tain to pray.
> And as he prayed, the fashion of his countenance was altered,
> and his raiment was white and glistering.
> And, behold, there talked with him two men, which were Moses
> and Elias:
> Who appeared in glory, and spake of his decease which he
> should accomplish at Jerusalem.
> But Peter and they that were with him were heavy with sleep:
> and when they were awake, they saw his glory, and the two men
> that stood with him.
> And it came to pass, as they departed from him, Peter said unto
> Jesus, Master, it is good for us to be here: and let us make three
> tabernacles; one for thee, and one for Moses, and one for Elias: not
> knowing what he said.

Lines 86–160: The fourth movement describes the enactment
of a masque showing the seven afflictions of the Church, the
early persecutions it suffered and its subsequent corruption in
the hands of contemporary popes. Witnessing the degradations
to which the Church has been subject throughout its history,
Beatrice – in terms of allegory – offers a constant image of all
that the Church should, properly, have sought to defend and

celebrate. The drama of the masque goes through seven acts, in which Dante continues to cite and modify Scriptural references, particularly to the writings of Ezekiel and Saint John. At each point he is especially interested in the often disastrous relationship between Church and State.

The first of these acts (lines 112–17) refers to the persecutions that the early Church suffered under Nero (AD 37–68) and Diocletian (AD 243–316). This is followed by the second (lines 118–23), with a reference to the early heresies – principally perhaps Gnosticism – by which the primitive Church was afflicted. The figure of false prophecy as a vixen (here driven away by Beatrice in the role of embodied truth) draws on Ezekiel 13: 4 and the Song of Solomon 2: 15. The third phase (lines 124–9) pictures the moment at which the Church received from Emperor Constantine (AD 272–337) the very equivocal gift of power and wealth, which Dante constantly sees as the source of an ill-judged mixing of secular and spiritual power. (See especially *Inferno* 19.) The chariot of the Church thus becomes confused with the 'feathers' of the imperial eagle. The voice from Heaven grieving over the Church may be that of Saint Peter, as recorded in the apocryphal Acts of Saint Peter. (Cf. the violent diatribe that Dante gives to Saint Peter in *Paradiso* 27.) The fourth assault (lines 130–35) on the Church probably refers to the sudden rise of Islam in the seventh century, and is connected to the second attack, in so far as Mohammed was thought to be a heretic and schismatic (see *Inferno* 28) – hence the emphasis upon the effects of splintering. The fifth phase (lines 136–41) probably refers to further grants of land and property by well-intentioned precursors of the medieval Holy Roman Empire: Pepin the younger (714–68) and Charlemagne (742–814), in 755 and 775. The further confusion of Church and State brought about by Pepin and Charlemagne prepares for the corruption that Dante vividly perceives in the Church of his own day. In general but graphic terms, the sixth act (lines 142–7) imagines the grotesque transformation of the Church, as bride of Christ, into a deformed, seven-headed monstrosity. Dante follows Revelation 13: 1 very closely: 'And I stood upon the sand of the sea, and saw a beast rise up out of the sea, having seven heads and ten horns . . .'

In the seventh and final transformation (lines 148–60), the Whore of Babylon (drawn from Revelation 17: 1) – the Church as the now-corrupted bride of Christ – is seen in dalliance with the kings of France, who in the fourteenth century came to exert a particularly strong ('giant') influence over papal policy. The seductive talk between the whore and the giant may represent the diplomatic negotiations between Pope Boniface VIII (*c.* 1235–1303) and Charles de Valois (1270–1325) which led to the invasion of Italy in 1301. The beating of the whore might refer to the humiliating treatment meted out to Boniface by the French. (Cf. *Purgatorio* 20.) The removal of the chariot to the wood probably refers to the removal of the papal seat to Avignon in 1309 – from where it only returned in 1378.

No reliable explanation can be offered for lines 154–6, where the whore casts her lascivious eye on Dante – though he is always aware of the malign effect that French interference has on the Florentine politics of his day. (See *Purgatorio* 20.) There is, however, significance in the grotesque comedy of this episode. Eyes and eyesight, cupidity and contemplation have been an issue throughout the last two cantos. Dante is now distant from all danger of sin, having passed through Lethe. It is an expression of contemplative confidence that he should be able to imagine, in the wandering eyes of the whore, a parodic reversal of that constantly shifting but always steady image of Christ that he saw at the end of *Purgatorio* 31 reflected in Beatrice's eyes.

97–9 The Aquilonian are northern winds and the Austral are southern.

109–11 In the fourteenth century, lightning was thought to be vapour that ignited by friction in a cloud and exploded from the cloud towards the earth. (Cf. *Purgatorio* 5: 37, 21: 49–53 and 28: 97–9.)

# CANTO 33

*Beatrice prophesies the coming of salvation for the world. Dante is refreshed in the stream of Eunoe.*

1–12 Two Scriptural references introduce the canto. The first is from the opening of Psalm 79:

O God, the heathen are come into thine inheritance; thy holy temple have they defiled; they have laid Jerusalem on heaps.

The dead bodies of thy servants have they given to be meat unto the fowls of heaven, the flesh of thy saints unto the beasts of the earth.

This refers to the destruction of the Temple in Jerusalem by Nebuchadnezzar (605–562 BC) in 587 BC, and contemplates the total defeat of God's chosen people. Yet, in the perspective of the New Testament, and particularly of Revelation, the absolute victory of evil is viewed as the direct preparation for the Second Coming of Christ in judgement. (Cf. *Inferno* 18–30 and notes to *Inferno* 17.) In that sense, the psalm is rightly to be read in conjunction with the second Scriptural reference, which recalls the words of Christ as recorded at John 16: 10–19. These same words, in anticipating the Passion and resurrection of Christ, speak of how utter hopelessness – waiting without hope – is the very condition of faith through which true hope will be renewed.

31f The following lines contain much that is (deliberately) enigmatic and allusive. Beatrice prophesies an end to the evils that were witnessed in the Masque of the Church. Referring to God's vengeance at lines 34–6, Beatrice's first target (lines 34–9) is (probably) the unholy alliance between the Church and the kings of France, which led eventually to the transferral of the papal throne to Avignon – the 'vessel that the serpent broke' being the Church. (See notes to *Purgatorio* 32.) Dante's phrasing here recalls Revelation 17: 8: 'The beast that thou sawest was, and is not; and shall ascend out of the bottomless pit, and go into perdition.' The beast of ecclesiastical corruption will be consigned eternally to Hell when salvation comes. The time of salvation is close at hand – but is designated by a ghoulish reference to medieval conventions of sanctuary whereby, according to early commentators, a murderer, if he succeeded in eating a sop of bread for three days in succession while seated on the grave of his victim, would escape revenge. God's vengeance cannot be eluded.

The agent of salvation that Beatrice speaks of may be Christ in judgement. But since, for Dante, the emperor is the representative of Christ's justice on earth, he speaks (at lines 37–8) of the Saviour as heir to the imperial Eagle. The eagle left its 'feathers on the cart' when Constantine ill-advisedly endowed the Church with temporal power (see notes to *Purgatorio* 32), making it into a 'monster' and laying it open, eventually, to the corrupting ambitions of France. The promised saviour who will destroy both the corruption of the Church and the pretensions of the French is referred to in an impenetrable piece of numerological symbolism: 'FIVE HUNDRED TEN AND FIVE' (line 43). From the

point at which (in *Inferno* 1: 100–105) Dante first referred to the
saviour of the world as the '*veltro*' or 'hunting hound', all such
references have been deliberately cryptic, and commentators
have expended great ingenuity on attempting to solve what
Dante has, in all likelihood, been at pains to make insoluble.
Most agree that the reference is to an imperial authority. Others,
however, reverse the Latin numerals DXV to yield VXD, and
see in this a liturgical acronym for the words that, in the Mass,
immediately precede the Canon – '*Vero dignum et iustum*' ('It is
truly fitting and just').

46–51  Themis, mother of Prometheus, is enraged by the success of
the Naiads in solving the riddle of the Sphinx, which she could
not solve, and causes their territories to be devastated, as Ovid
tells in *Metamorphoses* 7: 749–65. Dante has misread Ovid's
text, which refers properly to 'Laiades' not 'Naiades' (Oedipus
being the son of Laius).

67–9  The Tuscan river Elsa is rich in calcium carbonate, which coats
objects dipped in it with a mineral crust. In Ovid's *Metamorphoses*
4: 162–6, the blood of the dying lover Pyramus stains the white
fruit of the mulberry tree dark red. (Cf. *Purgatorio* 27: 37–9.)

85–90  Beatrice here mounts an attack – which has been implicit
since the disappearance of Virgil – on the competence of purely
intellectual understanding. The many deliberate enigmas that
punctuate this canto are an indication of the limits that need to
be recognized in confronting the workings of providence. Her
words recall the way in which Christ himself spoke of his own
enigmatic parables in John 16: 25: 'These things have I spoken
unto you in proverbs: but the time cometh, when I shall no more
speak unto you in proverbs, but I shall shew you plainly of the
Father.'

103–14  Dante now approaches the river Eunoe (see note to *Purga-
torio* 28: 1f) where he will refresh himself and recover the
memory of the good deeds he has performed in his lifetime.
Eunoe rises from the same source as Lethe but branches off in a
different direction, as if the two streams were friends parting
unwillingly. The reference to the Tigris and Euphrates at lines
112–14 recalls that they were thought to be two of the four riv-
ers of Eden (Genesis 2: 10–14) – the other two being Gihon and
Pison, identified by Saint Augustine as the Nile and the Ganges.

# PARADISO

## CANTO 1

*An invocation to Apollo. Although at the beginning
of the canto Dante is still in the Earthly Paradise,
he then begins to rise towards the heavens
and Beatrice explains why.*

1f The word 'glory' ('*gloria*' in Dante's Italian) has a richer meaning than
it possesses in modern English, carrying – as do cognate words such
as the adjective '*glorioso*' ('glorious') – biblical, theological, liturgi-
cal and also military associations. In Latin the word derives from
'*gloriari*' ('to boast') and thus can be associated with triumphal dis-
plays of power and merit (as in *Paradiso* 23: 139). In biblical terms,
the word refers to the display of God's power and beauty in the cre-
ated world, thus referring to the glory of God, his majesty, power
and light. These are the visible and comprehensible manifestations
of divine light (though distinct from God himself). Psalm 19: 1,
among many other psalms, uses 'glory' in this sense: 'The heavens
declare the glory of God; and the firmament sheweth his handy-
work.' The ancient hymn 'Glory to God in the highest' is sung early
in the liturgy of the Mass. (Cf. *Paradiso* 27: 1–2.)

From the *Vita nuova* 1: 2 onwards, Dante associates the word
'glory' with Beatrice, as when he describes her as '*la gloriosa donna
della mia mente*' ('the glorious sovereign lady of my mind'). In
the *Paradiso* the full meaning of such designations becomes
clear. Beatrice is the principal reflection of divine light to Dante
and the element in which his spiritual life is lived. She also reflects
the 'triumph' of the Creator over death, in that it is through her
death that Dante realizes the full significance of the Resurrec-
tion. In this sense, too, human flesh is referred to in *Paradiso* 14:
43 as '*la carne gloriosa e santa*' ('the glorious and sacred flesh').
Here, as in Beatrice, the human form is celebrated as God's
ultimate creation and triumph.

4–6 The Empyrean, the 'sphere' that Dante enters in *Paradiso* 30, is
the presence of God, a realm of purely intellectual light and love.
(See also lines 121–3.) However, before arriving at that height,
Dante imagines himself passing through all the intermediate
spheres of the created universe, visiting in turn each of the plan-
etary heavens. (See Plan of Paradise, p. lxv.) Note that the first

three planetary spheres – the moon, Mercury and Venus – lie within the cone of shadow that the earth casts into the universe.

13–36 In this formal invocation, though addressing himself to the Christian God, Dante does not hesitate to employ the language of classical mythology, defining his appeal to His wisdom and intelligence through a detailed allusion to the sun god Apollo. Virgil, as a character, has disappeared, but here as throughout the *Paradiso*, the classical culture that he represents (along with many others, most especially Ovid) continues to provide a source of elevated rhetoric. In these lines, Dante makes a fine distinction. Mount Parnassus (line 16) has twin peaks. One of these – Helicon – is sacred to the Muses, whom Dante has invoked in *Inferno* 2: 7 and *Purgatorio* 1: 8. The second – Cirra – is sacred to Apollo himself; and it is the ultimate power of wisdom and knowledge to which Dante now appeals at line 36. The labour, indeed self-abandonment, that is involved in receiving this inspiration is now evoked (lines 19–21) through reference to the myth of Marsyas. (See Ovid, *Metamorphoses* 6: 382–400.) The satyr Marsyas challenges Apollo to a flute-playing contest, loses and is flayed alive for his presumption. This has regularly been regarded as an account of inspiration – the flayed skin of the artist wholly infused by the in-dwelling spirit of the god. At lines 28–33, referring to the triumphal laurel crowns that are bestowed alike on poets and conquerors, Dante makes learned and very elliptical reference to the mythic origins of the laurel: Daphne is the daughter of the river Peneus – hence 'peneian' – and loved by Apollo. Fleeing, she is transformed into a laurel bush (see Ovid, *Metamorphoses* 1: 452–567), while new joy is born in Apollo whenever poets or conquerors show their devotion to him. (In Dante's Italian, lines 31–33 capture this cycle of flight, growth, rebirth and desire in a lyrical flow of alliterations and enjambments.)

37–45 Until this point, Dante is still in the Earthly Paradise; these lines calculate the hour of his ascent to Heaven. In Eden where Dante now is (in the southern hemisphere, on the summit of Mount Purgatory) it is noon; in Jerusalem in the northern hemisphere (at the antipodes of Eden) it is midnight. Dante rises from the Earthly Paradise to Paradise-proper in the propitious time of the spring equinox, though a little after the equinox itself, which was thought to be the time of Creation and of Christ's conception. The 'beacon of the world' is the sun which rises in the sky at a different point on each day of the year. These points are

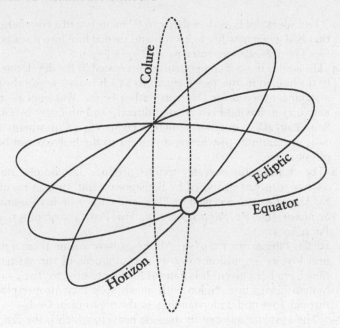

'foci' – outlets or 'estuaries' – the most favourable of which is 21 March. This brings together four circles ('spheres') and three crosses ('cruciforms') in the sense that the four circles that are traced in the track of the heavens here intersect the horizon, each forming a cross with it. (See diagram above.) The four circles are the horizon, the equator, the ecliptic and the 'colure' (the circle that passes the two poles of the heavens and crosses the ecliptic at Aries and Libra). Rising at this point, the sun is coupled with its best orbit, and the constellation Aries is the 'best' constellation. So at this point the sun has its best influence on the earth. (For this and other questions of astronomy, see P. Boyde, *Dante, Philomythes and Philosopher* (Cambridge, 1981), pp. 153–4.)

**49–54** These lines in Italian contain an untranslatable pun on the word *pelegrin*, which can mean both 'peregrine falcon' and 'pilgrim'. (Cf. *Purgatorio* 9: 16.) Both meanings contribute to the picture of light reflected back to its source. Pilgrims desire to arrive at the goals they have set themselves; falcons dive, then return to the sky. So, too, a ray of light is reflected from a mirror at the angle of 'incidence', the exact angle at which it first struck that surface.

67–9  Ovid speaks of how the fisherman Glaucus tasted a certain herb that had given new life to his fish and turned him into a sea god. (See Ovid, *Metamorphoses* 13: 898–968.)

73–5  The soul is the last component to be created in the development of the human foetus. (See *Purgatorio* 25.) It is also 'new' (always a significant word for Dante as author of the *Vita nuova* – the *new* life) in having been created directly and uniquely by God. Saint Paul asks a question similar to Dante's in 2 Corinthians 12: 2–4, uncertain as to whether an ascent to the heavens can be a physical one.

76–8  The idea that the heavenly spheres produce harmonious music as they turn was proposed by Pythagoras, and, though rejected by Aristotle, was accepted by Plato and Cicero (in his *Somnium Scipionis* (*De Re Publica* 6: 17)). For Plato's cosmology, see *Paradiso* 4.

103–20  Cf. *Purgatorio* 17: 91–4. All things have within them a natural love or impulsion towards the fulfilment of the existence they have been given. It is natural for Dante now to 'rise', since human beings in common with angels seek their proper place, through love and understanding, in the presence of God.

121–7  The absolute quiet of the highest heaven, which is the Empyrean – where presence of God is directly experienced – contains the *Primum Mobile*, the fastest moving of the heavenly spheres. (See also note to *Purgatorio* 28: 88f.)


# CANTO 2

*Dante and Beatrice ascend to the Heaven of the*
*Moon, where Beatrice explains why there are dark*
*patches on the surface of the moon.*


7–9  Minerva is the goddess of wisdom, Apollo (as in *Paradiso* 1: 13) is the god of the highest reaches of poetry. The 'Ursa-stars' are the constellation of Ursa Major and Ursa Minor (the latter containing the North Star, from which navigators take their direction). The 'nine bright Muses' are the goddesses of literature and art.

10–12  Cf. Psalm 78: 25 for manna as the bread of angels; cf. *Convivio* 1: 1: 6–7 for the 'bread' of wisdom.

16–18 The Argonauts, the mythic first navigators, seeking the Golden Fleece in Colchis, were astonished to see their leader Jason yoke two fire-breathing bulls to his plough and go scattering serpents' teeth as seed. (See Ovid, *Metamorphoses* 7: 100–48.) See also for references to Jason, *Inferno* 18: 83f and *Paradiso* 33: 96.

19–21 The sphere to which this line refers is that of the Fixed Stars which form the constellations, visible from earth. (See *Paradiso* 22–7.)

49f Folkloric explanations refer to Cain as the man in the moon – to which he had been banished for the murder of his brother Abel (Genesis 4: 1–16) – carrying a bundle of thorns on his back. (Cf. *Inferno* 20: 126.) Against this, the argument presented here enters an area of refined Scholastic debate, pitting the true opinion offered by Saint Thomas Aquinas (*c.* 1225–74) in *De Coelo* 2: 16 against the view which Dante had supported in the *Convivio* 2: 13: 9, drawn from the twelfth-century philosopher Averroes's *De Substantia Orbis* 2. On this account, dark and light spots are a result of a merely quantitative distribution of more or less of the same material on the moon. Now Dante insists, through Beatrice's words at lines 70–72, that this variation proceeds from the action of different formal principles, one producing white matter, the other black. So the emphasis falls upon difference, and the order of the universe which in *Paradiso* 1 was also seen to be mainly concerned with the quantitative distribution of light is now seen, here and throughout the rest of the *Paradiso*, as one which makes diversity and variety possible. Even blackness has its place in the dapple of the whole, and is in no dualistic way to be dismissed as evidence of lack or negativity.

67f The term '*virtù*', appearing in Dante's Italian text at line 68 and here translated as 'power of life', is perhaps the most significant single word in Dante's philosophical vocabulary. Repeated six times in this canto and forty-five times in the course of the *Paradiso*, it means not simply moral virtue but the power or principle of growth. 'Virtue', in modern English, is rarely an adequate translation. For Dante, the moral implications of the word are directly related to the inner strength and special qualities which God, as Creator, has instilled into every created being. Thus in *Convivio* 4: 16: 7, a *virtù* is defined as a 'principle of activity'. The perfection of every being or particular nature coincides with the achievement of its proper and specific *virtù*. (See also *Purgatorio* 18: 19f.)

73–8 Throughout this passage, defining the mistaken view, darkness
   is seen to result from a *lack* of material, from the inability of the
   rarer patches to reflect light back. (See note to lines 49f.)

94–105 Aristotle sanctions experimental method in *Metaphysics* 1: 1.
   The experiment with the three mirrors establishes that, even
   though lights at different distances from the eye will appear dif-
   ferent in size, the light that comes from each of the three is equal
   in intensity.

112f Here – once more enlarging the focus and sweep of his consid-
   erations – Dante provides an explanation of the whole operation
   of the cosmic order as designed to produce variety of existence.
   (Words signifying difference occur throughout this canto.) The
   intelligence of God is one and indivisible (lines 136–8), but
   through the angelic order (see *Paradiso* 28), then downwards
   from the *Primum Mobile* (see note to *Paradiso* 1: 121–7), the
   universe is designed to radiate these powers and principles into
   all things, setting a seal upon them as an artist or craftsman
   might mark his products (lines 127–32). (See also *Paradiso* 13:
   55–75.) The Fixed Stars of the constellations in particular (lines
   115–117) produce, by their various astrological conjunctions,
   innumerable permutations (line 138) in the lower spheres.

# CANTO 3

*Dante encounters Piccarda Donati, who speaks of
charity as the principle underlying the order of
Heaven and tells how she was prevented from
following her earthly vocation as a nun.*

16–18 Narcissus, as a punishment for rejecting the love of the nymph
   Echo, was compelled to fall in love with his own reflection in a
   stream. (See Ovid, *Metamorphoses* 3: 402–510.)

34f The 'shadow' is Piccarda Donati (*c.* 1270– *c.* 1298/9), cousin of
   Dante's wife, Gemma, and sister of his close friend Forese
   Donati, who appears in *Purgatorio* 23 and 24. Piccarda's other
   brother, Corso Donati (d. 1308), is numbered among Dante's
   bitterest enemies, having played a considerable role in the events
   leading to his exile, and (at *Purgatorio* 24: 82–7) is said to be
   heading direct to Hell. Here (as in *Paradiso* 8 and 9) Dante
   shows considerable interest in the way that members of the same

family on earth may exhibit very different moral characteristics. Piccarda, knowing from early childhood that she wished to become a nun, joined the Order of Poor Clares and entered a convent on the outskirts of Florence. But at some point between 1283 and 1288, Corso came to carry Piccarda away, so as to offer her in a political marriage to Rossellino della Tosa. An outline account of Piccarda's earthly life is given at lines 103–108.

70f In Piccarda's philosophical response to Dante and in the story she subsequently tells, at lines 97–114, of how she was abducted from her nunnery, there is an implicit contrast between the human will when it acts in violence against other human beings, and the will of God, with which the human will can cooperate in promoting free and intelligent modes of existence.

85–7 The famous line 85 may have its origins in Saint Augustine, *Confessions* 13: 9. Line 87 should be read in the light of *Purgatorio* 25 and will be seen in *Paradiso* 7 (see notes to these cantos). Dante here envisages two ways of coming into being. One is creation, where God acts directly in forming his creatures. The other is generation, where nature – the system created by God – produces according to its own physical and biological laws. Mankind is unique in being both 'created' and 'generated'.

97–9 Saint Clare of Assisi (1194–1253), who founded the Order of Poor Clares in 1212 in association with Saint Francis.

115–20 Empress Constance (d. 1198), daughter and heir of King Roger II, the Norman ruler of Naples and Sicily, married Emperor Henry VI, bringing with her the kingdom of Sicily as dowry. Her son the emperor Frederick II (see *Inferno* 10 and *Purgatorio* 3) thus inherited Sicily as well as the Holy Roman Empire. The Swabian storms are the three emperors of the Swabian dynasty, Frederick I ('Barbarossa') (1122–90), Henry VI (1165–97) and Frederick II (1194–1250).

# CANTO 4

*Doubts left unanswered by Piccarda concerning the
location of souls in Heaven and the keeping of vows
are resolved by Beatrice.*

1–12 Dante pictures himself faced, in intellectual terms, with a dilemma comparable to that of 'Buridan's ass', which, in a famous medieval conundrum, would starve to death if faced with two equidistant and equally attractive bundles of hay, having no way of deciding which bundle to go for.

13–15 In Daniel 2: 1–45, Nebuchadnezzar, king of Babylon, is angered by the ineffectiveness of his court advisers in interpreting his dreams, but is calmed by the divinely inspired words of the prophet Daniel. Beatrice, endowed with similar insight into the divine plan, proceeds to analyse Dante's two competing doubts in terms of their relative gravity.

22–7 Plato in the *Timaeus* (which Dante knew through an account offered by Saint Augustine in *The City of God* 13: 19) argues that souls pre-exist in the stars and return to these same stars at their death. Dante (like Aquinas) allows that the stars do have an influence on our characters. (See especially *Paradiso* 22: 112–17.) But Plato's view would deny that utter intimacy between the human creature and its Creator which, for Dante, is central to the Christian revelation. In that sense, Plato's is the more venomous of the two questions that assail him, in that it threatens a central conception of Christian belief.

28–30 The two Saint Johns referred to here are John the Baptist and John the Evangelist.

34–48 These lines are crucial for an understanding of Dante's plan in the *Paradiso*. At no point are we to suppose that the sights which Dante describes in this *cantica* are an exact representation of what he believes Heaven to be like. Since all souls are created directly by God, the final destiny of each one is to return directly to the presence of God, which in Dante's cosmology means that they will all be found, in an eternity beyond all spatial and temporal hierarchies, in the Empyrean. The apparent disposition of the souls of the blessed into 'higher' and 'lower' or 'more' and 'less' is nothing more than a scheme intended to accommodate the human mind, which necessarily functions according to the categories of space and time.

In traversing the planetary spheres, we are simply witnessing a series of metaphors or analogies. This is a familiar truth to all those who recognize that an infinite Creator must always be infinitely in excess of finite creation. It is in the same spirit that the Old Testament speaks of the 'hands' and 'feet' of God. It would be idolatrous (and thus contrary to the very spirit of the Judaeo-Christian tradition) to suppose that such phrases were anything more than metaphor. Our minds may be nourished by metaphor, but the point of this nourishment is to prepare us for that gymnastic leap of faith which carries us into the 'no-thing-ness' of divine existence. Indeed, the universe itself, so lovingly explored in Dante's text, is nothing more or less than a metaphor (like Dante's text itself), preparing us to recognize that, keen and serious as we must be in our pursuit of knowledge, existence in all its immediacy will be wholly different from anything we might anticipate. (See also *Paradiso* 30: 76–8.)

At lines 46–8, the third archangel is Raphael, who helped to restore the sight of the old prophet Tobit. (See Tobit 11: 1–15.)

64f The less venomous of Dante's two original doubts (see note to 22–7) is that of mistaking the nature of the vows made between the human being and God. A vow is seen as an act of free will and is to be contrasted with violence (such as Piccarda suffers) where the will is forced to abandon its freely formed intentions. Beatrice first of all asserts the absolute sovereignty of human will, recognizing that it is possible, even when confronted with the utmost violence, for the will to remain steadfast. That is demonstrated both by Christian martyrs, such as Saint Lawrence (line 83) – a deacon of the Church in Rome who was grilled to death in AD 258 – and classical heroes, such as Mucius Scaevola (line 84), who attempted, but failed, to kill the Etruscan Lars Porsenna and was about to be executed at the stake. His courage in holding his own hand into the flame earned for him a reprieve – and for Rome, too. (See Livy, *History of Rome* 2: 12; also *De Monarchia* 2: 5: 14.) Realistically, Dante admits that the will can frequently bend under external pressure and give partial consent to the act of violence in order to avoid worse dangers. This occurred in Piccarda's case, though her absolute will remained intact. And once that is understood, there is no discrepancy between her words and those of Beatrice (lines 109–14).

103–5 Alcmaeon was persuaded to murder his mother by his dying father, who had been urged to enter the Trojan War on the treacherous advice of his wife. (See Ovid, *Metamorphoses* 9: 408 and Virgil, *Aeneid* 6: 445–6; also *Purgatorio* 12: 49–51.)

# CANTO 5

*Beatrice discusses the freedom of the human will as a gift freely given to human beings by God, and goes on to discuss the conditions under which vows are to be taken. The ascent to the Heaven of Mercury.*

19f Beatrice, discussing whether vows can in any way be altered, extends the conception of free will that was first expounded by Virgil in *Purgatorio* 16–18. (See notes to those cantos.) A crucial difference between Virgil's words and Beatrice's is that she should first speak, in enthusiastic and even lyrical terms, of free will as a gift from God. Freedom is fully expressed in the free giving and returning of that gift. It is thus possible for human beings freely to sacrifice their wills to God's will (lines 28–30). Vows represent a form of that exchange in which God and the human being freely enter into a contract. Divine consent, in this particular instance, is at one with human consent (line 27), and this contract reflects the highest dignity that a human being can achieve. A sacrifice is involved in this (line 30), and for that reason it should not be supposed that all people are able to or need to commit themselves to vows. This, however, is a very different sacrifice from that which was required in the cases of Agamemnon and Jephthah. (See notes to lines 64–72.) In the first place, the fact that a contract with God, once made, cannot subsequently be erased, reflects the absolute dignity of the mutual consent which underwrites it – whereas Agamemnon and Jephthah were both overwhelmed by consequences that were wholly unforeseen. In the second place, while the fact that an agreement has been established – the '*convenenza*' (line 45) – can never be cancelled, the exact terms in which the agreement is fulfilled may (under certain conditions decided by the Church or judicial authority) be subject to variation (lines 46–65). Dante's terminology, and his citations of case law, are here technical and legalistic.

49–51 In Leviticus 27, rules are set down which govern the ways in which the contract between God and His chosen people can be both observed and modified.

64–72 The story of the judge Jephthah is told in *Judges* 11: 29f. Jephthah promises he will sacrifice to Jehovah the first person he meets at a feast to celebrate victory over the Ammonites. This person proves to be his daughter. Agamemnon, 'the chieftain of the Greeks', sought to placate Diana for a sacrilegious act by sacrificing his daughter Iphigenia. (See Virgil, *Aeneid* 2: 116; Ovid, *Metamorphoses* 13: 24–38; and Cicero, *De Officiis* 3: 25: 95.)

79–81 These lines possibly refer to the practice whereby certain corrupt priests and friars were willing, for a fee, to manipulate the terms under which a vow had been made.

121–39 The soul to whom Dante is now encouraged to speak is Emperor Justinian. (See notes to *Paradiso* 6.)

## CANTO 6

*The sphere of Mercury. The ambitious. Emperor Justinian tells the story of the providential mission of the Empire from Roman times to Dante's own day.*

1f The speaker throughout this canto is Emperor Justinian (*c.* 482–565), who ruled the Empire between AD 527 and 565 from Constantinople, formerly Byzantium, to which the emperor Constantine had removed the seat of imperial power in AD 324 (lines 1–3). In military terms, Justinian's Empire was largely successful, mainly through the military prowess of his nephew, the general Belisarius (490–565), who waged war in Asia, Africa and in the Italian peninsula against the invading Ostrogoths (lines 25–6). Belisarius's efforts, however, gave Justinian the leisure and confidence (line 27) to pursue his major work, which was the codification and clarification of Roman law – an achievement that was to provide a foundation for legal practice throughout the Middle Ages. For the importance that Dante attached to the Empire as the agent of divine providence, see his *De Monarchia*.

Lines 1–6 refer to Aeneas, the Trojan progenitor of Rome, who is here identified as the husband of Lavinia (his Italian second wife). He followed the sun from east to west from Troy to Rome. Constantine, whose actions Dante often deplores (as in *Inferno* 19 and 27), reversed this trajectory.

13–18 Dante may be reinventing history at this point to emphasize the importance of a proper understanding of Christ's human nature to the initiation of Justinian's enterprise. Justinian's codification of the law took place between 528 and 533; Agapetus was pope between 535 and 536.

31f The first reference here is to those who in Dante's own day have unjustly appropriated the sign of the Roman Eagle (the Ghibellines) or opposed it (the Guelfs). Justinian then outlines four main phases in the development of Rome (lines 34–54, 55–81, 82–93 and 94–111), emphasizing its divine sanction, providential diffusion and uninterrupted lineage.

Lines 34–54: Dante is concerned with the centuries in which Rome established its position in Italy and defended itself against Hannibal's Carthaginians. Fighting in the region around Rome, Aeneas was assisted by the native Italian Pallas (whose sister Lavinia he married). Pallas died in battle against Turnus and the Rutuli. (See Virgil, *Aeneid* 10: 479–89.) Alba Longa was founded by Aeneas's son, Ascanius, prior to the settlement of Rome and defended by the Curiatii, champions of Alba Longa, who were defeated by the three Horatii, and the Eagle's power transferred to Rome. (See *Aeneid* 1: 272.) The rape of the Sabine women, in the time of Romulus, brought wives to the earliest Romans. Lucretia, during the time of the seven kings of Rome, was raped by the son of Tarquinius Superbus, an event which led to the overthrow of monarchical rule and the establishment of the republic in 510 BC. The 'Brenner Gaul' (line 44) is Brennus, leader of the Gauls in the fourth century BC; Pyrrhus was the third-century BC king of Epirus. A list of exemplary ancient Romans follows. Torquatus condemned his own son to death; Quinctius, nicknamed Cincinnatus because of his 'unkempt' hair (line 46), was called to leave his austere life as a ploughman and become dictator. The Decii and Fabii died fighting for Rome. The Arabs are the North African Carthaginians who contested supremacy of the Mediterranean with Rome in the Punic Wars until Hannibal (247–*c.* 183 BC) was defeated by Scipio Africanus the Elder (235–183 BC) at the battle of Zama in 202 BC. (Scipio had first fought the Carthaginians at the age of nineteen at the battle of Cannae in 216 BC.) Pompey the Great (106–48 BC) fought successful campaigns in Sicily, Spain and Africa, and was defeated in the civil wars by Julius Caesar (100–44 BC). 'Those hills' are the hills of Fiesole thought to be peopled by Catiline conspirators against the true authority of Rome. (For Dante's continually aggressive attitude to Fiesole, see *Inferno* 15: 73–96 and *Paradiso* 16.)

Lines 55–81: The world was brought back to peace and justice (says Dante here and in *Paradiso* 7) in preparation for the coming of Christ. But near that time, Julius Caesar first conducted his successful campaigns in Gaul from the river Var to the Rhine, carrying his successes into the regions designated by all the tributaries of the Rhône and the rivers Isère, Loire and Seine. Caesar precipitated the civil wars by crossing the river Rubicon between Ravenna and Rimini in 49 BC, neglecting orders from the Senate. Caesar besieged Pompey at Durazzo (or Dyrrachium) in Illyria (on the western coast of the Balkan peninsula) and defeated him at Pharsalia in northern Greece in 48 BC. Atandros, close to the river Simois, was the port from which Aeneas set sail, near Troy where Hector's body is buried outside the walls. Caesar took Egypt from the Ptolemys and gave it to Cleopatra (69–30 BC) as queen. Juba, king of the Numidians, was an ally of Pompey. The 'western realms' (line 71) are Spain, where followers of Pompey (led by his sons) were finally defeated at the battle of Munda on 17 March 45 BC. The following 'stewardship' (line 73) is that of Octavius Augustus (63 BC–AD 14), who defeated Brutus and Cassius (see *Inferno* 34), Mark Antony at Modena, and Mark Antony's brother Lucius at Perugia. After the final defeat of Mark Antony, Cleopatra, who had become his lover, killed herself with an asp bite. When Augustus's victories were complete, the doors of the temple of Janus were closed as a sign of universal peace.

Lines 82–93: These lines speak of the providential dispensation that allows Christ to be crucified under Roman jurisdiction – in the reign of Tiberius (emperor AD 14–37) – and the subsequent vengeance that was taken on the Jews by the Empire in the sack of Jerusalem in AD 70 (a highly problematic contention, which none the less forms a link with Paradiso 7: 19–21), under the military leadership of Titus, later emperor (AD 79–81).

Lines 94–111: Dante speaks here of the medieval successor of Rome, the Holy Roman Empire, identifying its prestige under Charlemagne and its decline into the civil strife wrought by Guelfs and Ghibellines in Italy when imperial power came to be replaced by the disruptive ambitions of the French Angevin dynasty – of which much more will be said in *Paradiso* 8 and 9. The threat to Christendom offered by the Longobard invasions of Italy was ended by the victories of Charlemagne (742–814), whose aid was requested by Pope Hadrian I (d. 795) in 773, and who was crowned emperor on Christmas Day 800. But since Charlemagne's time, the Empire has been affected by rebellion and partisan strife. One group (the Guelfs – often in alliance with the 'tinsel lilies' (line 101), which are the emblem of France) directly oppose the Empire, while the Ghibellines claim to own the imperial sign themselves. Charles II of Anjou (1254–1309), who came into Italy in 1300 (and seems to have been implicated in Dante's exile), became the most powerful supporter of the Guelfs (along with the Church) against imperial rule. Charles is warned against assuming that the 'lily flowers' (line 111) of his coat-of-arms can replace the imperial Eagle. (See notes to *Purgatorio* 20.)

**127–142** Romieu de Villeneuve (1170–1250) rose from humble origins to become the seneschal of Count Raymond Berenger IV of Provence (*fl.* 1209–45). He arranged the marriage of Raymond's four daughters to four kings. Unjustly accused of embezzlement, Romieu was dismissed and died in poverty.

# CANTO 7

*Beatrice speaks of the role of imperial justice in avenging the death of Christ and offers an account of Christ's death as a just atonement for sin.*

**1–3** Dante here combines Latin and (rather suspect) Hebrew to produce, as Justinian's final words, his own version of a solemn acclamation of praise to the god of battles: 'Hosanna, holy God of hosts, who illuminates supremely with your brightness the happy fires of this realm.' (Contrast the invented languages of *Paradiso* 15: 28–30, and *Inferno* 7: 1 and Inferno 31: 67. Cf. also the rewriting of the Lord's Prayer that opens *Purgatorio* 11.)

**10f** The epic voice of Justinian gives way to the intimately lyrical meditation on the syllables of Beatrice's name. This in Florentine was 'Bice', though in the course of the *Vita nuova* Dante enriched this original form, to reveal a symbolic dimension: 'she who makes blessed'. The 'blessedness' that Beatrice now proceeds to bestow comes in the form of an answer to three doubts or questions, which, though unspoken, she reads in Dante's mind (lines 20–21, 55–7 and 124–9). All of her answers depend upon an exposition of the doctrine of the Atonement, which is central to Christian belief.

**19–123** The explanations offered by Beatrice are stimulated by a question (which the modern mind must rightly find offensive) that first arose in *Paradiso* 6: 92–3, as to why Christ's death – which was an act of justice in so far as it punished fallen human nature – should have been avenged 'justly' by the Roman attack on Jerusalem in AD 70 – which led to the massacre of the Jews and the destruction of the Temple. The argument at lines 46–8 is that, in so far as Christ was divine as well as human, his death on the Cross at the behest of the Caiaphas was as unjust as, from the human point of view, it was just – in being punishment for the sin of Adam. At lines 25–33, Beatrice speaks of Adam's disobedience as a sin that involves the whole of subsequent humanity in that original sin, until the *Logos* or 'Word of God' (which is Christ) chose, in an act of love, to unite itself totally with human nature. How, after the fall of Adam, can human nature ever again be at one with God? Some reparation or satisfaction is required. But it is not logical to suppose that a finite creature can ever compensate for an offence done to an infinite Creator, except that in Christ human nature is miraculously made one with the divine, and so in self-sacrifice on the Cross can make a just and fitting response. This argument draws on Saint Anselm's *Cur Deus Homo?* (see note to *Paradiso* 12: 130–41): 'No one save God can make it [reparation]. No one save man ought to make it. It is necessary for a God-man to make it' (chapter 6). In offering his own version of Anselm's teaching, Dante here, as in his *De Monarchia*, goes to extreme lengths in his devotion to the idea of Roman justice to treat Christ's death under Roman jurisdiction as not only retribution for the sins of Adam but an indication of the mission of Rome in bringing providential justice to the world. Dante now pursues Anselm's quasi-legal interest in the question of how compensation can be made to God. The word 'satisfaction' is constantly repeated (such as at lines 93, 98 and 102).

But why did God choose this way, of the many ways that might have been chosen, to redeem humanity? This is Dante's second unspoken question. The emphasis in lines 55–120 then begins to fall as much upon notions of God's freedom and generosity (or in Italian, '*bontà*') as upon his justice. The original act of creation was an act of pure freedom and generosity on God's part. (See lines 64–6 and cf. *Paradiso* 29.) In *Paradiso* 5: 19–24, Dante has already emphasized that God's intention in creating Adam was to endow humanity with its own freedom to participate (or not, if it so chose) in divine life. So, along with the question of how reparation can be made, goes that of how the human freedom which has been lost in the Fall should be restored. Had God simply offered an amnesty, this would not have recognized the potential dignity of the human creature. Yet human beings possess neither the freedom nor the resources to restore themselves to their former state (lines 91–102). So in his generosity, God chose to become Man, making use of all his divine powers (lines 103–118).

124f Dante's third question as interpreted by Beatrice is whether all
things in Creation are assured of eternal life. These arguments
depend upon a distinction, which is further explored in *Paradiso*
13, between the two ways in which creatures are brought
into existence. They can be 'created' directly by God ('*sanza
mezzo*'/'without intermediary' – translated as 'without a second
cause' at lines 67 and 70) or 'generated' by God working through
the agency of nature. (See also *Purgatorio* 25.) The angels, the
heavenly spheres and the human soul are created directly by
God. Physical things are created by the physical, chemical and
biological laws of nature. The human being, as body and soul, is
unique in being brought into existence by both direct and indir-
ect action. All generated things are subject to decay – save for the
human body which is associated with the 'created' soul. (See also
line 25 – where Adam is said be 'unborn'.)

133–8 For the distribution of *virtù*, or creative power in the universe,
see notes to *Paradiso* 2: 67f. This power works – in its many
different ways – on primal, undifferentiated matter, which has
the potential to assume any particular nature.


# CANTO 8

*Rising to the Heaven of Venus, Dante encounters
spirits whose earthly lives have been characterized by
sexual passion. Charles Martel discusses providence
and heredity.*

1–9 Venus, in *Convivio* 2: 13 and 14, is compared by Dante to the art
of rhetoric: just as the planet Venus is clear and sweet in its
appearance, so too is rhetoric, and just as Venus is both the
morning and the evening star, so rhetoric can offer both lucid
and darker or more hidden meanings. The opening lines (in com-
mon with *Paradiso* 8 and 9) display a high degree of rhetorical
elaboration, designating the planetary sphere at which Dante has
now arrived through a concise history of the pagan cult of Venus.
The goddess was brought ashore in Cyprus – hence the 'Cyprian'.
Her mother was Dione and her son, Cupid (whom Virgil
describes, at *Aeneid* 1: 685–8, as lying, disguised as Aeneas's son,
in the lap of Dido and thus preparing for her tragic affair with
Aeneas). In the course of this long, periodic sentence, Dante is

able to interleave scientific astronomy into these mythic allu-
sions, referring to the epicycle – the loop, or subsidiary orbit,
around a point on its major orbit – through which the planet
Venus was thought to move. (See *Convivio* 2: 4.)

**22–4** Dante here compares the movement of the souls in this circle to
the movement of winds which erupt from clouds compressed by
cold air. (In Dante's science, lightning or meteors are visible or
'seen' winds.)

**31–9** The speaker is Charles Martel (Carlo Martello) (1271–95), the
one member of the Angevin dynasty whom Dante speaks of with
unambiguous praise, lamenting how Charles's early death at the
age of twenty-four opened the way for a series of disasters that
then befell Italy. Son of Mary of Hungary and Charles II of
Anjou, Charles Martel was heir to the Angevin kingdom of
Naples and king of Hungary. Charles I of Anjou was his grand-
father and Rudolph I of Habsburg his father-in-law. (See
*Purgatorio* 7: 91 and 126 and *Purgatorio* 20: 64–9.) Charles
Martel visited Florence in 1294, a year before his death, and
Dante seems to have been involved in the chivalric celebrations
of the occasion. At lines 34–9, he makes reference to one of his
own *canzoni* (which appears as an introduction to *Convivio* 2)
in which, as at line 97 onwards, he is concerned with the order
of the angelic hierarchies and their role in communicating the
goodness of God's intentions to the universe at large. Between
the *Convivio* and the *Paradiso*, Dante has changed his view of
the exact order in which the angelic hierarchy is arranged. (See
also notes on *Paradiso* 28.)

**55f** Charles Martel's speech moves through three phases, interlacing
political concerns with issues relating to the providential govern-
ment of the universe. The first phase (lines 58–84) views the
territories that Charles, by natural inheritance, would have
ruled, had he lived to do so. The second phase (lines 97–111)
speaks of providence and the angelic orders. The third phase
(lines 124–35) compares the workings of the universe to those of
a city conceived in Aristotelian terms (see note to 115f).

**58–60** This geographical periphrasis designates the county of Pro-
vence, which lies to the left of the Rhône running south, below
its confluence with the river Sorgue. It came to the Angevins as
the dowry of Charles Martel's grandmother. (Cf. *Paradiso* 6:
133–4 and *Purgatorio* 20: 61–2.)

**61f** The three towns mentioned here demarcate the horn of Ausonia
(a classical name for Italy) and thus refer to the southern region

of the peninsula, corresponding to the kingdom of Naples. The rivers Tronto, on the eastern side of the kingdom, and Verde on the west, divide the realm of Naples from the Papal States. Sicily is designated by references to the Pachino (Pachynus) to the south and Peloro (the modern Cape Faro) to the north. The whole island is dominated by the smoke of Etna. The passage draws extensively on Ovid, *Metamorphoses* 5: 350–53.

64–84  Charles Martel's illuminating presence is celebrated in a reference (line 64) to the 'shining crown' of Hungary which he had already inherited through his mother, having been crowned at Aix in 1292. But this sovereignty would have extended to Sicily had it not been for the 'misrule' (line 73) that led to the revolt known as the Sicilian Vespers, to the loss of Sicily by the Angevins to the Aragonese and, subsequently, to the disruption of Italian politics by Angevin attempts to reassert their one-time position in the southern provinces. In Italy the presence of Angevin armies exacerbated the strife between Guelfs and Ghibellines, and Charles II of Anjou (1254–1309) is regularly attacked by Dante for the part he played in the poet's exile. This speech is syntactically sustained and studded with rhetorical devices (as, for instance, when Sicily is ornamentally referred to as 'Trinacria' (line 67)), but it ends with a violent report (registered in Dante's text in colloquial Sicilian) of the cry uttered by citizens of Palermo as they rose against their French overlords. There follows a recognition that lineage is no guarantee of moral rectitude, as Charles Martel attacks his younger brother, Robert of Anjou (1275–1343), who was acknowledged as king of Naples in 1297 with the connivance of Dante's great enemy, Pope Boniface VIII. Robert was held as a hostage for his father in Catalonia by the Aragonese from 1288 to 1295, and, when he succeeded to the throne of Naples in 1309, he brought Catalonian officials into his (generally mismanaged) government.

97–111  These lines direct attention away from history to the workings of providence. The account draws on the Aristotelian view (to be found in *De Anima* 3) which holds that nature never does anything in vain. In keeping, however, with the view of divine order that he is exploring in the *Paradiso*, Dante goes beyond Aristotle and proposes a fully Christian understanding: it is divine goodness which moves all the spheres through which Dante is passing (lines 97–9), and such goodness desires not merely that all things should exist but that, according to their nature, all things should move towards their own particular 'end' and fulfilment (lines 100–102).

115f Aristotle is also an influence upon the final phase of Charles
Martel's argument. (See note to 55f.) It is he who is the 'teacher'
cited at line 120. Here Dante employs the Aristotelian idea of a
city to define further the notion of ordered diversity in the cos-
mos: just as a city needs many different types of talent if it is to
operate effectively (Aristotle, *Politics* 1: 2, cited in *Convivio* 4:
4), so, too, does a perfect universe.

124-6 Solon (the Athenian lawmaker, 638–558 BC) is the typical
model of a statesman, Xerxes (the Persian emperor who reigned
485–465 BC) of a warrior and Melchizedek (from Genesis 14:
18–20) of a priest. The 'craftsman' here is the mythological
Daedalus, skilled inventor and father of Icarus.

130-32 Esau and Jacob (Genesis 25: 21–34), though twin brothers,
were entirely different, both temperamentally and physically: one
was hairy, the other smooth. Romulus, whose father was low-
born though his mother was royal, had a strength of character
that earned him the favour of divine paternity. Romulus founded
Rome on the Palatine Hill after murdering his twin brother
Remus in a quarrel over the site of the city. Here, as in *Paradiso*
9, Dante is concerned with the ways in which a single family may
produce members who are very different in character and merit.

145-8 Human ignorance and malice here distort the providential dis-
position of talents. Human beings are not determined in any
particular direction by genetic inheritance, but are guided towards
their end by providence. Yet, through making priests out of per-
sons who were destined to be warriors or kings out of preachers,
mortals confuse the providential design and contribute to the chaos
visible throughout the Europe which is depicted in this canto.


# CANTO 9

*Still in the sphere of Venus, Dante encounters*
*Cunizza da Romano (who forgives herself for her*
*erotic impulses) and the troubadour poet and bishop*
*Folco of Marseilles, who speaks of the redemption*
*of the harlot Rahab.*


1-6 The 'Clemenza' to whom these lines are addressed is probably
the wife (died 1301) of Charles Martel ('Carlo'). The 'treacheries
his seed would face' (line 3) refers to the tangled dynastic conflicts

which implicated the House of Anjou very deeply in the history
of the Italian peninsula in this period. The son of Charles Martel,
Charles Robert (1288–1342), had a legitimate claim to the
throne of Naples. But this right was waived in 1309, following
the death of his grandfather Charles II of Anjou, in favour of
Charles Martel's younger brother, Robert, whose succession was
confirmed that year by Pope Clement V. (See also note to *Para-
diso* 8: 64–84.) The pope, however, also confirmed Charles
Robert's claim to the throne of Hungary.

13–31  This is Cunizza da Romano (*c.* 1198–*c.* 1279), the four times
married mistress of the troubadour poet Sordello (who has an
important role in *Purgatorio* 6–8). At the end of her life, Cunizza,
having settled in Florence, is said to have granted freedom to all
the loyal slaves of her father and brother's household (thus con-
verting *eros* to *agape*). Cunizza was the sister of the despotic
Ezzelino III (1194–1259), who is the 'torch' referred to at line
31. The *'evil* part' of Italy (lines 25–7) is the march of Treviso.
(See note to lines 49–60.) Rialto is the highest of the islands com-
posing Venice.

46–8  In 1314, Can Grande della Scala (1291–1329), to whom prob-
ably Dante dedicated the *Paradiso* (see note to *Paradiso* 17:
70–77), defeated the Guelfs of Padua, who had held the city for
some fifty years. The river Bacchiglione, which forms marshes
around Vicenza, ran red with Paduan blood.

49–60  The rivers Sile and Cagnano conjoin at Treviso, which was, at this
time, ruled by the tyrannical Rizzardo da Camino, a militant Ghi-
belline who was assassinated in a Guelf plot of 1312. The 'Clink'
('*malta*' in the Italian) of line 54 may signify either a generically
squalid dungeon or a prison on Lake Bolsena reserved for bishops
convicted of crimes. The loss of 'Ferrarese blood' (line 55) refers to
the treachery of the Guelf bishop of Feltre, who in 1314 betrayed
four Ghibelline refugees to Ferrara, where they were executed.

61–3  The 'Thrones' are third in the hierarchical order of angels. (For
Dante's change of mind concerning the relative position of
Thrones and Principalities (mentioned at *Paradiso* 8: 34), see
notes to *Paradiso* 28.)

76–8  The six-winged Seraphim appear in Isaiah 6: 2. (Cf. *Purgatorio*
29: 94–6.)

82f  The second speaker in this canto is the troubadour-turned-bishop
Folco of Marseilles (*fl.* 1180–95), the third in a sequence of Occi-
tan poets that have been given prominence in the *Commedia*.
(Cf. Bertran de Born in *Inferno* 28 and Arnaut Daniel in *Purga-*

*torio* 26. See also *De Vulgari Eloquentia* 2: 6.) Dante does not reproduce the idiom of Folco's poetic voice as he did in the case of Arnaut. However, as if to signal a literary conversion on Folco's part to the classicism that Dante himself espoused in his devotion to Virgil, he does attribute to the troubadour a high degree of rhetorical skill (as in the periphrasis designating the Mediterranean sea at lines 82–7). Likewise, Folco's account of his amorous inclinations when young is marked by classical allusions to the story of Dido and Aeneas (cf. *Paradiso* 8: 9) and other stories of heroic love drawn from Ovid (lines 97–102). As to Folco's ultimate career after his entry (around 1195) into a Cistercian monastery, and subsequently as a bishop, Dante says nothing. This may seem surprising, for Folco was particularly involved in the crusade which the Dominicans pursued (see *Paradiso* 12) against the heretical Albigensians of southern France in 1209 – though at line 126 Folco does criticize modern popes for failing to crusade in the Holy Land. This was a peculiarly violent offensive, leading to the extermination of a culture that had contributed greatly to the development of modern vernacular literature. Yet the reasons why Dante may have sympathized with this crusade are implicit in this canto, and provide a subtext to Folco's speeches. The heretical aspect of Albigensian thinking lay in a certain dualism which sought to give priority to the spirit over the body and encourage a detachment from the earthly life in favour of perfections that human beings could themselves achieve through ascetic exercise. Such a view runs directly counter to the Christian emphasis on the Incarnation of Christ and the subsequent revelation of an intrinsic relationship (as pictured in *Paradiso* 8 and 9) between the workings of providence and the painful but essential involvement of Christians in the sufferings of history. (Cf. *Paradiso* 15 to 17.)

88–93 The Ebro is in Spain. The Magra flowed into the sea near La Spezia and divided Genoa from Tuscany. Bougiah, a port east of Algiers, falls on the same meridian as Marseilles. The massacre of the population of Marseilles occurred during the Roman civil wars when, in 49 BC, Pompey's supporters were slaughtered by Julius Caesar's navy.

100–102 The Thracian princess Phyllis, whose palace was near Mount Rhodope, hanged herself, supposing she had been deserted by her lover Demophoon, son of Theseus. (See Ovid, *Heroides* 2: 147–8.) Hercules (Alcides) deceived his wife Deianira when he fell in love with Iole (*Heroides* 9: 127f). (Cf. *Inferno* 12: 67–9.)

112–26 The last figure who appears in the Heaven of Venus is the
prostitute Rahab. Her story (told in Joshua 2 and 6) is central to
the providential history of the Israelites. As the Israelites
approach Jericho under the command of Joshua, two of their
spies are sheltered within the walls of Jericho by Rahab, who is
later saved from death when Joshua enters the city and destroys
its other inhabitants. In subsequent Christian writings, Rahab is
taken as the type of those gentiles who, through their faith in the
revelation granted to Jews and Christians, can be assured of
ultimate salvation (lines 118–20). She is referred to as a figural
example in Hebrews 11: 31 and James 2: 25.

118 A reference to the conical shadow that the earth casts into the cos-
mos, extending over the spheres of the moon, Mercury and Venus.

127–32 The gold florin coined in 1252 in Florence carried the figure
of Saint John as patron of Florence on its face and a lily on its
obverse. Though this coin played a crucial part in the inter-
national success of Florentine banking, for Dante its 'accursèd
flower' was a satanic parody of virtuous growth.

133–5 The Decretals are the texts of the canon law rapidly develop-
ing at this time as the Church's legal and bureaucratic exercise of
power was extended.

139–42 These lines refer to the Vatican Hill where Saint Peter was
crucified and to the early Christian martyrs who followed in his
footsteps. The canto concludes in the certain hope that the polit-
ical and ecclesial corruption that it has exposed will soon be
ended by divine intervention.


# CANTO 10

*Passing beyond the shadow that the earth casts into the
universe, Dante enters the Heaven of the Sun and
encounters Christian philosophers. From this point
until the end of* Paradiso *22, he will travel successively
through the sphere of the sun, Mars, Jupiter and Saturn.*


7–21 These lines refer to the time of Dante's journey around the
spring equinox, in the constellation of Aries, the Ram. (See notes
to *Paradiso* 1.) They meditate on the providential dispensation
of the heavens which ensures that the sun's heat nourishes rather
than desolates the earth. The two motions that coincide are the

daily movement of the planets on the celestial equator and the yearly revolution of the sun along the ecliptic. At the point of the Ram, the ecliptic crosses the celestial equator. The oblique circle is the Zodiac, an imagined circle around the Heaven of the Fixed Stars (18 degrees in width) within which the solar ecliptic keeps its path. The Zodiac lies at an angle of 23½ degrees north and south in respect of the equator, and this angle ensures an optimum distribution of celestial influences over the earth. The 'straight course' (line 20) is the equator.

28–39 The minister of nature is the sun, the movement of which round the earth – between the winter and summer solstices – can be represented as a spiral.

67–9 'Latona's daughter' is the moon.

82f The concluding phase of the canto is introduced by the figure of Saint Thomas Aquinas (1226–74, canonized 1323 – two years after Dante's death), who was in the avant-garde of those Scholastic philosophers who applied Aristotelian methods to the discussion of Christian truths and who, in Dante's time, still remained a controversial figure.

94–6 The significance of 'All grow fat who do not go astray' is explained at *Paradiso* 11: 124–39.

97f The figures who appear in the first of the circular dances are: the Swiss Albertus Magnus (1193–1280), otherwise known as Albert of Cologne, bishop of Regensburg, who was Aquinas's teacher and established Aristotle's philosophy in the Scholastic study of theology; and Saint Thomas Aquinas himself (see note to lines 82f), born into a family of southern Italian aristocrats. Francesco Graziano (Gratian) (b. *c.* 1090) is the Tuscan Benedictine who is said to have founded the field of ecclesiastical or canon law in his *Decretum* (1140–50), which attempted to reconcile the law of the Church with the civil law. Peter Lombard (d. 1160), born near Novara, became professor of theology and bishop of Paris, writing an extremely influential *summa* of Christian philosophy, the *Sentences*. (See notes to *Paradiso* 14.) The 'fifth light' (line 109) is Solomon, son of King David of Israel; the sixth light is Dionysius the Areopagite, converted to Christianity by Saint Paul in AD 52 (see Acts of the Apostles 17: 34), reputedly first bishop of Athens and author of a work on the hierarchy of angels, *De Coelesti Hierarchiae*, to which Dante makes important allusions in *Paradiso* 8, 9 and 28; then there follows (probably) the Spanish historian of the fourth to fifth century Paulus Orosius (*c.* 385–420), whose *Historiae Adversus Paganos*,

dedicated to Saint Augustine, was widely used by Dante. Next is
Boethius (d. 526) author of *The Consolation of Philosophy*, a
work cited and used by Dante from the *Vita nuova* onward (as,
for instance, in the depiction of Fortune in *Inferno* 7). After his
death in prison at the hands of Theodoric, king of the Ostrogoths,
Boethius was buried in the church of Saint Peter in Ciel d'Oro,
Pavia ('Golden Heaven Church'). Bede of Jarrow in Northum-
berland (d. 735) composed the *Ecclesiastical History of England*;
Isidore, bishop of Seville (d. 636), wrote an early compendium of
knowledge largely based around the study of Latin word struc-
tures, the *Etymologies*; Richard of Saint Victor (d. 1173) is
probably a Scot who, at the abbey of Saint Victor in Paris, was a
colleague of Peter Lombard and produced influential writings on
the contemplative life, notably the *Benjamin Minor*; Siger of Bra-
bant (d. *c.* 1283) was a scholar at the university of Paris who was
violently opposed by Aquinas.

112–14 The proposition 'no second ever rose who saw so much' is
specifically analysed by Aquinas in *Paradiso* 13: 46–111.

136–8 The medieval rue de Fouarre (Straw Alleyway) in Paris is now
the rue Dante.

139–44 This is one of the earliest known references to mechanically
chiming clocks, which began to appear in Europe at the end of
the thirteenth century.


# CANTO 11

*Aquinas, in the Heaven of the Sun, discusses an
obscure phrase that had arisen in an earlier speech. He
celebrates the virtues of Saint Francis and condemns
the present corruption of his own Dominican Order.*

25–42 Saint Thomas Aquinas refers to the two phrases that were
introduced at *Paradiso* 10: 96 ('All grow fat who do not go
astray') and 114 ('no second ever rose who saw so much'). He
proceeds to explain the first of these, praising the institution of
the Franciscan Order. (For his analysis of the second phrase, see
*Paradiso* 13: 46–111.) He speaks of how providence alloted to
the Church two champions or 'princes' (line 35), likened to the
Seraphim and Cherubim, angels of love and wisdom respectively.
The 'one' (line 37) is Saint Francis (1182–1226), canonized in

1228, the 'other' (line 38) is Saint Dominic. (See notes to *Paradiso* 12.) Aquinas (as a Dominican) will speak in praise of Saint Francis, and against the corruption of his own order, while, conversely, Saint Bonaventure (a Franciscan) will speak in *Paradiso* 12 in praise of Saint Dominic, and against the corrupt Franciscans. (See *Paradiso* 12: 112f.)

43–8  The position of Assisi in Umbria – Saint Francis's birthplace – is defined by reference to the river Topino and the river Chiascio, which has its source north-east of Gubbio, near the hermitage of Saint Ubaldo. The mountain above Assisi is Monte Subasio. Its west slope (less steep than the eastern one) faces Perugia. The Porta Sole or Sun Gate of Perugia is the one nearest Subasio. The town of Perugia feels the effect of sun and cold from the mountain. North-east of Subasio are the towns of Nòcera and Gualdo, which suffer, or weep, from the effects of Apennine weather.

52–4  Dante plays on the (fanciful) etymology of 'Assisi', which in the Tuscan of Dante's day was known as 'Ascesi', taken here to mean 'I rose'. (Cf. the etymologies at *Paradiso* 12: 79–81.) The only appropriate designation, however, would be 'Orient', derived from the Latin *'oriari'* ('to rise up').

58f  In 1209, at the age of twenty-seven, Francis formally declared his devotion to poverty in the bishop's court, in the presence of his father (*'coram patre'*), a wealthy wool merchant. It is the virtue of poverty – the acceptance of a universal order that transcends self-seeking individualism – that allows him to recognize the interrelatedness of all things as creatures of God and to express his delight in the brotherhood and sisterhood of all created things, in the form of a hymn to the sun that echoes Dante's own celebration of his union with the sun in *Paradiso* 10: 'All praise be yours, my Lord, through all that you have made, / And first my lord, Brother Sun, / Who brings the day; and light you give to us through him' (*Laudes Creaturarum*, stanza 2). In *Paradiso* 11, Dante stresses the notion of intellectual poverty, emphasizing the joy that comes, paradoxically, in the acceptance of limit and self-abandonment. Just as Saint Francis embraces Poverty as if she were a lover, so Poverty herself willingly leaps on the Cross with Christ (lines 58–75). The early and most influential records of Saint Francis's life were cast in the form of anecdotes and folktales, imitating, to some degree, the Gospels in the way that Saint Francis's conduct imitated Christ.

The relationship between Saint Francis and Lady Poverty (line 64 onwards) is portrayed as a courtly love affair. In terms of literary genre, this is in part a rather simplistic allegory (as the speaker confesses with something approaching comic irritation at lines 73–5) and in part a fable. The lady whom Francis loves is the widow of Christ and old and off-putting in appearance – partly a Mary Magdalene, partly a 'loathly lady' or magical hag. Yet, as some princess transformed by the attention of a lover, she attracts not only Francis but all his early followers, who (again in a passage of farcical energy at lines 82–4) fling off their sandals as they rush to follow, discovering riches in Poverty that are hidden to the world. Intertwined with these features, however, there is a highly chivalric diction, representing Saint Francis (against his own outward poverty of appearance) as a courtly lover or even as a king when he regally reveals his message to Pope Innocent III (line 92) or boldly enters the court of the sultan of Syria (lines 100–104).

67–9 This reference briefly recalls the example of the poor fisherman Amyclas (to whom Dante also refers in Convivio 4: 13), who was able to refuse the demands of Julius Caesar for transport across the Adriatic precisely because he had nothing to lose.

79–84 Bernardo da Quintavalle (fl. c. 1210), a prosperous merchant of Assisi, was the first follower of Saint Francis; Egidio was described by Tommaso of Celano in his Vita prima (c. 1228) as 'a poor and timorous citizen of Assisi'; Silvestro was a priest of the town.

91–9 In 1210, Pope Innocent III with some reluctance gave his oral blessing to Saint Francis's order. Official sanction of his Rule was given by Pope Honorius III (1148–1227) in 1223. In Greek 'archimandrite' (line 97) signifies the 'leader of a flock'.

100–102 In 1219, during the Fifth Crusade, Saint Francis visited Sultan Malek al-Kamil (d. 1238), who was reputed to be sympathetic to Coptic Christians, but proved disappointed with the results of his preaching.

103–8 On the very precipitous slopes of Monte La Verna, between the upper Arno and the source of the Tiber, Saint Francis received, mystically, the wounds of Christ on his own body, which remained visible for two years, as the ultimate sanction of his mission.

118 The 'other' is Saint Dominic. (See the note to Paradiso 12: 82–105.)

# CANTO 12

*A second circle of twelve philosophers appears, to
join the first. Saint Bonaventure tells the story of
Saint Dominic's life.*

1-30 The opening sequence (returning to the scene in Heaven)
describes the appearance of a further ring of twelve philosophers
who join in the dance with the first that Dante described in
*Paradiso* 10. The second ring includes the Saint Bonaventure
(1221-74), who became Minister General of the Franciscan
Order in 1257 (later to become a cardinal) and produced the first
extensive philosophical writings in response to Saint Francis's
example. In contrast with the writings of Aquinas, which are
strongly marked by Aristotelianism, Bonaventure's philosophy
tends to adopt a Neoplatonic emphasis, and a rich, sometimes
emotive rhetoric, drawing attention to the power of the mind to
rise up in love and contemplation to union with the divine, seek-
ing, as in the opening of his *Itinerarium Mentis in Deum* ('The
Journey of the Mind into God') (1259):

> the peace which our Lord Jesus Christ has proclaimed and has
> given; the renewer of whose preaching was our Father Francis,
> announcing at the beginning and end of all his preaching peace, in
> every salutation choosing peace, in every contemplation longing
> towards ecstatic peace as a citizen of that Jerusalem concerning
> which the man of peace speaks.

31f Bonaventure matches Aquinas's account of Saint Francis's life
with a eulogy to the founder of the Dominican Order of Preach-
ers, the Spanish saint Dominic (1170-1221, canonized 1224).
58-66 According to legend, before Dominic's birth his mother
dreamed that she would give birth to a black and white dog with
a flaming torch in its mouth. The Dominicans (on a false etymol-
ogy) were taken to be the 'dogs of God' ('*domini canes*') and
their religious dress is black and white. The torch represents the
energy that Dominic displayed in opposing heresy. The second
dream (lines 64-9) came to Dominic's godmother and showed
the saint with a star in his forehead - signifying his ability to
illuminate the world with orthodox doctrine.

82–105 These lines allude to the mature works of Saint Dominic whose dominant concern is faith. His devotion to poverty (in founding a mendicant order) is stressed, as at line 75 where he adheres to Christ's commandment to love the poor. His learning does not lead him to follow the example of canon lawyers such as Henry of Susa, bishop of Ostia (d. 1271), or rich physicians such as the Florentine Taddeo d'Alderotti (d. 1295), who founded the medical school in Bologna. (Cf. *Paradiso* 11: 4–9.) Nor does he ask for remuneration, diverting, as the Roman Curia did, the 10 per cent tithe intended for the poor to his own uses. At line 93 Dante adopts the curial Latin phrase for these tithes and these lines throughout are marked by a parodic use of the official jargon that was employed to justify the abuse of Church revenues. Instead he asks of the pope of the day, Innocent III, for a commission to combat religious error and is granted this in 1216 by Innocent's successor, Honorius III. This sanction leads in particular to Dominic's crusade against the broadly dualistic heresies of the Albigensians of southern France (see note to *Paradiso* 9: 82f), a violent 'torrent' (line 99) of activity which led to the extinction of Albigensian culture.

94–6 The twenty-four 'saplings' are the philosophers (see note to lines 1–30) who form the double dance.

106 For the Franciscans and Dominicans as the wheels of the true Church, see *Purgatorio* 29: 106f.

112f As Bonaventure turns in the final phase of the canto to attack the degeneracy of his fellow Franciscans, the language in Dante's text becomes especially dense, employing a rapid mixing of metaphors which was characteristic of some prophetic writings in the late Middle Ages. In a single *terzina* (lines 112–14) the Order is compared to a wonky cartwheel and musty wine, while subsequent *terzine* allude to bad harvests and poorly written pages. According to Bonaventure, the true Franciscans will not include figures such as Ubertino da Casale (d. 1338) and Matteo d'Acquasparta (d. 1303) (lines 124–6), representing the two warring factions among the Franciscans – the former an extreme ascetic 'Spiritual', the latter (General of the Order from 1287) a 'Conventual' who pursued a more conciliatory policy.

130–41 Illuminato da Rieti and Agostino di Assisi were among the earliest (and therefore truest) followers of Francis. Hugo of Saint Victor (d. 1141) was a Fleming, who became a canon of the Abbey of Saint Victor in Paris and contributed to the growth of an Augustinian form of mystic spirituality. (Cf. Richard of Saint Victor, *Paradiso* 10: 131.) Pietro Ispano (Peter the Spaniard)

(1226–77) became Pope John XXI in 1276; his twelve-volume *Summulae Logicales* (*c.* 1250) combats the neo-Aristotelianism of Albertus Magnus and Aquinas. Pietro Mangiadore (or Petrus Comestor) (d. 1179) was a Frenchman, chancellor of the university of Paris and author of a major commentary on biblical history. Nathan is the Old Testament prophet who spoke out against King David's adulterous liaison with Bathsheba (2 Samuel 12). Saint John Chrysostom (d. 407), Patriarch of Constantinople, preached against the corruption of the Church. Saint Anselm (1033–1109) became archbishop of Canterbury and wrote the very influential treatise *Cur Deus Homo?* (see note on *Paradiso* 7: 19–123). Donatus was a fourth-century Latin grammarian and probably teacher of Saint Jerome; his *Ars Grammatica* was a standard text throughout the Middle Ages. The German Rabanus Maurus (d. 856), archbishop of Mainz, wrote an extensive encyclopedia, *De Universo*, and biblical commentaries. Joachim da Fiore (*c.* 1145– *c.* 1202), Cistercian abbot of Corazzo in Calabria and founder of the monastery of Saint Giovanni in Fiore, developed a very influential philosophy of history – viewed in prophetic terms as the progressive revelation of God's truth – and was noted for his Apocalyptic vision of the Antichrist. His writings were at times viewed as heretical, and Bonaventure is sometimes said to have opposed their implications as vehemently as Aquinas opposed the teaching of Siger of Brabant. (See notes to *Paradiso* 10.) There is a case, however, for saying that Dante was influenced by Joachim's visionary and prophetic mode of thought, as well as by his interest in the providential workings of history.

# CANTO 13

*Aquinas explains why Solomon is to be seen as the wisest of all human beings, offering a detailed interpretation of a phrase used in* Paradiso *10. He provides a philosophical account of the structure of the universe to demonstrate how Solomon differs from Christ and Adam. The canto concludes with a warning against over-hasty judgements.*

1–18 To gain some idea of the brightness of the souls in the double dance (see *Paradiso* 12: 1–30), the reader is invited to think of the twenty-four brightest stars in the northern hemisphere: the fifteen major stars in Ptolemy's system, the seven stars of the Wain (or Plough), forming part of the Great Bear (Ursa Major), and two from the Little Bear (Ursa Minor), these two stars being at the mouth of the Horn and furthest from the North Star. Lines 14–15 refer (inaccurately) to the legend of Ariadne, daughter of Minos (Ovid, *Metamorphoses* 8: 176–82), who was deserted by Theseus and befriended by Bacchus, who set Ariadne's crown in the skies as a constellation to ensure her continuing fame.

22–4 The comparison is between the fastest moving of the heavenly spheres – the *Primum Mobile* – and a sluggish Tuscan stream, the Chiana.

25–7 'Peana' is one of the names for Apollo.

34f Aquinas here begins to address the meaning of the phrase 'no second ever rose who saw so much', first applied to an otherwise unidentified philosopher at *Paradiso* 10: 114 and now revealed as King Solomon. On this phrase depends a crucial distinction between Solomon, on the one hand, and Adam and Christ, on the other, in that while all three figures are fully human, they did not all 'rise', or come into being, in the same way. To clarify this distinction, Aquinas has first to explain (lines 52–90) the structure of the universe as it descends from the divine act by virtue of which all things, in one way or another, originally came into being.

However, there are two ways in which creatures can 'come into being'. (For an excellent account of this question, see P. Boyde, *Dante, Philomythes and Philosopher* (Cambridge, 1981) pp. 235–69.) 'Creation' is a term properly reserved for those things that are created directly or 'without intermediary' ('*sanza mezzo*' – cf. *Paradiso* 7: 67 and 70) by God, as in the creation of the angels or the human soul. At the same time, there is a 'generative influence' (line 66). Things are generated when they come into being through the *in*direct action of God, that is through the action of nature, which is the system of physical, chemical and biological laws that God has set in motion. Nature at the furthest remove from God's direct action produces the good but transient things to which Dante refers, at lines 63–4, as 'brief contingencies', which is to say generated things. Yet in the act of generation, nature is not always perfectly in control, but rather behaves like an artist whose hand at times trembles (lines 76–8), departing from the intended plan. Human beings are unique in

the cosmos, in so far as their souls are created – without inter-
mediate action – by God, while their physical properties are
generated by nature. The union of body and soul is indissoluble
and it is good that human beings should exist in this fashion.
(Cf. *Purgatorio* 25 and *Paradiso* 7: 124–48.) However, in two
cases – that of the first created man, Adam, and that of the
Christ, as the second Adam – providence ensured that the hand
of nature did *not* tremble but rather followed the divine purpose
exactly (lines 79–87). But this is true only in these two cases, so
Solomon is in no way comparable with either of them.

Once this is clarified, the argument returns to the word 'rose'
(line 106) and argues that this must be taken to indicate the
ascent to a throne and therefore to kingship. Dante now desig-
nates kingly wisdom as the highest form of philosophy. Referring,
at lines 95–6, to the Scriptural account in 1 Kings 3: 5–12, which
speaks of Solomon's prayer to God, Aquinas identifies the height
of Solomon's wisdom to be to ask for sufficient practical wisdom
to rule his kingdom for the greater good of his fellow human
beings. Unlike those concerned with the fine detail of theoretical
or speculative knowledge, Solomon sought only the practical
wisdom to benefit his subjects.

In developing this episode, Dante is able to draw attention to
many of the characteristics which make the historical Aquinas a
model of Christian rationalism. It was Aquinas himself who
wrote in his *Opusculum*: 'It would scarcely accord with the char-
acter of divine goodness were God to keep his knowledge to
himself without intimately disclosing himself to others, since to
be generous is of the nature of goodness.'

97–102 Parallel to the satirical account that opened *Paradiso* 11,
Dante now produces a parodic sequence of tags in Latin (lines
98–100), indicating the theoretical and speculative questions
that contrast with Solomon's political interests. In the uncertain
realm of generated existence – of 'brief contingencies' – there
will be a peculiar need for justice in the distribution of limited
goods, honours and rewards. The well-being of the human com-
munity depends on this, and the height of wisdom, on this
account, is to care for the human community, in the pursuit of
justice. (Solomon's words: 'Love Justice you rulers of the world'
(Book of Wisdom 1: 1) are elaborately quoted at the beginning
of the sequence in *Paradiso* 18–20 which is concerned with the
virtue of justice.)

This parody of Scholastic inquiry (into an issue also debated by Plato and Aristotle) points to the futility of questions such as whether, from an absolute premise and 'contingent' premise, one can draw a necessary ('*necesse*') conclusion. '*Si est dare primum motum esse*' ('Whether primal motion is to be assumed') indicates the question of whether it is possible to admit in the universe a primary motion independent of all others. The final speculation concerns the question of whether, given a semicircle, one can inscribe in it a triangle which is not a right-angled triangle.

124–6 Bryson, Parmenides and Melissus are Greek philosophers of the fifth century BC, mentioned in Aristotle's *Metaphysics*, as cited in Dante's *De Monarchia* 3: 4: 4.

127–9 Arius (d. 336) and Sabellius (d. *c.* 265) are heretics, the former exerting wide influence in his contention that Christ was not consubstantial with the Father, the latter calling into question the doctrine of the Trinity.

# CANTO 14

*Solomon speaks of the Resurrection of the Body.*
*Vision of Christ on the Cross. Transition from the*
*Heaven of the Sun to the Heaven of Mars.*

34–63 The 'modest' voice that now sounds, though unnamed, is generally taken to be that of King Solomon, who in the preceding canto was celebrated as the wisest human being who ever 'rose'. (See note to *Paradiso* 13: 34f.) For Dante, Solomon is of political significance, in his understanding the value of our temporal lives. (See also note to *Paradiso* 18.) But in *Paradiso* 14, as elsewhere, the biblical Book of Wisdom and the Song of Songs – both of which are attributed to Solomon – must also be prominent in Dante's mind. In his Book of Wisdom – a great influence on the Dante of the *Convivio* – Solomon repeatedly rejoices, as Dante does throughout the Heaven of the sun, in the orderly structure of the universe:

Within [Wisdom] is a spirit intelligent, holy, unique, manifold, subtle, active, incisive, unsullied, lucid, invulnerable, benevolent, sharp, irresistible, beneficent, loving to man, steadfast, dependable, unperturbed, almighty, all-surveying, penetrating all intelligent, pure and

most subtle spirits; for Wisdom is quicker to move than any motion,
she is so pure; she pervades and permeates all things. She is the
breath of the power of God.

                                                     Book of Wisdom 7: 22–5

At the same time, in the Song of Songs, Solomon takes a pro-
found delight in the value and significance of the human body:
'This thy stature is like to a palm tree, and thy breasts to clusters
of grapes. I said, I will go up to the palm tree, I will take hold of
the boughs thereof: now also thy breasts shall be as clusters of
the vine, and the smell of thy nose like apples' (7: 7–8). This
great erotic love song was frequently the subject of allegorical
interpretation, as in the hands of Saint Bernard of Clairvaux
(1090–1153), who saw human love as an expression of the love
between God and the Church or the human soul. Dante will take
Bernard as his final guide in *Paradiso* 31.

At lines 37–60, Dante attributes to Solomon the great hymn
of praise to the resurrection of the body. The Resurrection
assures of our return to the bodily nature, now glorified, in
which our temporal lives were lived. It is the height of Christian
wisdom to see this as the final expression of God's purposes for
us. And desire for the glorified body is now seen as the power
that motivates even the Christian philosophers, who long for the
restoration of their own 'dead bones' (line 63) and those of all
who were dear to them.

82f  Dante here enters the sphere of Mars, which is for Dante not only
the planet of war but also the planet of music. As Dante explains
in the *Convivio*, Mars resembles music in two ways: it instils
passion into the heart but it also produces harmony, since in the
planetary system Mars occupies the central position, holding the
rest of the planets in position. Thus, in lines 118–23, there occurs
the first of a series of references to musical phenomena in which
a melody runs through the Cross, holding Dante enraptured
even though he does not understand its meaning.

94–6  In a surprising neologism, Dante, in the Italian text, combines a
Hebrew word for God ('*Eli*') with the Greek for 'sun' ('*helios*')
in '*Eliòs*'.

# CANTO 15

*Entering the sphere of Mars, where the virtue of*
*courage is celebrated, Dante meets a twelfth-century*
*ancestor, the Crusader Cacciaguida.*

1–9 The Cross is here represented as a musical instrument. (See note
to *Paradiso* 14: 82f.)

28–30 'O blood of mine! O overflowing grace of God! To whom, as
to you, was ever the gate of Heaven twice flung open?' In these
Latin phrases, Dante brings together references to Virgil's *Aeneid*
6 (especially line 836) with allusions to the characteristic lan-
guage of Saint Paul's epistles. (The adjective *'superinfusa'*
appears to be constructed on models to be found in Romans 5:
20 and Ephesians 1: 8.)

31f The speaker in *Paradiso* 15 and throughout the following two
cantos is Dante's great-great-grandfather, Cacciaguida (1090–
1147), of whom nothing is known except that he was knighted
by Emperor Conrad III and died on the Second Crusade in the
Holy Land (lines 139–41). But Dante, in reinventing this histor-
ical figure, constructs an episode that reflects upon a wide range
of issues significant throughout the *Commedia*. These include
the themes of mutability and fortune (see *Paradiso* 16: 73–84),
as contrasted with the certainties of divine providence (see *Para-*
*diso* 15: 49–51 and 17: 37–42), the question of suffering and
heroism, where Cacciaguida's death is assimilated to the death of
Christ on the Cross – the image that dominates the Heaven of
Mars – while also providing a model that Dante holds before
himself in facing exile and the demands that his own poetic car-
eer impose upon him (see *Paradiso* 17: 106–42). Constant and
detailed contrasts are drawn between the nobility of Florentine
life in Cacciaguida's time and the decadence that ensues in
Dante's day through the rapid expansion of the city and the
development of its mercantile economy. (See especially *Paradiso*
15: 97–148 and 16: 85–154.)

46–63 God is celebrated as the Holy Trinity but also as the author of
the 'book' of providence, in which all temporal events are fore-
known, and as the principle of unity upon which all conceptions
of number depend.

73–5 God is the 'Primal Equipoise' in that all His attributes are infin-
ite and therefore all equal and balanced one with the other.

91–3 Cacciaguida's son adopted the name Alighiero (or Allagherius), which derived from the family name of Cacciaguida's mother. At line 137, she is said to have come from the Po valley, possibly from Ferrara, where at this period there seem to have been a family called Alighieri.

97–9 The walls, or 'ancient ring', were begun in 1078, extending the original city circuit. A further circle was begun in 1284. The reference is to canonical hours 9 a.m. and 3 p.m. ('terce and nones'), signalled by a bell rung at the tenth-century Benedictine church of the Badia in Florence (close to Dante's house and standing near the second line of walls). The city was at its best when still circumscribed by the radius of sound from these bells. The map on p. 642 shows the restricted extent of Cacciaguida's Florence and also the domicile of many of the families that Dante will refer to in the course of the present episode.

103–5 The age of marriage had not yet become unreasonably low nor dowries extravagant.

106–8 Sardanapalus, king of Assyria, was renowned for his luxurious tastes and decadence. (See Juvenal, *Satires* 10: 362.)

109–11 Montemalo (Monte Mario) and Uccellatoio (here translated as the 'Aviary') are hills overlooking Rome and Florence respectively. The implication is that Florence has now outstripped Rome in building high and ostentatious monuments.

112–15 Bellincion Berti dei Ravignani (*c.* 1150–*c.* 1200), the moral exemplar of ancient Florence, was the ancestor of the Conti Guidi, the Counts Palatine. Conte Guido Guerra spent his youth at the imperial court, but shifted his allegiances to the Guelf cause. He appears among the sodomites in *Inferno* 16. The Nerli and del Vecchio are, likewise, ancient Florentine families. The exemplary figures mentioned in the Mars episode, above all Cacciaguida himself, may usefully be contrasted with such Florentines of earlier generations who are consigned to Hell, as, for example, Farinata in *Inferno* 10, Brunetto in *Inferno* 15 and Mosca de' Lamberti in *Inferno* 28.

127–9 Cianghella della Tosa (*c.* 1260–90), notorious for her licentiousness, is also mentioned by Boccaccio in his misogynistic *Corbaccio* 228–30 (?1365). Lapo Salterello, a prominent lawyer in Florence in the late 1200s, enjoyed a high reputation, except among White Guelfs such as Dante and the chronicler Dino Compagni. Lucius Quinctius Cincinnatus (*c.* 519–438 BC), the ploughman ruler of Rome, and Cornelia Africana (*c.* 190–100 BC),

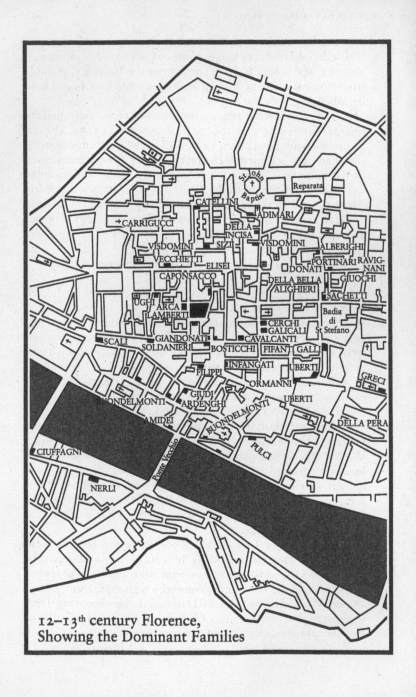

12–13ᵗʰ century Florence,
Showing the Dominant Families

the virtuous mother of the Gracchi, are also mentioned respect-
ively at *Paradiso* 6: 46 and *Inferno* 4: 128.

133–5 The name of the Virgin Mary, as invoked by women in labour.
The Baptistery in Florence – the foundations of which date
back, probably, to the fourth century AD – was the civic as well
as religious centre of the city in Dante's day. (See also notes to
*Paradiso* 25.)

139–41 Conrad III of Swabia (1093–1152) commanded the Second
Crusade of 1147–9, along with Louis VII of France.

# CANTO 16

*Cacciaguida speaks of the decline of the great families
of ancient Florence and of the subsequent decline in
the city's moral climate in the thirteenth century.*

1–6 In common with many city intellectuals of his time, Dante was
much concerned with the true nature of nobility, and argued
against any suggestion that nobility was a matter of rank or inher-
ited riches. In the *Vita nuova*, he claimed, along with other poets of
the '*dolce stil novo*' ('sweet new style' – see Introduction, p. xvi),
that a capacity for love must be included among the attributes of the
noble heart. In the *Convivio*, he demanded that wisdom, intelli-
gence and an interest in philosophy should likewise be regarded as
defining features of true nobility. These criteria are not abandoned
in the *Commedia*, but his interest in Rome, as the original founder
of Florence, leads to an emphasis upon the almost genetic connec-
tion between the past and the present. Here, specifically, in
constructing for himself the father figure of Cacciaguida, Dante
seems aware of, and even comically awkward about, the extrava-
gant claims he is making for his own lineage: nobility is a boast
even on earth, and he in Heaven – resuscitating the example of a
remote and scarcely visible forebear in the otherwise hardly illustri-
ous Alighieri line – has even greater reason to glory in his ancestry.
(Cf. the discussions of family characteristics in *Paradiso* 8 and 9.)

10–15 Beatrice's only contribution to the long conversation between
Dante and his ancestor is to note, with amusement, Dante's self-
aggrandizing use of the plural pronoun '*voi*'. This form of
address follows a Latin usage which was insitituted when Julius
Caesar made himself emperor, in place of the more intimately

colloquial *'tu'*. (This in translation needs to be registered by 'thou', as an instance of the slightly archaic features of, particularly, Cacciaguida's speech.) In drawing Dante's attention to his pompous *faux-pas*, Beatrice is compared to the Lady of Malhout, who in the Old French Romance of *Lancelot du Lac* (cf. *Inferno* 5: 127–38) is secretly in love with Lancelot and coughs to alert Guinevere to the danger of her own first meeting with him.

25-7 The sheepfold is either Florence, whose patron saint is Saint John the Baptist, or the Florentine Baptistery. (See note to *Paradiso* 15: 133–4 and *Paradiso* 25.)

37-9 Time is here calculated by the movement of planets and constellations: by the time of Cacciaguida's birth, the planet Mars had entered the constellation of Leo 580 times since the Annunciation.

40-48 Races were run annually along the Corso in Florence on Saint John's Day (24 June). The finishing line was located near the Mercato Vecchio. In Cacciaguida's time Florence lay within a semicircle of walls on the north bank of the Arno. The ancient statue of Mars stood at one extreme on the south side of the Ponte Vecchio, the Baptistery at the northernmost reach. (See note to *Inferno* 13: 147.) Of the men of arms-bearing age living 'Between the Baptistery and Mars' it is estimated that there were 30,000 in 1100.

49-57 Campi, Certaldo and Fegghine (now Figline) were country towns under Florentine influence, which produced many immigrants into the city. The villages of Galluzzo and Trespiano stood, respectively, about three miles south of the old city walls and four miles north. Aguglione is in the Val di Pesa, while Signa lies on the Arno, west of Florence. The 'peasant' and the 'cad' (line 56) are probably Baldo and Fazio Morunbaldini (*c.* 1280–1320), eminent lawyers whose ancestors had been immigrants. Contemporaries of Dante, these two men seemed to have attracted Dante's condemnation through their opposition to Emperor Henry VII, whom Dante supported.

58-60 Dante here, as usual, attacks the Church of his day for interfering with the Empire in its pursuit of justice, in particular for entering into financial alliances with the new Florentine mercantile classes to support its political ambitions.

61-6 This list of third-generation immigrants (sometimes subsumed into Florence by virtue of Florentine expansion) refers in turn to the Velluti family (probably) from Semifonte, a fortress town in the Val d'Elsa, south-west of Florence; and to those who came from the castle of Montemurlo, north-west of the city, which

Florence acquired by forced sale from the Ghibelline Conti Guidi (see note to *Paradiso* 15: 112–15) in 1254. The Cerchi were leaders of the White Guelfs, the party to which Dante belonged, in the tumultuous period around 1300, which ended (line 96) in the jettisoning of the party (including the exiled Dante) from power in 1302. Originating from Acone in the Val di Sieve, they bought the palace of the Conti Guidi in 1280. The Buondelmonti were Guelfs, credited with causing the thirteenth-century conflict in Florence. Their castle of Montebuono in the Val di Grieve had been taken by Florence in 1135. (On the immigrant expansion of Florence, see also *Inferno* 15.)

73–132 Dante now looks at the effect of fortune on Florentine families, noting how some once-great families have simply disappeared. Cities themselves (lines 73–5) can pass out of existence, through disease or warfare, as have Luni in Tuscany and Urbisaglia in the Marche, and as will Chiusi in the Val di Chiana and Sinigaglia. The families mentioned here have left little trace, save in Dante's praise of them – or at times his condemnation. The Ravignani (line 97) were the ancestors of the powerful Conti Guidi. The Della Pressa clan (line 100) held public office. The Galigai (line 102) were Ghibellines of chivalric rank – hence their sword and hilt. Again referring to chivalric and heraldic imagery, Dante identifies the Pigli family by the diagonal band of fur ('Pale of Vair' (line 103)) across their arms. The Sachetti (line 104) were an ancient Guelf family, while the next four families have sunk without trace, including the Chiaramontesi, who 'blush' to think of their ancestors who – when salt commissioners – used false measuring instruments.

At line 106, the 'stock' is that of the Donati family (still very influential in Dante's day – see *Purgatorio* 23 and 24 and *Paradiso* 3). But the Calfucci who sprang from them have gone, as have the Sizii and Arrigucci, who once occupied positions of authority. Those 'destroyed / by their own pride' (lines 109–10) and otherwise unnamed, are the great Uberti family. (See especially Farinata degli Uberti, who has a central role in *Inferno* 10.) Like the Uberti, the Lamberti – identified by the golden balls of their coat-of-arms – were of German descent.

The unnamed families of lines 112–14 were probably the Visdomini and the Tosinghi, who acted as (corrupt?) administrators of episcopal revenues when the See of Florence fell vacant. The 'bullying crew' (lines 115–20) were the Adimari. Their descendants included Filippo Argenti, who appears in *Inferno* 8 in

violent conflict with Dante. Ubertino of the noble Donati clan
was ashamed of even the remotest taint of relationship with the
crass Adimari: having married a daughter of the great Bellincion
Berti (see *Paradiso* 15: 112–15), Ubertino 'looked askance' when
Bellincione gave another of his daughters in marriage to the
Adimari.

The Pera family (line 126) originally gave its name to one of
the main entrances into the old city (now the Porta Peruzzi) but
has now utterly vanished, along with the families mentioned at
lines 121–3. At lines 127–32, Dante is once again concerned
with feudal chivalry. The 'great baron' (line 128) is the imperial
vicar, Hugh of Brandenburg, marquis of Tuscany, who died in
1001 on Saint Thomas's Day (21 December), and who is conse-
quently remembered and revered at every 'Thomas feast' in the
abbey in Florence where he is buried (one of seven that he
founded). A number of families (the Giandonati, Pulci, Nerli,
Gingalandi and Ciuffagni) not named in these lines were knighted
by Hugh and bear in their own arms references to the baron's
armorial bearings. One of these descendants, however, is Giano
della Bella (1250–1300) (referred to at lines 131–2), who in
1293 introduced the *Ordinamenti della Giustizia* (Ordinances of
Justice) which severely curtailed the privileges of the ancient
noble families.

133–44 Attention now begins to fall once again on the factional strife
that arose intially between the Buondelmonti and the Amidei,
spreading to include the whole of Florence. (See notes to *Para-
diso* 15.) The newcomers, the Buondelmonti, settled close to the
Gualterotti and Importuni – hence, by circumlocution, it would
have been better if the latter had not had 'the neighbours that
then came' (line 135). Best of all (lines 142–4) would have been
for God to drown Buondelmonte in the river Ema, which he had
to cross on his way from his original home into Florence.

151–4 The canto, having been much concerned with heraldic desig-
nations, concludes with a picture of the desecration, in the course
of partisan strife, of the Florentine flag. In 1251, when the
Ghibellines were driven out, the Guelfs altered the Florentine
standard, which originally bore a white lily on a red field, to a
red lily on a white field. The Ghibellines continued to use the
original design.

# CANTO 17

*Cacciaguida speaks prophetically of Dante's future
life, urging him to be courageous in the face of exile
and in writing his account of his journey through the
other world.*

1–3 Phaeton, supposedly the son of Apollo and Clymene, when told
that Apollo is not his father, seeks definite knowledge of his
paternity and subsequently exploits the sun god's indulgence to
wreak havoc with his misguided adventure in the chariot of the
sun – and thus makes fathers 'chary of their sons' (line 3). (See
Ovid, *Metamorphoses* 1: 748–56.)

31 The Italian word *'ambage'* – translated here as 'enigmatic words' –
picks up the phrase used of the Sibyl's song in Virgil's *Aeneid* 6:
99: *'Horrendas canit ambages'* ('She sings her dreadful enigmas').

37–45 See the connection with the 'brief contingencies' of which
Aquinas speaks in *Paradiso* 13: 63.

46–8 Hippolytus was driven out of Athens by the accusations of his
stepmother, Phaedra. (See Ovid, *Metamorphoses* 15: 493–503.)

49–54 The plot alluded to is that between Pope Boniface VIII (see
especially *Inferno* 19 and 27 and *Purgatorio* 20) and Corso
Donati (see *Purgatorio* 24) which led to the defeat of the White
Guelfs in Florence and to Dante's exile in 1302.

61–9 These lines probably refer to attempts at reconciliation made by
the White Guelfs in which Dante played no part. Dante's sym-
pathies with imperial policy tended to associate him with the
Ghibelline cause, although his interest was in the theory of
empire rather than the practical politics.

70–78 Dante in exile found refuge at Verona, under the protection of
the 'great Lombard' Bartolommeo della Scala, whose younger
brother was Can Grande della Scala (1291–1329), lord of Verona
from 1312, imperial vicar in the province of Vicenza (1312) and
captain-general of the Ghibelline League (1318). The Scaligeri
arms, referred to at line 72, displayed a ladder surmounted by an
imperial Eagle.

82–4 The 'Gascon' is Pope Clement V, who failed to support the
cause of the emperor Henry VII of Luxembourg, in whom Dante
had placed, prior to Henry's death in 1313, his hopes for a
revival of imperial power in Italy. (See *Purgatorio* 6 and 7 and
*Paradiso* 30: 133–48.)

# CANTO 18

*Rising from the Heaven of Mars to that of Jupiter,*
*Dante encounters the souls of the just, who form*
*themselves before his eyes in the shape of a great*
*emblematic Eagle.*

37–48 After the death of Moses, Joshua led the Israelites through the
   wilderness to the Promised Land (Deuteronomy 1: 38). (Cf. *Par-
   adiso* 9: 124–5.) In the second century BC, Judas Maccabeus
   liberated Israel from the tyranny of Syria (1 Maccabees 2: 66–9:
   22). Charlemagne (742–814), king of the Franks, was crowned
   as the first emperor of the Holy Roman Empire in Rome on
   Christmas Day 800. He was canonized for his defence of Chris-
   tendom against the Longobards and Moors in 1165. (Cf.
   *Paradiso* 6: 94–6.) Roland, one of Charlemagne's twelve paladins
   (and thought to be his nephew), is the hero of the eleventh-
   century French *Chanson de Roland*, which recounts his heroic
   defeat and death in fighting a rearguard action against the Moors
   at Roncesvalles. (See also note to *Inferno* 31: 16–18.) William,
   duke of Orange (who died as a monk in 812) and his brother-
   in-law Reynald (or Renoart – he was a Saracen converted to
   Christianity) also fought against the Moors and are celebrated in
   the French *chansons de geste* (songs of heroic deeds). (Reynald is
   probably a fictional character whom Dante took to be histor-
   ical.) Duke Godfrey of Boulogne or Bouillon (1061–1100) led
   the First Crusade in 1096 and was crowned king of Jerusalem.
   Robert Guiscard (*c.* 1015–85) was of Norman extraction and
   fought against the Saracens in southern Italy and Sicily. He
   was count of Apulia (1057–59), then duke of Apulia, Calabria
   and Sicily. In 1084 he saved Rome from attack by Emperor
   Henry IV and rescued Pope Gregory VII (*c.* 1020–85). (Cf. *Inferno*
   28: 14.)
82–4 The winged horse Pegasus struck Mount Helicon, the home of
   the Muses, with its hoof and produced the Hippocrene spring.
   (See Ovid, *Metamorphoses* 5: 250–93. For other references to
   the inspiration of the Muses, see *Purgatorio* 1: 7–12 and *Para-
   diso* 1: 16–18.)
88–114 The configuration of souls, as Dante now imagines it, con-
   trasts with the circularities and rectilinearities of the preceding

sequences, and suggestively establishes a connection between just-
ice and the use of signs and language. In the Romance languages
'*lex*' ('law') is etymologically connected to the act of read-
ing – '*leggere*' – as, logically, it must be, since a law which is not
comprehensibly *readable* cannot be just at all. Dante has already
made a similar connection in *Paradiso* 6, where Justinian's codifi-
cation of Roman law is associated with an emphasis on the notion
of a 'sign'. Now Dante goes further. The souls now appear to him
(at lines 88 to 93) as letters written in the sky, forming in Latin the
sentence: '*Diligite iustitiam qui iudicatis terram*' ('Love justice,
you rulers of the earth'), which opens the first verse of King Solo-
mon's Book of Wisdom. At every point, Dante emphasizes the
lexical and grammatical features of this act, its vowels, conso-
nants and verbs. Then the linguistic sign transforms into a visual
one. The final 'M' of the sentence, when written in cursive Gothic
script, reveals the shape, firstly, of a heraldic lily (line 113). This is
then subsumed into the form of the Eagle (lines 106–14) which
will henceforth act as the spokesman of justice in the episode.

121–3 Christ's attack on the money-lenders in the Temple is recorded
in Matthew 21: 12–13.

127–36 These lines refer to excommunication as a penalty imposed
by the papacy on political enemies. The target of Dante's polemic
are popes such as John XXII (1249–1334), who slyly pervert the
words of Scripture. John may indeed follow Saint John the Bap-
tist and know nothing of his predecessor, Saint Peter, but only in
the sense that he is avariciously devoted to the Florentine coin-
age, issued under the mark of the city's patron saint, Saint John,
and thus disregards the example of the apostolic fishermen.
Lines 130–32 refer to Saint Peter and Saint Paul, who both died
martyr's deaths after lives spent working in the vineyard of
Christ's service.

# CANTO 19

*The Eagle speaks of God as the unknowable source
of all conceptions of justice. Questions concerning the
fate of the noble pagan are raised. The faults of the
rulers of Christian Europe are laid open to view.*

1–3 'Frui' is the infinitive form of the Latin 'fruor', 'to enjoy or delight in', hence used here as a noun to signify 'delight'.

31–63 The question running through this canto and continuing into Paradiso 20 is whether it is just for virtuous pagans such as Virgil to be deprived of beatitude and relegated to Limbo. The answer that the Eagle gives is at first sight authoritarian. Ultimate justice is linked to the creative, infinite and ultimately incomprehensible act by which God first wielded His 'compass' (lines 40–45) to form out of nothing a world of determinate and finite beings. Such beings exist because of, and depend upon, the perfect geometry of this creation, and through this geometry God's purposes are indeed legible to the rational mind. But God remains, as an infinite being, in 'excess' (lines 43–5) of all finite creation. We may have comprehensible conceptions of justice, but these derive from depths we cannot comprehend (lines 58–63). Consequently, it is a condition of every act of human justice that it should be founded upon a just recognition of God's existential infinity. All conceptions of justice ultimately derive from God, and therefore to question God's justice, even in condemning the noble pagan, is self-contradictory, since we should have no conception of justice at all if God had not initially instilled it into us. This is the contradiction into which Satan fell, when, failing to realize his position as a finite creature (albeit the highest in all Creation), he sought prematurely to receive more light than he had been given, even though out of an infinity of light he would progressively have received more and yet more understanding. Satan's sin is as much impatience as it is pride (lines 46–8).

103f Dante allows that there are those who before Christ's Incarnation believed that he would come, just as there are those who believed in him after his coming. (See also Inferno 4 and Paradiso 32.) From line 115, the poet develops an acrostic on the letters L, U, E, which spell out the word meaning 'pestilence' in Italian (here translated as 'pox'), while each terzina alludes to events in contemporary history from Norway to Sicily which demonstrate how far the world is contaminated by injustice.

115–29 Albert I of Germany (1255–1308), son of Rudolph of Habsburg, was elected emperor (though never crowned) in 1298 and invaded the kingdom of Bohemia in 1304. (Cf. Purgatorio 6: 97.) Albert ruled as king of Germany from 1285 until he was assassinated in 1308. Lines 118–20 refer to Philip IV of France (1268–1314), who, after the battle of Courtrai in 1302, issued debased coinage to fund his wars against Flanders, to the detriment of the French economy (the 'Seine') He died in a hunting accident when his horse was tripped up by a boar. Lines 121–3 refer to the wars of Edward I (1239–1307) and Edward II (1284–1327) of England against the Scots under William Wallace (c. 1270–1305) and Robert the Bruce (1274–1329), which culminated in the battle of Bannockburn in 1314. Lines 124–6 refer to Ferdinand IV of Castile and León (1285–1312), who, with the help of Aragon, won Gibraltar from the Saracens in 1296 but subsequently took little part in the defence of Christendom. Wenceslaus II of Bohemia (1270–1305) resisted Albert of Austria's invasions of Bohemia, but won a reputation for lust and easy living. (See also *Purgatorio* 7: 101.) At lines 127–9, the 'Cripple' is Charles II of Anjou and Naples (1254–1309), titular king of Jerusalem, who was deeply involved in the political affairs of thirteenth-century Sicily. He is the target of Dante's animus against the Angevins at *Purgatorio* 20: 79.

130–38  A reference to Frederick of Aragon (1272–1337), king of Sicily and grandson of Manfred (see *Purgatorio* 3), who deserted the Ghibelline cause after the death of Emperor Henry VII in 1313 – hence Dante's disapproval. (Cf. *Purgatorio* 7: 119.) Frederick's brother James II of Aragon (1267–1327), surnamed 'The Just' by his subjects, ceded Sicily to the Angevin claimant, Charles II, on his marriage to Charles's daughter. (Cf. *Purgatorio* 7: 119–23.) At line 138, the 'two crowns' are those of Aragon and Majorca.

139–48  Line 139 refers, respectively, to Diniz, king of Portugal (1261–1325), known as 'The Farmer' for his promotion of agricultural reform – though why Dante opposes him is not clear – and to Haakon V, king of Norway (1270–1319), whose reign was punctuated by wars against Denmark of the sort that, for Dante, characterized the divided state of Christendom. The 'Rascian' is Stephen Uros II Milutin, king of Old Serbian Rascia (1253–1321), who issued a debased coinage similar in appearance to the *matapan* and *grosso* of Venice. The lament for the state of Hungary is precipitated by the dominance of the Angevin dynasty in that country from 1301 under the French monarch Philip IV, whom Dante detested. The son of Charles Martel (see *Paradiso* 8) was confirmed as king of Hungary in 1309 by Pope Clement V, thus ensuring the continuance of misgovernment. Navarre was united with the kingdom of France in 1305 under Louis X (1289–1316). Navarre would have been 'blessed' if the mountains between Navarre and France had proved a protection.

The Cypriot towns of Nicosia and Famagosta were suffering in 1300 from misgovernment (as in later years would Hungary and Navarre) at the hand of Henry II of Lusignan (d. 1324).

## CANTO 20

*Dante contemplates the souls who are found at the eye of the Eagle, who include the Trojan Ripheus and the Roman emperor Trajan.*

**31–6** Attention now falls on the particular named individuals who compose the eye of the Eagle, rather than its general form, a new emphasis that reminds one that the Eagle not only symbolizes the Roman Empire but is also the emblem of Saint John the Evangelist and thus represents an understanding of the revelation of divine love. In medieval animal lore, the eagle was believed (as Dante says at line 33) to be uniquely capable of seeing into the sun without suffering any harm, symbolizing an ability to see directly into the truth of God.

**37–72** The eye of the Eagle contains, at its pupil, David, 'singer of the Holy Ghost', and king of Israel; at lines 49–54, Hezekiah, king of Judah (2 Kings 20: 1–11); Emperor Constantine (see notes to *Paradiso* 6 and *Inferno* 19), who moved the seat of the Empire from Rome to Byzantium – thus becoming Greek (line 57) – and left Rome in the hands of an eventually corrupt papacy. William (line 62) is the Norman William II (1153–89), who as king of Naples (Apulia) and Sicily was renowned for his uprightness and compassion. At line 63, a contrast is drawn between the just King William and later rulers Charles of Anjou and Provence – a regular target of Dante's odium – and the Aragonese King Frederick II. In 1300, Charles and Frederick were, respectively, rulers of Naples and the kingdom of Sicily.

Dante daringly chooses to place two pagans, the emperor Trajan (lines 43–8) and the Trojan warrior Ripheus (lines 67–72), at the eye of the Eagle. The case of Trajan is not perhaps surprising. Throughout the Middle Ages legend had it that the emperor had benefited from the special prayers of Pope Gregory the Great on his behalf, and Dante had already taken Trajan as an example of humility in *Purgatorio* 10: 73–93. Ripheus, however, presents a much more complex case. A figure drawn from legend, all that is known of him is derived from three lines in Virgil's *Aeneid*, which declare that Ripheus the Trojan, slain in the last battle for his homeland, was the most just of all the sons of Troy, although the gods, in allowing his death, thought otherwise – '*iustissimus unus qui fuit in Troia (dis aliter visum)*' (*Aeneid* 2: 426–8). It may be said that Ripheus's passion for justice was so great that he was given special grace to see into the depths of the ocean of justice evoked in this canto.

94–9 The phrase '*Regnum celorum*' ('the kingdom of the heavens') adapts the meaning of Matthew 11: 12, in which the kingdom of Heaven is said to suffer the violence of violent men.

127–9 This refers to the pageant of the Revelation described in *Purgatorio* 29: 121–6, in which three ladies appear symbolizing Faith, Hope and Charity.

# CANTO 21

*Entering the sphere of Saturn, Dante sees a golden ladder rising to the highest heavens. He encounters the contemplatives, including Saint Peter Damian.*

4–6 Semele, daughter of Cadmus of Thebes, was one of Jupiter's lovers. Juno, jealous of her husband's liaison, persuaded Semele to ask that she should see her lover in all his majesty as king of the gods. When her request was granted, Semele was reduced to ashes by the sight of him. (See Ovid, *Metamorphoses* 3: 253–86; cf. *Inferno* 30: 1–3.)

13–15 Saturn was considered in medieval lore to be a cold and dry planet and hence is here associated with the moral virtue of temperance. The souls that Dante meets in the sphere of Saturn are all ascetics or members of monastic orders. In April 1300, at the date of Dante's fictional journey, the planet was located within the constellation of Leo.

25–7 Saturn as father of the gods ruled Crete in the Golden Age when crime was unknown.

28f The dominant image in the Heaven of Saturn is that of the Ladder of Contemplation. In Genesis 28: 12, Jacob sees a ladder stretching to Heaven, and monastic preachers used this image to signify the contemplative ascent to God.

**43f** The figure is Saint Peter Damian. Born around 1007 of poor parents, he began his career as a teacher of jurisprudence in Ravenna and Faenza before becoming a Benedictine monk in 1037 and, in 1043, abbot of Fonte Avellana. He became a cardinal reluctantly (lines 124–6) in 1057, a position which he later resigned, and died in 1072. Peter Damian's teachings (embodied in a large corpus of sermons, some 180 letters and a number of poems) resisted attempts to rationalize Christian faith. He is also known for the vehemence of his attacks on Church corruption – as in the *Gomorrhianus* (a treatise against sodomy) – which may be illustrated here by the following lines from *Epistle* 48, written in 1057 on his elevation to the position of cardinal bishop of Ostia:

> The office of bishop does not consist in peaked caps of sable or of some other wild beast from overseas, not in blazing red garments topped by collars of marten fur, not in flowing gold coverlets as ornamentation for their horses, and finally, not in the prancing lines of massed knights, nor in neighing horses champing at their spuming bits, but in uprightness of life and the practice of virtue.

These lines seem to have been in Dante's mind at lines 130–35.

**106–11** This geographical periphrasis (cf. *Paradiso* 8 and 9) describes the Apennine range which divides Italy. Monte Catria is a mountain in the Apennine range, north of Gubbio in Umbria.

**121–3** Though the exact reference of this *terzina* has been long discussed (without conclusion), it is known that Peter Damian was accustomed to sign himself 'Peter the Sinner'.

**127–9** Cephas is Saint Peter. The 'vessel' is Saint Paul.


# CANTO 22

*Still in the sphere of Saturn, with the contemplatives,*
*Dante meets Saint Benedict, who speaks of the*
*Benedictine Order that he founded and its decline in*
*modern times. Dante ascends the ladder to the sphere*
*of the Fixed Stars or constellations.*

**31f** The speaker who now appears is Saint Benedict (*c.* 480–*c.* 547), born in the Umbrian town of Nursia and educated at Rome when it was in the throes of its imperial decline and fall. Fleeing the city at the age of fourteen to become a hermit, Benedict later established a community of twelve fellow hermits (deciding initially on the apostolic number) which eventually became the monastic community of Monte Cassino. Benedict was moved by the conviction that the contemplative life is best pursued in an orderly society, with its own clear, comprehensible and mutually beneficial rules of conduct, and always under the guidance of an abbot who is required 'to profit his brethren rather than to preside over them' (*The Rule of Saint Benedict*, chapter 64). Under *The Rule*, provision is made for various kinds of productive work – some of it physical. But the main work of the monastery is the '*Opus Dei*', the liturgical performance of prayer and hymn pursued daily in the communal singing of the canonical hours (*The Rule of Saint Benedict*, chapter 5), from dawn to dusk.

49–51 In three deliberately austere but beautifully balanced verses, Dante emphasizes the inwardness ('*dentro ai chiostri*'/'within the cloister') of the monastic community – which is now replicated in the Heaven of Saturn. The intimate use of proper names indicates the recognition accorded to person and identity within the Order. And the moderation of the final line speaks of the poise and steadiness that the 'heart' achieves when the 'foot' comes to rest and ceases to dissipate its best efforts. All of which exactly reflects the sentiments expressed in chapter 4 of *The Rule*, which speaks of the 'stability' offered by enclosure in the monastic community.

'Maccario' – meaning the 'blessed' or 'sainted' – was a fairly common name, but here probably Dante means Maccarius the Younger of Alexandria (d. 404), who founded the traditions of monasticism in the East as did Benedict in the West. Romoaldus (*c.* 950–1027) founded a reformed and especially ascetic Order based on Saint Benedict's *Rule*. The Peter Damian of *Paradiso* 21 belonged to this Order and wrote a life of its founder. Romoaldus may have contributed to the idea of the Ladder of Contemplation by a vision recorded in the *Breviarum Romanum* (*c.* 1020).

70–72 See note to *Paradiso* 21: 28f.

94–6 A reference to the miraculous actions of God in which the Jordan is said to turn back against its regular course (Psalm 114: 3 and Joshua 3: 13) and the Red Sea parts as the Israelites flee from Egypt (Exodus 14: 21–2). Even such events are less extreme than the corruption of the modern monastic orders.

100–38 Here Dante and Beatrice rise to the Heaven of the Fixed Stars
(which will be the scene of the poem until *Paradiso* 27), entering
at the constellation of Gemini (the 'sign that follows Taurus'
(line 111)), under whose astral influence Dante was born in the
later part of May 1265. This passage can seem surprising, given
Dante's unfailing insistence on the freedom of the will. Yet at
every point since *Purgatorio* 17, where Dante most fully dis-
cusses the freedom of the will, true freedom is seen to reside not
in some impossible state of autonomy, but in a conscious align-
ment of the will with the existence which providentially it has
been given at the moment of its creation. In this perspective, it is
not deterministic for Dante to say that his specific identity and
'whatever talents that are mine' derive from the influence of
Gemini (line 114). Fulfilment of his existence depends upon his
willing recovery of the possibilities that were stamped upon him
at the time of his birth.

From line 133, Dante may well be drawing on Cicero's *Som-
nium Scipionis* 3, which speaks, with relief, of man's power to
transcend his earthly origins.

139–41 The 'daughter of Latona' is the moon. The dark patches on
the moon can only be observed on the side nearest the earth. (See
*Paradiso* 2.)

142–53 These lines pass in review the heavens surrounding the earth
through which Dante has passed to arrive at the Fixed Stars. The
son of Hyperion (see Ovid, *Metamorphoses* 4: 142 and 192) is
the sun, Mercury is the child of Maia and Venus of Dione. Jupiter,
standing between his son Mars and his father Saturn, moderates
the two extremes that these represent of heat and cold.


# CANTO 23

*Dante momentarily sees Christ, along with all the
members of the Church Triumphant. When this
vision has passed, his attention falls upon the Virgin
Mary, who is surrounded by saints, including Saint
Peter, who will examine Dante's faith in Paradiso 24.*

10–12 In the middle of the sky, the sun seems to move more slowly
than it does near the horizon.

25–7  Dante's Italian speaks here of '*Trivia*'. This is one of the names of Artemis (otherwise Diana), who is 'tri-form' in being the goddess of the moon, of the hunt and of death. The moon here is seen among a vista of stars – the 'eternal nymphs'.

37–9  Christ, in the phrase of Saint Paul (1 Corinthians 1: 24), is the 'power of God, and the wisdom of God'.

52–4  Cf. the opening sentences of the *Vita nuova* where Dante introduces the story of his love for Beatrice as written in the 'book' of his memory.

55–7  Polyhymnia is the Muse of sacred poetry, referred to here with her eight 'sister' Muses.

73–5  In traditional iconography, the Virgin Mary is the mystic 'rose'. The lilies or 'fleurs-de-lys' are the saints of the Church.

106–14  The allusions here are to the plan of the Ptolemaic universe. Beyond the Fixed Stars there is the *Primum Mobile* (here referred to as the 'regal surcoat' (line 112)) – which Dante enters in *Paradiso* 27. The Empyrean is the supreme sphere, the eternal presence of God, where Dante arrives in *Paradiso* 30.

127–9  '*Regina coeli*' ('Queen of Heaven') is one of the liturgical hymns to the Virgin Mary, particularly associated with Eastertime. (Cf. *Purgatorio* 7: 82.)

133–5  Life on earth is compared to the exile in Babylon suffered by the Jews. (Cf. Jeremiah 52.)

136–9  In the celestial rose (see *Paradiso* 32), Saint Peter, 'who holds such glory's key', sits at the right hand of the Virgin. The 'new and . . . ancient' courts are, respectively, the assemblies of those in the Christian era who believed in the Christ who had now come and those in the Old Testament who believed in Christ 'to come'.


# CANTO 24

*Saint Peter examines Dante in the virtue of*
*Christian faith.*

13–15  Cf. the simile here, which describes the workings of an early chiming clock, with the clock at *Paradiso* 10: 139–44.

46f  Here and in the following two cantos, Dante represents himself (sometimes comically) as a candidate undergoing examination in the medieval university system, where students were tested orally in methods of syllogistic argumentation (see also lines 76–7), though they were not expected (line 47) to provide definitive conclusions. Dante's responses throughout draw not only on argument but on frequent references to Scripture and the history of the Church. The first examination, in this canto, concerns the virtue of faith and is conducted by Saint Peter.

Where in *Paradiso* 10–22, Dante's theme was, progressively, the four cardinal virtues (wisdom, courage, justice and temperance), his subject now is the three theological virtues (faith, hope and charity). His understanding broadly follows Saint Thomas Aquinas, who, comparing the cardinal virtues with the theological, writes:

> When a man is admitted to citizenship, he should have the virtues ensuring that he loves and serves the State. Likewise, when by divine grace a man is set on sharing eternal bliss, which consists in the joyful vision of God, he becomes a citizen and a companion in the blessed society of the Heavenly Jerusalem: *ye are ... fellow-citizens, with the saints, and of the household of God* (Ephesians 2: 19). Definite virtues are required of a man thus enrolled. They are the infused virtues freely given to him, and their activity is prompted by love of the common good of that perfect society, namely the divine good which is the heart of happiness.
>
> Disputations, *De Caritate* 2

> The theological virtues are those that make us well-adjusted to our last end, which is God himself ... The theological virtues are therefore three – *faith*, which makes us know God; *hope*, which makes us look forward to joining him; *charity*, which makes us his friends.
>
> Disputations, *De Virtutibus in Communi* 12

61–9 These lines draw upon Hebrews 11: 1 and on Aquinas's discussion of faith in the *Summa Theologiae* 2: 2: 4: 1: 'Faith is substantial to the things we hope, the evidence of things we do not see' (lines 64–6).

73–8 The terms 'substance' and 'evidence' ('*sustanza*' and '*argomento*' in the Italian) are used technically, as in Scholastic philosophy, to mean 'foundational reality' and a 'reason for certainty'.

103–8 Saint Peter points out that Dante's arguments are tending to become circular – taking the Bible to prove what the Bible claims to prove. But Dante escapes this by looking to the history of Christian witness: if the world had been converted to Christianity without miraculous claims on the resources of faith, this would itself have been the greatest miracle of all.

124–6 Peter, older than the rest of the disciples such as John, ran more slowly to the tomb of Christ on the morning of the Resurrection, but was quicker to believe that Christ had risen. (See John 20: 1–9.)

133–8 The proofs offered by physics and metaphysics are those that Aristotle develops in his understanding of God as the unmoved first mover. Lines 136–8 refer to all the writings of the early Church, including the two epistles of Saint Peter, which were composed after Pentecost under the influence of the Holy Spirit.

# CANTO 25

*Dante expresses his fading hopes for a return to Florence. He is then examined in the theological virtue of hope by Saint James, whose brother John appears at the conclusion.*

1–9 Dante's hopes for a return from exile to Florence are expressed in very guarded terms, contrasting with the certainty of his hopes for Heaven. The Florentine Baptistery, where Dante supposes he might eventually receive due recognition as a poet, is regularly referred to in the *Commedia* as the true centre of both civic and religious life, a symbol of what Florence might be at its virtuous best.

13f The examiner in this canto is the Apostle James the Great, brother of Saint John the Evangelist. Saint John joins the scene at lines 103–11 and, in *Paradiso* 26, will examine Dante in the virtue of charity. The Epistle of Saint James is referred to at lines 76–8. Saint James does not speak explicitly of hope in his writings but rather of the rewards that will be given by God to those who suffer and who are capable, through love, of overcoming temptation (James 1: 12). Dante clearly derives from these words a particular understanding of the second theological virtue, applying them to his own case.

Hope is less a matter of doctrine than of an attention to the divine, sustained throughout the journey of earthly existence. At lines 52–4 Dante claims, through the mouth of Beatrice, especial adherence to this virtue. This claim goes back to chapter 40 of the *Vita nuova* where, meditating on the example of certain pilgrims whom he sees travelling through Florence, he defines the word 'pilgrim' – '*peregrino*' – as one who travels as a stranger far from his own land and, specifically, seeks to visit the tomb of Saint James at Compostela in Galicia. (Dante appears to have confused Saint James the Great, whose shrine is at Compostela, with the brother of Jesus who is taken to be the author of the epistle.)

25–7 The Latin phrase '*coram me*' ('in my presence') adds rhetorical elevation to the discussion.

31–3 The 'favoured three' are the Apostles Peter, James and John who witnessed Christ's Transfiguration (Mark 9: 2). (Cf. *Purgatorio* 32: 76–81.)

55–7 Egypt, as the land in which the Hebrews suffered servitude, is symbolic of life on earth.

67f Dante's definition of hope reproduces in Italian the Latin phrases of the major theological textbook of the period, Peter Lombard's *Sententiae* 3: 26 (1145–51). Prominence is also given in this canto to the words of King David, the author of Psalm 9: 10, twice quoted, in Italian at line 73 and in the Latin of the Vulgate ('*Sperent in te*') at line 98: 'And they that know thy name will put their trust in thee: for thou, Lord, hast not forsaken them that seek thee'.

79–81 In Mark 3: 17, Jesus nicknamed James and John 'the sons of thunder'.

82–4 James suffered martyrdom under King Herod in the year AD 44 (Acts 12: 1–2).

91–6 The reference is to Isaiah 61: 7 and 10. In Revelation 3: 5 and 7: 9–17, Saint John speaks of the 'white raiment' or 'robes' that will be worn by those elected to Heaven.

100–102 For a month in the middle of winter, the constellation of Cancer shines all night through. Were this constellation to contain a star as luminous as this 'crystal' throughout that month, then night would be as bright as day.

112–14 The reference is to Psalm 102: 6: 'I am like a pelican of the wilderness.' The pelican pecks its own breast to revive its young with its blood, and is thus a symbol of Christ's self-sacrifice. The Virgin Mary is given into Saint John's care by Christ as he hangs on the Cross.

121–3 Dante is hoping to see Saint John's body, on the erroneous expectation – refuted by Saint Thomas but supported by certain medieval theologians – that John, and also Elijah and Enoch, had been directly assumed to Heaven in bodily form as only the Virgin Mary and Christ himself had been.

127–9 The two 'robes' are the radiance of spirit and that of the resurrected body.

## CANTO 26

*Dante, now temporarily blinded, is examined
in the virtue of charity by Saint John the Evangelist.
When his eyesight returns, he encounters Adam and is
told about the conditions of the Garden of
Eden, in particular the language that was
spoken in the Garden.*

1f Saint John appears in this canto as author of the fourth Gospel and Book of Revelation. In medieval iconography he is frequently represented as the Eagle of God (lines 52–3), since eagles were supposedly able to see into the sun without being blinded. (See *Paradiso* 20: 31–3.) Charity in its highest form is to be understood as a God-given capacity for contemplation and vision which, once concentrated on God, brings delight at the presence of the divine, and permits, as Aquinas puts it (in *Summa Theologiae* 2a–2ae: 23.1), 'a union or friendship with the purposes of the divine'.

10–12 In Acts 9: 17–18, Ananias places his hands on Saint Paul's eyes to cure him of blindness.

16–18 Cf. Revelation 22: 13.

37–43 There is some controversy as to the authority which is referred to at line 38. Some recent commentators have argued that Dante is here alluding to the Platonic tradition, received into medieval thought particularly through the writings of Saint Augustine. Early commentators, however, cited Aristotle, or the *Liber de Causis* (supposed, in Dante's day, to be Aristotle's work). At line 42, Dante records God's words to Moses in Exodus 33: 19. He then alludes to the words with which his present interlocutor, Saint John, opens his Gospel, where the love of God expressed in the Trinity is announced.

64–6 The 'orchardist', or gardener, is Christ. (Cf. John 15: 1.)

**67–9** 'Holy, Holy, Holy' is the song of the Seraphim spoken of in Isaiah 6: 3, which is now sung by congregations in preparation for Mass.

**115–32** The fall of Adam is here seen as a matter not of appetite ('the tasting of the tree') but of disobedience, transgressing the conditions that God had placed upon human existence. Before Christ's coming (lines 118–23), Adam was confined in Limbo, the realm of Hell in which Beatrice found Virgil. (See *Inferno* 1.) Dante here follows a chronology established by Eusebius in his *Chronicle* (*c*. AD 325): the creation of Adam was 5198 BC; Adam's death and descent into Limbo occurred in 4268 BC. The mention of Virgil's name at this late stage in the poem is significant, especially as the discussion between Dante and Adam is largely concerned with questions relating to language that had occupied Dante throughout his career, particularly in the *De Vulgari Eloquentia* where he addresses the issues raised by the mutability of vernacular tongues. The mention of Nimrod at line 125 reminds one of the confusion wrought in human language at the building of the Tower of Babel. (See *Inferno* 31; also notes to *Purgatorio* 26.) Now, altering his earlier stance, Dante suggests that linguistic change need not be considered a disaster, nor even as a consequence of the confusion of tongues at Babel. Language is the product of human reason, and all such products are subject to change. We speak as pleases us, and there is not even one single or magically accurate name for God. So, long before Babel, Adam's original language had already been extinguished.

**133–8** The reference here is to the two names for God in Hebrew Scripture, '*I*' or '*Yah*' being the opening of '*Yahweh*', '*El*' being an alternative form.

**139–42** The length of time that Adam spent in the Garden of Eden before and after the Fall was seven hours, from 6 a.m., the first hour of the day, to the hour that follows noon.

## CANTO 27

*Saint Peter condemns the corruption of the modern*
*Church. Dante and Beatrice ascend to the* Primum Mobile.

**13–15** The hymnic elevation of the opening sequence disappears and is momentarily replaced by an extremely compressed astronomical fantasy: as Saint Peter's countenance turns from praise to polemic, Dante – in order to describe the blush of indignation that suffuses the saint – imagines a wholly unnatural transformation in the appearance of the planets, whereby Jupiter takes on the red hue – the 'plumage' – that is characteristic of Mars.

22–7 The usurper referred to here is Boniface VIII, who held the papal throne in the year that Dante set out on his fictional otherworldly journey, 1300. (Cf. *Inferno* 19: 52–7 and 27: 85 onwards.) The 'sod' (line 26) so pleased by Boniface's actions is Satan.

28–30 This much debated passage probably refers to the effect of light on clouds when the sun is below the horizon.

40–45 Saint Peter and his two immediate successors, Saint Linus and Saint Cletus, were martyred in *c.* 67, *c.* 79 and *c.* 90 respectively. Popes Sixtus I (d. 125), Pius I (d. *c.* 155), Calixtus I (d. 222) and Urban I (d. 230) also died for the faith.

46–54 Contemporary popes are here condemned for their involvement in secular politics, favouring on the 'right hand' the Guelf cause and condemning the Ghibellines. The 'keys' (line 49) – representing the keys to the kingdom of Heaven given to Saint Peter – now become emblems on the battle standards of warrior popes, as in their campaigns for influence over the Italian peninsula against Emperor Frederick II.

58–60 The inhabitants of Cahors in southern France were notorious as usurious bankers favoured by the anti-Pope John XXII, a native of that city. Similarly, Pope Clement V favoured his fellow Gascons.

61–3 Scipio Africanus the Elder defeated the Carthaginian forces under Hannibal that threatened Rome at the battle of Zama in 202 BC. This victory was decisive in ensuring Rome's dominance as a Mediterranean power.

67–9 The sun is in conjunction with Capricorn, the Goat, in midwinter, between 21 December and 21 January.

79–87 Dante has been moving with the very slowly moving sphere of Fixed Stars. He has passed six hours in this sphere. On his arrival, he was directly above the meridian of Jerusalem; now he is above the meridian of Cadiz, opposite Gibraltar. (See the diagram on p.644.) From his new vantage point, he can see westwards far into the Atlantic, following the track of Ulysses's voyage into the southern hemisphere. (See *Inferno* 26.) Eastwards he can see the shadowy coasts of Phoenicia, where Jupiter, disguised as a bull, carried off Europa, as narrated in Ovid's *Metamorphoses* 2:

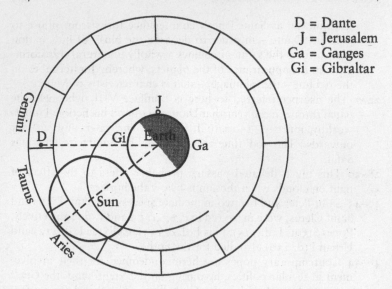

D = Dante
J = Jerusalem
Ga = Ganges
Gi = Gibraltar

833–75. (Cf. the reference to the rape of Leda at lines 97–9, as narrated in Ovid's *Heroides* 17: 55–6; see also note to lines 97–120.) The 'sign' referred to at line 87 is Aries, 30 degrees west of Dante's position.

97–120 Dante now ascends from the constellation Gemini – designated by reference to Leda, who bore the twins Castor and Pollux as a result of being seduced by Jupiter in the form of a swan – to the *Primum Mobile*, the unmoved mover, which communicates motion to all the lower heavens and from which all time and space are measured. The *Primum Mobile* is itself invisible to human eyes ('Its motion is not gauged by other marks' (line 115)), but all time 'takes root' there (line 119); and the movements of the lower heavens are visible through the movements of the stars and planets that they impel. Beyond the *Primum Mobile* (line 109) is a realm which is constituted neither by space and time, nor by cause and effect, nor by any supernatural version of earthly geography, but rather by intelligence and the desire to maintain the relationship of love between all existing beings.

121f Cupidity is here contrasted with the love that displays itself generously in the creation and sustaining of the universal system.

136–8 The white face of innocence turns black as adulthood
approaches. This much contested passage probably imagines the
attraction of worldly goods which seduce as the 'lovely child' of
the sun, Circe, seduced Ulysses. (Cf. *Purgatorio* 19: 1–24.)

142–4 The Julian calendar miscalculated the length of a solar year by
what Dante calls here the hundredth part of a day. Left uncor-
rected, January would eventually have become a springtime
month, when birds announce the end of winter with their song.
This long period of time is here referred to ironically, to indicate
how *soon* the Day of Judgement will come.


## CANTO 28

*Dante sees God as a point of light, infinitesimally
small, reflected first in Beatrice's eyes. He contem-
plates the hierarchy of angelic beings that move in
God's sight and in turn communicate to the material
universe His providential design.*

16f God, seen as point of light, is absolutely simple and eternal, and
wholly distinct from the order that is Creation. As such, the
point of light must cause the human eye that looks on it to close
in self-protection against its intensity (line 18), since human
minds work in the created order through the construction of
merely rational chains of observation and argumentation. The
angels, by contrast, are pure intelligences (see especially *Paradiso*
29: 76–84) and thus see directly and instantaneously into the
truth of God. The function of the angels, who are themselves
part of the created order, is to understand, enjoy and praise their
maker. But some of the angels – those whom Dante now sees
arranged in nine circles around the Single Point – also communi-
cate God's design in Creation to the material heavens through
which Dante is now ascending. Hitherto, Dante has seen (though
not described) the fulminating presence of Christ in Paradise.
(See *Paradiso* 14: 88–105 and 23: 19–33.) The present vision
emphasizes a fundamental understanding in theology which is
that, although we do not know what God is like, we must pro-
ceed on the understanding that, unlike his creation, God is
indeed utterly simple, single and eternal. And while the created

order may resemble God as circles around a central point – a point being itself a circle yet not a circle, a location and yet no location at all – no creature, even if it is an angel, is more than a cloudy halo around the original light (lines 22–4). At no subsequent moment will Dante attempt to leap the gap between divine existence and creaturely existence. But he is brought to realize the miraculous logic (line 76) by which the smallest and therefore most intense circle of angelic intelligence is related to the largest and widest of the physical heavens. He also reflects (lines 121–39) on how in theology human minds have, sometimes erroneously, sought to enumerate and give names to the nine orders of angelic beings – these nine (lines 98–126) being subdivided into three interrelated subgroups of three.

79–81 Boreas is the north wind, blowing from a 'milder', easterly direction.

91–3 To follow the sequence established when the first square of a chessboard equals 1, the second 2, the third 4, the fourth 8 and so on produces at the sixty-fourth square a number with twenty figures: 18,500,000,000,000,000,000,000. A legend – referred to by the Occitan poets Peire Vidal and Folco of Marseilles (see *Paradiso* 9) – tells of how a Persian king offered the inventor of chess a reward in which he placed one grain of corn on the first square of the board and followed the progression through to its unexpectedly huge conclusion.

94–6 The Latin *'ubi'* ('where') is a term from Scholastic philosophy, used as a noun.

109–14 Here (as also at *Paradiso* 29: 139–41) Dante enters a dispute, current in his day, as to whether beatitude depends upon sight (or knowledge) or upon love. Here he associates himself with Aquinas and the Dominicans rather than the Franciscans (cf. *Paradiso* 14: 40–41) in arguing that, while love is the ultimate condition of our relationship with God, we must first *see* what we love.

115–20 When the constellation Aries rises at night, the season is autumn and trees lose their leaves. But the angelic orders enjoy an eternal spring, singing as birds do at the end of winter. Dante here uses the word *'sberna'*, which has associations both in Latin and Occitan love poetry, signifying both the exit from winter and the springtime song of birds.

130–35 Dionysius the Areopagite, reputedly the first bishop of Athens, is mentioned in Acts 17: 34. He was thought to have been converted by Saint Paul and to have written a treatise on the angelic hierarchy, *De Coelesti Hierarchia*. The authenticity of this work was subsequently disproved and the treatise was therefore attributed to the Pseudo-Dionysius. Saint Gregory expounded his view of the angels in his *Moralia in Librum Beati Job*. The rankings ascribed to angels are, from highest to lowest, as follows:

| Dionysius and *Paradiso* | Dante in *Convivio* | Gregory |
|---|---|---|
| Seraphim | Seraphim | Seraphim |
| Cherubim | Cherubim | Cherubim |
| Thrones | Powers | Thrones |
| | | |
| Dominions | Principalities | Dominions |
| Virtues | Virtues | Principalities |
| Powers | Dominions | Powers |
| | | |
| Principalities | Thrones | Virtues |
| Archangels | Archangels | Archangels |
| Angels | Angels | Angels |

# CANTO 29

*Continuing to discuss the order of the angelic*
*hierarchies, Beatrice speaks of the creation of the*
*universe, in which God out of pure generosity*
*shares his own goodness with the created order.*
*Attention is given in particular to the creation of the*
*angels and the fall of Lucifer. Beatrice concludes with*
*an attack on false preachers and those who trust*
*speculation rather than Scripture.*

1-9 Astronomical and mythic references are employed here to designate a moment which is strictly out of time and indefinable within an astronomical scheme. As in the diagram on p.668, Dante imagines how the sun and moon might be balanced at opposite points on the horizon. The twin offspring of Latona are Apollo (the sun) and Diana (the moon), and the 'balance' between them occurs when the sun is in the sign of Aries and the moon in the sign of Libra. But, since the movements of sun and

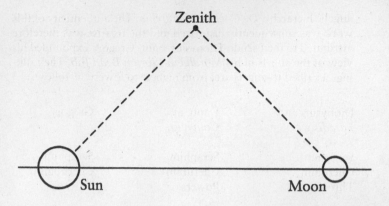

moon never pause, the time between the moment when they are in balance and when they are loosed from that balance is infinitesimally small. This instantaneity is matched by the reference to light speed at lines 25–7.

13–36 The terms 'subsist' ('*Subsisto*' in the Italian (line 15) – translated here as 'I am'), 'form' and 'matter' (line 22), along with 'act' (line 33) and 'potentiality' (or 'potency' (line 34)), are to be understood in the technical sense they possess in Scholastic, and ultimately Aristotelian, philosophy. To 'subsist', or to have substance, is to be endowed by God with the capacity for independent intelligent existence. 'Form' is pure form, or spiritual character without material extension – the angels are pure form. 'Matter' is pure potentiality, and should not be understood in terms of visible or quantifiable entities, but as a capacity for existence – for 'act' – which subsequently may become the elements of the physical universe (lines 22–4). When pure form is conjoined with pure matter, the heavens and heavenly bodies are created. These three modes of being – form, matter and their conjunction – are a direct expression of God's creative intention. (And God, in Scholastic philosophy, is understood to be pure 'act'.) They are, therefore, incorruptible. (The human being, as discussed in *Paradiso* 7 and 13, is, uniquely, a conjunction of God's creative will and the generative processes that operate in the physical universe.) Universal order was created simultaneously with the angelic hierarchies (line 31).

37–48 Jerome's view, expressed in his notes on the Epistle of Saint Paul to Titus, is that angels were created long before the physical heavens. Aquinas disagrees (see *Summa Theologiae, Prima* 59, Art. 3), as does Dante, who here argues that some angels have the function of moving the spheres of the physical universe and could not be perfect unless, from the moment of their creation, they were able to perform that function (lines 44–5). The creation of the physical universe was therefore simultaneous with the creation of the angels.

49–51 The fall of Lucifer and the rebel angels occurred in an immeasurably short time after the instant of Creation. (See also *Paradiso* 19: 46–8.)

64–6 The important point here is that grace, far from being given as a reward for merit, is itself given to make merit possible. Such grace is a response to love and the capacity for love is foreordained. (Cf. the implications of *Paradiso* 32.)

73–81 An important distinction is made between angels and human beings. Angels, seeing directly and constantly into the truth of God, do not have memory – though Aquinas tends to think otherwise. The soul of man – seeing with 'cut' or interrupted vision (line 79) – does have memory, along with will and understanding. Angels do not have 'split seeing' like human beings and so do not need memory (though some, possibly including Aquinas, fallaciously argue otherwise).

85f Beatrice now turns to attack misguided academics who prefer fashionable theories, drawn from popular science, to any serious meditation on the meaning of Christ's Passion (lines 97–102). In all of this, the human reality that underlies and gives depth to the Scriptures – which are founded on the blood of martyrs (line 91) – is tragically obscured. There are those, for instance, who argue that the darkness that came over the land at the Crucifixion (Matthew 27: 45) was seen by some as an eclipse caused by the moon wandering off course (lines 97–9). Dante, by contrast, sees it as a miracle.

109–11 Cf. Mark 16: 15.

124–6 Saint Anthony of Egypt is usually depicted with a hog at his feet – to symbolize his defeat of the devil in the form of carnal pleasure. The monks of the Order of Saint Anthony kept herds of swine but, as Dante suggests here, paid for the upkeep of these herds through the issue of spurious indulgences. These monks were among the most notorious abusers of pardons in Dante's time, becoming servants rather than masters of the carnal 'hog'.

**130–5** Angels are innumerable and, though Dante speaks of them in groups, strictly speaking each single angel is a species in itself, each being as different from another as a dolphin is from a delphinium or a dog from a diamond. (See D. Keck, *Angels and Angelology in the Middle Ages* (New York and Oxford, 1998).) The 'thousands' in line 134 is a reference to Daniel 7: 10: a 'thousand thousands ministered unto him, and ten thousand times ten thousand stood before him.'

# CANTO 30

*Dante ascends from the* Primum Mobile *to the true eternity of the Empyrean where all the souls are gathered whom, hitherto, he has seen distributed among the planetary spheres. He sees the court of Heaven shaped in the form of a rose and notes that there is an empty throne, awaiting the arrival of the emperor, Henry VII.*

**1–3** The following diagram may explain the astronomy behind this passage.

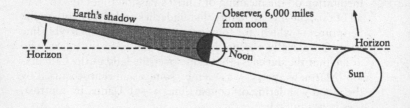

About an hour before sunrise at any point on earth, the sun, 6,000 miles to the east, will be at its noon-time point, below the horizon. At that same time, towards the west, the conical shadow that the earth casts into the cosmic system will be lowering close to the western horizon.

46–8 'Spirits' here is used in a technical and physiological sense, referring to the optical organ and the process of seeing.

94–6 The two courts of Heaven are that of the angels and that of those who await the resurrection of the body in the Empyrean.

133–41 These lines refer to Henry VII of Luxembourg, who was Holy Roman Emperor from 1308 to 1313. His death (before the composition of the *Paradiso*) disappointed Dante's hopes of a renewal of political justice in Italy. (Cf. *Purgatorio* 6 and 7.) The papacy and the Guelf parties were both opposed to imperial authority. In the attack on 'blind cupidity' (line 139) that concludes the canto, Dante voices polemically the contrast which has been central to his vision throughout the *Commedia*: where greed destroys both community and subtlety of understanding, *caritas*, which is contemplative love, refines our understanding (as exemplified in the imaginative delicacy that prevails in this canto) and restores a living harmony between the created order and its Creator.

142–8 This is a reference to Pope Clement V (*c.* 1260–1314). (Cf. *Inferno* 19: 83, where Clement is condemned to Hell as a simonist.) Clement initially supported Henry VII, but, under pressure from Philip IV of France, transferred his support, when Henry entered Italy, to the Angevin Robert of Naples. Simon Magus is the prototype of all corrupt clergy. The final reference to the 'Anagnese pope' is to the especially corrupt Pope Boniface VIII, who was born in Anagni. (See *Inferno* 19.)

# CANTO 31

*Dante views all the souls of the blessed gathered now*
*within the Empyrean. Beatrice leaves his side to*
*return to her place among the saints. Her position is*
*taken by Saint Bernard, who, as Dante's last guide,*
*points out to him the throne of the*
*Blessed Virgin Mary.*

31–6 The barbarians come from the north, the region of the constellations of Ursa Major and Ursa Minor. The nymph Helice (or Callisto) was transformed by Jupiter into the Great Bear, her son Arcas or Bootes into the Lesser Bear. (See Ovid, *Metamorphoses* 2: 496–530.) The Lateran had been the imperial palace in Rome until Constantine removed his seat to Constantinople. In Dante's day, it was the palace of the popes.

58f The figure introduced here, as the last of Dante's three companions on his journey, is Saint Bernard of Clairvaux (1090–1153). Bernard, living a century before Dante was born, was the most prominent churchman of his day. Successfully attempting to reform the monastic orders, he attracted much aristocratic support for the austere Cistercian rule which he first established in the monasteries of Burgundy. His power extended into the political arena, where he was able to convince his protégé, Pope Eugenius III (d. 1153), to embark (disastrously) on the Second Crusade, in which Dante's forebear, Cacciaguida, died. (See *Paradiso* 15–17). Bernard also did much to encourage an acknowledgement of papal supremacy. Yet Dante, despite his own political interests and suspicion of authoritarian popes, makes no allusion to this turbulent history. Nor does he mention the extent to which Bernard's theological position led him into controversial conflict with certain intellectuals of the period whom Dante himself might be supposed to have admired, notably Peter Abelard. Intellect itself, for Bernard, offers a less sure path towards the truth of God than *caritas* and contemplation. Dante does not always sympathize with this view, but he appears to find it appropriate in the final stages of a spiritual quest.

Dante seems to have seen in Saint Bernard someone who articulates two of his deepest concerns: a devotion to the Virgin Mary and a realization that desire – even erotic desire – can drive the human being towards an immediate encounter with the source of its own existence. In hymns devoted to the Blessed Virgin – and written in the luxuriant and emotive vein that also characterizes his prose and won for him a nickname as 'the mellifluous teacher' – Bernard makes a very significant contribution to the development of Marian devotion which gave so great an impetus to European culture around the turn of the millennium. (*Paradiso* 23 represents Dante's own most sustained and delicate contribution to this tradition.) It is thus appropriate that Saint Bernard's main function in the *Paradiso* should be to sing the 'Hymn to the Blessed Virgin' that occupies the first third of *Paradiso* 33.

The cult of the Blessed Virgin was closely connected with the changes in sensibility that also produced the courtly love tradition. Bernard shares with this tradition a dawning interest in

Neoplatonic thinking about the nature of desire. And the result, in his case, is the sequence of sermons on the Song of Songs (see *Paradiso* 14), in which the rich eroticism of the Scriptural original is maintained yet translated into an account of how the soul is driven by desire to union with Christ. The following example takes the opening verse of the Song and luxuriantly develops a parallel between erotic encounter and the exquisite pleasures of finding Christ in the text of Scripture itself:

> Tell us, I entreat you, by whom, about whom and to whom it is said: 'Let him kiss me with the kiss of his mouth.' How shall I explain so abrupt a beginning, this sudden irruption as from a speech in mid-course? The words spring out at us as if indicating one speaker to whom another is replying as she demands a kiss – whoever she may be . . . She does not, however, say: 'Let him kiss me *with his mouth*'; but something much more intimate: 'with the kiss of his mouth'. What a gorgeous turn of phrase this is, prompted into life by the kiss, with Scripture's own engaging countenance inspiring the reader and enticing him on, that he may find pleasure even in the laborious pursuit of what lies hidden, with a fascinating theme to sweeten the fatigue of research.
>
> Sermon 1: 3

103–8 Legend has it that Saint Veronica wiped the face of Christ as he went to the Crucifixion, and that the towel she used subsequently bore the image of Christ's features. This towel was displayed as a relic in Saint Peter's, Rome, annually on 8 March, attracting pilgrims from countries as distant (to Dante) as Croatia.

124–6 Phaeton, son of Apollo, who drove the chariot of the sun to wild destruction, is referred to on four other occasions in the *Commedia* – at *Inferno* 17: 106–8, *Purgatorio* 4: 72–5 and 29: 115–20, and *Paradiso* 17: 1–3. Dante's source is Ovid, *Metamorphoses* 1: 748–76 and 2: 1–366. The reference here is to the rising of the sun (the 'chariot pole') over the western horizon.

127–9 The 'oriflamme' was the red and gold battle standard (here, by contrast, 'a peace pennant') of the kings of France, first used in 1152 and last used at the battle of Agincourt in 1415.

133–5 These lines refer to the Virgin Mary.

# CANTO 32

*Saint Bernard indicates the places occupied in the*
*rose by those who have believed in Christ to come,*
*and in Christ once He has come. He speaks of*
*predestination and grace.*

**1f** The diagram opposite indicates the positions allocated to the fig-
ures who are now seen by Dante enthroned in the celestial rose.

**4–6** The wound that Mary cures is the wound of sin inflicted by Eve
at the Fall. The history of redemption is dominated by the Hebrew
women whose lineage leads to Mary. The diagram opposite
shows how the order of the rose is arranged around these women.

**7–12** Rachel was the second wife of Jacob (see Genesis 29). As a figure
for the contemplation of the divine, she had an important role to
play in *Purgatorio* 27. Sara was the wife of Abraham and mother
of Isaac. (See Genesis 12: 5–20.) Rebecca was Isaac's wife and
Esau and Jacob's mother. (See Genesis 25: 21; see also line 68.)
Judith was the Jewish heroine who beheaded Holofernes. (See the
apocryphal Book of Judith.) Ruth was grandmother of King
David, who was at 'fault' for sending Uriah, the husband of his
mistress Bathsheba, to his death in the forefront of the battle. (See
2 Samuel 11.) The *'Miserere mei'* is Psalm 51. (Cf. *Inferno* 2,
where Dante depicts the chorus of heavenly ladies who initiate
his journey through the other world.)

**19–21** A distinction is drawn between those who believed in Christ to
come and those who believed in Christ already come. (Cf. *Para-
diso* 19: 103–5 and *Paradiso* 20: 103–5.)

**25–7** A few places remain to be filled, implying that the end of time is
near.

**31–3** Saint John the Baptist, martyred two years before Christ's
crucifixion, had to wait two years for redemption in Limbo.

**34–6** This list of saints elsewhere applauded in the *Paradiso* includes
one of Dante's surprisingly rare mentions of Saint Augustine
(354–430), author of *The City of God.*

**43–8** The children referred to here are those who died before they
became competent to choose by their own rational powers
between good and evil. As throughout the canto, Dante empha-
sizes that salvation ultimately depends on the grace of God.

**52f** Dante uncompromisingly announces that the place of individuals
in the rose may be absolutely assured, but not by any merit or

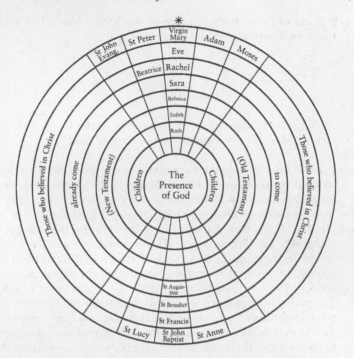

action of the human will. Rather, it is an effect of grace, which acts differently – for inscrutable reasons or no 'reason' at all – in producing differences between the standings of each of the blessed. All depends (lines 76–8) on the perception of God's grace that was given to them as the foundation of their existence at the moment of their creation.

67–9 The reference here is to Jacob and Esau, sons of Rebecca (see above) and Isaac (Genesis 25: 21). Though these children were twins, God chose Jacob over Esau.

79–81 Circumcision was instituted as a profession of faith in the time of Abraham.

94–6 This refers to the Angel Gabriel. (Cf. *Paradiso* 23: 103–5.) He is singing 'Hail, Mary, full of grace'.

127–32 Saint John the Evangelist, credited with the Book of Revelation, speaks of the sufferings to be endured by the Church in the last days before the Second Coming. (Cf. *Purgatorio* 32.) The 'lord' here is Moses, who guided his people from servitude in Egypt.

133–8 Anna or Anne is the mother of the Virgin Mary. For Saint
Lucy, see *Inferno* 2: 97 and *Purgatorio* 9: 55.

# CANTO 33

*Saint Bernard prays on Dante's behalf to the Virgin
Mary. Dante ascends to the vision of God.*

13–15 These lines reflect Saint Bernard's concern throughout his own
writings to represent the Blessed Virgin as the supreme interces-
sor between God and humanity.

64–6 For the Cumean Sibyl, see Virgil, *Aeneid* 3: 441f and 6: 74f.

94–6 To T. S. Eliot, these haunting lines demonstrate the 'combina-
tive power' of all true poetry (*Dante* (London, 1929), p. 000).
Suddenly, Dante introduces a verse that springs directly from his
reading of classical literature – producing incongruous refer-
ences to Neptune and Jason's Argosy. (Cf. *Paradiso* 2: 16–18.)
The probable meaning of the verse is this: that in the one moment
when Dante sees God, more truth and experience are contained
than in the twenty-five centuries that have passed since the Argo-
nauts – who mythologically were the first seafarers – amazed the
god Neptune by crossing his hitherto untravelled ocean.

115–17 Dante sees the perfected form of a three-fold rainbow arc.
There is a wonderful appreciation here of 'being' in its most rar-
efied form – of light and colour as the most refined of all physical
realities. There is also an appreciation of geometry – of that
which some might hold to be the underlying form of all being.
There is finally an allusion to the rainbow that came as a coven-
ant between God and Noah. This covenant carried with it the
assurance that the world, once created by God, was safe once
again for human habitation and, equally, that the realities of this
world could offer a reliable underpinning to human design.

133–8 Dante sees in God a human face, and the simplicity of this defeats
understanding in the way that the geometer is defeated in any
attempt to find the square of a circle. Saint Paul speaks of our see-
ing God 'face to face'. (See 1 Corinthians 13: 12.) Recent theology
and literary criticism, too, recalls the insistence placed by the rab-
binical philosopher Emmanuel Levinas on the encounter of faces,
which can be regarded as a metaphor for the originary moment of
creation: face looking into face will refuse to kill the other, and by

that refusal display its devotion to life. From this initial acknowledgement of reciprocity there derives the everyday repetition of ethical action in all our moments of regard or courtesy. (See David Ford, *Self and Salvation* (Cambridge, 1999), pp. 17–72.)

That said, however, the last lines of the *Paradiso* are characteristically tender towards the identity and even individuality of historical human beings, as Dante has always been in his praise of the existence of Beatrice or the Virgin Mary. The 'otherness' of our fellow human beings makes possible those conversations in which, individually, we discover and rediscover our own selves. Yet Dante now sees God as an 'other', and in this case encounters an otherness that is like no other. God has no place in any spatial geometry or system of binary oppositions. 'She is as much within as He is beyond' (Denys Turner, *Faith, Reason and the Existence of God* (Cambridge, 2004), pp. 154–68).

# PENGUIN CLASSICS

**LA VITA NUOVA (POEMS OF YOUTH)**
DANTE

> 'When she a little smiles, her aspect then
> No tongue can tell, no memory can hold'

Dante's sequence of poems tells the story of his passion for Beatrice, the beautiful sister of one of his closest friends, transformed through his writing into the symbol of a love that was both spiritual and romantic. *La Vita Nuova* begins with the moment Dante first glimpses Beatrice in her childhood, follows him through unrequited passion and ends with his profound grief over the loss of his love. Interspersing exquisite verse with Dante's own commentary analysing the structure and origins of each poem, *La Vita Nuova* offers a unique insight into the poet's art and skill. And, by introducing personal experience into the strict formalism of Medieval love poetry, it marked a turning point in European literature.

Barbara Reynolds's translation is remarkable for its lucidity and faithfulness to the original. In her new introduction she examines the ways in which Dante broke with poetic conventions of his day and analyses his early poetry within the context of his life. This edition also contains notes, a chronology and an index.

Translated with a new introduction by Barbara Reynolds

# PENGUIN CLASSICS

---

## PARADISO
## DANTE

*'And so my mind, held high above itself,*
*looked on intent and still, in wondering awe'*

Leaving Hell and Mount Purgatory far behind, Dante in the *Paradiso* ascends to heaven and crosses the planetary spheres that circle round the Earth, now guided by his beloved Beatrice. Here Dante encounters spirits, from Thomas Aquinas to Saint Peter, who engage him in passionate conversation about history, politics and Christian doctrine. Ascending finally to a sphere beyond space and time, Dante miraculously sees the faces of human beings with greater clarity than ever before and prepares to contemplate the face of God. The *Paradiso* is an account of the order, harmony and beauty of the universe in which Dante offers a deeply personal and unfailingly inventive exploration of divine truth and human goodness.

Robin Kirkpatrick's new translation captures the sublime imaginative power of the final sequence of the *Commedia* and the vigour of the original Italian, which is printed on facing pages. This edition includes an introduction, a map of Dante's Italy and a plan of Paradise. Commentaries on each canto explain the work's ethical, theological and political subtexts.

Translated and edited with an introduction, commentary and notes by Robin Kirkpatrick

read more ⟨Ⓟ⟩

# PENGUIN CLASSICS

## DANTE IN ENGLISH

'All in the middle of the road of life
I stood bewildered in a dusky wood'

Dante Alighieri (1265–1321) created poetry of profound force and beauty that
proved influential far beyond the borders of his native Italy. This new collection
brings together translations from all his verse, including the *Vita Nuova*, his tale of
erotic despair and hope, and the *Commedia*, his vast yet intimate poem depicting
one man's journey into the afterlife. It also contains extracts from many English
masterpieces influenced by Dante, including Chaucer's *Canterbury Tales*,
Milton's *Paradise Lost*, Byron's *Don Juan*, T. S. Eliot's *The Waste Land* and
Derek Walcott's *Omeros*.

Edited by Eric Griffiths and Matthew Reynolds, this anthology explores the
variety of encounters between Dante and English-speakers across more than six
centuries. Its detailed notes enable even readers with little or no Italian to
appreciate translations that range from the hilarious to the inspired. Eric Griffiths'
introduction explains how intricately Dante's work is tied to his own time, yet still
speaks across the ages. This edition also includes an account of Dante's life and a
list of further reading.

Edited with an introduction and notes by Eric Griffiths

and Matthew Reynolds

# PENGUIN CLASSICS

---

**THE DECAMERON**
GIOVANNI BOCCACCIO

'Ever since the world began, men have been subject to various tricks of Fortune'

In the summer of 1348, as the Black Death ravages their city, ten young Florentines take refuge in the countryside. They amuse themselves by each telling a story a day for the ten days they are destined to remain there – a hundred stories of love, adventure and surprising twists of fate. Less preoccupied with abstract concepts of morality or religion than earthly values, the tales range from the bawdy Peronella hiding her lover in a tub to Ser Cepperallo, who, despite his unholy effrontery, becomes a Saint. The result is a towering monument of European literature and a masterpiece of imaginative narrative.

This is the second edition of G. H. McWilliam's acclaimed translation of *The Decameron*. In his introduction Professor McWilliam illuminates the worlds of Boccaccio and of his storytellers, showing Boccaccio as a master of vivid and exciting prose fiction.

Translated with a new introduction and notes by G. H. McWilliam

---

# PENGUIN CLASSICS

## THE BOOK OF THE COURTIER
## BALDESAR CASTIGLIONE

'The courtier has to imbue with grace his movements, his gestures, his way of doing things and in short, his every action'

In *The Book of the Courtier* (1528), Baldesar Castiglione, a diplomat and Papal Nuncio to Rome, sets out to define the essential virtues for those at Court. In a lively series of imaginary conversations between the real-life courtiers to the Duke of Urbino, his speakers discuss qualities of noble behaviour – chiefly discretion, decorum, nonchalance and gracefulness – as well as wider questions such as the duties of a good government and the true nature of love. Castiglione's narrative power and psychological perception make this guide both an entertaining comedy of manners and a revealing window onto the ideals and preoccupations of the Italian Renaissance at the moment of its greatest splendour.

George Bull's elegant translation captures the variety of tone in Castiglione's speakers, from comic interjections to elevated rhetoric. This edition includes an introduction examining Castiglione's career in the courts of Urbino and Mantua, a list of the historical characters he portrays and further reading.

Translated and with an introduction by George Bull

# PENGUIN CLASSICS

**PARADISE LOST**
JOHN MILTON

'Better to reign in Hell, than serve in Heav'n ...'

In *Paradise Lost* Milton produced a poem of epic scale, conjuring up a vast, awe-inspiring cosmos and ranging across huge tracts of space and time. And yet, in putting a charismatic Satan and naked Adam and Eve at the centre of this story, he also created an intensely human tragedy on the Fall of Man. Written when Milton was in his fifties – blind, bitterly disappointed by the Restoration and briefly in danger of execution – *Paradise Lost*'s apparent ambivalence towards authority has led to intense debate about whether it manages to 'justify the ways of God to men', or exposes the cruelty of Christianity.

John Leonard's revised edition of *Paradise Lost* contains full notes, elucidating Milton's biblical, classical and historical allusions and discussing his vivid, highly original use of language and blank verse.

'An endless moral maze, introducing literature's first Romantic, Satan' John Carey

Edited with an introduction and notes by John Leonard

# PENGUIN CLASSICS

**TROILUS AND CRISEYDE**
GEOFFREY CHAUCER

The tragedy of *Troilus and Criseyde* is one of the greatest narrative poems in English literature. Set during the siege of Troy, it tells how the young knight Troilus, son of King Priam, falls in love with Criseyde, a beautiful widow. Brought together by Criseyde's uncle, Pandarus, the lovers are then forced apart by the events of war, which test their oaths of fidelity and trust to the limits. The first work in English to depict human passion with such sympathy and understanding, *Troilus and Criseyde* is Chaucer's supreme evocation of the joy and grief inherent in love.

In his critical introduction to this original-spelling edition, Barry Windeatt discusses the traditions, sources and interpretations of *Troilus and Criseyde*. The poem is provided with on-page glosses, explanatory notes and full glossary, and appendices explore topics such as metre and versification.

Edited with an introduction and notes by Barry Windeatt

# THE STORY OF PENGUIN CLASSICS

**Before 1946** ... 'Classics' are mainly the domain of academics and students; readable editions for everyone else are almost unheard of. This all changes when a little-known classicist, E. V. Rieu, presents Penguin founder Allen Lane with the translation of Homer's *Odyssey* that he has been working on in his spare time.

**1946** Penguin Classics debuts with *The Odyssey*, which promptly sells three million copies. Suddenly, classics are no longer for the privileged few.

**1950s** Rieu, now series editor, turns to professional writers for the best modern, readable translations, including Dorothy L. Sayers's *Inferno* and Robert Graves's unexpurgated *Twelve Caesars*.

**1960s** The Classics are given the distinctive black covers that have remained a constant throughout the life of the series. Rieu retires in 1964, hailing the Penguin Classics list as 'the greatest educative force of the twentieth century.'

**1970s** A new generation of translators swells the Penguin Classics ranks, introducing readers of English to classics of world literature from more than twenty languages. The list grows to encompass more history, philosophy, science, religion and politics.

**1980s** The Penguin American Library launches with titles such as *Uncle Tom's Cabin*, and joins forces with Penguin Classics to provide the most comprehensive library of world literature available from any paperback publisher.

**1990s** The launch of Penguin Audiobooks brings the classics to a listening audience for the first time, and in 1999 the worldwide launch of the Penguin Classics website extends their reach to the global online community.

**The 21st Century** Penguin Classics are completely redesigned for the first time in nearly twenty years. This world-famous series now consists of more than 1300 titles, making the widest range of the best books ever written available to millions – and constantly redefining what makes a 'classic'.

The Odyssey continues ...

*The best books ever written*

PENGUIN 🐧 CLASSICS

SINCE 1946

Find out more at www.penguinclassics.com